# Extreme War

# Extreme War

The Military Book Club's
Encyclopedia of the Biggest,
Fastest, Bloodiest,
& Best in Warfare

## Terrence Poulos

CITADEL PRESS
Kensington Publishing Corp.
www.kensingtonbooks.com

CITADEL PRESS BOOKS are published by

Kensington Publishing Corp.
850 Third Avenue
New York, NY 10022

Previously published in hardcover by the Military Book Club, 401 Franklin Avenue, Garden City, NY 11530.

All Kensington titles, imprints, and distributed lines are available at special quantity discounts for bulk purchases for sales promotions, premiums, fund-raising, educational, or institutional use. Special book excerpts or customized printings can also be created to fit specific needs. For details, write or phone the office of the Kensington special sales manager: Kensington Publishing Corp., 850 Third Avenue, New York, NY 10022, attn: Special Sales Department; phone 1-800-221-2647.

CITADEL PRESS and the Citadel logo are Reg. U.S. Pat. & TM Off.

First Citadel Press printing: January 2006

10 9 8 7 6 5 4 3 2 1

Printed in the United States of America

Library of Congress Control Number: 2005928273

ISBN 0-8065-2730-7

*Memoria in aeterna*
*Dena, John, and Christine*

# Contents

## The Medieval World  97

## The Early Modern Era 154

## Prelude to Cataclysm   260

# Modern Warfare   313

# Acknowledgments

The author has had a great deal of help in this project. His relatives helped him by reading their own instruction manuals, thereby leaving him alone. They hired contractors to redo their basements, kitchens, bathrooms, and bedrooms, thereby leaving him alone. The author's brother, Philip; sister, Cindy; and father, George, gave him all the material support he needed, and then left him alone. The author's friends promised martinis, moonlight, and Montecristos upon completion, and then left him alone. The following, freely gave advice when asked, made suggestions when prompted, and discussed points, general and esoteric—John Allen, Diane Paget Dellio, Jack English, Richard Helmstadter, Eugenia Kiesling, John Lynn, Margaret MacMillan, Robert Manson, Dawn Miller, Charles Morrisey, Sarandis Papadopoulos, Hew Strachan—and then asked to be left alone. The author apologizes, in advance, to anyone whom he has inadvertently omitted.

The author thanks the various institutions that provided images for the book. Greg Loughton of the Royal Canadian Military Institute in Toronto, and Bruce and Catharina Hogarth of the Hogarth House Museum in Elora, Ontario, freely gave of their time and images; Malory Truman of the Higgins Armory Museum of Worcester, Massachusetts, moved with dispatch to provide images; and Tina Poitras of Magma Photo/Corbis in Montreal is a gem.

Lieutenant Colonel Hugh Foster, USA (Ret.) contributed the article on the A7V tank and considerable information about WWI helmet designs for that article as well. Lieutenant Colonel Mark Reardon, USA, author of the justly-acclaimed *Victory at Mortain* (University Press of Kansas, 2002) contributed almost all of the article about the battle of Mortain; the only parts that are not his are the introduction and part of the conclusion.

The author thanks also his friend and co-founder of the Society of the Free and Easy Johns, Michael Strong of Los Angeles, for drawing the sketch of the Helepolis. *Ebibite!*

Lastly, this project would not have come about without the friendship of Lieutenant Colonel Kit Bonn (USA, Ret.) and Patti Bonn. They guided this project throughout with encouragement, technical expertise, and aplomb. They saved the author many mistakes. Kit also contributed the article about General Patch, as well as much of the information in the articles about the German tanks and WWI helmets. Kit and Patti's firm, Aegis Consulting Group, Inc., created the maps, which greatly aid understanding of the articles they support.

As for what mistakes remain, *faber est quisque fortunae suae.* Thus they are the responsibility of the author, alone.

# Extreme War

# The Ancient World

## Introduction

Much of what we know of the distant past we know from war. War is the most important of man's activities; all who participate in it are marked by it for the rest of their lives. The results of war are serious, the organization for and conduct of war consumes the time and treasure of countries and the best of their blood. War has been the concern of kings and preoccupation of poets for thousands of years. The line stretches from Thutmosis III of Egypt who put down rebels at Megiddo (1479 or 1469 B.C.); through the Persian empire of Cyrus the Great; the militarized state of Sparta; the greatest of all military commanders, Alexander of Macedon; to the Romans, whose genius for organization sustained their empire for hundreds of years. Homer immortalized war in *The Iliad*, Aeschylus fought the Persians at Marathon, Sophocles served as a naval commander in the Athenian navy, and Socrates was a hoplite in the phalanx and fought at Potidaea and Delium.

It was the Greek style of war which came to rule the Mediterranean and set the foundation for the western way of warfare. It is astonishing to think that the doings of these farmers and soldiers, politicians and poets so long, long ago shaped the way that we fight wars today, but it is so. The Greeks were not the first to impose discipline and doctrine, technology and tactics, public spending and strategy on warmaking, but they did it better than anyone before them and this established the foundation upon which the conduct of western warfare has been based ever since. The West has made war more effectively than any other civilization in history. The West has made it more deadly, more efficient, and, as a result, Western ways of war have been more emulated than any others. If modern states cannot fight in this way, then they are at the mercy of those who can and have the will to do so. The resort to terror

1

by groups or states cannot, in the end, be sustained against the unrestrained use of force by a Western-style military establishment.

We should begin, however, at what we think is the beginning; primitive man and primitive warfare. Was it organized? The author believes it to be so. The banding together of men to pursue some common goal is ingrained. How organized was it? Nobody knows. There are, however, fortifications at Jericho dating back at least to 6000 B.C., and this indicates that there were more than a few people wishing others ill and many others who were prepared to do something about it. This, in turn, indicates an organizing principle. To what extent did these ancient wars, campaigns, and battles reflect our modern notions of cohesion, maneuver, and discipline? We do not know. These battles could have been little more than huge melees and probably were for some time, but the author suspects that they did not remain so for very long. The human instinct for organization would soon extend to warfare and man would devote his ample imagination and energy to turning chaos into order.

Early weapons were fashioned out of wood, stone, and bone. Clubs were for hitting; rocks, of course, were for throwing. Primitive as they are, these weapons introduce two classes of arms which, in general terms, are still with us: shock and missile. Later, shock weapons developed to include lances, pikes, spears, swords, and a wide variety of clubs, including the mace and flail. Missile weapons were refined as well to include slings for throwing small stones farther, javelins, and eventually bows and arrows. There was also the introduction and the development of personal protection in the form of body armor. Shields were made from wood, wicker, and animal hide, and later embossed with metal. Helmets were made from leather, which were later covered with hard material such as animal teeth or metal. Breastplates and coverings for legs and arms were also developed. Once the first man took up a shield, no matter how rudimentary, to ward off an attacker armed with a club, another concept was introduced into warfare: the action/reaction cycle whereby developments in offensive weapons are met by countering developments in defensive weapons. The countering then inspires further refinement in offensive weaponry, which is eventually countered again, and so on.

About 3500 B.C., the Stone Age yielded to the Copper Age as man discovered how to work metal, and he then entered into the Bronze Age when copper was hardened with tin. The Iron Age began about 1000 B.C., and iron proved to be an even harder metal, which made even better weapons. The introduction of metal to weapons was a huge step forward in their effectiveness. Metal, bronze, and later, iron, was used for the points of spears—which came to have edges—axes and maces. Then came the dagger and the sword. They came later because of the technical requirements associated with the working of metal to produce long, thin, hard blades.

## Egypt

We start in that part of the world referred to today as the Middle East. Two civilizations which brought a higher level of organization to warfare were the Egyptian and Assyrian. By this it is meant that troops were disciplined and even maneuver was used on the battlefield. These are two features of a military which signify a sophisticated civilization. A few words about each people are needed to advance the story. The Egyptians enter the picture about 5,000 years ago (the reader should know that these dates are approximate and the details do not overly concern us). From the Old Kingdom, say around 2600 B.C., to the Middle Kingdom, circa 2100 to 1800 B.C., there is the usual expansion and contraction of influence. These include internal disorder and centralized response, civil war, foreign invasion, occupation, and suppression of indigenous people. The New Kingdom emerges about 1580 B.C. as the pharaohs introduce new weapons and—through a strong central government—an effective military. By the reign of Thutmosis III (1491–1449 B.C.), Egyptian rule has been extended to Libya, Nubia, Palestine, Syria, and into Mesopotamia. From this point, it is downhill for the Egyptian empire, but who knew? It is under Thutmosis' watch that we have the first recorded battle in history in 1469 B.C. (probably) and there is more on that later.

## Assyria

The next great military power is Assyria, whose peoples appeared about 5,000 years ago in northeastern Mesopotamia along the Tigris River. This is a flat country with little in the way of natural barriers. Given that this was also fertile country meant that there were trade routes up and down the valleys; that, in turn, meant invaders. To hold on to what they had, the Assyrians developed an effective military. By the time of Tiglath-Pilesar I (1116–1093 B.C.), Assyria was an important power in the area, having expanded into Anatolia and northern Syria to the Mediterranean. There then followed centuries of fighting as successive waves of invaders were defeated or absorbed and the empire's limits expanded. When the rulers were weak, revolts sprang up, and when the next strong ruler came along, the empire reestablished control.

Tiglath-Pilesar III (745–727 B.C.) was one such strong ruler. His campaigning was constant and extended Assyrian rule. He was able to do this because he had, beyond his own abilities, a military more advanced than any yet seen. The semi-regular militia of 400 years earlier had been provided with weapons and armor, but he established a standing army. All else flowed from the exigencies of having to maintain a force of fighting regulars. War was now the primary activity of the Assyrians. Society was ordered to further the war-making efficiency of the state. Soldiers were continuously trained and weapons were constantly improved. To do this, bureaucratic systems were refined, and finance and trade supervised. The Assyrian army of this time was made up of heavy infantry armed with spears, light infantry armed with bows, cavalry which included Scythian mercenaries, and charioteers. Infantry was the most numerous in this army and organized into sub-units. The officer corps was a distinct class and appointments were made in the name of the king. Archers used a strong bow and, with iron-tipped arrows, they had an advantage over their opponents. The battle tactics used are unknown, but it has been suggested that the bowmen opened the attack to soften up the enemy at range, inflict losses, and initiate chaos. Then the charioteers would charge en masse, perhaps with the cavalry to break up the enemy formation. The heavy infantry then would move into the attack and drive the enemy from the field, whereupon the charioteers and cavalry could take up the pursuit. The Assyrians also had a siege train consisting of heavy engines for battering down walls and movable towers from which their archers could attack the defenders on the walls of fortifications. The expansion of the Assyrian empire carried with it the seeds of its collapse. To defend itself, it had to incorporate captured and subjugated peoples into its army because there were not enough Assyrian peasants to do the job. This meant that when outside pressures and internal revolts had to be put down, the army may not have been particularly loyal to its masters. In the end, however, the Assyrians could not suppress all the peoples they conquered and internecine struggle took its toll as well. The Egyptians, Syrians, Cimmerians from the Caucasus, then Scythians, Babylonians, Elamites, Chadeans, and Medians exhausted the Assyrians. The end came in 612 B.C., when the Medians and Babylonians captured and destroyed the Assyrian capital of Nineveh. All that we have now of the Assyrians are artifacts and the dictionary being produced by the Oriental Institute at the University of Chicago.

As we leave this part of the world and this era, we enter into a period in which the historical record is more reliable and, although it is far from complete, it affords us a better picture of the times. We now turn our attention to the Greeks and Romans and their enemies. As we have a continuous record of events and personalities, it is possible for military historians to say that, starting about 600 B.C., war becomes something more than it had been in the past, and, by 400 B.C., it becomes an art. That means that through the application of some technology and a lot of intellectual effort, battles came to be more than glorified butchery by armed primitives. The squeamish and sensitive may think that an overstatement, and the author grants that, on some level, the latter element of killing may continue to seem that way, but now it is possible, because of the written record, to discern the animating spirit behind what happens on the battlefield. We can perceive the trends in warfare. We see maneuver enter the realm of tactics; doctrine is developed for the training of troops; weapons are refined; sophisticated treatises are written on the conduct of war; in short, historians can look back at fifth-century Greece and see directly the origins of our western military heritage.

## Persia

This part of the story begins with the first great power of the age, the Persian Empire. It posed a mortal threat to the Greeks, and in the clash of these two cultures, we can see how the superiority of the Greek way of war, with a little luck, worked over a period of 200 years to repulse Persian invasion and then conquer the empire.

So, who were the Persians and how did they make war? Into the vacuum created by the Median and Babylonian destruction of Assyria came Cyaxares of the Medes to found his own empire. His son, Astyages (585–550 B.C.), established the Median Empire between the Caspian and Black Seas, and this included a Persian principality centered around Anzam which was where the Elamites used to rule. Anyway, Astyages and Cambyses of Anzam arranged the marriage of their children and Cyrus was the issue. Such is the way of dynastic aspirations be they Mede and Persian, or mustard queen and hot dog king. Cyrus ruled from 559 to 530 B.C. and won a great empire.

The Persian military system employed all of the combat weapons of the day—the bow, the spear, swords, and axes—and all the delivery systems, too—horse cavalry, infantry (both light and heavy), and even chariots, although the latter had seen the end of their usefulness as engines of war. Most important, however, was the bow, and it was used by mounted and unmounted troops. The Persians favored tactics whereby they engaged the enemy at range with arrows fired by successive waves of horse-archers and light infantry. Once the enemy was disorganized and gaps were created in their formation, the Persians would close with the enemy. Their techniques, however, were flexible and suited to the terrain. For example, Cyrus's campaign in Lydia against Croesus (547–546 B.C.), which secured Asia Minor for him, demonstrates not only his flexibility and improvisational skills, but also an enlightened administration. After an indecisive battle, Croesus retreated to his fortress in Sardis. Lacking a siege train, Cyrus had no way to bring down the thick walls, so he decided upon stealth. One day, a Lydian soldier dropped his helmet outside the wall and went down to retrieve it and was observed climbing back in. His route was noted and a unit of Persians used the same way to get over the wall and stormed into the city. They seized the city and captured Croesus. Cyrus demonstrated his tactical skill at the battle of Thymbra in 546 where he defeated a larger force by forming a square with his army and taking advantage of gaps in the Lydian formation.

Cyrus then turned east in 545, and in 15 years of campaigning, conquered most of south central Asia and Babylonia, and was preparing to invade Egypt when he was killed fighting the Massagetae. His son, Cambyses, conquered Egypt and the Greek colony at Cyrene, but died in 522 on his way back to Persia to put down a revolt led by Gaumata who had usurped the throne, claiming to be Cambyses' brother, Bardiya. The revolt was put down by Darius, who took the throne. He was an excellent administrator and organizer who consolidated the conquests of Cyrus and Cambyses.

By 500 B.C., the Persian empire reached from Macedonia and Thrace through Asia Minor, Armenia, Egypt, upper reaches of the Nile, Libya, Palestine, Syria, Babylonia, Medea, Parthia, Bactria, Sogdiana to the Jaxartes River in the north, the Indus River in the east and the Persian Gulf and Indian Ocean in the south. Importantly, the Persians built a Royal Road from Sardis in Asia Minor to Pteria to Nineveh to Susa—a distance of about 1,600 miles. This greatly facilitated the transfer of messages, troops, and supplies in the empire, thereby also making the empire easier to administer.

Cyrus and Darius followed enlightened policies of occupation. They incorporated the conquered peoples into the empire, with each group providing men for the army. The empire was organized into 20 provinces, or satrapies, each administered by a governor, or satrap. Each satrapy had a military force, but it was commanded by a general who served the king and not the governor. The army is said by Herodotus to have had 29 corps of 60,000 men each. Ironically, the expansion of the empire and the method by which it was maintained cultivated the seeds of its weakness. The provincial contingents were not armed, equipped,

Darius I, who ruled the Persian Empire from 521–485 B.C.
© *Dave Bartruff/ CORBIS/MAGMA*

and trained in the same manner as the original Persian-Median army. This was a deliberate decision and ensured that the old, ethnically-pure army would retain an advantage if ever another usurper tried to steal the throne *à la* Gaumata. It also meant that the great kings had a lot of troops, but of inferior grade. Another criticism of the Persian army is that it lost combat efficiency by encouraging a lack of uniformity in equipment. The elite Ten Thousand Immortals consisted mostly of some 8,000 heavy infantry, which is to say men who wore some armor in the form of corselets of metal scales. They apparently wore no protective helmet, but opted for what appears to be a knit cap similar to the modern navy's watch cap. The Immortals' table of organization also included two bodyguard units of 1,000 men each—one of infantry and one of cavalry. The proper role of heavy infantry, as the Greeks would demonstrate to the Persians' discomfort, is shock. That is to say, they slam into the enemy and start spearing and stabbing. The Persians gave their infantry bows as well, thereby trying to create a hybrid missile-shock soldier. Obviously, a soldier cannot shoot arrows while holding a spear and a shield. The Persians would probably have to lay their spears on the ground—because Persian spears, unlike the Greek spears, had no butt spikes—and then fire away. Presumably these archers lacked shields as well because it was the role of the outer infantry to form a protective wall with their five-foot curved rectangular shields. The other pattern shield they used was a roughly three-foot long oval with cut-outs on the side to facilitate interlocking. Not all of the heavy infantry contingents wore armor; the Assyrians, for example, preferred a quilted tunic. The Persians also had six corps of heavy infantry.

Light infantry from the provinces consisted of two types of missileers, namely archers from the East who wore no armor and carried no shields, and unarmored spearmen and javelineers. Light infantry made up one-third of the army's 29 corps. Much of the light infantry was good only for skirmishing as they lacked armor, or even sidearms such as swords or daggers.

Cavalry consisted of pure horse archers and hybrid archer-spearmen. There was a camel corps as well, and it appears that the camels may have carried a driver and bowman.

All told, what we call the Persian army was made up of Bactrians, Scythians, Sogdians, Arians, Parthians, Libyans, Lydians, Mysians, Paphlagonians, Assyrians, Sarangians, Hyrkanians, Kashites, Babylonians, Egyptians, Ethiopians, Exiles, Medes, Persians, and others. The drawback of such a multiplicity of polyglot national troops is that each contingent was armed with different weapons and had different military traditions. If the Persian army were to face the traditional type of combat in which numbers counted for more than tactical expertise, then they would likely succeed, but if they faced a foe who fought differently from them, they might be in trouble. (Foreshadowing provided by the author for those who enjoy this literary device. . . .)

Periodic revolts erupted in Egypt and Babylonia, but the Persian leadership managed to beat back these challenges and others until the great king decided to do something about those pesky Greeks who, in assisting the Ionian Greeks on the Asia Minor coast, were promoting unrest.

## Greece

So what were the Greeks up to? The ancient Mycenaean civilization lasted from 1600–1100 B.C., when it collapsed under pressure from barbarian invaders, referred to as "Dorians" by later Greeks and as "sea peoples" by modern scholars. The end of this culture ushered in the Dark Ages of Greece (1100–800 B.C.), characterized by the disappearance of writing, population decline, and an end to centralized government. How did this come to be? Again it is a matter of one military system destroying another. The Mycenaean way of war is considered to have been akin to that in the Near East, and that is to say, combat by lightly armed troops and charioteers. The chariots were manned by archers and javelineers, who were armored. Society seems to have been ordered around a lord who controlled the surrounding lands from palaces with thick-walled fortifications. Patches of land were allocated, and the harvests from them brought to the palace and distributed. Weapons for the militia were also itemized and stored by the palace officials. The northern invaders fought as armored infantry spearmen in massed formations; the unarmored light infantry of the Mycenaeans could not stand up to them, even if they were supported by armored charioteers. The Mycenaeans did respond to the challenge and eventually, circa 1200 B.C., initiated a large-scale change in weapons and armor, introducing spears, swords, helmets, (shin guards), and round shields. The changes did not save the Mycenaeans—perhaps because they were put in use too late—and by 1100 B.C., the destruction of the palaces/citadels was nearly complete. This signalled the collapse of this ancient civilization.

Within this event we can see, dimly, the origins of our style of warfare, the lessons to be learned, and the foundations laid for the course Western warfare would take. First, and most importantly, is that the use of heavy infantry, however it was arrayed, was able to defeat the light infantry and chariots of the day. This would "put paid" or eventually signal the end of the oriental way of warfare which was based on light infantry and chariots, at least as far as the Greeks were concerned. Classical scholar Victor Davis Hanson tells us that once the Greek city-states emerged, circa 750 B.C., and based their military on heavy infantry, Greece would not be conquered by a foreign power until the arrival of the Romans. If we count the time between the Dorians and the Roman conquest of 146 B.C., we see that it is about 1,000 years, a full millennium of security made possible by the mastery of a way of war. The other lesson to be learned is that the only way to guarantee a long-lasting peace settlement on your enemy is to have killed a lot of their people, occupied their country, and imposed your culture. This the Dorians did. Granted, the sea peoples' culture was not as developed as the civilization it supplanted, but it was theirs. The writing of "Linear B," a Mycenaean feature, vanished. Big, thick-walled fortresses, were destroyed. Centralized social, political, and economic organization were gone. Welcome to the Dark Ages, Greek-style.

What happened in the evolution of warfare during the first several hundred years of this period? Self-deprecation aside, nobody really knows. There is no written record and archaeological evidence is skimpy. There is one battle of which we have some information and it is the battle for the Lelantine plain on the island of Euboea fought between the cities of Eretria and Chalcis before 700 B.C. The winner is unknown but there is reason to believe, from pottery, that heavy armored infantry had made its appearance by this time. We do know that by the end of the eighth century B.C., infantrymen are wearing metal breastplates, helmets with crests, greaves, and thigh and foot protection, which in total weighed about 70 pounds. They are carrying round shields and are armed with spears and swords. This is the hoplite as we know him and, with only minor adjustments to the equipment, it is how we will see him for the next few hundred years. This is not to say that all Greek infantry is necessarily heavy spear-wielding infantry by this time, but it is to say that the hoplite had emerged from the lifting mists of the Dark Ages. He would prove himself to be the most efficient and deadliest soldier the world had ever seen and he probably would have acquitted himself well on the battlefield up to the introduction of gunpowder.

The city-state emerged over centuries from the many local communities. Interestingly, the colonizing spirit of the Greeks remained and by the end of the Dark Ages, Greek colonies dotted the Black Sea, the coasts of southern Italy, Sicily, Spain, France, Cyrene, Cyprus, and most importantly for the future, Asia Minor. It was these Ionian Greek colonies and the support they received from other Greeks that would provide the catalyst for the Persian Wars. The Greek states would be ready for the Persians, however, because for the 300 years prior to 490 B.C., they would

A Corinthian helmet. Made of bronze, this one-piece helmet was typical wear for hoplites. *Higgins*

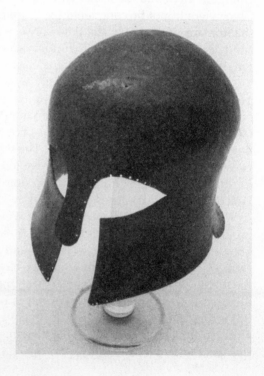

be periodically at war with each other. In war, there is no substitute for the hard lessons learned in the school of experience.

Armies are raised from their societies and the nature of the army depends a great deal on the nature of the society. Generally speaking, in Greece the eighth century B.C. saw the kings and warlords of various village groups of the Dark Ages replaced with oligarchies of the aristocracy. They, in turn, were supplanted in the seventh and sixth centuries B.C. by tyrannies in which rich and ambitious men became demagogic dictators or tyrants. The emergence of democracy, a reaction against tyranny, was the next stage and achieved only on the eve of the Persian Wars. Facilitating this evolution were changes in military tactics caused by the emergence of the hoplite—the Greek armored spearman. The origin of the word hoplite is not altogether clear. It is thought by some to refer to the shield he carried, the *hoplon*; others think that the term *hopla* describes all the battle gear. Whichever way one goes with this it is in its essence the same as the American soldier of the twentieth century being referred to as a "GI," or "government issue."

While cavalry seems to have dominated the battlefield in the past, the horseman was replaced by the heavy infantryman starting in the middle of the seventh century B.C., and by the sixth century, it was not in doubt: cavalry could not stand up to massed ranks of armored infantry which were trained to maneuver in formation. The hoplite fought in a phalanx (rows of men), a mass formation traditionally eight ranks deep, although it often varied depending upon the situation and terrain. The men held their shields on the left and spears in the right. They wore armor made of bronze, including breast plates, helmets, and greaves, the typical components of the hoplite panoply. In this era, they were armed with spears as short as seven feet and as long as ten feet. Later, the Macedonians would wield spears over 20 feet long. The spears had iron heads of varying shapes—but all designed to pierce—and a butt spike. The latter was important as it served as a secondary spear point when the shaft broke and it allowed the hoplite to stab downward against an enemy soldier on the ground as well.

Hoplites were farmers who owned their land and provided their own military equipment. This meant that the army was drawn from what would be later called the upper and middle classes. There were profound social implications. The aristocrat on his horse was no longer dominant in a society whose army and tactics depended for victory upon small landowners in the role of heavy infantry. Each member of the phalanx depended on his neighbor for survival, and because of drill, which subjected each hoplite to the same experience, a great sense of egalitarianism must have been fostered amongst these citizen soldiers.

The front ranks of a Greek phalanx.
© *Bettmann/CORBIS/MAGMA*

This seems to have resulted in a general societal disdain for ostentation and the notion of it as an oriental, or barbarian, sentiment.

This change in warfare wrought political implications as well. A city's well-being depended upon the size of its phalanx and this meant that the accumulation of land by wealthy individuals was a threat to the security of the state, as it removed potential soldiers from the muster rolls. This type of warfare was also economical as it did not require taxation to support a standing force, or to build fortifications, which were expensive to build and maintain, and then had to be manned as well.

As with everything in life there are exceptions, and ancient Greece was no different. Here the big exception to how the city-state was organized was Sparta, and it was *really* different. Sparta's army was the only professional force in Greece. It sprang from a thoroughly militarized society. In the eighth and seventh centuries B.C., Sparta fought a series of wars in Laconia and neighboring Messenia which led to their control of the people and territory of both areas. The Spartans, also known as Lacedaemonians, then enslaved the Messenians, had them work the land, and took what they needed to supply the army. Serfs, slaves, and subject peoples fell into several categories, but most of us know them collectively as *helots*. The *helots* worked and provided the necessities of life for the Spartans. This left the army free to train all the time. The army was composed of all able-bodied men and the training started at age seven. The training was rigorous and barracks life austere. The result was the most feared phalanx in Greece, one capable of cohesive maneuver in the face of the enemy. An elite force called the Spartiates protected the Spartan state, promoted oligarchic regimes abroad, and suppressed the vast numbers of the underclass, thought to be over 200,000. This last was accomplished in part by maintaining a secret police and periodic campaigns of terror. The Spartans were not invincible, but on occasion, the men opposing them in battle were known to break and run merely at the Lacedaemonians' approach. They wore red cloaks to distinguish themselves, they wore their hair long, and marched into battle at a measured pace to the sound of pipes or flutes playing music sometimes described as eerie. Their shields where distinguished by the Greek letter "lambda" (Λ) for "Lacedaemon."

So, how did these hoplites fight? What were their tactics, what were the shared assumptions of these deadly warriors? When Greek fought Greek, we believe that it went like this: first, find a piece of level land big enough to hold the combatants. Why level? Well, if you have even a gentle grade in your favor, it adds to your momentum as you go down hill and simultaneously retards your opponent's momentum. Accordingly, no one would willingly do battle at a disadvantage, so if you wanted a battle, you had to find a level field or pick a site that was important enough to your opponent to make him fight at a disadvantage. Level terrain was also important because it made it easier to keep the men in formation as they advanced. This was crucial for the strength and combat efficiency of the phalanx because it prevented gaps forming in the lines. Once gaps appeared in the line, the enemy could attack the resultant "seams" in the formation and attack men on their flanks while they were busy fighting to the front.

Once everybody arrived, it was time for the pre-battle rituals. These included a sacrifice to a god and a reading by a seer of what the sacrificial animal's entrails portended. Then the general, although leader or playing-coach better describes his status and function, would exhort the troops in a brief oration to help ready them for battle. Orders would be passed to the officers and then to the men and the watchword would be given and passed throughout the ranks. Then the signal would be given and the advance to combat began, often to music as it helped the soldiers keep together in time. The leader would also take his place in the phalanx and fight alongside his fellow soldiers because once things got underway, there was little a remote commander could do to influence the course of the battle. This is not to say that no communication was possible within the phalanx. In addition to the hoplites, there were supernumeraries attached to a company, or *taxis*, of about 128 men, assuming 8 ranks of 16 hoplites each. These supernumeraries included a herald, a signalman, a bugler, an aide, and a file closer. The herald would pass on commands vocally, but if the noise was too great, then the command would be passed by visual signal. If the dust was too great for the signal—a flag, perhaps—to be seen, then the bugler would sound the command. Presumably, these men were stationed close to the commander. And you thought supernumeraries were just in the opera holding stuff and not singing!

The tactics used in these frays were linear. That is, the two opposing forces faced each other arrayed in lines. Here is how it worked: You put your steadiest men on the right side of the formation because that was the exposed side. Everyone to the right of these men had a shield protecting his own left side and the right side of the man to his left. It has been observed by Thucydides that, as the phalanx advanced, it would drift to the right as each man instinctively sought the protection of the shield of the man to his right. If the reader is thinking, "does this mean that everyone in the phalanx was leaning on the outside guy?," he may be right. The depth of the phalanx varied depending on the situation. It has been reported as being as shallow as four men deep and as huge as 50 men deep. As mentioned above, however, the classical depth is considered to be eight ranks. At this depth, only the spears of the first three or four rows, depending on their length, would protrude beyond the front rank. The hoplites of rows five through eight held their spears angled forward above the heads of the men in front of them. As the phalanx neared the enemy lines, the hoplites would lift their spears into the attack position, which meant *above* the shoulder for those in the front ranks. This was done so that the men could thrust downward at whatever exposed parts they could find—neck, arm, groin, thigh—of their opponents. The phalanx would then break into a run, or maybe just a trot, as they prepared to slam into the enemy, shield to shield. The men would be shouting the war-cry rendered today as "Eleleu" or "Alala." At the moment of collision, spears could snap, men could go down, and everyone would push. In this regard, it was helpful to have experienced men at the rear, as file closers who kept the ranks closed up and who could provide sustained impetus. The key at this stage was to push *through* the enemy formation, breaking it apart. Thus, success depended on how things were going at the front. Was the front rank winning the struggle in what amounted to a vicious, armed scrum? It is thought that when a front rank soldier fell, or was wounded, or even just got tired, his place would be taken by the man behind him. From the excitement of the moment, the shouting, the stumbling over bodies, the slipping on blood, the heat, the dust, the confined and limited view from the helmets, eventually came movement. One side would begin to push through the other and if it continued, the tactical integrity of the other phalanx would fail. Fear and panic spread, then the men would break and the rout would be on. As the vanquished turned to run they were at risk, so the idea would be to get as far away as is possible as quickly as possible. Accordingly they would drop as much of their equipment as they could and flee. This makes sense, of course, because the victors still have their equipment and because they are carrying up to 70 pounds—the shield weighing at least 20—and they cannot run down men who have discarded theirs. It was at these moments of transition, however, that the losers were at their most vulnerable, and it was usually in the pursuit phase of a battle, once cohesion and formation had been lost, that the heavy casualties occurred. Cavalry is excellent for pursuit, but the Greeks did not have much of it during this era. It is also important to remember that if the war aims were limited, the desire for the wholesale slaughter of fellow Greeks was similarly restricted. Moreover, the Greeks seemed to believe it folly to die for a cause that was obviously lost and so there was no great shame in running away and living to fight on another day—Spartans excepted of course. They were expected to die.

After the battle, the dead were collected for burial, trophies taken for shrines, and the winning side erected a monument. It is important to all armies to retrieve their dead, and the ancient Greeks were no different. Given the nature of combat and the disfiguring wounds received, identification could be problematic, especially as the bodies were often stripped of their armor. With the use of muster rolls and the presence of family and friends in the phalanx, however, it was possible to identify most of the dead. Some Spartan soldiers introduced small pieces of wood which they affixed to their left wrists (some historians say necks) for identification. These were probably the first "dog tags." Curiously, it would be centuries, make that millennia, before other armies took up this example.

Nothing in human activity remains constant. The same is true of tactics, yet this mode of combat had a fairly long run, some 400 years. There are several reasons for this. The weapons used did not change much and this meant that there was no technological imperative driving tactical innovation. This type of combat suited the Greek mentality; after all, it was Greek in origin. The Greeks preferred a short bout of intense combat and terror. It suited their temperament, *vis-à-vis* than the type of campaigning which required the sustained discipline later displayed by the Romans. The Spartans had the discipline, but they did not usually campaign very far from home because of their constant concern over domestic rebellion. This type of combat also suited the terrain over which it was fought and that limited change as well. In essence it came down to this, "we are hoplites, we fight in a phalanx. Because we fight in a phalanx, we fight on level ground. We win our battles by breaking through the enemy's phalanx. We break through the enemy phalanx by maintaining alignment and pushing. If we try to maneuver —Spartans excepted of course—we risk opening gaps, and if we open gaps, we run the risk of losing."

The Spartans, because of their professional training, did have the ability to maneuver a separate detachment on the battlefield. Such units could launch a flank attack or, once the right side of the Spartan line had sufficiently overlapped the enemy's left, wheel the right part of the line and roll up the enemy flank. This made them formidable foes for 300 years. The Spartans also moved into battle at a slower rate than other infantry and this facilitated dressing their ranks and maintaining their formations. Their constant training made them formidable fighters, individually and collectively. They may have worn heavier armor, or rather more armor, and that is why they moved into contact at a reduced pace.

The Spartan phalanx was subdivided into several units, with each unit having a leader. In the early fourth century B.C., their phalanx was organized with 36 men in three ranks of 12, called an *enomotia*, and led by an *enomotarch*. This corresponds fairly closely to our modern infantry platoon, by the way. The *enomotarch* led one rank of 12 and there were two other rank leaders as well. Additionally, there were three half-rank leaders, whose place in the line was six files over. This made six leaders out of a group 36, and if the rank closers are considered leaders, you can add another three. This is a lot of leadership for 36 men and goes a long way to explain Spartan prowess. Two *enomotia* were combined to form a *pentekostys*, or a "fifty." Why would 72 men be called a fifty? The term is probably a holdover from when the phalanx was eight rows deep, so three files of eight times two (*enomotia*) would give 48. Each *pentekostys* was led by a *pentekonter*. Two *pentekostyses* were combined to form a *lochos* of 144 men, which was led by a *lochagos*. This was the basic unit of the Spartan army and fundamentally corresponds to our modern company. The leaders occupied the front ranks and right-most file of their unit. Four *lochoi* were formed into a *mora*, which was led by a *polemarch*. This unit of 576 men corresponds roughly to our modern battalion. Six *morae* constituted the Spartan army and was led by the king. There are deviations from this and they reflect, no doubt, different conditions in different eras, but the above provides a basic understanding.

# The Persian Wars

Eventually, the art of war would advance, but not until the Persians had been defeated, the Greek world had been convulsed by internecine fighting during the Peloponnesian Wars, and an ascetic tactical/strategic genius appeared from Thebes who would lead the first war of liberation in history. All this would set the stage for another military revolution and it would be led by a couple of Macedonians in the fourth century B.C.

The series of conflicts that became known as The Persian Wars ranged from 499 to 448 B.C. In the preliminaries, Darius campaigned against the Scythians beyond the Danube and north of the Black Sea to protect his rear and the long line of communications back to Persia from Greece. This done, the Persians then managed to stamp down the various rebels in their Ionian cities by 494 B.C. This included Miletus, a center of turmoil previously supported by Athens and Eretria with small contingents. Darius now decided to deal with Greece and sent Mardonius with a fleet to prepare the way for a major invasion. In 492 B.C., Mardonius conducted operations in Macedon and Thrace to prepare the region as a base for the invasion into Greece. A storm wrecked the fleet, however, and Mardonius withdrew to Asia Minor. Darius now decided upon a large amphibious operation against Greece. He gathered a large force, but the number given by Herodotus—100,000—seems unlikely. The Persian forces may have numbered 50,000, but they may have been fewer still. The Persians, under the command of Datis and Artaphernes, sailed across the Aegean and landed here and there, settling old scores and trying to pick up more recruits. When they reached Euboea, they landed part of the army and besieged Eretria. The Eretrians sent to Athens for help and the Athenians gathered a force of about 10,000 hoplites and another 1,000 from Plataea and sent word to Sparta for assistance. The Spartans said that they would be happy to help, but they had a religious festival and could not leave until the full moon some two weeks hence. The ten Athenian tribes sent 1,000 men each and each tribal contingent had an elected general, but effective command was vested in Callimachus and Miltiades. When the Athenians were on the march, word came that the Persians had landed at Marathon.

The bay at Marathon was ideally suited for landing ships. The Persian general, Datis, was advised to land there by Hippias, the deposed Athenian tyrant who had taken up with the Persians. When the Greeks arrived at Marathon, they deployed above the plain and between two rivers. The Greeks thereby blocked the route off the beach to Athens, which was some 26 miles away. Both sides then sat down and waited for reinforcements. The Persians may have had as many as 30,000 men there or they may have had only 15,000 or 20,000 infantry and about 1,000 cavalry. The Greeks had around 11,000 hoplites plus other troops, but no cavalry at all.

For eight days, a stalemate persisted, and the Spartans were still five days from leaving, when word arrived that Eretria had fallen. What happened next involves conjecture. Did Datis decide to re-embark his force and sail for Athens? That seems likely, but was it all of his force or just some of it? There was a battle, to be sure, and the Greeks won big, but as for details, we are lacking many. First, was the cavalry there or not? Was it already aboard the ships, was it off being watered over a mile from the battlefield, or did it participate in the battle but no mention is made of it? If the Persian cavalry was there, then the terrain chosen by the Greeks may have hampered its effectiveness. If the Persians were loading their cavalry aboard ship, then they may have sent out an infantry force to screen the withdrawal and this may be what inspired the Greeks to attack. It may be that some of the force was already dispatched to meet up with the Persian force sailing from Eretria to Athens. Datis' purpose then may have been to hold the Greeks at Marathon and after defeating them, march on Athens. If this were the case, then Miltiades may have figured it out and realized that the Greeks had to attack immediately, defeat the Persians at Marathon, and then speed to Athens to repel the other force. In any event, opportunity was knocking and Miltiades persuaded the others at a war council that it was time to answer the door. Here is what we do know: the Greeks lined up with the Athenians on the right and deployed along the line by tribe with the Plataeans on the left. The Persians had a larger force than the Greeks because the latter thinned the center of their line to only a few ranks to match the breadth of the Persian frontage. The Greeks also added to the depth of the wings of their army. Was Miltiades planning an envelopment? How thin was the center? Four rows rather than eight is a good guess, because at this depth at least all the hoplites could bring their spears to bear.

The Greeks advanced to battle and are reported by Herodotus to have run a mile or so before crashing into the Persians. This is highly unlikely and unnecessary in any case. The point at which the heavily-laden Greeks would begin running was probably the point at which they came within range of the Persian archers. This is considered to have been about 150 yards. By running—or trotting—through this gap, the Greeks would reduce the time they were subject to attack and they would diminish the effectiveness of the Persian fire. The Greek wings made contact before the center, thus bending the Greek line. During the fighting, the center of the Greek line was pushed back by the Persian heavy infantry who broke through at some point. The Greek center withdrew to high ground, presumably to reorganize. The wings, however, left and right, succeeded in driving back the troops facing them, whether they were cavalry or infantry.

The key action here was that rather than pursue the fleeing Persians, the wings wheeled inward and enveloped them, attacking the Persian flank and rear. Herodotus tells us that these Greeks then formed a line and attacked the Persian center from behind which, if the Greeks in the center had rallied, meant that the Persian heavy infantry was surrounded. Panic would have spread quickly at this point as the Persian center tried to retreat and instead ran into the remnants of their own flank troops, which the Greeks were already squeezing. Confusion would have reigned supreme in this situation and organized resistance by the Persians may have all but ended. Troops who could get away would do so; others would be slaughtered as they tried. The Persians would be heading for their ships and, while Herodotus does not mention it, Datis must have been able to organize some sort of rearguard action. This is because once the Greeks reached the beach, they were able to capture only seven ships. It was in this furious fighting that Callimachus was killed. Many notables took part in this battle and for some, it was the event which minted the capital they would later spend in public life; included among these is Themistocles, the politician, and Aeschylus, the playwright. In fact, Aeschylus's brother, Cynegirus, had his hand chopped off by an axe as he laid hold of a ship's stern and died of his wounds. Herodotus tells us that the epitaph on Aeschylus's tomb stated that the one thing of distinction he achieved was that he had fought at Marathon. Losses are set at 192 for the Athenians and 6,400 for the Persians while Plataean and other losses are unreported.

Ten years later, the Greeks and Persians were at it again. The defeat of the Persian fleet at Salamis in September 480 B.C., and the subsequent destruction of the Persian army at Plataea and the loss of their fleet at Mycale on the same day in 479 B.C. ended the Persian threat of invasion. From the Persian Wars, Athens and Sparta emerged as the premier powers of Greece. The former at sea as an imperial democracy, and the latter on land, an oligarchic power based on agrarianism. The wealth and expansion of the Athenians threatened the Peloponnesian states and it was only a matter of time before war came. What would come to be called the Peloponnesian War started in 431 B.C. and lasted, with an interlude of peace, until 404 B.C. The trouble for the Peloponnesians was that the Athenians would not fight this war as Greeks had fought wars for 300 years. There would be no battle of a single afternoon which settled things. Pericles, as smart a Greek as there was, realized that this war would be different. He would avoid pitched battle with the numerically superior and skillful Spartans and Boeotians. So, the question becomes, how do you fight a war when one side rejects the time honored methods?

Well if you are as talented as the ancient Greeks, it does not take long to come up with ways. If the enemy does not come out to fight, then take the fight to the enemy; besiege his cities, destroy his farms, range far and wide to attack his interests. Form alliances against him, encourage treachery within his cities, even ask the Persians for help. War becomes total: it debases man and his institutions alike. Civilians are attacked and driven from their homes, civil war is actively encouraged, and anything goes if it might further the cause and harm the enemy. Above all, war becomes very expensive . . . but not expensive enough to discourage going to war again a few years later.

In the first part of the war, 431–421 B.C., sometimes referred to as the Archidamian War, the biggest losses for Athens came from a plague (430 to 428 B.C.) which killed one-quarter of the population, including Pericles, and the battle of Delium in 424 B.C. The battle of Delium is notable for several reasons. The Boeotians were led by Pagondas the Theban and he stacked the Theban phalanx 25 deep on the right side of his line. In the center were, from right to left, the Haliartians, the Coroneaeans, the Copaeans, some others from the area in the center, and on the left were the Thespians, Tanagraeans, and the Orchomenians. Cavalry and light troops were arrayed on each wing. The Boeotian army totalled 18,000—7,000 hoplites, 1,000 cavalry, and 10,000 light troops. The Athenians had 7,000 hoplites and far fewer light troops than the Boeotians, although the number is unknown to us.

The Athenians drew up for battle in the customary eight-rank depth. Hippocrates, the Athenian commander, was addressing the troops, but before he could finish, Pagondas led his troops down from the crest of the hill on which they were deployed. The wings of the two forces did not come to blows due to intervening water courses, but the rest of the two forces met everywhere along the line. The heavy Theban right pushed the Athenians back steadily, but the Athenians got the better of the Boeotian left as far as the center of the line. The Thespians especially were hard pressed, then surrounded as the troops next to them gave way. So confused became the fighting here, Thucydides tells us, that Athenian came to blows with Athenian in the narrow space. In this part of field, those Boeotians who could fled back to their troops on the right.

Pagondas, seeing the distress felt by his allies, and knowing that if they fell, then he would soon have Athenian hoplites at his back, did something original. He sent two squadrons of cavalry around a hill so that they could not be seen, and ordered them attack the Athenian right. He brought cavalry into the battle to change the situation. In this sense, it acted as a reserve, and although it is not clear that it was designated for that purpose from the beginning, it worked that way nevertheless. The Athenians, thinking that a new army was attacking, panicked and fled. Many were run down in the pursuit by cavalry and light infantry and only nightfall saved the rest. Some say that 10,000 Athenians were killed in the process.

Hanson tells us that among the Athenians who got away was a 45-year-old hoplite named Socrates who determinedly led a group of men to safety. In the battle also was cavalryman named Alcibiades, then aged 26. Nine years later, it was his failed strategy to invade Sicily which led to Athenian defeat. On this point Hanson poses two questions to his reader; how different would things be if Athens had won the Peloponnesian War, and what course would Western philosophy have taken if its founder had been killed 25 years before his historical demise? This, in turn, raises two questions in the author's mind: 1) should more philosophers be in combat? and 2) would we be better off if more politicians died this way?

By 421 B.C., a stalemate existed and so the belligerents agreed to the "Fifty Years' Peace." The reader will not be surprised to learn that the peace was neither peaceful nor lasted 50 years. The Persians helped the Spartans build a fleet, the Athenians failed utterly in Sicily, losing a fleet and 40,000 men in the process. They rebuilt their fleet and went on for another ten years, but in the end, Athens was closely blockaded by the Peloponnesians and surrendered.

There were many sieges in this war and the necessity of prosecuting them resulted in advances in the design of siege engines and siegecraft. There was a lot more killing in this war, too, and more of it was aimed at civilians. War was also much costlier, with the belligerents expending tens of millions of *drachmas*. Arms did not change much, but armor did. Protective armor became lighter as mobility came to be valued more than protection, or perhaps better stated, it came to be that one could protect oneself better if, while being hostile, one was more mobile and agile. The metal breast and backplate, never universal, would give way to leather and even heavily woven linen tunics augmented by metal scales. The utility of maneuver on the battlefield had been demonstrated at Delium and it would continue to be developed.

The great demand for manpower was met by mercenaries. Light and heavy infantry were represented and light infantry tactics evolved rapidly as the utility of these professional troops was demonstrated. These unarmored men were known as *peltasts* for their small shield, the *pelta,* and were armed with a pair of javelins; they could operate over all manner of terrain. The shield is usually described as being a wicker crescent covered with animal hide. It could be slung over the shoulder by a strap or held with one arm. *Peltasts'* standard battle tactic was to run up, hurl their javelins, and then run away before anyone could come to grips with them. They were recruited from Thrace and other mountainous country. Their utility was clearly demonstrated in 390 B.C., when Iphicrates, the Athenian general, led a band of highly-trained *peltasts* in hilly terrain against the Spartans and killed about 250 of them, or half their number.

Now to move our story along more rapidly, the innovations of Epaminondas are described elsewhere; here it only need be said that he advanced the notions of maneuver and concentration on the battlefield, and demonstrated them with devastating resolve at Leuctra (371 B.C.). The other aspect of his army that is important is that his soldiers were imbued with a strong sense of mission.

The next great change in military affairs came from the Macedonians. It was professional, it was based on a national sentiment, and it was led by a pupil of Epaminondas, the Philip II of Macedon. Heretofore considered to be worse than country bumpkins by many Greeks in the south, the Macedonians developed a revolutionary military system. What mattered to this king was the skill of the man who served in his army, not his rank or status. The Macedonian Army was paid all year long; it drilled all year long; it was expected to fight all year long, on any and all terrain, in every and any kind of weather. It did not have the societal encumbrances of the Spartans, it employed mercenaries, engineers, armorers, and all the other trades necessary to produce the most formidable army the world had ever seen. The most obviously different feature of this army was its phalanx.

There were two types of hoplite in the Macedonian Army, namely the *pezetaeri,* who carried the 20-foot *sarissa,* and the *hypastpistai* who carried a shorter spear, as well as swords. These latter were the "Foot Companions" and the complement to the "Companions," the elite aristocratic cavalrymen. The *pezetaeri* wielded their pike two-handed about six feet from the butt end. For protection, they carried a shield about two feet in diameter which was slung around the neck by a strap. They wore armored headgear, breastplate, and greaves, but it was all much reduced in weight, probably being made of leather or composite material such as leather and some metal. In time, some of this equipment may have been discarded.

The *hypastpist* was distinguished from the more numerous *pezetaeri* by his shorter spear, say about ten feet, and lighter armor. The units comprised of this type of soldier were highly trained and very mobile. They functioned as the hinge between the Companion cavalry and the heavier part of the phalanx. The phalanx itself was usually 16 ranks deep and because of the extraordinary length of the *sarissa*, the first five ranks of the phalanx produced offensive power in the form of spear-points. The Companions were more heavily armored than the infantry and they usually charged in a solid wedge or rhomboid formation. The Companions were typically employed on the right and the Thessalian cavalry, which in this army was not as heavily armored as the Companions, was on the left. For offensive power, the cavalry carried ten-foot spears and swords.

There were also light troops in the Macedonian Army, including *peltasts*, javelineers, slingers, and archers. They often covered the advance of the phalanx and then retired to the flanks or rear. They may have worn some light armor. Additional light troops known as *psiloi* travelled with the army as armed servants. They were often detailed to scout or to guard the baggage train.

On the battlefield, the phalanx's purpose was designed by Philip to act as a base and pin the enemy formation while the cavalry charged and punched a hole through the enemy formation. This was a radical departure from earlier phalangial tactics. It was in a sense Epaminondian, however, instead of the deep phalanx breaking through, it would be the cavalry. The punching of a hole made a flank where none had existed before, and into this the *hypastpists* led the rest of the army. If the Companions wheeled left after the breakthrough, they would pound the enemy against the anvil of the infantry.

The phalanx was designed and drilled to be used with other arms, and in the Macedonian Army, all arms were represented. This included a precursor to field artillery, using lightweight siege engines such as the *ballista*, which shot very large arrows a great distance.

The key thing to know about the new way of war is that movement, supported by coordinated fires, was used to dislocate the enemy's alignment. The resulting gaps were exploited by the cavalry. Discerning the correct moment to charge is what makes a great cavalry commander and Philip's son Alexander was just that. He knew when and where to attack and he led them to that spot. Once he had broken through he was able to keep control of the unit, reorganize it and direct it to where it was needed.

The Macedonian Army was not just deadly, it was big and it was fast. Philip did not allow wagons to travel with the army. All baggage was carried by horses, mules, donkeys, and men. This meant that the army could cover ground at a rate unmatched by other armies.

In 338 B.C., the Greeks found out just how deadly this army was. The old and new met at Chaeronea. A Theban/Athenian-led army of some 38,000, including 30,000 hoplites, collided with the future, here represented by 32,000 Macedonians. Philip planned to defeat the Greeks by creating a gap in the Athenian line. The skill of the Macedonians was displayed once the battle started. The phalanx conducted the most difficult of maneuvers, a fighting withdrawal. By drawing back, they enticed the Athenian hoplites forward, and this created a gap. The Macedonian cavalry exploited the gaps and the Greeks gave way. Athenian morale broke and they fled. Alexander, 18 years old, led his cavalry through a gap and surrounded the Thebans; their elite Sacred Band of 300 fought to the last man. Then began the pursuit phase and in this as well the Macedonians differed radically from the past. They pursued and meant it. Annihilation of the enemy was the goal, and this was another break with the past.

Pursuit pursued beyond the battlefield had strategic implications and Alexander not only understood it, but mastered it. Immediately after his victory over the Persians at Gaugamela, for example, Alexander set out after Darius III and did not slacken his pace until nightfall. He rested a few hours and set off again. He knew that once he had Darius, he would have no more big battles to fight. Alexander and the Macedonian Army set the standard for war in the West (and even a big chunk of the East) for the next 160 years.

## Rome

The next and last aspect of this episodic survey of the ancient world is the Roman way of war. The Romans produced a military system of genius because it was just that, a system. It was one that did not need excellent commanders to win; one that could sustain huge losses and replenish them rapidly; one that harnessed Greek ingenuity to Roman aggression and dogged discipline. Centuries later, the army sustained the Roman Empire when there was little left of it that was Roman. They created a concept of order throughout their society which the chaotic Greeks, being Greek, did not favor. This is what made Romans Roman.

In the age of Servius Tullius (579–534 B.C.), the Romans fought in a traditional hoplite phalanx. Society was ordered into five military classes, from top to bottom. The wealthiest, Class I, were required to provide the full panoply, while the poorest, Class V, was kind of come just as you unfortunately are, with perhaps a sling and a few rocks. Men were organized in centuries of 100 and it is believed that there were enough Class men to produce 40 centuries. Beyond this, the details, such as they are known, do not concern us for it is some time hence before the Romans advanced the art of war.

The strength of the Roman Army of the Republic was its soldiers. Made up of farmers, which is to say of the middle classes, and led by men of similar class, the Roman legionary was a tough, well-disciplined, tactically-adroit fighter. Romans took war and their army seriously. Accordingly, it was these men who commanded the tactical units of the army and were elected by the soldiery. These early armies were not long-standing professional forces, however. They were made up of farmers who had to farm.

The singular feature about the Roman army of the Republic was its practice of regular castramentation. Male readers should not wince at this idea; this is not as painful as it sounds. Every day, at the end of the march, usually about noon, the army built a fortified camp, regularly laid out, with sentries posted around the perimeter at short intervals. To facilitate castramentation, each man carried among his roughly 80 pounds of equipment a couple of stakes which were used to erect a palisade on top of the rampart thrown up around the camp. The benefits of castramentation were many. The men could be easily accounted for, discipline was easily maintained, and the integrity of the force was preserved. If the coming day's battle did not go well, the army could withdraw to its camp and survive to fight again.

As a result of the reforms of Marcus Camillus, by about 250 B.C., the army had developed a new type of organization—the Legion. The youngest and least trained legionaries were the *velites,* recruited from the poor, who functioned as light infantry. They were unarmored, threw javelins, and may have carried a shield and sword. The *hastati* and *princeps* were equally-armed heavy infantry. They wore body armor, carried shields, a short sword (*gladius*), and *pila* (special spears, about which more later). The *hastati*—the term itself being a holdover from earlier times to describe soldiers who were armed with the *hasta,* a thrusting spear—were experienced soldiers in their early twenties who occupied the foremost deployed ranks of the legion. The second lines were made up of the *princeps,* who were men in their late twenties and early thirties. The third line, the *triarii,* were the most experienced and steadiest men; they wore armor, usually mail, and carried a thrusting spear of 10 to 12 feet, along with a shield.

The basic unit of a legion was the "maniple," formed from two centuries. The one in front was called the *prior* and the one behind call the *posterior.* By this time, a century was 60 to 80 men, so a maniple was 120 to 160 men for the *hastati* and *princeps.* The maniples of the *triarii* were 60 men. The next size up was the cohort, which consisted of three maniples or six centuries, 480 men. So far so good. There was also cavalry but not much of it; a *turma* was 30 horsemen. The confusing thing is that as Roman history progresses, the sizes of all these units change. The legion, for example, was 4,500 to 5,000 men in the Republic, but by the late empire, it was smaller. Anyway, those are all the names you will have to know. The astute reader may be wondering why the *princeps* formed the second battle line and not the first, and why the most experienced men, the *triarii*, were deployed in the back.

The men at the front are busy fighting and sword play is deadly serious, exhausting work; therefore, one wants the most physically-fit men starting off. The *princeps*, who are in the prime of life and experienced, are in a position to support the *hastati* morally and physically. The *triarii* are the most experienced and occupy the third line because they are the least likely to give way. The Romans understood that the basic material of war is man and a basic understanding of his nature was necessary to get the most out of him. In battle, it is not the men busy fighting who are the first to run away, it is the men in the middle and at the back who are *not* fighting and are imagining what is in store for them. It is on them that the terrible noise tells the most and because they cannot see very much, they have little idea of what is happening. It is they who have the motive and the opportunity to flee. Thus, the Romans wisely chose to employ their steadiest veterans in the third line. The author suspects that the *triarii* may also been used to push the columns or lines forward, in the fashion of noncommissioned officers in the Prussian and other professional armies of the eighteenth century. This is just speculation, of course.

Roman tactical formations remain somewhat unclear. How we are told they looked does not support how they apparently fought. Here is what we know: the heavy infantry, already described, was arrayed in three lines. The first line was about six ranks deep, which makes it 20 files across. The maniples, we are told, were arranged in a *quincunx* or checkerboard pattern, with the space between the maniples of the first line being equal to the area occupied by a maniple. Think of it this way, red are the maniples and black the spaces. Similarly to the checkerboard, the maniples of the second line cover the gaps left in the first line. The third line covered the gaps of the second line. In this way, a continuous line could be formed by the advance of the second line or the retirement of the first line. Why do it this way? The short answer is because it is easier to maneuver such a formation over broken ground and maintain alignment. Now one does not have to worry about gaps because they are built in to the system. It is possible to advance a line of troops in a straight line across a parade square, but across a field with some slope here and there, and the task becomes far more difficult.

This leads us to the next problem. How did this army fight? No one really knows that, either. Here is what some suggest: first, the *velites* ran out and threw whatever missiles they had and then run back through the gaps in the formation. The Romans advance, and at some point, they form a line to maximize combat power. The maniples of the *hastati* advance in column and the front maniple moves to the right, allowing the rear maniple to move up. Now a solid line is presented and it advances to *pilum*-throwing range. The men will be in open order and slightly offset to facilitate pilum hurling. As they move forward, they throw. The author would throw the light one first, then once a bit closer, the heavy one for more effect. Then collision occurred and the hard work of killing with the sword begins. Men from the second through sixth ranks circulate through the fighting line as necessary. It is also possible that the entire line would be withdrawn for rest. After a time, the *hastati* would retire back through the intervals between the *princeps'* maniples, first the *posterior*, then the *prior*. The *princeps* would then repeat the maneuvers of the *hastati* and engage the enemy. If the enemy has not been defeated by this point, then the *triarii* would be brought up either to force the issue or cover the retirement of the army. Now if this is how it happened, and it would be elegant if it did, it could only be possible with highly-disciplined troops and, perhaps, a cooperative enemy.

A counter suggestion is that the *quincunx* formation was an actual combat formation, although the size of the intervals may have varied. The risk of penetration was not an issue because of the coverage afforded by the second and third lines. Enemy troops who rushed through the *hastati*'s intervals would be engaged by the *princeps*, if the *princeps* were close enough. This interpretation assumes that the battles were not quick and furious, but long and drawn out. The exhausting nature of hand-to-hand fighting meant that it could not go on for long. If no decision was reached on the first clash, then the combatants would draw apart and rest before resuming, the battle thereby taking on an aspect of primitive ritualism. This, so the counter-theory holds, is the only way to prolong fighting which is by its nature short, stressful, terrifying, and tiring. Did the two battle lines jeer, gesticulate, and then resume fighting?

One advantage to the *quincunx* is that if the enemy fights in a continuous line, then he has to break his formation to push into the intervals and this opens up his flanks. If the enemy comes on at a rush, as did the

Gauls, then they have their attack channeled and possibly brought under counterattack from the flanks.

Eventually, starting in the second century B.C., the Roman armies did become professionalized. Marius reformed the army following the disastrous defeat at Arausio (105 B.C.). He made the cohort the basic unit of the army with ten cohorts of 400 to 500 men forming a legion. The cohort had a frontage of 50 men and so was eight to ten ranks deep. It operated in open and close order for fighting and maneuvering. The cohorts were arrayed in the checkerboard pattern with a cohort-sized interval between cohorts. The weapons of the cohort did not differ, however; the *pilum* and *gladius* were still used. The cohort made it easier to pass orders as well. There were only ten cohorts to a legion instead of 30 maniples.

Most importantly, the legions became permanent establishments and the men who served in them were the landless poor, for whom soldiering became a way of life. This allowed for the institutionalization of knowledge, and the result was an army that developed technical expertise and had a wide range of specialists. The only drawback was that the legionary was no longer a farmer with some place to go after he was discharged. He now depended on his general for his future . . . an arrangement which was to have dire consequences in coming years.

The Romans did not develop an adequate cavalry force and recruited foreign horsemen and auxiliaries such as archers and slingers. The heavy infantry which won the battles were Roman and after the Social Wars, the former Italian allies were made citizens of Rome. This, then, was the Roman army in the basic form it would keep for the next 400 years.

# Equipment

## Longest Spear: The Sarissa

The Macedonian *sarissa* is the longest spear used in antiquity and the longest ever used in war. It has been described as a pike by some scholars because of its length and that it was wielded with two hands. In this section, the terms "spear" and "pike" will be used interchangeably. The ancients are themselves fairly consistent in their descriptions of the weapon's length, stating it to be at its uppermost length between 14 and 16 cubits, or 21 to 24 feet. This has led to a lot of wrangling by scholars, which continues to this day, who believe that such a spear would be too big to be used effectively. Some scholars offer the theory that the ancient writers meant feet, not cubits, and over the years mistakes in copying have led to our misunderstanding. If this were the case, and the author does not believe it to be, a spear of 16 Greek feet would yield a spear 18.16 feet long, still pretty big. Be that as it may, in the Middle Ages, pikes, which we have today in museums, were nearly 19 feet long, so a sarissa of 21 feet is not a length too outrageous to contemplate. It has been suggested that the 24-foot sarissa was for training purposes only, and that makes a lot of sense when one considers that the Macedonians did a lot of training.

Here is what we *do* know: The *sarissa*, regardless of length, had two points, a spearhead made of iron and a butt spike. The latter was bigger than the spear point and provided a secondary weapon if the *sarissa* broke; it provided also about 2.33 pounds of weight at the end, which helped balance the spear. The weapon was held with two hands, as has been mentioned, and the pikeman's grip was about six feet from the butt end with the forward hand—which would be the left—and the rear grip would be two and one half to three feet from the butt. The weight of the sarissa depended upon its size, but if an 18-footer was about 15 pounds, then a 21-footer was close to 20 pounds.

The choice wood for this weapon was ash, which is very hard. The shaft's diameter at either end was just over one inch. Archeological evidence has revealed that the *sarissa* may have been made of two equal lengths of wood and fixed together at the mid-point by an iron cylinder. This tells us several things. The diameter, of what the author will call the joint cylinder, was the same as that of the sockets of the spear point and the butt spike. This would have made it easier to repair broken spears because one did not need to find extremely long pieces of straight wood to shape. It is also possible that the use of the iron joint cylinder and two shorter pieces of wood would cut down appreciably any vibration that the *sarisser* would experience when the spearhead crashed against its target. If the reader is wondering, "was the *sarissa* broken down for ease of transport?," the author thinks that a very good question.

The phalanx which formed up to use this weapon was traditionally 16 ranks deep and the compactness of the order would determine the number of ranks whose pikes poked out the front. If a man in the files had three feet between him and the man in front, then the spears of the first five rows could be brought to bear. Compared to the old hoplites with their seven- to nine-foot spears, the *sarisser's* pike gave him an eight to ten foot reach advantage. This meant that the Macedonian phalanx had two ranks more of spears adding offensive power. The next

11 ranks would keep their spears in the air slanting them forward. Additionally, the phalanx could be drawn up in various orders with the distances between the files ranging from two paces to half a pace. This would alter the frontage of the phalanx and it was done to suit particular tactical and geographical situations. Obviously, the *sarisser* (not a real term) could not carry the old fashioned round shield, but it is thought that he carried a two-foot diameter shield, which may have been slung on a strap around his neck or from the shoulder. Philip reputedly picked the tallest and strongest of his soldiers to carry the *sarissa*.

So how long was the *sarissa?* The author believes that the lengths would vary especially once repairs were made on campaign and men would have to rely on local resources. At the start of the campaign, therefore, when everybody had a nice shiny new *sarissa*, it was probably about 21 feet, or 14 cubits, or 6.3 meters (20 feet 9 inches); however you measure it, it was the longest spear ever used in combat.

## First Armored Fighting Vehicles: Chariots

Somewhere after the discovery of how to work copper and before the same was discerned for iron—that is, around 2,500 B.C.—Sumerians developed the chariot. By 1800 B.C., the chariot had been refined and it was widely used by several diverse armies. Egyptians had them, Hittites had them, even Assyrians and Chinese had them.

In modern terms, we would call the chariot a "platform" for "weapons systems." Depending on where they were used they were drawn by one, two, or three horses and were manned by a driver and a weaponeer. The latter discharged javelins or arrows and in some cases, a third man was involved holding a shield to protect the other two from attack from behind. Assyrian heavy chariots carried four spearmen and light chariots carried archers. Maneuverability and speed were essential for these vehicles to be effective. This meant that certain technological features had to be in place, namely spoked wheels, which were light weight, especially when compared to solid wheels, and they had to be mounted on a hub and axle in a way that reduced friction. It took a skilled wheelwright to make a wheel that was light, strong, and balanced. Some chariot wheels had sharp blades attached which, as we all know, is the favorite camera shot in all gladiator movies. The wheels and axle had to support several hundred pounds of chariot, men, armor, and weapons. A harness had to be developed which allowed the horse to carry some of the weight of the chariot. Weapon-wise, you had to have a weapon already deadly enough to make the whole expense of a

The world's first armored fighting vehicle—the chariot. This three-man team of Assyrians includes the driver, the weaponeer, and the man who held a shield to protect the other two from attack.
© Bettmann/CORBIS/MAGMA

chariot worthwhile. Enter the compound bow. Development of the bow added to the effectiveness of this system. The compound bow— made from wood, bone, and sinew—allowed the length of the bow to be shortened without sacrificing its power. This meant that the weapon could be wielded more easily in the chariot than a long wooden bow and the archer could deliver arrows faster and take cover quicker within the chariot. It was also harder to hit him when he was tearing across the land in a speeding chariot. Chariots and charioteers were most vulnerable was when the horses were unhitched, therefore, to protect themselves, they raised square earthen field works for shelter.

These were expensive machines to build and to operate—anyone who knows about horses realizes that they eat *a lot*—and required specific conditions for their use. Fabrication required raw materials including copper and tin (to make bronze), and these were rarely found together. Construction and even maintenance required the services of skilled artisans, including wheelwrights, bowmakers, fletchers, and metallurgists. Of course, good horses were also required, as were trainers who could make the teams work well together. The chariot was, in this period, an ideal weapon in the Middle East, Steppes, China, and India, but in forested or rocky areas, it was worthless.

Was their value in war worth the expense of creating them? Initially, it was. On the right terrain and against lightly-armed infantry which did not have metallic armor, it was, when used in sufficient numbers, a formidable weapon. Through its use, elites seized power in China, the Indus Valley, Egypt, and much of the Middle East. So what happen to end this happy state of affairs for the charioteer? Iron. The ability to make iron may have appeared about 1400 B.C. in eastern Asia Minor, and by 1200 B.C., it was starting to spread fast. Iron was easier to make than bronze, iron ore was more widespread and so it was cheap. All that was needed to smelt it was charcoal.

The availability of cheap metal transformed society in general and warfare in particular. Plentiful iron farm implements expanded agriculture and that created wealth. Plentiful iron-tipped weapons and armor meant that all kinds of people—farmers, herders, and assorted barbarians—could challenge the military elite, chariots or not. Simply put, the charioteers were overwhelmed by superior numbers of well-equipped raiders, and by about 900 B.C., by the first cavalry revolution. Think about it, two or three horses—expensive; a chariot—expensive; wheels for the chariot—they better be nice and round. The chariot could be armored and sometimes the horses as well, which was also expensive. For the price of two or three horses and two or three men, you get a weapons system that can only be used on flat or prepared ground and has only one guy throwing stuff at your enemy. If, on the other hand, you put a man on each horse, give him a bow and arrows, then you have multiplied the quantity of your "weapons systems," increased your tactical flexibility, and done it without shelling out the big *shekels* for a chariot.

These considerations, however, were either not readily apparent or they were ignored for reasons other than military utility. For example, the noble Greeks of the *Iliad* rode to the battle on chariot, dismounted, and fought on foot in heroic fashion. That this was so in Greece from the sociologic and geographic perspective should not be much of a surprise. There is not much terrain in Greece where massed chariots could be employed. In Greek warfare and the western tradition, fighting chariots, as opposed to limousine chariots, were the stuff of weird easterners.

The last time chariots were used in an important battle was Gaugamela (331 B.C.), when Alexander defeated Darius—and the chariots may as well have not showed up.

# Best Javelin of the Ancient World:
## The Roman Pilum

The most innovative of the javelins was the Roman *pilum.* Most Roman infantry carried two. The pyramidal, often barbed, head of the spear was made of soft iron and connected to the shaft by a slender neck which terminated in a socket. The length of the iron part of the javelin was two to three feet, the length of the wooden shaft was about four feet, making a weapon of up to seven feet in length. Plutarch tells us that the socket was affixed to the shaft with a wooden rivet.

Here is how this weapon worked: The small pyramidal point, because of its shape and the weight behind it, had good penetrative power. Once stuck in a shield, or person, or animal, the slender neck would bend or the weapon itself could break at the juncture of the socket and shaft. This explains the wooden rivet. Either way the weapon could not be thrown back, a definite plus. Moreover, if the pilum was

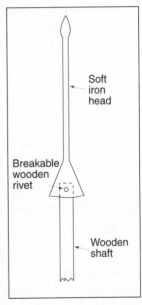

Roman legionary with with *pilum* and sheathed *gladius* (left)
© *Bettmann/CORBIS/ MAGMA*

Schematic of the business end of a pilum (below)

Soft iron head

Breakable wooden rivet

Wooden shaft

stuck in a shield or breastplate, it hampered the mobility of the victim. The length of the iron shank made it difficult for the opponent to reach beyond the metal part of the pilum to hack at the shaft. After the battle the pila could be repaired, the bent shanks straightened and the wooden rivets replaced.

This weapon served the Roman legionary for over 500 years. The *pilum* suited Roman offensive tactics which eschewed the long spears of the Greek phalanx and two-handed cutting sword of the Celts. The Romans preferred to throw their *pila* and close quickly with their short, double-edged cutting and thrusting swords. The maximum effective range of the *pilum* in the hands of an average legionary was about 30 yards, which means that the *pila* were probably thrown at less than that distance. It is reported also that of the two *pila* carried, one was heavier than the other. Which one would you throw first? Or would you throw the lighter one and keep the heavier one for jabbing?

## Best Sword of the Ancient World:
### Roman Gladius

Roman infantry formations were noted for closing with the enemy and killing with their swords. The *gladius* (yes, as in *gladiator*) was the sword of choice. The best known variant is the "Spanish" sword. The length of the blade varied, but it was no longer than two feet and less than two and one-half inches in width. It is characterized by a long tapering point and double edges, making it an effective thrusting and cutting weapon. It was made from high quality metal which retained a sharp edge. This sword served the legionary well from the third century B.C. Later versions, introduced in the first century A.D., were of similar dimensions, but the long tapering point was replaced with a shorter point and the blade's edges ran parallel to each other for more of its length.

Roman cavalry would have used a longer sword which allowed them to reach infantry or other horsemen. This version, known as the spatha,was as much as three feet long and an inch and three-quarters in width.

## Most Extreme Machine of the Ancient World:
### Demetrius Poliorcetes and the Helepolis of Rhodes, 305–304 B.C.—"Go Big or Go Home"

In the Helenistic Age, after Alexander, almost everything military got bigger. Armies got bigger, and the amount of money needed for armies got bigger. Siege engines got bigger and none was bigger than the

Helepolis, or "city-taker." We should expect this from Demetrius Poliorcetes because you do not get a nickname like "The Besieger" for no reason. During his siege of Rhodes, Demetrius constructed several siege engines. At first, he tried to capture the harbor. If he succeeded there, then he could cut off the city from its seaborne trade in grain and starve them into submission. He built two penthouses, one for his stone throwers and one for his bolt-shooters. Each of these was placed on two cargo boats which were fastened together. He also built two four-story towers which were similarly mounted on boats. The tops of these towers floated floated higher than the tops of the harbor walls. A long spike-studded boom was added to protect the siege engines and their platforms from enemy ships.

The Rhodians countered by building their walls higher, placing counterbattery catapults on the mole, and building platforms on some ships so that they could mount catapults on them. Demetrius enjoyed some

The Helepolis of Rhodes—
Most extreme machine of the
ancient world (Rendering by
Michael Strong)

early success by establishing an artillery battery on the end of the mole, then bringing the Rhodian wall-builders under attack from his ship-borne bolt throwers, and wrecking the enemy catapults with counter-battery fire from his stone throwers. The Rhodians, in their counterat-tacks, managed to destroy three of the floating machines, one by fire, including two by ramming. Demetrius must have sat down at this point and said to himself, "what I really need is a bigger floating weapon." So he constructed a huge floating battery, and huge means *huge*. It was three times as tall and three times as wide as the earlier models. Unfor-tunately, a storm wrecked it as he was bringing it into the harbor. The Rhodians took advantage of the storm to attack the mole and capture the battery Demetrius had established.

Demetrius was undaunted. He decided that the siege would have to proceed by land in the time-honored manner. At this point, Demetrius must have sat down again and said to himself, "I really gotta get a big-ger siege engine." Enter the Rhodian Helepolis—it was bigger than the previous big boy he had built for the siege of Salamis on Cyprus. This baby was *gigantic*. Converting from cubits, the machine was about 140 feet high, measured 72 feet square at the base, and tapered to 30-feet square at the top. It had nine floors and two internal staircases, one for going up and the other for coming down. The frame was built of squared timbers, tied with iron bars and the front and sides were planked and covered with iron plates. The structure moved on eight independently pivoting, solid wood wheels 15 feet in diameter and about a yard thick. These were covered with iron. On the bottom floor, he had three catapults, two firing 180-pound stones and one firing 60-pound ones. Floor two had three 60-pound catapults; floors three, four, five, six, and seven each had two catapults firing 30-pound stones. Floors eight and nine had two dart throwers each. The firing ports for each piece were mechanically operated and the shutters were padded with wool and covered in leather to protect them from enemy missiles. The weight of this magnificent machine? About 150 tons. It was manned by about 200 men. Did they call themselves Helepolisists? The cost? Well, if you have to ask, you can't afford one. One estimate is in the hun-dreds of thousands of *drachmas*. It was designed by Epimachus of Athens whose motto must have been "more is more." The ancients tell us that it required at least 3,400 men to move it, but it is unclear whether it was that many at once or perhaps that many in total working in shifts, some inside and others outside.

The purpose of this machine was to sweep the battlements and knock down the walls of the fortress. Covered galleries were built to protect the troops who had to move up to serve the machines and perform other functions. These galleries led to two penthouses which were built to house and protect the men serving the two battering rams. These were not your garden-variety battering rams by the way. Each of the rams was 180 feet long and manned by 1,000 men. The rams were capped with iron and moved on rollers. To those who question the dimensions of the rams, the author can only say that given the little you already know about Demetrius, how could you doubt it? The more men who pushed, the faster the ram could be accelerated; the heavier the ram and its acceleration, the greater the force that could be generated; the greater the force, the greater the damage to the target.

So, how did things go? Demetrius cleared a 650-yard approach to the walls to accommodate everything. The plan was to take on seven towers and the walls in between them. The Helepolis worked well in clearing the battlements, and the rams went to work. The usual mining and counter-mining went on as the Rhodians did everything they could to stop the Helepolis. They also built crescent walls inside the fortress to block any assault troops who might come through any breaches made by the machine.

The Rhodians managed, at one point, to dislodge some of the plates on the Helepolis which would have made it susceptible to fire. Demetrius withdrew the machine for repairs, and then sent it back in. The besiegers took down one tower and a section of curtain wall, but came up against the first crescent-shaped wall. As other parts of the walls weakened, the Rhodians continued to build crescent walls and dug a deep ditch to impede the progress of the siege engines into the city. The rams then brought down two more sections of curtain wall and isolated one of the towers. Its defenders fought on, however, and despite the losses the besiegers inflicted, Demetrius could make no headway. Demetrius tried one more assault by 1,500 men, but the Rhodians beat them back.

This operation against Rhodes was something of a private action on the part of Demetrius and those who hoped to profit from the sacking of Rhodes. Apparently, the Rhodians drew much sympathy from the Greek world for their courageous stand against this form of piracy. Whether he thought that this action was too unpopular to continue or that he just could not win, he called off the siege. The man who must have lived by the motto "go big or go home," went home.

What happened to the Helepolis and the other machines? Well the metal was collected and used to create the Colossus of Rhodes, of course. This statue of Apollo by the harbor entrance was over 90 feet tall or about the same size as the Statue of Liberty. Some 50 years or so later, the Colossus came down in an earthquake. One historian reports that in

672 AD., the Arabs, who had captured the island earlier, sold the statue to a Jew from Emesa who needed 900 camels to carry off the scrap.

# Personalities

## Greatest Tactician: Epaminondas

Epaminondas was the greatest tactician produced by the Greek city-states. He was Theban-born in about 418 B.C., and died in the battle of Mantinea in 362, at the moment of victory against the Spartans. So hated was he by the Spartans that they raised a statue to the man who killed him. Why was he so hated by Sparta? Epaminondas had made them look bad, not just on the battlefield, but in their own homes. As with most bone-deep enmities, there is a lot of history behind it, but rather than start in with the tactical and strategic excellence he demonstrated, let's turn to the personal.

Apparently, Epaminondas despised Sparta and all things Spartan, but none more than the practice of *helotage*. The Spartan subjugation of the Messenians, the enslavement of fellow Greeks, and the means by which they repressed these unfortunates, which included periodic culling, that is, killing, of the most able, was something he would not abide. Sparta had also occupied Thebes. Following victory in the Peloponnesian War (404 B.C.), Sparta established hegemony over Greece and then supported the Ionian Greeks against Persia. This came about because Tisaphernes, a loathsome customer from the Greek perspective, the *satrap*, or governor, of Lydia and Caria, was punishing the Ionians for their support of Cyrus "not the great," more commonly knows as Cyrus "the Younger." It was pay back on the part of the Persians.

To divert from our story for a moment, in 401 B.C., Cyrus the Younger led an army of about 50,000 to overthrow his brother Artaxerxes II, who had inherited the Persian throne. This army included 13,000 Greek mercenaries, of which some 10,600 were hoplites. This is the famous story immortalized by Xenophon in *The Anabasis*, or *The March Up Country*, one of the best military histories ever written. This force, made up mostly of Spartans, marched all the way to Cunaxa, near Babylon, where battle was joined. There, the Greeks won their side of the combat but Cyrus was killed and the rest of the army legged it. The Greeks then drove off the rest of the Persians at the cost of one wounded hoplite. Now they were 1,000 miles from anywhere friendly and their senior officers were murdered at a feast organized by Tisaphernes. The Greeks, therefore, decided to would march and fight their way back to the Greek colony of Trapezus on the Black Sea, and make their way from there back to Greece. When all this was going on, Epaminondas was still a teenager.

To return to story, the Spartans thus came to be at war with Persia from 400 to 387 B.C. During desultory campaigning in Asia Minor, in 395 B.C., the Greeks back home had had enough of Spartan arrogance and saw an opportunity to do something about it. The result was the Corinthian War (395–387 B.C.). Athens, Argos, Thebes, Corinth, and some other cities banded together to ally with Persia against Sparta. When it came to alliances, the Greeks were consistently inconsistent. As Athens started to recover some of her former colonies and rebuild her famous Long Walls, the Persians began to secretly give assistance to Sparta lest her allies get too strong and too soon. By 387 B.C., everybody had had enough and peace broke out. Persia was to be a nominal suzerain of Greece and the belligerents were to try and get along. Greeks being Greeks, this meant that from 387–379 B.C., Sparta tried to crush whatever challenges came along and placed occupation garrisons where she could. This is how Spartans came to be in Thebes and this gave the Spartans the opportunity to offend the Thebans so egregiously that they would foment a rebellion.

The opportunity came in 382 B.C., when the Spartans occupied the Theban *Cadmea*, a sacred place which represented the spiritual and political center of Thebes. A group of democracy-loving Thebans in exile in Athens began their planning and by 379 B.C., Pelopidas and Melon led a group of patriots who overthrew the garrison and eliminated of any collaborators they could find as well. Pelopidas, of whom we will hear more later, was Epaminondas's good friend and an exceptional general in his own right. Epaminondas participated in this uprising and helped establish a real democracy in Thebes, one that expanded the franchise and provided a dynamic drive that benefited Thebes immensely.

The expansion of democracy in Thebes (Boeotia, really.) had military ramifications. It meant that the Boeotians could field more hoplites than Sparta or Athens. To prevent a maturation of Boeotian power from her budding, broad-based democracy, Sparta launched four invasions of Boeotia, the last in 371 B.C. All failed.

Epaminondas was a Pythagorean. Followers of this way of life believed in the transmigration of souls: animals, as a part of human nature, were not to be eaten, for example. Pythagoreans' view of the cosmos was heliocentric, sort of, and metaphysically speaking, they believed that the essence of anything could be reduced to numbers. Harmony and higher truths about the universe could be discerned through mathematical revelation. The Pythagoreans believed in equality of the sexes, and were devoted to music, probably because of the mathematical implications. Private property did not exist between friends; they disdained materialism and avoided alcohol. Plutarch, however, tells us that Epaminondas drank vinegary wine when out to remind himself what he had at home. Epaminondas never married, was childless, and reportedly owned only one cloak. On the days it was washed, he stayed in his house, naked. He led an ascetic existence, never sought to enrich himself or kill any more men than necessary.

This gives us something of the man, now what about the general?

In the course of a summer day in July 371 B.C., near the town of Leuctra, Epaminondas led an underdog army of the Boeotian League against the Spartans who had invaded Boeotia, determined to destroy the Theban-led organization. In the course of the fighting, Epaminondas's troops killed 400 Spartans in one afternoon, more than had fallen in the wars against Persians or the Peloponnesian War combined. Furthermore, they did it with an army that was smaller than their opponents'. The Spartans would never forget something like that. (See page 72.)

So how did Epaminondas do it? He changed in hoplite tactics. Frank Adcock, the classical historian, noted that Epaminondas changed, "the face of hoplite battle by a tactical reform which ranks with, or above, the oblique order of Frederick the Great." (More about Frederick elsewhere.) Adcock concludes his assessment by saying that this innovation was, "like most great innovations in war, simple but demanding much skill in application." (Adcock, *The Greek and Macedonian Art of War*, p. 25) A deep column of phalangial infantry was not new, but Epaminondas made his 50 ranks deep and put it on the left side of the line, opposite the Spartans. He then echeloned his line back and to the right. Heretofore, the best troops occupied the right side of the line. Essentially, Epaminondas was betting that he could win the battle on the left side of his line before it could be lost on the right. He certainly had the raw material with which to make such a decision. The Thebans were noted in antiquity for their robust constitutions and great physicality. Their strength and prowess was developed through grinding farm labor and wrestling. Epaminondas was known as "Iron Gut" to his men.

Epaminondas had perceived the essence of tactics: he knew that the crucial place on the battlefield was opposite the Spartans. Crush them, and the battle was won. Crush them, and the image of Spartan invincibility was destroyed. With the Spartans' force destroyed, he would be one step closer to destroying Sparta itself. This is a departure from the warfare of the time. Leuctra was not to be an afternoon's battle fought by hoplites who then moseyed home to farm and hearth; it was the opening salvo in a clash of cultures. In this it was modern; indeed, it was *Western*. Just as the Allies in World War II imposed a lasting peace on the Axis by killing their people, occupying their countries, and imposing their culture, so, too, would Epaminondas.

The army with which Epaminondas and his right-hand man, Pelopidas, would do this was drawn from all aspects of Boeotian society. It was thus a democratic army and this makes it modern. Twenty-one centuries later it would be called a nation-in-arms. It would march for an idea, the liberation of the *helots*, and not for conquest. His campaign in the Peloponnesus would typify what would later come to be called "the indirect approach," which is now seen as the zenith of strategic achievement, that is, the dislocation of the enemy by maneuver.

How did it come about? Inspired by the defeat of Sparta at Leuctra and the death of all those Spartans, several cities in the Peloponnesus thought the time might be right to break away from Spartan control and establish democracies and federations. Epaminondas and Pelopidas thought that this was a good idea and as *beotarchs* (elected leaders), they were in a position to do something about it. In December of 370 B.C., Epaminondas gathered an army which eventually numbered 70,000 from various cities and marched through Sparta's province, Laconia, burning and looting as they went. The vaunted Spartan army did not oppose them. This was the first army to march into Laconia in 600 years.

After marching through Laconia to its southernmost point and destroying Sparta's harbor, Epaminondas took his army into Messenia in January and freed over 200,000 *helots*; they then proceeded to lay the foundations, literally, for the fortified cities of Messene, Mantinea, and Megalopolis. Once these places were walled, they could defend themselves against a Spartan resurgence. Messene, behind its five miles of walls, was laid out on a grid as befitted a city founded by a Pythagorean. The walls were paid for, in part, by the loot plundered from Sparta.

This campaign of liberation accomplished other objectives as well, namely establishing Thebes as the first city of Greece. This should not distract , however, from the greater significance of the event. Victor Hanson points out that this army represented four percent of the mainland population and when the *helots* and other Peloponnesians are added in, then one in six Greeks was involved. It was a quite remarkable force, which accomplished an unprecedented mission.

Sparta was not eliminated from the scene by the actions of Epaminondas, but its continued decline was assured. Thebes was now in its ascendency, but amongst the rest of the Greek states it was business as usual. Greeks being Greeks. Pelopidas was killed at the battle of Cynoscephalae fighting against the Thessalians when he advanced ahead of his troops in the melee. Epaminondas was killed at the battle of Mantinea in 362 B.C. fighting forces from Athens, Sparta, and disaffected members of the Arcadian League, a league founded by Thebes as a counter to Sparta. Once again, and for the last time, Epaminondas's tactics of the echeloned, or oblique, approach and the heavy left wing overwhelmed his opponents. He placed his cavalry in a deep formation as well as in front of his left wing and it seems that he placed the Sacred Band in a wedge ahead of the deep phalanx as well. The enemy was arranged in the following manner: the Mantineans—because it was their turf—had the place of honor on the right of the line; next came the Spartans; and then the Athenians. Each wing of this army was protected by cavalry. Epaminondas realized that the right, or unshielded, flank of his column was susceptible to attack by the Athenian left if they were to wheel to their right. The Athenians would have this opportunity because the center and right of the Boeotian line was stepped back a great distance. To guard against this possibility, Epaminondas sent units of cavalry and infantry well ahead of the main force to a rise in the plain, ordering them to attack the Athenians in the rear if they tried any funny business. They did not.

One would think that after Leuctra, the Spartans would have been able to figure out what was coming next, but they did not. The Theban cavalry drove off the enemy cavalry and Epaminondas led the hoplite wedge into the enemy line. They broke through, scattering the enemy. It was during this pursuit phase of the battle as he led his Thebans that Epaminondas was struck down by a spear thrust. When the news spread of his being mortally wounded, the drive went out of the army and the troops fell back. As he lay dying he asked for his successors, Iolaidas and Daiphantus. Upon being told that they had died in the fighting, he said that Thebes should make peace.

The uniqueness of Epaminondas, beyond his idiosyncrasies, rests in that he was a tactical innovator and strategic savant.

There is one last noteworthy item to be mentioned. In a bid to stop Athens spreading her influence into Macedonia, or rather, in making sure that the influence in Macedon was Theban, Pelopidas marched north and compelled Macedon to join the Theban alliance. To secure good behavior, some young Macedonian nobles were sent to Thebes for security. One of them was Philip, the future king of Macedon and father of Alexander the Great. He was schooled under Epaminondas himself and he showed, a few years later, that he was a keen student indeed of the Theban school of war.

## Greatest Military Leader:
### Alexander the Great, 356–323 B.C.

Describing Alexander encourages the use of superlatives—greatest commander, worst thug, cleverest tactical innovator, most loutish drunken killer, most brilliant strategic thinker, most loathsome mass murderer, and so on. Depending on whom one reads, these are the views presented. Of course, anyone who has spent 15 minutes reading a book on the ancient world will soon see that none of the men who fought the wars and led their states were sensitive, deeply caring types who were committed to genuine consideration for others.

Regardless of one's assessment of his character, however, Alexander was the greatest military leader of the ancient world, and probably the greatest in history. Is there a twentieth-century general one would rank above him? Who in the nineteenth century? Only Napoleon can be mentioned. Who in the eighteenth: Frederick? Marlborough? The seventeenth can boast Gustavus Adolphus, who was very good but not great. What about the centuries before that? True, there was Genghis Khan in the thirteenth. Charlemagne, ummh, Saladin or Suleiman, Attila, all preceded the Great Khan, but none of them rival Alexander. Julius Caesar was a very lucky fellow (up to a point), but is unlikely to have surpassed the Big A, even without Brutus and the boys. Hannibal, not quite: there's that unfortunate "L" he chalked up at Zama, and all that time spent fleeing from Roman pursuers afterward. No, Alexander made the most of his opportunities and ensured that all who came after him would be compared to him.

Aristotle was Alexander's academic tutor, but he was schooled in the art of war and diplomacy by one of the best, namely his father, Philip II of Macedon. At 18, Alexander led the critical cavalry charge at the battle of Chaeronea (338 B.C.), which decided the battle and delivered Greece to Philip. Upon his father's assassination in 336 B.C., Alexander became king. He moved quickly, which was customary, to secure his position with a campaign in the Balkans. When Thebes revolted, he headed south at great speed. He called for the two instigators of the rebellion to be handed over and offered a general pardon to all who came over to him. The Thebans declined his offer and fought instead. In a fierce battle, the Macedonians stormed the city and defeated the outnumbered Thebans. Alexander razed all the buildings, except some temples, the house of Pindar the poet, and those belonging to Macedon's supporters. Plutarch tells us that 6,000 were put to the sword and 30,000 sold into slavery.

The rest of Greece now saw that maybe it would be smart to go along with this young upstart. Although Greeks being Greek, you know that

would not last. So with his base secure, he left Antipater behind to keep an eye on things and he set out to conquer Persia, which was something that long concerned his father and him.

It was now 334 B.C. Alexander had gathered forces of some 40,000 infantry, a good portion of it Greek mercenaries, and 5,000 cavalry and crossed into Asia Minor. Now the Persians would find out what dealing with Alexander was like. This was an amazing undertaking: he pressed into the vastness of Asia and when he crossed the Hellespont, he did not have had the money to pay and provision the army for very long. Nevertheless, his first battle against the Persians was at the Granicus River. This was a battle he was advised not to undertake due to the position and the lateness of the day, but he led his cavalry across the river and up a steep, slippery six-foot bank amidst a hail of arrows. The Persians had made an error in deploying by not putting their Greek mercenary phalanx where it could directly oppose the Macedonians. The Macedonians pushed across and as they gained the other side, the fighting became frenzied and confused. In the melee on the other side, Alexander was nearly killed. Spithridates came up on the side of the king, raised himself on his horse, and struck him a heavy blow on the helmet with a battleaxe. The axe cleaved the crest and shell of the helmet and stopped just as it touched Alexander's head. The first blow stunned the king, and as Spithridates raised his axe to deliver the death blow, Alexander's comrade, Clitus, ran him through with a spear. As the Macedonian infantry came on, the Persians gave way. The path was now clear into Asia Minor. This is one of the great "what ifs" in history. What if Clitus had been delayed a second or two? Would Persia have been conquered? Would anyone have ever heard of Alexander? Almost assuredly, there would have been no rag-time band named for him.

Alexander campaigned during 333 and 332 B.C. in Asia Minor and along the Mediterranean coast. Along the way, he reduced Halicarnssus by siege, and in October 333 B.C., defeated Darius III at the battle of Issus. The Persians lost upwards of 50,000 men and the Macedonians a reported 450. Among the captured were Darius's family; equally important was the loss of the Greek mercenaries, for now Darius would have little in the way of heavy infantry. Alexander pursued for a bit and then returned to his task of controlling the sea coast.

Alexander demonstrated his exceptional strategic acumen in this campaign. He did not have a fleet that could defeat the Persians' and he did not dare risk leaving the Persian ships behind him as a force-in-being that could threaten his communications and potentially stir up trouble in Greece. He decided, therefore, to destroy the Persian fleet by controlling all its bases. In 332 B.C., he prosecuted a seven-month siege of Tyre which was on an island, half a mile off the coast of modern Lebanon. He built a 200-foot wide mole out to the island and, using captured ships, bottled up the enemy fleet in the harbor. Employing siege engines and towers on the mole, the Macedonians stormed the city through a breach they made.

After this, peace overtures came from Darius, but were turned aside. Alexander then occupied Egypt in early 331 B.C., and secured his rear from any raiding by the Persian fleet. Meanwhile, Antipater, who was protecting Macedonian interests in Greece, put down a Spartan-led, Persian-funded revolt by several states in the Peloponnesus. In April of that year, Alexander learned that Darius III was raising a large army. Alexander headed into Persia looking for the decisive battle that would deliver the Persian empire into his hands.

So anxious was Darius III to stop the inevitable that he made Alexander two offers to go away. The first, proffered during the previous summer, had been for 10,000 gold talents, the Persian empire west of the Euphrates, and his daughter in marriage. Alexander had turned that one down. The second was for 30,000 gold talents, half the kingdom, and his daughter. Alexander again declined. Instead, the two would bring their armies to battle on a plain near Nineveh; the stage was set for the "thrilla in Gaugamela."

This was the third set-piece between the two kings and their armies , but it was to be the last. Darius III had marshalled an army of at least 200,000 infantry and 45,000 cavalry, including a substantial quantity of heavy cavalry from the east. Additionally, Darius fielded elephants and chariots. The Macedonian army deployed only 40,000 infantry and

7,000 cavalry. The battle is detailed elsewhere, but what is important here is that this victory was the result of a superior military system applied by the most vigorous commander of the age. When the moment of decision came, Alexander recognized it, and led the Companion cavalry to the attack. He made straight for Darius; the latter's subsequent flight from the field demoralized the Persians rapidly. After that, Alexander led the cavalry to the left to relieve the pressure on his wing. When that was done, he took after the rest of the Persian army. It is believed that 50,000 Persians were killed in the battle and pursuit, and the Macedonian losses were about 500 killed and 3,000 wounded.

The Persian empire was his for the taking and all he needed to make it complete was to capture Darius III himself. He advanced into the heart of Persia, capturing Babylon, Susa, and more importantly, the Persian treasury; he later occupied Persepolis, the capital. In the winter, he pressed on to capture Darius, who he heard was at Ecbatana. When he got there, he found out that Darius had left, but he did confiscate 180,000 talents of bullion.

Determined more than ever to get Darius, Alexander assumed personal command 500 of his best men and in 11 days, he covered nearly 400 miles in pursuit. Just as Alexander was drawing near with a detachment of only 60 men, Darius was murdered by Persian nobles led by Bessus. The conspirators fled and Bessus tried to establish his own kingdom in Bactria. Alexander marched into Bactria, where he captured and executed Bessus. For two years, Alexander campaigned in central Asia where, by virtue of his energy, ingenuity, and daring, he subdued numerous mountain tribes. He also was wounded severely in some of the fighting.

In early 326 B.C., he reached India at the Indus River. After crossing, he advanced to the Hydaspes River, which was swollen and running fast from recent winter rains. Here, Alexander established a camp and prepared to fight what was to be his last major battle, against King Porus. Typically, Alexander again relied on deception and speed to unbalance the enemy. Porus's army numbered about 35,000 to Alexander's roughly 20,000. Porus knew that the Macedonians could not cross the river, but Alexander kept his troops busy making feints up and down the river as if they were going to attempt a crossing anyway. This activity kept the Indians on edge and it also desensitized them to the idea of a crossing. Eventually, the Indians became so used to the activity that they hardly noticed it. In May, he was ready to act and needed only the right conditions. It was literally a dark and stormy night when he set out with half of his army, including about 6,000 infantry and 5,000 cavalry. Proceeding upstream to a crossing and with boats that were already on hand—as well as locally-made rafts made from tents stuffed with straw—his army crossed the river at dawn.

Porus received reports that Alexander was crossing the river and sent his son with 120 chariots and 2,000 cavalry. The landing was ongoing when they arrived, but Alexander was already across with the Companions and some other troops, so he quickly engaged the enemy force and killed some 400 men, captured the chariots, and drove off the rest. Porus's son was among the dead. Those who escaped carried back the news that Alexander was across. Porus moved upstream to intercept Alexander, but left a small force behind to screen the Macedonians on the other side.

Porus arrayed his army with 100 elephants in front, knowing that the enemy horses might run away from them. Alexander put the right side of his army near the river to anchor this flank. From here, he echeloned his army to the left rear to prevent Porus from outflanking him. Alexander placed his light troops in front with orders to intercept, harass, and drive off the elephants. One of Alexander's subordinates, Coenus, was sent on a wide, circling movement which aimed at striking the Indian right flank. The Macedonian skirmishers succeeded in driving off the elephants and some of the beasts ran back into the Persian lines—by now, the reader can imagine what that means. Alexander then led the Companions forward. The Indians, seeing Alexander coming on, drew their cavalry from the other parts of the line and tried to attack the Companions. Coenus's approach foiled their maneuver, however, and they had to split this force and send some of it back to deal with Coenus. When Alexander saw the enemy cavalry change direction, he charged the enemy's left wing. These units broke and fled back into the elephants. The elephant handlers forced their beasts through the mass and tried to engage the Macedonian cavalry. Everybody knew back then that elephants were effective against horses because they spooked them. The archers and javelin-men poured their missiles against the elephants and their drivers. The Indian cavalry tried another charge against the Companions, but the more experienced and skilled Macedonians repulsed this attack, and the cavalry was forced back on the elephants. As the Indians jammed together, and the elephants took out their unhappiness on all and sundry, Alexander moved to surround them. The phalanx locked shields and advanced on the Indians. The Indian cavalry and infantry took grievous losses, although some managed to get away. Meanwhile Coenus was rolling up the line from the other side. Porus was wounded and captured. Craterus, Alexander's deputy who was commanding the army on the opposite bank of the river, crossed over and undertook the pursuit. Arrian tells us that 20,000

Indian infantry and 3,000 cavalry were killed, including two of Porus's sons. Macedonian losses were 80 infantry, 10 mounted archers, 20 Companions, and 200 cavalry.

Not long thereafter, Alexander's troops refused to participate in further conquests, and mutinied. He gave up his plan to push on to the Ganges, and instead sent part of his army home by the northern route through Kandahar. He took the other part down the Indus Valley. Here, they had to fight several times before reaching the sea, and Alexander was again seriously wounded fighting the Malli. He and his men then set out across the Gedrosian desert. This passage—which cost him three-quarters of his army of 87,000 infantry, 18,000 cavalry, and 52,000 camp followers—has been club which critics have used on Alexander to dispute his greatness. The passage was supposed to be coordinated with the fleet, but the monsoons which provided the army with water also kept the fleet from sailing. So whereas Alexander left in mid-July, the fleet could not leave until October due to unfavorable winds. Not knowing what had happened to his fleet, which was supposed to supply grain to the army, Alexander had to improvise and to keep his army supplied as best as he could. Donald Engels in his logistical study of the Macedonian army judges that Alexander's leadership and organizational skill prevented his *entire* force from succumbing in the desert. In the end, he saved one-quarter of the army and all of his navy. Anyone else would have lost it all.

For Engels, the Gedrosian episode is a *tour de force*. This march was one of the most gruelling and difficult in military history, and that is another superlative we can ascribe to Alexander. Although cold comfort (if that is the term one should apply to those baked in a desert) to the 118,000 that did not make it, it is a demonstration of Alexander's skill and tenacity under the most adverse conditions.

In three years, aged 33, Alexander would die in Babylon under circumstances which some thought suspicious. Many thought then and think now that he was poisoned. It is certainly possible. It is also likely that his body just gave up after years of abuse. He became an object of divine worship, in part through his own promotion, and he alienated many of his officers by taking on other oriental ways.

He has been criticized by modern historians for his conquests, his heavy drinking, and the needless misery he occasioned with his campaigning for glory. It has been pointed out that Alexander killed more Greeks than any other actor in the ancient world. About those Greek mercenaries who fought in Persian employ, can we just say, "they chose the wrong side and that determined their fate"? Alexander may have killed more of *everybody* in the ancient world. He was in the conquering business, and that meant killing. Did he have to kill so many? Does any commander? That he killed so many, we rightly find deplorable, but we should remember in our assessment of Alexander's character, and this should be especially important to those with a 1990s sensibility, that he was the product of a broken home.

Most of his critics, however, admit to his military genius and that is the point of this entry. To say "military" genius is to say that he had a synthetic, highly original, and unique comprehension and application of tactics, strategy, and logistics. He was successful when fighting in all manner of terrain because he could quickly adapt his force structure and his plans. On the plains of Persia, it was business as usual: the phalanx holds, the Companions charge, and everyone else hangs on until we win. In the mountains against tribesmen, he used light troops and missile weapons with equally effective coordination, flexibility, and mobility. Irrespective of the terrain or other conditions, he was a master of reconnaissance and was always thinking about the next move and how to get there. He was also a charismatic leader *par excellence* and that was extremely important to his success. He was in the van of the fighting force, leading by example, and as a result, he sustained many serious wounds, but such courage is often infectious.

In our time, the nearest thing to war known personally to the vast majority of people is sports. In terms of leadership, there are many parallels. On all successful sports teams, there is at least one guy who makes it all go. He is the fellow who never quits and will not let anyone else quit. He has the ability to win the game through sheer personal ability and will. All he needs is for the team to hang in there long enough until the opportunity for victory presents itself. Alexander was like this. With Alexander, the army knew that they would always win because he would find the way to win. It has been suggested by one historian that the Macedonian army, when led by Alexander, could have bested all armies up to the introduction of gunpowder. This is a proposition against which the author would not bet.

The other great advantage Alexander possessed was his army. A professional force which was the first combined-arms team in history, his infantry and cavalry worked together implicitly. Also, his army travelled light—there were no wagons to slow the baggage train. Everything was carried on horses, mules, and later, camels, as well as the most versatile of load-bearing creatures—men. Alexander's men could carry 80 pounds of gear, which is one-third of what a mule or horse can carry, but men can eat more types of food and still go on, and need a lot less food and water than animals. This meant that the Macedonian army could cover more ground faster than any other army, and in warfare that can be crucial. A commander who moves twice as fast as his opponent halves the time his enemy has to make decisions or correct errors. Movement becomes a weapon of itself and the Macedonians were faster than rapid. With this army, the greatest of its time, and his abilities, Alexander conquered more of the world than anyone before him, and only one man since can claim he has done the same.

## Most Impressive Fast March in the Ancient World: Antigonus I, 319 B.C.

Antigonus I was one of the Diadochi, the generals of Alexander the Great, who divided up the Macedonian empire upon Alexander's death in 323 B.C. They and their successors instituted four decades of warfare with their wrangling over whom should have what and should they be allowed to keep it. These men may have lacked the spark of genius which animated Alexander, but they were tough, resourceful, battle-hardened men. They had marched and fought from Greece to India with the greatest military leader of that or any age. They had accumulated the type of experience and military education which none had had before and few have had since. They also resorted to intrigue, treachery, bribes, and guile. After all, a win is a win.

In 319 B.C., Antigonus decided that he had to attack Alcetas and his army of 20,000. Alcetas was nearly 300 miles away with his army of 20,000. No matter. Antigonus moved his army of 50,000 the full distance and attacked Alcetas in only seven days and nights. The average of 40 miles every 24 hours over a week's time is easily an ancient record, and the best light infantry of *any* age would be extremely hard-pressed to compete . . . but Antigonus's feat becomes almost impossible to comprehend when considering that his army had horses and elephants, too!

## First Documented Association of Palm Hair with Military Life: Crassus in Parthia

When Crassus came out of winter quarters in Syria in 53 b.c., he received a delegation from the Parthian king, Hyrodes. Crassus was 60 but apparently looked much older. The ambassadors told the Roman that if he came to make war at the behest of the Roman people, then war it would be. If on the other hand, Crassus was up to no good on his own (which was, in fact, pretty much how it was—he was mostly seeking an easy victory and lots of treasure), then the king was willing to take pity on a man in his dotage and let him return home. Crassus replied that he would answer the Parthians once he was in Seleucia, a Hellenic city on the Tigris river, deep inside Parthia.

Vagises, the eldest of the ambassadors and obviously the Shecky Greene of Parthia, laughed, showed them the palm of his hand, and said that hair would be growing there before Crassus made it to Seleucia.

Not long after, Crassus and his 40,000 man army were beaten in one of the worst defeats ever suffered by Roman arms. Near Carrhae, in Syria, 20,000 Parthians rained arrows on the Romans for two days, ultimately killing about 20,000 and capturing (and enslaving) another 10,000. Crassus survived the battle, but he was overtaken and killed by a Parthian who Plutarch tells us may have been named Pomaxathres. This fellow then severed Crassus's head and his right hand, and sent them Hyrodes in Seleucia.

Having told us what happened to Crassus, Plutarch does not, however, tell us whether, or under what circumstances, any hair ever grew on Vagises' palm. Subsequent generations of lonely soldiers have, in fact, proven, that this never happens anyway.

## Heaviest Traveler in Style: Surena

Surena, the Parthian general who defeated Crassus at Carrhae in 53 B.C., was surely one of the finest commanders Parthia produced. He was blessed with personal bravery and a subtle mind, as his various opponents found out. He was not just the man who captured Seleucia, but he was the first man onto the wall where he fought off his attackers while his men clambered up behind him. It was his family which held the honor of placing the crown on the head of the king at his coronation. He was from one of the richest families in Parthia and he was adjudged to be in beauty, stature, courage, and intelligence, the first man of his nation. His features are reported by Plutarch as being delicate and he chose an effeminate style of dress. He wore make-up and his hair was parted in the Median fashion. Presumably this was a more refined look than the standard Parthian "do," which was shaggy and had the hair gathered on the forehead in the Scythian style. His sensibilities must have been very refined indeed, because he took great offense, after the battle of Carrhae, when he saw the pornography carried in the defeated Roman's baggage. Perhaps Crassus had been carrying it with him to give it to Vagises so the Romans could reach Seleucia after all.

He was also the heaviest travelling general of the ancient world. When he traveled privately, his entourage included 200 chariots for his concubines, 1,000 fully-armed men as a body guard, and more than that lightly armed. Add in his servants and attendants, and he had 10,000 horsemen with him. Just in case you are wondering how much baggage comes with all the above, Plutarch figured on at least 1,000 camels.

His accomplishments and stature did him in, however; he was killed by order of King Hyrodes shortly after defeating Crassus. The king, you see, was a bit jealous and envious of the accomplishment.

# Tactics

## Most Misused Term: Circumvallation

Well, it may not be, but this is a book about superlatives and there is no a term more wrongly used and more easily corrected. A look in the dictionary shows that "circum" means "around or round about." "Vallation" is the action of building a wall or bank of earth for the purposes of fortification. Thus, to "circumvallate" means to build a wall of some sort around something. This is done in the simplest way by digging a trench and piling up the earth. The pile of earth, by the way, is called a rampart. With enough shovels and enough time, a besieging army can circumvallate its objective. After building the rampart, the diggers would sometimes top the rampart with large wooden stakes for added defense; this is called a palisade. Wooden stakes can also be added to the wall of the trench to further impede attacks by the surrounded defenders, and other obstacles may also be constructed. So far, so good, right? Now the trouble starts because we have to introduce the opposite though complementary term—contravallation. Again, a look in the dictionary tells one that "contra" means "against or opposed." In no way should "circum" and "contra" be confused, but they are.

Contravallation means to build a wall or rampart directed against something. It is designed to stop what the enemy is doing. This does not mean the enemy we have already surrounded by virtue of circumvallation; it means the enemy relief force which may be marching to attack the besieger in order to raise the siege. The besieger constructs works of contravallation to prevent enemy forces from breaking through from the outside. In this way, there is one trench and rampart to keep the enemy on the inside from breaking out and another longer trench and rampart around the previous one facing outwards to keep the enemy on the outside from breaking in. Simple.

In both circum- and contravallation, sets of earthworks, redoubts, or little forts, may be constructed at intervals along the wall to serve as strongpoints which are manned to prevent surprise attack. The trick for

the besieging commander is to move his finite forces from place to place in response to enemy attacks.

One of the best examples of these tactics is the siege of Alesia in 52 B.C. wherein Julius Caesar captured the town and the great Gallic rebel, Vercingetorix. In his account of the Gallic Wars, Caesar describes in detail the preparations the Romans made. They included lines of circumvallation of a perimeter of nearly ten miles. After learning that Vercingetorix had sent his cavalry away to bring back relief forces, Caesar decided to build further entrenchments. His men dug a 20-foot wide trench with straight sides, then two more 15-foot trenches were dug. The trench nearer to the town was flooded with water diverted from a river. Atop the rampart, a palisade 12 feet high was constructed with breastworks and battlements. Large forked branches were placed where the rampart and palisade met; long trenches five feet deep were dug with sharpened stakes fixed in the bottom. In front of these were diagonal three-foot-deep, slope-sided trenches arranged in a checkerboard pattern with sharpened stakes, hardened by fire and as thick as a man's thigh. The earth in the pits was tamped down to a foot from the top and then brushwood was placed over the top to conceal the trap. These traps were set in groups of eight, three feet apart. In front of this was buried blocks of wood with iron hooks. The legionaries called the last two mentioned traps, "lilies" and "spurs."

Caesar also had his men build 23 redoubts, and towers every 130 yards for the length of the line of circumvallation. Once this was done, which is to say having built the lines of circumvallation, Caesar ordered the construction of similar entrenchments facing outwards of some 14 miles in length. These were the lines of contravallation.

Somehow or other, over the years these terms became confused in the minds of certain writers. There are many modern historians who persist in making this mistake as well. The author could list them and point out there errors but some of them are his friends. He has one friend, however, who has got it right and that is John Lynn in his *The Wars of Louis XIV, 1664–1714*. The rest of you are on notice that the readers of this book, if they believe the author, will, too, be watching you.

## First Use of Circumvallation and Contravallation:
### The Siege of Plataea, 429–427 B.C.

The Siege of Plataea (429–427 B.C.) is the first known use of lines of circumvallation and contravallation in war. This occurred during the third year of the Peloponnesian War fought between Sparta and Athens and their allies. The siege started in the summer, but the Peloponnesians, led by King Archidamus of Sparta, did not start out by building the lines. The Plataeans had sent away most of the non-combatants, including women, children, and the oldest men. Remaining in the town were 400 Plataeans, 80 Athenians, and 110 women to bake bread.

The Peloponnesians began the siege by enclosing the town with a palisade made from the fruit trees there. They then threw up a mound against one section of wall which, once it was high enough, would become a ramp that would enable them to assault the city. They brought in logs and arranged them in a lattice pattern on either side of the mound to shore up the ramp. They then used rocks and earth to fill in around and between the logs. The Spartans worked day and night for 70 days, raising the ramp and advancing it towards the city's wall.

In response, the Plataeans erected wooden scaffolding on their wall opposite the approaching ramp. They covered it with hides to protect the workers from flaming arrows and built up the height of the walls with bricks from nearby houses. As the wall was raised, so was the ramp. When the ramp reached the wall, the Plataeans pulled out some of their wall stones down low and took away the earth from the ramp into their city. When the Spartans discovered this, they blocked the hole with wattles of reed and clay, which prevented the Plataeans from carrying away the dirt.

The Plataeans then began a mine. They dug under their wall and came up under the ramp. They carried away the earth as before, so as the attackers piled up the dirt on top, the height of the ramp did not appreciably increase because the added dirt merely replaced what the Plataeans were excavating. This was not enough for them, however, and they stopped building up the height of the outer wall and undertook the construction of a second interior wall which spanned the width of the ramp. Thus, if the besiegers did manage to breach the outer wall, they would charge in and find an inner wall. The inner wall was crescent shaped, which meant that once the Spartans reached it and began erecting a second mound, the engineers would be subject to missile attacks on their flanks. This inner wall would become *de rigeur* for all siege and counter-siege operations throughout history.

With the ramp in place, the Spartans brought up battering rams and employed them against several parts of the wall. The Plataeans lassoed some of them and broke the ram off others by hanging great beams over the walls from two iron chains at the end of two poles and then dropping the beams on slack chains onto the engine. These tactics, by the way, date back to ninth century B.C. Assyria at least. Even though part of the mound was literally undermined, however, the besiegers did manage to shake apart some of the wall. Nevertheless, the Spartans were thwarted. They faced the prospect of a blockade and circumvallating the town, but they wanted to avoid that and tried to burn the city first. After all, they figured it wasn't such a big town.

The Spartans gathered brushwood into faggots and began lobbing the bundles into the space between the two walls. When that was filled, they threw the kindling into the town itself. Then the whole thing was set alight with sulfur and pitch (tar). The flames carried into the city, and the plan to torch the city might just have worked had not a thunderstorm arrived, drenched the city, and put out the fire.

The attempt to burn the city having failed, the Spartans decided that they had to starve the garrison. The Plataeans had anticipated this, so they had already cleared out the non-combatants, because they just eat up valuable food and divert resources. The Peloponnesians then dismissed a portion of the army and dug two trenches around Plataea, 16 feet apart. On the inside of each trench, a wall was built made from bricks made from the excavated earth. The inner wall to keep the

Plataeans in was the line of circumvallation and the outer wall designed to keep the relief force out was the line of contravallation. The Spartans did a pretty good job on this one. The span between the walls was decked and huts built underneath for living quarters. Battlements were built on top of the deck to afford protection; every ten battlements, perhaps every 50 feet or so, roofed towers were built to shelter the troops during bad weather.

During a moonless stormy night in winter, the Plataeans did manage to break out with 212 men using scaling ladders, stealth, and a diversion. Eventually, with no relief in sight, the garrison surrendered. After a trial, the 225 surviving men were slain and the women taken as slaves.

## First Man to Have Tactics Named for Him:
Quintus Fabius and Fabian Tactics

Quintus Fabius was appointed dictator by the Senate, and from May to October of 217 B.C., he skillfully conducted a campaign of harassment and delay, while avoiding battle. This earned him the opprobrium of the people and the appointment of M. Minucius Rufus as his co-equal.

Rufus, one of Fabius's former lieutenants, accepted battle with Hannibal at Geronium. He was on the verge of defeat when Fabius arrived in time to threaten the Carthaginian flank and force their withdrawal.

Fabius's gift to the world was Fabian tactics, a strategy of battle avoidance and harassment. The first man to give his name to a strategy which is based on delaying tactics, he gave Rome time to raise new legions.

## First Offensive Use of Field Fortifications:
Battle of Chaeronea, 86 B.C.

### First Mithridatic War, 89–84 B.C.

Sulla came to battle on Boeotia with 30,000 men to meet Archelaus who had 110,000 men and 90 chariots. These figures are from Sulla's account and there may have been more than a little self-promotion involved in reporting the numbers. Especially as Sulla, after his victory, reported 100,000 dead. The reader is free to take Sulla at his word of course. The author only wishes to add that should the reader one day meet the author, the latter would be pleased to recount the story of his 110-yard interception return.

Lucius Cornelius Sulla,
138–78 B.C.
© Bettmann/CORBIS/
MAGMA

It is odd to contemplate, is it not, that as recently as 86 B.C., people were still trying to win battles with chariots? Yet these weapons platforms give a Near Eastern tinge to Mithridates' army. The infantry element of this army was the good old phalanx.

Sulla, outnumbered to the extent he was, dug entrenchments to protect his flanks against envelopment by cavalry and built palisades along the front of his position to protect against the chariots. He posted javelineers and archers in front of his lines. Their enemy, it is reported, does not appear to have been well-trained.

Archelaus started off the battle with a cavalry charge. Naturally, the palisades diverted much of the attack but some cavalry did get through the entrenchments. Sulla's legions formed into squares to repulse the horsemen. The chariots, when they attacked, were engaged first by the skirmishers and turned back through their own phalanx spreading confusion and disrupting the order. We are also told that this part of the battle occasioned laughter and even applause from the Romans. Sulla took advantage of the enemy disorder and counter-attacked with his infantry and cavalry, carrying the day.

# Battles

## Most Famous Last Stand:
## Thermopylae, August 480 B.C.

Ten years after their defeat at Marathon, the Persians were again ready to invade Greece. Xerxes, now the king after Darius's death, gathered an army of 200,000 and made preparations for a combined land-sea invasion. The army crossed the Hellespont on two floating bridges built for the crossing. To isolate Greece, Xerxes even arranged for Carthage to attack Sicily, thereby denying the mainland Greeks any support from their colonies. The Greeks learned of the preparations and resolved to resist.

Well most of them. Sparta and Athens led those who were for defending Greece. Other city-states, especially those likely to be the first to be overrun by the Persians, opted to stay neutral or go over to the barbarians. The Spartans thought the defense should be conducted at the isthmus of Corinth and all of Greece north of there abandoned. They argued that the isthmus was only four and one-half miles wide and as Sparta was south of there, it made pretty good sense to them. The Athenians, led by that veteran of Marathon, Themistocles, argued that the Persian advance could be stopped north of the isthmus by a combination of sea and land forces and as they lived north of the isthmus, it made pretty good sense to them. The Spartans, who realized that a navy was needed, agreed. Powerful forces were on the move.

Northern Greece, Macedonia, and Thessaly were abandoned, as it would have required too many troops to defend the passes into those regions. Instead, it was decided to meet the Persians at the defile at Thermopylae. For this purpose, the Greeks gathered a force of around 7,000 hoplites. Herodotus tells us that the troops included 300 Spartans, 500 from Tegea, 500 from Mantinea, 120 from Orchomenus in Arcadia, 1,000 from the rest of Arcadia, 400 from Corinth, 200 from Philus, 80 from Mycenae, 700 from Thespiae, 400 from Thebes, 1,000 from Phocia, and others from the Locrians of Opus. Each contingent was led by its own commander, although Leonidas, a king of Sparta, was the overall army commander.

The pass at Thermopylae is ideal for defense. There is water on one side, mountains on the other, and the defile is less than 50 feet wide. Here, a force of determined men could hold off vastly superior numbers. Adding to the defensive strength of the position was the Phocian wall, which started with a tower at the top of the ridge and ran along in zigs and zags to level ground, ending next to the marsh, where their was most likely another tower.

The other route into central Greece is the Asopus valley to the west, but this passes through steep gorges and is defended by a fortress at Trachis. This is why the Persians decided to try pressing their advance through Thermopylae.

The Greeks established a supply depot at Alpenos, the eastern gate of the defile and took up their positions at the middle gate, Thermopylae. Leonidas placed the 1,000 Phocians atop the mountain where they could guard against any attempt by the Persians to turn their position by advancing up the Asopus valley. To say the Greeks here were outnumbered is understatement in the extreme. The Persians had about 1,200 ships to the Greeks' 380, as well as at least 200,000 soldiers.

Herodotus tells us that Xerxes sent a spy to see what the Spartans were doing. He reported that they were stripped, exercising, and combing their hair. Xerxes did not believe him and sent for Demaratus to explain. Demaratus told him that the Spartans were brave men preparing for battle, they were ready to die, and they were really funny about their hair. Xerxes found this all a bit absurd. Now if this story isn't true, it ought to be. Xerxes waited four days for the Greeks to come to their senses, realize that they were outnumbered 50 to 1, and go away. They did neither. On the fifth day, having had enough, he sent the Medes and Cissians with orders to bring all those pesky Greeks back to him so he could have a look at them. If the reader is wondering how to tell the difference between the similarly-armed Mede and Cissian, he need only look for the black turban worn by the latter. These troops went forward and battled for much of the day. They could make no progress against the Greeks, and were recalled after sustaining heavy losses.

Xerxes then sent Hydarnes and the elite bodyguard, the Immortals. This military unit was always kept at its full strength of 10,000. They made no more headway than the Medes and in time were withdrawn. The Greeks, by virtue of their longer spears, had the advantage in reach and offensive power. Moreover, fighting in a restricted space meant that the Persians could not exploit their manpower advantage. The Greeks took some casualties, but not many.

On Day Two, the Persians were back at it but the Greeks never slackened in their fighting. They rotated their national divisions in and out of the front line during the day and again inflicted heavy casualties on the Persians. The Persians withdrew. Later on, the bugbear, bane, and bugaboo of the Greek character surfaced, namely treachery. A certain Ephialtes from Malis told the Persians there was a path over the mountains which would put them behind the Greek lines, and he wouldn't

Xerxes, who ruled the
Persian Empire from
485–465 B.C.
© Bettmann/CORBIS/
MAGMA

mind a big reward for selling out his people. That night, Hydarnes and the Immortals followed Ephialtes along the Anopaea path, which winds its way through the heavily-forested mountain to come out at Alpenos and the eastern gate, behind the Spartan positions. The reader should note that it was probably not all the 10,000 Immortals who made it through the pass.

By early dawn, they came upon the 1,000 Phocians who were guarding the path. In this encounter battle, meaning that both sides were surprised at the other being there, the Persians let loose a storm of arrows and missiles, and the Phocians, apparently thinking that they were the main object of the attack, moved off the path to higher ground from which they could better defend themselves. The Persians, happy that they had come up against Phocians, and not Spartans, stayed on the path and went past as fast as they could.

On the Greek side, Day Two ended with still no relief force in sight. Leonidas had been calling for reinforcements, but realized that none were coming. Dawn came word that the Persians were in the mountains behind them. A war council was called and resulted in most of the Greeks leaving, while the Spartans, Thespians, and Thebans were to stay. Why? Interpretations vary on this point. Herodotus reports that it was said Leonidas dismissed them to spare their lives, but Herodotus believes that the real reason was that Leonidas knew that the men in these contingents did not have the heart for the fight and would be unwilling to share in the danger. The Spartans would stay because they could not desert their post. The Thespians stayed because they would not desert Leonidas and the Thebans stayed, so we are told, because Leonidas detained them as hostages.

There was also an oracle, which told them that for Sparta to avoid attack, a Spartan king must die. Herodotus puts much stock in this explanation and he believes further that it was Leonidas's desire to cover the Spartans in glory.

On Day Three, Xerxes held back until mid-morning waiting for the Immortals to make their way down the mountain. The Greeks, prepared for a fight to the last, moved out from behind the wall, and formed up and fought the Persians in front of them knowing that, at some point, the enemy would show up at their backs. Many Persians were killed and as the survivors fell back, they were whipped by their officers to keep them in the fight. In the course of this furious and savage fighting, most of the Greek spears were broken, but combat continued with swords.

Then Leonidas fell and a fearsome struggled developed over his corpse. Four times, the Spartans had to wrest it back from the Persians. Many notables on both sides died at this stage of the fighting, including the two brothers of Xerxes, Habrocomes and Hyperanthes. This went on until the Immortals came upon the scene with Ephialtes, at which point the Greeks moved back through the gate to a small hillock, where they formed into a tight circle and made their last stand. The Persians could not successfully assault this position, so they encircled it and reduced the pocket with missiles. By midday, it was all over; the 300 Spartans were dead. Total Greek dead over the three days are said to be about 4,000.

Herodotus recounts the deeds of some of the combatants. The Spartan Dieneces, when told by a native of Trachis that the Persian arrows will fly so thickly that they will block out the sun, retorted that if this was true it was good news indeed because it meant that they could have their battle in the shade.

There is, of course, no more interesting figure in this event than Leonidas. He was a descendant of Heracles through his father, Anaxandridas, and grandfather, Leon. His father was long childless and eventually the *ephors* (magistrates who advised the Spartan kings) advised him to divorce and take another wife. He refused to do so, but the *ephors* managed to push on him a compromise whereby he would take a second wife and establish a second household. Needless to say, this was, by all accounts, unprecedented in Sparta. Soon enough, the second wife produced an heir, Cleomenes. The first wife then became pregnant and gave birth to a boy named Dorieus. She then produced Leonidas (circa 540 B.C.) and Cleombrotus, and the second wife never had another child. When Cleomenes became king, Dorieus sought permission to take some Spartans and found a colony; he was, you see, not enamored of the idea of being ruled by his half-brother.

Dorieus met his death in Sicily after taking part in the destruction of Sybaris in 510 B.C. When Cleomenes died without an heir, Leonidas became king. When he married Gorgo, the daughter of Cleomenes, his step-niece, Leonidas was about 50 and she about 19. John R. Grant, the classicist, puts forth the idea that the first Mrs. Anaxandridas and her husband must have been deeply offended by the actions forced on them. This seems especially likely when one learns that the second Mrs. Anaxandridas was related to Chilon, one of the *ephors*. Did Leonidas dislike the *ephors* as much as his parents did? Probably.

When he became king, he followed the anti-Persian policy of Cleomenes, in contrast to the *ephors*, who had shown themselves to be fairly linguini-spined when it came to opposing Persia. Hence their tepid response to the Persian invasion. Was Leonidas determined to show up the *ephors*? Did the previous retirement without a fight of the Greeks from the pass at Tempe in Thessaly grate on him? Had he decided to show the Persians a thing or two about how Greeks fight and simultaneously show the Greeks how to do one's duty, even if it meant dying? If so, then Leonidas insubordinated [*sic*] himself into war's pantheon of heroes.

What became of the traitor, Ephialtes? Well, he fled to Thessaly, fearing what the Spartans would do to him if they caught him. The Amphictyons put a price on his head. Sometime later, he returned to Trachis and was killed by Athenades, although it was not for his treachery but on an apparently unrelated matter. The Spartans honored Athenades nevertheless.

## Biggest Hoplite Battle: Plataea, 479 B.C.

This battle between the Greeks and the Persians and their Greek allies was the last one they would fight in Greece. The forces involved were the largest the city-states would ever field in Greece. When it was over, the Greeks, united to a remarkable degree, would not be conquered by a foreign power until the second century B.C. Alexander the Great does not count as a foreigner, by the way. It would be centuries before the Macedonians became foreign.

Following the defeat of the Greeks at Thermopylae, the Persians went south. The northern city-states realized that the balance of power had shifted in favor of the Persians and, Greeks being Greek, they figured that they would have to make accommodation with the new Persian reality of Greece. The northern Greeks knew that if they opposed the Persians, they would be destroyed. They thus adopted a policy of hunkering down and waiting (and, presumably, hoping) for things to change in the Greeks' favor once gain; after all, wouldn't it be stupid to have one's house in cinders when the Persians left town again?

The usual terms of submission to Persia applied to the vanquished Greeks: as a conquered people, they had to send contingents to fight in the Persian army.

Meanwhile, the Greek fleets had withdrawn to the south. The Athenian navy evacuated Athens, with most of the women and children moving to the Peloponnesus, some to the island Aegina, and some, with the able-bodied men to the island of Salamis, a few miles west of Piraeus. At this same time, the Persians—army and navy—moved south, laying waste to the countryside. Athens was captured and the few who stayed behind to defend the Acropolis were killed after a tough fight. The temples were looted and burned, other buildings ransacked, and the Greek admirals discussed what to do next, no doubt at 100 decibels, which is three above the noise level of a boiler factory.

In the end, Themistocles prevailed and a united Greek fleet defeated the Persians at Salamis in September 480 B.C. The Persians lost at least 200 ships, the Greeks, 40. Xerxes, an interested spectator of the battle, left part of his army with his deputy, Mardonius, and headed back across the Aegean Sea to Ionia, lest the Greeks there be encouraged to revolt at the news of the victory their cousins had achieved. Mardonius withdrew north and went into winter quarters.

In the summer of 479 B.C., the Persians moved south again and reoccupied Athens, and people again moved to Salamis. Desperately, the Greeks tried to reach agreement over what to do. The Spartans had already started a wall across the isthmus at Corinth and were content to continue it, that is, right up to the point when the Athenians said that they would make an accommodation with Mardonius. That would have opened up the Peloponnesus to attack from the sea, and that the Spartans could not countenance. Now they acted and quickly. Pausanius, the Spartan king, was made the army commander. The Spartans contributed at least 5,000 hoplites plus 35,000 *helots* and other troops; these were joined by 5,000 more from Sparta's allies. There were also 1,500 Tegeans deployed with the Spartans. Athens sent 8,000 hoplites, and they deployed as a separate unit, as did the 3,000 hoplites from Megara. Additional Allied-Greek forces, deployed together on the battlefield, consisted of 5,000 from Corinth, 300 from Potidaea, 400 from Chalcis, 600 from Eretria, 200 from Pale, 500 from Aegina, 3,000 from Sicyon, 1,000 from Troezen, 200 from Lepreum, 800 from Leucas, 500 from Ambracia, 300 from Hermione, 800 from Epidaurus; 600 from Orchomenos; 400 from Mycenae and Tiryns, 1,000 from Philus; 1,800 from Thespiae; and 600 from Plataea. There were an additional 35,000 light troops as well. Herodotus places the entire contingent at around 110,000. Persian strength was perhaps 120,000 from all sources including subject Greeks from the northern areas. Some modern scholars place the size of the army somewhat smaller and some scholars place the size of the army *a lot* smaller. No matter, let the quibblers quibble. This was going to be one big battle.

When Mardonius heard the Greeks were on the move, he headed to Boeotia where the plain would give him room for his cavalry. He established a fortified camp north of the Asopus River. The Greeks arrived east of Plataea in July and took positions in the hills overlooking the plain. The Spartans and Tegeans were deployed on the right, the allies in the middle, and the Megarians and Athenians on the left. Here the Persian cavalry under Masistius came out to entice the Greeks down from the hills.

The Megarians were at a disadvantage in the terrain here and suffered terribly from the attacks of Persian horse archers. They sent a runner to the Athenians on their left to ask for help. Three hundred hoplites and some archers came to their aid. They took up positions in front of the Megarians and tried to break up the attack. They, in turn, were the targets of the archers. Masistius led the charges at the Athenians and, on one occasion, the last occasion for him, his horse was shot and threw him off. The Athenians closed in on him, grabbed his horse, and set about their deadly work. His armor, worn in Persian fashion beneath his purple tunic, was leather and gilded scales and impenetrable to the Greeks spears. He was then speared through the eye. The Persians tried mightily to retrieve the body but could not, so they broke off the attack. When the news reached the Persian lines, there was much consternation and disturbance in their camp.

The Persians had been raiding the Greeks' supply lines and poisoning water supplies, so to improve their logistical situation, the Greeks

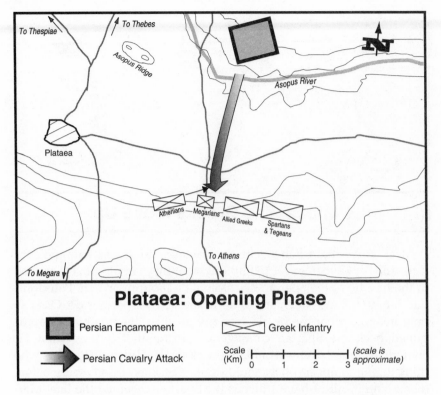

## Plataea: Opening Phase

Persian Encampment          Greek Infantry

Persian Cavalry Attack      Scale (Km) |—————|—————|—————| 0  1  2  3  *(scale is approximate)*

moved northwest about seven and one-half miles toward Plataea. The Greeks took up their second positions on the Asopus ridge north of Plataea, but this did not produce any results, so after three days of skirmishing, another war council was called and they decided to move back toward Plataea and see if this encouraged a Persian attack or a Persian mistake. They planned a night move and the expected happened: some Megarian and allied Greek units got lost, some units did not move, and opportunity reigned supreme.

By dawn, the units which had gotten lost were camped against the walls of Plataea. The Athenians, who were supposed to move to the center next to the Spartans, were still on the left and had not moved at all. The wings were ordered to withdraw and this led to more problems. On this occasion Amompharetus, one of the Spartan commanders, decided that since he had not been consulted about the move, he was not going to abandon his position. Pausanias did not want to leave Amompharetus and his men behind, so he and Euryanax tried to persuade him to get with the program. Accordingly, while this debate was going on, the Spartans were stationary.

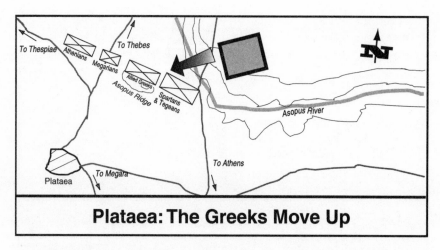

## Plataea: The Greeks Move Up

Meanwhile, the Athenians heard that something was wrong on the right and sent a messenger to find out what they should do. He arrived in the middle of the Spartan discussion, or shouting match. Pausanius told him to tell the Athenians to do whatever the Spartans do. One can only imagine what the herald made of all this. Eventually, Pausanius pulled back the Spartan contingent figuring that if they went far enough, Amompharetus would follow along. He did, too. (Readers who think this story apocryphal should think of Sickles at Gettysburg before dismissing it out of hand.) Just as the Spartans rejoined the line, Mardonius ordered a general attack, using his cavalry and infantry. He must

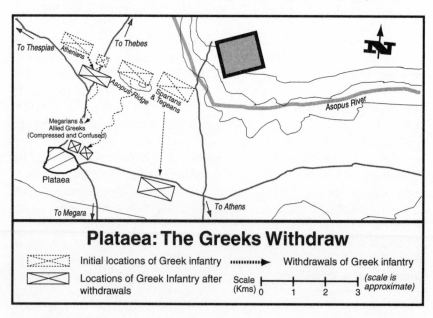

## Plataea: The Greeks Withdraw

have seen the evident chaos in the Greek army and decided that this was the time. Who can blame him? Unfortunately, he did not realize even after all that campaigning in Greece that the Greeks, being Greek, are at home in chaos.

Persian cavalry pinned the Spartans and Tegeans where they were. Mardonius's infantry moved forward against the Greek right, set their shields as a wall, and started firing arrows. Pausanius sent a rider to see whether the Athenians could close the gap in the center created by the lost units now in Plataea. The Athenians, however, were also pinned, and when the infantry behind them near Plataea came up to help, they, in turn, were attacked by Theban cavalry in the Persian service.

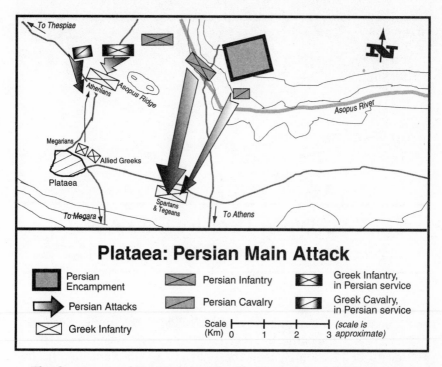

## Plataea: Persian Main Attack

| | | |
|---|---|---|
| Persian Encampment | Persian Infantry | Greek Infantry, in Persian service |
| Persian Attacks | Persian Cavalry | Greek Cavalry, in Persian service |
| Greek Infantry | Scale (Km) 0 1 2 3 | (scale is approximate) |

The Spartans and Tegeans crouched behind their shields and tried to wait out the storm of missiles being poured on them. Pausanius, meanwhile, was up on the hill sacrificing and praying for good omens. The superior discipline of the Spartans kept them in formation even though they were taking casualties. The Tegeans, in contrast, thought that enough was enough, and rose up 1,500 strong and charged. Pausanius saw this and realized that it was time for action. He declared the omens favorable—a very serious offense if they are not—and sped to join his troops. Upon reaching them, he gave the order to advance. The Spartans moved to the charge as the Persians discarded their bows and grabbed their spears.

Once contact was made, the Spartans gained the advantage. Their longer spears, heavier armor, and superior fighting ability soon told. Even though the Persians grabbed the hoplites' spears and broke them when they could, they could not hope to win this contest. The Persians were pushed back and Mardonius, astride his white horse, was in the midst of 1,000 select men, urging them along in the fighting. It was in this combat that Mardonius was killed. The Athenians were also winning the battle at their end of the field.

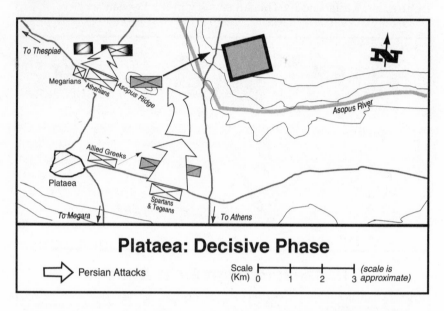

### Plataea: Decisive Phase

⇨ Persian Attacks

Scale (Km) — 0   1   2   3   (scale is approximate)

Meanwhile, word reached Plataea that, "there was a battle going on and things are going our way." The Allied-Greek units there then rushed to get to the battle, but it was just about over when they arrived. The death of Mardonius took the fight out of the Persians, the line broke, and the rout was on. The Persian cavalry, including the Thebans in the Persian service, covered the retreat rather than leading it, but the Greek light troops led the pursuit and the slaughter continued. The Greeks stormed the Persian camp, eventually forced their way in, and the killing persisted.

Mardonius's body was not mutilated, but it did mysteriously vanish and no one learned who buried it. Amompharetus died in the fighting and was buried with the other slain Greeks before the gates of Plataea. Casualty figures are, of course, as problematic as always. The 152 Greek

The Spartans drive the attack home at Plataea.
© Bettmann/CORBIS/MAGMA

casualties alleged by Herodotus are impossibly low. Plutarch gives a more believable 1360. Herodotus says only 3,000 Persians survived, once one takes away the 40,000 troops under Artabazus who never participated in the battle. Still, does this mean that there were 67,000 dead Persians? If that is too high, about 50,000 dead Persians may not be. In any event, it was a lopsided victory in every sense, and certainly proved the value of the Greek hoplite.

## Best Flip-Flop in a Battle:
### The Battle of Mycale, August 479 B.C.

Herodotus tells us that this happened the same day as the Persian defeat at Plataea.

A Greek fleet under the command of the Spartan Leotychides was lying at Delos, about 100 miles from Mycale on the Ionian coast. Three men from Samos, an island off Cape Mycale, arrived to appeal to the Greeks to come to Ionia. Lampon, Athenagoras, and Hegesistratus told the Greeks that they had been sent by the Samians without the knowledge of the Persians or Theomestor, the man they had set up as despot. They wanted the Greeks to help free them from Persian bondage and argued that the appearance of the fleet would inspire the Ionians to rise in revolt against their oppressors. The delegates offered themselves as hostages as proof of their sincerity. Hegesistratus, apparently, was doing most of the talking when Leotychides asked him his name. This was done either by chance or perhaps in the hopes that it could signal a favorable omen. It proved to be the latter as Hegesistratus means "leader of the host" and upon hearing this Leotychides cut short the debate and said the omen was good enough for him. So never ask, "what's in a name?"

After this, the oaths were administered, a verbal compact of mutual support was made, and Lampon and Athenagoras set off for Samos. Hegesistratus was ordered to sail with the Greek fleet because Leotychides knew that you don't let your good luck charm get away. The Greeks sacrificed the next day with good results and set sail.

The Persians, upon hearing of the Greek fleet appearing at Calami, made way for the Asian coast because they knew their ships were no match for the Greeks. They landed at Mycale, where they would have the protection of the 60,000 Persian troops left by Xerxes under the command of Tigranes to guard Ionia. The Persians beached their vessels and constructed a defensive position by throwing up a wall of wood and timber and adding an outer ring of sharpened stakes.

The Greeks, not finding the Persians where they thought they would be, decided to press on for the mainland. Here they found the Persian fleet, and Leotychides sailed in close to the shore and had a crier call upon the Ionians serving with the Persians to remember freedom when the battle started . . . and also to remember the password, "Hera." In doing this, Leotychides had possibly secured the assistance of some Ionians once the battle began, or if the Persians learned of the call to defect, then the Ionians would be suspected and Tigranes would have to divert men and spend time on preventing treachery.

Following this appeal to the Ionians, the Greeks put ashore and formed up their soldiers. The Persians disarmed the Samians fearing that they'd be too sympathetic to the Greeks. Then the Milesians, Ionians, too, were sent by the Persians to guard the passes which led up to the heights of Mycale. These precautions being made, the Persians drew up into a defensive line with their shields interlocked. The part of the opposite line occupied by the Athenians, Corinthians, Sicyonians, and Troezenians passed over the beach and flat ground, the Spartans and other contingents had to pass over a watercourse and high hills; accordingly they were still marching when the Athenians met the Persians.

The Persians repelled all the Greek assaults at their shield line and acquitted themselves well. The Athenians and their neighbors wanted to win the battle before the Spartans could engage and so they passed the word to make another big push, and pierced the Persian shield line.

The Persians and their other troops still held on for a time, but eventually they had to withdraw to their barricade. The Greeks were hot on their heels and forced their way into the Persian defensive works. Once the Greeks were inside, many of the enemy troops, save the Persians, fled. The latter fought on in scattered groups. The Persian naval commanders, Artayntes and Ithamitres, got away; Tigranes, allegedly the tallest and best-looking man in the army, was killed. The Spartans arrived at this point and joined in the fighting. The Samians did what they could to help the Greeks, but it is not clear what; they were unarmed, remember. The Milesians, whose knowledge of the hills was supposed to save the Persians if they had to retreat, used that knowledge to guide the Persians right back to their enemies and then they themselves joined in the attack. The Greeks burned the Persian ships and fort after removing everything of value.

## Best Example of Why Commanders Should Listen to Their Men: King Agis and the Hoplite Who Spoke His Mind

It was 418 B.C., during the Peloponnesian War, and Thucycides tells us that Agis, who was commanding the Spartans, had, in the minds of his allies, blown a big opportunity for subduing Argos, an opposing city-state. The Argives, truth be told, pulled off a good one here. They and their allies were surrounded on the battlefield, but managed to get Agis to agree to a four-month truce so that grievances could be addressed. Surprisingly, the Argives blamed their own guys, Thrasylus and Alciphron, for negotiating without permission and, besides, they thought that since the battle would have been held close to their city walls, they had a pretty good chance of winning.

Apparently, the fact that they were surrounded did not matter; to their way of thinking, they had the enemy right where they wanted them. Upon returning to the town, Thrasylus was stoned in the bed of Charadrus, the place where military cases were tried. He saved his life only by fleeing to the altar and gaining sanctuary. His property was confiscated, however.

Meanwhile the Spartans, were equally upset with Agis. They thought that his home should be razed and he should be fined 10,000 *drachmas*. Nowadays 10,000 *drachmas* will buy you four Big Macs in Athens, but in those days it was a lot of money. A day's wage was about one drachma, so that amount would field 1,000 hoplites for a week and a half, or pay for a trireme. Agis prevailed upon his critics to give him another chance and if it did not go better, then they could do whatever they wanted to him. They agreed to this, but assigned him ten counselors whose consent he needed even to go to the bathroom.

At this point in our story, word arrived that unless help arrived pronto the Tegeans, neighbors of Mantinea, would go over to the Argives. So calls went out to the various allies to get a move on and meet back at Mantinea as soon as possible. Meanwhile, the Spartans and their Arcadian allies encamped near the temple of Heracles and plundered the Mantinean countryside. The Argives and their allies found them and took up positions for battle. The position they chose was a strong one on a hill and would have proved difficult to assault. Agis, undeterred, drew up his army into battle formation and advanced against the enemy. When the two armies were within a javelin's cast of each other, one of the Spartans—an older soldier who recognized the strength of the enemy's position—called out to King Agis that he was trying to cure one evil with another. By this, he meant that Agis was trying to make up for the previous unseemly retreat with an untimely attack now. Agis thought it over and, if for this reason or another, he led the army away without engaging the enemy.

The Argive commanders were amazed, to say the least, and they watched the Spartans go. Then they came under criticism for once again letting the enemy get away, so they moved down onto the plain and tried to entice the Spartans to battle. The next day the battle was fought and the Spartans won, but it was very close.

What became of the courageous hoplite is lost to history, but it would be nice to think that he was promoted. After all, he got Agis out of the doghouse, prevented a likely defeat, and postured the Spartans for an important victory.

## Worst Defeat of Sparta; First Use of the Refused Flank and Echeloned Approach; Deepest Phalanx Used in Battle: Leuctra, 371 B.C.

The Thebans deployed a phalanx at Leuctra which was 50 shields deep, so we are told. This is in keeping with the Theban tradition of tactical innovation. The Thebans usually massed more deeply than the other phalanxes of the ancient world. Where most phalanxes adopted eight-deep formations in the fifth century B.C., the Thebans, after the battle of Delium (424), massed 16 to 25 deep.

At Leuctra, Epaminondas massed his phalanx 50 shields deep and 80 across. At such a depth, there were liabilities: a column that deep was susceptible to attack on the flanks and the offensive power of the column is much reduced in the sense that there are fewer spears brought to attack. In another sense, however, there is a lot of offensive power from that much weight and one should remember that quantity has a quality all of its own.

These may have been the tactics of a moment, but they suited the situation perfectly and Epaminondas is responsible for it. After the battle, others claimed that they had thought of it, too, but the author gives the credit to Epaminondas—he is deserving of it; after all, if the Thebans had failed, the blame would have all been his.

What led the Spartans and their allies north into Boeotia that summer was their fear of growing Theban power. Thebes was the leader of the Boeotian League and Sparta, while still the first state in Greece, was declining. Moreover, the events of the period from the end of the Peloponnesian War in 404 B.C. to now, 371, had demonstrated to many that Sparta was slipping. She had lost a few battles in the intervening years and that had set tongues to wagging, hopes to rising, and opportunity to knocking. The internecine world of Greek intramural relations was triangular in this era. Athens sought to make a comeback after losing the last big one. Sparta wanted to remain on top, and Thebes, as the up-and-coming power, was a threat. On the sidelines but making a name for himself up north was Jason, the tyrant of Thessaly. He had big plans and had he not been assassinated in 370 B.C., he may well have made a large impact on events.

In an attempt to head off hostilities, the Greeks sat down for a big meeting, but little was resolved and so Sparta marched north to deal with Thebes. The Thebans were ready for them. Thus, the first advantage went to Thebes. Epaminondas had chosen the battlefield and thereby taken the initiative away from the Spartans. In choosing his ground, he would have done so with an eye to securing the best terrain for his tactical plan and taken into account that he would be outnumbered. If he could keep one or both flanks from being turned, then he would be closer to victory, or at least farther away from defeat.

The Spartans and their allies, commanded by King Cleombrotus, numbered about 10,000 hoplites and 1,000 cavalry. The Spartans held the right of the line, their traditional place. Besides the 2,000 Spartans, literally, were 1,500 Phocians; then 1,000 Acarnanians; 2,000 Corinthians; 2,000 Arcadians; and 1,500 Achaeans, Eleian, and Sicyonians. The Thebans and allies under Epaminondas had 6,000 hoplites and 1,500 cavalry, including the elite Sacred Band of 300 commanded by Pelopidas, Epaminondas's right-hand man; in this battle, though, the right-hand man would be on the left. In addition, each side had assorted light troops, but they are not talked about and did not enter into the decision.

The Spartans drew up for battle in the traditional manner, occupying the right side of the line with their allies to their left. Cleombrotus put his cavalry in front of his right. The Thebans lined up in a decided break from tradition. Epaminondas placed the Thebans in deep column on the

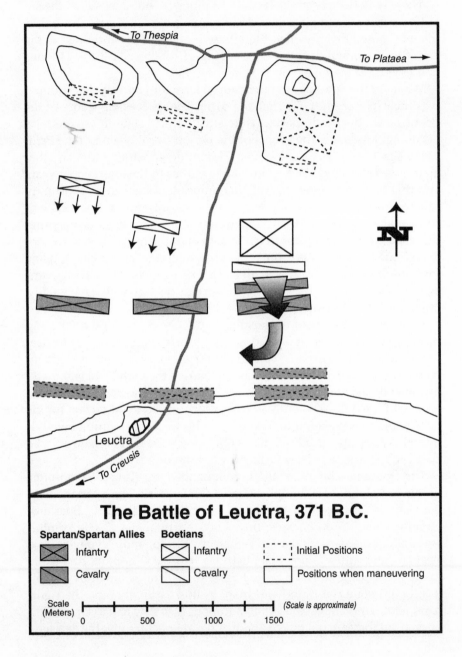

## The Battle of Leuctra, 371 B.C.

| Spartan/Spartan Allies | Boetians | |
|---|---|---|
| ⊠ Infantry | ⊠ Infantry | ⌐ ¬ Initial Positions |
| ⧄ Cavalry | ⧄ Cavalry | ☐ Positions when maneuvering |

Scale (Meters)   0    500    1000    1500   *(Scale is approximate)*

left and his weaker allies in the center and right. The cavalry was on the left wing, thus the superior Theban cavalry was opposite the Spartan horse. Epaminondas's idea was to win the battle on the left by defeating the Spartans by shock action before he lost it on the right.

Any description of the battle order introduces the question of the position of the Sacred Band, an issue of dispute amongst some historians. The Band has been placed by historians anywhere from at the back of the deep phalanx to the front of it or even beside it. Where one places it depends upon how one believes the battle to have been fought and how much expertise one wishes to ascribe to the Thebans in general and Epaminondas in particular. Clearly, the Sacred Band as an elite unit of 300 was well trained, and that meant that it could undertake and execute maneuver in the presence of the enemy. Accordingly, it could have been placed left of the deep phalanx, and in this position it could act in concert with the cavalry as a flank guard for the regular infantry—which in and of itself would be another innovation. The Band could carry out the flank guard function by interfering with any Spartan attempt to outflank the Thebans. If, for some reason, the Spartans could not outflank the Theban left—say, terrain prevented it or their attempt to do so went awry early on, as may have happened—then the Band could move to take a position at the head of the deep phalanx.

As anyone who has been in the military or even just coached a football team knows, simpler is better. Accordingly, the author places the Band at the head of the deep phalanx. From there, it could protect the flank of the deep phalanx if the Spartans tried to outflank it by turning left and coordinating with the cavalry. If it was not needed for this, then the Sacred Band would stay in the general assault. This puts the best men in the place where Epaminondas determined the key to victory laid. Some sources say that the Sacred Band was formed into a wedge and led the assault on the left into the Spartans. Some historians dispute this; others dispute the nature of the wedge itself. In all battles and in ancient battles in particular, there is a lot we do not know and that provides ample grist for the mills of historians, antiquarians, hobbyists, reenactors, and armchair generals in general. Who comes closest? The author would not discount the reenactors.

What we do know is that the battle began with a cavalry-versus-cavalry encounter. The Theban horse was sent against their opposite number and in the ensuing clash, the Spartan cavalry was driven off by the crack Thebans. Where did they go? It is unknown, but the only way to get away would be to ride back through the Spartan infantry or leave the field by some other route, if possible. As they were on the right of the Spartan line, however, it is unlikely that they would ride all the way across the front line. If there were *peltasts*—light infantry—on the far right of the Spartan line, then they may have been the unwelcoming hosts for the routed horsemen. It may have even happened that some of the fleeing cavalry ran into the Spartan phalanx, creating disorder.

At this point, the infantry moved forward and, according to Epaminondas's plan, his center and left would hang back. This is the echeloned, or oblique, approach which characterizes this battle. With his right refused, he accomplished two things. He kept that part of his army intact, and it was therefore a potential threat. The depth of the Theban phalanx shortened the length of the line, thereby subjecting the other Boeotians on the right to a possible outflanking. This was not the way to make friends and influence allies. The refused Boeotian right meant that the Peloponnesian left could not outflank them because there was too much ground to cover and not enough time—if things went according to plan—for the Spartan allies to cover it. In effect, Epaminondas was saying to the other troops, "instead of putting you on the left where the Spartans will cream you, I'm putting you on the right against the weaker guys and I'm holding you back so that the you may never even get into the fight. Meanwhile, me and the boys will handle the Similars (the Spartan elite)." This sounded good to them. Anyway, once the Spartans were beaten, the whole army was beaten, and everybody knew it.

Whether the Spartan right was dislocated after the cavalry action or not, the Theban deep phalanx came on at the trot and at perhaps a near run, crashed into the Spartans, and began to push ahead. The men had been told by Epaminondas that if they lost, their homes would be destroyed and their families enslaved. This pep talk undoubtedly riled them up and a ferocious battle developed as Greek fought Greek, just as they had for years.

The worst of the fighting was around Cleombrotus, and the superior push of the Theban farmers began to tell. The Spartans gave way and were shoved aside. In the ensuing carnage, Cleombrotus and 400 of the Spartan elite were killed—some in the phalangial collision, others in the retreat. The Peloponnesians made for their fortified camp with the allies never having engaged the enemy and seemingly none too worried about it. The next day, they went home.

Casualties are, as usual, difficult to calculate precisely, but the Peloponnesians probably suffered about 1,000 killed and maybe an equal amount wounded. Theban casualties probably amounted to no more than about 300 killed.

This was a famous victory. The Thebans, badly outnumbered, defeated a superior force of Spartans and killed their king. A Spartan king had not been killed in battle since Leonidas at Thermopolyae 109 years before. Four hundred Similars were slain. As the historian Victor Hanson has pointed out, this is more Spartans than were killed in the Persian and Peloponnesian Wars. And when one takes into account that there were only 1,500 to 2,000 of these men in Sparta's population, the reverberations were felt throughout Greece. In one afternoon, the muscular rustics of Boeotia had shifted the balance of power in Greece. How much they had done so was demonstrated the following year when in December 370 B.C., Epaminondas led an army of 70,000 into the Peloponnese and did so handily.

## First and Only Man to Have Modified the Word "Victory:" Pyrrhus and the Battles of Heraclea and Asculum, 280 B.C.

Roman expansion into southern Italy in 281 B.C. occasioned a nine-year war. Tarentum appealed to Pyrrhus, the King of Epirus, for assistance. He brought an army of 20,000 phalangial infantry organized along Macedonian lines, as well as 3,000 Thessalian and Epirote cavalry and some elephants.

In this battle, the Romans had an army of about 35,000 under the command of Publius Valerius Laevinus; the army under Pyrrhus amounted to about 30,000. This was to be the Romans' first encounter with elephants. A fierce struggle between the forces was resolved by Pyrrhus's use of his elephants against the Roman cavalry, which was routed. The allied army then drove the Romans into and across the river in great disorder. The losses were, for the Romans 7,000–15,000, and for the victors 4,000–11,000. Pyrrhus is said to have remarked after the battle, "One more such victory and we are lost."

Pyrrhus advanced north, but upon hearing that another Roman and allied army was moving to meet him, he retired to the south of Italy and recruited an army, with contingents from Samnia and other Italian and Greek cities; all told, he had perhaps 70,000 men. The Roman army was led by the consuls Caius Fabricius and Quintus Aemilius and was about the size of the Italo-Greek army.

The armies met in 279 B.C. at Asculum (modern Ascoli) in Apulia. This was to be a two-day battle. The results of the first day were inconclusive. On the second day, Pyrrhus again made good use of his elephants against the Roman cavalry and the Roman army withdrew, but in good order. The casualties were about 11,000 to each side. The Greek contingents from Epirus suffered especially in this encounter.

This was another hard-won victory for Pyrrhus, but the cost was too high. It is from these two battles that the term "Pyrrhic victory" was coined. It now means a victory which nearly ruins the victor.

Between 278–276 B.C., Pyrrhus was in Sicily assisting the Syracusans against the Carthaginians. He raised the siege of Syracuse and drove the Carthaginians into their strongholds in central and western Sicily. He did not have time to conquer the island as he was called back to southern Italy in 275. There, he fought another hard, close battle with the Romans at Beneventum. This one he lost, however, when the Romans, who had been pushed back to their camp, were joined by the camp garrison, which managed to drive Pyrrhus's elephants into his phalanx. In the resulting confusion, the Romans counterattacked and inflicted great losses. Pyrrhus returned to Greece and was killed in a street fight in Argos in 272 B.C. By 269 B.C., Rome was master of southern Italy.

Pyrrhus remains the only man in history to have a type of victory named for him. While exactly how Pyrrhus might have felt about this dubious legacy remains unknown, exhaustive research could not turn up a single person in the ancient world named "Overwhelming," "Crushing," "Decisive," "Spectacular," or "Lop-sided," so maybe he wouldn't have felt so bad about it after all.

## War with the Biggest Slaughters:
### The Second Punic War, 219–202 B.C.

This war was notorious for battles which produced immense casualties.

The first battle in Italy between the Romans and Carthaginians took place in November at the Ticinus River. The Romans lost what was mostly a cavalry-versus-cavalry encounter and Scipio was wounded. Meanwhile, Sempronius brought his army up the Po Valley to join Scipio's forces. Hannibal's army was now over 30,000 because of recruitment of Gauls. The Romans totalled about 40,000.

Sempronius, against the advice of Scipio, crossed the Trebia River and attacked. The two armies were arrayed with their cavalry on either flank. The Carthaginian cavalry drove off their Roman counterparts but the decisive action was that of Mago, Hannibal's brother. Mago led a mixed infantry-cavalry contingent, which was concealed in a ravine, against the right flank and rear of the Roman line. Only 10,000 Romans escaped by breaking through the center of the Carthaginian line. Hannibal lost more than 5,000.

By mid-March, 217 B.C., the consulship was in the hands of Gaius Flaminius and Gnaeus Servilius. They commanded armies of 40,000 at

Arretium (Arezzo) and 20,000 at Arminium (Rimini) respectively. From these positions, the armies blocked the two main roads into Central Italy. Hannibal spent March and April leading his 40,000 men through the Appenine passes north of Genoa, south along the seacoast, and across the supposedly impassable Arnus marshes, putting his army behind those of the Romans. It is in this portion of the march that Hannibal lost an eye to infection but, in modern parlance, gained a strategic envelopment. Hannibal had turned the enemy's flank. He was now between the Roman army and Rome, thereby cutting their lines of communication. When this happens, commanders get nervous.

Hannibal headed south, plundering the countryside and torching villages. Livy tells us that Hannibal was turning the area into a desert. One reason this was done, leaving out for the sheer fun of it, was to draw Flaminius on. Reconnaissance was not a strong point of the Romans and it did them in on this occasion. It is so with most armies that are weak in this tactic or which neglect it.

Flaminius rushed south to seek battle and restore his line of communications. Hannibal chose, as the site of the ambush, the main road next to Lake Trasimene, which was overlooked by hills. The interesting thing about this choice of terrain was that the ambush was to take place not at the natural choke point, the narrowest part of the defile where it would be expected, but on a plain to which the Romans would come before encountering the defile. This could, and apparently did, encourage some laxness on the part of the Romans. Hannibal made camp on a hill at the east end. The Romans arrived late in the day and camped to the west, perhaps eight kilometers away, and they may have been able to see the Carthaginian camp. During the moonlit night, the Carthaginians moved out of camp and deployed. This set the stage for the Battle at Lake Trasimene.

Hannibal placed his heavy infantry, the Spanish and African veterans, at the southern end on a spur with the lake behind them, thereby blocking Roman passage to the east. He may have also placed his slingers and javelineers with these troops and it is speculated that they were placed behind the heavy infantry on rising ground, which allowed them to shoot over the heads of the infantry. He concealed his light infantry and cavalry on the wooded mountain side and perhaps also in the small valleys. Above the western end of the trap, that is, the entrance to the ambush, he deployed his Celts and more cavalry.

The Romans entered the ambush at dawn the next day. Aiding the Carthaginians was a heavy mist on the lake, which obscured the Roman view of the hills. The Roman advance guard, the *Extraordinarii*, crossed the plain with the rest of the army following in column. As they made

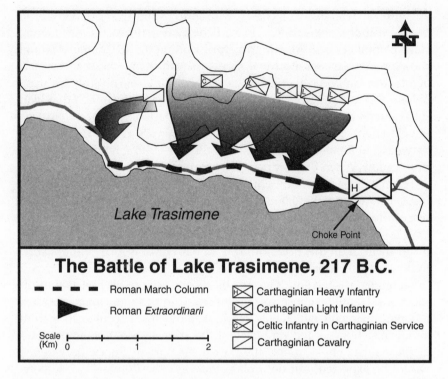

## The Battle of Lake Trasimene, 217 B.C.

■ ■ ■ ■   Roman March Column

◤   Roman *Extraordinarii*

Scale
(Km)  0          1          2

⊠  Carthaginian Heavy Infantry

⊠  Carthaginian Light Infantry

⊠  Celtic Infantry in Carthaginian Service

◻  Carthaginian Cavalry

contact with the infantry at the eastern end, trumpets were sounded and the rest of the Carthaginian army attacked from the hills and the north. The Romans, in march column and not in battle order, were beset from three sides with a lake on the fourth. The vanguard managed to fight its way through, but the rest of the army was trapped. Flaminius tried to bring order to his army and moved as best he could amongst his men, encouraging them, but noise of the battle was so loud that commands could not be easily passed, if at all. In the confusion and limited visibility, some men fled, some fought, and all around, men died. There was no escape, but the fighting raged on for three hours. Livy tells us that the combatants did not even notice the earthquake which occurred during the battle. Flaminius was cut down by an Isubian lancer named Ducarius, who was out to avenge the destruction of his town by the Roman. The consul's men fought furiously to prevent his body being mutilated, but the commander's death was the beginning of the end and the panic started. Everywhere, men were cut down—those who tried to swim for it, those who tried to gain the high ground, those who tried to fight their way out.

By the time the sun burned off the mist, the vanguard, which after fighting their way out and taking roost on some high ground beyond the ambush, was able to see the extent of the disaster. They then moved on the next day, before dawn, but they were overtaken by Carthaginian cavalry under one of Hannibal's deputies, Marhabal. They surrendered their arms on the condition that they would be free to go with one garment. This Maharbal accepted, but Hannibal later put them in chains.

Casualties are placed at around 15,000 dead for the Romans with about the same number captured. Somehow, approximately 10,000 made their way back to Rome. Carthaginian dead were estimated at only 1,550 to 2,500. Hannibal released all the allied prisoners without ransom because he was trying to undermine their alliances with Rome. Three days after this news arrived in Rome came word that 4,000 cavalry sent by consul Servilius to assist Flaminius had also been lost. Half were reported killed, the rest captured. After this bombshell had been absorbed, the Romans appointed Quintius Fabius Maximus as acting-dictator and Marcus Minucius Rufus as his Master of Horse. These two were given the task of strengthening the defenses of the city and defending Rome. Hannibal moved south to seek a base in southern Italy and to raise more armies from the cities and tribes, which were of dubious loyalty to Rome.

## Battle Against Which All Others Are Compared:
### Battle of Cannae, 2 August 216 B.C.

By the summer of 216 B.C., the Romans had an army of eight Roman and eight allied legions totaling 80,000 men and 7,000 cavalry. There were two new consuls as well, Aemilius Paulus and Terentius Varro. The former was cautious, the latter was not. Command alternated daily, as per Roman custom and Hannibal may have been counting on that when he decided to force the issue. The Carthaginians conducted a night march to Cannae and captured a supply depot and the granary of southern Apulia. The Romans followed and the antagonists established fortified camps six miles apart south of the Aufidus River. The Carthaginians numbered about 40,000 infantry and 10,000 cavalry.

Hannibal drew up for battle on the morning of 2 August; his back was to the river which curved at this point away from him. His left flank ran to a stream and was thereby protected from envelopment. He left 8,000 men to defend the camp. Hannibal placed his infantry, Spaniards and Gauls, in the center in a thin line; he placed his African heavy infantry on both flanks of these, arrayed in a deep phalanx. On the far left flank, he deployed his 8,000 Spanish and Gallic heavy cavalry under the command of Hasdrubal, while he deployed his 2,000 Numidian light cavalry on the far right.

Varro accepted the offer of battle and drew up the Roman army thus. He sent 11,000 men to attack the Carthaginian camp. As the Carthaginian flanks were well-protected, he decided to use his greater numbers to advantage by overwhelming the enemy. He doubled the depth of each maniple and reduced the intervals between them so that his force of 65,000 men occupied the same frontage as the Carthaginians. Varro placed 2,400 Roman cavalry on his right flank facing Hasdrubal and 4,800 allied cavalry on the left flank facing the 2,000 Numidians. Skirmishers were deployed forward of all Roman units.

Hannibal advanced with the central portion of his line forming a salient while his phalangeal wings stood fast. On his left, Hasdrubal led the heavy cavalry forward and attacked the Roman cavalry. In the ensuing combat, most of these Romans were killed and the rest driven off. On the Carthaginian right, the Numidians fought the more numerous allied cavalry to a standstill. Hasdrubal reorganized his horsemen and

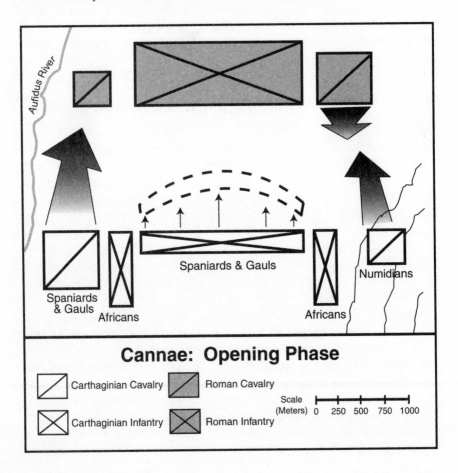

## Cannae: Opening Phase

Carthaginian Cavalry    Roman Cavalry

Carthaginian Infantry    Roman Infantry

Scale
(Meters)   0    250   500   750   1000

led them in an envelopment of the Roman lines, striking the allied cavalry in the rear. The allied cavalry broke and fled, with the Numidians in pursuit.

Meanwhile, the weight of the Roman infantry pushed forward and the Carthaginian center gave ground by design. As the Romans pushed ahead, the Carthaginian line became concave in shape and the already densely-packed Romans were even more compressed. At this point, the African heavy infantry wheeled inward and began to attack the Roman flanks. Hasdrubal again reformed his cavalry and led it into the rear of the Roman infantry, thereby sealing off the only escape route for the Roman infantry and ensuring that the Romans would die by the thousands. Panic spread through the surrounded soldiers who minutes

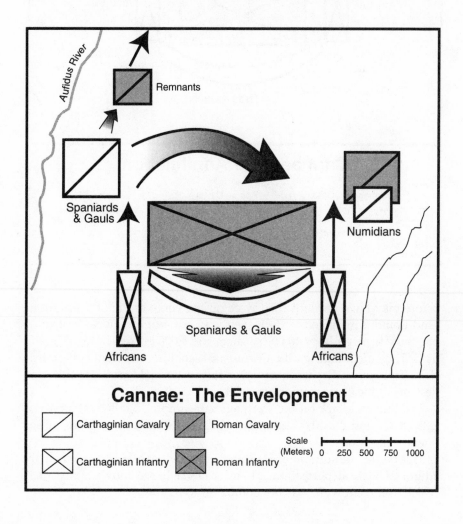

**Cannae: The Envelopment**

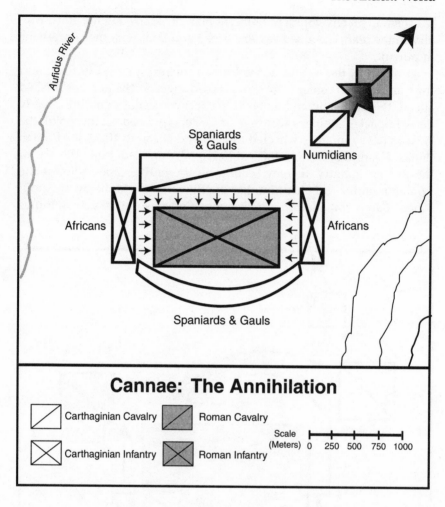

## Cannae: The Annihilation

Carthaginian Cavalry    Roman Cavalry

Carthaginian Infantry    Roman Infantry

Scale (Meters)  0  250  500  750  1000

before may have thought they were on the verge of victory. Ten thousand Romans managed to fight their way out, but by the close of combat, there were perhaps 40,000 soldiers and 4,000 horsemen dead on the field. They included Aemilius Paulus, 80 senators, and many other officials. The largest Roman army ever put in the field to this point was destroyed; the Carthaginians lost 6,000 to 8,000.

The Roman attack on the Carthaginian camp also failed, at a cost of 2,000 lives, and the 10,000 men guarding the Roman camp were subsequently captured.

This battle, the summit of Hannibal's military career, became the paradigm of tactical perfection. There is not a battle fought since then which, if it went well, was not compared to it.

## Worst Defeat of the Roman Army:
### Battle of Arausio, 105 B.C.

Although killing lots of enemy soldiers is usually a way to ensure winning a battle, it may not be the best way, nor does it always lead to decisive results in a campaign, much less a war. In 105 B.C., the migrating Cimbri and Teutones entered southern Gaul and defeated the army of M. Junius Silanus near the Rhône River. The Romans then dispatched Consul Mallius Maximus with an an army of 80,000 men to halt these wandering barbarians. At Arausio (modern day Orange, France), Mallius and his men confronted them in what quickly became easily one of the worst disasters ever to befall Roman arms. Not only were practically all of the Romans killed, but an additional 40,000 Roman non-combatants were slaughtered by the Germans, too.

This battle, while high in body count, is not reckoned by historians as being decisive; there was no long-term impact from the result of the battle. The Germans moved on to Spain and the Romans, under Marius, began wide-spread reform of the army. Seventy years later, the Romans came back with improved legions and thoroughly colonized the area. They literally had the last laugh, too: sometime around the early first century A.D., they constructed a theater that not only remains standing, but is still in use today for musical and dramatic festivals, most notably operas by Giuseppe Verdi.

## Victory Against the Biggest Odds:
### Battle of Tigranocerta, 69 B.C.

Lucius Licinius Lucullus, who was one of Sulla's subordinate commanders, invaded Armenia with only 10,000 men. At Tigranocerta, he attacked and defeated Tigranes, who had an army of about 100,000. Lucullus then marched into northeastern Armenia, where he again won at Artaxata in 68 B.C. From there, he returned to the Euphrates River valley in 67 B.C. because his men refused to go on after three years of campaigning.

## Most Decisive:
### Battle of the Teutoburg Forest, A.D. 9

When Octavian was named *imperator*, or emperor, in 29 B.C., one of the pressing questions of empire facing him was one which has subsequently vexed so many European and world leaders as well: "What to do about Germany?"

The border with the German tribes at this time was the Rhine River. From here, it was easy for the Germans to launch raids into Gaul, and by 27 B.C., the newly-proclaimed Caesar Augustus sought to establish a buffer zone along the Elbe River and Roman hegemony over these belligerent tribes. A series of campaigns by Augustus's stepsons, Drusus and Tiberius, succeeded in pushing the Germans back toward the Elbe River; indeed, in 7 B.C., Tiberius and his legions actually reached that barrier. The Romans, at this time, were perhaps justified to think that it was only a matter of time until Germany would become a Roman province.

Things turned out differently.

Periodic revolts by uncooperative German tribes began in the last year before the birth of Christ. Tiberius was sent in A.D. 4 to put out the fires. By the next year, he had pretty well suppressed the tribal upstarts, and in 6 A.D., he and his legions were sent further, down the Danube to deal with serious uprisings in Pannonia. This occupied him for the next three years. Meanwhile, command in Germany passed to P. Quintilius Varus, a man whose qualifications as a general in Germany seem to have been that he had been an experienced administrator in Syria. He then set out as governor to try to collect taxes, Syrian-style, from people who had little in the way of specie. Not surprisingly, the Germans took issue with this, and revolted again.

Varus commanded five legions in Germany plus a number of auxiliary units. One of these latter was commanded by a German chief named Arminius, and it was he who would lead the revolt against Rome. In the service of Rome, Arminius had gained military experience and had been granted citizenship and noble title. He ingratiated himself with Varus and convinced him that he was loyal. Being closely familiar with Roman tactics, and fully cognizant of the Roman superiority in battlefield discipline and flexibility, his plan to destroy the their legions was to ambush them in terrain that restricted their maneuver. To lure them into such a position, Arminius arranged for a series of revolts against the Roman garrisons, whereupon he would suggest to Varus that he put them down on the way to winter quarters on the Rhine. It would all happen in the autumn, by late September or early October. Having finished the summer campaigning, Varus and his men were marching back to Aliso on the Lupia (Lippe) River when he received word of the uprisings and a conspiracy against him. He refused to believe the latter and tasked Arminius to plan the route to put down the rebellions. Varus entered the Teutoburg Forest with three legions numbering about 20,000 soldiers, 10,000 non-combatants, and all the attendant baggage.

The exact route through modern-day Westphalia is unknown, but what is clear is that the narrow track on which the Romans moved wound through rugged, heavily-forested terrain. Heavy rains and high winds also impeded Roman progress. At some point, Arminius left the main force with his contingent, ostensibly to scout ahead; in fact, he rallied the German tribes to him.

The Romans were then beset by hit-and-run attacks during their difficult passage, which was made harder by slippery conditions. Worse, the dense woods severely degraded the effectiveness of missile weapons such pila and arrows, which the Romans used to keep the savage Germans at bay.

At the end of the first day, the Romans reached a clearing which gave them the opportunity to erect their traditional fortified camp. This allowed the Romans a brief respite. The next day, however, the Romans abandoned many of their wagons to speed their progress through the woods, but once they entered the forest, they again came under attack and continued to suffer heavy losses.

It is unclear for how many more days this went on, but the end was near. The Roman cavalry attempted to break away from the main force, but it apparently did not make it. On what is considered to be the last day, the Romans managed to erect some sort of earthworks for defense, but the Germans overwhelmed them. Varus and other wounded officers committed suicide; the survivors and non-combatants were butchered. Losses are unknown but sources say that only a few survived. A safe estimate of Roman losses probably approaches 25,000. Meanwhile, the garrison at Aliso fought its way out to the Rhine. With this, the Romans abandoned central Germany.

The results of this battle were extremely long lasting. While this was not the worst defeat of the Roman army in a tactical sense, it was the most significant one in which they had engaged in quite a while.

After the Teutoburg Forest, the Romans decided that the cost of pacifying Germany was be too high and they no longer pressed military forces into central Germany. They came to accept the Rhine as the northern border of the Empire. This meant that the future of Germany would not be a Latin one, nor would the regions beyond come under Roman control. This was decisive for the course of European history. The peoples beyond the Rhine would develop their languages and culture unhindered by the ablative case.

The battle demonstrated also that Roman tactics and discipline—while ideally suited for open terrain—could not be applied, or in this case adapted, to difficult terrain and an aggressive, persistent, and tenacious enemy.

## Battle That Ended the Dominance of the Infantry in War:
### Adrianople, A.D. 378

This battle, fought between the Goths and forces of the eastern portion of the newly-divided Roman Empire, is generally considered to signal of the end of infantry dominance in warfare and the rise of cavalry for the next thousand years.

There were two kinds of Goths, Visi- and Ostro-; think of them as West and East. These peoples, who originated in Scandinavia, marched around a good part of the world. Their migrations had taken them from northeastern Europe to Russia, to the Balkans, and beyond. Under pressure from the Huns coming out of the east, the Ostrogoths moved west from Russia and bumped up against the Visigoths, who pushed other Goths living in the Danube valley up against the eastern Romans. The Romans allowed these Goths to live in their territory if they gave up their arms and provided hostages. The Goths were subjected to indignities by the two Roman officials charged to administer them, who sought to enrich themselves at Gothic expense. Bribes and sexual favors were sought, and, apparently, reluctantly given, in return for allowing the Goths to keep their weapons. Into this scene entered the Ostrogoths, led by Alatheus and Saphrax, who requested permission to settle there. This was refused, but they crossed the Danube anyway, where they allied with the Visigoths under Fritigern, who had enough of the Romans' corruption.

Disturbed by the growing disobedience and in the light of there being no controlling legal authority, the Roman duo decided that assassinating Fritigern would solve their whole problem. They invited Fritigern and Alavivus, another Goth leader, to dinner, whence they would get them drunk and kill them. The Goths' bodyguard, who was in another part of the palace, was attacked, and this alerted the Goth leaders. Alavivus was killed, but Fritigern was able to draw his sword and make his escape.

This meant war. The Goths were an experienced and warlike folk, many of whom had previously served the Romans as mercenaries. The Goths carried all manner of weapons, including short stabbing swords, long cutting swords, battle axes, pikes, and bucklers. (A buckler is a small, round shield either carried in the hand or worn on the arm. The Gothic ones were made in part with iron.) The Goths traveled with large wagons which they formed into a circle or circles to create portable fortresses from which they could operate. These wagon cities are often referred to as *laagers*. What the Goths lacked was a siege train.

Initially, the campaign went well for the Romans. Gratian, the eastern Emperor Valens's nephew, brought his army from Italy and suppressed uprisings in Gaul before heading down the Danube. Valens's generals enjoyed similar success in Thrace against the Goths. Valens later placed Sebastiani, an Italian, in command; he believed that the war should be fought by small, mobile units of well-trained soldiers who would engage in hit-and-run tactics. In this way, the Goths could be worn down and once their supplies ran out, they would want to negotiate their withdrawal. If, in the process, the withdrawal sent the Goths east into the path of the Huns, well, so much the better. Valens decided against this for reasons of vanity, so Edward Gibbon tells us in *The Decline and Fall of the Roman Empire*. He wished for himself the glory which he perceived to be going to his nephew and generals.

On 9 July, a hot day in more ways than one, Valens led an army of 40,000 infantry and 20,000 heavy and light cavalry out of their camp near Adrianople against the Goth's camp, 11 miles away. Fritigern, when learning of the advance, sent for Alatheus and Saphrax, who were out foraging with their cavalry. He then played for time by offering to open negotiations. Valens agreed to negotiate, but ordered the deployment of his tired troops from march formation to battle order, with cavalry in the vanguard, then the infantry, followed by more cavalry. This took a long time and as the heat of the day built up, the men and animals became exhausted. In fact, both commanders were playing for time.

Valens, hoping to complete his deployment, sent the first Gothic emissaries back to Fritigern saying that they were not of sufficiently exalted stature. This was fine by Fritigern. Then the unexpected happened. When Valens's ambassador was on his way to negotiate with Fritigern, his escort of Iberian archers opened fire on the Goth's *laager* and then ran for it.

These Roman auxiliaries opened the fighting before the main body of their army was deployed for battle. The legions were still forming up, although the cavalry was ready on the flanks. At this point, probably sensing that being aggressive, if unprepared, was better than being passive and unprepared, Valens ordered a general attack. Alatheus and Saphrax returned with their cavalry at this time and charged the cavalry on the Roman right, routing them.

The Gothic horsemen rode around the back of the *laager* and assailed the Roman cavalry on the left flank. This assault was coordinated with the Visigoth infantry, which sortied from behind the wagon ramparts. This drove the remaining Roman cavalry from the field, leaving only the infantry, which was still deploying. The horsemen then swarmed

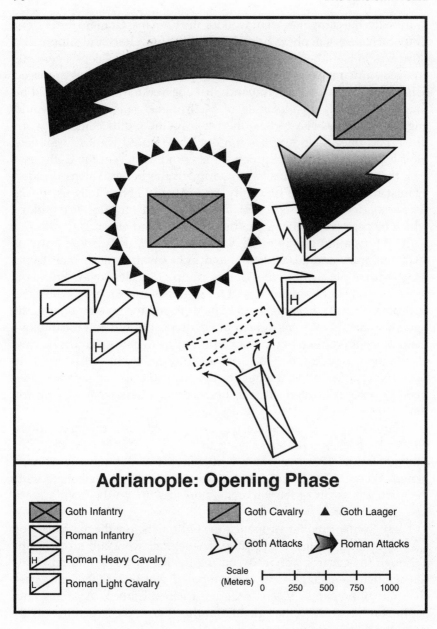

## Adrianople: Opening Phase

| | | | |
|---|---|---|---|
| Goth Infantry | Goth Cavalry | Goth Laager | |
| Roman Infantry | Goth Attacks | Roman Attacks | |
| H Roman Heavy Cavalry | | | |
| L Roman Light Cavalry | Scale (Meters) | 0   250   500   750   1000 | |

around the Romans' flanks and the Visigoths sallied from their camp
and engaged the legionaries, infantry to infantry. The Romans were surrounded and jammed together to such an extent that they could not
effectively use their weapons. The slaughter started and did not stop

until Sebastiani, 35 tribunes, and 40,000 other Roman soldiers were killed. Valens was wounded and his men managed to get him away from the battlefield to a cottage. Here the Goths surrounded the place and set it alight, not knowing that the emperor was inside. A youth from inside the hut managed to escape and relate the tale.

The disaster at Adrianople was as great as any which befell Roman arms, but it ranks with Cannae in its impact on the Empire, which

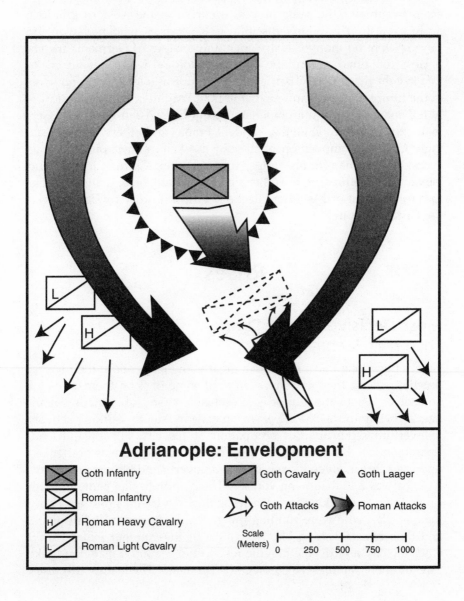

## Adrianople: Envelopment

| | | |
|---|---|---|
| Goth Infantry | Goth Cavalry | ▲ Goth Laager |
| Roman Infantry | | |
| H Roman Heavy Cavalry | Goth Attacks | Roman Attacks |
| L Roman Light Cavalry | | |

Scale (Meters) 0 250 500 750 1000

became panic-stricken. It not only indicated that the Teutonic hordes were in the ascendency, but also that infantry-centric tactics, evolved over the past 1,000 years, had now definitely been eclipsed. In their place was the new arm of decision in war—cavalry.

Theodosius succeeded Valens and instituted widespread reform in the Roman military establishment. As he campaigned successfully against the Goths, he incorporated them as mercenaries (*foederati*) into the Eastern army, thereby irretrievably changing the institution's character. Eventually, the same process occurred in the western Empire's army as well. The highly disciplined legionaries who had won the Empire were no more. Cavalry, including masses of Germanic mercenaries, remained ascendant until technology would again make infantry the master of the battlefield, but that was over a thousand years in the future. In the meantime, the Roman Empire in the West gradually fell apart under continuous hammering from Asian Huns and Germanic tribes including Goths, Vandals, Franks and others. The increasingly German composition of the did not help, either; on numerous occasions, "Roman" units simply followed their German leaders and joined their brethren on the other side of the battle line! Only the eventual recruitment of easterners in the late fifth century probably saved the Eastern Empire.

# Ruses

## Most Decisive Use of Drag:
### Thebes in Boeotia, 379 B.C.

Greeks have long had to endure a great many jokes about their sexual proclivities, but they may have brought some of it on themselves (or "ourselves," since the author is of exclusively Greek heritage). Pelopidas, a Theban (b. ?—364 b.c..), was in exile in Athens working actively to overthrow the Spartan occupation of his city. His great friend, Epaminondas, did not have to flee Thebes because he was not looked upon as a threat, given his self-imposed poverty and philosophical outlook; he was a Pythagorean you see. The plan the exiles came up with came down to sneaking into Thebes, going to a friend's house, finding the oligarchs who were running things for the Spartans, killing them, and thus re-establishing liberty. Twelve of the younger exiles would enter the city and do the job; the rest would remain outside and take care of their families if the worst happened. The exiles disguised themselves as hunters in short coats and had with them hounds and hunting poles.

Pelopidas and his fellow hunters entered the city during the day from different places and they were aided by a winter storm, which kept most of the people indoors. They were met by sympathizers who conducted them to the house of Charon, a prominent Theban who was in favor of the plot.

Their number now reached 48. The targets of the assassins were Archias, the *polemarch* or commander, Leontidas (no relation to Leonidas of Thermopylae fame), and Philip. They were men who Plutarch describes as rich, imbued of oligarchic principles, and immoderately ambitious. Phillidas, the secretary to Archias and Philip, was also in on the plot and it was he who made the arrangements that would deliver the tyrants. How? The usual way, of course: they were to be plied with abundant alcohol and immediately available women.

The victims arrived for the party and the wine flowed, but before Archias was drunk, he received word that the exiles were in the town. Phillidas tried to deflect the conversation but Archias called for one of the guards to go to Charon's house and bring him back. The guard arrived and informed Charon that he was wanted by the *polemarch*. Trepidation swept over the conspirators—were they discovered? Was a trap set for them? Charon, in consulting with them, said that he had to go or it would create suspicion. Before leaving, he offered them his young son as a guarantee of his fidelity to the cause. If he was proved a traitor to them, then they should kill the boy. The would-be killers of Archias and the others protested that they could do no such thing.

When Charon arrived, he talked with Archias and Phillidas. Archias said that he had heard that there were some men lurking in town and they had some supporters. Charon asked after their identity and more information about their activities. Archias said he had no specific information but he would look into it because these kinds of things had to be taken seriously. Phillidas said, "That is a great idea, Archias. Have another drink. I think the women will be here soon." Charon returned home and told Pelopidas and his men what had transpired, but to the others, he made up a story. The plan would go ahead.

About the time the storm blew over, a messenger with a letter arrived in Thebes. He had been sent from an Archias in Athens with a letter for Archias in Thebes. The letter detailed all the aspects of the plot. The messenger said to the drunk Archias that the writer of the letter desired the recipient to read it at once as it was urgent business. Archias said, "Urgent business tomorrow," and put the letter under his pillow. The plotters were now on the move in two groups. Charon and Melon had the task of killing Archias and Philip. They put woman's clothing on over their breastplates and wound garlands of fir and pine around them to hide their faces. When they came into the party the men clapped and cheered until the assassins, or freedom fighters, if the reader prefers, revealed themselves. They went for Archias and Philip, and any drunk guest who tried to interfere was dealt with as well. Pelopidas and his party had the harder task of killing the sober and strong Leontidas and his neighbor, Hypates. Leontidas's house was shut and it took some time for a servant to come and unbar the door. The instant he did, the assassins/freedom fighters rushed in. Leontidas had time to draw his dagger and he stabbed the first man, Cephisodorus, at the bedroom door. The second man was Pelopidas and he engaged Leontidas in the narrow passageway with the Cephisodorus' corpse between them. In a fast and deadly furious fight Pelopidas killed Leontidas.

The men then went to Hypates's house and similarly broke in, but Hypates fled to a neighbor's house. The group followed and Hypates was caught and killed. Now the conspirators all joined up and sent word to Athens for all the exiles to speed to Thebes. They then called upon the citizens to fight for their liberty and they broke open all the armorer's shops and equipped all who came. Epaminondas and Gorgidas came in already armed with a group of young men and capable older men. Confusion and excitement was spreading throughout the town but as the citizens did not appear to be massing, the Spartan garrison of some 1,500 did nothing. The next day, the armed exiles from Athens appeared and a general assembly was called. Epaminondas and Gorgidas praised Pelopidas and the others and presented them as the deliverers of Theban liberty. Pelopidas was chosen as the chief captain of Boeotia and he, Melon, and Charon led an assault against the citadel where the Spartans were barricaded. It was crucial to dislodge them before the Spartan relief force could reach Thebes, and it was close. The Spartans surrendered on terms and left. On the way back, they met the Spartan force. The Spartans executed two of their governors in Thebes and fined a third.

Over the next few years, 379—371 B.C., there followed a series of battles by which Theban and Boeotian freedom was preserved.

## Best Example of Fighting Fire with Fire:
### Eumenes the Diadoch, 317 B.C.

Antigonus I, that fast mover of the Diadochi (successors of Alexander the Great), resolved in 317 B.C. that he had to attack Eumenes, a fellow Diadoch. Eumenes was in Persia with his army dispersed into winter quarters. In a rapid approach, Antigonus estimated he could be there in nine days. He ordered that fires could not be lit because it would alert the enemy to their approach.

On the fifth night of the march, the soldiers had had enough of the cold and lit their fires. Villagers on the line of approach saw them and sent word back to Eumenes. He needed time to get his army together, so he sought to convey the impression that his army was already assembled. To this end, he had his men light fires at night every 30 feet on some high ground to simulate the perimeter of his army. The fires were brighter at the first watch, then burned less so at the second watch and dimly at the third watch when all but a few were allowed to go out, indicating to the informed but misled observer that an army was cooking supper, going to bed, and leaving a few fires for the watch. Antigonus inferred from this that the enemy was assembled and so he checked his advance, thinking that the element of surprise had been lost, and giving Eumenes the time needed to concentrate his forces. To refresh his troops, Antigonus decided to reduce the pace of the march through the villages and towns. During this time, there was no skirmishing with the other army and this was the dog that didn't bark as far as he was concerned. When two armies are this close, it is expected that patrols will meet and blows be exchanged. The locals told Antigonus that no army had been seen in the country for some time. Antigonus realized that he had been fooled.

In the battle which finally followed the great campfire ruse, Eumenes' phalanx, composed of Philip's and Alexander's veteran Macedonians, routed the infantry of Antigonus. Antigonus's cavalry, however, had captured the baggage of the *Argyraspids*, or Silver Shields. They wanted it back, so Antigonus told them that if they turned Eumenes over to him, he would allow them to retrieve their baggage. In a stunning display of treachery, the Silver Shields agreed, and it was done. Apparently embarrassed by his own underhandedness, Antigonus could not face Eumenes when he was brought to his camp. He gave orders to make him comfortable and allowed his friends to visit. He was undecided about what to do with his former pal, and while some argued in favor of keeping him alive, there were more voices calling for his death. Ultimately, Eumenes was executed forthwith, because apparently, there was not enough time to starve him to death, which was the preferred method. His friends received permission to cremate his remains and they sent Eumenes' ashes in a silver urn to his family. Whether Antigonus was overwhelmed with guilt at his actions or just acting on the principle that there are certain things troops should not be allowed to do, the Silver Shields were delivered to Sibyrtius, the governor of Archosia, with orders that by any and all means they must be destroyed and exterminated so that not one man of them would ever set foot in Macedonia or even come within sight of the Greek Sea. This Plutarch tells us.

# The Medieval World

## Introduction to the Middle Ages: 400 to 1500

The era begins with the end of the Roman Empire, leaving only the Eastern Roman Empire (later referred to as the "Byzantine Empire") defending Christendom and western civilization. As said before, the trend of incorporating barbarian *foederati* cavalry into the Roman armies continued, and cavalry's dominance of the battlefield was not reversed until the fourteenth century. The Roman army of the west had been for centuries an infantry-based army. As the empire expanded, it moved into regions where cavalry dominated. The Romans had to make accommodation with the type of warfare practiced in the east and other places, warfare which took account of different geography, traditions, and assumptions. The Romans took to the horse and by the beginning of the third century A.D., the army was one-quarter cavalry, with an even larger percentage of Roman forces in the East consisting of mounted units. The army also increased the role of missile weapons in its tactical system. This led to the adoption of the Persian-style heavy cavalryman, the *cataphract*. An armored horse-archer who carried a bow, sword, and shield, this was the best trained of the new Roman cavalry. He could be used, as circumstances permitted, in missile or shock roles.

Belisarius (505–565) of Byzantium, one of the best generals the New Rome produced, relied heavily upon cavalry in his battles. He had three types, namely the *cataphracts*, light horse-archers recruited from the Huns, and heavy spearmen recruited from the Lombards and Goths. Belisarius defeated a Persian-Arab army of 40,000 with his army of 25,000 at the battle of Daras in 530. He positioned his army behind a deep trench with the infantry in the middle and cavalry on the wings. There were passages across the trench so that the cavalry could move unimpeded. The Persians came on in two lines and when their infantry in the center came to the trench, it lost contact with the cavalry on its wings, creating two gaps. Belisarius then led the cavalry reserve through a gap and drove off the Persian left wing before attacking the center on the flank and rear, and inflicting huge losses. This is an example of a counterattack culminating in an envelopment with devastating results, and it is indicative of good generalship and a good army.

The only real infantry in this period—and by that, what is meant is the inheritors of dismounted shock tactics—is of the Franks. They were noted for the vitality and vigor of their attack in a dense, disorganized mass. They wore little, if any, armor and carried a javelin or francisca (a heavy throwing axe), and a sword. They were physically imposing, rude barbarians with little regard for the Roman way of war. This is demonstrated by the fact that despite years of contact and combat, they had taken on none of the discipline which characterized legionary infantry. Clovis, who ruled the Franks from 481–511, instilled discipline to a level unknown by the Frankish army and his forces consistently performed well in a series of successful wars. He defeated the Alemanni, and advanced his empire to the upper Rhine. He intervened in a dispute in Burgundy to his advantage. He fought and defeated the Visigoths at Vouillé (507), personally killing King Alaric II. This expanded the Frankish kingdom to the Pyrenees. He also converted to Christianity as his wife had done earlier, and at the time of his death, the Frankish kingdom—the basis for France—incorporated much of Gaul and western Germany. It would fall to the successors of Clovis to protect western Europe from expansionist Arab Muslims just over a century later.

There was nothing new about the Muslims' system of warfare; it relied upon horse-archers and lancers. What was new was the religious fervor associated with it, and it carried these armies in a dynamic wave of conquest. Fortunately for them, the temporary exhaustion of the Persian and Byzantine empires, which had been at war for 26 years, provided a good place to start. Persia was overrun, but the superior discipline, training, and talent of the Byzantines checked the Arab advance to the north. The Byzantines also had an ace in the hole, a substance called "Greek fire." This napalm-like mixture, composition now unknown, was the miracle weapon of the time. It was squirted under pressure, probably powered by an instrument resembling a giant syringe, from a tube filled with water. It was water, by the way, which ignited this mixture which only vinegar, sand, or urine could put out. The Muslims' first assault on Constantinople (also known as Byzantium) came in 673 with a joint land-sea force. The Byzantines withstood a four-year siege ending in a climactic battle that killed 30,000 on sea and on land. The Muslim invaders withdrew and agreed to restore all conquered lands and pay an annual tribute of 3,000 pounds of gold. In June 717, the Muslims were back again with a force of 80,000 men led by Maslama. In September 717, Suleiman arrived with an armada of 1,800 ships and another 80,000 men. The Byzantines under Leo III again managed to keep the enemy at bay. In the spring of 718, the assaults renewed but Leo had some surprises in store. In June, Leo's fleet attacked the enemy fleet in the Bosphorus and used fire to destroy an enemy squadron at anchor. With the way clear, he landed an army on the southern side of the Bosphorus and defeated part of the Muslim army. Previously, he had arranged with Terbelis, the king of Bulgaria, to attack Maslama's army camped south of Adrianople. In July, Terbelis did just that, and handed the Muslims another defeat. In August 718, the Muslims called off the siege. Part of the army marched through Asia Minor, where it was harassed by the Byzantines, and the rest departed on the fleet. During its voyage, a terrible storm wrecked all but five of the ships, and only 30,000 men made it home. Once again, the Byzantines had saved Christendom, for if the Muslims had succeeded in capturing Constantinople, it is unlikely that any of the western Europeans could have stopped them. The result of this siege was momentous for the West.

The basis for this victory was the Byzantine military system and its leadership. It is successful military systems which keep all empires in business. The keys to success are the same throughout history—discipline, organization, arms, *esprit de corps,* and tactics that are better than those of the opponents. If you have all this, all you need is competent leadership which will not throw away victory. The Byzantines, in addition to the education they received on the battlefield, institutionalized their experiences in military manuals, the best known being Maurice's *Strategikon,* and Leo the Wise's *Tactica.* The Byzantines maintained infantry as well and found uses for a combined arms team, which is the hallmark of a superior military. Officers were trained in staff and command duties. They also employed siegecraft, engineers, field fortifications, and an ambulance corps. (It would be the seventeenth century before Europe saw one of the latter!)

The Byzantines were usually outnumbered in their wars, but through superior training and highly adaptable tactics, they were able to prevail over a number of different foes. This was the best army of the Middle Ages and for over 500 years, it consistently "punched above its weight class"—to use a boxing metaphor—and won most of its bouts. At the heart of Byzantine grand strategy was the desire to retain the land they had, rather than going crazy trying to gain more. This defensive strategy served them well. They also used diplomacy, propaganda, all manner of ruses, intelligence networks, and bribery—some would say subsidies —to keep potential and real enemies off balance. In this way the Byzantines, whose political intrigues still inform the workings of Chicago politics, developed an integrated approach to war.

At the other end of the European continent, some years later, the Muslims suffered another setback. In 732 (some say 733), at the battle of Tours (some say Poitiers), the Franks, under Charles Martel (all agree on that), scored a victory over the Muslim army of Abd er-Rahman, which had invaded Frankish territory from Spain. Gaul would remain under the Franks, and remains Christian to this day.

The first empire to be built on the ruins of the Roman one was that of Charles the Great, better known as Charlemagne. Born in 742, he was king of all the Franks from 771 until 814. His military system was not perhaps as integrated as the Byzantine, but it did not need to be. When one is surrounded by anarchy, even two tablespoons of organization will work wonders and Charlemagne was of greater capacity than that. He harnessed Frankish vigor and imposed discipline on it; the result was that he created an empire which stretched from north of the Pyrenees to the Danube and the Elbe Rivers, and included one-half of the Italian peninsula. He established a standing army and the logistical organization necessary to support it without ravaging the countryside. The army was supplied with men in an orderly fashion from society based on the individual's or group of individuals' ability to provide an equipped man. Charlemagne maintained a siege train and sought to bolster his army in areas he deemed lacking, such as heavy (mailed) cavalry. The Lombardian cavalry was superior to his, so he brought it in and used it as a model to improve the Frankish cavalry. To control the newly-conquered territory, he established fortified posts or *burgs* along the frontier, and connected them with roads. Typically, another road connected each *burg* to the old frontier, thus facilitating movement along interior lines. The *burgs* were storehouses as well, and this made them good bases from which to launch attacks into enemy territory. Charlemagne also attempted to introduce the bow into his army, but this effort did not succeed. Through his imperial ordinances, he established the criteria for a standardized military system, tactical doctrine, and staff training. These elements are represented still in all efficient and professional military organizations.

Although there was much strife in the years after Charlemagne, there was not much new in the way of tactics. In the eighth and ninth centuries, swooping down from Scandinavia, the Vikings raided the

European continent and the British Isles, and even made their way up several rivers to penetrate deeply into Russia. Incredibly, they attacked Constantinople by way of Russia in 860. In the ninth and tenth centuries, the Magyars burst out of the area that is modern-day Hungary, invading and raiding their way into central Europe at one end, and into the Byzantine Empire at the other. The Turks, a nomadic horsepeople from central Asia, moved west, bumping into the Muslims moving east. Eventually, the Muslims subdued the Turks and enslaved them by the hundred thousand; these slaves were then used to form armies much larger than would have otherwise been possible using Arab manpower alone. The Byzantines expanded their holdings and then tried to defend them against depredations by European Christians and Muslims alike.

If these continuous threats did not spur significant innovations in tactics, they did, nevertheless, motivate European nobles to advance the art of fortification. Castles advanced from simple earth and wooden motte-and-bailey refuges to enormous stone wonders of engineering that constituted the first truly significant structures to be built in Europe since the demise of the western Roman empire more than 600 years earlier. As the feudal system evolved, these castles took on great importance beyond their military purposes, but throughout the Middle Ages, their use as defensive bastions against invaders was undiminished.

After centuries of being purely on the defensive, western, southern, and some central Europeans united, sort of, in a series of counteroffensives in the Middle East. In 1095, the call went out from Pope Urban II for a crusade to the Holy Land; this not only strengthened the power of the church over the rising nation-states, but it also provided an excellent opportunity for a little cross-cultural military interaction. There is always a benefit from such exchanges, even if they do end up with thousands of dead. The battles with the Muslims demonstrated that the heavily-armored European cavalry could annihilate anything it could catch, but catching highly mobile Muslim light forces was not easily accomplished. The Crusaders came to realize that the coordination of cavalry and infantry could produce victories, as Richard I, the Lionheart, demonstrated.

The Crusaders, as the most backward of the military organizations involved in these wars, gained the most from the interactions. Tactically, they learned to use light cavalry for screening and reconnaissance, thus helping to protect their main force. Improvements in castle design came as the Crusaders absorbed the lessons and examples of Byzantine fortifications. The Crusaders also learned the hard way to appreciate the importance of logistics. After all, the Middle East was not Europe, where armies took the field for only a season, sustain themselves, and

A full set of chain mail
armor.
*Higgins*

then go home when the food ran out. In the Middle East, preparations had to be made in advance, or men and horses died from lack of food, water, and fodder. In fact, more did so in the first two crusades than from combat. Richard the Lionheart is again our example of how to do it right with his march from Acre to Ascalon.

In terms of tactics, cavalry still dominated the battlefield, but infantry—heavy infantry—was soon to make its comeback. Cavalry came in three types. Heavy cavalry in Europe was the mailed knight armed with lance and shield and sword; shock action was his reason for being. The heavy Byzantine cavalryman was a horse-archer and a lancer capable of missile or shock action. The Muslim light cavalryman was lightly armored and either an archer or lancer.

New weaponry appeared in the eleventh century—at least it was new to Europe—in the form of the crossbow. A hand-held version of the ancient *ballista*, it propelled a heavy arrow, dart, or bolt with a force so great it could penetrate the armor of the day. Now *that* was not going to go over well with the armored classes. Of course, much worse news would come before the end of the Middle Ages.

Another infantry weapon which entered service was the halberd, a modification and improvement on the pike. The halberd's head combined the spear point of the pike with the cutting blade of an axe on an eight-foot shaft. Armor became heavier as the mail was modified and protection extended. It was all part of the still-ongoing endless duel between lethality and protection, which, after all, only mirrors the action-reaction nature of offensive and defensive tactics themselves.

Few developments were made in siegecraft during this period, and the techniques used by commanders besieging fortified areas were strikingly similar to those used by Romans a millennium earlier. One new weapon was introduced into siege warfare in the thirteenth century, however—the trebuchet. Relying on a counterweight rather than torsion, it was the best siege engine yet designed for throwing rocks to batter down enemy walls, or suppressing (or killing) defenders.

The thirteenth century also brought advances in armor, with plate armor gradually supplanting mail. Improvements in metallurgy and the armorers' skills created the beautiful suits of armor with which we are most familiar. The armorer was able to construct armor which gave the wearer a full range of motion and protection while still being able to fight effectively. This included protection for hands and feet as well.

The last weapon which rose to prominence in the thirteenth century was the longbow. A Welsh weapon, this mighty bow surpassed the crossbow in range, power, and rate of fire. In the following century, it was to figure prominently in the battles of Crécy (1342), Poitiers (1356), and Agincourt (1415), which demonstrated that infantry had returned to prominence on the battlefield as the senior partner of the combined arms team. Prior to this, however, in the thirteenth century, there arrived on the scene the greatest cavalry force the world would ever see, and it would conquer the largest empire ever known to man—the Mongols.

At the end of the twelfth century (1190), the Mongol chief Temujin (later known as Genghis Khan) started to co-opt some neighboring tribes. By the time he was finished in 1227, he had conquered all the land he wanted between Korea and Hungary. This left out India and Indo-China. It took him until 1206 to unite all the Mongolian tribes. He then started his wars against the Chinese and by 1215, he sacked Peking. In 1218, he turned west and invaded central Asia, defeating the Muslim Khwarwezmian empire of Mohammed Shah in a series of campaigns lasting five years. They also advanced into the Caucasus in 1221 and Russia in 1222, wintering by the Black Sea. In 1223, the Mongols

Bronze handcannon.
*Hogarth*

defeated a large Russian-Cuman army and then returned to Mongolia in 1224. In 1225, the Mongols returned to China to deal with the Hsia and Chin empires which had formed an alliance against Genghis. By 1227, the Mongols had secured victory over the Hsia, but rejected overtures from the Chin.

Genghis, having a premonition of his own death, set out for Mongolia, but died en route. His successors completed the conquest of China and his grandson, Kublai, established the Yuan Dynasty in 1279. Prior to this, from 1237 to 1240, Ogatai, Genghis's son, sent his brother, Subotai, to campaign in eastern Europe. He was successful in these campaigns and in 1241, he invaded Central Europe with about 120,000 men. Advancing with four separate armies, the Mongols invaded Poland, Silesia, and Hungary. By the summer, they were in control of Europe from the Baltic to the Danube and the Dnieper to the Oder, with more conquest planned for 1242 in the Balkans, Italy, Austria, and Germany. Before this could happen, word came to Subotai that Ogatai had died, and Mongol law required all of Genghis's descendants to return home to elect the new Khan. It was a lucky thing for western Europe. Russia remained under Mongol control—the "Golden Horde"—until 1380. The rest of Asia was divided up into Khanates and over the course of the fourteenth century, the Empire fragmented. Now you know why so many eastern Europeans have high cheekbones and almond-shaped eyelids. Those with blond hair or blue eyes can thank the Vikings, who had ravaged their way around coastal Europe and down the Volga a few centuries before. Who said military history is just about the boring mechanics of battles and details about weapons?

The Mongol military system was entirely cavalry based and organized into *toumans* of 10,000 men. These were further subdivided decimally, that is, into 10 units of 1,000 which, in turn, were divided into 10 units of 100, which was formed from 10 units of 10 men. The army was composed of heavy and light cavalry. Heavy cavalrymen wore armor of leather with some iron scales added; they carried a lance, a scimitar and wore a helmet. The light cavalrymen were archers carrying three

A woodcut depicting the use of crossbows, longbows, siege engines, and handcannon in an attack on a castle.
*Hogarth*

quivers of arrows, and assorted other weapons including a javelin, an axe, and a rope. The Mongols were well-trained, growing up in the saddle and experiencing a hard, outdoor life which gave them ample training with their weapons. Discipline was fierce; their mobility was unmatched. They always had riders out scouting and reporting back to a central headquarters, which, in turn, disseminated the information to all parts of the army on the march. The army advanced on a broad front in several columns, and once a column encountered the enemy, it would either attack or retire, depending upon the situation. The other columns would continue the advance and surround the enemy. The enemy would be showered with missiles from the light troops and at the right moment, the heavy cavalry would be sent in on a coordinated charge, preferably striking on the flank or rear.

The Mongols had no indigenous siegecraft, so they acquired it from the Chinese. The Mongols gathered intelligence on their victims and developed a plan of advance designed ahead of time. They kept records of their own and the enemy's dead, the latter by apparently cutting one ear from every dead soldier and tossing them in bags for counting. This provides an indication of the Mongol penchant for psychological warfare based upon cruelty. Terror was a valuable commodity to the Mongols and they knew that killing a few thousand here and a few more thousand there could amount to a persuasive argument for surrender. Once a territory was subdued, an administration was put in place and peace was enforced by force of arms. Then, the inhabitants of the area were taxed.

To return to Europe, the fourteenth century also saw the start of the Hundred Years' War. This is the longest-named war in history—which is to say that there is no war named the Hundred and One Years' War—even though it actually lasted from 1337 to 1453. It was a series of conflicts fought between the French and English over dynastic and political issues, and was punctuated with truces, some lasting for years. The truces were, 1340–41; 1343–45; 1347–54 (mainly due to the Black Death); 1360–67 was the Peace of Bretigny, which meant that the English only besieged Auray and seized it in 1364 while a war was ongoing in Brittany over the succession. Otherwise, the peasants had only to deal with the disbanded mercenaries. In 1368, peace having been given a chance, warfare resumed. The next truce was 1375–83, with only sporadic fighting. From 1389 to 1396, there were truces and some fighting, and in 1396, a 30-year peace was signed. Then in 1398, a 28-year truce was agreed upon by the French and English which lasted until 1415, when Henry V invaded France. The next truce, for two years in 1444, actually lasted until 1449. In 1450, the war resumed and lasted three years.

Things did not go well for the English. Aiding the French in this rapid conquest of the English possessions was their artillery, which made short work of the English castles. The fall of Bordeaux on 19 October 1453 was the end of the war. That makes 54 years of peace or almost-peace out of 116 years of war . . . so it really wasn't a 100(+) year war, after all.

The Middle Ages ended in the fifteenth century, at least as far as historians are concerned. Several factors contribute to this: The Hundred Years' War ended; the walls of Constantinople were breached by a monstrous bombard; and the Byzantine empire was finally destroyed.

By the end of the century, body armor was largely obsolete because of the capabilities of early guns. Small arms developed rapidly in the century. Starting out as iron tubes stuck on a pole, by mid-century they were barrels attached to a stock with a sophisticated firing mechanism called the matchlock. The weapon was loaded at the muzzle, with a powder charge held in place by tamping, and then the projectile was shoved down the barrel. The matchlock was an S-shaped piece of metal which held a slow-burning cord, the match. It was mounted on the side of the piece next to the pan and touch hole. Once the gun was loaded, priming powder was placed in the pan. When the firer pulled the trigger, the match swung into the pan and ignited the priming powder, which flared through the touch hole into the chamber and ignited the powder charge. The ensuing explosion propelled the projectile from the muzzle of the piece. In the latter half of the century, these weapons were fitted with a curved shoulder stock and set on a hooked stick at the front to support it. The French term was *arquebus* and it had an effective range of less than 100 yards.

Large gunpowder weapons developed apace as well and the French readily used artillery. The king established a permanent establishment for artillery under the Bureau brothers. This marks an institutionalization of a technical arm and that, too, is a sign of growing professionalism. In this period, improvements were also made for the carriages which carried these pieces. This made *field* artillery—as opposed to siege artillery—possible. The carriages had strong axles and wheels, and were built with long trails which made them more stable. The barrels were made with trunnions, two stout projecting pins on either side of the piece placed at or near the center of gravity. The trunnions held the tube to the carriage and allowed the weapon to be raised or lowered by pivoting it on the pins.

In tactics, trained and disciplined infantry was being combined with *arquebusiers* to produce combined missile and shock formations. The Swiss fielded the best infantry of the fifteenth century, and just behind them in proficiency were the German mercenaries called *Landsknechts*. These infantry formations were essentially phalanxes with massed pikemen. The Swiss could adapt their formations to suit conditions, but most often fought in deep column. They marched in this formation and so were able to go immediately on the attack without reforming. They came on in three columns, either in wedge or echelon, with each column ready to come to support of the other. The Swiss, in particular, were noted for the ferocity of their attack and the speed of their movement. It is easier for infantry in column to maneuver than it is for infantry in line. Additionally, the Swiss, because they were lightly armored, could march farther and faster than their more heavily-armored opponents.

# Equipment

## Most Powerful Bow: Crossbow

The crossbow originated in China in the sixth or fifth centuries B.C. Archeological evidence in Chinese tombs finds crossbows in the fifth and fourth centuries B.C. William McNeill tells us that the first great improvement came in A.D. 1068, when Li Ting invented the foot stirrup. The author poses a question, "why is it that if the Chinese were smart enough to invent the crossbow in the sixth century B.C., it took them 1,500 years years to invent the stirrup?" Maybe those Russian mathematicians are right and this is only the year A.D. 937. Leaving that aside, the weapon was powerful as was demonstrated when east met west at the battle of Sogdiana (Bukhara) in 36 B.C. Roman legionaries, possibly from Marc Antony's Parthian campaign, where shot down by crossbowmen from the Han empire whose bolts penetrated Roman armor and shields without difficulty.

The crossbow dominated archery for the last two-thirds of the medieval period. This weapon is characterized by a bow transversely affixed to a stock. The string, once pulled back, is held in place by a stop called the nut. A trigger mechanism, when actuated, releases the string from its stop and the arrow or bolt travels along a groove in the stock. The earliest triggers were simple levers which protruded through the bottom of the stock and were squeezed to release the string from the stop. The early crossbow strings were drawn by hand or by a claw which hooked onto the archer's belt; when the shooter stood up, he drew the string. The crossbow was also more accurate than the long or

The medieval crossbow.
*Higgins*

short bow. In fact, so devastating was this weapon and so brutal the wounds it inflicted that the church condemned its use by Christians in 1096–97 and 1139. Naturally, anybody headed for the battlefield was inclined to ignore these pronouncements. The church then decided in 1200 that it was all right to use the crossbow against non-believers and wrong-believers and in any just war.

As this weapon's deadliness increased, its use spread. Adapting the composite bow to the crossbow made this weapon more efficient. Made up of laminations of wood, bone, horn, and sinew, and glued together, the composite bow allowed an increase in power. A bow that cannot be cocked, however, is of little use, and it took especially strong, fit men to not only cock these weapons, but to do it repeatedly under battle conditions. Once the stirrup was added to the front of the stock, by slipping a foot through it, bowmen could anchor the stock to the ground and pull with their legs. This innovation allowed the construction of even more powerful bows.

Clearly, beyond the technical limits of the materials themselves, the limitations of the power of these weapons was the ability of bowmen to cock them. To facilitate this, by the fourteenth century, a windlasses were fitted to the butt end of the stocks. By winding the mechanism, the string could be drawn and and locked onto the stop in 12 seconds, according to the authority, Kelly DeVries. The pull of this weapon (pull constituting the force with which the arrow is launched), is given at about 1,200 pounds. By way of comparison, the same authority gives the pull of the longbow at about 50 pounds. The final cocking system developed was the *cranequin*, which was a ratchet-type affair. It required very little strength to use, but took 35 seconds to operate.

Improvements were also made to the trigger mechanism and aiming was assisted by the attachment of a rear-mounted notched sight. By the fifteenth century, the crossbow was made of steel and the range improved to as much as 500 yards. The bolts were made from ash or yew wood and tipped with a sharp tetrahedral-shaped metal point. Its length varied, but some samples are about 15 inches long. The bolt was stabilized in flight by feathers and it could penetrate plate armor.

One of the great advantages of the crossbow was that it did not require a lifetime of training to use it effectively as did the longbow. Once the bowman learned how to draw the bowstring and lock it in position, all he had to do was learn to aim. The longbowman had to develop his strength and dexterity and constantly practice a great deal to be effective. Interestingly, the best mercenary crossbowmen came from Genoa and Gascony.

Ironically, and not for the first time in history, the crossbow had reached a high state of sophistication when it was eclipsed by gunpowder weapons.

The trouble with crossbowmen was they took the fun out of war. There are examples of them being ridden down by their own cavalry.

## Best Infantry Weapon: Halberd and Pole-axe

The distinguishing feature of these hafted weapons was the shape of their steel heads. They combined two or three different ideas in their deadly business end. The halberd head combined a spear point with an axe blade attached part of the way back, and sometimes a hook as well for pulling riders off their mounts. The pole-axe was similar to the halberd; it, too, had a spear point, but sported a smaller axe blade. Where the halberd had a hook, the pole-axe had a hammer. The pole-axe permitted the aggressive user to spear, smash, and cleave his way to glory. Obviously, to be effective, the heads of these weapons had to be heavy.

The heads of the weapons were attached to a wooden pole by two or four metal straps forged together and running up to a yard in length along the shaft. The pole-axe emerged in the early fourteenth century and by the early fifteenth century, it was the weapon of choice for the

The halberd, weapon of choice for the medieval man-at-arms.
© *Historical Picture Archive/ CORBIS/MAGMA*

medieval man-at-arms. The overall length of these weapons was seven to eight feet. The halberdier and pikeman made up the shock component of the Swiss phalanx.

## Most Destructive Non-Gunpowder Artillery:
### The Counterweight Trebuchet

The trebuchet originated in China sometime between the fifth and third centuries B.C., and from there moved west. By the end of the seventh century A.D., the trebuchet was in use by the Muslims; by the thirteenth century, the Europeans had adopted it. It remained in use until the fifteenth century, when it was supplanted by gunpowder artillery.

The weapon was a stone thrower which was built in several versions, differentiated by each design's respective type of propulsive power. In the first version, called the traction trebuchet, propulsive power was provided by teams of men who pulled on ropes to get things moving. It is reported that as many as 250 men were used to pull on the ropes and they could generate enough momentum to throw a 120-pound stone over 400 feet. The machine was large and the heart of it was a long beam or pole which rotated on an axle that was off-centered two-thirds to three-quarters from the end. The axle was supported on a trestle-style tower which allowed the short end of the beam to swing through. A sling was attached to the long end of the beam. The projectile was placed in the pocket, and the open end of the sling was looped over a rod at the end of the beam. One could alter the distance the projectile traveled by adjusting the angle of the rod. By making this adjustment, one changed the point at which the sling came off the beam and that determined range. As the short end of the beam swung down, the sling was dragged along from underneath the trebuchet and the stone was released as the sling reached the top of its arc.

Some historians disagree about when the first traction trebuchet was used in Europe, but as their dates are only 600 years apart, we will not bother trying to resolve the dispute. What is clear is that by the twelfth century, the trebuchet was part of the siege warfare business anyplace Europeans were besieging. The drawback of the traction trebuchet was that the pullers could not provide consistent force to the ropes from shot to shot, so range was somewhat unpredictable.

The search for a consistent propulsive force ended when someone whose identity is sadly lost to history came up with the weighty idea of using weights. The counterweight trebuchet apparently appeared in the mid-twelfth century, although the traction trebuchet remained in use for some years more. Why should this be? The author suspects that it may have to do with simple economics. The earliest counterweight trebuchet had fixed weights, say lead plates, attached to the short end of the beam. How much weight?` Ten thousand to thirty thousand pounds, depending on the size of the machine. It may not have been easy to acquire that much metal, whereas guys pulling on ropes could be acquired most anywhere. On one occasion, the roofs of many churches were pulled down to secure enough metal to power a trebuchet. This machine could fire stone projectiles weighing up to 200 pounds over ranges of 300 yards. Two further refinements increased the power of this machine: the swinging basket and wheels.

The swinging basket was affixed to an axle at the short end of the beam in place of the fixed weights. The basket allowed more and different type of weighty material to be used simply because of its capacity. Besides more weight, it had the added benefit of lengthening the

Trebuchet (lower right corner) being prepared for firing during a siege.
© Bettmann/CORBIS/MAGMA

effective distance of the drop of the weight and this meant that more
momentum was delivered to the beam.

The use of wheels on the trebuchet is a matter of discussion among
many historians. The author's view is that wheels helped the efficiency
of the machine when firing by directing forces imparted to the carriage
into backward motion. This had to save on trebuchet wear and tear.

These engines were very effective against fortifications, especially
rubble-filled masonry curtain walls. The Muslims used 92 counterweight trebuchets when besieging the Christians at Acre in 1291, and
that has to be a record. Edward I used three trebuchets in 1296 when
besieging Holyrood abbey and secured their surrender after three days
and 158 stones. Of course, human ingenuity being what it is, the trebuchets were not restricted to just firing stones. Crocks of Greek fire,

which would shatter and ignite on impact, were favorite projectiles for those who had them. There are also accounts of rotten or diseased animal carcasses being thrown, or even human bodies or parts of bodies launched over the walls. These are early examples of not only biological warfare, but of psychological operations as well. After being bombarded with cow and pig (and human) innards, who would want to stick around long enough to be infected by their germs?

While the trebuchet continued to be used after the advent of gunpowder artillery, it was on the way out by the middle of the fourteenth century. Cannon were easier to build and more accurate, even if their ability to shoot sheep's entrails was pretty limited. It would be another six centuries before artillery could again effectively deliver biological agents, which was good news for man and beast alike.

## Greatest Castle of the Middle Ages:
### Krak des Chevaliers ("Castle of the Knights"), Syria

What is a great European castle doing near Safita in southern Syria? It all started in November 1095, when Pope Urban II called for a crusade to retake the Holy Land from the Muslims, who had stolen it from the Christian Byzantines in a mid-seventh century *jihad*, or holy war. The next year, an assemblage of Crusaders set off by various routes and agreed to meet at Constantinople. By the spring of 1097, all who had made it were ready to move and Alexius Commenus, the Byzantine emperor, was happy to see them move on. In two years of campaigning, the Crusaders captured Antioch and Jerusalem, and established four Christian kingdoms with elected monarchs at Edessa, Antioch, Jerusalem, and Tripoli. With the capture of the Holy Lands, most of the Crusaders returned home. Those who remained behind had to defend what they had won.

Castles, similar to the ones which had been springing up all over Europe in response to the invasions of Vikings, Magyars, and Muslim— not to mention neighboring European nobles—were rapidly built atop difficult terrain, at strategic points, in mountain passes, along the frontiers, along the sea coast, and inland to serve as bases for raiding and other offensive operations.

Some castles were built in the then-current European style of a rectangular keep and surrounded with a stone wall. These castles were expensive to build and the fortified keep, which was the castle's primary defensive feature, took the longest to construct. The majority of the

The Krak des Chevaliers.
© Bettmann/CORBIS/MAGMA

castles were built on the Byzantine pattern. This style was easier to erect, could be built more quickly, and lent itself to physically larger design. The last was an important factor because the European-style castle was too small to house the number of troops and stores required for the missions and garrisons required. The Byzantine-style castle had reinforced walls and towers where needed. Inner buildings, absent the keep, were used for stores, barracks, kitchens, magazines, and so on. This style of castle depended first on perimeter defense.

The *Krak* was built on a hilltop over 2,000 feet in elevation and could only be approached over steep slopes. Expanded and strengthened continuously over a century and half following 1110 by Crusaders, especially the Knights Hospitallers, the castle eventually covered an area approximately 682 feet by 455 feet. Semi-circular towers were arrayed along the walls at intervals to provide extra opportunities for observation and fires to be directed at the enemy. The gate was protected by two towers and the narrow entrance into the fortress passed through three gateways. There were also inner defenses which included a deep ditch, a stronghold with five large towers, and all the buildings in the inner area were built from solid stone with firing slits for launching arrows. The inner defenses of the *Krak* were not only strong, but cunningly arranged. For example, behind a gate of mundane appearance lies a ramp that leads up past two sharp bends. Archer's ports were arrayed with point-blank fields of fire along the ramp; a series of portcullises and rock-falls could trap any invading foe in kill zones where there was no escaping the arrows fired through the slits in the walls.

The castle was attacked often and besieged at least ten times between its construction in the early twelfth century and 1270. Its garrisons never succumbed to force of arms. Ultimately, the *Krak* was captured in 1271 by Mameluke forces under Sultan Baibar of Aleppo, after most of its garrison had been tricked into departing.

## Greatest Invention of War Ever:
### Gunpowder Weaponry

Gunpowder is made from saltpeter (potassium nitrate), sulfur, and charcoal. The best ratio is roughly 75 to 12 to 13. From this simple mixture was produced the longest lasting and most important invention in the history of warfare. Gunpowder eventually made every combatant, on the battlefield and beyond it, a missileer. Allowing him to kill at ever-increasing ranges and in larger numbers, these weapons respected no class and killed all manner of aristocrat, up to and beyond King James II of Scotland; one of his cannons exploded while he was standing next to it.

Will it come as a surprise to the reader to learn that gunpowder was a Chinese invention from the eighth or ninth century? At least, most historians accept the Chinese as the inventors. One Frenchman, the Marshal de Tavannes, believed gunpowder to have been a German invention. After all, to such a key player in the St. Bartholomew's Day massacre, most evil things in the world came from Germany, and he had the existence of Protestantism as proof.

Naturally, there is no agreement as to how and when gunpowder made it to Europe. Nor is this solely attributable to the contentious nature of historians; there is simply no conclusive evidence to be had. The Chinese, it is said, initially used gunpowder as an explosive in various bombs and rockets. It was not until the late thirteenth or early fourteenth century that gunpowder was used in a gun as a propellant. What is clear is that by the middle of the fourteenth century, there was some type of gunpowder weaponry being used at sieges and on the battlefield. The author is not convinced that the Chinese invented gunpowder. He falls more in line with those, most notably Charles Oman, who say that just because the Chinese had an incendiary substance, that is not the same thing as saying they had gunpowder. Could Roger Bacon, a thirteenth-century Englishman, be our boy? History is, of course, an argument without end and we may never know definitively.

Innovation, modification, and invention came quickly to this weapon, spurred on by monarchs who wanted wall-busters in a big way. They saw the dazzling possibility that sieges, which were expensive and took months, could be brought to favorable conclusions with a few cannons. Nor should we dismiss the appeal of making all that smoke and fire and noise.

In the earliest representations of cannons, they appear as a large vases. The projectile is an arrow and a gunner is igniting the powder at the touch hole. Before too long, cannons were made with tubed barrels and they fired spherical projectiles. This made for a more efficient weapon, as the gas from the exploding powder had a greater opportunity to accelerate the shot along the tube.

Medieval castle walls were particularly susceptible to cannon fire. Their walls were high which made easy targets. The ballistic impact of cannon balls easily damaged the walls. Who was the first to bring down a fortress's walls? Philip the Bold, Duke of Burgundy gets the nod. In 1377, his army besieged the fortress of Odruik which was defended by the Englishman William de Weston. Philip had 140 cannon, some of which fired 200-pound projectiles from cannons with a bore of about 16.5 inches. An additional first achieved in this event is the first surrender of a castle due to cannon fire.

This is not to say that the trebuchet was immediately superseded by the cannon. The trebuchet remained effective into the fifteenth century. It was capable of firing equally large stones, but the telling difference resided in how they were fired. Trebuchets launched their stones in high parabolic arcs, cannons fired their stones on a flatter trajectory and at a greater velocity. This resulted in a greater destructive kinetic energy being imparted to the target. The reader will undoubtedly remember the formula from high school physics: *kinetic energy* = *.5 times mass times velocity squared (KE=.5mv2)*. Thus, even a slight increase in velocity produced substantially more trouble for the defenders.

These earliest cannons had low velocities, and this was probably a good thing, given their construction. Built up from strips of iron which were fused together and bound with iron hoops, just like a barrel, this method did not produce a very strong weapon. It is probably just as well that the earliest guns were charged with finely ground powder, too, which caused a slow combustion rate. How big did these weapons become?

The biggest of the cannons were known as *bombards*. Kelly DeVries tells us that the biggest of them were almost 17 feet in length, had bores

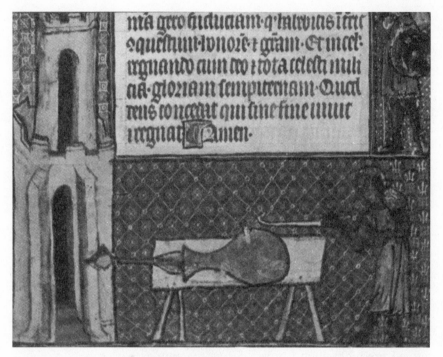

Earliest known manuscript depicting cannon
*Hogarth*

of 28 inches, fired cannonballs of 850 pounds, and weighed as much as 18 tons. Nevertheless, the desire for bigger and heavier shot led to bigger and heavier cannon, as well as the quest for higher velocities. This, in turn, led to bursting barrels. William McNeill tells us that the solution, within the technical means of the day, was to change metals and cast the barrels. Bell makers were already adept at casting bronze and brass and so the gunpowder age helped usher in the second Bronze Age (1453–1543). Of course, copper, tin, and zinc were no more plentiful or found together than they were before, and this became a strategic concern for those desiring cannon. The ingenuity of man, and Europeans in particular, was up to the challenge of finding solutions to the problem of how to dispatch their fellow man more efficiently. By the middle of the sixteenth century, cannon were again being made of iron.

Before the end of the Middle Ages, two more advances were made in gunpowder weaponry. The first was the discovery that smaller diameter tubes firing smaller, but heavy, iron shot could produce as much damage as the huge bombards firing stone shot. (Even if they didn't know that $KE=.5mv2$, they empirically discerned the concept on the battlefield.) All that was needed was a sufficiently strong barrel, especially at the chamber. The second was the "corning" of the propellant. Gunpowder was formed into small pellets of varying sizes which provided more surface area for ignition when packed into the barrel. This meant that the powder burned more evenly and quickly than before and thus more quickly generated more gases to propel the shot. More explosive power translated into the higher projectile velocities they sought. As they say in high school, physics is indeed phun.

Regardless of its shortcomings during the various stages of design development, cannon figured in several sieges in the fourteenth and fifteenth centuries: Oudenarde (1382), Maastricht (1407–1408), Bourges Ham (1411, 1412), Harfleur (1415), Lagny (1431), Fortepice (1433), Bourg (1451), Bouvignes (1466), Dinant (1466), Rhodes (1480), and so on. There were setbacks as well for gunpowder weapons in this period, but this was, and is, overwhelmingly a success story.

Men at arms using handcannon and long-bows.
*Hogarth*

Guns also became smaller. When hand-held guns were developed is problematical, but at the beginning of the fifteenth century, they were appearing on the battlefield, and by the middle of the century, they were well represented.

As the fifteenth century progressed, it became clear that one could not be a proper or effective ruler and not have an artillery park. To support this new and costly weapon, Charles VII of France added new taxes. The French under Charles and then Louis XI and Charles VIII developed the best artillery system of the century which was institutionalized in a bureaucracy and run by professionals. French artillery helped win the Hundred Years' War and subdue Italy in 1494. How much longer would the Byzantine Empire have lasted if the Ottomans had not had artillery?

Is it too much to say that gunpowder changed everything about war and thus about society? The Middle Ages were at an end; the modern age was beginning. The weapons which had served man for thousands of years were on the way out. Archers had only a few decades at most. Spearmen had a few more, but not many. At the apogee of the armorer's art, the knight in plate armor became obsolete. As fortifications, castles became obsolete, although the military engineers' art did eventually adapt and new types of fortresses that could withstand shelling eventually evolved into enormous undertakings such as the Maginot Line, the *Westwall* (or "Siegfried Line") and the Atlantic Wall. Overall, no other single technological development more profoundly changed the nature of war than the introduction of gunpowder in firearms.

Italian tester pistol. The powder tester, a simple but ingenious device, determined the strength of gunpowder so that the user knew how much to load into his firearm. The tester was loaded with a blank charge and fired, the discharge moved the gauge, thus providing a reading of the strength of the gunpowder. *Hogarth*

## Most Important Piece of Other Equipment:
### The Stirrup

Here is how to tell the difference between a smart guy and a genius. If, after talking to someone who solved a problem you'd been working on, you said to yourself, "oh yeah, I could have figured that out," then you were talking to a smart guy. If, on the other hand, after talking to someone who solved a problem you'd been working on, and you said to yourself, "I never could have dreamed up that approach," then you were talking to a genius.

Was the person who came up with the stirrup a genius? We do not know, nor does it matter, but the solution to the problem of how to better sit on a horse in combat was arrived at instantly, and seemingly so obviously. Does the reader not wonder why, when man had created all manner of bits and bridles for horses in the ancient world that it took him so long to come up with the stirrup? Yes? Join the club.

The stirrup, once it appeared, spread widely and rapidly. Different authorities place the invention at various places and times. Acknowledging that no definite answer is possible, here is what we know: the stirrup appeared at the turn of the fifth–sixth, late seventh, early eighth centuries in Europe. In Korea, Japan, China, and India, the stirrup appeared earlier and spread to the Middle East in the seventh century and from there to Byzantium and the Franks. Is it possible that we are all wrong? Possible, but we will never know. If the reader wishes to know how to recognize a brave medievalist, look for one who places a date on the stirrup and expounds a treatise on the societal consequences of its invention.

The stirrup gave the horseman a firm platform from which to operate. He could stand on his irons and lash out at the enemy without falling from his mount, and he could do so at speed. The stirrup, when combined with an improved saddle with a pronounced pommel and high cantel (front and back of the saddle), virtually locked the rider to the horse. The knight no longer relied on a thrusting spear to deliver his attack. Instead the lance came to the fore, and with it, the rider could deliver a blow with all the force a charging horse and rider could impart. The cavalry lance now had to be heavier than the spear of old to stand up to the stresses placed on it. It was over 12 feet long and had a flat, double-edged, pointed head at the business end. A crosswing, or pennon, was added behind the lance's head to stop the weapon from penetrating too deeply into the enemy's body and thereby running the risk of it getting stuck. The shaft of the lance had a handgrip and was flared in front of the grip to prevent the hand from slipping forward at

The stirrup in use (foreground) and being crafted (shop in background). Italian engraving, created 1650.
© Historical Picture Archive/CORBIS/MAGMA

impact. Lastly, it was now possible for the knight to carry his lance in the couched position against his body and under his armpit. This anchored the lance to the rider just as the saddle and stirrup anchored him to his horse. By the mid-twelfth century, we are told, all this was in place and no cavalryman in the world could deliver an attack with the sheer shock that could be mustered by the mounted armored knights of western Europe.

## Most Unusual Weapon:
### The Flemish *Goedendag*

Of the array of hafted weapons used in the Middle Ages, the whimsically-named *goedendag* was at the opposite end of the ubiquitous halberd and pole-axe. Used exclusively by Flemish infantry in the fourteenth century, the *goedendag* (which means "good day" or "hello") was a combination of a spear, a club, and a mace. About the size of a fat baseball bat, the narrow end came to a spear point, useful for unseating mounted adversaries, or, conceivably, stabbing as well. The thicker end of the weapon was flared and topped with a mace-like finial which could be used to bash, smash, and mash an opponent's armor and bones. Or, the mace could be used to knock the rider off his horse and then the spear used to finish him off. In any event, if this is how the fourteenth-century Flemings said hello, what happened with "goodbye?"

The Flemish infantry used this pike at the battle of Courtrai, 11 July 1302. It played a key role in this battle in which an infantry force comprised overwhelmingly of peasants and merchants defeated a large force of mounted French knights. (See page 129) Clearly, whoever invented the *goedendag* had produced something unique and especially effective.

Pikeman's armor
*Hogarth*

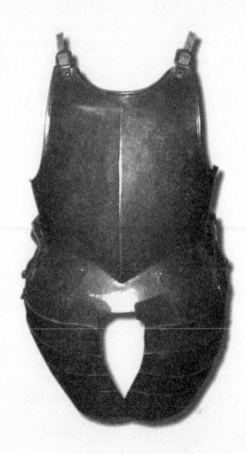

# Personalities

## Worst Army of the Middle Ages:
Peter the Hermit and the First Crusade
(or "Why War Should Be Left to the Professionals")

### The People's Crusade of 1096

The man responsible for this debacle was Peter the Hermit (1050–1115). Reasonably well born in Amiens, he became a holy man, possibly inspired, so Edward Gibbon tells us, by the fact that his noble wife was aged and ugly. Thus, his move from family man to hermit may not have been such a great sacrifice. He was a small, ugly man, nearly emaciated, who survived mostly on fish and wine. He was known as "*Kuku* Peter" or little Peter. He wore little more than a rough wool shirt and mantle and went sleeveless and shoeless. Whatever alms he received, he quickly dispersed to the needy. He was, by all accounts, a gifted and dynamic speaker who drew large crowds wherever he spoke.

He had visited the Holy Land 20 years before and become highly enthused about the notion of restoring it to Christian control. When Pope Urban II called for a crusade, Peter the Hermit was front and center agitating the people for the cause, calling upon all Christians to help free their enslaved co-religionists. A mania set in among the would-be pilgrims and swept along many. They all demanded of Peter that he lead them to the Holy Land as the first crusaders. The real crusaders—knights, men-at-arms, etc., were gathering to leave in August, but such was the enthusiasm that the "People's Crusaders" departed in March 1096. Peter led 60,000, some say 100,000, people out of France. (The reader will note here that the numbers are always a problem).

The military leader of this peoples' army was Walter the Penniless, who led a force of 8 knights and 15,000 foot. Walter was, by all accounts, a well-known soldier of the day and well-regarded for his valor. His moniker accurately describes his finances. The pilgrims' route would be along the Danube and the Rhine, thus passing through modern Hungary, thence into Bulgaria, and on to Constantinople. They were followed by another group of 15,000 German peasants led away from their villages by a monk named Godescal. Behind the German contingent came another 200,000. Gibbon tells us that this mob was an endless parade of human debris, indulging in theft, prostitution, rapine, and drunkenness. Apparently, this mob believed that the Holy Spirit resided in a goose and goat which led the way, and had been designated as the real leaders of the effort. Accompanying all were the expected groups of opportunists out to rake in the loot. Will it surprise the reader to learn that virtually no preparations had been made for the journey? The absence of military discipline meant, to put it too mildly, that there would be misunderstandings along the way. Pillage was not unknown to these people and many areas were ravaged, the inhabitants killed, and among the hardest hit were the Jews who happened to live along the route.

It was not long, therefore, before Walter was detached from the main group and sent on ahead to make whatever arrangements he could. He did well, in fact, and secured from King Coloman of Hungary permission to transit his kingdom in peace, and to trade there. Walter then pressed on to Bulgaria where his reception was hostile, but he made it through, albeit with sizable losses. Peter's passage was not as smooth. Enmity was engendered with the Hungarians and rightly so, as the rear of Peter's mob killed 4,000 Hungarians at Semlin. King Coloman raised his army and the Bulgarians did likewise. They pursued the People's Crusaders relentlessly and it is reported that only one-third of those who started out made it to Constantinople.

The Byzantine emperor, Alexius, advised Peter that his army should wait for the professionals to arrive before setting out to do battle with the Turks. Peter had lost some control of his army by this time, and two national faction leaders had emerged: Rainald, leading the Germans and Italians, and Geoffrey Burel, leading the Franks. Meanwhile, the People's Army behaved no better outside Constantinople than it had anywhere else. Alexius shipped them across the Strait.

Once across, they raided villages populated by Christians, but under Muslim Turkish control. The two national groups then set off in search of greater plunder. The Germans under Rainald marched beyond Nicaea to seize the empty fortress of Xerogord. They were promptly besieged by the Turks, who cut off the water supply. After eight days, Rainald and many of his men surrendered, and those who did not wish to convert to Islam were killed. The rest were enslaved.

The other part of the people's army was destroyed with equal ease. This part was in much tumult over the news about Xerogord and wanted to march on the Turks and force a battle. Walter and some of the other commanders urged delay, but Geoffrey Burel reproached them so much that they changed their minds.

The next day, they marched out with 25,000 infantry and 500 mounted knights. The Turks met them on a plain and killed most of them. So ended the command of Walter the Penniless, pierced by seven arrows.

The Turks then pursued the survivors to their camp and slaughtered men, women, and children alike, unless they were worth keeping as slaves. The only soldiers to escape were those—a few thousand we are told—who had dispersed into the mountains. Some of them made their way to the coast and holed up in an abandoned fortress near Civiote. There they held off the Turks until the Emperor sent a naval force to rescue them.

Where was Peter the Hermit during all this? Unable to influence his army any longer, he had gone to Constantinople. Gibbon puts the dead of the People's Crusade at 300,000. Such can be the force of an idea and such can be the folly of people, or of an army.

# Tactics

## Largest Army of the Fourteenth Century:
The English at the Siege of Calais, September 1346– August 1347

### "There is no arguing with a pregnant queen"
Following his victory at Crécy, Edward III moved to exploit it by gaining territory. In this instance, he marched on to Calais and laid siege. His army, which eventually reached just over 32,000, is said to be the largest ever assembled in the fourteenth century.

The choice of Calais made ample sense at that time. It was near Dunkirk, which was controlled by the friendly Flemings; it was the closest French port to England; and it was the center of privateers who preyed on English merchant shipping. Edward arrived at the city on 4 September and circumvallated the place. He contacted the Flemings, let them know what he was doing, and arranged for ships to come from England to take off the wounded.

To accommodate his forces, Edward III essentially built another city. Known as Ville-à-Neuve, it was built, along with the siege works, on the former suburbs of Calais. "Former," as in "pull down the French suburbs and build our stuff." In addition to the siege works, Kelly DeVries tells us that the English built towers around the harbors and a market place. The latter provided for English soldiers' needs and included a large population of prostitutes. Sanitary conditions were obviously not what they should have been, as dysentery incapacitated half the army and many deaths came from disease.

Securing the surrender or reduction of the fortress was not going to be easy because the approaches were covered either by wet ditches or marshes. This would eliminate at least two types of siege techniques from Edward's repertoire, mining and large siege engines such as the trebuchet. That did not mean, however, that Edward III, one of best battlefield commanders of the Middle Ages, would not try. After all, he could always try starvation.

Calais was blockaded from the sea and then all concerned settled down for a nice, old-fashioned game of "who has the most food"—at least for the winter. After a time, it became obvious that the garrison was not going to be starved out anytime soon. This presented the spectre of the French coming to raise the siege. Edward called for, and started receiving, reinforcements from England. He also began digging lines of contravallation to fend off any relief force. He also called for all the cannon he had to help cover the approaches to these lines.

By mid-summer, Edward had about 32,000 men participating in the siege. This force consisted of 5,340 noblemen and 26,963 others. It was expensive to keep such a large force in the field. Charles Oman tells us that the Prince of Wales received one pound a day; earls and bishops six shillings eightpence; down to the lowly Welsh pikemen, who received two pence per day. To add to Edward's problems, the French relief force showed up by mid-summer.

On 18 July, this French force was spotted south of Calais. Having heard about the formidable nature of the English contravallation, King Philip called on Edward to come out and fight in the open on 2 August. Way too smart to accept such an offer, Edward explicitly declined. In what may have been a show of good judgement or a demonstration of rank cowardice, Philip promptly marched off and left the garrison commander of Calais on his own.

The commander of the garrison, Jean de Vienne, seeing how this game was being played, and the citizens nearly starved, surrendered two days later. Edward required that the six leading citizens of Calais be brought to him, bare-headed, stripped to their shirts, shoeless, with rope halters around their necks. They were also to have with them all the keys to the town. At the gate, they were met by Sir Walter Manny, the king's envoy. He brought them before the king, who ordered them beheaded immediately. Sir Walter and the other nobles called upon the king to exercise clemency and do nothing so dishonorable, but he was adamant. The king replied that the people of Calais had killed many of his men, and caused him much pointless aggravation and expense. The queen, who had come to visit with her court despite her advanced state of pregnancy, interceded and begged the king to show mercy. After a time, the king relented.

The six burghers were given clothes and food and safe conduct to Picardy. Edward, who intended to re-populate Calais, ordered all inhabitants to leave, taking nothing with them. The King of France, by the way, did not see fit to compensate these unfortunates either. Eventually over 300 families came to Calais to take advantage of the benefits the king bestowed on those who went.

# Battles

## Smallest Important Battle in the Middle Ages, If Not Ever: Badr, 15 March 624

Mohammed, yes, THE Mohammed, led 300 men representing Medina against the forces of Abu Sufyan, 900 men from Mecca. Mohammed had taken to religious teaching after receiving his visions, and in his prose-lytizing, he had been critical of some of the methods used by the Meccan merchants. This had gained him and his tribe some enemies. In 622, he moved to Medina, 200 miles north of Mecca, at the invitation of some followers who believed him to be the prophet. The Meccans worried that in Medina, Mohammed would be free to build a following without there being anything they could do to curb it. Mohammed's following did, in fact, grow in Medina, and they made a living raiding Meccan caravans. The Meccans countered by establishing an intelligence network in Medina, which gave them information about when the caravans were going to be raided. Precipitating things was the raid made on a Meccan caravan during a month when fighting was proscribed. The Meccans decided to draw Mohammed and his followers into battle by setting up a ruse in the form of—what else?—a caravan. The caravan was owned by Abu Sufyan and he received the assistance of a force from Mecca of 1,300 men led by Amru bin Hasham. This force included 600 heavy infantry, 700 camels, and 100 horses. Mohammed's force consisted of 300 men, 70 camels, and 2 horses.

Sufyan, travelling with the caravan, learned the location of Mohammed's force and diverted his caravan so that it arrived safely in Mecca. He then sent word to Hasham's force that the caravan had arrived safely and upon hearing this, 400 of them decided to go home. Hasham, however, decided to do battle with Mohammed anyway. They set out for the wells at Badr, 25 miles southwest of Mecca. Mohammed was already there and ready for them. Knowing that the Meccans would be in need of water, he stopped up all the wells but one, and there he established his force. Mohammed watched the ensuing battle from a tent and ordered his men to attack first with arrows from their superior positions on higher ground. As the attack began, a sandstorm struck the Meccans, just as Mohammed's vision said it would, and it was later reported that angels on horseback had intervened. As the Meccans faltered, Mohammed's men attacked and routed the enemy. Hasham was wounded and captured. He was beheaded after failing to acknowledge that the victory belonged to Allah. Thereafter, he became known as Abu Jahl, father of folly.

This battle victory, which has been declared a "holy miracle" in Muslim tradition, made Mohammed's reputation and after this, he won two more battles, Medina (627) and Mecca (630), versus one defeat, Ohud (625). Followers flocked to him after Badr and his power and influence grew. This was the very thing the Meccans had hoped to prevent. Mohammed died in 632 and Abu Bekr became Caliph. Under his reign and subsequent rulers, Islam experienced a rapid expansion across much of the known world. But it all started with Badr.

## First Defeat of Cavalry by Infantry in the Middle Ages: Courtrai, 11 July 1302, The Most Written-About Battle of the Fourteenth Century

At the beginning of the fourteenth century, 1300–1302, France renewed its war with England and Flanders. This two-year struggle apparently resolved little, but it is the end of it, the battle of Courtrai, which concerns us.

Count Robert of Artois, Philip IV's brother, led an army into Flanders to suppress a revolt. His enemy consisted of an army of heavy infantry with some mercenary crossbowmen. In a clash of classes, the aristocratic mounted knights of France were to meet the plodding infantry of the emerging merchant class of Flanders, here represented primarily by the money of the burghers of Bruges.

The French readied for battle at 6 A.M. on 11 July. The French army had about 2,500 nobles arranged into 10 units of knights and squires, plus infantry, crossbowmen, and light infantry javelineers, totaling about 7,000. Flemish army strength is put at 8,000 to 10,500, consisting of foot soldiers, knights, and some crossbowmen. The tactical calculus of the time reckoned that one mounted French nobleman was equal to ten foot soldiers, so the French were deemed to have the advantage in combat power. To counter that, Guy of Namur, one of the Flemish commanders, chose a battle site which could not have suited them better.

On the left front, the Flemings' position was protected by the *Groeningebeek* (Groeninge Brook) and on the right front by the *Grote Beek* (Big Brook). Behind their army was the River Lys and the water obstacle that protected the fortified city of Courtrai. The water to the front and sides would seriously impede any cavalry maneuver by the French. The flanks were protected by the city moat on the left and a cloister on the right. The Flemings had also prepared the ground by digging *trous-de-loup*, or ditches, in front of their lines, some of which they had filled with water. With water behind the Flemings, there was nowhere for them to run if things went against them. They knew this, and the commanders had purposely chosen a position from which there was no retreat. This sort of thing focuses the mind, and reinforces the will.

The French apparently held a council to consider their battle plan and the advice given to the Count of Artois was varied. For one thing, it was recognized that once the cavalry was across the brooks, the consequences would be ruinous if they had to come back with the Flemings in pursuit. The commander of the crossbowmen argued for a preparatory bombardment with crossbow bolts to soften up the Flemings, followed by a French cavalry charge to destroy the confused and disorganized foe. One commander argued in favor of the boldest and bravest course of all—do nothing. Let the Flemings stand all day under the hot sun without relief, and then see what happens tomorrow. The majority opinion of the council was that battle should be given that day.

The Flemings deployed for battle with the infantry behind the brooks, to put as much distance between them and the enemy's crossbows as they could, but not so much as to give the French cavalry room to form up and maneuver once they were beyond the brooks and ditches. How far was too far for the Flemish soldiers? Well, where you stood on that question depended on where you stood. The Flemings arranged their positions as follows: the left side of their main battle line was commanded by Guy of Namur and the right by William of Jülich. The reserve, deployed not far behind the line, was commanded by John of Renesse. The Ypres militia guarded the sally port from the Courtrai castle, lest the royal garrison should attempt to sortie and take the Flemings from behind.

Once they were drawn up, the commanders addressed the troops and offered encouragement. John of Renesse told the frontlines that the reserve would move up to support them if they were in trouble.

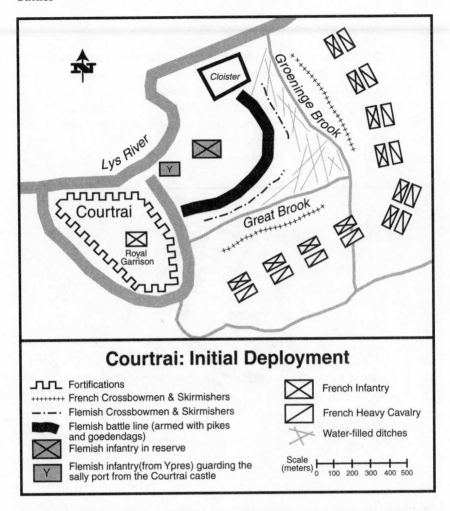

## Courtrai: Initial Deployment

| | | | |
|---|---|---|---|
| ЛЛЛ | Fortifications | | |
| ++++++++ | French Crossbowmen & Skirmishers | | |
| — · — · | Flemish Crossbowmen & Skirmishers | | |
| ▰ | Flemish battle line (armed with pikes and goedendags) | ⊠ French Infantry | |
| ⊠ | Flemish infantry in reserve | ⬱ French Heavy Cavalry | |
| Y | Flemish infantry(from Ypres) guarding the sally port from the Courtrai castle | ⤬ Water-filled ditches | |

Scale (meters) 0  100  200  300  400  500

Furthermore, they should not let anyone break through, but if there was a breakthrough, the reserve would deal with it. Renesse told them to attack the horses and push the knights into the ditches. The troops were also told that any soldier who collected booty, surrendered, or fled would be killed. Additionally, they were to give no quarter and take no prisoners. When this was done, the nobles dismounted and took their places in the line, with their troops. The infantry was armed with pikes and *goedendags* (which means "good morning" or "hello"), the unique Flemish fusion of spear point and mace. (See page 122) Then the Flemings waited . . . and waited.

Finally, around noon, the French sent their Genoese crossbowmen forward and an exchange of missiles ensued. They were taking the measure of the Flemings, which is military-ese for killing some of them but maybe not enough of them. What happened next depends on which version of events one favors. One version is that the Genoese fire was telling on the Flemish *arbalesters*, or crossbowmen, and so they were drawn back out of range. This movement exposed the heavy infantry to the rain of crossbow bolts and so they withdrew. How far? Some scores of yards, says Charles Oman. The other version is that the arrow attacks had no real effect. Then the French infantry went forward, crossed the ditches, and engaged the Flemings.

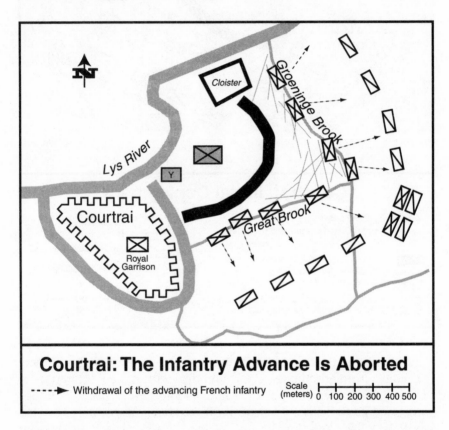

## Courtrai: The Infantry Advance Is Aborted

----▶ Withdrawal of the advancing French infantry      Scale ├─┼─┼─┼─┼─┤
                                                      (meters) 0  100 200 300 400 500

Either the French infantry failed to discomfit the Flemings to the point that they would quit or the French were doing very well and clearly winning the battle. Regardless of motivation, at this point, for some reason, the French cavalry charged. The explanation is either because their infantry was losing or because it was winning. In the first circumstance, the charge was made to try something else, even though the ground was bound to make things difficult for the French horse. In the second circumstance, the charge was made because the infantry had to be denied the honor of winning the battle. In both circumstances, the signal "Recall" was given by the Count of Artois and the infantry came back to the French lines. What is agreed upon is that the first line of French cavalry charged. How many of their own men they rode down is a point to be disputed.

There is one note to be made here about the ditches. Some chroniclers have said that the French did not know about the ditches. That notion is absurd. Artois bought a map of the ditches before the battle and the price he paid for it is entered in his accounts. Moreover, the French army had just watched their infantry cross these same ditches. The French cavalry, the finest in Europe, made it over the ditches and through the water courses. As to their disarray, one is free to imagine. Either the knights made it across, had time to reform and attack the Flemish battle line, which repelled them, or the Flemish infantry attacked the cavalry as they were forming. The latter makes more sense to the author, but what is clear is that the French cavalry was being pushed into the ditches. At this point, Artois led the French cavalry reserves forward to support the struggling first wave. There are reports that the French

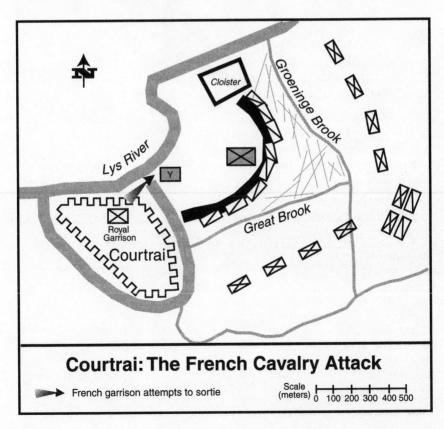

## Courtrai: The French Cavalry Attack

French garrison attempts to sortie

Scale (meters) |—+—+—+—+—+—|
0  100 200 300 400 500

managed a penetration in the center, but Renesse brought up the reserve and restored the integrity of the Flemish line.

The Flemings gave no quarter and as they cut, smashed, and stabbed rider and horse alike. The French gave way and many of those who were pushed into the ditches were drowned. The Flemings were reportedly astounded at how effective the ditches were. Artois, beset on all sides in the fighting, defended himself very well. Then Willem van Saaftinge cut down his horse and Artois fell to the ground where he was bludgeoned and slain by a *goedendag* even as he tried to surrender. "Hello," *Monsieur Le Comte*, indeed. The uncommitted French cavalry, watching these horrors unfold, left the field.

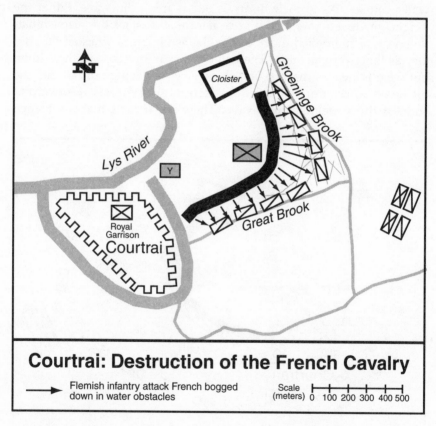

## Courtrai: Destruction of the French Cavalry

→ Flemish infantry attack French bogged down in water obstacles

Scale (meters) 0  100 200 300 400 500

Great numbers of French knights were slaughtered after they were unhorsed. In the end, the Flemings hung up 700 pairs of spurs in the nearby church as a victory offering. The Flemish losses amounted to a few hundred. The final tally of French dead included Artois; Raoul de Nesle, the Constable of France; 2 marshals; 63 counts and barons and bannerets. A banneret, by the way, was a knight who was allowed to bring vassals onto the field under his own banner, so he ranked above a regular knight.

Lest the reader think that memories are not long after something this catastrophic, picture the scene 80 years later. Froissart tells us that the French King, Philip, came to Courtrai on 1 December 1382, after no longer being able to stand the stench arising from his victory at Rossebeke. His arrival coincided with the killing of the Flemings who had retreated from Rossebeke. When the king learned that Courtrai was the site of the stunning massacre of so many French nobles and the church was the repository of all those spurs, he gave orders for the spurs to be retrieved and the town torched.

For the first time since Adrianople (378), as the historians are wont to say, infantry had defeated cavalry in a pitched battle. Courtrai presaged the return of infantry to dominance on the battlefield. This was not a clear-cut victory of infantry over cavalry, however, because of the nature of the ground, but it *was* the first in a long time. News of this victory flashed across Western Europe and created shock and consternation. That mere infantry, consisting overwhelmingly of common burghers and peasants, had bested the nobility of the best army in Europe was too much for some to bear. They had to write treatises and chronicles and invent reasons about how it had happened. Courtrai became the most written-about battle of the fourteenth century. It would not be long before the result was repeated.

## First Defeat of Cavalry by Combined Arms:
### Crécy, 26 August 1346

Cavalry was defeated by infantry in a dramatic fashion for the first time in the Middle Ages at Courtrai in 1302. At Loudon Hill in 1307, Scottish infantry defeated English cavalry in a battle similar to Courtrai. In 1314 at the battle of Bannockburn, Scottish infantry did it again to the English cavalry on the second day of fighting. These battles have striking similarities. In each case, the victors were formed up in defensive formations with their flanks and rear protected by terrain features or manmade barriers. Additionally, the infantry commanders had had the time to prepare the ground in front of their positions by digging ditches and pits and flooding some of them. In each case, moreover, the victors had also had the luxury of time and had chosen their ground carefully. For these reasons, commentators and even nobles could excuse the losses suffered by their horse-borne peers due to "special circumstances."

Miniature illustration of the Battle of Crécy from Jean Froissart's (c.1337–c.1410),
"Chronique;" a history of western Europe from 1300–1400.
© Bettmann/CORBIS/MAGMA

The English, after experiencing two such affairs, took note and decided upon another course. In battles after these against the Scots at Dup-
plin Moor (1332) and Halidon Hill (1333), we see the English dis-
mounting their knights, using archers, and staying in defensive positions. Kelly DeVries points out that the archers were not the decisive
killers of men in these battles, but served a subtler purpose. It was the
massed archers on the flanks of the English formations who, through
rapid volley fire of arrows, broke up the cohesion of the charging Scottish infantry formations. They did the job of ditches and pits. The long-
bowmen also served to narrow the frontage of the attackers, as the
assault troops would naturally veer toward the center to avoid the
storm of arrows coming at them from the sides. In modern parlance, we
would say that the archers canalized the attack. When the attackers—
whether they were infantry or cavalry—reached the English line, their
formation was somewhat disorganized and slowed, thereby less likely
to deliver a telling blow.

Although, as is often the case, there are varying estimates of the two sides' strengths, some put the total English strength at 12,000, consisting of 2,000 knights and men-at-arms, 6,750 English and Welsh bowmen, 2,750 spearmen and 500 or 600 others. Some put the English at 8,500 total, of which 6,200 were archers. At the high end is the figure of 20,000 for the English. For the French, the upper limit is 60,000 of which 12,000 to 20,000 were knights, although even larger numbers are advocated by some medieval chroniclers. Whichever numbers the reader chooses, the English must have had fewer participants than the French or their victory would not be as stunning. All accounts agree, however, that the French army was massive and as impressive a gathering of bluebloods as warfare had known.

Edward III had chosen his ground well. The English lined up on the forward edge of a little plateau between the villages of Crécy and Wadicourt; the right of the army was protected by the Maye River, which runs past Crécy; the left was secured by the village of Wadicourt. The archers also dug ditches and potholes in front of the English positions. The rear of the formation was protected by woods and the baggage was enclosed in a wagon fortress.

The English drew up for combat with their cavalry dismounted in three battles or lines in the middle of their formation and the archers on either flank. Some historians place a third unit of archers in the center of the line. All the archer formations were in the shape of a "V" with the point facing the French. Froissart (c. 1337–1410) tells us that the archers were drawn up in the *en manière de herse* and this is where the trouble started. What exactly did Froissart mean? The author has no particular axe to grind when it comes to the formation and location of the archers, but the reader may be interested to learn that this debate has gone on for over a century in terms of modern scholarship alone.

The author's position is this: the maps of the battle depicting the English with a frontline of two divisions of dismounted men-at-arms, with two V-shaped projections of archers on either side and a third in the middle and a second line of men-at-arms as a reserve with archers on either side, are definitely "cooler" to look at. This formation, however, is inherently weaker than the alternate one, of infantry massed together in a dense line with archers on the flanks. Otherwise, what would happen to the archers in the middle of the line when the French came up? We know that they could not stand up to heavy cavalry or infantry. Thus, the French would be able to penetrate the English formation and that is often the prelude to defeat. What then would the archers do? Would they, after firing their arrows, face about and march out of (or through) the formation to their rear, thereby leaving a gap for the reserve infantry to fill? In the middle of combat, that makes for a dicey proposition. The task of moving several hundred archers and their equipment to the rear and then filling the gap with reserve infantry, which would then have to dress the new line and prepare to absorb the shock of the charging French cavalry, is just too complex and risky. No leader asks for more problems. Thus, given the choice between equally valid historical evidence, the simpler, decidedly less cool, but more practical formation depicted on the diagram is the more likely deployment.

This battle was to be a star-studded affair. The majority of the nobility in either country seems to have accompanied their sovereign.

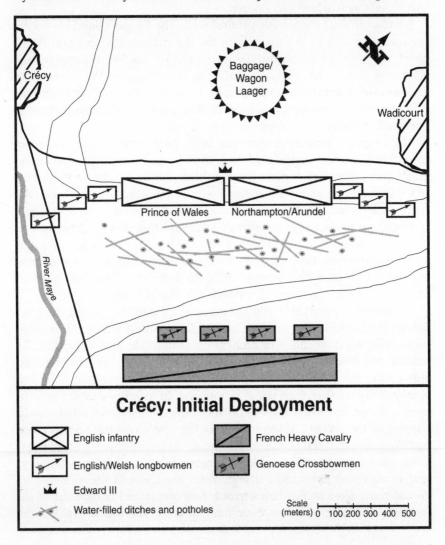

## Crécy: Initial Deployment

| | English infantry | | French Heavy Cavalry |
| | English/Welsh longbowmen | | Genoese Crossbowmen |
| | Edward III | | |
| | Water-filled ditches and potholes | | Scale (meters) 0  100 200 300 400 500 |

Included in the French contingent of nobles was the King of Bohemia, also known as John of Luxembourg.

The Prince of Wales commanded the right battle, or division; the Earls of Northampton and Arundel commanded the left division; and the King took his place in the center. The French army was strung out over many roads for quite a distance. Upon locating the English troops, the French scouts reported to the king that the enemy was drawn up for battle and waiting. A council was held and Philip VI was urged not to attack on this day, but wait for his entire army to come up and then rest. Philip agreed and ordered the vanguard to halt where it was and await the consolidation of the army. Arguing also for delay until the morrow was the fact that it was already late in the afternoon. That seemed to be sound advice to the king, but the noblemen were not of a mind to listen. The vanguard apparently was ready to halt, but when they learned that those following on refused to stop until they could see the English, too, then the vanguard moved forward as well. Thus, Froissart tells us that pride and vanity took command of the situation and the French army arrived on the battlefield in no particular order and with no particular plan. They were, however, supremely confident about securing victory.

It was about 6 P.M. by now and the order was given to send the crossbowmen forward. They are usually described as Genoese, but they probably were not all Italian. They numbered about 6,000 and forward they went, just as they did a thunderstorm swept in and drenched everybody. As quickly as it came, it went, and the sun again shone. This rain had two effects impinging on the coming battle: it made the ground muddy and slippery (although to what extent we do not know) and it affected the archers' bowstrings. The English had quickly unstrung their bows and put their strings under their helmets to keep them dry, the crossbowmen apparently did not and wet bowstrings did not perform optimally in this era.

French drums and trumpets and other noisemakers sounded and the Genoese went forward. The idea was that they would close within range of the English and let loose a volley or two of arrows to disorganize the English and then retire, leaving it to the heavy cavalry to finish the job. On they came, stopping twice to dress their formation and shouting to unnerve the enemy. The English, we are told, stayed silent and waited. It should be mentioned at this point that the Genoese were fatigued, having marched 18 miles, or over six leagues, and "fatigue," as Vince Lombardi once said, "makes cowards of us all." That and, of course, superior enemy weaponry will do it every time. On the third halt, they shouted once again and then leveled their crossbows and let loose their bolts from extreme range. The English archers took one step

forward and began to shoot. Whether the Genoese were just too far
away or the wet bowstrings were now to fail them, their bolts fell short
by some yards. The longbowmen shot their cloth-yard arrows into the
enemy archers at a furious rate. Froissart says the English arrows fell
like snow on the Genoese, so rapidly and evenly were they fired. The
powerful arrows penetrated wherever they struck and within seconds,
the Genoese were reeling from the attack and soon broke. Some cast
aside their weapons, others cut their strings, but all who were still
standing took to their heels.

The retreating Genoese were then cut down by the French knights
either on orders of the king, who was disgusted by their performance,
or, perhaps, on the orders of the Count d'Alençon, who was disgusted
by their performance, or maybe at the convenience of the charging
knights, who were collectively disgusted with their performance as a

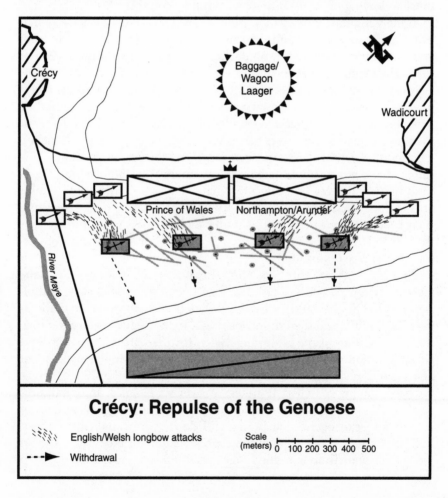

## Crécy: Repulse of the Genoese

English/Welsh longbow attacks

Withdrawal

Scale
(meters) 0   100 200 300 400 500

matter of principle. Meanwhile, the English were still shooting arrows. The first cavalry charge was delivered by this group of knights who were obviously slowed and further disorganized by their own madly retreating crossbowmen, as well as the losses they suffered from the archers. "Charge" may be overstating their rate of progress, but they did make it to the English line. Once there, they engaged in brutal combat with the English knights. The battle, as best we can tell, from this point on became a series of charges. How well coordinated they were is unclear. The first attackers were not clear of the field or even disengaged when the second charge went in. The English men-at-arms held their lines against multiple assaults and the archers were apparently never seriously challenged during the battle. The Prince of Wales distinguished himself in the fighting on the right, which was hard and prolonged.

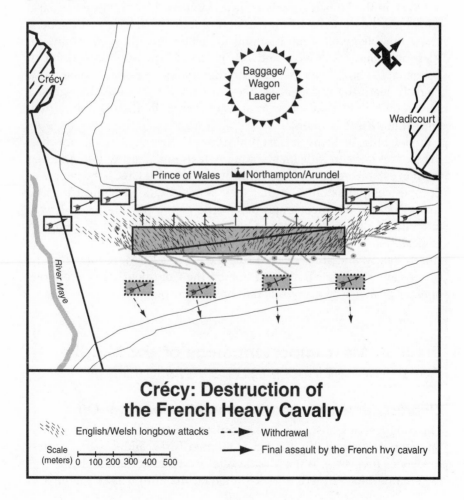

## Crécy: Destruction of the French Heavy Cavalry

⫶⫶⫶ English/Welsh longbow attacks      - - -▶ Withdrawal

Scale                                                       ▶ Final assault by the French hvy cavalry
(meters) 0  100 200 300 400 500

Bravery was on display as ever, including the blind King of Bohemia requesting to go forward and land a blow. He was accommodated by his lords who tied the bridles of their horses to his and took him into the bloody combat. King Philip does not seem to have made it to the front-line, but he is reported to have been wounded in the neck by an arrow and to have had one horse killed from under him.

The lack of a plan, of proper alignment, and of firm tactical control now spelled ruin for the French. Telling also was the approaching darkness; the late start of the battle meant that the scattered French would not be able to regroup and thus would be at the mercy of the English. As darkness fell, men began to leave. Combat continued until midnight we are told, but long before that, it was clear that the battle was lost. Philip was led from the field by John, Count of Hainault. The extent of the French dead would not be known until daylight.

Dead on the French side: 11 princes, about 1,500 knights, and 16,000 others. As Edward had forbade looting and the taking of prisoners, many notables were found among the slain, including the counts of Alençon, Flanders, Savoy, and others. Dead also was King John of Bohemia; his body was treated with dignity and returned to Germany. English dead: the numbers for the notables are given as 2 knights, 1 squire, and 40 men-at-arms. Total dead for the English is unreported, one estimate is 200 others.

In defeating an army at least three times its size, the English now had the tactical basis to inflict a stunning defeat on any army that attacked them in established positions. When it happened at Crécy, the people of Europe were so astonished that they stopped talking about Courtrai. Crécy became the most important battle of the Middle Ages. It was more than just a great victory—Crécy was the debut of the new English tactical system on the Continent. From here on out, infantry—if it was smart, steady, and sure—would rule the battlefield. More immediately, Crécy gave the English a reputation on the Continent. They were recognized as a deadly army, one that merited respect.

## Biggest, Most Important Siege of the Middle Ages: Constantinople, February–May 1453

### Unprecedented Massed, Massive Cannons Pay Off

The conquest of Constantinople by Sultan Mehmet II ended the Byzantine Empire, opened Europe to the Ottoman Turks, and saw the greatest display of firepower in the Middle Ages. Some historians style the Sultan's name Mohammed, others Mahomet; the author uses Mehmet to

Conquest of Constantinople by the Turks. Undated engraving.
© Bettmann/CORBIS/MAGMA

avoid confusing the Sultan with the Prophet, and it is easier for him to type Mehmet.

The Turks, with over 80,000 men, attacked a city defended by 10,000 (Sphrantzes, the chronicler, says fewer than 5,000). Mehmet was a highly intelligent, educated, and cruel man. In war, he relied on the weight of numbers and had dreamed from boyhood of conquering the city. Facing him was Emperor Constantine XI, who had made the unpopular decision of accepting Papal superiority in return for military assistance. Constantine certainly got less than he bargained for when only 200 archers showed up. The reader can rightly conclude from that meager number that the two major Christian churches had issues, and had for hundreds of years. This is not to say that western Europeans were not to be represented in the last act of the Eastern Empire. Constantine had hired Giovanni Giustiniani and his 700 knights and archers, and the German military engineer Johann Grant—who may have been Scottish and just "John Grant"—to help in the defense. Mehmet had the services of Urban the Hungarian, a gun-founder who supplied him with 70 pieces for the siege.

The object of all this attention was Constantinople and her walls, which by this time, were in need of some attention, but were still formidable. The landward wall stretching from the Sea of Marmara to the Golden Horn in the north was a triple wall built in the fifth century. The innermost wall was 40 feet high with 112 towers that were 60 feet in height. The outer wall was 25 feet high with towers. The third wall was fronted by a ditch 60 feet wide and 15 feet deep in which the back wall was incorporated into the third wall. The distance between each wall was about 20 yards.

The Byzantines would have to defend over 11 miles of outer wall, by the author's reckoning, if they were completely surrounded and attacked on all sides. A boom chain stretching across the Golden Horn to Galata prevented Turkish naval forces from entering the Golden Horn. Later, Mehmed succeeded in transferring ships overland from the Bosphorus to the Horn by leveling a road north of Galata, planking it over, covering it with ox and ram fat, and in a single night moved his 30 triremes and biremes. This was quite a feat, but not decisive. Nevertheless, Turkish ships operating in the Golden Horn would bear watching and that could strip troops from the land wall.

The real story is the numerous assaults from the landward side mostly directed at the Gate of St. Romanus. The largest gun that Urban cast for Mehmet was a bombard called "Basilica." Cast of iron and bound with hoops, its barrel had a circumference of 96 inches and a length of 27 feet. The stone balls it fired were reported to weigh over 800 pounds, some say perhaps as much as 1,400 pounds. It required 60 oxen 42 days to pull this cannon from Adrianople to Constantinople. Several lesser bombards were built as well, firing five 100-pound balls and 50 cannons firing 200-pound stone shot. The "Basilica" was not an easy weapon to operate. It took two hours to load and what with everything else one had to do, it had a rate of fire of only seven rounds *per day*. Even this proved too much for it, as it began to crack on the second day. It was repaired and fired some more, then burst. The other guns fared better.

The bombardment from 14 batteries began from on 2 April. The battery opposite the St. Romanus Gate produced results after ten days when one of the towers came down. The rubble fell into the moat but the Turks were unprepared to storm the breach. The defenders moved quickly to block the gap with rubble and whatever else they could find. The Turks kept up the firing on the wall in an effort to prevent repairs and to increase the size of the breach. Turkish artillery efficiency was improved when another European suggested that the guns should concentrate their fire on specific sections of the wall and not disperse their shot. Byzantine efforts to mount cannons on their own walls failed because the structures could not withstand the vibrations caused by the firing.

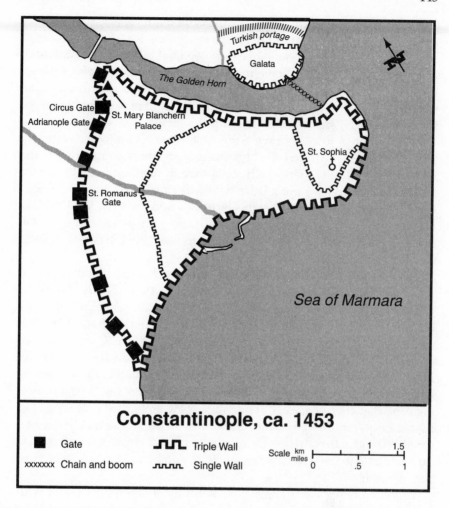

**Constantinople, ca. 1453**

| ■ | Gate | ⊓⊔⊓ | Triple Wall |
| xxxxxxx | Chain and boom | ⊓⊔⊓ | Single Wall |

Scale km / miles

On 18 April, the Turks launched two assaults, one on land against the St. Romanus Gate and the other, a naval attack on the boom chain. Both failed. Giustiniani beat back the assault at the gate using handguns, crossbows, bows, and catapults to inflict great losses on the Turks. Mehmet was furious at the failure and only with difficulty was he restrained by his commanders from loading his trebuchets with his dead and sending them over the wall. Yes, there were still trebuchets in action, and they were still potentially dangerous to whomever might be the chosen object of their use. Mehmet was somewhat high-strung, too: after an earlier naval defeat in March he had wanted, at one point, to impale his admiral.

In fact, Mehmet simply was not a pleasant man. He rarely smiled, we are told, but one incident did tickle his fancy, so J. F. C. Fuller tells us. It seems that Mehmet had sent envoys to see Drakul, Prince of Wallachia. The envoys, upon being shown in to see Drakul, refused to remove their turbans. Drakul's response was to nail the turbans to their heads. One supposes that Drakul was giving the envoys good reason not to remove them again. The sultan, upon hearing this news, was so taken with it that he adopted it as his own form of torture. On another occasion, Drakul impaled the heads of all his Turkish prisoners, numbering in the thousands. The sultan reportedly exclaimed in admiration that it would be impossible to drive out a ruler who was capable of such grand gestures. The author suspects that this is the one and the same Vlad Drakul, also known as Vlad the Impaler, but the reader can decide. If it is not the same, it makes one wonder just how many heads one has to impale to earn a nasty moniker?

The Turks kept up the bombardment day and night. The dynamic of the siege became, in essence, a race between how readily the Turks could blow a breach and how rapidly the Byzantines could repair or block it. On 6 May, the outer wall breach was rendered irreparable. The artillery fire continued throughout the day and on 7 May, another assault was made at the Romanus Gate. Giustiniani had erected an inner wall to meet the assault and in a three-hour battle, the Christians again repelled the Turks. On 12 May, The Turks then assaulted a breach near the Blanchern Palace, but once again the embattled defenders, led by the Emperor, drove out the attackers with great loss of Turkish life. On 18 May, the Turks wheeled up a helepolis, or city-taker, and from it poured fire into the city. Giustiniani blew it up by rolling barrels of gunpowder at it.

Turkish attempts at mining were skillfully countered by Grant who detected the mines and destroyed them with counter-mines, or blew them up with powder, or suffocated the miners with smoke-pots, or drowned them with water, or burned them with liquid fire, or simply fought them hand to hand.

By 26 May, Mehmet was doubting victory was possible. He heard rumors of an approaching Papal fleet and a Hungarian army. The Turkish camp had, in fact, heard the rumors and all were thinking that the siege would have to be raised. The sultan called a council and the issue was debated. He was ready to quit, we are told, but was eventually convinced to continue the siege. Both sides prepared for what they felt would be the culminating event. On the night of 28/29 May, Constantine addressed his troops of both Christian persuasions, calling on them to work together and defend their faith. After this, the Emperor, such men and notables as could be spared, and everyone else who could fit, went to St. Sophia for the divine liturgy. Here, in the most beautiful place in the Christian world, the defenders of a dying empire gathered to say farewell.

On 29 May, the final assault was made at the Romanus Gate. The Byzantines defended from behind a stockade. Starting at 2:00 A.M., the Bashi-Bazouks threw themselves at the defenders for two hours, but were repulsed. Next came the Anatolian regular troops and another two-hour assault, which was thrown back. A third wave, the Janissaries, then surged forward. Again, the thinning ranks of the defenders held back Mehmet's most fanatical troops. Now chance entered and set in motion a series of events which led to the fall of the city. The Circus Gate, north of the Romanus gate and formerly walled up but recently opened, was discovered by a party of 50 Janissaries. Either partly open—which seems unlikely—and lightly defended, or closed and undefended, the Turks rushed it and got inside the inner enclosure. They attacked the defenders there and successfully stormed the wall. They plundered a bit, and ran up their flag. Some Byzantine reinforcements arrived, however, and restored the situation. The intruders, unable to stay where they were, moved south looking for a way out or more of their comrades.

At the same time, Giustiniani was wounded by a projectile and left for medical attention over the remonstrances of the emperor to remain. This created confusion amongst the defenders, but they fended off a fourth assault at the Romanus Gate. Sometime after this, the wandering Janissaries had passed southward, past the Adrianople Gate, and reached the Romanus Gate. They attacked that gate's defenders from their right, or northern, flank. Mehmet then launched a fifth assault and carried the inner enclosure. Panic began to spread from the rear—it usually does—and cries rang out that the city had fallen. No doubt the Turkish flag helped that along.

The situation was, perhaps, retrievable and the Emperor galloped up with some men to try. They engaged the invaders in close combat and the Emperor fought bravely, with several of his retainers and military advisors directly at his side. They shoved Turks from the walls, cut down others, and repelled two assaults. The Emperor and all with him knew that they must win here or die in the attempt. It must have been quite a sight, the last emperor of the empire fighting on, covered in blood, perhaps only discernible as the emperor by the imperial eagles on his armor. Eventually, he and his men were struck down, and with no one left to defend the city, the remaining walls were easily penetrated by the attackers. With the fall of the Emperor, the city and a thousand years of history fell as well. Mehmet, true to his word, allowed his men to sack the city for three days.

It is estimated that 4,000 people were killed while the city was looted. Fifty thousand people were delivered into slavery. Thus ended the most important siege of the Middle Ages, victory made possible by massed gunpowder artillery. The Turks moved into the Balkans after this and were hammering, periodically, on the gates of Vienna until 1683. How much different the world would be today if Constantinople had remained in Christian hands is left to the musings of the reader.

## Best Heavy Infantry of the Middle Ages (or "How to Make a Reputation"): Swiss Infantry at the Battle of St. Jacob, 24 August 1444

Tactically, the Swiss were the best infantry of the era. The characteristics they displayed in abundance are the same as those shown by the Macedonian phalanx of Alexander the Great, the Roman legions of the Republic, and all other successful armies throughout history. The Swiss pikemen were highly disciplined and well trained. These traits provided the foundation for their tactical excellence, which was highlighted by their ability to maneuver rapidly on and off the battlefield. Additionally, there was a national impulse for the Swiss based on their devotion to liberty. Yet the fervor of patriotism they displayed in defending their country seems to have transferred to their mercenary practices as well. If you had the money and wanted the best, you hired the Swiss.

The ruthless Swiss were noted for sanguinary victories. On 15 November 1315, at the battle of Morgarten, the Austrian Habsburg army of 5,000 or more heavy cavalry and infantry under Duke Leopold I was wiped out by 2,000 Swiss pikemen and archers. The Austrians were caught in a position similar to the Romans at Lake Trasimene; that is to say, they were in a defile between a mountain and a lake with nowhere to run. The Swiss blocked the far end of the defile with a rubble wall and rolled boulders and logs down on the Austrians and then went to work with their halberds. At least 1,500 were killed, mostly nobles.

On 21 June 1339 at Laupen, the Swiss defeated a Burgundian-Austrian army, first driving off the infantry and then withstanding the cavalry. The Swiss took up positions on a hill and waited for the Burgundians to deploy because they had decided to fight a defensive battle. The ground being steeper on their left, the Burgundians put all of their cavalry on the right opposite the gentler slope. They put their men-at-arms—

dismounted knights—on the left. Additionally, the Burgundians had a large body of unreliable infantry, up to about 20,000 in all. Knights, on the other hand, were said to number 1,200. The Swiss—and here that is meant to mean the Bernese and their allies—numbered 6,000 and were under the command of Rudolf von Erlach, an experienced general. The Burgundians included the Count of Kyburg, who had lost two towns to the Bernese, as well as the Count Neufchâtel and Count Gruyères; the battle had all the makings of a cheesy affair.

It should be noted at this stage of the story that the Council of Bern had secured the assistance of their allies from the mountain states, or Forest Cantons, as they were called, by offering them an alliance which could have proved useful in the future, and the Bernese also offered a good whack of money, which the Swiss, being Swiss, accepted.

The soldiers from the Forest Cantons, placed on the left opposite the Burgundian cavalry, numbered about 1,000 and were supported with some other small contingents. The Bernese formed the center and right of the line opposite the Freiburgers and other infantry. Once everybody was ready, the Burgundians sent heralds to make offer of a parlay; it was rejected. Then they decided to have a knighting ceremony for some squires. Finally, individual riders went forward to taunt and jeer at the Swiss. One can only imagine the deep emotional damage this caused, perhaps necessitating years of therapy and costing millions of francs.

Finally, the battle started. The Burgundians and Austrians came on while the Swiss waited. As they started up the slope, Rudolf set his columns on the right in motion. The Bernese had momentum on their side and they would need it because not all of their column moved forward. Apparently a good number of the unarmored men and some with armor thought that this was not such a good idea after all. The defections occurred at the back, however, which is usually bugging out starts, and so the front part of the phalanx had no knowledge of it. They drove into the Freiburgers and broke apart their formation. At this point, the unreliable infantry on both sides is supposed to have legged it, although, one must say, at least they had hung around this long. On the other side of the field, the cavalry had surrounded the Forest Canton troops who had formed into an all-around defensive position, or hedgehog, formation. As these men were armed with halberds and not long pikes, they could not keep the cavalry at bay, but they maintained their cohesion, which is key, and fought resolutely. They inflicted and received nasty wounds, but stood by their comrades until Rudolf came up with the Bernese infantry and fell on the cavalry, flank and rear. Now the surrounders were becoming the surrounded. The horsemen made one attempt to attack the Bernese, but whether they were tired or had

had enough, they quit the field. In the immediate pursuit, many horsemen were drowned when forced into the Sense River. Among the dead were three counts; Louis of Savoy's only son, John; 80 barons; and hundreds of knights and men-at-arms. Total killed for the Austrian- Burgundian army was perhaps 1,500. Swiss losses were light, with most of the casualties being among the Forest Canton contingent, who had fought off the cavalry. In so doing, they graphically demonstrated that disciplined infantry, even less than optimally armed, could withstand the cavalry charges. This was telling for future tactical developments. It also helped further the moral ascendency of Swiss infantry. Napoleon once noted that the moral was to the physical, as three is to one. The author notes that the character of men usually counts for more than the quality of their weapons.

On 9 July 1386, at the battle of Sempach, 6,000 Austrians and mercenaries under Duke Leopold III of Austria (the nephew of his namesake who lost big at Morgarten) came up against 1,600 Swiss. Leopold had waited until a good part of the Swiss troops were out fighting somebody else's battles. He had read the playbook from the past and he was determined to try something new. Just as the English had done at Crécy (1342) and both sides at Poitiers (1356), the Austrians dismounted their cavalry. More recently, the French had done the same at Roosebeke (1382) and prevailed over the Flemings. The difference was that the English had archers at these battles, and good ones.

This was an encounter battle, which is to say that the two forces came upon each other unwittingly while on the march. The Swiss vanguard was the Lucerne contingent, which was apparently considerably advanced from the main Swiss force. The Lucerners took up a position on a slope with a narrow, level space in front of them. Duke Leopold ordered his first corps to dismount and sent the armored knights forward. Their formation was not in as good order as the Swiss, but on they came. The more heavily armored Austrians outfought the Lucerners, and the latter began losing ground. There are several versions of what happened next. In one, it is stated that the Swiss hero of legend, Arnold Winkelried, gathered up several Austrian spear points in his arms and held them to his chest. In sacrificing himself thus, he opened up a gap for his comrades to exploit. The other version is that just as the Lucerners were fought out, the main Swiss column came up. The Lucerners moved to the flank as the fresh infantry charged into the Austrians. The latter were now at quite a disadvantage, tired from fighting in heavy armor, so they gave ground and called for support. The Duke, with the second Austrian corps, immediately swung out of his saddle, and calling on the others to do the same, led these nobles forward. They hurried on in loose order, but before they could reach the first corps, the Swiss broke through the line. The disorder of the retreating Austrian knights further upset the cohesion of the second corps and the Swiss had the advantage in this combat. At this point, Count Hohenzollern and Baron Oberkirch, who commanded the third corps, made two decisions: 1) things were not going so well, and 2) discretion was the better part of valor. They pulled on their reins, turned, and rode away. Duke Leopold fought on valiantly until he and all with him were cut down. Of the 1,400 nobles in the Austrian army, perhaps 900 had been engaged in the fighting. Of them, the Swiss counted 667 dead, all of noble birth. The Swiss lost about 120, with more than half of them Lucerners.

If the fourteenth century had not convinced Europe of the fighting prowess of the Swiss, the fifteenth surely did. In any fight, whether army versus army or individual versus individual, it helps to have a fiercesome reputation precede one. There is only one way to gain such a reputation, however, and that is by doing. Do it enough and word gets around. The terror inspired by the Spartans, by the Macedonians, by the Mongols, and then by the Swiss was all premised on doing. The Swiss, like the Mongols, gave no quarter whether fighting invaders in their homeland or other mercenaries in foreign lands. This extended, on occasion, to prisoners.

It was at St. Jacob, near Basel, on 24 August 1444, that the Swiss infantry showed all of Europe of what it was made and what it would take to defeat it. The French, under the Dauphin Louis (XI), invaded Switzerland with an army of 30,000. The Swiss met them with a force reported at 1,500 to 2,000. The Swiss, being Swiss, immediately went to the attack. They broke through the French center and then were surrounded. They deployed into their hedgehog and in the open withstood charge after charge by the French cavalry. Charles Oman tells us that the Swiss then moved to a nearby ruined leper hospital and formed around it. The cavalry charges continued, which were followed by attacks by crossbow bolts and other missiles. As the day wore on, the Swiss dead piled up, but not as quickly as the corpses of the French. The Swiss fought to the very end, and by evening, when resistance ended, there were 3,000 dead French. Louis had lost one-tenth of his army at the hands of a force one-fifteenth the size. The French realized that Pyrrhic victories were still as costly in 1444 as they had been in 280 B.C. at Heraclea. They went home.

Henceforth, any commander who came up against the Swiss had it in his mind that these guys would fight anybody, anywhere, anytime, regardless of the consequences, and do so to the death. Troops facing the Swiss would think that they could not defeat such men as these.

Anytime an army goes into a battle thinking that way, it is halfway to defeat.

Why didn't the Swiss conquer Europe? There was no one leading all of Switzerland. The cantons were independently oriented and decisions were made by war councils; the appointment of a supreme commander was rare. The Swiss were always ready to fight, which explains their tactical prowess, but they had no great generals, no one with the opportunity to display strategic vision. The conduct of war eventually surpassed the Swiss in the sixteenth century, in part because they refused to change.

Lastly, and slightly off the point of the Swiss, there has been confusion on the part of some historians as to which Leopolds led Austrian forces in these battles. Here is the rundown. Charles Oman states that the Leopold at Sempach (1386) was Duke Leopold the Valiant, the nephew of the Leopold killed at Morgarten. This is half right: nephew yes, "the Valiant," no. The Leopold at Sempach was a Habsburg and seems to have been quite valorous indeed, but he was not "Leopold the Valiant." Leopold III "the Valiant" was, in fact, not a duke but a margrave (count and military governor), and was a member of the House of Babenberg, which, although an illustrious and famous clan, was definitely not the Habsburg family. Leopold III Babenberg, "The Valiant," Margrave of Austria, lived from 1073 to 1136, and was canonized in 1485. He is the patron saint of Austria, and his line died out in 1246, when one of his descendants, also apparently valorous, was killed in battle.

# Ruses

## Most Effective Forgery in Medieval Military History: Duping the Defenders of the *Krak des Chevaliers*, 1271

The *Krak des Chevaliers* withstood attack for over seven score years. It was built in the early twelfth century by Crusaders and Knights Hospitallers on top of earlier fortifications created by Kurds and successfully withstood attacks by Arabs, Saracens, and other Muslim warriors in 1125, 1163, 1167, 1188, 1207, 1218, 1229, 1252, 1267, and 1270. Besides the best attempts of humans to capture it the *Krak* also withstood two earthquakes. What brute force had not been able to achieve, however, ingenuity did.

In 1271, Sultan Baibar of Aleppo led an Egyptian Mameluke army along with other contingents against the *Krak*. The fortress, which had the capacity of holding up to two thousand knights, was garrisoned by only 300 at this time. The siege had gone on for a month and the attackers had reached the fourth line of defenses, but the inner walls were still holding. The defenders knew that if they could hold out long enough, a relief force would come from Tripoli in Lebanon. In due course a letter came from Tripoli advising the defenders that no relief would be coming and they should negotiate the best terms they could for surrender.

The Knights Hospitallers were offered safe passage to the coast and they took the deal. The *Krak* was immediately occupied by the Mamelukes, and the most formidable Christian fortress in Palestine was in the hands of its enemies. Later the Knights found out that no letter had been sent from Tripoli; it had been forged. Sultan Baibar had pulled a fast one and taken the fortress by trickery. Odysseus would have been pleased.

# The Early Modern Era

## Introduction to the Early Modern Era: Sixteenth Century to 1815

We leave the Middle Ages with the start of the Italian wars of the late fifteenth and early sixteenth centuries. This series of wars was fought between the French, the Italians, and an alliance of Habsburgs (those who ruled Spain and the Holy Roman Empire). It was in these wars that the transition from medieval to modern warfare occurred. Here was the breeding ground for siege artillery, professional troops, modern fortifications, and the new infantry formations and drill.

Before addressing the technical and tactical aspects of this revolution, a few of the broader cultural trends of the era should be remembered. The wars of the sixteenth and seventeenth centuries in Europe were ferocious affairs, largely involving the passions springing from religious disputes and arising from the struggle between ecclesiastical and political authorities. These continual wars, which seemed in many ways to be practically continuous from about 1525 to 1648, spread destruction, famine, and disease over much of western—and especially central—Europe. Whether it was Protestant hacking at Catholic, Christian parrying the persistent blows of successive waves of Muslim invaders, or the internecine slaughter between Roman Catholic Bourbons and Habsburgs, even the Europeans were sick of war by the middle of the seventeenth century. Additionally, the attrition of the nobility in these conflicts and the inevitable, endless subdivision of family lands left the feudal system in ruins. Sadly, the days in which a king could gather his vassals, their men-at-arms, and the peasant fyrd armed with pruning hooks and pitchforks were gone forever.

Throughout the early modern period to the end of the eighteenth century, armies were increasingly professionalized. The roving bands of looting, pillaging mercenaries which replaced the feudal armies during the first part of the early modern period were despised and distrusted by an increasingly war-weary Europe. Mercenaries, in turn, were replaced by better-trained, better-equipped, standing armies of paid soldiers who were disciplined and controlled by rising nation-states and led by aristocratic warrior-leaders as opposed to warrior-fighters such as had been the case earlier.

Against this backdrop of great cultural trends occurred what Michael Roberts termed a "military revolution" brought on by new technologies and developments in the art and science of war. King Charles VIII of France invaded Italy in 1494 to make good his claim to the Kingdom of Naples. He took with him the new artillery that was to batter down the old medieval forts so easily. These bronze guns shared three design characteristics. First, the tubes were stronger than the earlier bombards and their bores were smaller. This allowed denser iron shot to be used rather than stone shot. The advantage of this was that the destructive power of the guns remained the same, but the guns themselves were one-third the size, hence, they were lighter. Also, iron balls were cheaper and easier to make than stone balls and did not shatter on impact. Second, the invention of corned powder allowed for uniformly-mixed gunpowder to be used. By making the powder into grains, the proper ratio of ingredients was maintained and the powder burned more rapidly in the chamber. Consequently, muzzle energy was increased. Third, changes in carriage design allowed for a team of strong horses to pull these eight-foot-long guns anywhere heavy wagons could go. Artillery was now more mobile.

The impact of this artillery was great. Old fortifications fell willy-nilly. This new artillery was expensive, however; only wealthy states could afford it. The response to this artillery, in time, was a new style of fortress with long, low walls; ditches; bastions for counterfire; and star-shaped designs called the *trace Italienne*. A state that could afford such fortifications could go a long way toward preserving its independence, and only states, not individual nobles, could afford them.

These wars were also the proving ground for infantry tactics. Previously, heavy cavalry and heavy infantry in the form of dense squares of pikemen dominated tactics. Light infantry was represented by long-bowmen in England, and crossbowmen and *arquebusiers* on the continent. Light cavalry—that is to say, missile-armed riders—was not prominent in this era and field artillery was nonexistent during the Middle Ages.

The *arquebus* and its successor, the musket, began the process which ended the dominance of non-gunpowder weapons on the battlefield. The *arquebus* was fired by a match and was, at first, a fairly unreliable weapon. It actually discharged a projectile only about half the time it was fired and its .75-caliber ball found its target—say a line of men 100 yards away—only half the time as well. Eventually, the hand-held gun would outrange the crossbow, but what kept the firearm around as a viable weapon at this time was the fact that the *arquebus* and its ammunition was cheaper and easier to produce than the crossbow with its windlass and bolts. The rate of fire was the same for both weapons and the *arquebus* had equal hitting power. Until the widespread use of rifled muskets in the nineteenth century, the essential element to this usage would be rate of fire, not accuracy.

The issue for commanders in these wars was how to combine the three types of units at their disposal—heavy and light infantry, and

Soldier with *arquebus* and
aiming fork
© *Bettmann/CORBIS/*
*MAGMA*

heavy cavalry—into an effective force. The Spanish were the first to do it with their development of the *tercio* (for a diagram, see page 181). They surrounded rectangles of pikemen with *arquebusiers*. These two types of infantry, along with a dwindling number of "sword and buckler" men—partially-armored troops wielding swords and small shields for close combat—worked together and supported each other. The *arquebusiers* were protected from heavy cavalry by taking refuge amidst the forest of pikes and they, in turn, helped defend the formation with their firepower.

The Spanish replaced their crossbowmen with *arquebusiers* fairly rapidly and the catalyst for this change seems to have been the battle of Pavia in 1525. Here Spanish *arquebusiers* were employed as skirmishers who used the natural cover available on the battlefield and fired from prepared entrenchments. The *arquebusiers'* skirmishing greatly inhibited the effectiveness of the French cavalry and German mercenaries, while their use of field fortifications halted an attack by Swiss pikemen. Both actions were important to subsequent Spanish thinking; by the end of the sixteenth century, *arquebusiers* and pikemen were equally represented in the *tercio*. A steady fire could be maintained by having the *arquebusiers* fire by alternate rank and this, too, was practiced. In substituting *arquebusiers* for crossbowmen, the Spanish were changing light infantry missile men, but not initiating a great tactical revolution.

Cavalry tactics also changed because of technology. The heavy cavalryman armed with a lance gave way to the more versatile *Reiter* who was armed with a pair of wheellock pistols and a sword. The wheellock mechanism—though expensive and delicate—allowed a rider to hold the reins with one hand and shoot with the other. The tactic developed to employ this mobile firepower was the caracole, by which a formation of *Reiter* would marshall just beyond effective range of the enemy's *arquebusiers* (perhaps 100 meters), then charge. Due to their slow rate of fire and limited range, the *arquebusiers* would get off at most one shot before they would have to retire behind a wall of pikemen, who thus masked their fire. Just before crashing into the infantry, the *Reiter* would abruptly halt their steeds, fire point-blank shots with each of the two pistols they carried, turn about, and ride as fast as they could out of *arquebus* range. In theory, this uneven duel would continue until the infantry withdrew or were sufficiently weakened that an all-out charge, all the way into the defensive line, would break the defense. Thus a square comprised purely of pikemen could not defend itself against *Reiter* unless it had *arquebusiers*, because the *Reiter* could ride up to a pike formation, stay well away from the pikes, and blithely blast away. Thus did the *arquebusier* became a valued performer on the battlefield, even if the caracole could give him fits.

The last point to be made here concerns casualties. Archer Jones, in analyzing 20 battles between 1495 and 1600, gives us the following information. The defeated typically lost 38 percent of their men and the victors only 6 percent. Jones explains that the great disparity existed because the losers were disorganized and had no effective means of regrouping and rallying. From this, one can see why commanders were reluctant to risk battle unless there was a high chance of victory.

In highly-fortified areas, battle became exceedingly unlikely. The defenders would lodge themselves in their modernized forts and could successfully resist a huge army for months. This is, in fact, what the Dutch did when they revolted against their Spanish masters. The Dutch had several advantages, however, the foremost of which was money from their extensive overseas trade. It allowed them to build forts, maintain a navy, and pay soldiers regularly. In the sixteenth and early part of the seventeenth centuries, they also controlled a great deal of the east Indian saltpeter (potassium nitrate) trade; of the three basic components of gunpowder, this one was exceedingly rare in Europe, so the Dutch position was not only helpful to their logistical situation, but tremendously profitable. They brought back thousands of tons, typically as ballast in their ships.

The great contribution of the Dutch to the evolution of tactics was the reforms of Maurice of Nassau. Using their own ideas and receiving inspiration from the writings of the ancients, Maurice and his cousin, William Louis, introduced the next stage in tactical evolution: the establishment of the linear firing line. Maurice replaced the 2,500 strong, dense blocks of pikemen with smaller units deployed on line. Pikemen

Fifteenth-/sixteenth-century sword.
*Higgins*

Queen Anne pistol
*Higgins*

were now only 5 to 10 ranks deep with a front of 50 men, and *arque-busiers* were arranged in three groups, four abreast and ten deep, on each side. An additional group of 60 *arquebusiers* were used as skirmishers. These units, comprising battalions of 450 or so, were deployed in three lines, thereby enabling the commander of an army to establish one line as a reserve. To control this "looser" formation, the number of officers was increased. The men were taught volley fire by rank with each rank marching to the rear of the formation to reload while the next rank fired.

Volley fire from a linear formation spread out armies on a battlefield, in effect, adding more guns to the offense and less density to the defense. The shallow pike and musket formations now had the challenge of remaining steady under attack with less mass. Consequently, each man had to be a better individual soldier than his predecessor had been. Due to their size, these formations were more maneuverable and mobile than the larger *tercios.* If all these advantages were to be achieved, however, then the men in them would have to be well-drilled in all aspects of their responsibilities.

Drill not only enhanced individual and collective proficiency, it improved cohesion. It developed better soldiers and that made for better armies. Dutch wealth ensured that the men would be paid regularly, and this checked wasteful and destructive pillaging and ensured that the units would remain together year-round. These practices established the basis for professional armies. Maurice also started to standardize firearms and his cousin, John, standardized drill by creating illustrated manuals. So, as drill was making men more responsive to a broader variety of commands, drill manuals were making the commands uniformly understood. Maurice also made it a common practice for his men to dig. They dug entrenchments to defend themselves and to circumvallate the enemy in his defenses.

The linear tactics of Maurice were to be refined in the seventeenth century during the Thirty Years' War by Gustavus Adolphus. The Swedish king put a great emphasis on firepower as his tactics demonstrated. The adoption of lighter muskets and the use of paper cartridges with pre-measured charges allowed his well-drilled infantry to maintain volley fire with only six ranks. He also shifted his musketeers sometimes to three ranks and had all of them fire simultaneously. This was accomplished by having the front rank kneel and the second rank stoop. Gustavus eliminated the caracole from his cavalry's repertoire of tactics in favor of the charge on line with swords. This returned shock action to the cavalry, which had been getting out of that habit. Lastly, he introduced a small field gun to his battalions to increase firepower.

During the Thirty Years' War, the role of the musketeer grew, due in part to the changes in cavalry. Light infantry (first bowmen and then hand gunners) needed the support of heavy infantry to protect it from cavalry. What spelled the decline of the pikemen and the sword and buckler troops was the rise of light cavalry (*Reiter*), which did not have to close with the infantry to inflict casualties. The pikemen and swordsmen then needed the light infantry musketeers to outrange the light cavalry's pistols and the musketeers needed the pikemen to protect them from armored heavy cavalry charges.

Developments in technology upset this fine, symbiotic relationship. Once improvements to the hand-held gun and the conduct of drill increased, not only the musket's power but its rate of fire and its superior range made it the weapon of choice. Technologically, improvements in musket design increased the rate of fire to two or three rounds per minute. The flintlock replaced the matchlock/*arquebus* and with it increased to 66 percent the likelihood of the musket firing, eventually firing 85 percent of the time. Better metal for the barrel, moreover, allowed a higher muzzle velocity for the one-ounce ball (1,000 feet per second), which increased the range. This development also brought forth smaller, lighter, more compact designs. The decrease in weight allowed shooters to dispense with the hooked stick, and less space was required to handle and operate the weapon. Accordingly, soldiers could stand closer together when firing, which meant more guns per unit frontage for the firing line. Once cavalry gave up the lance, the density of pikemen was decreased. Sword-armed cavalry, which was discarding much of its armor due to its weight and susceptibility to firearms, did not have the shock value of lance-armed cavalry. If financial considerations are any standard of merit and worth, by the end of the seventeenth century, musketeers were being paid twice what pike-men received.

The drawback of this system was that the shallow battalion-sized formations lacked the capacity for effective all-around defense. The flanks and rear were vulnerable to attack; innovators like Gustavus used a second line to support the first. The other weakness of linear deployment was that it was difficult to keep the alignment of battalions straight. Overall, however, the advantages exceeded the liabilities, especially as the flexibility of mercenary pike formations, of the kind recruited in the Thirty Years' War and the type most readily available, was not up to Swiss standards.

Artillery was growing in power, but heavy-caliber guns were still not sufficiently mobile to take an effective part in offensive operations in the field. On the defensive and protected by infantry, it was formidable indeed, and for siege work or defense, it was indispensable. The rest of the century saw no great changes in the linear tactical system described above and technological innovations would reinforce the trend of raising infantry to the dominant weapons system on the battlefield.

The advent of the bayonet, particularly the socket bayonet, introduced in the 1690s, allowed infantry to function in light and heavy roles simultaneously. This, in turn, spelled the demise of the *Reiter* who was now outclassed by infantry. His pistol was significantly out-ranged by infantry muskets, and the firepower to which he was exposed during his galloping approach was significantly more effective. No longer did firearm-equipped infantry have to hide behind pike-equipped infantry; they were one in the same. Thus, charging cavalry, especially attempting a caracole, might even be subject to two volleys en route, or, worse, a volley at close range, which would be devastating. His saber could not outreach the small pikes the infantry could create for themselves with the bayonet. Now, three ranks of infantry could withstand a cavalry charge.

The infantry line, however, was still vulnerable to attacks on its flanks and rear, but to counter these threats it could deploy into a hollow square. This maneuver took time and if it was not accomplished expeditiously, cavalry could exploit the gaps in the formation. Nevertheless, the bayonet reduced western Europeans to employing two basic types of combat soldiers—musket and bayonet-armed infantry and cavalry intended for shock action. Homogeneity, that is, commonality, of weapons made battles more even and the casualties of the defeated relatively smaller than before.

In the eighteenth century, three approaches were taken to tactics. In the first approach, some Frenchmen experimented with and debated the merits of columns and shock action. In the second, others sought to use skirmishers and infantry arrayed in a line (hence the term which survives to this day, "line infantry"), and the third one involved improving a combination facilitated by infantry drill. The Prussians became masters of the third. The advantage of speed in war is paramount. The Prussians' constant and uniform—that is, consistent—drilling allowed them to maneuver and deploy for battle more quickly than anyone else. Drill allowed them to keep their lines dressed and their homogeneous battalions meant that they were in battle array even when marching. Furthermore, by marching in platoons with platoon-sized gaps between each unit, they needed only to halt and execute a right face to be in full-battle formation. (See page 194)

This movement technique was used by Frederick the Great often, most notably at the battle of Leuthen. Here he used the superior mobility of his columns to put his battle line at nearly right angles to the Austrian line. He then advanced in "echelon right," thereby bringing his stronger right wing in contact with the enemy well before his weaker, and "refused" (physically unassailable) left was engaged. Another Prussian advantage was their iron ramrod. As it was stronger than the wooden one, it did not break under the stress of rapid loading.

The foundation of Prussian supremacy on the battlefield was based upon tactical excellence. This was the response of Frederick William I and his son, Frederick the Great, to the security problem of Prussia. States need armies to defend them. Prussia, as she had no easily defensible frontier, needed the best army in Europe and the bigger the army the better it would be for the king. This quest for excellence and size did not come without economic consequences for the state and the people, but what concerns us here is the military manifestation of the sacrifices and policies. Prussia, as a relatively poor state with an expensive army to maintain, did not desire to fight long-term wars. Of course, who does? For Prussia, however, what this meant was that she needed an army that could win wars rapidly, or least get out in front quickly and then hold on. Fortunately for Frederick the Great, he had just the right kind of genius and he ruled over just the right kind of people for this to be possible. Through a system of drill, imposed by the severest discipline in Europe, Frederick produced an army which had many of the hallmarks of the modern age: professionalism, flexibility, and doctrine. The other thing to note is that the Prussian army was mostly German. In 1740, the army of 76,000 contained 26,000 foreigners; by 1763, at the end of the Seven Years War, the army was 103,000 Germans and 37,000 foreigners. Nevertheless, the presence of mercenaries and foreign troops meant that Frederick had to limit their opportunities to desert.

Also limited was Frederick's amount of light infantry. His army was mostly line or heavy infantry. Prussia did not have troops available from the Balkans, as did Austria with the Croats, soldiers with a tradition of irregular fighting and independent action.

For Frederick's army, as it has been for all armies, the character of men counts for more than the quality of their weapons. This calculus meant that in Frederick's army well-drilled troops would compensate for material shortcomings, particularly in artillery. Rigorous training could turn raw recruits into adequate soldiers in a few weeks, which is to say, men able to march in formation, stand in close (22 inches allotted per man) and shoot it out, or even charge with bayonets. It was not enough time to make them independent-minded skirmishers. The Prussian soldier had to fire more shots per minute and to maneuver across the battlefield in formation faster than his adversaries. Frederick recognized that he had to be offensive-minded from the onset of hostilities. He also had no qualms about engaging a numerically superior enemy. His goal was to bring the issue to a decision as quickly as possible and because the stakes for Frederick were so high, he was prepared to attack against the odds and to fight a battle for as long as it took to win.

Frederick's favored method of deployment was in echelon and he utilized an oblique approach to deceive and confuse the enemy. His purpose was to place the bulk of his force on the enemy's flank and rear. Thus he would attack the weakest part of the enemy formation with the strongest part of his army. Even if outnumbered overall, he had the local advantage where he wanted it. The Prussian cavalry contributed to this asymmetrical maneuver with its flexibility, attacking whenever there was an opportunity. This is an important point to make, as the offensive action of Frederick's cavalry often decided the battle and his subordinates were prepared to exercise their initiative.

In essence, what Frederick was doing was perfecting the existing system of warfare: faster marching, more offensive-minded, and better drilled in the intricate mass motions of battlefield deployment. The quest for improvement naturally extended to the musket. Aimed infantry fire was not prized as much as a large volume of fire. Thus, a more durable iron ramrod replaced the wooden one, a conical touch hole was introduced, and the barrel's bore was sufficiently large so that loading was facilitated at each stage of the process. These changes cut the loading time from 11 seconds to eight or nine. A minor improvement on the surface of things, but in practical terms, this was a major development. A battalion of 576 men could, in theory, now deliver five volleys a minute instead of four, sending an extra 576 musket balls into the enemy's ranks. Even if combat conditions reduced the fire effectiveness of the men, the new musket increased the weight of metal delivered. Lastly—and speaking of weight—the musket, with the bayonet permanently fixed and the heavier iron ramrod, was purposely designed to be muzzle-heavy to counter the well-known tendency of men under pressure to fire high.

The French army of the eighteenth century until the French Revolution was an army with a great deal of intellectual activity. Its defeats— at the beginning of the century by Marlborough and Eugene of Savoy, and at mid-century in the Seven Years' War—made it an army diligently trying to understand the reasons for its defeats. From this debate, the army emerged with the basic tenets that Napoleon would use so brilliantly and vigorously that it seemed to observers that a whole new way of war had appeared. The debate proceeded along two lines: the proper composition of the battalion, which was the basic infantry unit; and second, the apportionment of the army into divisions. The former affected tactics and the latter, strategy. The central issue of the debate was whether the battalions should deploy in column and rely on shock, or deploy in line and rely on firepower. The former was termed the *ordre profond*, and the latter, the *ordre mince*. In the end, a compromise was reached. The resulting *ordre mixte* was more *mince* than *profond*. That it turned out this way reflected the fact that missile weapons were more important to a favorable tactical solution than shock action. In fact, the *ordre mixte*, which combined columnar and linear formations, was most useful for battlefield mobility; it did not represent a desire to return to the tactics of the Swiss pikemen.

The new French deployment went from column to three-deep line by having the separate units march diagonally to take their places in the line or, if the head of the column was still moving, the deploying units ran to their places. Any gaps between units could be covered by fire. The impact of this on the battlefield was potentially great because it was faster than anything else. The ordered advance of a long thin line of men formed of units 200 by 3 deep, even over level ground, was difficult and slow. In contrast, the movement of a battalion 24 files by 25 ranks was relatively rapid. Heretofore, the deployment from columns to line had been a cumbersome process. The Prussian method of Frederick the Great was only possible because of the open order of the column.

Tactical speed and flexibility were not the only things increased as a result of these changes; so too was strategic maneuver. This was accomplished by breaking an army up into four similarly constituted divisions of 10,000 men. An army of divisions could move faster than a massed force because it could move along more roads, and obviously, it is easier to handle 10,000 men and their equipment and supplies than it is to handle 40,000. Later, divisions would be grouped into corps.

Adding also to the increased speed in the tactical-strategic mix were the developments in field artillery, most notably under Jean-Baptiste Vaquette de Gribeauval, a French artillery and military engineering officer. Improvements in boring techniques allowed barrels to be bored out to more exact tolerances. This meant less wastage of propellant, and smaller charges could thus be used to achieve the same velocity. This meant an increase in range, too. Smaller charges also meant barrels could be shorter and thinner, so guns became lighter. Carriages were better balanced because of improvements in design, and new styles of harnesses were developed for draft animals so that the guns could now keep up with the rest of the army. Gribeauval also standardized the calibers and this made for fewer types of equipment that had to carried along. Together these advances increased not only the tactical and strategic mobility of artillery, but its rate of fire as well.

The impact of commonly-armed infantry on strategy was remarkable, but before that impact is discussed, it should be noted that the increasing professionalism of armies and more sophisticated tactics did give rise to a diversification of subtypes of infantry and cavalry. By the end of the eighteenth century, musket-armed infantry had variegated into light infantry (for skirmishing and scouting); line infantry (for mass maneuver and blasting away); and grenadiers (for missions requiring special shock or tenacity). The French, naturally, had exquisitely beautiful names for them such as *voltigeurs, fusiliers,* and *grenadiers,* respectively, and different armies had their own special variations, but they were essentially the same three types. Generally, each regiment of the line possessed single companies of light and grenadier infantry, and several companies of line infantry. There were exceptions, such as whole regiments of light infantry or *grenadiers,* but most regiments (800–1,200 soldiers) were organized this way.

Similarly, cavalry was now split into light cavalry (for reconnaissance, pursuit, and liaison missions) and heavy cavalry (for shock action). There was even a hybrid mounted infantry, which moved on horseback, but carried infantry muskets and bayonets to be able to fight on foot. As always, these sound more impressive in French as *hussars* (light cavalry trained for reconnoitering and liaison missions); *lanciers,* or lancers (ditto, trained for pursuit of a fleeing enemy and equipped with long lances for obvious purposes); *cuirassiers* (partially-armored heavy cavalry armed with straight swords and trained for close combat); and *dragons*,or dragoons (mounted infantry). Generally, each regiment of cavalry (300–600 soldiers and horses) consisted of a single type.

Cavalry's mobility has never been in question. Cavalry was highly useful for scouting in advance of the main body, exploiting gaps in the enemy line, pursuing a fleeing enemy, or for just plain devastating the countryside by arson and pillage.

In the seventeenth century, cavalry was restored to the role of shock by Gustavus Adolphus who armed his horsemen with sabers and ordered them to charge the enemy. In the eighteenth century, however, innovation in infantry equipment, specifically the bayonet, led to the decline of cavalry for shock action. Men on the ground with muskets and bayonets, assuming they were not running away, had little to fear from men on horseback armed with pistols and sabers. In terms of unit tactics, infantry in line was still vulnerable on the flanks and rear to cavalry attacks, but once infantry formed a square, they could resist very effectively. In direct combat, cavalry was best used against other cavalry or unformed infantry. Cavalry had, relatively speaking, little defensive power.

Frederick the Great noted that his cavalry must be ready to attack the enemy sword in hand and, after driving off the enemy cavalry, it should attack the enemy infantry's flank and rear. So important was offensive action to Frederick that cavalry officers, who allowed themselves to be attacked by, rather than first attacking, the enemy, would be cashiered. Frederick directed that to be effective, the cavalry charge would begin at a walk and then move to the trot; when the line was 200 paces from the enemy, the horses were given free rein and galloped at full speed. The entire line had to follow this procedure because piecemeal attacks, whereby one regiment followed the other, robbed the assault of its power. Once the enemy cavalry was driven from the field, a part of the attack force was assigned to prevent the scattered enemy from returning while the rest reformed to attack the enemy infantry's flank and rear. Before this was done, however, an officer had to ride to the Prussian infantry and tell them that such an attack was pending so that they would not fire on their own riders. During the attack horsemen, even if dragoons, were not to use their pistols or carbines but only their swords.

The cavalry's primary roles through the eighteenth century remained exploitation and pursuit, but it never dominated the battlefield again. The offensive power of infantry grew throughout this era as their weapons improved and as the theoreticians of tactics devised methods for the more rapid movement of troops across the battlefield.

Dividing the army into divisions, consisting of several regiments of infantry and cavalry, and supported by a variable number of artillery batteries, presented the opportunity for a new strategic concept. Each division was a combined arms team, so it could hold its own against a superior force while the other divisions marched to support it. The French deployed from column to line so quickly, moreover, that they enjoyed a multi-faceted advantage in speed. The division moved faster than the army and the column moved faster than the line. If one can move twice as fast as one's opponent, one halves the time one's foe has to react. In war, this is a tremendous advantage. Now a commander could hold an enemy to his front and maneuver onto his rear; he could cut his supply line; fall on his flank; or do all three. Furthermore, because the route of advance was dispersed, it was harder for an opponent to determine the exact approach. Foraging for supplies was easier as the army could draw from a larger area. The result of all this was that battle would be harder to refuse. Previously, if a commander did not want to fight he could refuse battle and march away, terrain and supplies permitting.

Thus, strategy came to be ever more influenced by logistical concerns. In the recent past, commanders eschewed battle under less-than-certain circumstances because armies were expensive and the price of losing was too high to pay. It was safer and, given the high desertion rates, easier, to compel the enemy to retreat by cutting his supply lines rather than trying to defeat him in battle. The new mobility introduced the combat element to strategy. This French system of war—which owed much to the efforts of Bourcet, Broglie, and Guibert—was, by the end of the century, ready to prove itself. It needed only a genius to demonstrate its potential. Europe would not have long to wait.

The wars inaugurated by the French Revolution and sustained by Napoleon were unprecedented in scale. It was not tactics that set them apart, however. The Napoleonic revolution was strategic in nature. Napoleon relied upon the French army's superior mobility and, at least initially, on the maintenance of interior lines to turn upon his enemies in quick succession. His armies lived off the land and so were housed mostly at the expense of the vanquished. He was able to do this because his troops were not the mercenaries of old or the so-called dregs of society. They saw themselves as citizens committed to the ideals of the Revolution—liberty, fraternity, and equality. This made them more reliable as soldiers and less likely to desert. The Revolution's concept of the nation-in-arms, wherein all citizens were put at the service of the state, assured the army of a large manpower supply. It became easier, therefore, to make armies bigger.

Once the French lost their monopoly on this manner of fighting, things evened out. While the genius of Napoleon could not be captured, the essence of his strategy could. The allies, united in their efforts and plans, were able to defeat Napoleon as they showed at Leipzig in 1813 and the subsequent campaign of 1814.

The most important thing about this era, however, was the way in which battle established itself as a feature of strategy. This was so because tactical organization had made it possible. Interestingly, even though battle became more and more a feature of war, the percentage of casualties from battle did not substantially increase. Jones observes that in this period the proportion of battle casualties rose 1 percent, to 13.5 percent for the winners and 22.9 for the losers, from the the levels at the beginning of the eighteenth century. When compared to the 60 percent casualties the French suffered at Blenheim, one can see that the consequences of losing a battle were far less severe, and as soldiers were more easily replaced, generals became inclined to fight battles more often, which was just as well, for battles were now easier to arrange. Battles were not deadlier because of the reasons stated elsewhere. Armies were similarly armed, more maneuverable, and thus better able to withdraw from a lost battle. Better-trained soldiers meant also that an army was more resilient in dealing with retreat. Furthermore, with large armies fighting in western Europe, a high force-to-space ratio existed, making it harder to avoid an opponent. When Napoleon invaded Russia, he had a low force-to-space ratio and so he could not bring Kutuzov to battle on terms unfavorable to the Russians.

The last point to make about the Napoleonic wars is that artillery continued to increase in importance. Hew Strachan notes that artillery was the least disturbed arm of the army during the Revolution because of its bourgeois officers, with 80 percent of the junior officers being of long standing. Napoleon introduced civilian draft team drivers into the army in 1800 and in 1803 eliminated regimental artillery. This permitted the infantry to move faster. He then augmented the number of guns in higher formations. The calibers of guns were increased as was the number of artillery pieces. In 1805, the French army had 286 field pieces; in 1812 it took 1,146 to Russia. Napoleon also concentrated his artillery on the battlefield in large numbers. Artillery, while strong on the defensive, also showed great destructive power when it could be used offensively. Given that the effective range of the musket was about 100 yards, artillery could unlimber well beyond that and still deliver devastating fire. At the battle of Friedland in 1807, for example, in 25 minutes, 30 French guns firing canister and moving forward in stages inflicted 4,000 casualties before redeploying to stave off a cavalry attack.

# Equipment

## First Examples of Modern Fortification:
### Italy, Artillery, and the Action-Reaction Cycle

The development of siege artillery ended the effectiveness of medieval castles as defensive bastions, and the castle owners were not going to take this lying down. Human ingenuity, being what it is, would soon find a solution to the challenge presented by iron projectiles flung at high speed against vertical stone walls.

The first one was inventive and temporary, but effective. At the siege of Pisa in 1500, the French, assisting the Florentines, battered down a section of the wall but found, to their surprise, another line of defenses. The Pisans had thrown up what was, in essence, field works inside their fortress. They dug a ditch and used the earth to throw up a rampart. The rampart was broad enough to mount cannons and was protected by other means as well. Shortly after the French confronted this second line of defense, they gave up the siege.

Christopher Duffy makes two points about this from the technical side. The first concerns the nature of the breech itself. If the battering was done with large stone balls at low velocity, as it had to be from bombards, then the rubble produced was of large pieces of masonry. On the other hand, if the breech was made by small caliber guns shooting iron shot at a high velocity then the rubble produced was smaller. Smaller rubble was easier to scale and this facilitated the assault. The second involves the rampart's construction and what came to be known as the double Pisan rampart. The rampart did not press against the outer wall and this was important because when the outer wall came down, it did so solely as a heap of sharp stones. This made the rubble more difficult to traverse. Moreover, if the earthen wall was against the masonry wall then it, too, would have been shaken apart by the pounding. Using this system of interior ramparts, Padua successfully held off a French and Habsburg siege in 1509.

The next step was the creation of more permanent elements of fortification designed to defeat the advantages of artillery. In medieval forts, the high walls were protected by towers, in modern forts the walls came to be protected by bastions, ditches, and other manner of outworks which were low and spread out. The key element, however, is the bastion, which is a four-sided angular projection with two faces and two flanks. Think of it as an irregular pentagon with two long sides—the flanks—and then two short sides which attach to the wall. The fifth side or bottom of the pentagon is the wall itself. These bastions projected out far enough to permit the mounting of guns on the bastions which could cover the length of wall between any two bastions. This allowed for mutually supporting bastions to engage in crossfire defense along the ditch before them. Lastly, the angular shape eliminated the dead ground which existed before, which is to say, in front of the old round and square towers.

So who was the first to design and build a bastion? Duffy favors the Sangallo family of Florence who were reshaping fortress walls in Tuscany in the middle of the fifteenth century into something bastioned. The pace of bastioning obviously picked up in the fifteenth century and before long, refinements to the bastion appeared. Most recognizable was the *"orillon,"* similar in looks to an earlobe. Think of the ace of spades in a deck of cards. It was placed where the face met the flank and thereby provided more protection to the guns on the flank. This was important because these guns were to sweep the ditch clear of attackers. From *orillon,* to *redan* and *glacis,* the language of fortification is varied and opaque to the uninitiated. The reader should beware of buying a book on early modern fortifications without a glossary.

A *redan* is a pointed outwork, apex toward the enemy, built up to a height necessary to protect its defenders from direct fire. Often, two more walls were added, one to each side parallel to the one opposite, to protect the defenders from being taken in flank. The *glacis* is the forward slope of earth, stone, or masonry that faces toward the enemy. It is constructed so that the enemy will come under fire from the

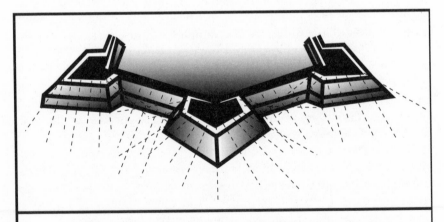

**Typical Early Modern Bastions and Their Fields Observation and Fire**

defenders atop the slope without any "dead space," or locations from which he cannot be observed or engaged by fire as he advances. The sloping face also cuts down the angle of impact of incoming cannon balls, and thus reduces their effectiveness by deflecting them over the heads of the defenders. Often, a separate glacis was built up on the enemy side of the ditch which surrounded the main fortress; this further protected the walls from direct fire by siege artillery.

It did not take long for these new and especially effective designs to proliferate. The Sangallo "Family," Duffy says, built and collaborated on 38 works of fortification. The design is known as the *trace Italienne*, so-called because the design of the fort is traced on the ground and it started in Italy. The designs were very geometric in form. Moreover, because these fortifications used a lot of earth, defense became a question of how many shovels do we have and not how many skilled masons can we lay our hands on. This is not to say that skilled workers were unnecessary, plenty of skilled workers were needed for the latest in fortress building. The reader may find it reassuring to know that, long before the nuclear age, survival for some people under attack was simply just a case of having enough shovels to go around.

## Best Examples of Gunpowder's Gift to Language: Siege Warfare Leads to Metaphor

### *"Hoist with his own petar"; "a flash in the pan"; and "making the rounds"*

Some readers may recognize that the first line is from Shakespeare. They are correct, too, if they say that it is from Hamlet and if they know it as Act III, scene iv, they are obviously devotees and perhaps too smart to be reading this book. If there are any who know that it is line 207 (2nd Quarto) then they have already stopped reading this section.

The element in question, the petard, to give its usual spelling, was an explosive device designed to bring down gates, doors, or thin walls. It was in its essence, a bell, usually of bronze, with a good strong pole sticking out of the top. The pole was secured to the bell by whatever means the engineers could fashion, and the contraption was placed against the target in such a way that when it went off the pole was driven into, and hopefully through, the wall. Christopher Duffy tells us that the charge was calculated at 12 pounds of powder for every 100 pounds of petard weight. It was fired by the petardier who lit the fuse and then ran to safety. There are many assumptions in this type of work. First, that the petardiers made it to the wall safely and managed to bring up their equipment. Second, that they were able to set it up without being injured. Third, that they properly set the fuse. Fourth, that they lit the fuse and the gadget did not blow up right away. Fifth, that the petardier was able to get away safely. Henry of Navarre, we are told, was the foremost practitioner, if not the inventor of this weapon. He first used it on the night of 5–6 May 1580 at Cahors, prosecuting, Duffy states, a private feud against the town. The sixteenth century must have been a great time to be a man, or at least a rich and powerful one. Henry was, in fact, quite accomplished in siege warfare and innovative.

To be "hoisted by one's petard," therefore, now means to receive a comeuppance but one at the hands of the device by which one meant to destroy others. Interestingly, the next line of Hamlet's speech, "and it shall go hard, but I will delve one yard below their mines and blow them at the moon." Is the reader ahead of the author in recognizing the reference to counter-mining?

A "flash in the pan" refers to the firing mechanism of the flintlock musket. When it operates properly, the hammer with the flint falls forward and strikes the steel which creates sparks. The sparks light the gunpowder in the pan, which sets off the charge in the barrel. If there is flash and no discharge of the weapon then we have a flash *in,* and *only in,* the pan, and that is ineffectual. Hence, his phrase refers to anything that starts brilliantly and fails quickly or a person who does the same. The author must admit that he heard the terms used a lot more when he was younger. He calls on the readership to actively promote these metaphors and to stop smirking.

"Making the rounds" comes to us from fortifications and were it not for gunpowder, this particular form of fortification would not have appeared. Ian Hogg tells us that the term originates with the Dutch system of bastions. The high water table in the Low Countries resulted in numerous uses of wide—but not deep—wet ditches in front of low thick earthen ramparts. The open space behind the ramparts was known as *"chemin des rondes."* Thus "making the rounds" came to mean, the officer going about and checking the men in the various *chemin des rondes.*

## Most Ubiquitous Firearm in History:
### The "Brown Bess"

The Land Service musket was a smooth-bore flintlock musket developed in the 1720s. It had a caliber (diameter of the projectile) of .75 inch (thus called "seventy-five caliber" in military parlance). This weapon was produced in five versions or patterns. The Long Land Service musket had a 46-inch barrel and was in production from the 1720s until 1790. The Short Land musket was produced from circa 1745 to 1797 and had a barrel of 42 inches. The Marine and Militia service muskets were versions of the Short Land musket. There were additionally an India pattern and a New Land pattern musket, the last two in production until 1815. The reason for its nickname is unknown, but it may stem from the fact that the Short Land musket had a walnut stock, which distinguished it from earlier muskets that had stocks painted black.

This musket took a socket bayonet about 14 inches long and weighed about 11 pounds. If a soldier could fire two to three rounds a minute, he was doing pretty well. In this regard, he was aided by the paper cartridge. The cartridge was made up in rolled paper with six to eight drams of powder and the ball. If the reader is wondering, it is 16 drams

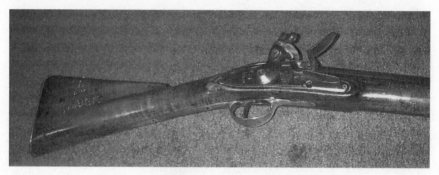

The flintlock, trigger, and butt end of a "Brown Bess" (above). *Hogarth*

Powder flask (right). *Hogarth*

to the ounce, *avoirdupois*. The soldier would bite open the cartridge, use the powder to prime his pan and then load his weapon. The paper was used for the wadding, to ensure the ball fit snugly against the interior of the bore, and did not just roll out the muzzle.

The weapon was not accurate beyond 100 yards and it was best at ranges 80 yards and under. It fired a one-ounce lead ball at relatively low velocity, and this created horrific wounds in the human body because the heavy ball tumbled as it passed through the body. The large caliber of the Brown Bess meant that all sorts of bullets could be used in the musket. This weapon was in use until the percussion cap superseded the flintlock in the nineteenth century, circa 1830. The Brown Bess continued to appear in battles throughout the nineteenth century, however, especially with armies from technologically retarded societies.

# Personalities

## Best Example of Why You Shouldn't Drink and Shoot: Oudenarrde, 1582

### "Gee, thanks Mr. Parma. It sounds like a real blast, I'd love to come for dinner"

His Grace, the Duke of Parma, was born Alessandro Farnese in 1545 and he died in 1592. The Duchy of Parma had been created for Alessandro's grandfather by his great-grandfather, Pope Paul III. Alessandro's mother was the illegitimate daughter of Charles V (1500–1558), the Holy Roman Emperor. If only more of us could start life with advantages such as this family of mercenaries.

Alessandro married Maria of Portugal in 1565 and, like Peter the Hermit, preferred to be away from home. He learned the trade of war from Don Juan of Austria, one of the great military commanders of the sixteenth century. In 1571, Parma served under Don Juan at the battle of Lepanto, one of the most important naval battles in history. He spent the rest of his military career fighting the Dutch rebels. This conflict, also known as the Eighty Years' War (1567–1648), was occasioned by religious differences arising from the Reformation and attacks on the unofficial religion of Europe, money. The opposition to Habsburg rule coalesced as Philip II and his general, the Duke of Alba, engaged in repressive measures to stamp out Protestantism. These actions and the assault on the other religion of Europe, and here the author speaks of the ten percent sales tax Alba imposed, led even Catholic merchants to join the rebels.

Parma succeeded to the command of Habsburg forces in the Nether-lands after the death of Don Juan in 1578. Parma proved an apt pupil of Don Juan's, and combined skilled diplomacy with military ability. He brought the southern Catholic provinces back into the Habsburg fold and began his campaign against the northern Protestant states in 1582.

During the siege of Oudenarrde, a drunken Spanish gunner mistak-enly, we presume, aimed his piece at his own camp and fired. The ball hit a dinner party being hosted by Parma. The dead and dying were removed, the dinner went on, and Alessandro treated it as if nothing untoward had happened. Such aplomb stood him well as he conducted a skillful campaign of sieges against the Dutch Protestants, which including the 13-month siege of Antwerp, which ended in August 1585. It should be mentioned that Parma knew that to cut off the city, he had to control the Scheldt River. The reader should take note of this because not every general has been so smart in the same situation.

## Best Innovator of the Sixteenth Century:
### Maurice of Nassau, Prince of Orange, 1567–1625

Maurice came to the throne following the assassination of his father in 1584. The sixteenth century was the era of the mercenary; all armies employed them and, at some point, all army commanders regretted having done so. There are numerous examples of mercenary units leav-ing *en masse* when not paid, or threatening to leave—on the eve of a bat-tle is the best time—if not paid more. Just before the battle of Pavia in 1525, King Francis of France lost the services of his 2,000 Italian merce-naries when they left after their leader died of wounds. Two days later, 6,000 Swiss left after learning that their borders were under attack by a Milanese force. The reader will not be surprised then to learn that after losing 8,000 infantry in three days, things did not go well for Francis. He was captured in the subsequent battle; but let us return to our subject at hand.

Maurice, now commanding the rebellion of the Netherlands against the Habsburgs, had to do all he could to counter the superior forces and generalship of the Duke of Parma. Thus, Maurice had ample motive for change. Moreover, he and his cousin, William Louis, were devotees of ancient military systems, particularly that of the ancient Romans. As such, they believed that flexibility and smaller units that were rigorous-ly drilled were keys to military proficiency. With the power of their con-victions, the two men began experimenting. They were also fortunate to

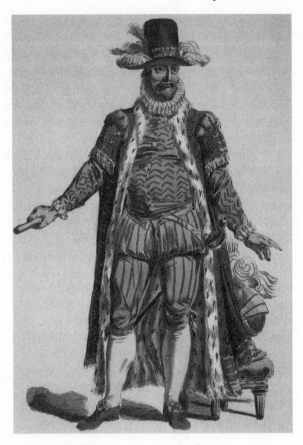

have some respite to do so. In 1587, the preparations for the Spanish Armada (1588) occupied the resources which could have been used for continued campaigning. In 1589, Parma was called away from the Netherlands by Philip II, who sent him to fight the forces of Henry IV of France. In August 1591, Parma was back in the Netherlands, but was called away again by Philip in September. Maurice made great use of Parma's absences and recovered lost territory. Parma was never to return; he died of wounds in December 1592.

The first feature of Maurice's reforms was discipline and drill. Maurice had foreign troops in his army, but he realized that the way to get the most out of them and his other troops was to impose discipline, pay them regularly, and sign them up for long terms of enlistment. This set the basis for professionalization. Constant drill created proficiency with arms, built morale, and led to troops who would fight hard under all conditions. The creation of a disciplined military force meant that

Maurice could get all his troops to do the other important thing for success in warfare in the Netherlands—dig. This war was, after all, mostly one of sieges, and when entrenchments were combined with the natural obstacles of waterways and permanent fortifications, the United Provinces was turned into one vast defensive sector.

Maurice's tactical reforms were bound up with the continuing improvement in gunpowder handguns and the proper role for them. Throughout the sixteenth century, the ratio of firearms to pikemen was increasing, and the challenge for any commander was how to resolve the desire of unit security with the desire for more firepower. One such improvement was the introduction of the musket. The musket had an effective range of 200 yards and was more powerful than the *arquebus*. It was also lighter and faster to operate than the *arquebus* and the shooter could discard the fork-shaped support required for the older system.

Maurice also steadily reduced the size of his companies from 250 men down to 115, and even to 80 by some reports. At the same time, Geoffrey Parker tells us, the number of officers increased in absolute terms from 11 to 12, and in relative terms this meant that the number of officers doubled, going from approximately 1 for every 23 men to 1 for every 10.

As the depth of the company was reduced, its width was increased. This was done to bring more guns to the front of the formation and thereby increase offensive power. If the reader is wondering, "was Maurice paying attention to Xenophon regarding the proper depth of a phalanx?," the reader may be right. Maurice grouped his companies into larger units—the equivalent of our battalion—made up of 250 pikes, 100 muskets, and 200 *arquebuses*. The formation now had pikemen in the middle and musketeers and *arquebusiers* on the wings. The pikemen now maintained three-foot intervals and the musketeers were ranged 10 deep. Why ten ranks? The handgunner would discharge his weapon and then move to the back—countermarch, it is called—to reload. It was determined that ten-ranks depth was the minimum necessary to give the gunner the time needed to move, reload, and then be back in position to fire. In this manner, a continuous or rolling fire could be maintained. Volley fire had arrived, and it was the brainchild of William Louis who, while reading Aelian on tactics, came up with the idea and explained it to Maurice in a letter written on 8 December 1594. The spreading out of the pike formation was a sure sign that dispersion on the battlefield was seen as one way to diminish the deleterious effects of concentrated gunfire. When troops are deployed in more open order, there is an increased need not only for more leaders, but for better-trained soldiers.

Maurice also instituted several changes to improve his army's effectiveness in the prosecution of siege warfare. He improved the quality of his artillery and standardized its calibers, which made logistical support easier. It was Maurice who first classified guns by the weight of their projectiles, and the reader should know that guns were still referred to by this metric (that is, "25-pounder") in British forces well into the 1960s. Maurice also provided training and education for his technical troops. He then moved to institutionalize his reforms.

All this was accomplished because Maurice could pay his men and it was the wealth based on seaborne trade which made it possible. Maurice died in the siege of Breda, which was under attack by Spinola, another Habsburg commander who, like Parma, seemed to get the best of Maurice in their encounters.

The great legacy of Maurice is not as a commander in the field but as the man who demonstrated how to make an army and its components better, how to make them more efficient, more controlled, and thus more professional. It was a Swede named Gustavus Adolphus who built on the work of Maurice and produced the next advance in the art of war.

## Best Commander of the Seventeenth Century:
### Gustavus Adolphus, 1594–1632

Gustavus became king at age 16 in 1611. His country was at war then and would remain at war for most of his life. He was to be the greatest military innovator of his time. By the time of his death—which, for the reader who does not know, came in battle—he had changed warfare. As the king of Sweden, Gustavus was involved in wars against the Danes and the Russians in the Baltic. He fought off a Danish invasion and warred with Russia until 1617. In the 1620s, he campaigned south of the Baltic, capturing Riga, in modern Latvia, in 1621. His wars with the Poles lasted from 1626–29, and ended in a truce which was brought about by Habsburg intervention against Sweden.

By the end of seventeenth century, only vestiges of medieval warfare remained. The pikeman, who was more or less on a par with the musketeer at the beginning of the century, was all but gone from the battlefield, his effectiveness long over. Those few who carried the halberd did so, in some cases, as an indicator of rank. Artillery was now integrated with the infantry and cavalry on the battlefield. Improvements in design to the guns, carriages, and harnesses made genuine field artillery a reality. Now the heavier firepower of guns could be maneuvered on the battlefield and brought to bear where the commander wanted it. Tactical formations changed as well; the columns of pike infantry

The Death of Gustavus Adolphus in the Battle of Lützen.
© Bettmann/CORBIS/MAGMA
Date Created: November 1632

became lines of musketeers. Cavalry had given up the lance and even relegated the pistol to a secondary role; swords were again in vogue as a primary weapon. This all came about because of the fertile mind and daring of Gustavus who built upon the reforms of Maurice of Nassau. This is getting ahead of things, however, as Gustavus actually had important work for his pikemen.

As the basic building block of any army is its manpower, let us begin there. Gustavus employed mercenaries to augment his army, but he designed a system of conscription and pay for the Swedes which was tied to the land. All Swedish males between 15 and 60 owed military service if they were without a settled dwelling. Gustavus recruited one tenth from the rest of the male population drawn by lots. Certain trades were exempt from military service. He preferred land owners, of course, but who did not? An officer served for 20 years or until he was 50, at which time he received a farm. A serving private received a wage, a cloth allowance, and one-eighth of the homestead where he lived. The farmer paid him his wage from money otherwise earmarked for taxes and the soldier helped work the farm. On campaign, the army was paid in cash, ideally. Gustavus, a deeply religious Lutheran like most of his countrymen, had prohibitions against inebriation, looting, cursing, and fornication. What? No camp followers? No, but the wives and children were permitted to follow the army and the children were educated in regimental schools. Well, travel does broaden the mind.

Montross tells us that on the march, the army was provisioned from magazines established on the route. These magazines received supplies from Sweden and forced contributions from the areas through which they moved. The army either bivouacked in fortified camps or was billetted with the population. In the latter case, the rules and regulations were that the soldier was entitled to salt, vinegar, and a bed. He also had the use of the cooking fire. Anything else was considered looting. In time, Gustavus established a system of payments from conquered areas and subsidies from allied governments. This income reduced the amount the army used from the annual revenue to one-sixth of the total.

The strength of his army was the character of the Swedes themselves, and they became famed for their tenacity in battle. The Swedish soldier was integrated with society in peacetime and served with his countrymen in war; this enhanced cohesion and morale. Although this system provided an annual national core of some 10,000 men for his army, Gustavus had to hire mercenaries to get the numbers up to the point where he could fight the big dogs. The Swedes did well for a while in the Thirty Years' War, but they simply did not possess the manpower and wealth to sustain their effort against the Holy Roman Empire of the German Nation. Once Gustavus was killed, there was no genius to replace him. In the end, Sweden did not have what was necessary to effectively oppose the far wealthier Habsburgs and their much more numerous minions.

Gustavus's contributions, to the art and science of war, however, are what make him noteworthy. Organizationally, he reduced the size of his companies from 250 to about 140. As his basic unit, he established squadrons (sometimes referred to as "half-regiments") of 408 men plus officers and extra musketeers. Of this 408, 216 of them were pikemen and 192 were musketeers. The pikemen formed the middle of the formation six ranks deep and the musketeers were on either side, also six ranks deep. Thus, the pikemen were 36 across and the musketeers 16. The musketeers could fire in a variety of modes. They could, after all men had loaded, reduce their formation to three ranks by filling in the intervals between men. Then the front rank would kneel, the second rank would slouch—stoop is probably a better word and less likely to draw criticism from one's mother—and then all three ranks would fire. Alternatively, the musketeers could fire by rank and then countermarch to the rear to reload. Or, the first two ranks could close up and fire as one and then countermarch, followed by rows three and four doing the same, and so on. The reason for the intervals between the ranks of musketeers existed because each man needed room to tend to the match on his musket. While the gunpowder boys were reloading, the pikemen provided protection. Gustavus's idea was for the continuous gunfire to create weak points in the enemy's line, and then to punch through with pikemen. In this, each squadron was aided by the integration of three light artillery pieces.

When three regiments were brigaded together, the formation of roughly 1,200 men was, at times, arranged in a modified "T." This formation had many advantages over the large *tercio* or Spanish square. It

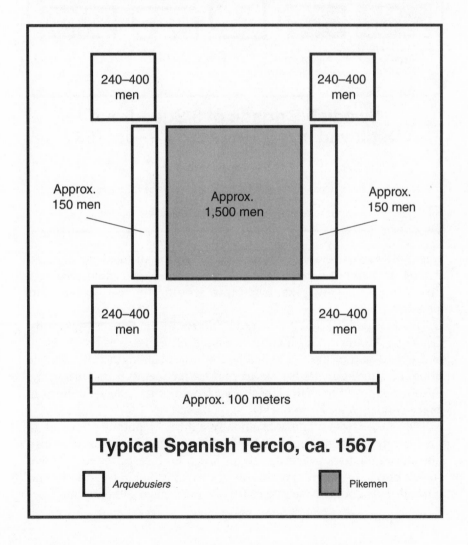

240–400 men

240–400 men

Approx. 150 men

Approx. 1,500 men

Approx. 150 men

240–400 men

240–400 men

Approx. 100 meters

**Typical Spanish Tercio, ca. 1567**

*Arquebusiers*   Pikemen

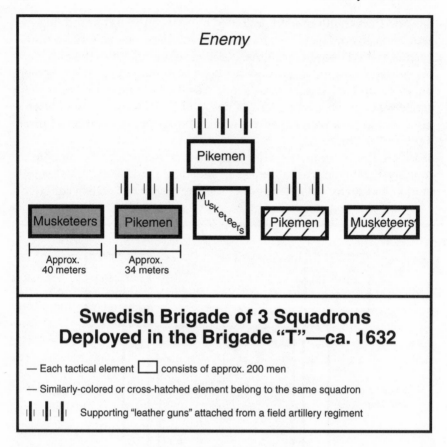

Enemy

Pikemen

Musketeers    Pikemen    Musketeers    Pikemen    Musketeers

Approx.
40 meters

Approx.
34 meters

## Swedish Brigade of 3 Squadrons
## Deployed in the Brigade "T"—ca. 1632

— Each tactical element ☐ consists of approx. 200 men

— Similarly-colored or cross-hatched element belong to the same squadron

Supporting "leather guns" attached from a field artillery regiment

was more maneuverable because each squadron of musketeers could deploy and fire and then retreat to reload, all the while receiving protection from the pikemen. How would the reader sally his squadrons?

This is as good a point as any to talk about the Swedes' weapons. Gustavus modified both infantry weapons. The pike was cut down to 11 feet and part of the shaft sheathed in iron to strengthen it. Like the pilum of old, the metal served to prevent an enemy from cutting the business end off the shaft. The shorter length of the pike—down from 16 feet—made it easier to wield.

The musket was made substantially lighter, 11 pounds. Even at 11 pounds, the musket would need the fork for support. Gustavus also introduced the paper cartridge to his army. Each cartridge had a measure of powder—the right measure of powder, it should be added—and the ball. This doubled the rate of fire, Dupuy tells us, to one round per minute. One historian says that this cartridge is a myth—should we believe him?

Cavalry was armed with the pistol and sword, but Gustavus preferred that they charge with their swords (called the *arme blanche*) rather than perform the caracole. The reader will recall that the caracole saw horsemen ride up close to a formation, discharge their pistols, and then ride back to reload. He, Gustavus that is, placed musketeers with the cavalry to provide a more effective missile capability and cover their retiring. Gustavus also insisted—and being the king he got his way—that only the first rank of the cavalry fire their pistols and only one shot per man, then all draw sabers and charge. The other ranks of the cavalry would use their pistols only if necessary. The resort to the charge was the result of Gustavus's campaigning against the Poles in the 1620s. The Poles had charged his formations with the lance to good results and Gustavus recognized a good thing when he saw it, especially if it was coming right at him.

It was Gustavus's artillery which really set him apart. His assistant, that is, artillery chief, was the 27-year-old Lennart Torstensson. The artillery was organized into regiments of six companies each. Within each regiment were four companies of gunners; one of sappers—which is to say, the combat engineers of the day; and one of explosives experts dealing with grenades and such. The fact that Gustavus made these permanent establishments meant that excellence was institutionalized.

Much experimentation was done with the guns and the results were stunning. Gustavus wanted to introduce more firepower to the battlefield, and to that end, he created field artillery in a usable and deadly form. The key, of course, was mobility and for guns to be mobile, they had to be light. He began experimenting.

First up was the so-called "leather gun." It was made from copper and the brass breach was bound with iron hoops. The copper tube was then covered with goop—experts would say mastic—wrapped in cords, covered in plaster, then covered with leather. Who thought this up? This piece was so light that it could be man-handled by two men, but it took only a small charge. This gun was replaced with two more successful pieces: a 4-pounder and a 9-pounder (some historians say 12-pounder). The 4-pounder (the term describes the weight of shot), weighed in at about 500 pounds, which meant that two horses could pull it. Each regiment received two 4-pounders to add firepower. Manned by crews of three, these guns were loaded with pre-packaged cartridges which combined the powder and shot. This sped up the rate of fire considerably as it reduced the number of steps involved in loading. Gustavus also increased the number of guns in his army. The previous average had been one gun per thousand men; under Gustavus, it reached just over 9 per thousand. He massed his guns on the battlefield to concentrate his fire.

After campaigning in eastern Europe and the Baltic, Gustavus decided to join the Thirty Years' War, and unlike those other numbered wars of previous centuries, this one really did last 30 years, although the warfare was not continuous during the entire period. His system is best revealed at the battle of Breitenfeld in 1631 for which there is another entry on page 212. In this and a subsequent battle (Lech River) against Tilly, Gustavus's army displayed displayed the highest levels of steadiness in the ranks and flexibility in maneuver. Gustavus was killed at the battle of Lützen, 16 November 1632, at the point of victory.

The legacy of this great innovator lasted far beyond him. He was, of course, not the sole innovator of the seventeenth century, but he was the best. Among all the others, he was able to translate best his theories into practice and it helped that he had good theories. After his death, other armies tried to emulate his system. He brought cavalry shock action back to the battlefield, although it was best against other cavalry. He added to, or boosted yet further, the ascendency of infantry on the battlefield and here we speak of handgunners or light infantry. The *arquebus* and musket gave the light infantryman a larger role on the battlefield. Their shot was needed to repel cavalry and to help protect the heavy infantry pikemen. So effective had their shot become that the medieval armored knight was long gone. Thus with no heavy cavalry to confront, the pike formations did not need to be as large and as deep. This, in turn, meant that more infantrymen equipped with firearms could be used. Gustavus's infantry deployed in two lines, which gave him a reserve, and armies which can use reserves are decidedly advanced tactically speaking. They have, if they are as well-drilled as Gustavus's men, more articulation or flexibility on the battlefield and the ability to adjust to the unexpected, either on the battlefield or the gridiron, is often the key to victory.

## Best Artillerist of the Sixteenth Century:
### Lennart Torstensson, 1603–1651

Torstensson is considered by many military historians as the father of modern field artillery. Along with his King, Gustavus, Torstensson made the Swedes the leading innovators, for a time, in artillery design and tactics.

At 15, Torstensson became a page to Gustavus and as such, he participated in the campaign of 1621–23 in Livonia (modern Estonia and Latvia). In 1624, he was sent to study for two years with Maurice of Nassau and he must have learned much from the great Dutchman's military mind. Upon his return to Sweden, he served in the Prussian campaigns against Poland (1626–1629). One could not have been better placed to participate in the artillery reforms which Gustavus instituted. Significantly, Gustavus created a permanent artillery regiment and made Torstensson its first commander. This unit was formed from the six existing companies of artillery in the army and was the first artillery regiment in Europe. Constituting artillery as a permanent force meant that its excellence was institutionalized. Thus, Swedish artillerymen would have an expertise available to them which exceeded the memory and experience of any one man.

The Swedish army previously had 16 types of cannon in its inventory. Gustavus cut that down to three types: siege, field, and regimental. Regimental guns were the 4-pounders. Siege and field guns came in three calibers: 24-pounder, 12-pounder, and—here is where the trouble starts—some authorities say the third size was a 9-pounder, others a 6-pounder, or a 3-pounder. The reader can make up his own mind. The goal, regardless of type, was to make the guns lighter and thus easier to move and thus reduce significantly the problems of transport and supply. As to the caliber of these weapons, the reader should imagine the 24-pounder at about 5.8 inches, the 12-pounder at about 4.6 inches, and the 6-pounder at 3.7 inches, the 4-pounder at about 3 inches, and the 3-pounder at roughly 2.9 inches.

The field guns probably had shorter barrels than the siege guns because they did not need the range or power corollary to higher velocity. Obviously, a lighter gun is an easier gun to move, and if one's guns only take three sizes of ammunition, then more of what you need for each type of gun can be brought along. Mobility was enhanced also by improvements in gunpowder. Technical advancements in powder meant that less of it had to be carried to achieve the same results in terms of range and velocity. This made for lighter wagon loads and happier horses.

Mobility on the field was matched by rapidity in loading. The new regimental guns—we will continue to call them 4-pounders—were loaded with a revolutionary new item—the cartridge. The powder was measured and placed in a bag, possibly flannel, and wired to the shot. It was carried in wooden ammunition cases, which was another first. This improved the reported rate of fire of these guns to eight rounds for every six from a musketeer; in other words, the artillery could fire more quickly than the opposing infantry. At Breitenfeld, the Torstensson's gunners outshot the Habsburg's three to one and moved up to support the infantry late in the battle.

At the battle of the Lech River (April 1632), Torstensson's guns provided sufficient fire support to deceive the Imperial Habsburg forces regarding the direction of the attack. Here, Torstensson gathered 72 guns and unleashed such a bombardment that the enemy took cover and could not observe therefore the Swedish army crossing the river. The river crossing was further obscured by creating a smoke screen by burning damp straw. Torstensson also covered the crossing with 18 guns. He was captured at the battle of Alte Veste in 1632 and spent a year as a prisoner until coming home in a prisoner exchange.

Torstensson returned to campaigning in 1635 as chief-of-staff to Johan Baner, a career soldier and the army commander (probably no relation to John Banner, who played the role of "Sergeant Schultz" on *Hogan's Heroes*). He reluctantly became commander of the army in 1641 when Baner died. The army had developed discipline problems by this time because of the high numbers of mercenaries it included. Torstensson restored proper order. He won the battle of Leipzig (1642) in ruthless campaigning there, as well as in Bohemia (1644) and also a notable victory at Jankow (Jankau) (1645). His artillery moved about the field during the battle and poured fire at various targets and helped win the day.

Torstensson, who had been made a field marshal in 1641, retired in 1646, with his health broken, it is said, from many hard years of campaigning. Given the prevalence of disease across war-torn Europe, as well as the dangers inherent to exposure to the elements and life in the field under primitive circumstances, that is not surprising.

## Most Famous Military Engineer of the Early Modern Period: Sebastien le Prestre de Vauban, 1633–1707

The best-known engineer of the early modern period was Sebastien le Prestre de Vauban (1633–1707). Ask anyone to name a military engineer and if they can name one, it will probably be Vauban. Vauban was the engineer who most successfully incorporated the prevailing ideas and features of fortifications and siegecraft into a system. So often we see in life that it is the innovator who, by combining existing methods in a unique way, re-orders the manner in which things are done. This usually leads to success in any endeavor, and it certainly did for Vauban. He

built 33 new fortresses in his career and at least five naval bases. He also remodeled hundreds more. He was apparently rarely home in his long working life.

Equally notable, however, is Vauban's expertise in siege warfare. He worked both sides of the street and did so from the beginning of his career. Hogg tells us that in 1652 Vauban was assisting in the construction of the fortifications at Clermont-en-Argonne and then participated in the siege of St. Menehoud. In 1653, he was responsible for repairing the works at St. Menehoud, after which he took charge of the siege of Clermont-en-Argonne. Any veteran can understand how that happens; in Vauban's case it may have had something to do with the fact that he started out on the side of the Fronde in 1651 fighting against the king' s forces. In 1653, he was captured and prevailed upon by Marshal Ferte-Senneterre to change sides. This demonstrates, in part, the regard with which his talents were held even early in his career. This led to other commands and in 1655, he was appointed as the "King's ordinary engineer." If you are a guy who wants to build your own fortresses and capture others', this is the job to have.

Vauban introduced what soon became the standard method of siege warfare: the construction of parallels and pushing the lines forward by approach trenches, or saps. This system made its debut in 1673 at the siege of Maastricht. John Lynn, in *The Wars of Louis XIV*, describes it well. Step one was to dig the first trench parallel to the fortress's wall at a distance of about 600 yards, depending on the circumstances. Here the first siege batteries were also set and began to batter the walls. The first trench was widened and even covered to offer improved protection to the attackers. From here, the trenches were dug to the second parallel. These zig-zagged forward so that a single cannon ball from the fort could not take out an entire column of men moving up a trench. Once the saps reached about 250 yards, a second parallel was dug and new batteries erected. From here, the saps were pushed forward again to the third parallel where the breaching batteries were erected at a distance of 30 to 60 yards. These trenches zig-zagged more acutely to further mitigate the possibility of cannonade. To lessen the effects of gunfire, the trenches were dug at night. Further protection was provided by filling large baskets (called gabions) with earth and positioning them where needed. There could, of course, be more than three parallels dug in a siege depending on conditions. The last parallel was dug into the glacis and stopped at the last ditch. At this point, there were a couple of options. The troops could fill the ditch with material or use ladders to then climb the walls, a maneuver called an escalade. The other way was to batter the walls at some point and have the infantry storm the breach. The hard work of digging the approach saved lives and so was well worth the effort. Vauban believed strongly in this.

Another innovation of Vauban's was ricochet fire. The idea was that even with its energy dissipated by deflections, a solid iron ball could still do a lot of damage and reach a lot more targets by bouncing. For example, a cannon ball could be skipped over various outworks and still have enough force to damage whatever it hit. Ricochets were particularly effective when they could strike closely packed targets from the side, such as a column of infantry in a trench or guns on a rampart. The dates and locations of the first use of purposeful (as opposed to accidental) ricochet vary from historian to historian. The earliest places it at 1688; the latest at 1696.

Vauban also developed the socket bayonet which fitted over the end of the barrel and still allowed the musket to fire. This quickly superseded the plug bayonet and turned every infantryman into a pikeman and handgunner simultaneously. The plug bayonet was a sword with a plug on the end which fit into the muzzle of the musket thereby turning the gun into a pike and the gunner into a pikeman.

Vauban used three systems of fortification in his career. The first was essentially that developed by Blaise François, Comte de Pagan (1604–1648). Pagan's approach to fortification construction was: first, look at the terrain, then figure out where the bastions have to go, and then work outwards. Vauban is most renowned and, apparently, misunderstood, for his second system. Hogg tells us that it was developed to improve existing fortifications. It is uniquely characterized by the two-tiered bastion. The lower level is casemated so that guns can cover the ditches to the flanks and the upper tier had embrasures cut into the parapet for guns. The third system added more to the second in terms of defensive strength and included more internal elements to impede the besiegers once they were in amongst the defenses.

## Greatest Commander of the Enlightenment:
King Frederick II of Prussia (1712–1786)—the Vince Lombardi of the Eighteenth Century

Frederick was born 24 January 1712 to Frederick William I of Prussia and Sophia Dorothea of Hanover, she being the sister of the British king, George II. Frederick's youth was unhappy. He had to cope with an overbearing father who did not, and apparently could not, understand him. His father was a typical bully who happened to a have good army and a bad temper. Frederick William preferred the company of men, and hunting, drinking, and soldiering. He was brutal to those whom he felt deserved it. Two examples: Frederick sent some small presents to the 16-year-old daughter of a school principal. Frederick, you see, very much enjoyed her singing. Even though there was nothing more to it and the girl was innocent, Frederick William had her publicly whipped and sent to a workhouse.

The most notorious example came when Frederick, 18, tried to flee Prussia with the help of his best friend, Katte. They were caught and Frederick was put on trial for desertion by his father. His father threatened to have him executed in the hope that Frederick would renounce the throne in favor of a brother. He did not, probably sensing that his father would not go through with it, but more real was the threat of imprisonment for life. Even this, however, he came to dismiss as infeasible for the long-term. What he could not dismiss was the king ordering the execution of Katte and seeing it carried out. After this, Frederick

suffered a profound psychological crisis and eventually decided to accept his father's will, at least outwardly.

He received instruction in his father's brand of Protestantism, but did so for the practical purpose of improving his situation, not because he sought a religious conversion. In a testament to his resilience but perhaps also indicative of his detachment from all others, he was said to have recovered in a few weeks. He was then sent to Küstrin to learn the minutiae of administration. He mastered it quickly, given his lively and intelligent mind and his highly energetic nature.

At 19, he was forced into a dynastic marriage with the minor House of Brunswick; no Habsburg princess for him! He went along with it because it was the best way to his goal of gaining his father's trust and the throne. He did not care for his wife and this seems to be a theme in the lives of many great commanders. Invade Silesia? Sure, anything to get out of the house.

One thing Frederick did take to was his military education. In 1734, he had the opportunity to be tutored by one of the best. In that year, he accompanied Eugene of Savoy on his Rhine campaign. Frederick later wrote that Eugene was the greatest warrior of the century. In 1735 came his real opportunity for education. He was allowed to establish his own court at Rheinsberg. Frederick surrounded himself with culture, learned men, and books on all subjects. He corresponded with the best minds available, including Voltaire. He had four years of this and like a truly educated man, he maintained his quest for knowledge throughout his life. This is, of course, what people who have never been to university think it is like.

When he ascended the throne in 1740, his father finally succumbing to dropsy, he had an army of 80,000 men and an adequate treasury, reportedly eight million thalers. His father had doubled the size of the army, and improved its organization and equipment. He set out to use both. His army was noted for the iron discipline imposed on it and as a result of this, its speed of movement. Frederick believed that his soldiers had to fear their officers more than they feared the enemy if he was going to get the best out of them. He favored the offensive and sought as early decisions on the battlefield. Battles, not sieges, were what he pursued. He did so because he had faith in the abilities of his army, and because his own personality quickly shook off setbacks. Frederick also had certain advantages in deciding what to do; as the king he could do pretty much anything he wanted.

Frederick's original contribution to warfare was the enhancement of horse artillery. The requisite components are: light-weight guns; horses; and the carriages and limbers necessary to move all the accoutrement. Frederick organized his first batteries of horse artillery in May 1759 at Landeshut. The artillerymen wore blue coats, which were lined with red. Straw-colored waistcoats and breeches completed the ensemble. The horse artillerymen were differentiated by their white plumes and riding boots, as Frederick had the bright idea of mounting the gunners on horses as well; Polish horses were preferred because of their strength. The point should also be made that these horses were the horses of the unit and the guns were the guns of the unit. Thus they had organic equipment and transport and that made them self-contained. The mounted gunners acted as a mobile reserve for Frederick's army. The guns could thus move during the battle and closely support the advance. The rapid movement of artillery about the battlefield facilitated the exploitation of enemy weaknesses. Frederick treated his horse artillery as a secret weapon, however. In one of his treatises, he wrote that the horse artillery should only be used occasionally and at the most important moments—if used more often, then the enemy would be able to copy it. One such moment, he tells us, was at Reichenbach, 16 August 1762. The piece of choice was the six-pounder and it was accompanied by seven artillerists, each on his own horse. Generally, Frederick used his artillery to bombard the key point he wanted to attack. He concentrated his fire against the infantry because he thought that led to the best results.

Christopher Duffy tells us that the first brigade of horse artillery—or light artillery as Frederick referred to it—was lost at Kunersdorf on 12 August 1759. Of course, what wasn't lost? This was his greatest defeat. Briefly, in this battle, Frederick came up against the Russians and Austrians who had managed, contrary to his efforts, to unite against him. Frederick had about 53,000 troops and the Austro-Russians about 90,000. The combined army had entrenched on the sand hills at Kunersdorf, four miles east of Frankfurt an der Oder. The Russian commander, Field Marshal Saltykov, in the hope of countering the Prussian oblique approach, had concentrated much of his force in the middle of his formation so that he could reinforce either wing. Frederick planned on a double envelopment of his enemy's wings, but things did not go his way. His columns had to march through woods on their approach and some of them got lost. As a consequence, Frederick's attacks did not go ahead at their full strength or fully coordinated. The first attack failed, but Frederick did not attain his position or reputation by by lacking determination. More attacks went in and they too were repulsed, and each repulse created more casualties, and each casualty created more disconcertion. Frederick's master of cavalry, Friedrich Wilhelm von Seydlitz, tried to reverse the trend of the battle, but the enemy infantry was far from being disconcerted. Seydlitz's attack failed as well and when he was wounded, the Prussians were out of cards to play. Soon there after, the Austrian cavalry charged and the Prussians fled. Frederick could not stop his troops as they headed west for the Oder River. Eventually, he did gain control of his army and he was fortunate that the Austrians and Russians did not pursue. In six hours of battle, the Prussians lost over 20,000 men, 178 guns, 28 colors, and their horse artillery. The victors lost 15,700 men.

Frederick reconstituted his horse artillery in August after the battle of Kunersdorf and continued with his experiment. Regrettably for him, the replacement unit of ten pieces was captured at the battle of Maxen, 21 November 1759. On this occasion, Frederick had sent General Friedrich von Finck with 12,000 men to envelop the Austrian force of Field Marshal Count Leopold von Daun which was in Dresden. The count was a very able commander, however, and this was unfortunate for the Prussians. Von Daun withdrew his army south to Maxen where he managed to assemble some 42,000 men. He surrounded von Finck's army and after two days of fighting, the Prussians, including the horse artillery surrendered. The saying, "the third time's the charm" certainly applied here; in 1760 Frederick again established a battery of horse artillery and it made it to the end of the war in 1763 when Frederick disbanded it, probably so no one else could capture it. This was not the end of the experiment, however. Duffy tells us that Frederick built up the horse artillery again. By 1768, it consisted of 20 guns and 4 howitzers. In March 1773, a training battery was established in Potsdam through which Frederick ran his regular artillerists. By the time of the War of the Bavarian Succession (1778–79), he had six brigades of nine guns each.

Frederick is most renowned for his oblique order of battle. It should be pointed out here that Frederick is not regarded highly in the realm of strategy by some historians; rather, it is the tactical brilliance of the Prussians and the implacable determination of Frederick to keep attacking that they say carried them to victory. The Prussians drilled more than other armies; their soldiers were disciplined than those of other armies; thus, they fought harder than other armies. They could carry out rapidly the maneuvers on the battlefield that other armies could not match. As a result of their training, the Prussians did not suffer the degradation of performance under fire to the same extent that other armies did. And fire it was, for in the eighteenth century, the European infantryman was musketeer and pikeman, all in one thanks to the socket bayonet.

Frederick's emphasis on drill and some improvements to the equipment combined to increase the rate of fire of his infantry. Heretofore, the depth of musket infantry formations was dependent upon the length of time it took to load the weapon. Commanders wanted to maintain a constant fire. Hence, the longer the time to reload, the deeper the formation. Frederick's men, it is reported, could fire five or six rounds a minute at their best. In combat, this rate of fire would certainly decline, but it would still be faster than that of their enemy. As Frederick's men could fire almost twice as fast as their opponents, however, Frederick could halve the depth of his line to three ranks and still deliver the same weight of metal.

By thinning his ranks, Frederick could extend his line and this gave him more tactical possibilities to exploit and it also made it more difficult for his flank to be turned. Frederick, in turn, wanted to turn his enemy's flank and this is how he went about it. The key was, as always, to move faster than one's opponent to diminish the time he had to react.

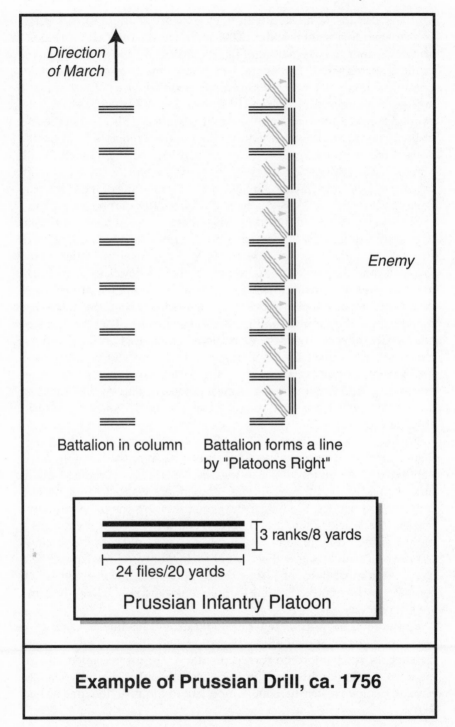

Direction
of March

Enemy

Battalion in column

Battalion forms a line
by "Platoons Right"

3 ranks/8 yards

24 files/20 yards

Prussian Infantry Platoon

**Example of Prussian Drill, ca. 1756**

The Prussians would march onto the battlefield in columns, which is the fastest way to move, and the easiest to control, and deploy into line across from the enemy, to allow maximum firepower to be brought to bear. The simplest way to do this would be to march onto the battlefield in a column of three firing files and execute a "column left" or "column right," but this takes a long time to bring all guns to bear, and also exposes one's men to the enemy's fire throughout the process. It is also difficult to control three enormous, continuous firing lines. The Prussians' solution sounds simple, but was very difficult to execute on the battlefield, and thus required iron discipline borne of endless practice. They organized their march columns by platoons into battalions. Each platoon of 72 men was ordered in three ranks and there were eight platoons in each battalion. The interval between each platoon was equal to the width of the platoon. When the battalion halted and its commander wished to deploy from column to line, each platoon would execute its own right or left 90 degree turn and be in a line. Thus the Prussians could march across the enemy's front, deploy beyond their flank, and attack before the enemy could reorder or extend his line. To develop these capabilities was the purpose of Prussian drill.

Frederick realized that when he faced armies of equal size or larger, he had to do something to prevent his off-flank being overwhelmed. His answer was the same as Epaminondas's: an echeloned or oblique formation. By refusing one wing and reinforcing the other, Frederick intended to defeat the enemy at one point of the line while protecting his own weaker wing. This approach works best when the enemy is uncertain about where the attack will fall. Thus Frederick had to fake out his enemy or surprise him. Which ploy he employed in deploying his forces depended on the specific circumstances of each battle and the terrain. At Leuthen and Rossbach, his approach was masked by hills and this resulted in two great victories. In situations where the enemy could see the Prussians coming and were prepared, things did not go Frederick's way. Gerhard Ritter, in his biography of Frederick, points out rightly that the generals commanding the refused wing of the army must not get too involved in the attack or they would turn the oblique attack into an uneven parallel battle, and that created other problems.

Frederick realized that it was imperative to keep things simple or make them simple. Complicated maneuvers in the face of the enemy invariably led to trouble. Success in any physical endeavor starts with doing the basic things better than the other guy. Even if he knows what is coming, he may not be able to stop it. The Lombardi sweep of the Green Bay Packers came as no secret to defenses, but they could not stop it because of the Green Bay players' perfect execution . . . which was possible because Vince drilled the players until they could perform their respective duties in their sleep. Frederick proved himself highly adept at translating his theories of war into practice. By drilling and drilling his troops so that they could accomplish the basic things in dangerous and confusing circumstances, and by imposing severe discipline on them so that they were more afraid of their officers than the enemy, Frederick knew that he could get more out of his men than any other commander. He also knew that men were the most important commodity in war.

## Best of the Nineteenth Century (and Maybe the Only One to Rival Alexander the Great): Napoleon, 1769–1821

Well, who else can one consider? There are some able candidates, of course, but no one really comes close. Sherlock Holmes described Moriarty as "the Napoleon of crime," not the Robert E. Lee or Helmuth von Moltke. Anecdotal perhaps, but apt, as Napoleon was described during his life as a monster and as a criminal. To be compared to Napoleon is to be accounted exceptional, but also to be considered ruthless. Some may think that the misery alone occasioned by his drive for conquests qualifies him as a criminal. Here is what our statistically-driven friend, Gaston Bodart, said of Napoleon, "No other man has sacrificed so many human victims to the god of war as did Napoleon I; no other man has sowed death broadcast on such a scale; no commander ever cared less for the lives of his soldiers than he." Bodart's study was prepared in 1913, he hadn't seen anything yet. Irony aside, let us make some use of Bodart's scholarship and see why he came to his conclusions.

The Napoleonic Wars, properly considered, were fought between 1805 and 1815. In those ten years, the French fought 221 land battles in which the losses for both sides exceeded 2,000 men, and they waged 91 sieges. The French and their allies lost 12,343 officers killed and 39,879 wounded in this time period for a total of 52,222. This list is incomplete, however, so the total could be 60,000. As one would expect, the greatest losses came in the infantry which suffered 34,622 officer casualties. The safest spot to have was in the supply train (262 casualties) although the ratio of killed to wounded was 1 to 2.7, which was not much better than the infantry's 1 to 2.9. The *total* number of soldiers killed and wounded for the French and their allies in these ten years was 1,334,750. The breakdown for the French alone was 306,000 killed and 764,000 wounded. These figures include naval losses and encompass only battle casualties. Clearly, the total losses of European manhood were much, much higher. Bodart estimates that 15 to 20 percent of the wounded may have been permanently disabled. These are some of the simple statistics, let us now examine Bodart's chief perpetrator of misery.

When one reads of Napoleon, three words keep occurring; genius, energy, and determination. These qualities allowed him to make war as no one else had before. He did not invent new means of making war, he did not invent any new weapons; rather, he took what was available, organized it in a certain manner, and transformed Europe. At the zenith, he controlled more of Europe than any man since the Roman emperors. Foremost of Napoleon's traits was personal magnetism. He made an impact on all who met him. He knew its affect on people and used it to secure what he wanted. It drew people to him, which is why they call it *magnetism*. We have all met people like this, but Napoleon had a much bigger dose of it than most; it is always remarked upon by those who met him. It conveyed his confidence, his intellectual power, and it did so authoritatively and forcefully. It made him charming; it made him captivating; it made one want to *follow* him. An aspiring leader who starts out with these advantages will have little trouble inspiring men to do his bidding or to follow his orders, even unto death.

Tied to this was his intellect, described as wide-ranging and powerful, which operated at high speed and could find the core of any issue. Thus he was unlikely to sidetrack himself with extraneous musings. His powers of concentration meant that he could jump from one topic to another and be wholly absorbed in it until it was resolved in turn or he had to turn to something else. He could then come back to an earlier matter and pick up where he had left off.

Napoleon's tremendous memory meant that few details would escape him. He seemingly could recall details, facts, and figures from years before. One story told of him is from 1805 when he came across a commander whose unit had become separated from its division. The officer had lost his orders and did not know where his parent unit was. Napoleon came upon the scene and while the staffs pored over all available papers in an attempt to sort things out, the emperor proceeded to rattle off the location of the division, its location for the next three nights and then threw in a thumbnail portrait of the divisional commander for good measure. This remarkable ability also extended to faces and the ability to recognize individual soldiers and recall a couple of details about their past. This is a marvelous tool for recognizing talent and for promoting morale, and it never deserted Napoleon, no matter how many battles he fought or how difficult his situations later became.

In his study of the Leipzig campaign, Anthony Brett-Jame provides this example. On 12 October 1813, General Sebastiani of the cavalry

corps sent Second Lieutenant Calosso of the 24th Chasseurs to carry an
urgent dispatch from Torgau to Napoleon at Düben. Calosso and a Polish lancer covered 20 miles during the night, evading the Cossacks in
the forests, and arrived at Napoleon's headquarters in the morning.
Calosso was brought into the study of the house. There he found the
emperor kneeling on the floor pushing wax-headed pins of two colors
into the campaign map. Napoleon told Berthier to take the dispatch and
then asked Calosso from where he had come, by what route, and how
he had avoided the Cossacks. Calosso provided short answers. At this
point, Berthier asked Calosso a question and as he turned to answer
him, Napoleon saw the regimental number on the hunting horn of the
Lieutenant's cartridge pouch.

"You from the 24th Chasseurs?"

"Yes, Sire."

"That's it, I've seen you before. You were senior sergeant of the elite
company at my review in Gorkum."

"Yes, sire."

"Were you in the Russian campaign?"

"Yes, sire, with the 2d Corps."

"Good."

Napoleon then turned to his chief-of-staff and said, "This officer must be tired. He will rest here for two days, and will then rejoin Sebastiani, who by that time will be in Leipzig."

Then Calosso was given a room in the house and he noted for posterity that he was "overcome with admiration for the prodigious memory which enabled Napoleon to recognize so insignificant a person as myself amid so many happenings and all his day-to-day preoccupations."

How good was he? Napoleon was the kind of commander who could take his'n and beat your'n, and then take your'n and beat his'n. And he could do it on consecutive days. No one has matched him since and he is the only one with a chance to equal Alexander.

Napoleon, as all of you know, was born in Ajaccio, Corsica, on 15 August in 1769. He was the fourth of thirteen children and the second son born to Carlo and Letizia Buonaparte. At the age of nine years and four months, he was sent to France to learn French first and then to train at military school. He would not return home until he was 16. The term "military school" undoubtedly conveys a meaning to the reader which did not exist at the time. Brienne, where Napoleon went, was run by priests along monastic lines. Mass every day, French, Latin but no Greek, German, English, music, dancing, fencing, history, geography, writing, and mathematics. Napoleon excelled at mathematics and geography and found great interest in history and biography, particularly Plutarch.

Napoleon was a proud Corsican although six of his eight great grandparents were Ligurian. His French, in those days, was elementary, and he had little money. These factors isolated him from the French boys at school. Forced into himself he developed self-reliance and developed an independent way. He sought escape in study and defended Corsica's honor against all comers. He greatly resented that France ruled over Corsica, but it was this same fact which secured for his father the status of minor nobility and tuition paid for by the King.

Not only did Napoleon want to study, he *had* to study because he was slated for a career in one of the technical branches of the armed forces: the navy, artillery, or engineers. Students destined for the infantry, cavalry, or non-military careers had a much easier time of it. All students had to stay in school for six years and were not allowed to leave. Napoleon's first visit from his parents came when he was 12, in June 1782. He would see his father once more, in 1784. Carlo died of stomach cancer in February 1785. Napoleon did not secure admission to the navy or engineers, so it was the artillery branch in which he would find his destiny. In the fall of 1784, he and four others were sent to the Military College in Paris for a year of training.

Now this was a college! It aimed at turning out gentlemen officers of judgment rare. The faculty, Norwood Young tells us, consisted of 24 professors plus riding and fencing masters plus dance instructors. The subjects taught were mathematics, history, geography, French, German, English, fortification, drawing, and writing. Food was plentiful and of high quality. The surroundings were luxurious with a large support staff of cooks, porters, grooms, dormitory custodians, managers, accountants, hall-keepers, secretaries, and more, totalling 111. Napoleon passed the examinations at Metz, site of the chief artillery school, in September 1785 and was commissioned a second lieutenant in the bombardier company of the La Fère Regiment of artillery. He had been the first Corsican to attend a French military school.

It was the perfect time for a man of limitless ambition. Great change was afoot and that meant opportunities abounded. Revolution, and the armies of revolution, would destroy what was, and whoever led the armies would create what would be. Napoleon seized the opportunity. It was said of him that he could pour everything he had into what he was doing and that gave him an advantage over others. Therein lies one of the reasons for his success. He also required little sleep, and held a great capacity for work. Marshal Marmont tells us that Napoleon went to bed at six or seven in the evening and arose around midnight. He then read reports as they came in and sent out orders so that they reached the units at reveille. Napoleon maintained himself with cat-naps. This is not to give the impression that he was super-human in matters of his health. He suffered his share of ailments, but he could push himself and his staff unceasingly for days before he had to make up the deficit.

Like Alexander, Napoleon had a grand vision for his part of the world and as his notion of a Continental empire ran counter to England's interests, it was inevitable that there would be war—years and years of war. This was fine for Napoleon as he had the most talented chief of staff and operations officer in history—himself. The armies he led were animated by a romantic sense of glory, and universal conscription made the armies bigger than ever. Napoleon was prepared to have them live off the land and this made them more mobile. Mobility, in turn, made victory more likely. In his book, *Napoleon's War Maxims*, Lucien Henry provides this insight from the emperor, "The strength of an army, like the quantity of motion in mechanics, is estimated by the mass multiplied by the velocity.* A swift march enhances the *morale* of the army and increases its power for victory."

---

*In modern physics, as in modern sports or war, this is known as *momentum*.

Napoleon was brave and unafraid to lead from the front. He admired Frederick the Great's audacity and, like him, he preferred to attack rather than defend. A disadvantageous disparity, even a large one, in force sizes would not dissuade him from attacking an enemy. He saw all he could for himself by day and worked on orders at night. Strategically, he was unsurpassed and it all came down to timing, which is why he insisted all his generals have carriage clocks. He knew that time lost could not be recovered.

How was it that Napoleon was so good at strategy? He thought things through as far in advance as he needed and he did it better than anyone else because he knew his business in every respect. By immersing himself in the minutiae of his profession, he came to understand the whole in a profound way.

Napoleon's memory gave him remarkable recall of terrain and an eye for the ground is necessary for success in the war business. Napoleon was always thinking ahead as well. Chandler tells us that, to mislead the enemy about his intentions and strength, Napoleon employed widespread deception operations integral to his tactical maneuvers. Information in the press was suppressed, the borders were closed, surveillance was stepped up by the secret police, and secondary operations such as feints and demonstrations were mounted to mislead the enemy. Once on the march, Napoleon used his cavalry as a counter-reconnaissance screen and juggled his order of battle. He would move divisions from one corps to another, and draw a few divisions together to form a provisional corps for some purpose and then disband it. In this way, he made it difficult for the enemy to construct an accurate picture of his army and even when they did, the picture soon changed.

Even as he was confusing the enemy, Napoleon was also gathering intelligence on him by every means possible. Once contact was imminent, Napoleon gained further advantage over the enemy by virtue of the faster speed at which his army moved, and when they had to, they could move very fast. There are many examples from which to choose: take Davout's corps before Austerlitz. One division covered 95 miles in 48 hours, and only 24 miles of that was traveled on roads. Normally the army covered 10 to 12 miles per day but when he needed speed, inspired by his personal charisma, Napoleon's soldiers gave it to him as no other soldiers of any other army could or did.

Napoleon's style was also especially flexible. He fully recognized that the plan was a guide and not a rigid set of instructions. In essence, Napoleon prepared himself to expect the unexpected. He constantly wargamed situations with himself. "What would I do," he often asked, "if the enemy appeared now on my flank or at my rear?" More than one commentator has mentioned that when they brought him news of a reversal, he would take in the information and then issue orders accordingly, almost as if he had expected it.

The one area in which he has been criticized is in failing to develop a staff system. It did not matter so much when the armies were relatively small and he could see all and do all himself, but even all his genius and hard work could not impose his will on huge armies and expansive battlefields. When he could not do it all, he had to rely on the officers available. Here a developed, institutionalized staff system would have helped immensely. This is not to say that he did not have talented officers, but no one could come close to equaling his personal brilliance.

The other area of criticism is that Napoleon never had an effective logistics system. His men did not live off the land completely, but the supply columns of the day could not keep up with the speed of movement of Napoleon's troops. The *Grande Armée* moved fast, and won decisive victories because it moved fast. It also had to move fast to avoid starvation. When the army had to resort to foraging, however, the breakdown in discipline was inevitable. This made for trouble with the indigenous population and could lead to large-scale desertions, both of which affected combat power. These elements figured prominently in the logistics failure of 1812 which destroyed most of what remained of the French army after the battle of Borodino.

The basis of Napoleon's military system was the *corps d'armée*, a formation of two or more divisions of infantry, a brigade or more of light cavalry, several batteries of artillery, and support troops that included engineers. Usually, when the divisions and corps moved, they were separated from each other by one day's march or less. Each division was a smaller version of the army in terms of its composition and the corps was a force which could hold its own against a much larger-sized army. With support only hours away, every commander was thus encouraged to hang on. The method by which the the terrain was assessed, the routes of march determined, and the time computed for where each unit would be at any given moment was all done by Napoleon and stored in his magnificent Corsican brain. All was thought out to achieve the object of the campaign, which was, usually, the destruction of the enemy's army. Napoleon planned it out so that his forces came together on the battlefield in numbers greater than the enemy and in a manner and from directions which the enemy did not expect. Napoleon would seek to isolate his enemy through a combination of terrain and the interposition of his army. Then part of his army would pin the enemy from the front while the rest of the army maneuvered onto the enemy's flank and rear. This added psychological dislocation to the enemy's physical unease, and thereby made the subsequent battle easier to win.

The exact makeup of the corps depended upon circumstances. In 1805, the *Grande Armée* was composed of seven corps. Rothenberg tells us that the reserves were Napoleon's to command: the famed Imperial Guard, an artillery reserve of one-quarter the guns available, and the cavalry reserve of six heavy divisions.

Think of it as this: Imagine an army of four corps arranged in the pattern of a baseball diamond. The corps at second base led the formation. The distance along the base paths could be covered in a day's march or less. If the corps at second base found the enemy, then it pinned him in place while the corps at first and third maneuvered and came up in support. The corps at homeplate came up in reserve. If the enemy appeared instead at third base, then the corps at second and home came up in support with the corps at first acting as the reserve.

Even with all this planning and foresight, the unexpected still happened. But when it happened to Napoleon, he had the capacity to adjust his plan. The ability to do so was the product of his genius. The disposition of his forces, not quite dispersed, not quite concentrated, granted him the flexibility he needed to counter the unforeseen without major dislocation of his plan. He did this according to specific circumstances, of course, but the intent was always to confuse the enemy regarding his intentions, his strength, and his location. As the author has commented elsewhere, in confusion there is opportunity and nothing creates opportunity better than moving faster than one's opponent. The genius of Napoleon was the way he moved his dispersed forces, always knowing how long it would take to concentrate some or all of them for the maximum effect.

Generalship on the battlefield, in this era, was inextricably tied to grand tactics. The term is unused today but in Napoleon's time it was, Jomini tells us, "the art of posting troops upon the battlefield according to the accidents of the ground, of bringing them into action, and the art of fighting upon the ground. . . ." Thus, "the maneuvering of an army upon the battlefield, and the different formations of troops for attack, constitute Grand Tactics." What Napoleon did—generally speaking— was pin the enemy at the front and then maneuver onto his flank and rear. In this sense, it was the same as his campaign, or operational, plans which sought to isolate the enemy, cut his lines of communications, and place him in as disadvantageous a position as possible. Here is how it went, ideally.

The first units in contact with the enemy would attack. This held the enemy in place while supporting units came up and were fed into the battle line. The enemy would have to respond in kind or retreat, and the more troops he committed, the harder it was to disengage. Napoleon wanted additional enemy troops involved as it made their ensuing defeat more decisive. Meanwhile, Napoleon's flanking force was moving into position. Screened from the enemy by terrain and/or cavalry, this force's sudden appearance on the enemy's flank or rear would spread consternation at the least and panic at best. Timing was crucial. The flanking force would have the biggest impact if the enemy had already committed his reserves to the costly battle to their front. To meet the new threat, the commander would have to strip troops from that side of the line to create a new defensive line which, in turn, created a potential weak spot. Regardless of the timing, however, the enemy now faced the unsettling prospect of being cut off from his base and surrounded. If the commander chose retreat at this point, he still had to contend with the French to his front.

Napoleon believed that it was not possible to surprise the enemy enough in a battle. His next move was to attack the weak point with shot and shell and then surprise the enemy with fresh troops. Up to this time, Napoleon, having husbanded his reserve forces and concealed their movement, now brought them into action. This was another issue of timing, and recognition of the moment was critical to success. Napoleon's superior perception made him aware of when the extra effort was needed and, heedless of the cost, would win the battle. Preceded by horse artillery to blast open the way, the infantry, supported by cavalry, would surge forward and break through. Once the enemy line was rent, the cavalry would pour through the gap and the pursuit phase began as the enemy formations fell back or were routed outright. The vigor with which the enemy was pressed determined the extent of the victory: how many muskets thrown away; how many cannon abandoned; how many soldiers ridden down and cut up or speared with lances; how many units destroyed; how many miles covered before dark?

To summarize, Napoleon is what each generation and each culture chooses to make of him—monster, genius, embodiment of French greatness. Napoleon knew that his genius and understanding of war gave him the ability to do it better than anyone. As he once said, "one engages, and then one sees." One's success, in this circumstance, is the product of how well one has prepared, and how capable one is in using the instruments at hand. In the last millennium, no one was better at this than Napoleon.

# Tactics

## Best Infantry of the Fifteenth Century:
### The Spanish *Tercio*

The development of this fighting formation is credited to Gonzalo de Córdoba (1453–1515), later known as *"El Gran Capitán,"* and rightly so—he reportedly lost only one battle in his career. This tactical system was the result of the knowledge and experience he gained in his years of successful campaigning in Italy. (For a diagram of the typical tercio formation, see page 181) The Spanish *tercio* was made up of *arquebusiers* and pikemen. The latter carried an 18-foot weapon, which weighed about ten pounds. It was handled with two hands, carried chest-high, and aimed at their enemy's face.

*Tercio* means "third" and the name derives from the older military practice, which divided an army into three parts: the vanguard, the main body, and the rear. Thus a *tercio* came to be a unit large enough to represent one of these divisions. In 1534, when we first hear of the *tercio*, its size, on paper, was 3,096 all ranks. Composed of 12 companies of 250 men each, it was commanded by a *maestro de campo*, whom we would today style a colonel. He got the big bucks, 40 *escudos per mensem*. After him came a *serjeant mayor* (major, we would say), and then other grades of officers, including a captain, a lieutenant, a *municiario* (quartermaster), physician, surgeon, apothecary, chaplain, drum major, and eight halberdiers. This was just the staff for the *tercio* and it drew 194 *escudos per mensem* in total. The company was commanded by a captain who was paid 15 *escudos*, which was three more than a staff captain. Assisting the captain was a lieutenant, a serjeant, ten corporals, a quartermaster. Add in 240 privates, a drummer, a fifer, and a chaplain and a page for the captain, and you have, for 900 to 950 *escudos*, a unit you can take anywhere. The number of officers in the company would increase over the years to include a lieutenant and four sergeants. The reader should note that the paper strength of the *tercio* was not a hard and fast rule. It was more usual for an actual *tercio* to be smaller because of wastage from all sources and even problems in recruiting. For example, in 1536, the two *tercios* for the Italian war against the French were 5,000 together. There were also 28 companies which were not combined into a *tercio*.

Interestingly, the *arquebusiers* were paid more than the pikemen, 4 versus 3 *escudos*, as a result of bonuses for superior shooting and other distinctions. This demonstrates the rising importance of gunpowder weapons in warfare in general and within the Spanish system in particular. Modern readers may wonder about the role of musicians in these companies; it was not just to play music in the park. The drummers and fifers would communicate commands on and off the battlefield. Soldiers, or anyone for that matter, can march farther and feel less fatigued, if it is done in unison and to music. Something to remember for later.

The *arquebusiers* and pikemen formed a symbiotic partnership on the battlefield. The former were effective for only as long as they were protected. In entrenchments, *arquebusiers* could defend positions more extended than before and they were protected while reloading. The Córdoba solution to how they were to be protected in the open field was to place them with the pikemen. The *arquebusiers* could fire and even retreat, if need be, into the *tercio* to reload. Otherwise, they would march to the rear after firing and reload. The *tercio* combined missile fire with shock action. As in the Middle Ages, the idea was the same: the *arquebusiers* served the same role as the archers in softening up the enemy at a distance. Once this was done and, if the situation was right, a resort to shock action by massed pikemen could sweep the field with their 18-foot weapons. This system would perform well for much of the sixteenth century, although as time passed, the number of gunners in the *tercio* expanded. They also came to be massed in several ranks so as to present an almost constant gunfire.

Lastly, the Spaniards, after centuries of combat against the Moors, were tough soldiers and fierce fighters. They had *élan* and a morale strength that convinced them that victory was theirs. The value of this cannot be overestimated.

# Battles

## First Victory by Small Arms Gunfire:
Cerignola, 26 April 1503

The battle at Cerignola was one of the many fought in the Italian Wars from 1495 to 1515. For some reason, successive kings of various countries all thought that taking over parts of Italy was the thing to do. This is understandable when one learns that Italy was wealthy, but not unified, and was unable to defend herself adequately. Charles VIII of France started things off in 1495, and when Louis XII succeeded to the throne in 1498, he kept things rolling. Spanish interests were well represented by Gonzalo de Córdoba (*"El Gran Capitán;"* see page 205). On 11 November 1500, Louis and King Ferdinand partitioned the

Kingdom of Naples under the provisions of the Treaty of Granada. The peace lasted for two years, or until the former belligerents were ready for more war. The war resumed in the summer of 1502.

The Duke of Nemours, representing France, had a force of 1,000 lances (which works out to about 6,000 men, once all the support troops are accounted for); 3,500 French and Gascon infantry; and 3,000 Swiss pikemen. Córdoba had 1,000 horsemen and 3,000 foot soldiers. Córdoba, being a smart commander, withdrew from Naples to Barletta, a seaport in Apulia. There, the situation remained static for some months as the French maintained a loose blockade of Barletta. In April 1503, Córdoba received some 2,000 Swiss as reinforcements, and because of this and his weakening supply situation, he decided to give battle.

On 21 April, he took up positions on a hillside at Cerignola and prepared his ground. The hill was covered with vines and there was a ditch along his front, which he deepened. The earth from the digging was thrown up to form a parapet and stakes were embedded in it. The infantry took their positions behind the fieldworks and 13 artillery pieces were emplaced. The heavy cavalry was held in reserve. The light cavalry, javelineers or *genitours* (not to be confused with doctors who operate on your prostate or guys who clean up after you at school), were sent ahead to screen the French advance and prevent any meaningful reconnaissance. Nemours arrived late in the afternoon and was urged to go into battle without too much waiting. The French artillery was still moving up.

The French attacked in three "battles," or tactical groupings, each with infantry and heavy cavalry. The Duke led the first "battle" on the right and the other two were echeloned to the left. The Spaniards opened fire with their artillery, but it did not fire for long. Their gunpowder supply blew up, probably touched off by a stray spark. The French came on, not knowing about the ditch. Apparently, the first in were the horsemen and when they came to a halt, so did the rest. Nemours was looking for a gap to redirect his attack when he was shot by an *arquebusier*. The French and Swiss in the middle "battle" were stopped by the ditch as well and then came under *arquebus* fire. An attempt to maneuver to the left by the third and rearmost "battle" to clear the ditch if possible was also halted by gunfire.

The attack was now bogged down, with their commander and many of their other leaders dead. The infantry began to give way and Córdoba ordered his heavy cavalry to sweep in from both flanks and the infantry to advance. The French left the field in disorder. The French artillery train was captured, and the infantry was pursued by the *genitours* for some distance. French losses have been placed at 3,000.

# Youngest Commander of the Fifteenth Century:
## Gaston de Foix

and

# First Battle in Which Artillery Played a
# Central Role: Ravenna, 1512

Gaston was the new Duke of Nemours and nephew of Louis XII. When he took over the command of the French forces in 1511, he was 21. The scene of action was Italy. The French seemed to be on the way to controlling northern Italy and this, as you might expect, gave rise to opposition. Pope Julius II formed an alliance of the Papal States, the Spanish, and the Venetians to drive out the invader. The Pope also had his eye on the holdings of the Duke of Ferrara, who was aligned with the French.

Boulogna, which the French had captured, was besieged by Spanish and Papal forces. Gaston acted quickly. He marched the army to Boulogna, drove off the enemy forces, and raised the siege. He then marched to Brescia and laid siege to it. The city was captured in February 1512. He then moved south in March to engage the Spanish-Papal army in battle. Gaston intended to lay siege to Ravenna and force the allies to give battle. It worked. Ramon de Cardona, the allies' commander, brought his army to Ravenna and, on the advice of Pedro de Navarro, took up a position two miles south of the besieged town.

The Spanish-Papal army took up positions by the Ronco River. They deployed with the river behind them, dug entrenchments, and prepared obstacles in front of them on the night of 10 March. Cardona's army included approximately 16,000 men and 30 pieces of artillery. Cardona's army deployed with infantry in the middle; cavalry on the wings, which were refused; a body of cavalry in the middle behind the infantry; and his artillery in the middle, in front of the infantry.

The French army, including Ferrara's forces, consisted of approximately 23,000 men and 54 pieces of artillery. That same night, 10 March, the French built a pontoon bridge across the Ronco, which would allow the movement of artillery. The French held about 2,000 men at Ravenna to guard against a *sortie* from the city. At dawn on 11 March, the French drew up in a semi-circle, including (from right to left): the French cavalry men-at-arms; the French guns; the Gascon infantry; the 8,500-strong German *Landsknechte* (mercenary pikemen); French foot; French cavalry; Italian infantry; the *Ferrarese* (Italian) guns; and finally, about 2,000 French light cavalry composed of Italian horse-*arquebusiers*, mounted crossbowmen, and *genitours*.

The battle opened with the French and Italian guns and the allied guns engaging in hours-long bombardment. The Duke of Ferrara maneuvered his 24 guns far over to the left to enfilade the allied lines. Heavy casualties were inflicted on both sides, but it seems that only the Spanish infantry laid down to protect themselves somewhat. The German *Landsknechte* reportedly sustained 2,000 losses in the artillery attack. For the first time, two armies engaged in an artillery duel on the battlefield, designed to either prepare for an infantry attack or to prevent one.

Eventually, the Spanish cavalry on the right, no longer able to stand the pounding, decided that enough was enough and, without orders, charged the French light cavalry on the French left. The French drove off the Spanish horse and pursued. Gaston sent up the Gascon crossbowmen and some Picard pikemen to protect them against pike troops. These troops were met with heavy *arquebus* fire and pulled back with losses. Gaston then ordered a general advance and the two sides fought fiercely at the entrenchments for about an hour, during which the Germans were pushed out of the ditches with more losses. The German and French infantry regrouped and went forward again; this time, they got across the ditch, but the Spanish still would not give way. The French cavalry on the right, however, took on and eventually defeated the cavalry force opposite it when more troops, including crossbowmen and infantry, were sent in. These French troops then broke in on the allied left and inflicted heavy casualties.

While all this was going on, a French detachment under d'Alègre had moved two cannon across a pontoon bridge over the Ronco and taken up positions on the far side of the river opposite the Spanish rear. Their fire greatly disturbed the allied army. The French cavalry, which had pursed the Spanish horsemen, then returned to attack the Spanish army at the rear. Now the allies were beset by cavalry on both flanks and rear, and renewed pressure from the front. It was too much, and the infantry formation began to disintegrate. Panic set in, the rout began, and cavalry rode down the enemy troops.

In pursuit of the enemy, Gaston was killed in a rearguard skirmish. Pedro de Navarro, the Spanish infantry commander, was captured. The French victory was spoiled by the loss of their dynamic young commander. French casualties: about 4,500. Papal-Spanish losses: 9,000 killed, and wounded unknown.

Gaston saw that against an entrenched enemy, superior artillery was needed, and in this battle he had it. The Papal-Spanish army suffered from its choice of position. Navarro's suggestion of a position had put

Cardona's army in box with water behind and, after the entrenchments were dug, only one narrow way out. No wonder his own side refused to ransom him back; he eventually joined the French. One is left to wonder what kind of career Gaston would have had and how it would have made an impact on French arms if he had lived.

## Biggest Battle of the Sixteenth Century:
## St. Quentin, 10 August 1557

This battle came about because a Spanish army was besieging St. Quentin and a French army tried to lift the siege. Charles Oman provides us with the details.

The Spanish army of Philip II was under the command of Emmanuel Philibert, the Duke of Savoy; it numbered about 50,000 and included 7,000 English. Yes, the English joined the Spanish cause because Queen Mary, a Catholic, was married to Philip. The French, under the Duke of Montmorency, could raise only 26,000 men because the better part of their army was in Italy. The garrison in St. Quentin was commanded by Gaspard de Coligny. He had just made it into St. Quentin on 2 August with reinforcements (two companies of infantry, three companies of heavy cavalry) before the enemy closed the ring around it. As it was, not all of his troops made it inside—a quarter of his horse and one-half of his infantry got lost during the night approach. On the north bank of the Somme River, St. Quentin has its south side protected by water, marsh, bog, and mud. The only access from the south was a road, or causeway, which crossed two small islands. The Spanish troops barricaded the causeway and took up positions in a mill on the south shore.

Savoy surrounded the town, began to dig entrenchments on the north side, and erected emplacements for his artillery, which was still moving up. On 3 August, Montmorency tried to send in relief troops under the cover of darkness and had arranged with Coligny for guides for his force of 2,000 infantry who would fight their way in. They were to slip through a thin part of the Spanish lines while attacks were made at other points to distract the besiegers. Unfortunately for them, the plan was revealed to Savoy's men by some prisoners captured that day. An ambush was prepared by entrenched *arquebusiers*, who shot up the column and broke up the attempt.

A second relief attempt was made by Montmorency, whose nephew, by the way, was in the town. On this occasion, the French commander's plan was to send men in boats across the clear water parts of the Somme on the south side of St. Quentin. He thought that he could move sufficient forces into the town by *coup de main* before Savoy could respond. Aiding him, he thought, was the terrain. The nearest crossing over the Somme was a ford at Rouvray, which was unguarded. Moving at night on 9 August from La Fère, the French arrived unopposed on the south side of St. Quentin at 8:00 A.M. Presently, the Spanish troops guarding the southern causeway were driven onto a small island, the Faubourg d'Isle, and contained there. The movement across the water was slow because of the difficulty of getting the men in the boats, and the fact that there were only seven boats available for the movement. After two hours, some 450 men had been moved across and into the town. The French had also brought 15 artillery pieces. They set up a battery by the mill and, at long range, engaged the Spanish camp on the east side of the town.

The Duke of Savoy realized that opportunity was knocking and so he gathered up his cavalry—in which he had a sizable advantage—and set off for the Rouvray ford. The French noticed the movement and Montmorency sent the Duke of Nevers with three companies of cavalry to support the *Reiter* who were guarding the ford. It was now a race to the ford, and the Duke of Savoy's cavalry, some 4,000 to 5,000, won. They drove off the *Reiter* who were intercepted by Nevers and they told him that the enemy was coming on in force. Nevers decided against trying to block the crossing and returned to Montmorency.

The Duke ordered the crossing stopped and the boats abandoned. He sent off his infantry and artillery and rode forward with his cavalry to slow down the enemy horse. Savoy's cavalry set a measured pace, deploying into a long line to outflank the French, if possible. Montmorency tried to organize a defense between some woods and a village, but as he tried to do this, some of the non-combatants broke from the rear and others went with them. Then the Duke galloped to a little hill to get a better view of the attackers and gave the impression that he was fleeing the field. This set off the general exodus. Montmorency, who was the Constable of France, refused the offer of a fast horse and charged the enemy, hoping to be killed in battle. He was wounded but not killed, because his aide identified him to the enemy. The majority of the French cavalry were killed or captured. The infantry was then caught in column and attacked before it could properly deploy. It was cut up and those who made it into a nearby village were slaughtered in the streets.

It is estimated that two-thirds of the French army was killed, wounded, captured, or just went home from this, the biggest battle of a century full of big battles.

# First Test of Gustavus's System:
## Battle of Breitenfeld, 17 September 1631

### Modern Warfare Arrives in Europe

The machinations of the politics of the day—and here what is meant is politics and religion—do not concern us overly. A little background is in order, however.

On 4 July 1630, Gustavus crossed the Baltic with 13,000 men to spread his influence and defend the Protestant faith. Gustavus was a pious man who led his army in prayers and even wrote some hymns. The Emperor Ferdinand was not very interested in this development and for six months, neither of the Habsburg armies paid him any mind. These armies, by the way, were commanded by Tilly and Wallenstein, the great entrepreneur of early modern warfare. With a free hand, here is what the Swedish king did: he advanced from Usedom, his landing place, to Stettin and thence to Mecklenburg. Just as a storm picks up power as it sweeps over the ocean, so did Gustavus's army; it reached 24,000 men during the summer. He captured scores of towns in Pomerania and Mecklenburg.

The expected support from the Protestant princes of Germany, however, did not manifest itself. This is because they were meeting in an attempt to convince the Emperor to dismiss Wallenstein. The Princes were concerned that the great man—and this means Wallenstein—would try to carve out his own principality and become one of them. Ferdinand came to think the same way and he dismissed Wallenstein. The emperor was trying to garner support and removing an irritant seemed a good way to do it. Wallenstein was an able general, however, and in retrospect, the best time to remove him may not have been with a Swedish king rampaging on the Continent. Time would tell. It always does. Anyway, on 24 August, Wallenstein was out.

Gustavus was not without friends—perhaps supporters would be a better word. Cardinal Richelieu, he of Catholic France and Louis XIII, had a liaison officer with the Swedish king ever since he had landed, and in January 1631 a deal—which is to say, treaty—was struck. The Treaty of Bärwalde provided Gustavus with 120,000 rix-dollars and 400,000 annually for the next five years. In return, Gustavus would keep an army of 30,000 infantry and 6,000 cavalry in the field, and he would respect the Catholic faith wherever it was already established.

Meanwhile, Pappenheim, commanding the Emperor's army, had besieged Magdeburg from November to 20 May and ravaged the countryside in the process. This was nothing compared to what the army did when it finally got inside the city—25,000 of the 30,000 inhabitants were killed and the Elbe was choked with bodies. The sack and subsequent burning of Magdeburg spread fear and loathing in Protestant Germany and Gustavus reaped the benefit of more allies. Gustavus had tried to raise the siege in two ways. The first was to march on Frankfurt and pull Tilly's army away from Magdeburg, but the wily Walloon would not bite and marched on to join Pappenheim. The second way was by marching directly to Magdeburg's aid, but to do so he had to secure the permission of the Electors Georg Wilhelm of Brandenburg and Johann Georg of Saxony, or risk being attacked by them. Eventually Georg Wilhelm agreed, but Johann Georg would not, and so Magdeburg was left to its murderous fate.

Things changed A.M., "After Magdeburg." Gustavus, with his army at the gates of Berlin, strongly suggested to Georg Wilhelm of Brandenburg that he give up neutrality and join him. Georg Wilhelm saw the wisdom of it and agreed, then threw in the fortress of Spandau. Also signing on was Wilhelm of Hesse-Cassel and Prince Bernhard of Saxe-Weimar. Gustavus moved his army to Werben and into entrenchments. They were lacking supplies and fighting off disease. It was here that Tilly came with his army of 22,000 and launched attacks against the Swedish positions. Two assaults by his army were driven back with significant losses as the Swedish guns loaded with case shot cut down the attackers. Tilly had come to Werben with a hungry army and left with a starving army and 6,000 dead and wounded, which represents just over 27 percent casualties.

Tilly moved into Saxony, heretofore neutral and untouched by war, to procure supplies. His army laid waste to all and sundry. He told Leipzig that unless the city surrendered, they would get the Magdeburg treatment. They surrendered. Johann Georg of Saxony, who had been sitting on the fence reading "The Lives of Famous Protestant Moderates and Neutrals," came off the fence fully on Gustavus's side. He and his army of 16,000 joined the Swedish king and his 26,000. They met at Düben, which is about 25 miles north of Leipzig, and decided to march north. Tilly knew that he could not easily extract his soldiers from all the plunder they were enjoying, so he would probably have to stay put and fight a siege. Pappenheim, who apparently thought the 72-year old Tilly to be of diminished faculties, considered that the better course of action would be to meet the enemy away from Leipzig. Accordingly, he sent word to Tilly on 16 September that the Protestants were moving south, and Tilly had to come and support him because he could not withdraw safely. All told, it might have been better for Tilly to have stayed put, but it did not happen that way.

The combined force of Tilly and Pappenheim was about 36,000 men. Tilly may have been a septuagenarian, but he had learned the trade of war from the Duke of Parma. Is the reader wondering along with the author, "was Tilly at Parma's dinner party at Oudenarrde in 1582?" (See page 174) It is possible. Tilly would have been 23 at the time.

We are told that 17 September was a sunny, hot day. Tilly had drawn up his army just north of Breitenfeld on a gentle slope. His army deployed in the customary manner of the times, seventeen *tercios* with about 1,500 men each in the center of the line, cavalry on the wings, and the guns before all in the middle.* Pappenheim commanded the left wing of 5,000 cavalry and Tilly took his place in the middle. Gustavus's army marched onto the field after the Imperial forces were deployed. The king's officers had been well-briefed in the desires of their king. He had discussed with them what he wanted and what they should do in certain circumstances. Tilly sent 2,000 cavalry to interfere with the deployment, but they were driven off by the Swedish dragoons (mounted infantry) and some Scottish mercenaries. Gustavus deployed his army in two lines, infantry in the middle, cavalry on the right and left. The Saxons were in one line, with the infantry in the middle and cavalry on each wing.

The battle began at noon with trumpets blaring, drums beating, and cannonballs flying. The Swedes had 100 guns, which was more than what Tilly had, but how many more is a good question. Torstensson, Gustavus's chief of artillery, was commanding the gunners and they poured out fire at a rate three times that of the Imperials. The length of the artillery duel is given as two and one-half hours, by which time Pappenheim had had enough. He led his cavalry forward at the trot to deliver the caracole. The one problem with this was that Tilly had not ordered it. The king's cavalry on the right was commanded by Johann Baner. Interspersed with it were musketeers who were well placed to add defensive strength to their cavalry. The musketeers had the range advantage over the Imperial cavalrymen, who were armed only with pistols. In an effort to produce a result on his left, Pappenheim charged six more times, each time moving the thrust of his attack further to the left in an attempt to outflank his enemy. Each time, the Swedes adjusted to meet them and all the while the musketeers shot into the thick formation of horsemen. On the seventh charge, Baner sent his reserve cavalry at the Imperials and drove them from the field.

---

*In response to the greater flexibility of their long-time Dutch opponents, the Spanish had made their tercios progressively smaller since their initiation as 3,000+ man units a century earlier.

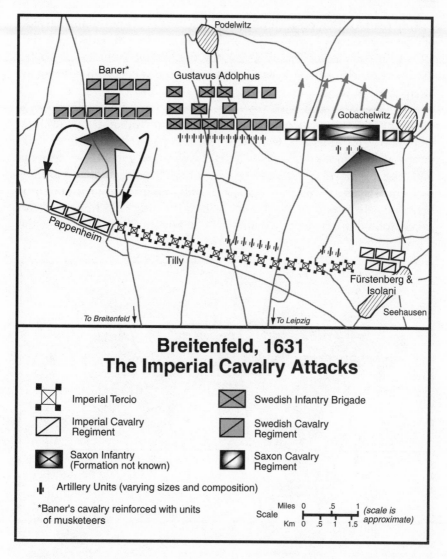

## Breitenfeld, 1631
## The Imperial Cavalry Attacks

Imperial Tercio

Imperial Cavalry Regiment

Saxon Infantry (Formation not known)

Swedish Infantry Brigade

Swedish Cavalry Regiment

Saxon Cavalry Regiment

Artillery Units (varying sizes and composition)

*Baner's cavalry reinforced with units of musketeers

Scale
Miles 0          .5          1
Km 0    .5    1    1.5
(scale is approximate)

Pappenheim's unauthorized action had encouraged the Imperial cavalry on the right—led by Fürstenberg and Isolani—to believe that the signal must have been given for an advance and so forward they went. Now Tilly had two unauthorized attacks on his hands. The result of the second attack proved very favorable, however; the 16,000 Saxons, broke as the Croatian cavalry came at them. Leading the reverse charge was Johann Georg himself. The retreat—headlong flight perhaps a better descriptive—was checked only by the Swedish baggage camp, which the Saxons stopped to pilfer.

Tilly realized that opportunity was knocking and loudly: the left side of Gustavus's army was exposed and his forces were already beyond it. He sent his tercios obliquely across the field to the right to gain more reach over the Swedish left and then had them wheel to the left in an attempt to roll up the line with 20,000 infantry and 2,000 horse. At this point of the battle and with any other army, it would have been Tilly's victory. The Swedish army, however, was not any other army and they were about to demonstrate why. This part of the Swedish line, 4,000 strong, was commanded by Gustav Horn, as able a general as Gustavus had. The high level of skill and training of the Swedes and their superior tactical system was put to the test and came through it superbly. Horn wheeled his units to the left to face the attacking Imperials and called for reinforcements. Gustavus sent him two brigades from the

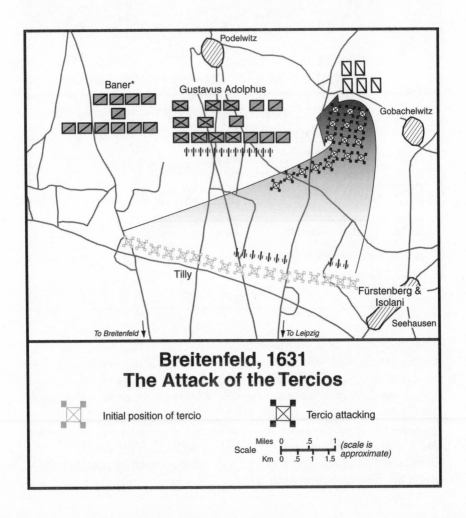

## Breitenfeld, 1631
## The Attack of the Tercios

Initial position of tercio          Tercio attacking

Miles 0    .5    1    (scale is
Scale                  approximate)
Km   0   .5   1   1.5

reserve. The firepower of the Swedes told on the Imperial infantry and Torstensson's reserve guns cut down large numbers of men. Here the combined arms team fought for the first time. Musketeers came out to shoot and then withdraw to reload, cavalrymen charged, and the pike-men came on and crashed into the *tercios*. And all the while, the maneu-verable regimental cannon were blasting away.

It was now some five or six hours since Pappenheim had attacked. The moment of decision was approaching, and it is the recognition of it and the ability to do something about it which makes great captains. Gustavus saw it. He took command of four squadrons of horse from the right wing and swept across the field to Tilly's emplaced 24-pounders. He captured the guns and, as they were already pointing at Tilly's men, he had them open fire. The *tercios* were now beset by enfilade fire and continued assault from the front. They began to disintegrate. The final blow was the charge of the Swedish cavalry from the rear. Fleeing Impe-rial soldiers were ridden down and killed.

The final casualties for the Imperials amounted to at least 7,000 killed and 6,000 wounded and captured, although the total casualties may have been closer to 19,000. Casualties for the Swedish army came to about 2,000. Tilly was wounded three times and got away with 600 men, while Pappenheim had 1,400 left. All the Imperial guns were captured and all of their baggage was taken along with 90 flags.

This was not the end of it, however. Gustavus led 1,500 cavalry in hot pursuit for four days more and captured even more prisoners. In this pursuit, we see Alexander the Great's purpose. Gustavus had fought a battle aimed at the annihilation of the enemy and he did so for strategic purpose. The only way little Sweden could maintain her position of dominance in the Baltic was to destroy as much of the empire's military power as was possible. Then, once establishing a physical and moral dominance, it had to grab as much territory as could be held. This was a strategy for a man in a hurry. This need for speed was reflected in all aspects of the Swedish army and its tactical system: lighter guns; pre-pared artillery cartridges; improved muskets; simpler drills with fewer motions to load prepared cartridges and fire them; decisive shock action, not wimpy caracoles, from the cavalry; reduced baggage trains; winter campaigning; and smaller tactical units. Above all, disciplined, well-trained leaders making decisions of their own accord, within guid-ance laid down by the Soldier-King. The smaller the unit, the more important the choice made. Does any of this not resonate with the mod-ern reader?

The Imperial forces at Breitenfeld fought separately by branch—artillery, then cavalry, then infantry. They were beaten by an army

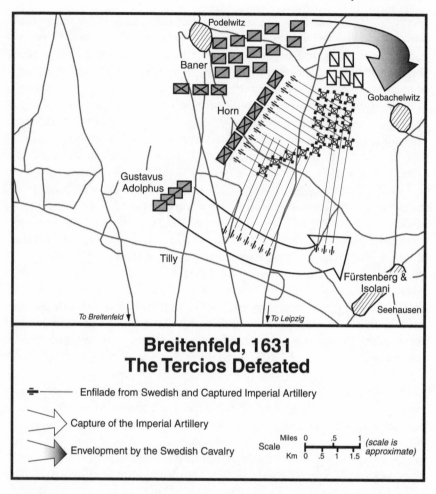

# Breitenfeld, 1631
# The Tercios Defeated

══──── Enfilade from Swedish and Captured Imperial Artillery

⟩ Capture of the Imperial Artillery

⟩ Envelopment by the Swedish Cavalry

Scale  Miles 0    .5    1  (scale is
       Km 0  .5  1  1.5   approximate)

which fought with all its weapons simultaneously. Thus were Pappenheim's cavalry driven off, and the *tercios* from the last century dispatched. This is why Breitenfeld is an important battle. It establishes the baseline parameter for modern warfare. If you want to know when modern warfare started, this is it.

## Highest French Losses by Percentage in a Major Battle: Blenheim, 13 August 1704

Two of the greatest generals of this age fought together in this battle at Blenheim, which was part of the War of the Spanish Succession 1701–1714, so perhaps a little background is in order. This was Louis XIV's final war as well, so, for sentimental reasons, let us set the stage for the final act of the fightingest monarch in French history.

The king of Spain, Carlos II, was dying, childless. The big question then was who gets the throne? Not surprisingly, there was more than one suggestion as to what to do, and these these smart men of Europe had not left this matter until the last minute to resolve. The main princes of Europe had worked out an agreement in 1698 which partitioned Spanish holdings in a way with which all could live. Unfortunately, one of the princes, Josef Ferdinand, elector of Bavaria, died in 1699 and this upset the apple cart. The main contenders now as before were Louis XIV, King of France, and Leopold I, the Holy Roman Emperor. Obviously, no one with an army was going to let either of them rule Spain and they had recognized this long ago. They were pushing claims, therefore, on behalf of their respective descendants, Louis for his second grandson Philip of Anjou, and Leopold for his second son, the Archduke Charles. You see, Josef Ferdinand had been picked to receive Spain and the Spanish Netherlands, and the colonies. Now, with him gone, who was to inherit the lion's share? Louis, having just finished the Nine Years War (1689–98) was not ready for another. He offered generous terms, stating that Josef Ferdinand's share should go to the Archduke Charles, except the Duchy of Milan which should go to his son. Leopold said, "Hey, I've got a better idea, everything should go to Archduke Charles and I refuse to negotiate."

The Spanish king, however, was not to be without some say in how things went. He made a will naming Philip of Anjou his heir. Upon Carlos II's death on November 1700, a courier left Spain headed for France. He asked Louis if he accepted the will. If he did not, then it was next stop: Vienna. Louis had no practicable option other than acceptance. Either way it would have been war, and accepting meant that he had some definite advantages. This point, however, is one of dispute amongst historians. The author's view is that, given the way Europeans generally behaved, there would have been a war over something soon enough, so why not now? Well, with Louis in charge, it did not take long. He ordered, then compelled, the Dutch out of some forts in the Spanish Netherlands which the latter had occupied with King Carlos II's permission. Now the Dutch were mad and then Louis brought the English into the act. He recognized James II's son as the legitimate king of England. This did not go over well with the Protestants and then the new Philip V of Spain froze the English out of the slave trade to the Spanish colonies.

The alliance formed up and the fighting had already started. With Louis were Spain, Savoy, Portugal, for a time Bavaria, and some Hungarian rebels. Opposing Louis were England, the Dutch United Provinces, the Austrian Habsburg Empire; the new-styled King of Prussia, Frederick William I, father of the Great One; and some other

German states. Once the war was started, some changes were made. The Duke of Savoy switched sides in October 1703. Meanwhile, Marlborough and Eugene demonstrated why they were the two best generals of this era, although Eugene erred when he raided Cremona on 1 February 1702. In command of Louis's army in Cremona was his favorite general, François de Neufville, the Duke of Villeroi. He was an amiable man and a gifted conversationalist, but a mediocre general. Eugene came out of winter quarters and launched a lightning raid on Cremona. His troops attacked and caused a lot of damage, but were pushed out of the town. In the process, they captured Villeroi! Military historians refer to this as a *"coup de main"*; for Louis, it was bad luck. Villeroi's replacement was the Duke of Vendôme, one of France's best generals. Vendôme and the new king of Spain and Naples, Philip V, held off Eugene in Italy for the rest of the year and recaptured lost territory. The author contends that Eugene should have sent Villeroi back to his troops or concocted some elaborate ruse to allow him to escape. He was more valuable to Eugene at head of his own army than as Eugene's guest, but there you have it. The same holds true in football. A defensive back you can beat all the time should not be beaten all the time so that he is replaced. He should be beaten only when you have to beat him, then he will be around when you need to pick on him. The guy who replaces him could be better. The moral is, never draw your opponent's attention to his weaknesses; however, this theory is not universally accepted by military men, historians, or coaches. Eugene eventually saw the truth in this as Villeroi was exchanged by the Austrians after six months and by the spring of 1703, Villeroi was again leading the French army.

In the event the reader is wondering, "when shall we return to Blenheim," it is now. The strategy for 1704 was this, the French were going to launch an attack toward Vienna under Marsin and reinforced by Tallard. Villeroi was to keep Marlborough in Flanders. The allied plan for 1704 was to mount diversionary operations against southern France where there was religious conflict and against Spain from Portugal. Marlborough would then take his army south and unite with Eugene's forces on the Danube in order to save Vienna, and, in the process, take Bavaria out of the war. Marlborough left 60,000 men in the Netherlands and headed south with 35,000. During the march south, he was shadowed by Villeroi who made no attempt to interfere. Marlborough deceived the French and the Dutch as to his intentions and headed for the Danube. There then followed a period of march, maneuver, and a battle or two between May and August. During this time, Marlborough and Eugene kept Villeroi in the dark as to their

Eugene of Savoy.
© *Bettmann/*
*CORBIS/MAGMA*

*EUGENE* Prince of *SAVOY.*

intentions and in the end, he was merely stopped at Strasbourg and missed the opportunity to reinforce the army of Marshal Marsin and Maximillian, the elector of Bavaria. Attempts to bring Maximillian to battle failed even though Marlborough and Ludwig of Baden devastated the Bavarian countryside. Marsin and Maximillian were waiting for the reinforcements of Tallard's army. Tallard marched off to join Marsin and Eugene left some of his army behind and went off after him. Villeroi stayed where he was and so took himself out of the campaign.

Ludwig of Baden went to besiege Ingolstädt and Eugene and Marlborough joined their armies on the afternoon of 11 August near Donauwörth. From there they moved west toward Munster. The Franco-Bavarian army of Tallard, Marsin and Maximillian moved east from Hockstädt. Both armies were north of the Danube and only a few miles apart on 12 August. Separating the armies was the Nebel River. The Franco-Bavarian army's strength is given at 60,000 and Marlborough's and Eugene's at 56,000 by most of the newest historians. The more experienced historians tend to place the numbers at 52,000 for Marlborough and Eugene and 56,000 for the French and Bavarians. By now the reader is well aware that nailing down numbers is a problem. In terms of battalions and squadrons, the French had 79 battalions of infantry, 143 squadrons of cavalry, 12 of which were dismounted. The allies had 66 battalions of infantry and 166 squadrons of cavalry.

The Nebel River, more a brook perhaps, divided the battlefield. The British and Austrians were north of the river and the French and Bavarians were south of it, however, a tributary also cut through the French position. In any event, the Nebel and the marshy ground around it did not prove an insurmountable obstacle. Marsin's left was secured by a hill. The guns of both armies were placed along the front line; the British and Austrians had 60 and the Franco-Bavarians had 90.

The British and Austrians had set out at 2:00 A.M. and arrived at the Nebel after five hours of marching. The appearance of the allied armies started the skirmishing and the French who had not thought battle on 13 August likely, began to form their battle lines. The British and Austrians deployed as well, but it was some hours before the armies were in place. In the meantime, casualties were inflicted by an artillery duel. The battle lines stretched some 6,000 yards. Tallard was in overall command of the Franco-Bavarian army. His right flank was anchored on Blenheim. Here Clérambault was in command of 9 battalions of infantry and 12 dismounted squadrons of cavalry. The French had maintained a strong position here. This part of the front was about 1,000 yards. From Blenheim to the next fortified position at Oberglauheim was about two miles. Tallard covered this stretch with 76 squadrons of cavalry. In Oberglauheim, Marsin had 14 battalions of infantry, and 19 battalions of infantry in two lines to the left of Oberglauheim. The extreme left of the French line was covered by a hill and nine battalions. The remaining squadrons formed a second line along with the remaining infantry, much of it behind Blenheim.

The British and Austrians set up with Eugene on the right opposite Marsin, Marlborough in the middle and Lord Cutts on the left opposite Blenheim. Eugene had 18 battalions and 80 squadrons. Marlborough had 48 battalions and 86 squadrons. Marlborough came up on the Nebel about 8:00 A.M. and started to deploy. Eugene's deployment took longer due to the greater distance his army had to march. Marlborough, upon observing the French dispositions at Blenheim, strengthened his left by bringing Cutts's force up to 20 battalions and 15 squadrons for their assault. Marlborough had arranged his units in four lines for the purpose of crossing the Nebel. The first line was infantry, the second and third lines cavalry and the fourth infantry. The idea was that the first line would cross the river and take up positions to permit the next two lines to cross. The fourth line was to act as reserve. Tallard, seeing the size of Marlborough's force opposite Blenheim, reinforced Clérambault's troops to 19 battalions, and a cavalry unit.

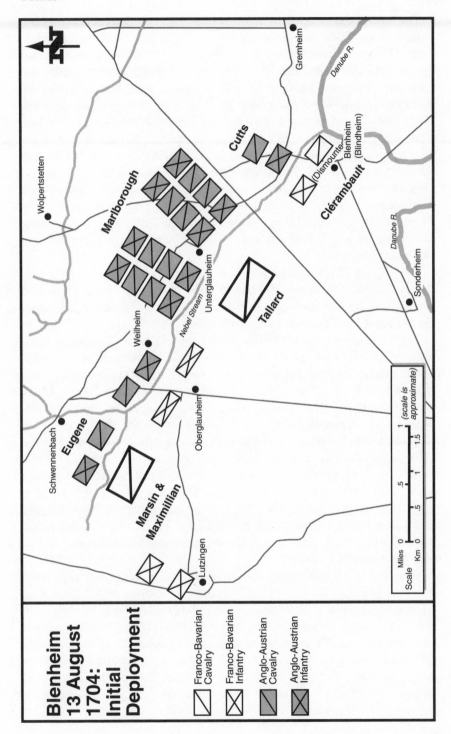

Blenheim
13 August
1704:
Initial
Deployment

Franco-Bavarian Cavalry

Franco-Bavarian Infantry

Anglo-Austrian Cavalry

Anglo-Austrian Infantry

Scale

Miles 0

Km 0

.5

.5

1

1

.5

1.5

1 (scale is approximate)

Gremheim

Danube R.

Blenheim (Blindheim)

Blenheim

(Dismounted)

Clérambault

Cutts

Marlborough

Danube R.

Sonderheim

Wolpertstetten

Unterglauheim

Tallard

Nebel Stream

Weilheim

Oberglauheim

Eugene

Schwennenbach

Marsin & Maximillian

Lutzingen

The battle commenced sometime after 12:30 P.M. with action on both wings. Cutts's first assault came forward against the French at Blenheim. Winston Churchill, in his biography of his ancestor, tells us that the French held their fire until the British troops were only 30 yards distant. Building on this, Archer Jones reports that the 2,400 British infantry men received the volley of 4,000 defenders and suffered 800 killed and wounded. The British pushed on until they reached the barricades and then fired. They could go no further, however. They were then supported by more infantry and in extending their attack to the left renewed their assault. The allies were able to gain footholds here and there on the edge of Blenheim. Marlborough's persistence here caused Clérambault to order in more troops, so he stripped off the reserve on the right. Tallard could not countermand this order as he was at the other side of the battlefield and he did not give any order later to retrieve them.

Meanwhile, Marlborough was building up his forces in the center on the south side of the Nebel. His first line of infantry was across and some of his cavalry as well. On they came across the pontoon bridges the engineers had erected while under fire.

The British had some cavalry across the Nebel by the water mills which were north and a bit west of Blenheim. Clérambault, at this point, saw the utility of interfering with these forces and sent eight squadrons of *gendarmerie* (elite cavalry) to envelop the enemy. The French attack was broken up by five squadrons of English cavalry. The English cavalry under the command of Colonel Palmes struck the French horse on both flanks and wheeled inward, thus driving the *gendarmes* from the field. Clérambault then decided, wisely, that he had to interfere with the build-up in the center as Marlborough had most of his first three lines across the Nebel. He ordered a cavalry charge against Marlborough's left. Unfortunately for the French, not everyone received the order. The attack succeeded in disrupting a few of the English squadrons, but it was halted by the infantry's fire. Marlborough continued to pour troops across to the other side.

Speaking of the other side, at this point, Eugene's attack was moving slowly. The plan Marlborough and he had developed called for him to envelop the enemy's left wing, however, the French and Bavarians were not cooperating. Eugene, nevertheless, was reporting some progress and this was against superior numbers. Marlborough's other attack, at Oberglauheim, was not succeeding but it was accomplishing its purpose, however; this attack, and more so, the one at Blenheim, had stripped off most of Tallard's infantry reserves. At both places, Marlborough had forced the defenders into decisive commitment and he

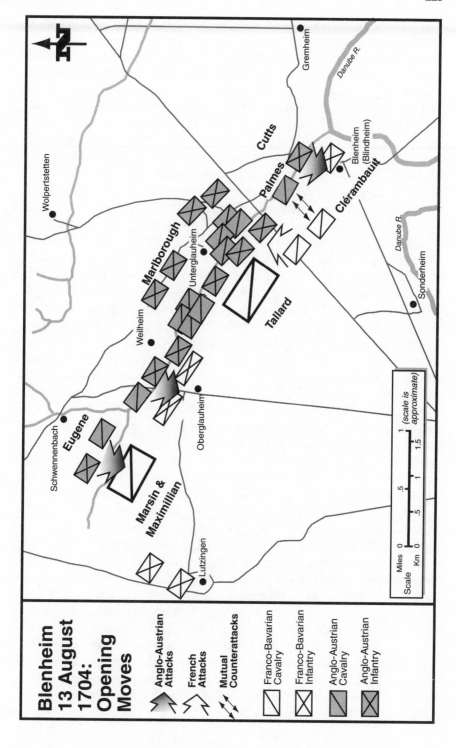

Blenheim
13 August
1704: Opening
Moves

Anglo-Austrian
Attacks

French
Attacks

Mutual
Counterattacks

Franco-Bavarian Cavalry

Franco-Bavarian Infantry

Anglo-Austrian Cavalry

Anglo-Austrian Infantry

Scale

Miles 0 .5 1 (scale is approximate)
Km 0 .5 1 1.5

Gremheim

Danube R.

Cutts

Palmes

Blenheim (Blindheim)

Clérambaut

Marlborough

Unterglauheim

Danube R.

Sonderheim

Wolpertstetten

Weilheim

Tallard

Eugene

Schwennenbach

Oberglauheim

Marsin & Maximilian

Lutzingen

was advancing his cannon. At 3:00 P.M., Tallard called for infantry from Marsin who, pressed as he was by Eugene, did not send any.

By 4:30 P.M., Marlborough was ready to make the main effort in the center. He called for, and received, cavalry support from Eugene and he massed 109 squadrons of cavalry and 16 battalions of infantry opposite Tallard's 76 squadrons and 10 battalions. The reader will not be surprised to learn that there is some dispute over the number of squadrons and battalions. It is important to note that most of the allied troops were fresh—not all of the French were—and, regardless of absolute numbers, the allies enjoyed a force superiority ratio of at least 1.45 to 1 to as much as 1.75 to 1. Marlborough ordered a general attack all along the line.

The allied cavalry, now the first line, was halted by the French infantry's musketry and drew back. Marlborough brought up his infantry and some guns and blasted the French infantry where it stood. The fighting lasted for an hour before the next stage of the battle began. Marlborough ordered his lines once more and sent the cavalry forward. This time the French cavalry broke and fled. Some headed toward Marsin and others for the Danube. Tallard tried to bring infantry from Blenheim to establish a new defensive line, but he was captured. Marlborough sent part of his cavalry to the right while he joined the cavalry swinging left. The 3,000 French were so jammed together in their panic-stricken flight that one participant, Mérode Westerloo, said that his horse was lifted from the ground and carried along for 300 yards before it could put a foot down and they were heading for the 15-foot-high bank of the Danube. Over it they tumbled, into the marsh and the deep river beyond, where most of them drowned.

At Blenheim, the defenders fought on for two more hours before surrendering, but not without some acrimony amongst the various commanders. On the other side of the field, Marsin and Maximillian retired before Marlborough could bring his forces across the field to complete their envelopment. Nevertheless, the great victory had been won.

The British and Austrians lost about 12,000 killed and wounded. The French killed and wounded total was about 20,000. Add in drowned, deserted, and captured, and the total loss was perhaps 39,000. As a minimum, the French lost 50 percent of the force engaged and, at a maximum, 64 percent and a lot of prestige. The immediate results of the battle saw the French withdraw to the Rhine with what was left of three armies. The allies occupied Bavaria, taking her out of the war. Louis XIV lost an ally and the Austrians gained a resource. Portugal and Savoy left Louis and sided with the Imperial Habsburg forces and the British. The war went on for another ten years and Marlborough would score more victories, but this was the most famous.

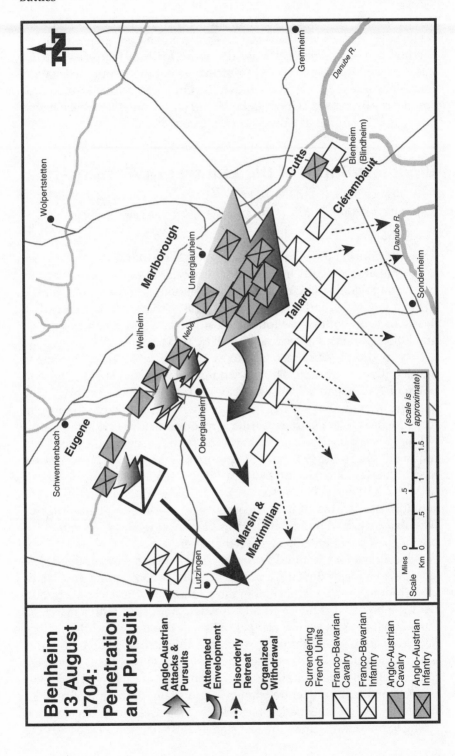

**Blenheim
13 August
1704:
Penetration
and Pursuit**

Anglo-Austrian
Attacks &
Pursuits

Attempted
Envelopment

Disorderly
Retreat

Organized
Withdrawal

Surrendering
French Units

Franco-Bavarian
Cavalry

Franco-Bavarian
Infantry

Anglo-Austrian
Cavalry

Anglo-Austrian
Infantry

Gremheim

Danube R.

Wolpertstetten

Cutts

Blenheim
(Blindheim)

Clérambault

Danube R.

Sonderheim

Marlborough

Unterglauheim

Tallard

Weilheim

Nebel

Eugene

Oberglauheim

Schwennenbach

Marsin &
Maximilian

Lutzingen

1 (scale is
approximate)

.5    1    1.5

.5    1    1.5

Miles  0
Scale
Km   0

The reader may be aware that John Churchill, the Earl of Marlborough, was later made a duke and given a grand house, palace really, by a grateful nation. They certainly did more for him than they did for Alanbrooke after World War II, but that is another story. The palace, Blenheim, is the seat of the Churchills. One supposes that the battle could have been called Oberglauheim, but who would have been happy to say that they dine at Oberglauheim once a week?

## Bloodiest Battle of the Eighteenth Century: Malplaquet, 11 September 1709, Marlborough's and Eugene's Pyrrhic Victory of the War of the Spanish Succession

This was, indeed, the bloodiest and biggest battle of the century. In fact, it was the biggest battle in European history until the Napoleonic wars when Napoleon failed to defeat the Russians at Borodino in 1812. Malplaquet was Marlborough's last great victory; by the end of it, 36,000 men on both sides would be lost, Eugene and Villars wounded, and allied casualties exceeding French by two to one.

So why did so many men (some say 200,000; others 161,000) come to a little village in France? Strategy and geography, of course. The campaign of 1709 began, as most campaigns did throughout history, in the spring, although this one began a little later than usual due to the winter hardships. The Flanders theater was of particular concern to Louis XIV because of its proximity to Paris and because several garrisons had mutinied over a lack of food. In command was Villars, by whom we mean Claude Louis Hector, Duke of Villars (1653–1734), one of Louis's (XIV and XV) best. He was sent by Louis XIV to Flanders to thwart the activities of that duo of military excellence, Marlborough and Eugene, who had bested Vendôme in 1708 at Oudenarrde and Lille and occupied a good part of the Spanish Netherlands.

What Louis had in mind was that Villars would stay on the defensive, avoid a major dust up, and maybe manage to keep the duo at bay. Unfortunately for the French, the duo had a plan. They wanted to outflank the French fortified zone and threaten the French with a march on Paris. This, in turn, would compel Villars to come out and fight. Once he was beaten, so the thinking went, the allies would march on Paris. The fortified zone, known as the Lines of La Bassée because of the location of Villars's headquarters, was a mixture of field fortifications, rivers, marshy ground, entrenchments, and so on, running east from La Bassée to Douai to Valenciennes. These defenses were deemed too strong to breakthrough, so the first step in outflanking the Lines was the capture of Tournai; the second step, the capture of Mons. In pursuit of the former, Marlborough laid siege to Tournai on 28 June. Tournai, by the way, was one of Vauban's fortifications. The perceptive reader has undoubtedly realized then that the longer Tournai held out, the shorter the time the allies would have to implement the rest of their strategy. Thus, there was an opportunity early on for the French to defeat the allied strategy. This, then, may explain Louis's initial passive approach to the campaign. Moreover, given the weak condition of the French forces, this may have been the only practicable strategy. The French hopes—that Tournai would hold out through the summer and possibly into the fall—fizzled on 29 July when the city surrendered, although the garrison retired to the citadel and continued to resist until 3 September. It was not an easy siege, however; rain was incessant and the discipline so severe in the allied camps that 500 to 600 men deserted and took up with the enemy. Eventually, the allies brought up 112 heavy guns and 70 mortars, using them to batter the defenses. One-third of the 6,400 defenders were wounded and another one-third killed. With Tournai in the bag, the allies moved against Mons. Villars had not been idle during this time; he had his men hard at work extending the Lines of La Bassée and fortifying them in depth as well. Louis, who, up to this time, had ordered Villars not to give battle, told his commander to do whatever he had to do to prevent Mons from being captured.

About this time, Villars was joined by Boufflers, by whom we mean Louis François, Duke of Boufflers (1644–1711). Boufflers, created marshal in 1693, had distinguished himself throughout his military career. At the beginning of the war, he had campaigned in the Spanish Netherlands against Marlborough and he had had early successes, although later, Marlborough reclaimed what he had lost. Even though Boufflers had just recovered from illness and was 65, he came in to act as Villars's second in command. The French would be glad he did.

Villars marched with some 90,000 men towards Mons intending to prevent the allies from surrounding the city. The allies, however, had been moving units from Tournai even before the surrender. Mons, which is two marching days from Tournai, was invested by 6 September, or three days after the surrender of Tournai. Marlborough, we see, was getting the best out of his army, especially as the rain was still falling and turning the roads into mud trails. When Villars arrived on 7 September, it was too late to do anything substantial to help Mons, nor is it clear that he would have tried. Mons lies between the Haine River to the north and the Trouille River to the south. It is east of the junction of these two rivers and Villars was south of the rivers using the line of the Haine and Trouille to bolster his defense. The relief of Mons was thus not worth the effort it would take.

The armies of Marlborough and Eugene were separated at this time,
but Villars opted to fight from a good defensive position, so he moved
his army to Malplaquet, which he reached on 9 September, and waited.
Here, amidst rolling hills, lies the village of Malplaquet and beyond it
are dense woods with two gaps in the forests. Villars's left was protected by the town of Montreuil on the Haine. Between the river and the
dense woods, known as the Forest of Taisnières (also known as the Forest of Sars by some), was a gap of clear terrain, then east of the forest
another gap of some 1,500 meters, and then the small woods of Tiry,
then another gap of about 2,000 meters, and then the woods of Lanière.
Marlborough gave Villars the opportunity to advance into one of the
gaps and attack the allies beyond them, but he said, "No thanks, Mr.
Smarty-Pants." Villars recognized the trap for what it was and knew
that his army's best chance at avoiding defeat was to remain on the
defensive.

On 10 September, as the allied armies moved into the area, the French
were raising fieldworks to strengthen further their positions between

the woods. Villars did not leave it at that, however; he also dug trenches and constructed abatis in the woods blocking the roads through them. Abatis are obstacles created by felling trees and sharpening the branches facing the enemy. The adage that a pint of sweat saves a gallon of blood must have been on Villars's mind. There was some cannonading on the part of the French to which the allies could not respond as their guns had not yet been brought up. There has been comment by historians ever since the battle that Marlborough and Eugene dawdled one or two days in commencing the battle and this gave Villars the time he needed to reinforce his position. We have seen, however, that the allies were hoping that the French would make a mistake and attack. When it was apparent on the morning of 10 September that the French would not attack, Marlborough and Eugene decided that they would wait until all their forces came to launch their attack. Troop movement was made more difficult by the weather—it was still raining. At this point, the belligerents were racing each other to make preparations. How much earth could the French dig? How many men could the allies bring up and how quickly? The commanders were calculating this equation hourly, knowing that mistakes in computation could be paid for in lives and territory. At a council of war on 10 September, Marlborough, Eugene, and Goslinga, representing the Dutch, agreed that battle would be given on 11 September at daybreak. The firing of the British cannon would be echoed by the Dutch guns and that would signal the start of the battle. Were the allies one day away from defeating the French army and thereby acquiring the opportunity to win the war?

The delay in the attack has caused much discussion from historians ever since the battle. Should the attack have gone in on the 10th? The French had worked wonders with their fieldworks since the 9th. The allies may have had their best chance on the 9th; by the 10th, the French defenses were so advanced that the allies—and here we mean Marlborough and Eugene—decided that they would need all their forces to carry the day and it would take until 11th to get them in place. In addition, Marlborough had diverted men to St. Ghislain to capture a bridge there over the Haine River to secure a retreat route for the allied army if the battle went against them. In the end, too many troops were detailed for this as the force in St. Ghislain was only 200 men. The size of this allied force is variously reported from 2,000 to 9,000.

Villars's men had constructed nine redans, aligned laterally from the Taisnières Forest toward the Lanières Woods, which covered all but 600 meters of the gap between the two forests. The remaining distance, on the right, was covered with three lines of entrenchments. In the woods, the French had dug trenches and constructed abatis to block the allied

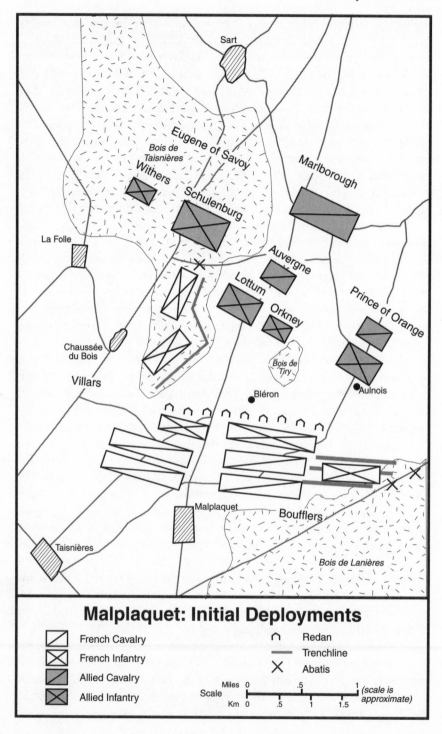

## Malplaquet: Initial Deployments

French Cavalry

French Infantry

Allied Cavalry

Allied Infantry

Redan

Trenchline

Abatis

Miles  0                    .5                    1
Scale                                                      (scale is
Km  0        .5        1        1.5              approximate)

infantry. Further entrenchments were dug behind Malplaquet as well. There is always more that a defender would like to do and the French dug all night, but time was up. With the coming dawn, it was time to fight the battle.

The allies were, in fact, up long before dawn; they were under arms and on the move by 4:00 A.M. The allied plan was Marlboroughian in design. The allies would attack both flanks and when Villars stripped his center to support his wings, the weakened center would be attacked and penetrated. If either of the flank attacks succeeded, however, they could roll up the French line and possibly inflict a devastating defeat. The Prince of Orange commanded the troops on the left of the allied line, with Goslinga as his second in command. The Dutch troops numbered 31 battalions of infantry, the Scottish Brigade which was part of the Dutch force, and the cavalry of the Prince of Hesse-Cassel with 10,000 horses. The left was about one-third of the allied strength. On the right was more than one-third of the army. Three forces would contest the woods: General von der Schulenburg's 20,000 Austro-Prussian infantry, Lord Lottum's 10,000 infantry, and General Henry Withers's mixed infantry-cavalry force. The remaining 6,000 infantry were in the center under the Earl of Orkney, George Hamilton, and the bulk of the cavalry as well. Additionally, Marlborough had established a great battery of 40 guns in the center of the line to support the attack upon the redans. The major attack would go in on the right under Eugene. Schulenburg and Lottum would strike into the Taisnières Forest and drive out the French; Withers would circle wide through the same woods and come out beyond the French left at La Folie Farms. They would join up with Schulenburg's and Lottum's men and threaten the French flank. Marlborough commanded the center and left of the allied army.

The French plan was to stay on the defensive, and their dispositions were as follows: the front line was manned by infantry and the second and third lines were manned by the cavalry. Gaps had been left in the redans in the center to allow the cavalry to pass through, if needed, to attack the allies and the gaps were covered by infantry. On the French right, the troops in the Lanière Woods and as far as the point of the line in front of Malplaquet were commanded by General Boufflers. Included here were the Swiss mercenaries and the Navarre Brigade, which was considered the finest unit in the army. In the center were German mercenaries, the Irish Brigades, the Bavarians, the Alsatians, and the Laon Brigade. The Taisnières Forest contained French Marines, regiments from Picardy, Champagne, and many others. Villars commanded these troops in the center and on the left.

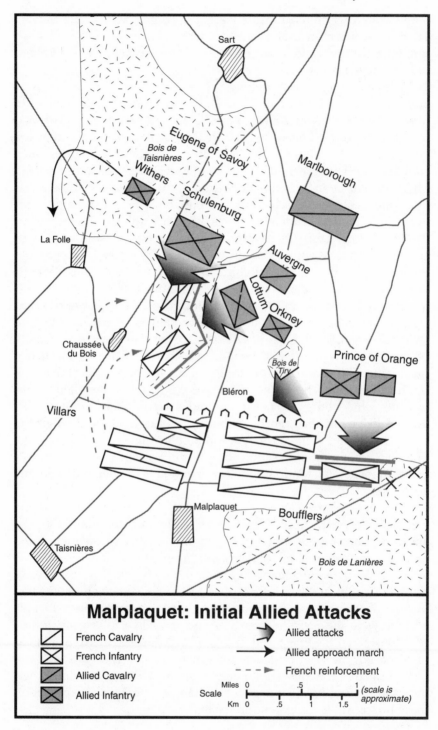

# Malplaquet: Initial Allied Attacks

French Cavalry

French Infantry

Allied Cavalry

Allied Infantry

Allied attacks

Allied approach march

French reinforcement

Scale

Miles 0 .5 1 (scale is approximate)

Km 0 .5 1 1.5

The French, on their right, were arrayed south of the Tiry Wood and the Bléron Farm. Their infantry was in the Lanière Woods on the right and covered the gap from the woods to Bléron and from Bléron to the Taisnières Forest. This is called the Aulnois gap because the village of Aulnois is in this gap level with the Tiry Woods. The Taisnières Forest projects southward here as it narrows down to about 400 meters across and the French infantry, behind its entrenchments, touched the woods at this point. The left of the French line ran from these woods to the village of Chaussée du Bois and 500 meters beyond. Additionally, the French had five brigades of infantry under Albergotti in the Taisnières Forest aligned roughly from north to south on the eastern edge of the forest. From here, they could attack the right flank of any allied force moving past them to attack the center of their line.

At first light, a heavy mist covered much of the battlefield, but this was going to be a nice sunny day for a change. Before long, the sun burned off the mist and the guns opened up around 7:30 A.M. The attack began at 9:00 on the allied right under Eugene and, as planned, Orange would launch his assault 30 minutes later against the Lanière Woods.

Both sides had put a substantial part of their forces in the Taisnières Forest and if Eugene's troops, which outnumbered the defenders, could make good headway, then Villars would have to strip off troops from the center or the right to prevent his army being dislocated. Such was the denseness of the woods and its position far beyond the French center that neither Villars nor Marlborough would have any true idea of what was going on. Once the Dutch attack went in, and provided that it was succeeding, then the French would not be able to move troops from the right to replace those taken from the center.

The allied commanders all went in with the initial attacks, but both allied attacks were stopped at the edge of the woodlines. Schulenburg's second line came up and his men did force back one French brigade, but the rest of the French formations stood firmly. Similarly, Marlborough led a second advance, reinforced with the Duke of Argyle's brigade, but he gained the woods.

The attack on the Allied left went in 30 minutes later. It was led by the young Prince of Orange and Goslinga, and included the Scottish Brigade on their left. At this part of the battlefield, the allies were outnumbered in infantry two to one. Modern military theory holds that the attacker needs a three to one advantage to overcome an enemy in defensive positions, but here is how the attack went: The Scots first and then the Dutch came under severe fire as they advanced. Orange's horse was shot out from under him and most of his staff was shot as well. As many as five generals may have fallen in this advance. Orange moved forward on foot. Unbeknownst to them, the French had concealed 20 cannon in a salient with a clear field of enfilade fire. As the Dutch neared the French entrenchments, the battery opened up. Whole ranks went down, but still the attackers came on. Orange and Goslinga reached the French lines, cleared the obstacles, and captured the works. Unfortunately for them, they were pushed out of the positions by the French reserves and were compelled to retreat.

Orange rallied the Dutch and Scots and led them forward a second time. Again, they gained the enemy's works, but the Navarre Brigade was brought up and pushed the allies out of the position. This time, reorganization was out of the question and the French left their positions to chase them, but their pursuit was cut short by the Prince of Hesse-Cassel who prepared to charge the French.

It was now 11:00 and the allies had been soundly repulsed on their left, taking heavy casualties in the process: some 5,000 men were dead or wounded, including several high ranking officers, and Orange had had his second horse shot out from under him. The Dutch had also lost many of their colors and the guns which had accompanied the advance. Their attack on the Bléron Farm, moreover, had also been repulsed.

On the other side of the battlefield, the allies had pushed a good way into the Taisnières Forest, but the fighting had been fierce and the going slow due to the obstacles and the denseness of the trees. Marlborough was called from Lottum's forces and asked to come to the Dutch. Marlborough could not have anticipated the sight he saw: this part of the battlefield was strewn for over a mile with dead and dying. He ordered a halt to offensive operations here and changed his plan; he would now attack in the center. Villars had helped Marlborough in this regard because he had been steadily pulling troops from the center to reinforce his positions in the Taisnières Forest, especially when Withers's progress became known. Villars had initially called for men from Boufflers, but that call came when the fighting with the Dutch was at its height and the marshal did not think he could spare any men for his commander. By noon, there were few men left manning the redans in the center of the French line. In this fighting, Eugene was wounded when a bullet grazed him behind the ear, but he refused to leave the field. Finally, the superior manpower of the allies was beginning to tell in the Taisnières Forest as Eugene's men fought countless individual battles amongst the trees, abattis, and trenches. Meanwhile, Marlborough ordered Lord Orkney to advance to the redans with as many Dutch as could be had.

It was now 1:00 P.M., and the French were being driven out of the Taisnières Forest. Villars then drew up what forces he could to attack the

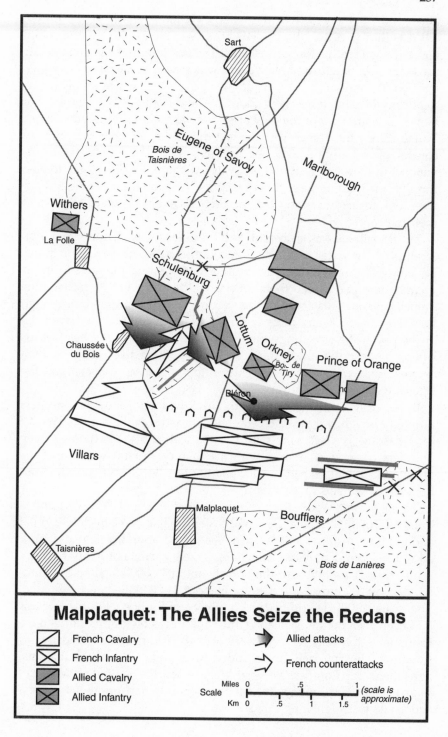

# Malplaquet: The Allies Seize the Redans

Sart

Eugene of Savoy

Bois de
Taisnières

Marlborough

Withers

La Folle

Schulenburg

Chaussée
du Bois

Lottum

Orkney

Bois de
Tiry

Prince of Orange

Bléron

Villars

Malplaquet

Boufflers

Taisnières

Bois de Lanières

| | French Cavalry | | Allied attacks |
| --- | --- | --- | --- |
| | French Infantry | | French counterattacks |
| | Allied Cavalry | | |
| | Allied Infantry | | |

Miles 0 .5 1 *(scale is*
Scale *approximate)*
Km 0 .5 1 1.5

allies as they emerged from the woods. He led a charge to disrupt the allies as they tried to form up. His horse was shot out from under him and as he gained his feet a musket ball struck him in the leg just below the knee. Villars refused to leave and was placed in a chair from which he tried to continue, but he eventually lost consciousness and was carried from the field. It was now about 1:30 and Boufflers had learned that he was in command of the only army between Marlborough and Paris. Worse yet for the French was the fact that Orkney's men were now in control of the all-but-abandoned redans. With these defenses in his hands, Marlborough sent up his cavalry, perhaps 30,000 in total, to pass through the gaps in the earthworks and reform on the other side. Boufflers took to his horse and led the French cavalry forward to prevent their reforming.

The first attack was successful and the allies fell back upon their own infantry in the redans, but the French attack went no farther as it was broken up by musket fire. Marlborough brought up the guns from his great battery and placed them on either side of the line to enfilade the French cavalry. This broke up the second French charge. Marlborough then led a fresh cavalry force against the French and he may have been at the point of succeeding when Boufflers charged at the head of his troops against the allied flank and drove them back. Eugene then arrived with yet more cavalry, the Imperial horse, and charged the French who had to withdraw.

It was now 3:00 P.M., and both sides had had enough. Boufflers ordered his right wing, which was still in control of the Lanière Woods, to withdraw. The left wing withdrew as well and the battle was over. Boufflers covered his retreat with his cavalry. Pursuit was out of the question as the allies had lost too many men. Boufflers had pulled out his army intact and saved France.

The bloodiest Wednesday of the century was now recorded and it must be remembered that the huge casualties had come in close combat and not the a result of a rout. The allies stayed upon the field and tended to the wounded, rested and reorganized; it was not ready to move until Friday. Casualties for the French: about 12,000 killed and wounded, only 500 captured. For the allies: about 24,000 killed and wounded. The casualty figures stunned the populace of Europe. Nothing like this had been seen before. Winston Churchill, in his biography of his illustrious ancestor, tells us that Marlborough was much affected by the slaughter. He sent back the wounded Irish, and called, without formal agreement, for Boufflers to send wagons for the wounded. Marlborough even used the money from his war chest to pay for relief. For these actions he was highly regarded.

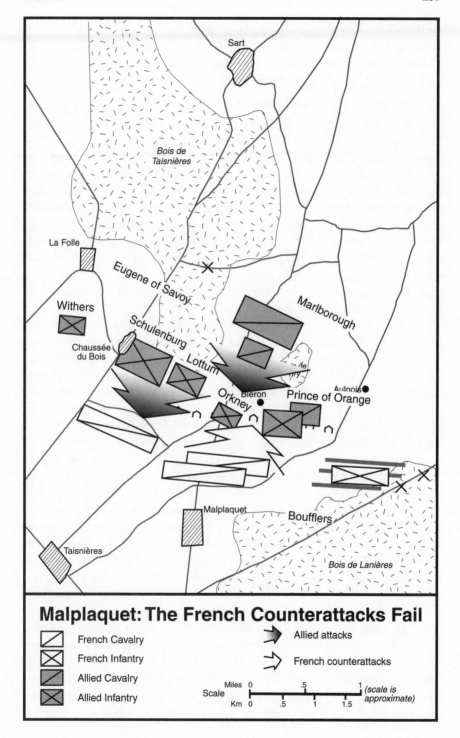

## Malplaquet: The French Counterattacks Fail

| | |
|---|---|
| ▨ French Cavalry | French Cavalry |
| ⊠ French Infantry | French Infantry |
| ▨ Allied Cavalry | Allied Cavalry |
| ⊠ Allied Infantry | Allied Infantry |

➤ Allied attacks

⇨ French counterattacks

Scale
Miles 0 — .5 — 1 *(scale is approximate)*
Km 0 — .5 — 1 — 1.5

# France's Most Unlikely Dragoon and the Last Battle of the War of the Spanish Succession:
## Denain, 24 July 1712

### *"Walk like a man, talk like a man . . ."*

The siege of Lille in 1708 was full of incidents. The *"affaire des poudres"* is referred to elsewhere, but what concerns us here is the story of Madeleine Caulier. John Lynn tells us that Madeleine worked at an inn near Lille and she was given leave by the familially-inclined allies to cross the lines so that she could visit her besieged brother in the garrison. In due time, the French realized that messages could be smuggled out by Madeleine and she obliged them. As payment for her services, she asked only that she be allowed to enlist in a dragoon regiment and serve as a man. This was granted her and she served France well, we are told.

This brings us, four years later, to Denain, the last major battle of the War of the Spanish Succession.

Eugene of Savoy started the summer of 1712 determined to take the offensive against the French forts in Flanders. In early July, he forced the surrender of Labadie and then moved on to Landrecies. Eugene's situation was weakened by two factors. First, the British departed. Second, Eugene's supply line was vulnerable. Marshal Villars determined that his army, superior in numbers, would exploit the situation. In a nice bit of misdirection, Villars demonstrated against Landrecies from 20 July until the night of 23 July, which convinced the enemy that the attack was coming there. Then Villars marched his army off in the night, crossed the River Scheldt over a pontoon bridge and arrived in front of Denain, some 26 miles away. The Dutchman, Arnold van Keppel, the Earl of Albermarle, was in command of the forces here but he was outnumbered 24,000 to 10,000. Eugene, realizing what had happened, was on the way with help but he would not arrive in time. By eight in the morning, Villars was across the river, and by lunch, the French and Spanish were at Denain. Villars had stolen a march, cut the allied supply lines, and a victory here would undo Eugene's position in Flanders.

The Dutch were entrenched next to the fortress of Denain. The French attacked early in the afternoon. The French did not, seemingly, at this point, overly concern themselves with battlefield maneuver, but there may not have been much room for it anyway. As they advanced in their lines, they took losses from Dutch artillery and then musketry but they kept coming on and reached the ditches. Once there, they forced Albermarle's men out of their positions and drove them toward the Scheldt.

The French took 2,100 casualties while inflicting 2,300 killed and wounded on the Dutch and capturing 4,100 men and 12 artillery pieces. French dead totalled just over 500 men and one woman.

Most of the belligerents agreed that it was time for peace and on 11 April 1713 they signed the Treaty of Utrecht. It has been estimated that this war cost the French and allies half a million casualties each. Civilian casualties are unknown. Interestingly, Louis XIV's wars cost him 222 generals killed, and of that total, 92 died in the War of the Spanish Succession.

## Most Embarrassing Debut for a Commander:
Frederick the Great at the Battle of Mollwitz, 10 April 1741

Upon the death of Emperor Charles VI in 1740, Maria Theresa, 23, inherited the Habsburg empire. Also newly enthroned was Frederick II of Prussia, 28, not yet "the Great." He instituted certain liberal reforms upon his ascent, but Frederick realized what his more philosophically inclined well-wishers did not, and it was this: the world is populated with carnivores. He was not alone in thinking that this would be a good time to grab some Austrian land. The French, Bavarians, Saxons and Piedmontese were all considering it, but Frederick was the first to act.

Frederick had done his calculations well. The larger Habsburg army was spread out and had commitments elsewhere, so all he had to do was get in, grab up as much of Silesia as he could, and hang on to it. At this time, Silesia was anchored on the east by the Oder River and it ran from about 50 degrees north latitude to about 40 miles south of Frankfurt an der Oder. It was about 50 miles across at its narrowest point nd over 100 at its widest. After World War II, the Allies gave it to the Poles in compensation for the land stolen by the USSR in eastern Poland (and retained by them after 1945) in 1939.

The invasion began on 16 December 1740 when Frederick led an army of 27,000 into Silesia. By February 1741, he had occupied the Habsburg province save for a few strongpoints. In March, he led his army out of winter quarters with the idea of capturing Neisse, but he was forced to change his plan when the Austrian army made a surprise move toward Ohlau, thereby threatening his supplies. Field Marshal Neipperg had arrived with 18,100 men of the Imperial Army and a less-than-stellar military reputation. Nevertheless, the Austrians were camped at Mollwitz and Frederick moved to the attack.

The Battle of Mollwitz
© *Bettmann/CORBIS/MAGMA*

On 10 April, on a snow-covered field, the Prussians, 22,000 strong, arrived and began to form up in two lines, with infantry in the middle, cavalry on the wings and 60 cannon in front. While they were forming up, the Austrian cavalry attacked the Prussian cavalry on the right. Frederick's cavalry could not hold up against the assaults. Duffy, citing Meyer, tells us that their commander, von der Schulenburg fought extremely bravely in this action. His horse was shot out from under him; a sword cut to his face left one eye hanging half-way down his cheek which he treated merely by putting a handkerchief to his face; and as he was swinging back into the saddle, he was shot through the head and killed. Things were not going well at this point and Marshal von Schwerin urged the king to leave the field to avoid risking capture. Frederick spurred his horse and rode for 30 miles.

Meanwhile, the superior training of the Prussians began to impose itself on the battle. After withstanding cavalry attacks with their musketry, the Prussian infantry advanced across the field and engaged their Austrian counterparts, who were mostly untrained. The Austrians suffered severe casualties and they cowered behind each other to avoid being shot. Neipperg retired his army in fairly good order, we are told, with the oncoming darkness. Prussian losses were about 4,800 or 22 percent and the Austrian losses just over 4,500 or 25 percent. De Catt tells us that Frederick later said, "I could not allow myself to be taken. What a humiliation for the first step I had taken on the path to glory."

# Biggest, Most Important Battle of the Nineteenth Century—Well, in Europe, Anyway: Leipzig, 1813

When one takes into account that the other name of this battle is the Battle of the Six Nations, then one can see why it was the biggest of the nineteenth century. Bigger than Gettysburg? That was only one nation. Bigger than Waterloo? That one got all the press, but not as big. Bigger than Borodino? In spite of the music, yes, bigger than Borodino.

## The Background

After the Big Defeat in Russia in 1812, Napoleon headed for Paris. The *Grande Armée* was down to about 93,000 from 655,000. The main army was at 25,000, down from 450,000. Napoleon had lost 370,000 who had been killed or died from disease and exposure. A further 200,000 had been taken prisoner, including 48 generals and 3,000 officers. On top of all that, 200,000 horses were lost and 929 guns captured. Napoleon needed to raise a new army, and fast. This was something new, by the way. The Revolution and conscription made it possible to raise armies at the drop of a shako. They were inexperienced armies, of course, but still armies. In January 1813, the Prussian contingent under Yorck von Wartenburg left the French alliance and this signalled a general uprising in Prussia. Yorck led his troops to join the Russians and Schwarzenberg decided to make a left at Warsaw and take his Austrian army to Bohemia. Hence, scratch another army from the French alliance. Speaking of alliances, the Russians, Prussians, Swedes, and British formed a new coalition aimed at ending Napoleonic domination of Europe. What would the Austrians do?

By the end of April 1813, Napoleon was back in Germany with an army of about 200,000, heading for Leipzig. He had the idea that he might be able to get the enemy before they could get him. This led to the battle of Lützen on 2 May. Marshal Ney's corps was surprised by Wittengstein's army as it approached Leipzig. Napoleon, who always told his commanders to march to the sound of the guns, heard the cannon and came a-running. He took command of the situation and defeated the enemy armies by pounding them in the center with artillery. The allied forces were split and they withdrew. At this point, this Lützen might have become another famous Napoleonic battle of encirclement and destruction except for one thing: there was no effective pursuit or turning movement. This army did not have the necessary cavalry for such a mission. Casualties were about 18,000 for each side.

Napoleon moved forward when he could and took Dresden five days later. He split his army at this point and gave Ney 100,000 men and told him to outflank the enemy position. Ney swung wide, 50 miles north of Dresden while Napoleon, with 115,000 men, attacked the Russians across the Spree River. He drove them back and waited for Ney to come down from the north and attack the enemy's flank and rear. Was a great victory was in the offing?

The Battle of Bautzen, 21–22 May, was ready for prime-time status, right up to the point that Ney blew it. He attacked late and not far enough east to threaten the enemy's line of communications. Instead of maneuvering onto the enemy's right flank and rear, Ney involved two corps in frontal attacks against prepared defenses. Wittengstein beat a hasty retreat, avoided the trap, and each side settled for another 20,000 casualties. F. N. Maude does provide some mitigation for Ney's tardiness through an examination of the orders sent to him, but he does not clear Ney for what happened once he reached the battlefield.

By the beginning of June, the allies were gaining strength. The man who had been Marshal Bernadotte of France and now was the Crown Prince of Sweden arrived leading an army of Prussians and Swedes against Berlin. Blücher was getting his army in shape and Schwarzenberg was loitering with intent in Bohemia with an army of 240,000.

If Napoleon had not been on his game before, he may have thought it was coming back to him with Lützen and Bautzen; nevertheless, he now committed what some say was one of the greatest mistakes of his career. He asked the allies for an armistice on 4 June and they said, "Thank you, Mr. Emperor. Is there anything else you can do for us?"

Was it a mistake? Napoleon later said it was. Is it unreasonable to disagree with Napoleon when he says he made a mistake? That depends. It is understandable that some people would read what Napoleon said and then go with it. It is, however, suspect, in the mind of the author, to wholeheartedly agree with Napoleon *post facto*. At the time he made the decision, he said that a lack of cavalry prevented him from securing strategic victories, and Austria was inclining more and more towards hostilities with France.

Let us examine his situation. The battles of Lützen and Bautzen had showed that the French lack of cavalry was seriously impairing their ability to secure strategic victories. Besides the importance of cavalry for reconnaissance, it was essential for pursuit. The French infantry, even when led by Napoleon, could not pursue fast enough far enough to cut off the enemy retreat. This was especially so given the allied predominance in horsemen and the allied reluctance to face Napoleon. The emperor needed time to raise more cavalry, train more troops, and fill up the ranks. F. N. Maude points out that as of the first week of June, the French had 90,000 men—sick men. Also, everything was not going France's way at the time; if it had been, then it is unlikely that there would have been an armistice. The Cossacks had captured a French artillery convoy and the French troops in Leipzig were in the process of being pushed out when the news of the already completed armistice arrived. The French were also running low on ordnance.

There was another reason for the armistice and it falls in the realm of grand strategy, as we speak of it today. Maude points out that strategy serves national policy, and in this instance, it all revolved around the question of Austria. Napoleon was not fooled into believing that the Austrians would not come in against him at some point, but he was trying to delay that event for as long as he could. Remember, at this time, Austria was not at war with France. Her army in Bohemia, moreover, was a potential threat to the long, unguarded, French line of communications. To guard the line would use up even more troops and Napoleon did not have enough at the time to surround the allied forces. If Austria could stay out long enough for Napoleon to rebuild his army, accumulate more cavalry, and score a decisive victory over the allies, then Austria could be dealt with later or perhaps cowed altogether. What Napoleon did not know at the time was that the allies were in worse shape than he thought they were and that they had decided to stand and fight, regardless of the consequences. Thus, Napoleon may have been on the verge of securing a battle which could have proved decisive. Instead, he gave the allies breathing room. So both sides benefitted from the armistice and perhaps the allies gained more. Was it a mistake then? In the author's view, no. Napoleon decided what was best for his army at the time with the information he had at the time. There was no guarantee that another battle with the allies would end in a decisive victory, but he did know that if he improved the condition of his army, he would have another opportunity to inflict a wholesale defeat on the allies.

Napoleon used the period to train his troops. Austria came into the allied fold. On 12 August, they declared war on France and that kind of brought an end to the armistice. Besides Schwarzenberg's 230,000, the allies had Blücher with 195,000, Bernadotte with 110,000, a few British soldiers, and thousands of British pounds sterling. Napoleon had about 300,000 men as well as Davout's corps in Hamburg, St. Cyr's corps in Dresden, and Rapp's corps besieged in Danzig.

Realizing that if they avoided Napoleon, they would not get into trouble, the allies decided that they would fight his subordinates where they could, but they would studiously advance in another direction when Napoleon moved toward them. This led to the Leipzig Campaign.

The Allies spent two months marching about Germany, avoiding Napoleon, but chasing his subordinates when feasible. Schwarzenberg, for example, attacked St. Cyr in Dresden on 26 August and Napoleon showed up in time to save the day. The next day, Napoleon turned the enemy's flank and inflicted 38,000 casualties on them, taking 10,000. Again an encirclement was avoided when Schwarzenberg rapidly withdrew. Napoleon had been called elsewhere and only Vandamme had the wherewithal to move his corps across the mountains and cut Schwarzenberg's line of communications. This was a Napoleonic maneuver and the possibility of encirclement and destruction loomed; only Vandamme, alone of Napoleon's commanders, however, had recognized the opportunity and attempted to capitalize on it.

On 29 and 30 August, he and his 30,000 men fought the battle of Kulm against the 100,000 men of the Austrians, Russians, and Prussians, and was wiped out. Vandamme was captured. On 6 September, Ney lost his Saxon divisions and the battle of Dennewitz to Bernadotte. In early October, the Bavarians joined the coalition against Napoleon. The allies began to move in on the French around Leipzig. The stage was being set for the battle of Leipzig.

A little about the geography of the place may prove helpful. Leipzig's population was about 30,000 in 1813; the city's defenses are described as antiquated and unlikely to hold up to attack by a modern army. Four rivers pass through or around Leipzig and merge—the Elster and the Pleisse from south to north, the Parthe to the northeast, and the Luppe to the northwest. In addition, there are other rivers and streams in the area. To the west of Leipzig are substantial marshes, so the only way out of Leipzig in that direction was along the causeway to Lindenau, and over a single bridge two miles hence.

On Friday, 15 October, Napoleon performed a personal reconnaissance around Leipzig and made his dispositions. Blücher, dogged as ever, was approaching Leipzig from the north with his Prussians. To the south was Schwarzenberg with the Army of Bohemia. Napoleon still had a chance to defeat the Austrians and Russians in the Army of Bohemia before Blücher came down from the north. In this, the French were aided by Bernadotte. Bernadotte, formerly of the French army and now created Crown Prince of Sweden, led an army of 65,000 Swedes and Russians. It was a rule, apparently, that the commander of the Army of the North had to have lead feet and eat chicken every day. Were it not for Blücher's aggressiveness, Bernadotte would have legged it for home by now. The author is not kidding—well, maybe just the chicken thing. Napoleon's plan was to hold Schwarzenberg's army on the west-to-east line between Connewitz and Liebertwolkwitz, then swing on Liebertwolkwitz to roll up the right side of the enemy line. The breakthrough would be effected by massed artillery bombardment followed by a cavalry assault. Was another strategic victory in the offing? Once the Austrians and Russians were driven off, then Napoleon could deal with Blücher. Interestingly, Napoleon did not expect much from Blücher on 16 October and his underestimation of the Prussian bulldog was to upset his plan. Blücher's nickname was "Alt vorwärts," or "Old Forward," and throughout his career, he demonstrated that it was apt. More than one historian has commented on Napoleon's continual underestimation of Blücher and why the Emperor would so view the fightingest man in the allied camp is a mystery.

The allied plan was as follows. Blücher, leading the Prussian Army of Silesia, would come at Leipzig from the northwest with his 54,000 men. Three other allied forces would also move on Leipzig. From the south, between the Elster and Pleisse Rivers, the Count von Meerveldt would move as best he could with 28,000 men. The bulk of the allied army, the Army of Bohemia, totalled about 203,000 men and was led by Prince Karl von Schwarzenberg. It would attack from the southeast and east.

This plan essentially broke the allied attacks into three separate and most likely uncoordinated attacks. It did not sit well with the Russian Staff and they went to Schwarzenberg and told him. He did not see it that way and he declined to modify it. The Russian Staff—which included the Swiss Jomini, who was formerly Ney's chief of staff, and Barclay de Tolly, a Livonian of Scottish descent who had made a name for himself fighting the Turks for the Russians—had a real advantage when it came to going over their commander's head. Tsar Alexander was with the army. They went to him and explained their concerns. Alexander called in Schwarzenberg and passed them on, but Schwarzenberg remained unmoved. Alexander then informed the commander, who had been picked by the various monarchs, that he was inclined to change the disposition of all the Russian troops. That settled matters. Of course, the subordinate commanders would have to redeploy and that would take some time. It has been said of Schwarzenberg that he was the only man who could have held this command. He had to deal with three monarchs who had accompanied their armies and outranked him, a mere prince. He had to lead a large coalition army and take on the greatest military genius since Alexander. He recognized, in contradistinction to Napoleon, that he would be controlled by events and in the end, it would be up to God how things ended.

Napoleon had a force of 177,500 men, nearly 700 guns, and the advantage of operating on interior lines. French engineers had destroyed many of the bridges in the area, impeding the movement of the allies, whereas the *maestro* could gain local superiority over whatever part of the allied armies he could reach. In theory.

## The Battle

The main action of the first day of the battle occurred southeast of Leipzig. As 16 October dawned, the battlefield was covered in a heavy mist left by the rain. There had been a lot of rain over the last few days. Barclay de Tolly entrusted the offensive of the right wing of the Army of Bohemia to Wittgenstein. The battle started early, as Wittgenstein attacked at 7 A.M. No one was ready—on either side. As events were to show, that was not necessarily a bad thing for the allies. The first attacks on the French left were repulsed, but the attackers maintained their positions as best they could and became rally points for the units still marching up to the front lines.

The allied attack in the center and left of their lines came from four separate columns. The center of the allied line was focused on Wachau. Two miles west from Wachau was the Pleisse River and the village of Markkleeberg and beyond there Meerveldt's column This was end of the line, moving as best it could through the marshes between the Pleisse and Elster Rivers. To the right of Meerveldt and east of the Pleisse was the corps column of General Kleist advancing against the French VIII Corps under Poniatowski at Markkleeberg itself. Next to Kleist was Prince Eugen of Württemberg. His column was moving on Wachau, which was defended by the French II Corps under Victor. The fourth column was commanded by Gortchakoff and was to the right of Eugen. It was headed for Liebertwolkwitz, east of Wachau.

The battle at Wachau started at 8:30 A.M. with a large bombardment. The Austrian troops were still moving up at 11:00, even though they had started attacking with little success at around 9:00. The other attacks failed to produce results; that is to say, results favorable to the allies. By 9:30, a gap—which Chandler tells us was large—opened up between Eugen and Gortchakoff. The French could not counterattack, however, as the troops needed for this—Sébastiani's cavalry and Marshal Macdonald's XI Corps—had yet to arrive in the sector. The weather was complicating everyone's movements.

By 11:00 A.M., the allies attacked Markkleeberg, but no ground could be gained against French artillery fire. The fighting around Wachau was fierce, but Eugen could not gain an advantage over Victor and hold the village. Meanwhile, Meersveldt's men had pushed, one author says splashed, as far as Connewitz near the Pleisse, nearly two miles *behind* Markkleeberg. They were stopped there, however, and could not cross the river. Gortschakoff's troops were stopped by the artillery of

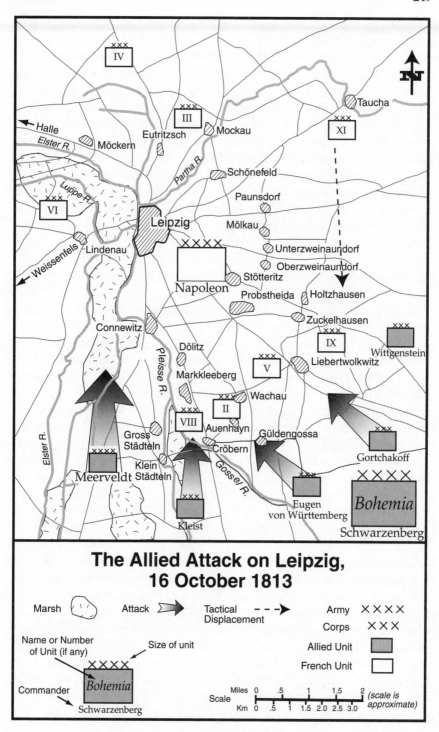

# The Allied Attack on Leipzig, 16 October 1813

Marsh        Attack        Tactical     - - -▶       Army    ✕ ✕ ✕ ✕
                                         Displacement        Corps    ✕ ✕ ✕

Name or Number
of Unit (if any)          Size of unit          Allied Unit

                          ✕ ✕ ✕ ✕          French Unit

Commander        *Bohemia*

          Schwarzenberg

                             Miles   0     .5      1     1.5     2   *(scale is*
                    Scale                                         *approximate)*
                             Km    0    .5    1   1.5   2.0   2.5   3.0

Lauriston's V Corps at Liebertwolkwitz. Macdonald's XI Corps had finally reached their start line. Napoleon's plan was to effect a break-through in the center from Wachau and drive to Güldengossa. While this was being done, Macdonald's XI and Souham's III Corps, whose arrival was still pending, would outflank the allied right and collapse the enemy wing onto the center. Now, where was Souham? As the French pondered that, the allies tried to restore the impetus to their attack. Tsar Alexander and his staff made the following decisions: the Russian reserve would be moved up; the Russian Guards would be brought up to Güldengossa; the Austrians would be urged to bring up their reserve; and everybody else who was on the way to Leipzig would be told to get there with all possible speed. Napoleon also brought up the Young Guard and Old Guard and Drouot massed 150 guns between Wachau and Liebertwolkwitz to blast an opening.

At noon, Macdonald began his attack *sans* Souham. He made pro-gress to Kolm Berg, which had been occupied by Klenau, and pushed him off.

By 2:00 P.M., Souham still had not shown up and Napoleon would wait no longer. The French attack in the center was led by Murat's cav-alry, 12,000 in number, with infantry waiting to exploit their success. It started well. Drouot's guns pounded the positions of Kleist and Eugen and Murat carried all before him. Macdonald's XI Corps was driving for Seiffertshayn; Victor's II Corps and Oudinot's Guards were attack-ing toward Auenhayn and Cröbern; and Lauriston's V Corps was head-ed for Güldengossa. Murat's horsemen made it almost to Cröbern, but their horses were blown. At this point, they were attacked by Austrian cavalry and chased back to the French lines. Here the enemy horse came under fire from Drouot's guns and were repulsed with heavy casualties. It was only 2:30 P.M. Napoleon heard the thunder of cannons from the direction of Möckern to the northwest and as things seemed to going well enough here, he galloped off.

A few minutes later, the unexpected came upon the battlefield in the form of General Doumerc, the commander of the 1st French Cavalry Corps, and settled things for the day. Napoleon was not the only man who could hear opportunity knocking. On this occasion, it was the hammering of a Russian battery. The guns were inflicting severe casu-alties on the the advancing French infantry columns and Doumerc chose to do something about it. He ordered General Bordesoulle to take his division of 18 squadrons of *cuirassiers*—about 2,500 men—and charge Eugen's flank. The *cuirassiers* cut their way through two battal-ions of infantry, which broke under the assault. They captured 26 guns and kept on going. They rode on to the rear of the allied lines and had

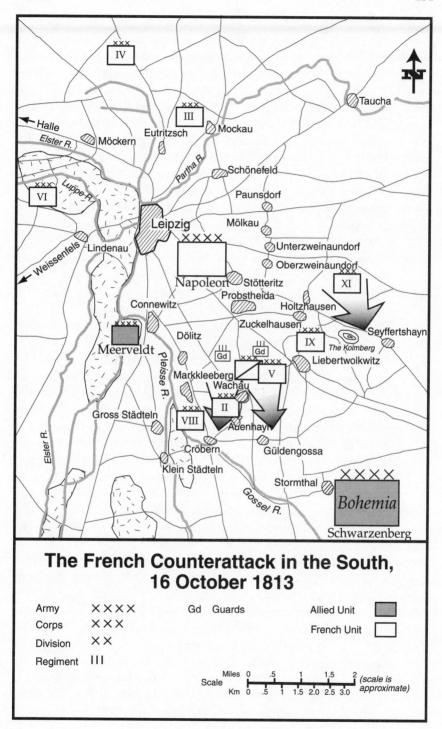

# The French Counterattack in the South, 16 October 1813

| | | | |
|---|---|---|---|
| Army | ×××× | Gd Guards | Allied Unit |
| Corps | ××× | | French Unit |
| Division | ×× | | |
| Regiment | ||| | | |

Scale  Miles 0  .5  1  1.5  2  *(scale is*
Km 0  .5  1  1.5  2.0  2.5  3.0  *approximate)*

almost reached the Tsar's command post when the counterattack came. It was 3:30. With blown horses, the French could do little, and as more and more enemy cavalry from both sides showed up to join the mêlee, the disorder in the formations spread. By 4:00, the French had pushed the line a mile or more forward. This was not to last, however, as Austrian reserves on the left began to make their weight felt. Meerveldt managed to get troops into Dölitz, a village midway between Markkleeberg and Connewitz on the Pleisse. Markkleeberg was also entered by the Austrians. It now appeared that the French right was in trouble, and it was. The Old Guard now made its presence felt and bucked up the line. At this moment, guess who else showed up? Some of Souham's III Corps. General Richard came up and helped push the Austrians back on Markkleeberg. To round things out, Meerveldt was captured and his force pushed back across the Pleisse.

More than one historian has wondered what would have happened if Napoleon had been around to reinforce Bordesoulle's charge. We all figure he would have won the day. So, the question is, "why did he go to Möckern?" And, "where is Möckern?"

Möckern is just over two miles northwest of Leipzig. Here the other great action of the day was fought, although Napoleon did not think it would be. The campfires of Bernadotte's army at Mersburg, west of Leipzig, convinced Napoleon, late on 15 October, that this army would come by the Weissenfels Road southwest of Leipzig, and not the Halle Road northwest of Leipzig. Napoleon did not expect Blücher to be in action on 16 October; the allied plan, as revised by the Tsar, did. Gyulai's corps of 19,000 would march from Markranstädt and attack Lindenau. Blücher would march via the Halle Road and attack at Möckern.

In Napoleon's assumption is found the reasons for the wandering of Souham's III Corps. Initially, Napoleon had placed Marmont's VI Corps northwest of Leipzig between Lindenthal and the Halle Road. As he did not expect much action there on 16 October, he moved the corps southwest of Leipzig. From this position, it could march to defend Lindenau in that unlikely event or—and what Napoleon though was more likely—join Macdonald's and Sebastiani's forces in outflanking the right wing of the Army of Bohemia. Marmont was in a difficult situation, he could see the Prussian campfires, but he had orders to move and at 10:00 A.M., he did. Blücher was also moving at 10:00 and, as the reader will expect, he was heading for the French lines. Marshal Ney was in command of this sector and he realized that Marmont could not just march off, so he ordered Marmont to take up positions near Möckern. Ney then ordered Bertrand to take IV Corps, which was about three miles directly north of Leipzig, to assume the original VI Corps mission.

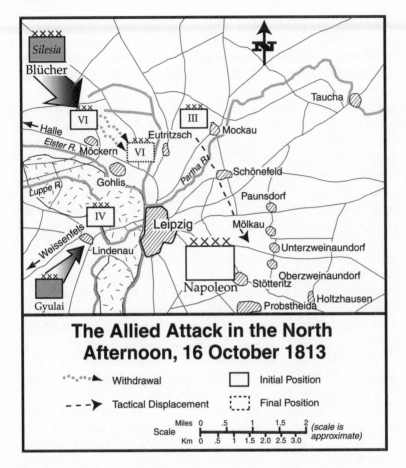

## The Allied Attack in the North
## Afternoon, 16 October 1813

| | |
|---|---|
| ◂···▸▲ Withdrawal | ☐ Initial Position |
| – – –▸ Tactical Displacement | ⌐ ¬ Final Position |

Scale

Miles 0 .5 1 1.5 2 *(scale is*
Km 0 .5 1 1.5 2.0 2.5 3.0 *approximate)*

Bertrand's men duly set out, but as they did, Gyulai's attack along
the causeway at Lindenau began to show results. Frantic calls for support at Lindenau were sent by Arrighi, the French commander on the
scene. Ney decided to divert Bertrand's Corps to Lindenau. David
Chandler points out that this was probably unnecessary as the allied
attack had been contained, but it was done. Now Ney still had a problem: Napoleon was expecting a corps from up north to show up down
south. Ney sent Souham's III Corps, northeast of Leipzig down south.
Well, not all of it actually, just the two divisions on hand. A third division, under Delmas, was escorting a column of vehicles. Nevertheless,
off they went. How far would they get?

By all accounts, the fighting at Möckern was the most severe of the
day. The Prussian attack was led by Yorck and they were up against the
best soldiers in the French army, under Marmont, and Dombrowski's

battle-hardened Polish division. It was 2:00 P.M. Two attacks were made and repulsed by the French. The Poles on Marmont's right, however, were pushed back, grudgingly. Ney decided to recall Souham, and back he went. Some time later, Ney decided that he did not need Souham after all, and sent him south again. This march and countermarch was, as Napoleon said, the great calamity of the day. Langeron, who was fighting against the Poles, was about to advance on the retreating troops when Delmas and his division of 5,000 men came into view. This apparition spooked Langeron and he believed a larger force than it was was about to descend on his flank. Accordingly, he pulled back. This gave Delmas the time he needed to get over the Partha River although many vehicles were abandoned. By 5:00 P.M., Marmont was poised to defeat the Prussians. Chandler tells us that their leading division had been routed and it needed only the cavalry to charge and make it complete. Marmont called on the Württemberg cavalry to attack, but they declined. What? "We don't feel like it. You know there are Germans over there and we've got issues with that." (In fact, the Württembergers literally changed sides on 18 October.) Marmont sent infantry forward alone to try and win the day and came close, but Yorck threw in all the cavalry he had. In the end, it was the French who fell back. The Prussians occupied Möckern. Marmont managed to restore some order to his troops on line between the villages of Gohlis and Eutritzsch. Darkness gave the exhausted troops an opportunity to rest.

The casualties were heavy. Marmont lost about 10,000, Yorck about 7,100, and Langeron about 1,500. Yorck's losses represented over one-third of his strength. Overall, the French lost 25,000 on the day and the allies 30,000. Thus ended the first day of the battle of Leipzig, yet things were shifting in favor of the allies. They had more reinforcements on the way than did the French. It was altogether possible that Bernadotte would show up with some 65,000 and Benningsen with another Russian corps. In contrast, Napoleon could count only on Reynier's 14,000. This would put the French at about 195,000 and the allies at around 300,000 with over 1,400 guns. Napoleon was aware of this. This was obviously the time to clear out of town. It *could* have started on 17 October, it *should* have started on 17 October, but it *didn't* start on 17 October. Had it started on 17 October, he could have pulled out most of his army from around Leipzig. Instead he obstinately remained in the area. The allies were content to hang around as well; consequently, there was little fighting on this day. Was Napoleon expecting them to make a big mistake? If so, they did not. He did.

A rainy Sunday was spent with both sides making preparations. At some point during the day, Napoleon decided to withdraw and he sent word to Bertrand to be ready to move IV Corps. During the early hours of Monday, 18 October, Napoleon was on the move. At 2:00 A.M., he was in Probstheida, three miles southeast of Leipzig. He then went to see Ney. They discussed things for three hours, then the emperor went to Lindenau and gave orders to throw some more bridges across the Elster, but there would not be enough time to complete them. At this time, there was only one bridge over the Elster. At 8:00 A.M., he was back at his headquarters in the tobacco mill at Stötteritz, about one and one-half miles southeast of Leipzig. Napoleon sent Bertrand his orders to move west. Through the heavy rain, the French lines began to pull back leaving only their outposts.

The allies decided that they would converge on the French from six directions. Gyulai would try to block the way west at Lindenau. Blücher would attack from the north and northwest. Bernadotte, finally realizing that only he believed his argument that the communication lines to Berlin were in danger and he should hang back to protect them, would attack to the left of Blücher. Prince Hessen-Homburg would attack Connewitz, Lösnig, and Dölitz from the south. Barclay would attack from the southeast on Probstheida, and to his right Bennigsen would march on Zuckelhausen.

Things were moving the French way in the morning of 18 October. Bertrand leading IV Corps, which was west of Leipzig, shoved Gyulai's blocking force aside and made for the Saale River to secure crossings for the rest of the army. Poniatowski's Corps repelled the allied attack once it reached Connewitz. Barclay was halted by heavy artillery fire and waited for Bennigson's Corps, which was still on the march, to come up in support. To the north, Bernadotte, who would rather have cut off his feet and been called "Stumpy" than face Napoleon, had still not arrived.

At 2:00 P.M., Poniatowski, Victor, and Lauriston still held their lines against allied attacks. Bennigsen, however, made the best use of his larger forces and pushed Macdonald and Sebastiani from Zuckelhausen, Holtzhausen, and the Zweinaundorfs. When Bernadotte finally showed up at 3:00 P.M., his forces joined Bennigsen and they pushed the French out of Molkau and Paunsdorf. Reynier's Corps, which had come up the day before, was fighting next to Macdonald. The Young and Old Guards arrived on the scene and pushed the enemy out of Paunsdorf, but Ney pulled them out of the village when he shortened his lines. At 4:30 P.M., things started to go the allies' way when two brigades of Saxons and an artillery battery in Reynier's Corps realized that they were on the wrong side and promptly defected. We are told that the French troops cheered them as they marched off, thinking that they were going on the attack. Ney now had to negate the negative impact of the Saxon

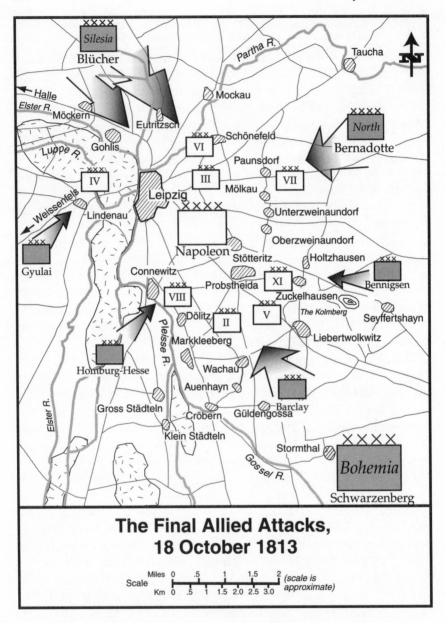

## The Final Allied Attacks,
## 18 October 1813

Scale
Miles 0   .5     1      1.5    2   (scale is
Km  0   .5   1   1.5  2.0  2.5  3.0   approximate)

switch. Just before dark, Bennigson, Bernadotte, and Langeron's Corps
pushed Marmont's VI Corps out of Schönefeld and the rest of the
French line northeast of Leipzig was pulled back to the outskirts of the
city. South and southeast of the city, the French still held their lines two
miles or so from Leipzig. By the end of the day, Ney, Souham, and

Poniatowski had all been wounded. Napoleon made Poniatowski a marshal in recognition of his service. The brave Pole had half a day of life remaining.

That night, Napoleon dictated the orders for the withdrawal. Last out would be VII, VIII, and XI Corps; these troops would constitute the rear guard. Schwarzenberg decided that tomorrow's attack would be more of the same, everybody at it. The only concession to stopping the French withdrawal came courtesy of Blücher who, upon hearing belatedly of Bertrand's success against Gyulai, sent Yorck to get to Mersburg and Halle on the Saale River before the French did. He would have to hurry because Bertrand's men reached Weissenfels, some 35 miles away before the allies started their attacks. At 2:00 A.M. on 19 October, a Tuesday, the French started to pull out of their positions south of Leipzig. The allies did nothing to interfere with the movements. Leipzig that night was jammed with men, matériel, animals, and baggage. The sky glowed red from the flames of the day's battle as the wet and hungry men, whole and wounded, struggled westward to the one bridge over the Elster at Lindenau.

The allied attacks began at 7:00 A.M. and they were as uncoordinated as before. Negotiations to save the city from attack were ultimately unsuccessful, but they did buy the French three more hours.

Leipzig proper came under attack and the rear guard fought determinedly to keep the enemy out. Napoleon crossed the bridge at 11:00 A.M. and fell asleep in the nearby mill.

The lack of new bridges had created a large bottleneck, but things were going according to plan for the French—more or less. One of the subsidiary bridges had already collapsed, but the main one was still standing. The job of blowing the bridge had been given to General Dulauloy who understood that what this task really required was a colonel. He, accordingly, passed the job to Colonel Montfort. The colonel duly put a corporal in charge of the demolitions and the reader can guess what is coming next. There is some dispute as to why Montfort did what he did. Chandler says that the Colonel found the action too hot for his future well-being and thus passed the job on. Fuller states that the Colonel had ridden forward to find out what troops would be the last across before the bridge was blown. Regardless of motive, the corporal panicked about 1:00 P.M., and blew the bridge. Needless to say, it was crowded with troops when it exploded. It also trapped 30,000 men in Leipzig; there was no way across now. Officers and men plunged into the river and tried to swim across. Marshal Macdonald made it; General Oudinot made it; Pontiatowski, weak from his wounds, did not. He had been a marshal for 12 hours. The forces left in

Leipzig surrendered in the late afternoon and among the prisoners were Lauriston and Reynier.

Estimated casualties on the day Fuller tells us was about 25,000 to each side. For the four days of fighting, the allies lost 54,000 killed and wounded, although one source puts their losses at 75,000. The French killed and wounded came to at least 38,000. To this we add 30,000 prisoners taken in Leipzig, plus deserters, plus sick in hospital, and we come out at almost double. What is almost double? If one adds the various numbers available regarding French losses, the number is at least 70,000. Of their best generals, the French lost 6 killed, 12 wounded, and additionally, 36 were captured. In terms of equipment, the allies captured 325 guns, 900 ammunition wagons, and 40,000 muskets. In four days of battle, the French cannons fired over 200,000 rounds.

This was the end of the battle. The French army reached Weissenfels on 20 October. It defeated a Bavarian army of 40,000 under von Wrede in a three-day battle ending on 31 October. The garrison in Dresden surrendered on 11 November and that ended the campaign.

# Ruses

## Worst Way to Deliver Gunpowder:
Siege of Lille, 28 September 1708,
*"L'affaire des poudres"*

Following the battle of Oudenarrde (1708), Marlborough and Eugene moved on to besiege Lille with 100,000 men. The garrison of 16,000 was commanded by Boufflers. The conduct of the siege was the responsibility of Eugene and duly the first parallel was dug and the lines pushed forward. Lille was well defended in the modern method of defense—bastions, ditches, glacis, and the rest. Marlborough's army defended the besiegers. Such was his position and such was his reputation by this time that the French relief force avoided battle. This is not to say that the French had no successes. The Chevalier de Luxembourg and 2,000 horsemen attempted to deliver gunpowder to the garrison by bluffing their way through the enemy lines. How were they to do this? John Lynn supplies the answer. The horsemen were ordered to wear Dutch insignia in their hats and act, well, *allied.* Each carried a sack of about 100 pounds of powder strapped to the back of the horse behind the saddle. They had almost made it through when the alarm was given. Half of the horsemen galloped on and made it into the town, but only about half of them made it in with their precious cargo. The remaining men met a grim fate. Jean Philippe Eugene, Count of Mérode-Westerloo, courtesy of David Chandler's translation (*The Art of Warfare in the Age of Marlborough*, 1976, pp. 261–62), tells us in his *Mémoires* what happened next:

> Our men seized their arms and opened fire; this made several sparks to set fire to some of the enemy's powder-bags; in an instant several hundred of them were hurled into the air amidst a terrifying explosion which shook the earth . . . . [the rest] turned about and made for Douai. As their powder-bags were made of linen and not leather, several sprang leaks, leaving a trail of powder along the road behind them. As they rode, their horseshoes made the sparks fly up, which set fire to the powder trail and this, in turn, ignited the sacks, blowing up a number of men with an infernal din. It was a horrible spectacle to see the remains of men and horses, whose legs, arms, and torsos even had been flung into the trees.

All told the French would lose 14,000 men killed, wounded, and captured in the siege of Lille between 14 August and 11 December.

# Prelude to Cataclysm

## Introduction
## 1816–1913

In the nineteenth century, technology's impact on tactics and industrialization's impact on society remade the way wars were fought. After the Brown Bess, the next advance in small arms was the development of the percussion cap, which ensured that the musket could be fired in all weather. This was followed by the Minié rifle, which allowed a rifled barrel to impart spin to an expandable, pointed bullet. This was the standard infantry weapon well into the second half of the century, and dominated the American Civil War. Despite these improvements, the weapons were still muzzle-loaders, which meant that infantry had to stand to load them. Nevertheless, the slaughter inherent to so many battles between Federal and Confederate troops clearly showed that tactically, the defensive had become the dominant mode of combat.

Despite all of the evidence from places like Fredericksburg and Gettysburg, the major change in infantry tactics took place in the period after the American Civil War when breech-loading rifles only further enhanced the havoc wrought on mass formations on open ground. The first army to have them was the Prussian, and in 1866, the Dreyse-manufactured "needle-gun" shot to pieces the European notion of Napoleonic mass.

The Dreyse had two advantages over other rifles: it could be loaded while lying down and its rate of fire was 6 to 7 rounds per minute, which was 50 to 75 percent faster than the rate of the Minié. These advantages more than compensated for the fact that the Minié could outrange it (1,000 versus 700 yards). The Dreyse was to have its first real test in the Austro-Prussian War of 1866, or Seven Weeks' War.

Tactically, this war was characterized by deep lines of skirmishers who used available cover and concealment, but this is not to say that the column was a thing of the past. In theory, Prussian doctrine still called for infantry companies to attack in column after the initial exchange of fire. In practice, Prussian officers had difficulty keeping the men in columns as they preferred to use cover and join the relative safety of the skirmish line. Cavalry, while still of some use for reconnaissance, was finished as a shock weapon on the European battlefield, although the horse soldier would be around for many more years. Artillery was as deadly in defense as ever, but in the Six Weeks War, it was still too immobile to provide a real offensive punch. This war showed also that tactics were becoming increasingly slanted in favor of the defender. The ability to fire from a protected, prone position against those advancing over open ground is obvious.

If defensive tactics were becoming dominant, however, strategy was becoming more offensively oriented and it was due to the railroad and the telegraph. Again, the potential of these two technologies was demonstrated clearly during the American Civil War, but it appears that only the Germans were really watching. Moltke saw to it that a railroad net was built across the coalescing German Empire that facilitated rapid assembly of his armies on the battlefield despite their origination from diverse initial locations. Thus, just as the recent American experience foreshadowed, the art of war was being transformed into a matter of getting to the best terrain first, then forcing your opponent to attack you there.

In the Franco-Prussian War of 1870–71, the French were armed with the Chassepot as the basic infantry weapon. It was a breech-loader that was effective to about the same range as the Dreyse and had a more effective seal at the breech than its German competitor. Prussian artillery, which had not performed well in the Seven Weeks' War, had converted to Krupp's steel breech-loaders. This war reinforced the tactical lessons of the last war. Attacks by close columns were stopped dead, literally. This happened to the Prussians at St. Privat where the Guards advanced in half-battalion columns covered by a skirmish line up an open gentle slope and sustained 30 percent casualties from French rifle fire. Not long after that, the Prussians resorted to rushing by bounds in loose lines and using cover.

Prussia had fielded an army of almost one million men, and she and France had been able to keep their troops supplied. This was done, by and large, in the old way of living off the land, a task made easier in a rich agricultural country like France. Supplies were moved by rail during the war, but while huge amounts were moved with facility out of

Germany, there was no efficient way to get them from the railhead to the front line in France. Ammunition supply was not a problem, however; small arms expenditure was about 56 rounds per man and that of artillery 200 per gun. The former was easily carried and the latter readily brought forward.

The deciding factor in this war, though, was superior leadership. The Prussian General Staff and Moltke had triumphed over French mediocrity. Where the Prussians had planned and calculated, the French had offered only insufficient improvisation. Larger armies had created a high force-to-space ratio; when combined with rail movement and the electric telegraph, that gave the capable commander the opportunity to use Napoleonic-style turning maneuvers to force battle on a grand scale. This happened to the hapless French at Sedan and Metz.

The casualty consequences of battle continued to evolve. In the Austro-French War of 1859, the victorious French lost only 10 percent of their force and the Austrians 17 percent. In the Franco-Prussian War, the Prussians lost 9.4 percent and the French 16 percent of their troops. Then again, this is somewhat misleading because as the importance and quantity of support and technical troops (signallers, railroad troops, ordnance specialists, and so on) rose, the percentage of soldiers directly exposed to the dangers of the combat fell. Hence, one should be careful about assuming that the battlefield was becoming a less lethal place. If anything, it was becoming more so, at least in comparison to the battlefields of pre-Napoleonic Europe. One need only read the accounts of some of the very first battles in which both sides possessed repeating rifles—in the Spanish-American War or Second Boer War, for example—to sense that defense from prepared positions in the hands of competent commanders had already become *the* overwhelmingly dominant tactical mode. Unfortunately for millions of Europeans, very few statesmen or generals comprehended this.

The progress in weapons design moved rapidly from the mid-nineteenth century to the eve of WWI. In ammunition, for example, all metal cartridges with hardened bullets appeared on the scene. They facilitated loading, burned new powder which ignited nearly simultaneously, left no smoke to reveal one's position and little deposit to foul barrels. By the 1880s, the major powers had armed their infantry with magazine-fed bolt action rifles and Hiram Maxim had invented the machine gun.

Artillery underwent similar refinements. Slow-burning powder, here a relative term, allowed for a constant acceleration of a shell in the barrel. This increased the range and velocity of guns, and at the same time, it diminished the strain on the chamber. The use of steel, which was stronger than iron, allowed higher muzzle velocities and guns could be made of larger calibers. The other great improvement in gun design was the recoilless carriage. This mechanism absorbed the gun's recoil without imparting it to the carriage. As the gun crew did not have to re-aim their piece after every shot, rapid fire was possible. Moreover, a shield could be added on the front of the carriage to protect the crew from small arms fire.

Although sporadic conflicts in southeastern Europe smoldered on, no combat occurred in Europe while all of these technologies progressed. There was no shortage of opportunity to test them out elsewhere, however. During the exact same period that Europeans decided to stop killing one another at home, warfare in their overseas colonies hit an all-time high. The British killed Afghans, Sudanese, Zulus, Burmese, and many others with their Martini-Henry rifles, Gatling guns, and Nordenfeldt machine guns; the French mowed down Tuaregs, Berbers, Annamese, Chinese, and Dahomeans—to name a few—with their *mitrailleuses* and Chassepots; and, in southern Africa; the Germans slaughtered Hottentots and Hereros with Mausers and Maxims. Of the great (or soon-to-be-great) powers, only the Russians and Americans lagged behind, killing their respective inconvenient natives or neighbors with breech-loading muskets well into the 1890s.

These colonial conflicts nevertheless provided valuable experience for the European armies which fought them, and they were by no means all walkovers, in the modern sense. British forces, for example, suffered major defeats at Isandhlwana (South Africa, 1879) and Maiwand (Afghanistan, 1880); even when the European powers won (which was almost all the time), the proportions of losses were nowhere nearly as lopsided as they have been in some late twentieth-century wars. In the Zulu War of 1879, for example, in which, for all purposes, the British forces possessed state-of-the-art firearms while the Zulus used spears and clubs, the total losses were about 8,000 for the Zulus and 1,100 for the British, for a casualty ratio of roughly 7.2 to 1. At the battle of Omdurman (Sudan, 1898), the Dervish losses amounted to 15,000, while the Anglo/Egyptian forces lost about 500, for a 30 to 1 ratio. These ratios, stunning as they are (especially for the losing side), pale beside the ratio of combat losses in the Persian Gulf War of 1991. According to American sources, in the sands of southern Iraq in early 1991, 606 American soldiers were killed or wounded in action, against about 400,000 Iraqis (not counting 160,000 Iraqi soldiers who deserted or surrendered). This is a ratio of about 660 to 1. At the dawn of the twenty-first century, one must be very careful about dismissing the technologically unbalanced wars of the second half of the nineteenth century as simple slaughters, unworthy of careful study or consideration of the valor displayed by soldiers of all sides!

# Equipment

## Longest-Lived Uniform Part Named for Someone (or, Who in the Sam Hill was Sam Browne?):
### The Sam Browne Belt

The eponymous crossbelt was the invention of Sir Samuel Browne. *The Dictionary of National Biography* and *Who Was Who* gives us the following profile of Samuel Browne. Browne was born in India in 1824 and educated in England. Upon his return to India in 1840, he was commissioned as an ensign in the 46th Bengal Native Infantry Regiment. He participated in the Second Sikh War (1848–49); served as adjutant and commanding officer of the 2nd Punjab Cavalry Regiment (1851–63); and was promoted to captain (10 February 1855). During the Indian Mutiny, Browne commanded the 2nd Punjab Cavalry at the siege of Lucknow (1858). After the city was captured, he served with Sir James Hope Grant against the rebels at Kursi (22 March 1858) and subsequent actions. Browne commanded the force which defeated the mutineers at Mohunpur. At daybreak on 31 August 1858 at Sirpura, he led 230 of his cavalry and 350 native infantry in a surprise attack. He reached the enemy's artillery at the rear of their position and, almost single-handedly, charged the gunners who were trying to reload their pieces to fire on the advancing infantry. He prevented them from reloading, but in the melee and violent hand-to-hand fighting, most of Browne's left arm was severed and he was wounded twice in the knee. Only the quick application of a tourniquet prevented him from bleeding to death. For this act of heroism, Browne was awarded the Victoria Cross in 1861.

Overall, Browne's exemplary conduct in the Indian Mutiny earned him the thanks of the Commander-in-Chief and Indian government, the War Medal with two clasps, and he was mentioned in dispatches three times. Browne achieved brevet rank of major on 20 July 1858, lieutenant-colonel on 26 April 1859, and colonel 17 November 1864. He married in 1860. He reached the rank of major-general on 6 February 1870, and in 1875 accompanied Edward, the Prince of Wales, on the latter's India tour. It must have been a good tour because at the close of it in 1876, Browne was nominated for Knight Commander of the Star of India (K.C.S.I.) and became a lieutenant-general on 1 October 1877.

As a military member of the governor-general's council, he advised Lord Lytton that in the upcoming Afghan War (1878–79), it would be very difficult to achieve much. His advice was disregarded. Browne commanded the 1st Division of the Peshawar Field Forces at the Khyber

Pass. Although he was continuously hampered by inadequate preparations for transport and commissariat through the government's mishandling, he managed to capture the fortress of Ali Masjid with little loss of life on 21 November 1878. He then advanced to Jellalabad and occupied it on 20 December. Lord Lytton wanted the British to push on to Kabul in 1879, but Browne and Haines, the Commander-in-Chief in India, argued that it was impossible, especially as Browne was already having trouble keeping his lines of communication open due to the Khyber tribesmen. Browne was able to reach Gandamak due to Gough's victory at Fatehabad in April 1879. A treaty was signed with the Afghans in May and the British withdrew. Lytton, a politician through and through, tried to hang his failures on Browne. Browne was created a Knight Commander of the Bath (K.C.B.) in 1879. For his efforts in Afghanistan, Browne received the thanks of the government of India and both Houses of Parliament.

The Afghan War reopened after the massacre in Kabul in September 1879, but Browne was unavailable for service, having already retired from active duty. In December 1888, Browne was made a general and Knight, Grand Cross of the Bath (G.C.B.) in 1891. Browne retired to the Isle of Wright and died in 1901.

If the reader thinks the author has forgotten the purpose of this entry, he has not. Sam Browne invented the cross-belt for a very practical reason. It was, and still is, worn from the right shoulder to the left hip and its original purpose was to secure Browne's scabbard and sword to his side so he could draw it with one hand. In the First World War, the officers of the American Expeditionary Forces adopted the "Sam Browne" of their allied counterparts so that the latter could more easily distinguish the American officers from their men. The "Sam Browne" is worn still in armies and many police departments use it as well. It is all due to the bravery, perseverance, and right-handedness of one man.

There were some other uniform parts named for people during the nineteenth century, but none were as pervasive or long-lasting. Let us begin with the shako. The historic trend in military uniforms has been for armies to copy the style and headgear of the dominant army of the day. Here we are concerned with the Wellington Shako, as in the Duke of Wellington. The British infantry shako was copied from the Austrian shako which was introduced in early 1800. The Wellington version was probably introduced in October 1806. The earlier version of the shako was pretty much like a stove pipe or cylinder with a flat crown and a short, flat brim. The front of the hat had plenty of room for a badge and a plume. Made of black felt, the Wellington Shako was cylindrical but the crown was slanted, being higher at the front that at the back. The brim was short but curved. The frame, or head band, of the hat was also slanted like the crown; thus the back of the cylinder leaned in a bit, which added to the jauntiness of the presentation. The height of the hat in the front was seven inches and in the back, six inches. The plume was affixed on the left side of the shako, near the top, in contrast to its predecessor which had the plume in the front. The Wellington Shako was supplanted starting in 1816 with the Regency Shako which had quite a bit more flare, literally, as the crown was 11 inches across and curved down on the left and right. As the century progressed, the shako decreased in height and was scrunched forward. The last 25 years of the nineteenth century were dominated by German influences and that means the funny little fore-and-aft brimmed leather hat with a spike or ball on the top. After the Franco-Prussian war, many armies—such as the Americans, Russians, and British—all adopted similar helmets similar to the German *Pickelhaube* for dress purposes. In the most bald-faced demonstration of who they thought was the best, the Americans dumped their French-style kepis less than a year after the fall of the Second Empire and adopted helmets very similar to the Germans'. In any event, the Wellington Shako was obsolete scarcely a year after Waterloo, and the Iron Duke's name remains associated today with a type of non-military rubber boot and, probably irrelevantly, with a preparation of beefsteak and goose's liver.

Another British general also had a uniform item named for him, and this piece of military apparel remained in service far longer than Wellington's. Field Marshal Viscount Garnet Wolseley, one of the most experienced colonial fighters the British had and commander in chief of Her Majesty's Army from 1895-99, introduced a new sun helmet just as he retired. It had a much broader brim, especially in the back, and a lower crown than the previous ones. Wolseley so embodied all of the martial attributes admired in a Victorian soldier that the expression "All Sir Garnet" came to mean roughly the same as "squared away" or "strac" means to modern American soldiers. His sun helmet was finally removed from the British Army inventory after World War II, so his hat can't compete with the Sam Browne belt's longevity, but British soldiers even today still know what "All Sir Garnet" means, and that is a compliment indeed.

The Americans also have an entry in this category. In 1855, Jefferson Davis, in his capacity of Secretary of War, created two cavalry regiments and convened a board to decide on the equipment. Among the recommendations was the call for a distinctive hat. The result was a broad-brimmed black felt hat with a raked, round crown. The hat is known by two names, the Jeff Davis and the Hardee. The latter appellation was for

William Joseph Hardee, a cavalry officer. The Hardee Hat came into service in 1855 and in 1858 it was issued to the entire army, replacing the shako-style cap. The felt hat was looped, that is, pinned up on one side or the other (depending on regulations' requirements) with a circular pin featuring an eagle in the middle, with the insignia in the front. The hats were issued for the enlisted ranks with colored hat cords representing the branch of the soldier. The hat cords for officers were black and silver and for general officers, gold. Officers purchased their hats and they had a ribbed black silk edging on the brim. This design, although both jaunty and practical, was very short-lived. The Hardee proved not to be as popular as the forage cap, and this hat (a.k.a. the kepi or bummer) all but replaced it during the Civil War. Thus, it was extremely short-lived, and has been completely forgotten by American soldiers. If you ask one about "the Hardee hat" today, he is most likely to think you are asking about the paper affairs worn by the folks who serve him sausage biscuits at the hamburger place just outside the main gate of his post.

Finally, for several decades, there has been an item of US Army apparel that is named after a nineteenth-century British general. The pathetically unmilitary cardigan sweater is named after Lord Cardigan, the incredibly brave, toweringly stupid fellow who led the Light Brigade to disaster during the Crimean War. (See page 273) Although no one in the US Army today associates its name with the bungler of Balaclava, the sooner the Army outlaws the wear of this miserable excuse for a uniform item, the better. That it has lasted longer than the Hardee hat or the Wellington Shako is inconceivable; hopefully, some future Chief of Staff will come to his senses and eliminate this bad looking, wimpy sweater, named after an infamous incompetent.

# Personalities

## Best Battle Report Never Rendered:
### Peccavi

General Sir Charles James Napier, 1782–1853, has the distinction of sending the best battle report of all time—except that he never did. Napier was in India in 1842 and was tasked to destroy the emirs of Sind. He did so in 1843 and annexed Sind amid controversy. Upon conquering the area, he telegraphed the message "*peccavi*," which is Latin for "I have sinned." Very clever, very erudite, very . . . very. The satirical magazine *Punch* reported this as sent by Napier to Lord Ellenborough, the Governor-General of India. The pun was, in fact, created by Catherine Winkworth (1827–1878) and submitted to the satirical magazine. Let us look at our two principals from the perspective of the *Dictionary of National Biography*. Catherine Winkworth was born on 13 September 1827, in London and raised in Manchester. She was educated by governesses and the Reverend William Gaskell and Dr. James Martineau. In the spring of 1845, she went to Dresden to stay with an aunt who had gone there to educate her daughters. Miss Winkworth stayed until July 1846. In 1853, she published her translation of German hymns and the book was hugely successful. It went through 23 editions and her second series of German hymns went through 12. She was active also in securing higher education for women. She died suddenly from heart disease in 1878 near Geneva, where she had gone to care for a sick nephew.

Charles James Napier was born in Whitehall, London on 10 August 1782 to Colonel the Honorable George Napier and his second wife, Lady Sarah Bunbury. Napier, due to an accident at birth, was sickly as a child and never attained the physical stature and beauty that characterized this family. Horace Walpole said of his mother that she was, "more beautiful than you can conceive. . . . She shone, besides, with all the graces of unaffected but animate nature." Napier was short-sighted, but he had a robust constitution. He entered the army on 31 January 1794 (yes, that's right—age 11), when he was commissioned as an ensign in the 33rd Regiment and promoted to lieutenant 8 May 1794. He made captain on 23 December 1803 and major on 29 May 1806, then was posted to the 50th Regiment. In August 1808, the regiment was sent to Lisbon and thence to Spain to take part in the Peninsular War against the French. As a colonel was on leave, Napier was placed in command of a battalion and he handled it well. On 16 January 1809, in action at Coruña, Napier was wounded five times, the *DNB* states that, "his leg was broken by a musket shot, he received a sabre cut on the head, a bayonet wound in the back, severe contusions from the butt end of a musket, and his ribs were broken by a gunshot." Captured, he was taken to French headquarters where he was cared for and released on parole on 20 March when Marshal Ney learned that Napier's mother was a widow, true, old, and blind. Napier promised not to serve again until he could be exchanged and that occurred in January 1810. Napier's strong constitution was again needed. In battle at the Coa on 10 July 1810, he had two horses killed beneath him. He then joined Wellington's staff and at the battle of Busaco on 27 September, he was shot through the face, had his jaw broken and his eye injured.

Napier finished out the Napoleonic Wars serving in North America against the Americans, as well as the Caribbean and Canada. He was put on half pay in 1814 and attended military college, but when Napoleon escaped from Elba, Napier volunteered for service. He went to Ghent, took part in the assault of Cambrai, and later marched into Paris. After the war, he was made a C.B. (Order of the Bath). His other honors were: mentioned in dispatches, gold medal for Coruña, and the silver war medal with two clasps. He nearly drowned on the way home when his ship sank in the harbor mouth. In 1817, he returned to finish military college at Farnham, which provided a broad education. In the 1820s, he saw service in Greece, where he became friends with Lord Byron. Napier was considered for, or sought the command of, the Greek army on two occasions, but he could not come to terms with the Greeks. And, the Greeks being Greek, Napier knew enough not to accept the post unless he had full autonomy.

He married in 1827, the year after his mother's death. His strong constitution again saved him in 1833 when he suffered an attack of cholera. His wife's death, however, at the end of July laid him low. He remarried in 1835. His military career continued to go well: he was promoted to major general on 10 January 1837, made a K.C.B. in 1838, and in April 1839, he was given command of the northern district of England. Here he had to deal with the Chartists and he managed to keep the peace in the area, which is no small accomplishment. In 1841, he was posted to India.

The controversy that surrounds Napier's Indian campaigns does not concern us directly, nor does it seem worthy of extended discussion. In the author's opinion, Napier acted in concert with his instructions and certainly with the support of Lord Ellenborough, the governor-general. Napier's mission was to confiscate the lands of the emirs of Sind who were violating not only the terms of the treaty they had signed, but were negotiating with other tribes to attack the British.

On 17 February 1843, Napier led a force of 2,800 against an enemy force of some 22,000 Baluchis at the Fuleli River near Miani, about six miles north of Hyderabad. The enemy was entrenched in the dry riverbed and had both flanks anchored on heavy woods. Napier sent 200 men off to the set fire to the woods and left 250 horse of the Poona cavalry and four companies of infantry, totaling 400 men, to guard the baggage. He had 12 guns to the enemy's 18. At this point, the river curved away from the British, and the enemy left—besides being anchored on the woods—had a wall to protect it further. Here the enemy disposed 6,000 Baluchis. Napier noticed a gap in this wall and posted a company of infantry from the 22nd and one gun to cover the opening. He ordered a Captain Tew and his 80 men to block the gap at all costs. If they succeeded, they would bottle up 6,000 men with a mere 80. The remaining 2,200 men of Napier's force, of which only 500 were European, advanced in echelon under heavy fire to the enemy battle line. The British deployed into line as each regiment neared the riverbank. They could go no farther, however, as the riverbed was jammed with enemy troops. The British resorted to advancing to the edge of the riverbank, firing into the massed enemy, then falling back to reload. The enemy made attempts to move forward against the British, but its attacks were uncoordinated and the British managed to force them back each time. During the battle, Napier rode along his line encouraging his men and exposing himself to fire. For two hours, the battle went on like this while Captain Tew and his company contained the Baluchis at the wall. Eventually, Tew fell, dead, but his company, even though it was taking losses, fought on.

Napier then sent his cavalry against the enemy right and they overran the enemy guns and struck the enemy's rear. The Baluchis began to waver and a frontal charge by the infantry settled things. There was no pursuit; the battle of Miani was at an end. The British lost 20 officers and 250 men and the Baluchis lost at least 6,000 killed and wounded. Six of the emirs surrendered and Napier gathered forces to go after Shir Muhammad, the Lion of Mirpur.

On 24 March, Napier led 1,100 horse and 3,900 men against the Lion's 26,000 in battle at Hyderabad, the capital of Sind. Napier had 14 guns and 5 pieces of horse artillery to the enemy's 15 guns. The British used their cannon well and a heavy bombardment of the enemy positions prepared the way for the British storming of the city. The fighting around the village of Dubba was hard indeed, and Napier was surprised by the presence of a second enemy line of troops. Napier led the charge, nevertheless, and was lucky to escape alive, let alone unscathed. At one point, a field magazine exploded and killed everyone around Napier. The only damage to him was that his sword was broken in his hand! The enemy lost some 2,000 men killed and 3,000 wounded and the British 256 killed and wounded. Muhammad got away, but the British finally defeated his army in June and the war was over. Napier had conquered Sind and then proceeded to demonstrate his talent for administration. He built the port of Karachi and imposed a fair civil administration. He was made a G.C.B. in November 1843 and received a letter of congratulations and praise in the House of Lords from the Duke of Wellington. Similarly, Sir Robert Peel lauded Napier's accomplishments in military operations and in civil administration. The rest of Napier's career, while of interest, is not germane to this discussion.

That he could have come up with *"peccavi"* was entirely believable. He was a man of letters who authored several works, many of them dealing with aspects of military affairs, but also administration. He also wrote a historical romance about William the Conqueror. Catherine Winkworth, however, as the translator of German hymns would surely know the Latin for "sin." The *Oxford Dictionary of Quotations, Third Edition*, tells us that she submitted the pun to *Punch* on 13 May 1844 and it was published on 18 May 1844 in Volume 6. *Punch* in those days appeared twice a year and was well over 200 pages. The entry on page 209, under the subject of foreign affairs, reads:

> It is a common idea that the most laconic military despatch ever issued was that sent by Caesar to the Horse-Guards at Rome, containing the three memorable words "*Veni, vidi, vici,*" and perhaps until our own day, no like instance of brevity had been found. The despatch of Sir Charles Napier after the capture of Scinde, to Lord Ellenborough, both for brevity and truth, is, far beyond it. The despatch consisted of one emphatic word—"*Peccavi,*" "I have Scinde [sinned]."

There is in this the added level of inference with regard to Napier's undertaking of the campaign. Many people, in and out of officialdom, thought that Napier acted without proper orders and with force incommensurate to the threat. Thus, the reference to having sinned, also reflects the notion that he had done wrong. This includes Captain James "out, out, damned spot" Outram, the British resident in Hyderabad. He believed that the situation could have been negotiated. Napier reckoned that as the use of force had been authorized by the Governor-General, and as the Afghan War was on-going and not going well from the British perspective, it was encouraging the tribes to make trouble. Thus, it was time for action, in the best Victorian sense.

Napier, despised by some, adored by others, returned to England in 1851. He remained active with his writing even though he was fighting liver disease contracted in 1846. He was one of Wellington's pall-bearers in September 1852 and he caught a severe cold then and never recovered his health. He died on 29 August 1853. He was honored in death with a statue in St. Paul's Cathedral and one in Trafalgar Square, and a portrait in the National Gallery, London.

## Most Famous Female Soldier of the US Civil War—Sarah Emma Edmonds

Sarah Emma Evelyn Edmonds (1841–1898) was a Canadian woman from New Brunswick who served in the Union Army as a nurse, as a spy, and as a soldier. When the war started, she changed her clothes, cut her hair, and enlisted as Frank Thompson (she was a very good shot by the way) in the 2nd Michigan Regiment and served for three years until she contracted malaria. Knowing that a medical examination would reveal all, or at least enough, she deserted. In 1864, she published a best-selling account (over 175,000 copies) of her life as a nurse and spy, leaving out the part about soldiering. She donated the money from the book to a charity for soldiers.

After the war, she married Linus Seelye of New Brunswick and settled in the United States. They wished to found a home for Civil War veterans, so to raise money, Emma decided to write another book and to claim her army pension from the army. For the pension, she needed letters from men in her old unit, so she went to one of them as a woman and revealed the truth about herself. Twenty years had passed, but she was still remembered at a veterans' reunion she attended as a woman. Letters were written on her behalf to the President and Congress. On 5 July 1884, President Chester A. Arthur signed into law her pension. In 1886, another bill was signed by the president rescinding the charge of desertion. She was the only Civil War woman soldier to receive a full army pension.

As a spy, and obvious master of disguise, she made 12 forays behind enemy lines collecting information for intelligence. Once she assumed the identity of a male slave to infiltrate the defenses around Yorktown, Virginia, as member of a work detail. She fought at the battles of Bull Run, Antietam, and Fredericksburg. Unfortunately, the manuscript about her life as a soldier was lost.

# Battles

## Best-Known Cavalry Charge in History and the Biggest Blunder of the Nineteenth Century:
### The Charge of the Light Brigade, 25 October 1854

There are three phases to the battle of Balaclava, which includes the famous and disastrous charge of the Light Brigade.

Interestingly, the whole battle was watched by the British commander, Lord Raglan, from the heights at the west end of the North Valley. Raglan was as well liked as any man in England. He had lost his right arm at Waterloo while serving as an aide to Wellington. After undergoing a battlefield amputation, he had famously called out to the surgeon to please remove his ring from the severed arm before it was carried away. He had spent his career as a staff officer to Wellington. He was not the man for the Crimea job, for he was a classic number two man, diplo-matic and used to facilitating things for a forceful leader. Raglan was over 60 and completely lacking in command experience.

Given the strong-willed, eccentric, and often-incompetent subordi-nates he had under him—none more so than the long-feuding brothers-in-law, the Lords Lucan and Cardigan—he never should have gone to the Crimea.

As our story is to be about the most famous cavalry charge in histo-ry, we should say a bit about our leading protagonists. Lord Lucan was in command of the Cavalry Division, the only cavalry division the British had in the Crimea. The Division was composed of two brigades plus horse artillery—the Heavy Brigade under Brigadier-General James Scarlett and the Light Brigade under Major General James Thomas Bru-denell, the Seventh Earl of Cardigan. The brigades were so styled because of the different equipment, weapons, and roles they had.

Scarlett's Heavy Brigade, about 1,500 strong, consisted of the 1st Royal Regiment of Dragoons, the 2nd Royal North British Dragoons (later called the Royal Scots Greys), the 4th Royal Irish Dragoon Guards, the 5th Princess Charlotte of Wales's Dragoon Guards, and the 6th Inniskilling Dragoons. Equipped with carbines and heavy, straight sabers, these troopers were to be used for missions requiring shock and firepower.

Cardigan's Light Brigade, with about 700 troopers and officers, con-sisted of the 4th Queen's Own Light Dragoons, the 8th King's Royal Irish Light Dragoons (Hussars), the 11th Prince Albert's Own Light Dra-goons (Hussars), the 13th Light Dragoons, and the 17th Light Dragoons (Lancers). These were units designed for reconnaissance, screening, and, especially in the case of the 17th, for pursuit of fleeing enemy units.

Since these units, combined, represented the total British cavalry in the Crimea, they were absolutely crucial to the success of the campaign. Any commander worth his salt would realized that he needed leaders who were at least competent, if not top-notch, to command these criti-cal assets. Thus, a good commander would have fired both Lucan and Cardigan long before they arrived in the Black Sea; in fact, he never would have brought them out in the first place. This was not to be, however. Lucan had not commanded troops for many years and did not know the current cavalry drill or even the commands for it. Cardigan had the best drilled cavalry in Europe, he was personally courageous beyond measure, and quite possibly as stupid as they come.

Both Lucan and Cardigan had prodigious tempers, arrogance in abundance, and petulance enough for a season's worth of bratty debu-tantes. The two men did not speak to each other during the campaign until minutes before the charge. If the military stage was ever set for disaster, this was it. One thing to remember in all this is that Raglan was perched on the heights at the western end of the North Valley. He had a bird's eye view of the battlefield and could see almost everything on the two-by-three-mile battlefield, albeit at a some distance; his subordinates on the ground had no such advantage. The undulating and rolling terrain meant that the belligerents could not see each other even when they were fairly close. One more thing: the Allies had been suffering from cholera long before they even arrived in the Black Sea, consequently the armies were nowhere near their allotted strength.

So, what did happen on 25 October? The first phase of the battle began just after 8:00 A.M., with the Russian attack on the Allied redoubts on the Causeway Heights, which was a Russian success. They drove the Turks from four of the six redoubts before destroying the fourth and manning the first three.

Phase two, part one, was the defense by a battalion of the 93rd Highlanders (Argyle & Sutherland). This force of 550 men and 100 invalids under the immediate tactical command of their brigade commander, Sir Colin Campbell, was the only thing between the Russians and Balaclava. The 93rd was deployed on a hillock, which blocked the entrance to the gorge, which led to the port of Balaclava, the sole supply line for the Allies. A large force of Russian cavalry, under Lieutenant-General I. I. Ryzhov, some 3,000 or 4, 000 strong, came down the North Valley. Four squadrons broke off, swept down from the Causeway Heights north of Campbell's position, and made for Balaclava. The rest of the Russian cavalry headed over the Heights and into the South Valley. Campbell had deployed his force into a line four men deep and had them lie down on the reverse slope of the hill. Up to this time, Campbell had been supported by some Turks, but when they saw that the Russians were coming, they skedaddled. Campbell told his men that there was no retreat possible and they had to die where they stood. As the four Russian squadrons neared the hillock, they moved to the gallop expecting to sweep into Balaclava. Instead, they encountered the unexpected—up stood the red-coated infantry, who then fired a volley. Mr. William Russell of *The Times* described them as, "that thin, red streak tipped with a line of steel," the *bon mots* from which the expression "Thin Red Line" later developed. The first volley of Minié balls slowed the charge, but the Russians still came on. The second volley told as well and the Russians wavered. From the 93rd's ranks, eagerness started the men to move forward, but Campbell shouted, steadying the impulse. A third volley was fired and the Russians veered to their left. Campbell, seeing that the cavalry may have been trying to outflank his

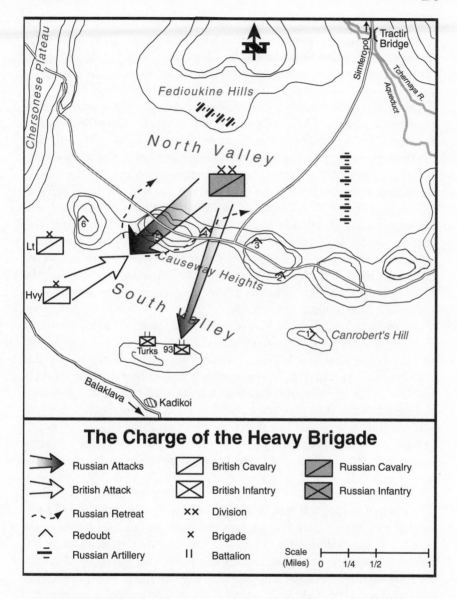

## The Charge of the Heavy Brigade

| | | |
|---|---|---|
| ➡ Russian Attacks | ▨ British Cavalry | ▨ Russian Cavalry |
| ⇨ British Attack | ⊠ British Infantry | ⊠ Russian Infantry |
| ⌁ Russian Retreat | ×× Division | |
| ∧ Redoubt | × Brigade | |
| ⚌ Russian Artillery | ‖ Battalion | Scale (Miles)  0  1/4  1/2  1 |

position, reacted quickly. A grenadier company, drawn back at 90 degrees on the right flank of the 93rd, swung round and poured fire into the Russians' flanks. The cavalry wheeled left and returned to the Causeway Heights. The phase two, part two, of the battle was the charge of the Heavy Brigade and was more or less concurrent with part one. Brigadier-General, the Honorable James Scarlett, led his troopers in the greatest cavalry feat of the nineteenth century. Scarlett was also lacking in military experience, but at least he had the good sense to be aware of it. Thus, he relied upon the advice of two of his subordinates, Colonel Beatson and Lieutenant Elliot, both of whom had seen action in India and had stellar reputations as cavalry commanders.

The reader will recall that 3,000 or so Russian cavalry were coming over the Causeway Heights. Prior to this, part of the Heavy Brigade had been in action there, helping to cover the withdrawal of the Turks fleeing from the redoubts. The brigade had just arrived at the western end of the South Valley when its leaders received orders to displace to Kadikoi, a village west of the 93rd's position, to support their defense. This required the Brigade to move around a ruined vineyard and through the Light Brigade's camp. Scarlett led the Brigade, but was unaware of the Russian cavalry on the Causeway Heights, now to his left near the Number 5 redoubt. He was probably concentrating on the 93rd to his right. The Heavy Brigade was moving in columns at the time when Elliot noticed the Russians a few hundred yards away and alerted Scarlett. It is axiomatic in cavalry warfare that cavalry on the move is harder to defeat than cavalry standing still, regardless of the odds; also, charges are usually most effectively delivered by units deployed on lines, not in columns. Impetus is everything in the charge, so the idea is to be moving faster than the enemy's horse. Scarlett immediately gave the order to left wheel into line. Lord Lucan came up at this time and had ordered the rearward cavalry to form on line as well. He told Scarlett that he had received word from Raglan that the Russian cavalry was on the move. Lucan agreed with Scarlett that the Russian cavalry column should be attacked. The Light Brigade was ordered to maintain its position.

The initial attack would be made by the Greys and the 2nd Squadron of the Inniskillings; the rest of the Brigade was to attack the flanks as soon as they were ready. Scarlett was raring to go, but the officers of the Greys and Inniskillings all but ignored him as they dressed their formations. They knew that their attack had to be well formed or it would be smothered by the superior weight of the Russians. What must have seemed agonizingly slow to onlookers was performed with seeming disregard to the advancing Russians. When all was ready, Scarlett led the first 300 of his 500 horse. They became known as Scarlett's "Three Hundred" and are gloriously described in Tennyson's poem, "The Charge of the Heavy Brigade."

The Russian cavalry came down the slope at the trot and then the canter, but then remarkably came to a halt. Their first line, Russell tells us, was twice as long as Scarlett's and three times as deep, and their second line equally so. They then swung the ends of their line forward to better surround the attackers. This series of movements by the Russians gave the Greys time to pick their way through the detritus of their camp and the Inniskillings slowed their advance to allow the Greys to catch up. Once together, they moved to the charge—uphill. All spectators who could see the action stopped to watch. French generals, officers, Zouaves, and other infantry sat down as if at the theater. More than one commentator has commented on the charging red horsemen and the sea of long grey-coated cavalry that awaited them. The Russians wore shakos, the Greys their bearskins, and the Dragoons their crested metal helmets. Scarlett was surrounded by Lieutenant Elliot, his orderly, and his trumpeter. In a display of leadership and masculine bravery customary of his class and era, Scarlett charged into the center of the Russian line, some 50 yards ahead of the Three Hundred, with the Inniskillings on the right and the Greys on the left.

Scarlett immediately began fighting his way through the Russian column. Seconds later, the rest of the British horse slammed into the Russians. The Inniskillings are reported as cheering loudly as they came to blows with the enemy and the Greys issuing a growling moan. Scarlett veered to the right and, swung his sword to both sides, emerging with minor wounds. Elliot drew more attention than Scarlett, perhaps because of the cocked hat Scarlett had insisted that he wear. Elliot ran the first man through to the hilt of his sword. Elliot was then struck in the forehead, had his face cleaved in two, and sustained a dozen other wounds before he made his way out of the fight. From a distance, it looked as if the entire Three Hundred had been swallowed up. The wings of the Russian formation now began to close on the British. The right wing was closing on the Greys when the 5th Dragoon Guards hit the Russian right wing. The 1st Squadron of the Inniskillings came up on the British right and pierced the flank and rear of the Russian left wing as it wheeled in on the their 2nd Squadron. Then the Royals, without orders, charged home on the British left, but caught only a part of the Russian wing. By now, elements of the Three Hundred were reaching the rear of the Russian formation and trying to rally themselves. Last to charge were the seething, impatient 4th Dragoon Guards, whom Lucan finally ordered forward at this point. They wheeled into line and smashed into the right flank of the main Russian formation and cut their way all the way through to the left flank. This was it: the Russian mass, now pierced in five places, disintegrated. The whole action had taken just eight minutes, it was not even 10:00 A.M. Casualties? Far less than one would think: 78 for the British and more for the Russians, but not much more. Russell reported 70 casualties total in the action, but this seems too low. Credit for the low loss of Russians is given to their uniforms. The heavy coats and stiff shakos warded off many blows that could have done serious damage.

This was the perfect time for an all-out pursuit of the fleeing Russian cavalry. The unit perfectly suited for the job, indeed, designed for it, was the Light Brigade, and they were fully available, not even half a mile away.

They did not move.

The finger pointing as to "why" started almost immediately. Cardigan said he wanted was ready, willing, and able, but he had been ordered by Lucan not to leave his position. As far as it goes, this was true. It was Raglan, however, who had placed the Light Brigade there and given the orders to Lucan. Lucan had told Cardigan that the Light Brigade was placed there by Raglan, but Lucan also told Cardigan to attack anything that came within reach of him. We all know what a great or even competent cavalry commander would have done when faced with such an opportunity, and we know that Cardigan was urged by a least one officer, Captain Morris, temporarily commanding the 17th Lancers, to pursue. After all, pursuit was the Lancers' *raison d'être*. Cardigan had the option to follow Lucan's modification of the orders, but he chose not to do so. Ultimately, it is Raglan's fault. He was fearful of losing what cavalry he had, he placed constraints on its commanders, and then complained when his subordinates followed his orders. Had the pursuit gone ahead, then the author would be writing an account of a great victory; instead, he now proceeds to phase three and the destruction of the Light Brigade.

The fleeing Russian cavalry headed north and then east along the Causeway Heights and their horse artillery unlimbered their guns at the east end of the North Valley. As they did so, they had little idea of what was to happen next.

The situation was this at about 10:00 A.M. The Russians occupied Redoubts 1, 2, and 3 on the Causeway Heights, but had nothing in the South Valley. Their beaten cavalry had taken up positions at the eastern end of the North Valley and provided the link between them and the Russian forces on the Fedioukine Heights, which ran parallel to the North Valley. The Light Brigade had moved to a position at the western end of the North Valley where it awaited the infantry it was told was coming. Thus, the North Valley had cavalry at either end, but nothing in between. At 10:50, the French commander, General Canrobert, and his staff met with Raglan to discuss the day's operations. Five minutes later, the *Chasseurs d'Afrique*, mounted infantry accustomed to fighting in mountainous terrain in North Africa, was on its way down the North

Valley and took up positions on the ridges of the Fedioukine Heights. Raglan's intention was that his infantry, specifically the slow-moving 4th Division, should retake the redoubts. The Russians, seeing that their troops occupying the redoubts could not hold them against a concerted attack, decided to take off the guns. This, of course, could not be allowed because it would give the Russians a legitimate claim to a victory on the day. Moreover, these guns were British naval property and one does not give the enemy useful equipment. Raglan resolved that as the 4th Division was not yet on the scene, he would send the Light Brigade.

The two orders which Raglan had sent previously that morning to Lucan had been vaguely worded and thus liable to misinterpretation. Predictably, they had been. This created frustration on the part of all concerned. The third order told Lucan to advance and take any opportunity to recover the heights and in this he would be supported by infantry. Lucan duly waited for infantry to show up, but what Raglan *really* meant was, "get along to the Heights." When Raglan's staff saw the Russians preparing to take off the guns, another order was sent to Lucan. The message was written in pencil by General Richard Airey, Raglan's Quartermaster General. The QMG was a job similar to today's chief of staff. This order, the fourth, read, "Lord Raglan wishes the cavalry to advance rapidly to the front—follow the enemy and try to prevent the enemy carrying away the guns." The task of delivering the order was taken by Captain Edward Nolan, a well-regarded horseman and the author of two works on cavalry and training. He also hated Lucan and Cardigan. As he prepared to ride straight down the 600-foot height to Lucan, Raglan called out that Lucan was to attack immediately.

Lucan received the order and read it slowly, Nolan was in a highly agitated state from his precipitous ride and his desire to see the Light Brigade do something that day. From his position, Lucan could see no guns and said that it was folly for unsupported cavalry to attack artillery. Nolan could not keep his temper and neither could Lucan. Raglan said later that the third and fourth orders were meant to be read together and had Lucan done so, he would have known to attack the Causeway Heights. Nolan, sinning above his station, shouted that Lord Raglan wished the attack to go immediately. Lucan shouted, "Attack? Attack what? What guns?" Nolan, reportedly, flung out an arm and said, "There, my lord, there is your enemy, there are your guns, sir, before them it is your duty to take them." Now the thing of it is, Nolan was not pointing to the Causeway Heights when he said it, he was pointing to the end of the North Valley. Moreover, from his position

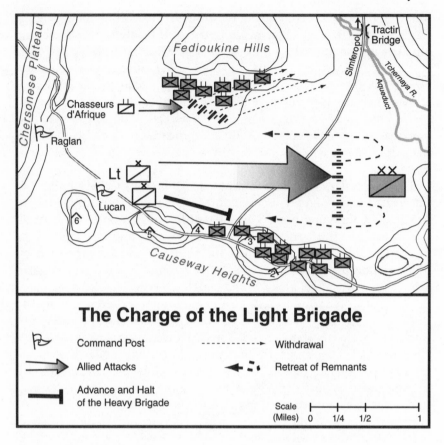

# The Charge of the Light Brigade

🏴 Command Post                    ┄┄┄┄▶ Withdrawal

➡ Allied Attacks                    ◀┄ ∴ Retreat of Remnants

⊢ Advance and Halt
of the Heavy Brigade

Scale ├──────┼──────┼──────────┤
(Miles)   0      1/4    1/2              1

Lucan could not see what was happening on the Heights, a factor that
Raglan did not take into account from his perch. In her book on the war,
*The Reason Why*, Cecil Woodham-Smith argues that Nolan had misunderstood Raglan's intent and order, and believed that the guns at the
end of the Valley were the ones to be attacked. Other authors see it that
Nolan did know it was the Heights that were to be attacked and had
gestured wildly without knowing where. This author is inclined to
think that Nolan knew it was the Heights which were to be attacked.

Lucan went to Cardigan and gave the order to attack the guns at the
end of the Valley. Cardigan mentioned that the Valley was covered by
guns and infantry on three sides, to which Lucan responded that he was
aware of it, but Lord Raglan had ordered this attack and they must obey.
Cardigan saluted his longtime antagonist and turned to his task. He
wheeled his horse around and rode over to Lord George Paget, his
second in command, to pass the order. As he did so, he said, "Well, here

goes the last of the Brudenells." Cardigan ordered the Brigade to draw up in two lines, he would command the first and Paget the second. Paget had just lit a cigar and resolved to keep it until it went out. Cardigan placed the 13th Light Dragoons, 11th Hussars (his own regiment), and the 17th Lancers in the first line, and the 4th Light Dragoons and the 8th Hussars in the second line. Lucan then came up and removed the 11th Hussars from the first line and placed them between the two lines. This was an affront to Cardigan on two levels, first, the 11th was Cardigan's regiment and now it was taken from its place of honor in the front line, and second, Lucan did not ask him to make the change. but ordered it himself. Conspicuously Lucan's old regiment, the 17th, was left in the front line. That done, Cardigan took his place in front of the Brigade, raised his sword, a trumpet called out, and Cardigan gave the order, "The Brigade will advance." "Brigade" is overstating the size of the formation. The five regiments, due to disease, totaled only some 673 men. The enemy on the Fedioukine Hills had 14 guns, eight battalions of infantry, and four squadrons of cavalry. On the Causeway Heights were 11 battalions and 30 guns, and at the end of the Valley were 12 guns, the defeated cavalry, and six more squadrons of Lancers. The Valley was less than a mile across and the Light Brigade was a mile and a quarter from the Russian guns. It was 10 minutes after 11.

Woodham-Smith tells us that as the Light Brigade moved a sudden silence fell over the battlefield and it was possible to hear the jingling of the equipment. Cardigan sat erect and tall in the saddle and never once during the whole attack did he turn round to check on his men and thus convey uncertainty. The Brigade started at the walk and then moved to the trot as well as if on parade. At 50 yards, they started to take fire from the Russian guns and when they had covered about 200 yards, there occurred another dramatic event in a day already filled with them. Nolan, who had been riding with his friend, Captain Morris, in the 17th Lancers, realized that the attack was heading in the wrong direction. He resolved to do something and so he galloped diagonally in front of the formation. Morris thought Nolan had let his excitement take hold of him and called to him to steady himself. Nolan continued to the right and crossed in front of Cardigan and began waving his sword and shouting. Cardigan considered this an egregious display and believed that Nolan was trying to take over the Brigade. The noise of battle had built up now to the point that Nolan could not be heard, and in the next instant, a Russian shell exploded near Cardigan and a fragment tore through Nolan's chest. Nolan's arm, we are told, went rigid although he dropped his sword, his horse wheeled, and ploughed to the rear through the 4th Light Dragoons. As it did so, Nolan kept his seat but emitted a blood-curdling shriek which disturbed all who heard it. When the horse had cleared the Brigade, Nolan, fell from his saddle, dead.

As the Brigade progressed down the Valley, it became clear that they were not going to take the redoubts, but were heading for the guns at the far end. The full realization of what was happening chilled onlookers. The Russian fire poured into the valley and the cavalry instinctively quickened the pace. Cardigan did all he could to check the Brigade so the horses would not be blown. He picked the center point of the guns as his goal and he continued to ride on, steady and erect, as if on parade. Meanwhile, the numbers of the Brigade dwindled as shot and shell found their mark. Reflecting their training and superb discipline, the troopers closed up the ranks whenever a gap appeared. On the Light Brigade came and smoke clouded the end of the valley.

Men and horses were ripped apart by the enfilade firing, John Selby in Balaclava relates the account of Sergeant Talbot of the Lancers whose head was ripped from his body by round shot and how the headless body remained in the saddle for 30 yards, with the lance still couched. Finally, after minutes of horror, which must have seemed like hours, the first line came within range of the guns at the end of the valley. The Light Brigade had covered just over half the distance.

The Heavy Brigade was also in the attack and led by Lucan. Some distance back of the Lights due to their heavier equipment and tired horses, the Heavy Brigade came under fire from the enemy on the flanks. Seeing the pounding the Light Brigade sustained and that the Heavies were now taking, Lucan made the decision not to throw away the brigade. Wounded in the leg and having lost 21 Greys, he called a halt and pulled the men out of range. They would wait to assist the return of the Light Brigade. Also helping where they could was the *Chasseurs d'Afrique* under General Morris. He led an attack against the Fedioukine Hills and drove off the Russian artillery and infantry. Now the Light Brigade would receive fire from only one flank on its return.

Closer and closer came the Light Brigade and slaughter continued. Riderless horses, mutilated and crazed, careered about the field, wounded men cried out for relief. The first line of the Brigade was broken into many pieces and the second line came up to close the gaps. It was now 11:18 and the British were nearly upon the guns. At 80 yards, the faces of the gunners were recognizable as the Russians fired. All but 50 of the first line went down. Then those following on made it into the gun line, Cardigan first. The smoke was so thick in spots that men could not see beyond their steeds. Speaking of smoke, it was at this point that Paget's cigar went out.

The fighting around the guns was fierce, but not confined just to the guns. Twenty lancers of the 17th pushed beyond the guns and struck a stationary body of Russian cavalry and cut their way through as the Russians broke and fled. In pursuit, the Lancers saw a large force of Cossacks making for them and so they turned about and had to fight their way back to the guns. As what was left of the rest of the regiments reached the guns, the Russian gunners stilled tried to drag off their pieces and the 4th Light Dragoons killed all who remained. Those who penetrated beyond the guns and smoke saw that a large mass of Russian cavalry was waiting for them and so they did what they were trained to do—formed up and prepared to attack. There were 70 of them from the 4th Light Dragoons and 8th Hussars led by Paget. Word came, however, that Russian Hussars were forming up as well some 500 yards behind them. Paget decided they had to retire, so they wheeled about and fought their way through the Russian Hussars.

The question on the minds of many of the troopers, commanders, and, no doubt, some readers, was, "where's Lord Cardigan?" He had cleared the guns, pressed on through the smoke, and come out the other side. There, he saw the Russian cavalry about a hundred yards away. He tried to rein in his horse, but by the time he did so, he was only 20 yards from the startled Russians. Cardigan had not stayed to fight amongst the guns because he did not think it proper for the commanding general to melee among privates. Nor had he any real idea about what was going on behind him as he had not looked back. Here is what happened next: One of the Russian officers, Prince Radzivill, recognized Cardigan from various social events in London, so ordered some Cossacks to capture him alive. Cardigan managed to break free of the Cossacks and vanish into the smoke at about the same place he came out. He crossed the gun line and, rather than try to rally his men and bring as many of them out as he could, he rode slowly back up the North Valley. Upon reaching Scarlett, he began complaining about Nolan's behavior.

Others of the Light Brigade made their way back as best they could. Paget's group of 70 made it unscathed through the Russian Hussars, who offered only indifferent opposition. The sight of what remained of the Light Brigade must have been heart-rending to see. Five hundred horses were dead and of the 673 men who fought in the battle only 195 made it back. The 13th Light Dragoons mustered 2 officers and 8 men out of 150. The 17th Lancers had 37 men left, although they made it up to 50 men and 3 officers after a couple of days.

The Light Brigade had been in action for 25 minutes.

General Bosquet, as he watched the Brigade ride down the Valley, said, "*C'est magnifique, mais ce n'est-ce pas la guerre*" which is the most famous. There was another French comment, "*Je suis vieux! J'ai vu des battailles; mais ceci est trop*" which I translate as "I am old, I have seen battles; but this is too much."

## Biggest Battle Ever Fought in North America:
### The Battle of Gettysburg, 1–3 July 1863

The Civil War—which everyone knows is the US Civil War, or the War Between the States, or the War of the Rebellion—was a conflict that introduced all the elements of modern war to the world. Oh, there were hints of these elements starting with the revolutions of 1848 in Europe, and real indications of them in the Crimean War 1854–56, but it took the Americans to give them life properly. This should not come as a surprise to the reader, as the author has mentioned elsewhere, the Americans are a resourceful, enterprising, and inventive people.

Take, for example, the railway and telegraph; both had a tremendous impact at the strategic level. The ability to move soldiers and materiel quickly by rail was first demonstrated in 1839 when the British moved troops to put down the Chartists. Through the 1840s and '50s, more states used railroads to move their soldiers, Prussia, Austria, and France being the foremost in Europe. In the Austro-Franco War of 1859, the French still managed to move 604,000 men and 130,000 horses into Italy in 86 days.

The Civil War could not have been fought effectively without the use of railways. After all, the war was fought over an area equal in size to that of Europe. Christopher Bellamy tell us in *The Oxford Companion to Military History* that with the railroad, the Union could move 23,000 men and associated guns and ammunition 1,200 miles in one week, a journey which previously took three months. Obviously, anything this important was likely to be attacked and, just as obviously, it was important to repair the damage as soon as possible. The North was particularly adept at this, and developed special equipment for the purpose. It also had special bridging equipment as well. Bellamy tells us also that the first attack against a railroad for military purposes was in 1848 when the Venetians destroyed an Austrian rail line. In the Franco-Prussian War 1870–71, the Prussians used 100,000 troops to protect 2,000 miles of track in France from sabotage by civilians.

Similarly, the telegraph allowed information—right and wrong and a lot of it—to be transmitted between the commanding general and his government, which meant that closer political control could be achieved and more staff officers kept busy. It was not possible, however, for the telegraph to be used in an operational capacity, although

General Joseph Hooker, when in command of the Army of the Potomac, attempted to use the telegraph to maintain communications with elements of his army. The first use of the telegraph in war was the Crimean War 1854–56, when a line linked the Crimea to England. In the Civil War, both sides used the telegraph extensively. The North developed special telegraph wagons that linked to the civilian lines to send messages. It was possible, however, for the army commanders to receive orders from the Commanding General of the Army in Washington, D.C., Henry Halleck, advising them as to strategic movements.

The Americans learned from the Europeans, but the reverse was not true. When France and England went to war against Russia in 1854 to defend Turkey, that illustrious Secretary of War, Jefferson Davis, sent a commission to Europe to study the latest trends in warfare. The resulting reports to Congress by Major Delafield are a trove of information and describe the status of the military art at mid-century. The Europeans, however, did not display an equal interest in events in North America.

To say that there are a great number of books written about the most important event in American history since the promulgation of the Constitution is a vast understatement. Quite literally, a book has been published about the Civil War for every day that has passed since the end of the war. Now let us turn to that town in Pennsylvania.

The battles preceding this one do not concern us, but it should be stated that the Confederacy under Robert E. Lee had won a string of victories over Union forces. Lee's combination of offensive strategy and defensive tactics had permitted his numerically-inferior forces to confound, drub, lick, rout, repulse, and rebuff the Federal army. Lee was considered the best American soldier of his time.

The Confederacy was faced with a pressing strategic problem in the spring of 1863. What were they to do about the pressure the Union armies were applying on all sides? Particularly threatening was General Grant's campaign against Confederate strongholds in the vicinity of Vicksburg, Mississippi, which, if taken, would cut the Confederacy in two as Vicksburg was the last important fortified city in Confederate hands on the Mississippi River.

A conference was held on 15 May in Richmond, the Confederate capital, to discuss strategy. President Jefferson Davis met with his cabinet and General Lee. Lee proposed that rather than take troops from his army and send them on a thousand-mile trip to reinforce the garrison at Vicksburg, it would be better to invade Pennsylvania and inflict a great defeat on the enemy. Such a campaign—and do not believe anyone who calls it a raid—would be a real attention getter on many levels. It would move the war out of Virginia, thereby allowing southern agriculture to rebound; Lee's army could feed on Pennsylvania for a change; and such activity on the North's home soil could encourage not only northerners who were looking to end the war, but also show the Europeans that the Confederacy was worthy of official recognition and material support. It could have even forced the Federal government to offer terms.

After his victory at Chancellorsville in the first week of May, another offensive-defensive demonstration, Lee and the Confederacy were

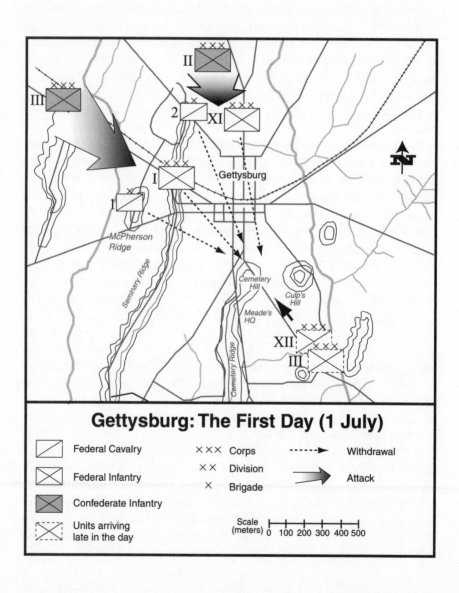

## Gettysburg: The First Day (1 July)

| | | |
|---|---|---|
| Federal Cavalry | ××× Corps | ------▶ Withdrawal |
| Federal Infantry | ×× Division | ▬▶ Attack |
| | × Brigade | |
| Confederate Infantry | | |
| Units arriving late in the day | Scale (meters) 0  100 200 300 400 500 | |

riding high. Lee's argument won the day, but did it set the stage to lose the war? As for the US government, the response to Chancellorsville was another change in command of the Army of the Potomac. Lincoln relieved Major General Joseph Hooker and replaced him with Major General George Meade.

On the morning of 1 July, Meade had been in command of the Army of the Potomac for three days when there was a clash just west of Gettysburg. By the time the battle ended, the Confederates had pushed some 75,000 men into the fight and the Federals somewhere between 88,000 to 95,000.

Confederate troops from Heth's division, part of A. P. Hill's III Corps, bumped into skirmishers belonging to the 1st and 2d Brigades of Brigadier General John Buford's 1st Cavalry Division at about 9:00 A.M. and the shooting started. Buford's men fought well, outnumbered as they were, until more Southern troops of Lieutenant General Richard Ewell's II Corps arrived from north of Gettysburg. Buford pulled his men back into Gettysburg and then south of the town, ultimately taking up positions on Cemetery Ridge. Lee ordered Ewell, Stonewall Jackson's replacement, to take the ridge if practicable, but Ewell hesitated and lost the opportunity. Meanwhile, Union reinforcements arrived to bolster the defense of Cemetery Ridge, which Major General Winfield Scott Hancock of II Corps decided was a good defensive position. He also sent elements of Major General Abner Doubleday's division to take up positions on Culp's Hill to the east. Hancock turned control of the field over to Major General Henry Slocum of XII Corps and rode to report to Meade who was coming on with the remainder of his army. Lee established positions opposite them there and also parallel to Cemetery Ridge on Seminary Ridge, a mile to the west. The Confederates sustained about 7,000 casualties on this day, and one of their brigade commanders, Brigadier General James Archer, had been captured. The United States Army lost one of its finest and bravest leaders, Major General John F. Reynolds, who was shot and killed while personally leading a critical counterattack.

There was a discussion of strategy on this occasion between Lee and Major General James Longstreet, the Confederate I Corps commander, as to what should be done next. Longstreet argued that what they should do is move the whole army south of their current positions and place themselves between Meade and Washington, D.C. Then Meade would be forced to attack the Confederates in prepared positions and that would be good for the boys in gray. Longstreet understood that the paradigm of the era was to conduct strategic offensives to arrange advantageous tactical defensive operations. Lee declined to take this advice and assigned Longstreet the task of attacking the lengthening Union left.

This leads us to the next series of mistakes. Major General Daniel Sickles, the first man to get off murder charges on the basis of temporary insanity, was given the task of defending part of the Union left with his III Corps. Rather than staying on Cemetery Ridge, he decided to occupy positions just over half a mile west, which is to say closer to the enemy and disconnected from contact with Hancock's II Corps to the north. Longstreet decided to follow his orders and at 4:00 P.M., engaged Sickles's exposed force rather than try to occupy the vacant Little Round Top. This piece of key terrain was behind—which is to say east of—

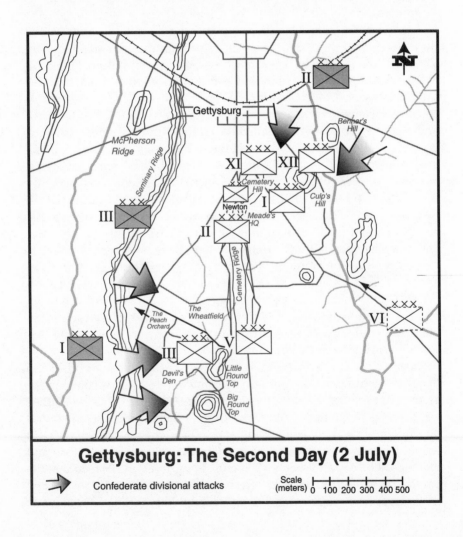

## Gettysburg: The Second Day (2 July)

Confederate divisional attacks

Scale (meters) 0  100  200  300  400  500

Sickles's line. From this cleared steep hilltop, the Confederates could have turned the entire Union line.

As Longstreet's men grappled with Sickles's, however, the Union Army's leadership caught their own error on their left flank. Major General George Sykes, commanding the V Corps which Meade had ordered forward to support Sickles' exposed units, ordered Colonel Strong Vincent's brigade to quickly establish defensive positions on Little Round Top. It fell to the 20th Regiment, Maine Volunteer Infantry under the command of Colonel Joshua Chamberlain to anchor the end of the Union line there. Longstreet's men succeeded in forcing Sickles's units back to Cemetery Ridge, and some of the terrain features which saw the fiercest fighting—places like "Devil's Den," "the Peach Orchard," and "the Wheatfield"—became legendary in American history. Although the Confederate forces under Brigadier General E.M. Law fiercely assaulted the 20th Maine, they could not dislodge them; a spectacular last-ditch bayonet charge by what was left of Chamberlain's regiment completely demoralized the exhausted Confederates. The second day of battle ended with another Confederate failure to turn the flank of the Union Army, although they came close at Culp's Hill, at the opposite end of the line from Little Round Top. At the end of Day Two, the armies on the field had sustained a combined total of about 35,000 battle casualties.

On the evening of 2 July, Lee held another conference with his staff. Longstreet suggested that they try again to turn the Union left, but Lee decided that they would launch an attack on the center of the Union position; once they broke through, he would exploit the breach. He mistakenly thought the flank attacks had skimmed men from the center, which should, by that reasoning, now be significantly weakened. Here he would send divisions commanded by Major Generals George Pickett, Isaac Trimble, and James Pettigrew across a mile of gently-rising, open ground. They would charge into history on foot against prepared positions and massed artillery.

At 1:00 P.M. on 3 July, the two sides opened fire with artillery for two hours, thus occasioning the largest artillery duel in North America. How many cannon? The author reckons that the total number of guns at Gettysburg was around 600: as of 1 June, Lee's army had 190 guns and the Union army of Hooker/Meade, as of 10 June, 410 guns. The number of guns involved in the artillery duel preceding Pickett's charge is problematical. As the reader has come to expect, various writers give different figures, your author has determined that the Confederates had about 150, perhaps 159 guns, and the Union about the same. He can live with 300 in total. About 3:00 P.M., the Confederate assault began. About

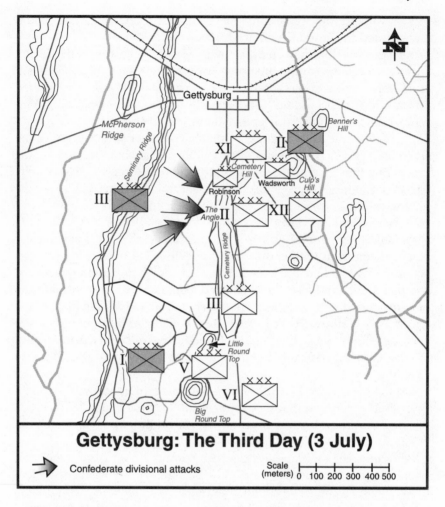

# Gettysburg: The Third Day (3 July)

Confederate divisional attacks

Scale (meters) 0  100 200 300 400 500

12,000 men, with a frontage of 1,600 yards set out for the Union line about three-quarters of a mile away; only one-half would return.

The Union artillery opened up with shot and shell fire with devastating results, and then switched to canister, but on the Rebels came. At effective rifle range, say about 200 yards, the Union infantry fired and Union infantry on the left and right of the attackers swung out to pour in flanking fire. Still the Rebels came on and one of Pickett's brigades under Armistead made it just across the Union lines at a point called "The Angle" with 100 men, but got no further. The Confederates had no reserve and the Federals did. Pickett ordered a retreat. The Rebels crossed the field again and returned to their lines. They covered themselves in glory and no small amount of blood, but the attack was a colossal mistake. Lee moved amongst his shattered men telling them that it was all his fault. It surely was. Two-thirds of Pickett's men were lost and three of his brigadiers and 13 colonels laid dead or wounded.

The next day passed without fighting, and that evening, Lee pulled back under the cover of a rainstorm and crossed back into Virginia. On the same day, Grant captured Vicksburg. The Mississippi River was now under Union control, the Confederacy was cut in half—the thing that Jefferson Davis had feared had come to pass, Lee's strategy had failed. Meade did not vigorously pursue; had he done so, he may have trapped Lee against the rain-swollen Potomac and overwhelmed him. The officially-reported but incomplete losses for the Confederates were: 2,579 killed, 12,709 wounded, and 5,150 missing for a total of 20,438, but more likely Southern losses were 28,000. Union losses are more reliably reported: 3,072 killed, 14,497 wounded, 5,434 missing, a total of 23,003.

There was also one Gettysburg civilian killed in the battle; Jennie Wade. She was baking bread for Union soldiers on the morning of 3 July at the home of her sister, Mrs. McClellan. A bullet came through the door and killed her as she kneaded dough.

## Bloodiest Battle in History:
### Nanking, July 1864

The battle of Nanking, which nowadays is spelled Nanjing to confuse people, was the climax of the Taiping Rebellion. This rebellion, 1850–64, was the bloodiest civil war in history. It resulted in the deaths of at least 20 million people and, although the final number is unknown, 30 million is thought by some to be the more accurate figure. These numbers represent two to three times the death toll of the First World War and are exceeded only by the Second World War.

In *God's Chinese Son*, Jonathan Spence provides us with the background. The whole thing was touched off by Hung Hsiu-chaun (Hong Xiuquan in the modern rendering). He was named Hong Huoxiu when he was born in 1814 into a farming family in the Hua County village of Guanlubu, about 50 miles north of Canton. As a young man, Hong studied to take the civil service examinations and taught school. He made it through the first set of exams and thus was called to sit the second set in Canton in 1836. He failed to gain a spot, but these exams were very competitive and not many made it from the thousands of candidates. It was on this occasion that he received a copy of a Christian text from two men, a Chinese translator and another man who was almost certainly the American Edwin Stevens. The book was not the Bible, however, but the understanding of the Bible reduced to nine chapters by Liang Afa, a Chinese Christian. Hong failed his civil service exam, but he did not let that get him down. The next year, he sat the preliminary exams and passed the first round and so set off again for Canton. Unfortunately for him and for China, he failed.

On his way home, he became seriously ill and hired a sedan chair to get him home. Once there, he collapsed. He was beset with delirium and he and his family thought him near dying. Sometimes he lay still; at other times, he cried out. He was in heaven, he thought, and he fought demons, driving them out. At times, he acted out his combats and his family stood guard to prevent him from leaving the house and doing harm to a villager. Under Chinese law, the family was responsible for the violent acts of any insane family member. Eventually, Hong came out of it and recovered. He had a new name, however—he was now the "Heavenly King, Lord of the Kingly Way," or Hong Xiuquan. God gave it to him, you see. Hong also now had another older brother, a fellow known as Jesus, the Christ.

In 1843, Hong failed to gain a place with the civil service for the fourth time. He also turned to Liang's book after being encouraged to read it by a friend, Li Jingfang, to whom he had lent it. Visions of good and evil mixed with incomplete Bible stories; this, in turn, mixed with his apocalyptic dream of six years ago; and the result was a true believer in a new, vaguely Christian religion. He and Li baptized each other and began to preach to their families and convert them. They also attacked the false idol represented by Confucian tablets. Hong soon lost his job, so in 1844 he took to the road with a few family members to preach and make his way selling ink and writing brushes. Over the next six years, more and more people were converted to this religion and the authorities began to worry. Hong's followers, known as "God worshippers," came to control four areas, and soon the followers were spoken of as an "army." They fought local bandits and defeated them. Nevertheless, the Imperial forces, the Qing (pronounced "Ching"), could not allow a large group of armed true believers to roam around, and so by 1850, the two were on a collision course. They banged together in early December 1850, and 50 or so of Qing soldiers were killed. On 1 January 1851 at the battle of Jintian, the Heavenly Army of about 10,000 met a Qing force and inflicted over 300 casualties. Hong's "Taipings" won. Taiping, by the way, means "great peace." This movement was just filled with irony.

In March 1851, Hong officially declared the existence of the Taiping Heavenly Kingdom. The younger brother of Jesus was now going to drive the Manchu demons from the throne and establish a Heavenly

Kingdom on Earth. China was about to change. By September 1851, the Taiping had captured the city of Yongan and that was just the start. Here are some of the highlights.

They instituted a new calendar. Here we have the author's first query for assessing revolutions: Has the new regime instituted a new calendar? Nothing indicates the bloody intentions of a regime better than a new calendar. Just ask the French or the Russians.

Another aspect of the regime was that they used women in the army, but the sexes were not to mix throughout the new society. The penalty for lust, lewdness, or adultery was decapitation. This applied to all unless you happened to be the Heavenly King—Hong's list of wives, although suppressed, topped out at 88. Now, one could argue that chastity need not apply to anyone who has been to Heaven and wants or needs a lot of wives; the penalty, however, for gossiping about the Heavenly Father's in-laws or his private life was . . . decapitation. The beheading was immediate, moreover, but this just saved on lawyers' fees. Some may think this betrays Hong's touchiness on the subject, but it serves also to demonstrate the author's second query for assessing regimes: Is the leader in it just to get babes? If so, then the followers are nitwits. This second undeniable truth of revolutions also applies to cults. And while he is on the subject, the author offers the third query, which tells the undeniable truth of revolutions: Has the leader changed his name? (Like Ulianov, aka "Lenin," or Djugashvili, aka "Stalin") and if so, then the new name may as well be spelt m-u-r-d-e-r.

Nanking, which became the Heavenly Capital, was captured in March 1853. The course of the rebellion and the varying fortunes of the Taipings and Qings do not concern us. It should be noted that the Taipings were beset at times with internal feuding which did, on occasion, turn quite deadly, and on a large scale. There were also inefficiencies and gross mistakes. Fortunately for them, the Qing were equally inept. Hong continued to receive messages from God and Jesus through various people who went into trances.

By the fall of 1863, the Imperial Forces advanced on Nanking and other Taiping strongholds. Li Xiucheng, the general defending Nanking, was in as bad a predicament as a commander could be. He had a split command authority on the forces available, he had a demented commander-in-chief who thought he was a Supreme Being, and, as such, the earthly concerns of the general were not really the Heavenly Father's problems. The advance planning Li made for supplies had not been followed and the closest relief force was 200 miles away, which its commander thought was just fine. Li, moreover, couldn't just leave because his mother, who lived in Nanking, didn't feel like moving.

General Li's attempts to secure supplies failed as the Qing moved toward the city and steadily applied pressure. Of course, Li was not at all aided by Hong's relatives who—in their capacity as high-ranking Taiping officials—insisted that for people to buy grain, they first needed to buy a permit; then they had to buy a passport so they could go get the grain; then, once they had the grain, they had to pay a tax on the grain when they brought it back to Nanking. And whom, perspicacious reader, do you think was in charge of collecting those taxes, and selling those permits, and passports? Bingo.

By November 1863, the Qing begin the siege of Nanking. In the confession that Li wrote after the battle, we are told that from December on, he arranged for people to be let out of the city secretly and contrary to the government edict. This served to ease the drain on the city's stores and perhaps gave the escapees a chance at survival. He estimated that 13,000 to 14,000 were let out of the city. The approaching doom and the lack of food produced the usual response in the trapped populace— thievery, robbery, looting, murder, and general mayhem. In December, the Qing blew down part of the wall near the south gate, but the Taiping troops and a strategically-placed creek kept the besiegers out of the city. After this, the usual response set in amongst some of the leaders— they began treating secretly with the Qing. The next response of repression and paranoia then followed and no one, not even Li, was above suspicion.

More attempts at resupply failed and the besiegers constructed lines of circumvallation and contravallation, and the reader by now knows which one points in and which one points out. The lines were 300 yards apart and there were 120 forts spaced around the perimeter, one every one-quarter to one-half mile.

The situation by late spring was this: Hong's solution to the supply problem was for the people to eat manna or "sweet dew." Anyway, he said, the people were supposed to have been stockpiling it for years by then. He even demonstrated how to get it. Every morning, you gather some weeds, form them into a ball, and eat them. In April, Hong fell ill. Li said it was from eating "sweet dew." Hong's health rallied in May, but he relapsed soon thereafter, and died on 1 June. There is some question about how the Heavenly Father died. It is most likely that the report of a maid is correct and he committed suicide. His 14-year-old son, Tiangui Fu, became the "Young Monarch" on 6 June.

The Qing had driven their lines forward, at some points only 30 yards from the walls. Qing engineers and miners had dug over 30 tunnels. The usual mining and counter-mining had gone on, and the grim business of breaking into the enemy's galleries had produced some gruesome fighting. The defenders had flooded Qing mines with water and sewage, and the Qing had countered with blowing poison gas into the mines. On 19 July, the mines were blown and 60 yards of wall came down; the Taiping soldiers could not contain the breaches. The Qing poured into the city and the sack of Nanking began. The reader also knows that when cities are sacked, the time-honored tradition is that houses, shops, palaces, and temples are looted and burned, and the women are raped. In the three days of fighting and ensuing massacre, 100,000 people were killed, making this the deadliest battle ever.

General Li, the Young Monarch, and a few hundred supporters disguised as Qing troops made it out of the city late at night through one of the breaches. Left behind in the confusion were the king's two younger brothers who were killed in the general slaughter. Li gave his best horse to the king and he rode a weak horse. In consequence, Li's horse collapsed after a few miles and he was forced to shelter for the night in an abandoned temple. He was robbed and later turned over to Imperial troops.

Spence tells us that the king managed to avoid capture and made it to Hozhou, 80 miles southeast of Nanking, where a Taiping army was based. They were driven out by Qing forces and the king became separated from his bodyguard. He managed to avoid capture and when he was near collapse from hunger, he received a biscuit from a tall snowy white man, which gave him the strength to keep going. The man vanished as quickly as he appeared. Was this a heavenly biscuit? He shaved his hair—all Taiping had to have long hair—and he worked for a few days for a farmer. After he left the farmer, a man robbed him of his clothes, and he later met another man who tried to compel him to carry a load of bamboo. He was arrested on 25 October.

In his confession, he stated that what he really wanted to do was become a scholar and possibly qualify for the civil service. The civil war was his father's idea and he wanted no part of it. All true, the officials said, and all irrelevant. The Young Monarch was executed by lingering death on 18 November, one week shy of his birthday. The fate of his four wives, whom he shook off, literally, during the final assault on the city, is unknown to the author.

After his capture and subsequent interrogation, General Li wrote his confession. Seven thousand words a day for seven days, during which he wore out one writing brush. It ends in the middle of a sentence where he is asking rhetorically why did he follow Hong and why was it that he was the man who had taken charge of affairs when there were so many other capable men who could have. "Why was it that they did not take charge of affairs and I alone did? Truly I do not understand this. . . ." is the translation in Franz Michael's book. One presumes that at this point, on 7 August 1864, Li was taken out and executed. And what of the Heavenly Father, the man who had started all of this? His corpse was dug up, decapitated, of course, and burned.

## Most Disastrous War of the Nineteenth Century: The War of the Triple Alliance, 1864–70— The Eponymous Lopez War

On 16 September 1862, the Paraguayan assembly met to elect a new president to succeed his late corpulence, Carlos Lopez; nearly all the 200 members were present. A few, about 20, who might have opposed what was going to happen, had been arrested on the orders of the vice-president, Francisco Lopez, the son of the late president. Francisco was angling to become the next president and wished to leave as little to chance as he could. Before the end of the day, Francisco was the new president for a term of ten years; he would need only eight to destroy his country. Prominent, and or smart, people who could leave the country, did. Anyone who stayed was liable to arbitrary arrest and torture and summary execution.

This is our portrait of the elected dictator. He was born in 1826, he was short, probably less than five foot four inches, bandy-legged, stout, and full-bearded. He was of dark aspect physically, reflecting the fact that he was of mixed race—Guarani and Spanish. As a boy, he was looked down upon by the Spanish nobility of Paraguay and many authors write of the negative effect this had on Lopez. The story of Lopez cannot be adequately told without telling that of Elisa Lynch, his mistress. She was born in 1835 and lived in Ireland until the Potato Famine drove the family to France. Her five uncles, named Crook, had served with Nelson at the Nile and Trafalgar. At 15, she married Monsieur Xavier Quatrefages, a veterinarian for the French army. They were posted to Algeria and there she drew the unwanted attention of the commanding officer. Her husband did not protect her, but another man did. A titled Russian officer, who had become acquainted with Elisa while riding, fought a duel with the Colonel and mortally wounded him—all this within two weeks of meeting her. Elisa left her husband of three years and returned to France. The Russian followed. She learned then that her father had died in the interim and her mother had returned to Ireland. She decided to stay in Paris and do whatever she had to do to make a life for herself. She is described as a tall, handsome woman, blonde with blue-gray eyes, and a marvelous figure. Her clothes accentuated her shape rather than hid it. She was smart, spoke three languages, sat a horse well, and showed that she did not care for public opinion by riding astride. She was ambitious and capable of charming every man she met. She was also courageous.

She became a courtesan and ran a gambling den in her salon. In 1853, Lopez arrived in Europe on a mission for his father to encourage emigration to Paraguay, make a name for Paraguay, and place orders for Paraguay. He did all this, and in Paris he met Elisa Lynch. Lopez crossed from England to France on 3 January 1854, a day on which events in the Straits signaled that the war between Turkey and Russia would soon expand into the Crimean War. Within a few days, he ended up at the gambling salon of Elisa Lynch. The war was important to Elisa because she knew that when war came, her Russian lover and benefactor would be sent away. She would need a non-belligerent replacement.

She saw that if she played it right, Lopez would take her away and she could swap her salon in Paris for a palace and an entire country. She was too experienced in handling men not to get it right. Lopez had quite an appetite for women, but he had never met one like Elisa. She apparently kept him dangling for a week and by the end of it, Lopez was hooked for life. Never underestimate the ability of a woman with a tight body and loose morals; she played Lopez like a fiddle to whatever tune she wanted (with apologies to Raymond Chandler).

The question one must answer when examining Lopez and Lynch is: What were they really like? Could they be guilty of every heinous act attributed to them? Probably not. Is there evidence enough to condemn them? Even giving them the benefit of the doubt, the author comes down in the "Lopez-was-a-psychopath and Lynch a dragon-lady" camp. They relied on each other, encouraged each other, and thought nothing of the consequences for those who followed them.

This war started on 26 December 1864 when Lopez led his army of 80,000 to the upper Paraguay River and invaded Brazil at Corumbá. The area was disputed and Lopez succeeded in isolating the area from eastern Brazil.

On 18 March 1865, Paraguay, which is to say Lopez, declared war on Argentina after the latter refused to give the former permission to cross its territory to invade southern Brazil. The Paraguayans went anyway. Moving down the Parana River, Colonel Antonio L. Estigarribia captured Corrientes at the confluence of the Parana and Paraguay Rivers on 13 April. He then headed east along the Parana and invaded southern Brazil via Encarnación.

On 1 May 1865, the Triple Alliance was formed by Uruguay, Argentina, and Brazil to destroy Lopez and his government and opening the Paraguay and Parana Rivers to free navigation. Of course, the reappropriation of some territory might just have been a fringe benefit, as well. This war would be fought on the rivers and on land.

Estigarribia's force reached the Uruguay River and penetrated to Uruguayana where he came up against the allied force of 30,000. Part of his force was destroyed and he surrendered the rump of his army on 18 September. The allies advanced north and the Paraguayans abandoned Corrientes rather than have their communications cut. Lopez established his 25,000-man army below, which is to say south of, the fortress of Humaita. Such was the situation at the end of October. It is estimated that the Paraguayans had lost about 20,000 men in combat up to this point, with 50,000 more dying from disease. Lopez took personal command of the armed forces in the field.

Starting in January 1866, the allies crossed the Parana but moved slowly with their army of 45,000. A Paraguayan attack was repulsed on 2 May at the battle of Estero Bellaco in the Paso de Patria zone. The Paraguayans, with about 5,000 troops under the command of Diaz, intended to halt the allied advance in the marshes and swamps of the area. They attacked the allied vanguard and drove them off, capturing artillery and equipment in the process. Pushing on against the allied main body, they were checked by superior numbers and retreated. The Paraguayans lost most of the equipment they had captured. The Allies lost about 1,600 men, but they continued to advance into Paraguay.

On 23 May, the allied army contacted the Paraguayans who were entrenched at Tuyuti. This area is marsh, swamp, mangroves, and lagoons. The Paraguayans had positioned themselves covering the passages out of this terrain and the allies would have to fight their way past a determined and brave army in prepared positions. Then Lopez decided that rather than stay in his entrenchments, the Paraguayans would launch a surprise attack the next day while the allies were still setting up their camp. In this way, they might sweep them into the Parana River, which was at their backs. The plan called for a double envelopment—the paradigm of tactical genius. General Barrios would lead 7,000 infantry and 1,000 cavalry on the Paraguayan right and General Resquin would lead his 8,000—one should say Lopez's 8,000 for it was not healthy to speak of Paraguay's soldiers as one's own—against the left. Major Jose Diaz and Hilario Marco would attack the center with 4,000 infantry and cavalry.

The allied commander, Mitre, ignored the signs that the enemy had been up to something since dawn, but he did order the troops to ready themselves for an attack in the afternoon. One thing the allies did right was to dig a ditch in front of their position. The attack was supposed to begin at dawn or thereabouts, but the difficulty of moving units along the tracks through the swamps delayed things until 11:30 A.M. or later. The actual battlefield was an area of raised ground.

The Paraguayans had early success on the wings, but the Argentines on the left eventually halted Resquin's attack with the use of reserves and artillery fire. On the right, Barrios pressed the Brazilians hard, but he did not have the reserves he needed to defeat their superior numbers. The frontal attacks were also beaten back and the as the afternoon wore on, the ditch in front of the allied position filled with dead and wounded soldiers. By mid-afternoon, it was over. The allies sustained about 4,000 casualties and the Paraguayans 5,000 dead, 8,000 wounded, and 350 taken prisoner. Some historians write that the war had been lost here in 1866 and yet there was four years more of suffering to come. Perhaps, but one could say more safely that, at this point, the Paraguayans were unlikely to win the war but they had not yet lost it. That would come later.

The disposal of the dead tells us more about the condition of the Lopez's army. The allies buried their dead, but decided to cremate the Paraguayans. They stacked the corpses with wood in alternate layers in piles of 50 to 100 and set fire to them. So thin were the Paraguayans that it was reported that they were difficult to burn. George Thompson, who was there and tells us this, was also there six weeks later. There were still bodies in the woods and the spaces between, but the bodies had not decomposed, rather they had been mummified as the skin had dried on the bones.

These were very heavy losses for Lopez—how heavy is the question. The Paraguayan strength is variously given as between 20,000 to 25,000. One source places them at under 20,000, but even at best, Lopez had lost over half his army in four hours. Particularly telling was who had been lost. Men from the Spanish aristocracy of Paraguay had been mown down. Scarcely a family from this class had not lost someone and very many families had lost all their men. Now Lopez was no fan of the higher classes of Paraguay; as a man who was part Spanish and part Guarani, the dominant Indian tribe—or, if you prefer, indigenous personnel of the region—he had been snubbed by much of Asunción's society for being a half-breed. Still, it was not good policy to lose what trained officers you had. Interestingly, only the higher-ranked officers in the army were allowed to wear shoes, everyone else went barefoot.

The allies failed to follow up their victory, however, and Lopez was allowed to slip away. There was to be a lot of failing to follow up victories immediately in this war and it came on both sides. After Tuyu-ti, the allies sat. Charles Kolinsky cites a letter General Flores wrote to his wife which illuminates why. Flores was the commander of the 1,400-strong Uruguayan contingent. He complained that delay was the rule in the alliance. Nothing was done until every aspect of a movement was calculated *ad infinitem* and then the thing was put off. The most activity was demonstrated when there was a holiday. Then the bands tuned up, regiments paraded, and everybody turned out for the festivities. The thing that irked Flores was that there always seemed to be some occasion! When *mañana* is added into the mix of incompetence, mistakes, and the fog of war, it should not be surprising that hard-won opportunity was abandoned. It should be remembered, however, that these battles were fiercesome events and that inertia afterwards was natural, especially in any army without a competent officer corps and a driving commander. This was neither the first time nor the last that these criticisms could be made about armies.

The allies opted to establish a base and then to push on. From 16 to 18 July 1866, the allies took 5,000 casualties to Lopez's 2,500, an action which we cannot consider minor, but the next major battle was two months away. Nevertheless, from 1 to 3 September, the allies forced the unfinished Paraguayan defenses at Curuzu, above the confluence of the Paraguay and Parana Rivers. The allies lost one ironclad, the *Rio de Janeiro*, to a torpedo during the attack on the river battery, the only such loss of the war. No matter, though; the naval commander, the Brazilian Admiral Tamandaré, could respond with more caution; no Farragut he. The Brazilian 2d Corps, consisting of 14,000 men under General Pôrto Alegre, stormed the defenses and carried them, albeit with heavy casualties. Once again, pursuit was not on the table. Had it been, the allies may have been able to reach the fortress of Humaita up river in one bound. The battle of Curupaity would have to be fought on 22 September.

Between the two dates, the world was treated to a peace conference. The Paraguayan army was suffering from disease and heavy losses and while it still had some punch left, perhaps it was time to do some talking. On 12 September, Lopez and Mitre met in a palm grove at Yataity-Corá to discuss the future. For the meeting, Lopez wore his full Parisian-made uniform modeled on that of Napoleon III. This consisted of gleaming, knee-high boots, spurs, and a scarlet poncho with gold at the collar. Mitre, never the clothes-horse, dressed down for the occasion. He wore a simple military frock coat and a broad-brimmed, flat-crowned hat known as a "Jim Crow." The two leaders exchanged greetings, sat on chairs, made toasts and talked for five hours. What they said exactly is unknown as they were alone. What we do know is that in accordance with the terms of the Triple Alliance, there had to be no more Lopez in Paraguay as a condition of ending the war. Lopez, now calling himself the "Marshal President," had the prospect of life in Europe in exile with enough money. He countered, apparently, with the offer that he would stay away for two years and then return. What happened next depends upon which version of events one believes.

In one account, Mitre turned down the deal and the meeting ended with a couple more drinks of brandy from each other's flasks and an exchange of riding whips. In the other account, Mitre was about to accept Lopez's offer, but before he could, Lopez had second thoughts of life without power and people to torture and announced that he could never leave the sacred soil of Paraguay. The readers should note that if they find themselves overseas and the national leader, especially a despotic one, begins talking about "sacred soil" and identifying himself as the "embodiment of the country," then it is a good time to be on the next boat, plane, or train out. In any event, if Lopez had left Paraguay, it is unlikely he would have been welcomed back by his people and the author suspects that he knew it. If the allies had succeeded in sending him into exile, the war would have been over and thousands of people would have been spared. If Mitre turned down the offer, he blew the deal of the century. Lopez decided to cap off the day by arresting the two aides-de-camp of Mitre who had been given permission to talk with some Paraguayan officers. They were sent to Paraguay and starved. He followed this up by arranging the ambush of some Paraguayans who had emigrated to Uruguay to escape his tyranny. These hapless individuals had taken advantage of the ceasefire to visit old friends on the day of the summit and promised to come back the next day. When the trap was sprung, one of the men got away, but the other two were wounded and arrested. Lopez had them flogged to death. With these amusements out of the way it was time to return to full-scale violence.

On 22 September 1866 at the battle of Curupaity, the allies attacked Lopez, who was entrenched at the bend of the Paraguay River where it makes a hard right turn. Things did not go their way. The allies numbered about 11,000 Brazilians and 7,000 Argentines. They began the action by shelling the Paraguayan positions with the fire from eight ironclad monitors in the river. They attempted to storm the defenses, but they were repulsed with heavy losses. Colonel Thompson, an English officer in Lopez's employ, had ordered a trench dug in front of their position. It was 2,000 yards long, 11 feet wide and 6 feet deep. Revetments were made from all the trees cut down to provide clear fields of fire and pointed stakes were fixed in the trench wall. Adding to the strength of the positions was the swampy terrain, which broke up the assault formations. The defenses were 30 feet above the river, so the pre-assault naval bombardment had little effect upon them.

Attack after attack failed and the bodies piled up as the infantry was torn apart by grape, cannister, and, when close enough, musket fire. Some Paraguayans, by the way, were still using the Brown Bess. The allies suffered 9,000 casualties, to the Paraguayans' 54. The losses were severe enough to put Argentina out of the war for a time. Lopez ordered the murder of all nonambulatory wounded who were left on the field. This time, it was Lopez who did not follow up the success, but his army probably could not. It was undeniably a great victory, but it would be his only one in the war.

A stalemate existed for the rest of the year and both sides had to fight cholera as much as the enemy. In fact, disease would carry away thousands upon tens of thousands in this war. The Brazilians, camped in swamps, suffered from malaria as well as cholera. By May 1867, Gilbert Phelps tells us, the Brazilian army had 13,000 in hospital and new patients being admitted at the rate of 280 a day.

For the benefit of the uninitiated, which thankfully is most of us, cholera is an infectious disease characterized by vomiting and purging of a rice-water-like fluid. It has an incubation period of two to five days although distress in the host can accelerate the onset of the disease. It starts with these symptoms and death can follow within 1 to 24 hours. If one makes it past this point, there is a chance of recovery. The mortality rate is 30 to 80 percent. It is known as "Asiatic cholera" because it originated in the East Indies. The cause of the disease is the *vibrio cholerae*, a comma-shaped bacillus, which can survive temperatures from −15 degrees F to 104 degrees F. The bacteria live chiefly in the intestines. Some people are immune to the disease and may be labeled as carriers. The disease is contagious and the two most common methods of transmission are through ordinary flies which have picked up the bacilli through the usual activity of flies and convey it to food and drink, or through polluted water.

There are three stages for the disease; invasion, collapse, and reaction. In the first stage the victim suffers from diarrhea, perhaps with fever or pain, vomiting, headache, and depression of spirit. In stage two, the diarrhea continues, but more painfully. The stool, which was at first yellow, becomes whitish like rice water and contains blood and mucus. There is great exhaustion, sub-normal temperature, cold sweats, and a barely perceptible pulse. You also do not look too good; ghastly is more precise. If, up to this point, you were afraid that you were going to die, you may now be afraid that you won't. In the third stage, normal body temperature returns, normal coloration, a perceptible pulse and other normal functions. Even the diarrhea eases off. Relapses are not uncommon, however, which may be characterized by uremia, loss of consciousness, and death.

Needless to say, the stalemate continued through 1867. An attempt by the Brazilians to invade northwest Paraguay through the Matto Grosso ended in abject failure. Over the course of 1867, Lopez also took ill. His Irish mistress, the redoubtable Elisa Lynch, came to his camp and nursed him. Lopez recovered and to celebrate, he released his old tutor, Father Maiz, from prison. Father Maiz would go on to bigger and better things and become one of Lopez's best interrogators and torturers. His advancement may have been assisted by the article he wrote upon his release which favorably compared Lopez to Christ (although he did not go as far as naming him his younger brother). Phelps adds that July, Lopez's birthday, was styled the month of the Christian Lopez. What did that make the decade of the 1860s?

As the cholera subsided in the late autumn, it was time for another offensive. Aerial reconnaissance made its debut in South America. Two American brothers, James and Ezra Allen, made several ascents to a height of 50 feet. The resourceful Paraguayans drove off the balloonists by lighting fires which produced noxious smoke. By July, General Mitre had just returned from Argentina where he had put down provincial revolts, and effective command was now exercised by the Brazilian Marquis de Caxias. The plan was to surround the Paraguayan forces in the defensive zone known as the *quadilatero*, the key to which was Fortress Humaita, and this they managed to do.

In August, the allied army of about 45,000 was slowly moving north up the Paraguay River. The replenished Brazilians numbered about 40,000, and the Argentines, 5,000. The Paraguayan army was about 20,000, but half the force was made up of boys and old men. The iron-clads were able to force passage at Curupaity, but stopped at the boom of chains which Lopez had strung across the Paraguay River just above its confluence with the Tebicuary. If the allies had pushed on to the fortress of Humaita, they would have found the greatest fort in South America quite undermanned and lacking artillery. Unfortunately, they did not. They chose to bombard Curupaity for months, to little effect.

The second battle of Tuyuti on 3 November was inconclusive, although it could have produced some dramatic results. A furious dawn attack by 8,000 Paraguayans succeeded in overrunning the allied lines, but the drive ended when the troops stopped to pillage the camp. This was, in fact, part of the orders issued to the army and it was superbly executed. The earlier plan was designed to capture enemy guns, but had been amended. Still, the Paraguayans managed to carry off 14 cannon, which were more modern than the ones they had. The break for the looting permitted the allied commanders to rally their troops. The 63-year-old Brazilian, Pôrto Alegre, managed to stem the panic and reform the fleeing soldiers. He then launched a counterattack, in the course of which he had two horses shot out from under him and, Kolinsky tells us, his uniform pierced by bullets. By 09:00 A.M. the Paraguayans under Barrios were in retreat back to their lines. The haul of booty did much to improve morale, however. Losses to each side were about 2,400. On 2 November, the allies captured the Paraguayan fort of Tuyi, some 15 miles north of Humaita. As November ended, the allies had finally surrounded the *quadrilatero*, more or less.

In 1868, Mitre returned to Argentina to head up the government and to suppress the revolts in the provinces. Caxias continued in command of the allied, mostly Brazilian, army. In February, the allied fleet steamed over the river boom when the water level was higher than normal. Lopez ordered Asunción evacuated. The ironclads ran the guns at Humaita and reached Asunción on 24 February. They bombarded the capital for a short while and left. The Paraguayans, meanwhile, removed the guns from Curupaity, but made it appear that it was still fully armed and manned. At the beginning of March, Lopez led his army of 10,000 to a new base at San Fernando, north of the Tebicuary. On 21 March, the allies finally got around to taking a look into Curupaity, but the defenders repelled the attack. The next day, they retreated to Humaita.

Lopez left behind a garrison of 3,000 to defend the fortress. Before moving on, he ordered the massacre of several hundred prisoners, but not the officers. He also ordered the defenders of Humaita, Colonels Martinez and Alén, to hold out to the last. The garrison held out for months due to its defenders' own doggedness and allied inactivity. They faced numbers ten times their own and, although they were starving, they managed to repel a couple of assaults. They telegraphed Lopez that they were at the end of their resources and surviving on roots; he told them to hold on for five more days and then withdraw. Martinez opened discussions with the Argentines to surrender. Being of Spanish descent, he identified with the Argentines. Alén, who had no such affinity, was at the end of his rope. He tried to blow out his brains rather than face the squalor and putrefaction and hopelessness that was his command. He missed. He destroyed one of his eyes, but lived. When Martinez surrendered himself and his fort on 5 August, he was down to 1,300 men. When Lopez heard the news, at breakfast with Elisa we are told, he went ape. Elisa could not restrain him. Martinez's wife and mother were tortured and shot. Alén managed to get through the swamps with some other officers and reached Lopez. If the reader is wondering what Alén was thinking, then he is at one with the author. Alén was clapped in irons, tortured for months, and finally shot.

The allies continued up the Paraguay River with the Brazilians on the east and the Argentines on the west. They were escorted by the Brazilian Navy's gunboats and monitors. The whole thing came to a halt at the Paraguayan defenses at Angostura. The next stage of the fighting lasted through December and is known as the "Lomas Valentinas" (Valentine Hills) campaign. The details do not concern us but the fighting was heavy at times and the losses significant. In the end the superior numbers of the allies told; they even out-flanked the Paraguayans on occasion.

In December, the Brazilians scored a desperate, hard-fought victory at the bridge at the battle of Torero. Caxias, who at 65 took personal command of the reserve troops at Torero and led the frontal assault which captured the bridge. The allies then nearly completely destroyed Caballero's force of 4,000 at Avay.

The Paraguayan army was not much over 3,000 by 21 December when the battle of Itá-Ibaty, or Lomas Valentinas, was fought; the allies were about 25,000. From 12:00 P.M. to 6:00 P.M., the allies assaulted the semi-circular, shallow defensive entrenchments of the Paraguayans. They were unable to break through, although they did haul off 14 guns, including the modern 32-pounder Whitworth which the Paraguayans had captured at the second Tuyuti. Lopez had prized this piece, which was more accurate than anything else in his army's arsenal. The allies lost 4,000 killed and wounded at this battle, and Paraguayans 1,000. They fired shot and shell at the Paraguayans for two more days and asked Lopez to surrender on 24 December; he answered that he would fight on until God decided things. God did not speak on 27 December, but He cleared his throat at least, and the Paraguayan line collapsed. Lopez fled east to Cerro León, but he was not pursued. The forces of Colonel Thompson at Angostura surrendered on 30 and 31 December; the allies were probably wondering whether the war was over. Had they pursued Lopez and caught him, then it would have been over. It was, after all, one of the stated goals of the alliance that Lopez leave Paraguay.

The allies reached Asunción on 1 January 1869. That the Marshal President did not care about the condition of his men is by now obvious to the reader. This unconcerned attitude extended to the civilians as well. Perhaps this is a good place to explain how and why so many people died in the course of this war. The blockade of Paraguay was producing great shortages and even though there was a fair amount of improvisation regarding the production of salt, gunpowder, and other necessities, the populace was suffering. Most cattle had been consumed and Paraguay was not a big producer of cattle anyway. Kolinsky tells us that whereas rations once equaled one cow for every 80 people, during the war it became eventually one cow for every 500. The continued stripping of the country for manpower had resulted in women, children, and the old being responsible for farming. Food production, consequently, fell; with hunger came disease, and the death-rate climbed. Cholera killed about one-quarter of the population, we are told. Later, when Lopez ordered his countrymen out of Asunción, fewer than one-quarter of them found sufficient shelter. The rest were outdoors—in the rainy season. You pick the disease, they had it. Why evacuate Asunción? Lopez probably feared that the allies would not massacre the populace.

The call ups of 1867 demonstrate the already sad state of manpower. The area of Villa Rica was a heavily-populated area; in November 1867, it was reported that there were 563 men in the district. The breakdown was as follows: 238 boys aged 12–14, 5 slaves, 8 librettos (slaves going to be free), 29 wounded soldiers, 260 militia men over 50 years old, and a few completely unsuitable for service. In Yutí, it was the same sort of thing, 249 of the 371 men were either around 12 years old or over 60 and the remaining men were suffering from various illnesses. At San Joaquín, it was 19 men aged 60 to 90, 12 men aged 40 to 59, 2 men 30 to 39, 7 men 12 to 19 and no men aged 20 to 29. By the end of 1868, it was worse. In fact, Elisa raised a woman's corps which, on one occasion, she led in battle against the Argentines at Villeta—successfully.

Maing it worse, after the fall of Humaita, Lopez became convinced that there was only one reason why things were going so badly for him. It was not the size of the army, or its lack of training, or its generally inferior weapons, or its generalship, or any of the monumental mistakes he had made that had seen things go against him. It was, obviously, the vast foreign and domestic conspiracy which was doing harm to him and to Paraguay. Elisa Lynch supported him in this conviction. It is the way of most despots, or the despotically inclined, to blame their misfortunes on a conspiracy. Elisa just didn't have the opportunity to announce it on "Good Morning Paraguay."

As to the conspiracy—there wasn't one. Well, O.K., his immediate family was up to something, but it came to naught. Not that a conspiracy was not warranted. Lopez was a monster and it is tragic that he did not have a knife stuck in his back or a lead ball sizzle his brain matter before this. In the course of this murderous rampage, Lopez had about

1,000 people arrested. On occasion, the victims, foreign and domestic, were brought before a drum-head military tribunal, "tried," tortured, and then shot. It is reported that one interviewee died under torture and this so infuriated Lopez that he had the corpse shot. Among those arrested and executed were Lopez's two brothers, his brothers-in-law, numerous military officers, and a bishop. The bishop and the others had been conspiring. Lopez even had his mother beaten and, on the day he was killed, he was ready to sign her death warrant. Nor had Lopez waited until now to show this side of his character, his brutality had been well-established in his youth when he carried out assignments his father had given him. How many were executed? At the least 500.

On 12 January 1869, Caxias declared the war over, prematurely. The Brazilian leadership decided that the war must continue until Lopez was captured. Caxias went home to explain his announcement, but he was honored also, made a duke, and retired from the army. After he left Asunción, the troops became bored and started to loot. A new commander was appointed, one with no real military experience, but he was the son-in-law of the Emperor, and grandson of Louis Philippe. Kolinsky gives us this thumbnail portrait of the Conde d'Eu also known as Luiz Felipe Maria Fernando Gastão d'Orléans. He was 26, blonde, blue-eyed, and bearded, partially deaf and not exactly at home in the Portuguese language. He was given a top notch staff, however, which the reader will recall, is the first rule for such appointments. By June, the allied army—and here it must be said that the army was essentially all Brazilian—numbered 26,000. The men were well equipped and divided into two corps under Generals Polidoro and Osório. The latter was now considered Brazil's greatest military figure. He returned to campaign even though he had been shot through the jaw and used a black silk scarf to bind his chin and conceal his wound. Also in June, a provisional government was put in place in Asunción. Now the only thing left to do was get Lopez.

The Marshal President had not been idle, however. He managed to scrape together 13,000 men and 13 pieces of artillery that had been cast by an improvised foundry. Infantry weapons were harder to come by. The new capital of Paraguay, at least of Lopez's Paraguay, was Piribebuy. The state treasury was under the care of Elisa Lynch and it traveled with Lopez and the four four children they had had together.

The Brazilians decided upon a campaign strategy and the Conde d'Eu executed it well. They outflanked Lopez at Piribebuy and captured the town on 12 August 1869. Among the dead, wounded, and those taken prisoner were the women and boys who were now fighting in the army. The Conde d'Eu, much to his credit, had heard of pursuit, and on

13 August, he moved north after Lopez. At Caacupé on 15 August, the Brazilians found 1,200 wounded. Generals Osório and Polidoro were replaced at this time as the former, in his sixties and still not recovered from his wounds, was exhausted, and the latter was ill. The First Corps was now commanded by General Barreto and the Second Corps by General Monteiro. The Marshal President quit his camps at Azcurra and moved northeast to Campo Grande.

The Conde d'Eu continued to push the pursuit of Lopez and at Campo Grande, the Brazilians came upon the rearguard of the Paraguayans. Moving quickly to the attack, they Brazilians defeated Caballero's force. The sadness of the battlefield was made worse when it was discovered that many of the defenders were boys as young as ten. They were wearing false beards to appear older and thus more formidable.

The lack of modern infantry weapons on the part of the Paraguayans was apparent and telling in combat. They were still relying on flintlocks. Lopez's army was now down to about 2,000 and without its baggage. As a fighting force, it was finished. Lopez headed for Caraguatay, the Conde d'Eu headed for Caraguatay; they missed him by a few hours. Lopez moved and the Conde d'Eu followed; the pressure was maintained. Along with what remained of Lopez's force was a large contingent of civilians, mostly women. Most were loyal to him, and some had evacuated their homes when ordered to and followed him on this death march. Others were suspected of loyalty and were, in effect, prisoners. As Lopez drove further into the wilderness of northeastern Paraguay, the privations increased. Starvation was rampant; those who could defect to the other side, did. On and on it went, and the army, Kolinsky tells us, was down to 1,000 by December; by February 1870, it was 500. Lopez and his group reached Cerro Corá and the Marshal President commemorated the six-month trek with a medal for the soldiers. The food supply was no better, however, as there were no farms in the region.

The end came on 1 March. Acting on intelligence from deserters and captured soldiers, a Brazilian cavalry force converged on Cerro Corá. The outpost was tossed aside at dawn and by 6:00 A.M., the word had reached headquarters that the enemy was near. Lopez had 400 men with him, but the Brazilians were in on the camp and scattered the defenders. Lopez fled, but was mortally wounded by José Lacerda's lance thrust to the abdomen. He managed, with assistance, to reach the Aquidaban-Niqüí River. There are several versions of Lopez's last minutes, but in essence they are the same. Lopez was called upon to surrender, but he would not. He shouted, "I die with my country!" Truer words were never spoken. João Sores, a cavalryman, fired his percussion lock Spencer carbine and Lopez was dead. Kolinsky tells us that

Lopez is the only chief executive in South America to die in battle against his country's enemies. It was not really much of a battle.

Elisa Lynch, meanwhile, had fled in her coach with her children. The horses could not make much speed, however, and she was overtaken. Her eldest son, Juan, 15 and already a colonel in the army, was sitting opposite her. He refused to surrender and from inside the coach fired a shot at the Brazilian lancers. A thrust from one of the lances pierced his heart and he fell forward into his mother's lap, dead. Elisa Lynch sought permission to bury her dead and, we are told, she, her sons, and Isidora Díaz had to scoop out the graves with their hands.

The US brokered a peace treaty on 20 June and Paraguay lost 55,000 square miles of territory to Brazil and Argentina. Lopez lost the war and 84 percent of the population of his country. In six years, the 1,400,000 Paraguayans were reduced to 21,000—29,000 adult males, 106,000 women, and 86,000 children. The allies lost about 1,000,000 men.

Lopez's mother and sisters denounced him, cited their arrest as proof of their opposition, and lived out their days in Asunción in comfort. Elisa Lynch pursued the settlement of Lopez's holdings for herself and her sons, but in the end she received nothing and spent most of the money she had on lawyers. She spent time in England, Ireland, the Holy Land, but she ended up back in Paris. She fell back into her old life, we are told, but in a much lower-rent district. She died in July 1886 and was buried at the expense of the city.

## End of Napoleonic Mass on the Battlefield:
St. Privat, 1870

The dilemma for tacticians to solve with the advent of the breech-loading rifle and later, the smokeless cartridge firing, magazine-fed rifle, was how to maintain offensive drive in the face of effective fire. Fire was seen as defensive as it stopped maneuver. So how to keep one's men moving? By early mid-century, the Prussians saw the answer as being to get the men across the battlefield more quickly, hence they devised a tactical scheme based on company columns. This was a break with the tactics of the past 150 years or more which relied on maneuver by battalion columns. This is not to say that all armies followed suit. In the Austro-Franco War of 1859, the French maneuvered by battalions that were screened by skirmishers. During the Six Weeks War between Austria and Prussia in 1866, the latter maneuvered their company columns into the skirmish line by platoons and relied upon the superiority of the Dreyse needle gun to defeat the Austrian attackers. The French saw that this was the way to go and changed their tactical scheme in 1867. This was not the end of it, however; before too long, maneuver by company columns would be shown to be equally impossible.

At St. Privat, the Prussian Guards Division advanced against the French, who were in defensive positions and armed with breech loading Chassepot rifles and *mitrailleuses*. The Prussian infantry was in columns of half battalions with skirmishers out front. At about 1,000 meters, the Prussians came under heavy fire. The Prussians pushed on, but in the first ten minutes, they sustained nearly 6,000 casualties. The attack managed to push forward to 600 yards from the French line and stopped. On the day, they lost 8,000 officers and men, sustaining 50 percent casualties. This was demonstration enough for the Prussians. Two months later at Le Bourget, they advanced in loose lines by bounds and using cover. At Plevna, during the Russo-Turkish War of 1877, Russian columns were similarly shot up to the tune of 35 percent casualties by the entrenched Turks. The problem then became one of training troops to operate effectively while dispersed and still maintain discipline and control. This was much more easily said than done, and the armies of countries whose military cultures were able to adapt profited significantly over the coming century.

## Last Triumph of Shock Tactics over Gunpowder:
Isandhlwana, 22 January 1879

At Isandhlwana, 20,000 Zulu warriors armed with spears (*assegais*) and a handful of rifles overwhelmed a force of 1,800 British (meaning Europeans) and 2,500 native troops. The news of the defeat arrived in England like a thunderclap and stunned all who heard it.

When the British laid claim to Zululand, they found that they would have to back it up with an invasion. King Cetewayo of the Zulus was determined to resist. The British army was led by Frederick August Thesiger, who is better known as Lord Chelmsford. Born in 1827, he had served in Canada, the Crimea War, the Indian Mutiny, and the Abbysinian War. In 1879, he commanded a force of 5,000 Europeans and 8,000 Africans against a Zulu army of about 40,000. The Zulus were a warrior tribe which had conquered their way across much of southern Africa over the previous five decades, and were not about to back down in the face of any threat. Indeed, much of their culture depended on conduct of more-or-less constant warfare.

On 11 January, Lord Chelmsford divided his force into three columns and invaded Zululand. The plan called for the three columns that would converge on Ulundi, the Zulu capital. Chelmsford personally commanded the center column and crossed the Buffalo River at Rorke's Drift, a place soon to be synonymous with heroic defense against great odds. By 22 January, Chelmsford's force was camped at Isandhlwana, some ten miles from Rorke's Drift. Before dawn on that day, Chelmsford had taken about half of his force to support one of his reconnaissance parties. This left the defense of the camp to six companies of the 1st and 2nd Battalions of the 24th Regiment of Foot, the 2d Warwickshire Regiment, along with some colonial troops, and two artillery pieces.* In command was Brevet Lieutenant-Colonel Henry Pulleine, but he had no real combat experience. Disconcerting to some officers was the fact that the camp had not been fortified according to standing orders, which called for entrenchments and breastworks.

At 11:00 A.M., Pulleine received news that a large force of Zulus had been spotted. At noon, another report came that the Zulus were moving, possibly away from the camp. They were moving, indeed; they had taken up positions in a large ravine near the camp. Chelmsford was eleven miles away, looking for them. Meanwhile, Pulleine was preparing his defenses. One of the mounted riders on patrol then stumbled upon the ravine about five miles from the camp; he wheeled about and raced for the camp. Behind him, the Zulus started for the camp. Pulleine spread out his riflemen rather than concentrate them in the camp. Word had been sent out earlier to Chelmsford regarding the situation.

The Zulus attacked in their classic pattern of left and right horns followed by the attack of the chest at the weak spot, which is to say, the Zulus attacked first with the two wings of their army and then the central part. The attack began as the horns closed around the camp. The left horn was checked by Brevet Colonel Anthony Durnford's troops, which consisted of mounted and foot soldiers. In this they were assisted by the crossfire coming from Captain Pope's G Company of the 2nd/24th. The Zulus were driven to the ground by fusillades of .45-caliber lead from G Company's Martini-Henry rifles some 1,100 yards from the British line. A lack of ammunition, or better said, a problem with ammunition circulation, however, caused fatal problems for the defenders. It is said that Durnford's men were refused ammunition from the 1st/24th wagons. Durnford had to pull back his men when they ran out of ammunition, and as a result, Pope also had to pull back. This created a 700-yard

---

*After the Cardwell Reforms of 1881, the 2nd Warwickshire was renamed "The South Wales Borderers." However, even at the time of the Zulu War, the regiment was heavily populated with Welsh, as the regiment's designated recruiting area was in Wales. In fact, according to official information provided by the regiment's modern day descendant organization, the Royal Regiment of Wales, there were only two soldiers from Warwickshire present at Rorke;s Drift!

gap between him and the 1st/24th. Accordingly, Pulleine ordered a retirement to close up the line. The Zulus poured through the gap, however, and eventually overran the position. Those defenders who could took flight, the ones with horses stood the best chance. Interestingly, except for a small and ineffectual bunch equipped with obsolete muskets and rifles, the Zulus were overwhelmingly equipped with two types of *assegais*—one for throwing and one for thrusting—as well as wooden clubs, called *knob-kerries*. They also carried cowhide shields. Their weapons were essentially about as sophisticated as those used by various minor clans easily subdued by Alexander the Great. At Isandhlwana, poor logistical practices combined with ineffective leadership on the part of the British/colonial force, and exceptional valor and aggressiveness on the part of the Zulus to bring about a stunning victory despite a grossly lopsided technological disparity.

Casualties are unreported for the Zulus, but they must have been very substantial. For the British force, 21 officers and 534 men of the 2nd Warwickshire Regiment, or 100 percent of those present on the battlefield, were killed; in total, 1,645 Europeans and 2,200 Africans lost their lives. Byron Farwell tells us in *Queen Victoria's Little Wars* that this number includes all the wounded who remained on the battlefield, and that the Zulus killed their own severely wounded tribesmen as well.

# Modern Warfare

## Introduction

By 1914, all the ingredients were in place to produce a destructive stalemate of the highest order. Thanks to widespread universal male conscription, armies numbered in the millions. Railroads were set to move tons of supplies rapidly over long distances, while telegraphs and early radios allowed long-distance communications at the speed of light. Rapid-fire weapons, coupled with long-range artillery firing high explosive shells, were guaranteed to deliver fire in a volume previously unimagined.

The First World War as it was waged in Europe was actually two kinds of war. In the east, a war of movement was still possible because of the low force-to-space ratio. In the west, a new kind of siege warfare soon set in, and a continuous fortified front sprang up from Switzerland to the English Channel. Various methods were tried to break the stalemate that barbed-wire entrenchments and firepower had created. The essential problem was that the defenses were so deep that an attacker, even after penetrating two of the enemy's lines, still had not effected a breakthrough. Moreover, the overwhelming artillery barrages that were used to create these penetrations could not range far enough to support the attackers when they needed firepower the most. In short, attacks were doomed to fail because the infantry outran its artillery and was then at the mercy of his opponent's artillery. Large guns were still not mobile enough to keep pace with the progress of foot soldiers.

The major combatants attempted to terminate this murderous impasse by a variety of technological responses and innovations in the art of war. At intervals, all of the major combatants (except the Russians) reintroduced personal armor—in the form of steel helmets—to reduce casualties. The British sought to make men bulletproof by developing the tank. The Germans sought the wholesale extermination of their enemies by introducing poison gas to the battlefield, and their local eradication by using flamethrowers. (The other sides soon followed suit.) The Germans also sought to make men invisible by developing their infiltration techniques.

In the latter case, the German efforts reflected the extent to which infantry tactics had become decentralized. The basic unit was now a squad of roughly ten men and a leader. They were armed with rifles and a light machine gun. These "stormtrooper" (actually "*Stosstrupp*" or "strike troops") tactics basically entailed bypassing strong points and reconnoitering all along the line looking for the weak spots. Penetration was achieved by sudden, violent attacks, heavily reinforced; attacks that ran into heavy opposition were halted, and the carefully-trained and specially-equipped *Stosstruppen* were saved to fight another day in a more promising location. The Germans hoped that in this manner they could rupture the allied line, then fall upon lines of communications and restore movement to war. In addition, special artillery tactics were developed which consisted of a sudden "hurricane" bombardment fired without ranging and delivered through the depth of the assault area. In contrast to the infantry tactics, these fire tactics required centralized control of the guns. Using these tactics, the German attack launched in March 1918 came close to succeeding, but in the end, it, too, ran out of impetus. The logistics of the age, which could keep a static army supplied with vast amounts of stores, could not keep up with an army that consumed vast amounts of stores and moved forward rapidly. Reversely, the allied armies were falling back, ever closer to their supply sources. In the end, the superior numbers of the allies and their superior logistics defeated the German army which had "shot its bolt" in the spring offensives.

The issue for military theorists in the inter-war period was how to avoid the killing stalemate of the Great War and restore mobility to the battlefield. The answer had already been revealed to them by 1918, but in 1939, only the Germans had embraced the solution, and even then, only partially. The answer was coordinated mechanized warfare, in which all arms, including artillery, were able to move about the battlefield by means of armored or motorized vehicles; careful coordination with tactical air forces, to create a sort of "flying artillery," was also critical. In other words, it wasn't just a matter of having lots of tanks (the allies had more than the Germans in 1940) or the best tanks (the French had those in 1940 as well), but of how they were organized and employed in battle.

In developing the panzer division as a combined arms team that also contained motorized infantry and artillery, the Germans produced a force with unprecedented flexibility in offensive and defensive operations. Its capabilities were further enhanced by the close cooperation of the *Luftwaffe*, which was dedicated to playing a major ground support role. Greater control of all these forces was now possible due to truly practical tactical radios, and this provided tactical flexibility previously unachievable. By 1940, once through the line, the panzers and their follow-on infantry were able to dislocate the entire enemy position. French attempts to close off the Ardennes were uncoordinated and beaten back. French heavy tank divisions, which were lacking in infantry, could not sustain themselves against the panzer divisions.

The critical thing is that the Germans were able to move a part of their army—only 10 panzer divisions in 1940—at a speed that the French and British could not match. When Guderian broke through the lightly-held Ardennes, the Germans had the opportunity to use their outstanding speed and flexibility to destroy their enemy's morale and will to fight. In this regard, it must be said that Hitler was lucky in his choice of opponent. The French fought at a slower pace than the Germans and it cost them dearly.

Motorized/mechanized units never comprised more than 15 percent of the *Wehrmacht*'s ground forces, however. Although they achieved spectacular successes in the summers and autumns of 1941 and 1942 in the Soviet Union, by early 1943, it was apparent that the armored tip of the German Army was not up to the challenge of defeating the Soviet juggernaut; after all, the vast bulk of German ground forces was still foot-borne or horse-drawn. Once the Soviet war machine was operating at capacity, and given the enormous size of the country, the German armed forces and those of their allies were completely unequal to the task of depriving the Soviets of their will to fight.

Once Hitler had invaded Russia and the United States entered the war, it became the largest global conflict in history. Battles were fought on land; on and under the sea; and in the air. All of the basic weapons systems had been present in 1918, but to say that the scale of the war was greater does not begin to describe the difference. It is important to state, however, that in WWII, most armies were still equipped and armed as they had been in WWI, only with some number of motorized and mechanized units added. Thanks to the latter, tactics became dispersed and on defense, the entrenched line—already giving way in WWI—evolved into the temporary strong-point defense, between which mobile units conducted counterattacks. The battlefield became more fluid, but remained a highly deadly place.

# Equipment

## Most Protected Brains: The Western Front, 1915–18

Although their tactics—running back and forth across No Man's Land directly into the final protective fires of massed artillery and machine guns—may not have been the brainiest way to win a war, World War I saw more protection offered to more brains than any war to that time.

Steel, or at least metal, helmets were nothing new, but their use had never been universal among the soldiers of any major war. The most armored army of ancient times, the Romans, employed thousands of auxiliaries, such as archers, slingers, and spearmen, who never had the luxury of much more than the hair on their heads to protect their brains from the damage caused by flung spears, flying arrows, barbarian axes, swords, daggers, and rocks. Their "barbarian" Germanic, Celtic, Persian, or Semitic foes had far fewer metal helmets still. The mounted knights and dismounted men-at-arms of even the wealthiest medieval lords were accompanied into battle by masses of poorly-protected peasants whose armament—scythes, pruning forks, and sharpened hoes—were high-tech ordnance compared to the pathetic cloth caps that adorned most of their heads.

As the penetration power of battlefield weapons soared with the increasing pervasiveness of firearms, it seems as if the designers of military protective fashion pretty much gave up trying to protect the skulls of the common soldier. As the era of pikemen and *arquebusier* gave way to the epoch of musket-armed fusiliers, grenadiers, and voltigeurs, headgear design became increasingly dictated by martial chic, and less devoted to the preservation of the bony integrity of soldiers' heads. The Thirty Years' War was the last general conflict in which most of the combatants, on all sides, wore metal helmets; even in that war, artillerymen rarely wore metal headgear, and many cavalrymen exhibited a fondness for broad-brimmed, feathered fedoras. Although, due to the high likelihood of shock action, cavalrymen of many armies continued to wear metal headgear, and even breastplates, throughout the centuries, infantrymen, field artillerymen, and other combat residents of the early modern battlefield gradually eschewed the wear of metal helmets in favor of felt bicorns or tricorns, leather shakos of diverse designs, cloth caps of a variety of shapes and sizes, or, in the second half of the nineteenth century, leather or felt helmets adorned with decorative finials of varying shapes. Generally, the headgear of western armies between the end of the wars of religion and the beginning of the twentieth century were decorative, attractive, and utterly useless for protecting the head of the wearer.

This absolute irrelevance of headgear to personal protection in the 250 years leading up to the twentieth century stemmed from several factors. Surely, the mass nature of western armies—beginning with the *levée en masse* of Napoleon Bonaparte—contributed to it; what prince could afford to universally equip the hundreds of thousands of soldiers under his command with metal helmets? Beyond that, what was the point? For most of this period, the state of military medicine was such that a hit from a musket ball, bullet, or shell fragment almost anywhere on the body could prove fatal, and the human trunk and limbs were far more likely targets for the inaccurate firearms of the day than the head. Why go to the outrageous expense of protecting the head, when a much more likely hit almost anywhere else could do just as much harm? As the period progressed, the climbing velocities of bullets and accuracy of common rifles completely obviated the metal helmet as a practical choice for headgear. It would take the widespread implementation of a weapon that could do especial damage to the head, coupled with innovations in military medicine and industrial capabilities, to profoundly change the military milliner's art.

The Great War saw the first widespread use of high-explosive artillery shells in warfare. Although shrapnel, canister, grape, and other varieties of projectiles that spread deadly submunitions around the battlefield had been around for well over a century, high-explosive shells were much more deadly. Powered by compounds many times more potent than the black powder that had propelled previous missiles, high-explosive shells swept the battlefield with shards of steel traveling at hyper-velocities far greater than those of bullets. Hits by even tiny pieces of jagged steel at these speeds caused enormous damage to human tissue, and easily penetrated bone.

Fortunately for the soldiers exposed to the ravages of these weapons, medical advances made many wounds survivable at a rate previously thought impossible. These fragments, which not too long before would have killed just as surely, if more slowly, by the sepsis that would have resulted from their presence anywhere in the body, were now far more likely to be discovered, thanks to the development and increasing pervasiveness of X-ray technologies. If slivers of metal did not destroy key body organs, they could thus be detected for removal, and the soldier had a very good chance of recovery. Thanks to the simultaneous development of aseptic surgery, in large part made possible by the increasingly common use of autoclaves to keep surgical instruments sterile, the removal of these fragments was progressively safe and effective.

The one human body part, however, to which fragments flying at many thousands of feet per second were still practically always lethal was the head. If a steel fragment penetrated the skull, the victim was almost always a goner. For the first year of the war, the cloth service caps of the British Expeditionary Force, the képis of the French armies, and the leather *Pickelhauben* of the Kaiser's soldiers were shredded daily by the torrents of steel flying around Flanders' fields . . . with predictable and devastating consequences for the wearers. World War I developed very differently from the way most military leaders imagined it would. While many thought the warfare triggered by the web of treaties that bound the European powers to or against one another would be over in a matter of months, the war dragged on. As it did so, in the West, the initially fluid lines gradually congealed into a mammoth warren of trenches and obstacles from the English Channel to the Swiss border. Inevitably, new weapons were introduced in attempts to break the deadlock and achieve decisive results. These, in turn, prodded new countermeasures. Poison gas forced the introduction of gas masks; the machine gun caused the development of the tank; and the high-explosive artillery shell compelled the development of a means by which the vulnerable heads of combat soldiers could be protected from fragments. In fact, the very nature of trench warfare compelled special attention to be paid to protecting the head and neck areas from fragments coming from above because these were clearly the body areas most often exposed on soldiers occupying a trench. Fortunately for the soldiers at the front, the same vast expansion of industrial capacity that allowed the production of millions of high-explosive shells also facilitated the production of tens of millions of steel helmets to provide the most protection ever afforded heads in harm's way.

The French, whose zealous dedication to offensive tactics and operations was obviously poorly advised, nevertheless were the first to issue steel helmets to their soldiers. This was particularly wise, since they started out the war wearing mostly red kepis, which made Gallic crania particularly obvious targets. The Model 1915 Adrian pattern helmet (named after the designer, General Adrian) was made of a soft manganese-steel alloy, and patterned after common French firemen's helmets. Undeniably the most aesthetically pleasing of the helmets introduced during the Great War, it was enthusiastically received by the troops. The shell was stamped out in three pieces (dome, rim, and crest), and manufactured in three basic sizes, designated "A" (approximately $6^7/8$), "B" (approximately $7^1/8$) and "C" (about $7^3/8$). For a better fit, each size of helmet was fitted with four different-sized linings, each of which could be further adjusted by means of a drawstring in the crown. The lining, made of goatskin, was separated from the shell by an alu-

French troops, ca.
1916, wearing their
Adrian helmets.
*National Archives (NA)*

minum band, which allowed a certain amount of ventilation, under the rim of the helmet, through a perforation in the helmet's dome, which was protected by the steel crest. The sheepskin chin strap was fastened to the sides of the helmet through metal bales (loops) attached to each side of the rim. A metal insignia was affixed to the front, the most common of which, worn by most infantry and cavalry soldiers, was a flaming bomb with the letters "*RF*," for *Republique Française*. Many members of the AEF posited an alternative meaning, but that is beyond the scope of this article. The helmets, which weighed about 1 pound, 10 ounces (.74 kg) were usually painted in *bleu horizon*, the color of the French Army uniforms from 1915 on.

The British were next to provide protection for the skulls of the sons of their Empire. British and Commonwealth troops began the war in Europe wearing a variety of cloth caps, including primarily the visored service cap, but also the glengarry and balmoral bonnets that were the distinctive headgear of Scottish troops. The "Brodie" helmet (named after the inventor, John Brodie) resembled those worn by medieval men-at-arms, and provided good protection from rain and fragments coming in over the lip of a trench. It provided very little protection from the sides, however. Nevertheless, early versions went into service with British and Commonwealth troops in late 1915. At first, it was issued in limited numbers—about 50 per battalion—and were to be used only by the soldiers who were most exposed to fire at any given moment. This changed in 1916, and a new design (the "Mark I") was also introduced in the spring of that year. This helmet, which featured a folded (less sharp) edge, two-piece lining, and roughened khaki finish, was churned out of British factories by the millions and used by British and Commonwealth forces all the way through WWII and beyond. The US Army

British infantry in the trenches, ca. 1916. From 1914 until just after this photo was taken, the cloth service cap was the standard head gear for most units. Note that the soldiers third and fifth from left are wearing cloth glengarry caps, unique to Scottish units. *NA*

American troops man a French Hotchkiss machine gun on an antiaircraft mount, ca. 1918. By 1916, British and British Commonwealth troops serving on the Western Front adopted this "Brodie" pattern helmet, which the Americans adopted when they entered the war in 1917. The US Army wore this helmet well into 1942, and British Commonwealth troops wore it well into the 1950s. *NA*

bought and issued 400,000 of them during the Great War, and began manufacturing its own after the United States entered the war in 1917. American forces used this virtually-identical design into 1942, when it was replaced by the M1 steel "pot." The major difference between the British and US designs were in the details of the linings and chin straps, but both were made of manganese-steel alloy and weighed about 2 pounds, 4 ounces (1.02 kg).

The British issued cloth or burlap covers after a while, and a wide variety were available for private purchase. Many soldiers painted unit insignia on the front, sides, and even backs of their helmets, and some units had their men drill holes in the helmets to affix regimental badges. This latter practice was officially forbidden, as it corrupted the integrity of the helmet, and contributed to fragmentation. Privately produced helmets were also available, and although most closely resembled the issue Brodies, the domes of some were noticeably deeper, or the brims narrower; some were actually made of soft steel and fluted, and as such resembled the Portuguese trench helmet. These privately-acquired helmets, however, were generally made of soft steel, and were also often banned because when hit, they shattered and were not only extremely dangerous to the wearer, but also to those around him.

The Kaiser's troops were the last to receive metal helmets. Although about 1,500 privately-acquired metal skull caps were issued by General Hans Emil Alexander Gaede to his troops fighting in the Vosges Mountains in 1915, it was not until the end of that year that a small number of government-produced steel helmets were first issued. Designed by *Hauptmann der Landwehr* (Captain of the Home Guard) Friedrich Schwerd of the Hannover Technical Institute, these helmets resembled a coal scuttle worn upside-down, and were distributed to German troops near Verdun in early 1916. They were so successful in reducing the number of head wounds that by the summer of that year, most of the German units on the Western Front had received the new helmets, although, like the British, they were initially issued for use only by soldiers operating in the most exposed positions. (It would be another full year before all German units on the Eastern Front were similarly equipped.) Due to this phased introduction, the old leather *Pickelhaube* continued being worn on both fronts long after the Allies abandoned their soft caps.

Three main models of the *Stahlhelm* saw service during World War I, namely the Models 1916, 1917, and 1918. With the exception of the very earliest helmets—which had a slightly more pronounced angle at the point where the rear flange dips from the front brim—all three were virtually identical in shape, and differed only in the details of their linings, leather chinstraps, and chinstrap attachments. Stamped out of

German soldiers in field gear, wearing cloth-covered leather Pickel-haube. They are armed with a Mauser 98s, to which standard issue "butcher knife" bayonets have been affixed. Royal Canadian Military Institute (RCMI)

chrome-nickel steel alloy, the helmets were manufactured in even sizes from 60 ($7\,^1/_2$) to 68 ($8\,^1/_4$). Lest anyone think that World War I German soldiers had exceptionally enormous heads, it should be remembered that the lining reduced the sizes by about six centimeters. Thus, the size 60 helmet actually fit a man who took a size 54 ($6\,^3/_4$) hat or *Pickelhaube*, and the 68 accommodated a noggin that would normally require about a 62 ($7\,^3/_4$). The smaller-sized helmets, sizes 60, 62, and 64, were manufactured with an extra step at the base of the helmet lugs, to allow the helmet plate, which only came in one size, to be properly fastened to helmets of all sizes.

A steel helmet with a wavy cutout near the ears was produced at the end of the war, and specialists still argue over the purpose: some say it was to reduce the shock of concussion on the ears; others say it was to allow the wear of a headphone for radio men; still others insist that it

German machine gun crew, manning MG 08, circa 1918. The *Stalhelm* replaced the *Pickelhaube* beginning in 1916, and provided the basis for German helmets that would be worn through the end of WWII . . . and in East Germany, until German reunification in 1990! *NA*

was designed for wear by cavalrymen. In any event, relatively few were issued, and the most familiar venue for them in photos seems to be on prominent Nazis, such as Sepp Dietrich, during formal occasions such as parades or inspections, during the early Third Reich.

Although it depended on their exact size, German helmets weighed about three pounds (1.4 kg). Glare and glint were a problem, just as they were with the Brodies, so in 1917, cloth covers were issued. These were expensive and tended to wear out quickly—neither constant wetness nor things like barbed wire and steel fragments are conducive to maintaining the integrity of cloth—so painted-on camouflage became the solution. Although initially issued painted in a flat field gray to match the German uniforms, later *Stahlhelme* were painted in a huge variety of camouflage patterns. The official policy pronounced by General Ludendorff in the summer of 1918 was to paint geometric designs, using shades of brown and drab green as appropriate for the vegetation in the area, and to separate them by black border stripes. Given that each soldier had to paint his own, variations inevitably developed, most typically foregoing the black borders or even adding stripes.

Perhaps the most striking feature of the German helmet was the twin lugs, one on either side of the helmet, about two-thirds of the way forward and a quarter of the way down from the top of the dome. These

Post-WWI *Reichswehr* troops parade wearing the "cut out" pattern steel helmet. During the early years of the Third *Reich*, this helmet was often favored for wear by Nazi Party and *SS* high officials. *NA*

hollow steel protrusions both allowed hot air to escape from the helmet, and also allowed the attachment of a thick, steel brow plate (*Stirnpanzer*) that provided protection against direct hits by rifle slugs—something that no mass-issued helmet in the Great War could do. The plate was notched so that it could fit over the lugs, and was bound to the helmet with a leather strap that fastened at the back. This appliqué armor was used mainly by soldiers whose heads were particularly exposed to direct fire from the enemy, such as sentries or machine gunners.

Other countries generally adopted the designs of these three major powers, at least if they were fighting in the West. The Italians, Belgians, Romanians, and even Russians and Czechs fighting in France wore Adrian-pattern helmets. The Austro-Hungarians wore German helmets, although the Austrians also had their own variation, called the Berndorfer. Manufactured in 1916–17 by the Krupp Berndorfer factory, it featured a brim with a much less-pronounced "skirt," or flange; the brim appears to encircle the helmet with a more consistent, less "stepped" look.

Interestingly, a variety of factors led to helmets being less prevalent on other fronts. Western and colonial soldiers fighting in East Africa and the Middle East generally wore sun helmets of varying designs or traditional head dress. The Germans fabricated about 5,500 helmets for use by their Turkish allies, with the brims thoughtfully cut off. This was done allegedly to allow Turkish soldiers to better heed their five-times daily calls to prayer, which required them to touch their foreheads to the ground in the direction of Mecca. The Germans' sensitive celebration of this rich multicultural diversity never paid off, however; the war ended before any of these helmets were delivered. It is not known exactly how many Turkish soldiers were hit by steel shell fragments in the head while praying, but it is well documented that many of these "Turkish helmets" were used by members of several *Freikorps* militias during the civil wars that plagued Germany after the Armistice.

While there is no doubt that the brains of the Western Front in World War I were the most protected in history to that point—Germany alone produced 7,500,000 steel helmets before the Armistice—it is also true that the largest Army in the war had the least protection of any of the major powers. Perhaps it is no coincidence that that army also sustained the most casualties in the Great War, and did so in significantly less than the four years of combat seen by the combatants on the Western Front. At least, it might be argued that its leaders' failure to provide this minimal measure of protection essential on the modern battlefield was symptomatic of the profound problems that beset not only that power's military establishment, but its entire culture. It might even be that the product of over three years of modern combat without helmets was the worst idea of the twentieth century: the institution of communism in Russia.

## Most Important Weapon of the Twentieth Century: The Machine Gun

Since their beginning, over six hundred years ago, improvements to firearms have sought to extend their range, to improve their accuracy, to enhance their mobility, and to increase their rate of fire. This has been, and is, the desire of all users of missile weapons from pea shooters to guns. The author, for example, scored particularly well in the rubberband wars by possessing an elastic-firing Gatling gun. In the era of muzzle-loaders and flintlocks, multiple shots could only be achieved with multiple barrels. Beyond that, it was the skill of the shooter and the quality of his equipment that determined how many rounds would be fired over a given time. The developments that made the machine gun possible were breech loading and the metal cartridge that contained the bullet, the propellant, and the primer to set it all off. The desire to kill as many men as possible in the shortest amount of time needed no similar gestation.

Everyone knows what a machine gun is; or do they? The author begins this section with a mild admonishment. In the *US Department of Defense Dictionary of Military Terms* (1988 edition), the machine gun is undefined. There are allusions to it, of course; for example, we are told that the M-48A3 and M-60 tanks each carry a .50-caliber and 7.62mm machine gun, but nowhere is there even a of definition of "caliber." Undaunted, the author plunged onward. He looked up submachine gun—no entry; automatic weapon—no dice. "Perhaps," he thought, "by weapon designation,". . . alas, the closest we come to "general purpose machine gun" is "general purchasing agent." Have things changed since 1988? However, the *United States Air Force Dictionary* of 1956 did come through. The machine gun is defined as:

1. Specif. A full-automatic small arm mounted on wheels, in an aircraft, etc. 2. Originally, a gun, esp. a small arm, designed to deliver successive shots rapidly, utilizing a crank-operated or lever-operated machine or mechanism built integral with the gun to accomplish this purpose. 3. By extension, any recoil-operated or gas-operated full-automatic small arm, including full-automatic rifles, machine pistols, submachine guns, and full-automatic mounted weapons.

The term "machine gun" was first generally applied to such weapons as the Gatling and Lowell guns, literally fired by crank-operated machines. The first important operational use of such machine guns was in the American Civil War. The first full-automatic and modern machine gun was a recoil-operated gun built by Hiram Maxim in the year 1884.

Some authors contend that the first machine gun is far older than the nineteenth century and here they refer to a firearm known as the "organ gun." For once, no wisecracks, please. Frederick V. Longstaff, writing in 1917 in *The Book of the Machine Gun*, described it broadly as a small-caliber firearm of one or more barrels fitted with a mechanical contrivance to produce rapid fire. The quest for a rapid-fire weapon goes back a lot farther of course, to the earliest days of the firearm, say the fifteenth century. Enter the organ guns, also known as *ribaudequins* or *orgues*. These weapons were multi-barrelled assemblages on a stand of some sort, hence the resemblance to an organ. The barrels could be fired simultaneously, more or less, by some mechanism. Organ guns were usually used in siege work. Longstaff tells us that the first and perhaps only use of the organ gun in the field came in 1467 at the Battle of Piccardina when the Venetian general Coleoni brought them into action with the advance guard cavalry. So if one accepts the organ gun as an embryonic machine gun, then one has the first use of the weapon in a tactical situation some 536 years ago.

By the mid-nineteenth century, the Nordenfeldt gun was the latest version of the machine gun. It was essentially an organ gun, but breech-loaded and operated by a manually-operated lever. The back and forth movement of the lever loaded the shells, fired them, and ejected them in turn. This assemblage was usually mounted on a carriage of some sort. The better known machine gun of the mid-century, the Gatling gun, the brainchild of Richard Gatling, was invented in 1862. The Gatling gun also featured several barrels, but they were arranged around a central axis and rotated. The cartridges were fed in from a hopper at the top, and as the barrel rotated, cartridges were loaded into the chamber of each barrel. When the barrel/chamber reached the bottom of the rotation, its shell was fired. On its way back up, the spent cartridge was extracted and the chamber vacated in preparation for the next round. This gun was also manually operated, in this case, by a rotary crank.

The Europeans waited until the Montigny *mitrailleuse* to look towards a machine gun. The word *"mitraille"* has the following meanings in French: one is scrap iron; another a soldering alloy; and the one with the most relevance for us is case shot, canister, or grape shot. Thus

The Gatling gun was a progenitor of the twentieth-century machine gun. It was used in the Indian Wars in America and various colonial wars abroad. *RCMI*

a *mitrailleuse* is a gun which fires a lot of bullets just like grape shot. The weapon was secretly manufactured in 1869 and introduced into the French army by Napoleon III in 1870. Secrecy continued to attend the *mitrailleuse* to the extent that only the officers and men who operated the machine were allowed to see it. The guns were transported to the front under tarpaulins and guarded in camp. Needless to say, this was another one of those secrets that all sorts of people knew.

The *mitrailleuse* was the invention of Captain Fafchamps, a Belgian officer. He came up with the designs around 1851 and offered them to Montigny, a Belgian engineer who had a gun-making business in Brussels. This led to a few guns being installed in Belgian forts for the purpose of sweeping the ditches clear of attackers. The *mitrailleuse* was also discussed in professional journals and it was considered by the Indian army in 1868. Moreover, the French press made mention of a secret weapon that would mow down Germans in the coming war. That is not all, however; many officers of different armies had inspected the gun in Brussels and the Austrian government had received one for testing. The really big secret was how the French army was going to employ a weapon that few of its soldiers had seen and with which none had tactical experience.

Here, in general terms, is how the weapon worked. The gun was mounted on a field artillery carriage and had multiple barrels. These were inside a larger, wrought-iron tube, thus giving the *mitrailleuse* the appearance of a field gun. The gun was speed loaded by fitting an 11mm-thick plate, which held the cartridges in position at right angles to the plate, to the breechblock. The loading lever advanced the plate and the breechblock, and introduced the cartridges into the chambers. The firing handle, which could be rotated in one second, would fire all the barrels. The gun could also discharge the bullets singly. The discharged plate could be removed and a new plate fitted in under four seconds. This gave a 25-barrel *mitrailleuse* a rate of fire of 300 shots per minute under perfect conditions. The extreme range of the gun was about a thousand yards, its effective range more like 400 yards. The gun and limber carrying 2,100 cartridges weighed 3,960 pounds and was accompanied by a caisson carrying 6,000 cartridges. A battery consisted of six guns, six caissons, a travelling forge, two baggage wagons, and horses.

The French decided that since the *mitrailleuse* looked like a field gun it should be given to the artillery. To make room for it, they took one battery of artillery of the three they usually grouped together and replaced it with a battery of 10 *mitrailleuses*. There were two consequences to this, neither good. The French reduced the firepower of their batteries by one-third and put a potentially very lethal weapon in a position where it would be outranged by artillery opposed to it. Thus, the French give us the best example of misuse of a weapon in this century. *Mitrailleuses* were blasted by Prussian guns in 1870 and were unable to respond adequately.

When the *mitrailleuses* were used against infantry, they performed with deadly effect. One example is at the battle of Gravelotte on 18 August 1870. In the center of the Prussian line, the Prussian's had artillery on a spur south of the Bois de la Cusse in an exposed position. The 4th Heavy Battery in particular had come under fire from French infantry. Sometime after 1:00, the French managed to bring a *mitrailleuse* battery from Amanvillers into the infantry line. At this effective range, the French machine guns inflicted heavy casualties on the Prussian gunners. The official German history tells us that in a few minutes, the *mitrailleuses* killed and wounded several officers, five gun commanders, 40 men, and destroyed nearly all the horses. French infantry then charged the hill and captured all but two pieces; the only artillery that the Prussians lost in the war. Meanwhile, on the left of the French line at Montigny-la-Grange, elements of the German 3rd Division came under French fire. The Germans were trying to cross a valley and push their forces into the woods on the other side. French infantry used their chassepots to good effect and significantly, they were supported by two batteries of *mitrailleuses* at either end of their firing lines. Sweeping the open ground with their fire, the French riddled the companies of the German 36th Regiment. Antulio Echevarria in *After Clausewitz*, tells us that in other actions against *mitrailleuses* and rifles, the second battalion of the 48th Infantry Regiment (Brandenburg) lost all its officers and over 600 men in fifteen minutes and the 52nd Infantry Regiment lost 1,054 officers and men. This represented 73 percent and 42 percent, respectively, of the strength of these units. The celebrated attack of the Prussian Guards up a gentle slope before St. Privat exacted a terrible toll on the Germans. They covered some 2,500 yards in their columns before the attack lost its drive 750 yards from the French line. In the first ten minutes of firing, the Prussians took 6,000 casualties.

The successes of the machine gun in the Franco-Prussian War went unnoticed in the post-war period for the most part as critics seized upon the great failures of the weapon when it was used as a form of field gun.

Gatling's system was later surpassed by the Maxim gun invented in 1884 by Hiram S. Maxim, but the principles of the Gatling gun would be resurrected in the 1960s when the rotary gun and the chain gun came into being. These updated versions of the Gatling gun spew bullets at cyclic rates of 2,000 to 6,000 per minute. The "cyclic" rate is that of the mechanism when properly functioning and continuously fired. Rarely does any automatic weapon fire continuously for a full minute, as tactical considerations do not often require it; it is very difficult to provide ammunition on this basis; and very few machine guns—especially air-cooled modern ones—can withstand the heat generated by such use. Barrels would melt, mechanisms would jam from overheating, and so on. Much more useful rates are the "rapid" rate, which is the rate at which a machine gun can fire for several minutes, and the "sustained" rate, which is the rate at which a machine gun can fire indefinitely.

The first true automatic gun was the brain child of Hiram Maxim. A genius of invention, Maxim was born in Maine in 1840. He was a skilled wood turner, draftsman, and self-described engineer. He was always reading and learning, and in the course of his life, he secured 122 American patents and 149 British patents between 1866 and 1916, the year of his death. Besides patents for firearms, cartridges projectiles, powders, and explosives (which one would expect), he also had patents for gas generators, inhalers, aeronautics, gun mountings, carburetors, the treatment of coffee, bombs, curling hair, the steam-powered vacuum cleaner, and many others. The vacuum was a flop by the way. Hiram Maxim could seemingly solve any technical problem to which he turned his active mind. Maxim got the idea of the machine gun after firing a U.S. army rifle and feeling the heavy recoil. He began thinking about using the energy of the recoil to load and fire a gun. The first mock-up fired six shots in half a second. His first patent towards this weapon was granted in June 1883 for a "mechanism facilitating the action of magazine rifles and other firearms." He continued to work on this project and Maxim had a tremendous capacity for work. He built the first machine gun himself. The cartridges for the Maxim gun were placed side by side between two layers of tape; this was known as the belt. The cartridges were belt-fed and were fired off at the rate of eleven per second. This is what Maxim's machine gun did: it fed a cartridge belt into the gun; pulled a cartridge from the belt and put the cartridge in the barrel; closed the breech; cocked the hammer; pulled the trigger; fired off the cartridge; extracted the cartridge, ejected it from the gun; and fed a new cartridge into the barrel. This is how it did it. The recoil of the barrel and breechblock provided the energy for extracting the spent cartridge, and cocking the hammer. It also stored energy in a spring. This energy was used to chamber a new cartridge, close the breech, and pull the trigger while advancing the next cartridge into position. All in one-eleventh of a second. The nature of warfare had just changed—dramatically. By 1884, the Maxim Gun Company was in business and every person of influence, from the Prince of Wales and General Garnet Wolseley on down, who stopped by Maxim's Hatton Garden workshop came away mightily impressed. The gun put round after round on target as it did not jump about when fired. Maxim stated that 200,000 rounds were fired for the benefit of visitors and with each trip of the hammer that much more doubt about Maxim's claims was shot away. It was Maxim, by the way, who brought the Vickers brothers into the new gun company and thus the armaments business.

In 1886, Hiram Maxim sailed for England with his secretary, the woman who would become his wife and future Lady Maxim. Maxim, although he did not say so, was moving to England. He would only visit the United States periodically after this date. It was altogether fitting that the future Mrs. Maxim should live in England. There were already two women in America believing themselves to be Mrs. Hiram Maxim, three would have pushed superfluity into farce.

What made this weapon such an advance over its predecessors was that the firing of the gun continued as long as the trigger was pressed and the ammunition supplied. The cyclic rate of fire was about 450 rounds per minute. The best a trained man with a bolt-action rifle could manage was about 15 rounds per minute. Given the "cyclic rate vs. practical rate" issue, perhaps a more useful comparison still would be the observation of a *Hauptmann* Fleck of the Imperial German Army. During the Russo-Japanese War of 1904–1905, Fleck noted that four machine guns, crewed by 20 men, firing over a period of five minutes, could place 3,600 rounds into a target at typical battlefield ranges. During a similar period, Fleck reckoned that a 100-man company using bolt-action, magazine-fed rifles could only manage 500 rounds into the same target.

The Colt, Gatling, and Maxim machine guns were used to significant effect in many colonial wars. In the Sudan at the battle of Omdurman, for example, the Maxim guns of the Kitchener's forces inflicted 15,000 casualties on the Khalifa's men. Machine guns were even used in the Spanish-American War in Cuba in 1898. Few military commanders, however, fully appreciated the profound impact that mass employment of these weapons would have on warfare. When the Great War broke out, a typical British brigade or French regiment possessed six or eight machine guns; by 1917, that number increased to about 150. In *On Infantry*, Lieutenant Colonel Jack English tells of a tactical situation in which the lethality of the machine gun became obvious. At Loos, Belgium, in 1915, two British divisions mounted an attack on entrenched Germans on a ridge. After a 20-minute artillery preparation—which had practically no impact on the dug-in defenders—10,000 British infantry made their way up the gentle slope toward the outer belts of

German barbed wire. German Maxim guns opened up at 1,500 yards, and in three hours and forty-five minutes, inflicted over 8,000 casualties. By 1918, the distribution of machine guns in the British Army was such that the infantry battalions of a British division had a light machine gun to cover every 27 yards of their doctrinal defensive frontage, and a heavy machine gun for every 41 yards. The killing power was devastating.

The main drawback of the machine-gun designs of the First World War was their weight and bulk. The German Maxim MG08 weighed 124 pounds with its sled mount, and the Austrian Schwarzlose 88 pounds with its tripod. Among the Allies' weapons, the French Hotchkiss—one of the very few air-cooled designs of the war, and therefore without a heavy water jacket—still weighed a ponderous 117 pounds with its tripod, while the British Vickers Mark I and its tripod weighed in at a sprightly 84 pounds. The Russian Model 1910 Maxim weighed a whopping 162 pounds with its armored shield and wheeled mount. A later entry, the American M-1917A1—which went on to serve through-out the Second World War and Korea—weighed 93 pounds, complete. Obviously, these guns were not terribly mobile and served mainly as engines of slaughter for mass formations of infantry charging across No Man's Land.

The machine gun determined, in large part, how the First World War would be fought and it produced a murderous stalemate on the Western Front. Both sides in the Great War sought means of breaking the tactical deadlock by developing new weapons such as flamethrowers, poison gas, and tanks (armored mobile machine gun platforms), and by

German troops man an
MG08 in 1914. NA

refining existing weapons such as airplanes (airborne machine gun platforms), high-explosive artillery shells, and the machine gun itself. The
idea was that the machine gun would be modified so that it could support offensive operations. The attempts resulted in three new genres of
weapons, namely, the light machine gun, the automatic rifle, and the
submachine gun.

The first category included both incredibly cumbersome guns such as
the German MG08/15, which was really not much more than the MG08
fitted with a shoulder stock and a bipod in lieu of the clumsy and heavy
sled mount. While this weapon could, indeed, lay down the same kind
of heavy firepower as its heavier brother, its weight of 36 pounds and
its employment of a belt feed did much to limit its utility in the assault
role. The British Lewis gun was closer to being a truly useful assault
weapon, as it fed from a convenient rotary magazine which was much
easier to use while moving or firing from a hastily-occupied position.
This arrangement also obviated the need for an assistant gunner to feed
the belt into the chamber. At 25 pounds, it was considerably lighter, too,
and thus allowed the gunner to more easily run, hit, and roll with the
gun during assaults. Most light machine guns were air-cooled, which
also saved weight by substituting a perforated metal cooling jacket
around the barrel in lieu of a water-filled one.

Besides their weight and congruence with the requirements for agility in the attack, the other thing that differentiated light machine guns
was their range. This was not a ballistic or barrel-length issue, but rather
one of sights and elevating mechanisms. Without the sled/tripod/
wheeled mounts of heavy machine guns, it was impossible to use the
sophisticated mechanical sights and traversing and elevating mechanisms that made heavy machine guns so effective at ranges out to 2,000
yards. Light machine guns, therefore, were accurate to about the range
at which the gunner could easily adjust fire using "Kentucky windage,"
which was about 800 yards.

The main difference between the automatic rifle and the light
machine gun is the amount of ammunition available in a magazine and,
therefore, the amount of firepower that the weapon can produce. Belts,
of course, can be of any length, and the two types of magazines used by
light machine guns such as the Lewis could hold 47 or 97 rounds. Automatic rifles such as the French Chauchat or the Browning Automatic
Rifle (BAR) weighed only about 20 pounds, and used magazines holding 20 rounds. Even with their typically lower cyclic rates of fire, the fre-
quency with which these weapons' magazines had to be changed limited their effect in suppressing the enemy on their users' tactical objectives. Still, the grossly reduced weights made automatic rifles much

more flexible in the offense than heavy machine guns. They could literally be used by a single gunner to dominate a trench once inside the enemy's galleries.

The only submachine gun to see extensive service in the Great War was the German Bergmann Model 1918. Firing the 9mm pistol cartridge from stick magazines of 32 rounds, it weighed only about 10 pounds and was easily wielded by a single soldier. Although extremely limited in range by its ammunition—about 50 yards—it was the ideal weapon for sweeping a trench. Bergmanns were used to especially great effect in consonance with the infiltration tactics employed by specially trained *Stosstruppen* (shock troops) in the last year of the Great War.

As has been demonstrated elsewhere in this book, although the breech-loading rifle should have brought about the end of mass infantry maneuver by the middle of the nineteenth century, it did not. It even took most military minds of the early twentieth century four years of mass slaughter to recognize that the machine gun had absolutely ended such tactics. Unfortunately, a huge part of a full generation of European manhood died in the process. Most of the machines and tactical techniques that characterized warfare in the rest of the twentieth century were inspired or enabled by the machine gun.

The tank, which became the dominant war machine of the Second World War and several later twentieth century conflicts, was developed specifically to protect soldiers from the effects of the machine gun and the high-explosive artillery shell, the two greatest killers of the war. Although only crudely developed by November 1918, the tank's subsequent evolution, along with entirely new tactics for its employment, profoundly changed the western way of war by 1939. Interestingly, for a while in the earliest stages of World War II, extremely large-caliber machine guns, such as the American .50-caliber Browning, were thought to be the best protection against tanks, given their thin armor plating. In fact, the .50-caliber or 12.7mm round was developed during WWI for antitank use. Of course, quickly-evolving armor technology soon ended the antitank efficacy of even the heaviest machine guns. Machine guns became important secondary weapons for tanks, however, supplementing the cannon by providing effective firepower for engaging unprotected infantry.

The war plane, used for reconnaissance at the outbreak of war in the summer of 1914, became devastatingly effective with the integration of machine guns and, later, large-caliber machine guns called "machine cannon." Forward-firing machine guns, firing first over, then through, the propeller arcs of fighter aircraft also made plane-to-plane "dogfighting" possible. By the Second World War, with six to eight machine

guns and machine cannon firing from the wing roots and through propeller hubs of individual aircraft, strafing also became an especially
deadly technique. Machine guns, sited obliquely in flexible mounts or
even in revolving turrets, gave bombers protection against attacking
fighters, thus making strategic bombing possible.

During World War I and continuing throughout the rest of the century, machine guns also provided protection against attacking aircraft.
From the single guns mounted on extended tripods with sights specially designed for "leading" the speeding aerial targets, to the multiple
mounts that appeared during WWII, such as the German triple- or
quad-mounted 20mm machine cannon or the American quadruple .50-
caliber machine guns, the machine gun was *the* weapon of choice for
close-in air defense for most armies throughout the rest of the twentieth
century. Even the automatic cannon, such as the ubiquitous Bofors
40mm, clearly had its roots in the machine gun.

Even with the advent of assault rifles, grenade launchers, and so on,
machine guns continued to provide the preponderance of infantry firepower. By World War II, the Germans had recognized that the machine
gun was the absolutely dominant infantry weapon, and they distributed them more widely than any other army in that conflict. Every German infantry squad had its own machine gun, and in most infantry
organizations, there were even more machine guns at the company and
battalion levels. A typically-organized German infantry company possessed 15 machine guns, and a battalion had 54. What's more, these
were the MG-34 or MG-42 designs which had singularly high rates of
fire (cyclically, 800–1200 rounds per minute, compared to 550–600 for
the average American, British, or Russian equivalents.) Thus, the comparative firepower a German infantry company or battalion could generate was awesome. An American infantry company, for example, possessed just two machine guns (Browning M1919A4s or A6s) and nine
BARs. As any veteran of infantry combat will confirm, the possession of
the semi-automatic M-1 rifle or M-1 carbine by each member of an
American infantry company was only very partial compensation for the
lack of sustained-fire machine guns. Those who argue that the Germans
relied on maneuver while the Allies relied on firepower are plain
wrong. Given that the definition of maneuver is "the integration of fire
and movement," it is obvious that firepower *enables* maneuver. The
Allied infantry could never match the Germans in firepower . . . and this
was because of the far greater distribution of machine guns in German
infantry formations.

From World War II forward, along with radio-coordinated mortars
and artillery, the proliferation of machine guns has changed infantry

combat into a hide-and-seek affair involving sophisticated techniques of fire and movement that would have astonished most commanders of WWI or earlier. As of this writing, US Army infantry platoons possess no fewer than *eight* machine guns (six M-249 Squad Automatic Weapons, or "SAWs," and two M-240 general purpose machine guns) in addition to the semi-automatic and three-round burst capability of the M16A2s or M4 carbines with which the rest of the platoon is armed. Obviously, this kind of firepower dwarfs even the German WWII infantry platoon at the height of its effectiveness.

Infantry tactics since 1939 have put much greater demands on small infantry units and even individuals because the machine gun has, to a significant extent, democratized ground warfare. The days of masses of rudimentarily-trained conscripts being lined up and ordered to charge into the opposition ended largely because of this highly lethal weapon. Far more decisions now devolve to platoon leaders, squad leaders, and individual infantrymen because of the flexibility required to fight on the modern battlefield in the face of automatic weapons. The training required to produce soldiers who can fight this way has, in turn, made warfare far more expensive. While none of this has ended war, it has certainly changed the political, economic, and military dynamics of warfare. More than any other weapon, it was the machine gun that was responsible.

# First Combined-Arms Armored Vehicle:
## The *Sturmpanzerwagen* A7V—Too Little, Too Late, and Too Many Cooks

The machine gun, more than anything else, led to the brutal, bloody trench warfare of the Great War. Massed infantry and horse-mounted cavalry were no match for the sweeping death of Hiram Maxim's invention, so both sides dug in, extended their trenchworks from the English Channel to the Swiss border, strung millions of miles of barbed wire, and began blasting each other to smithereens. The tactical concept employed by both sides was simple: bombard a segment of the enemy's line to rubble; push masses of infantry through the smoking, cratered landscape of twisted wire, caved-in trenches, and body parts; follow up with cavalry to exploit the breakthrough; feed even more infantry into the chasm; and continue the advance until the enemy established new defensive positions. Then start over.

There was a problem, though—it didn't work. The lengthy bombardments necessary to obliterate a prepared defensive position served to announce the exact point of attack, allowing the enemy to evacuate that area, mass counterattack troops nearby, and ready hordes of the very mobile machine guns on the flanks of the devastation. As the barrages slackened to allow the infantry to advance, the enemy moved in his machine guns and cut them down in windrows.

The tank was designed as a means to slow the slaughter of the infantry. In concept, armored, heavily-armed, track-laying vehicles could negotiate the cratered moonscape of the battlefield, drive straight across the trenches and deliver close-range cannon and machine-gun fire against the relatively exposed machine guns of the trench-rooted enemy, while at the same time being impervious to most enemy fire. As is the case with most weapons designed to end wars (such as TNT and the machine gun), the invention of the tank, however, served only to advance the art of warfare in a new direction.

Britain fielded the first "standard" tank in history, the trapezoid-shaped Mark I, unleashing 32 of the monsters on the unsuspecting Germans on 15 September 1916. There were some gains, but the British infantry was too slow to follow up and German counterattacks regained most of the ground lost within a few days. Several disabled Mark Is fell into German hands. Having literally been hit on the head by this good idea, the German army demanded tanks of its own.

In mid-November 1916, the German War Ministry instructed its Motor Vehicle Testing Commission to develop a German tank for use on the Western Front. The project to develop a *Gelaendespanzerwagen* (armored all-terrain vehicle) fell to the *Allgemeine Kriegsdepartment 7, Abteilung Verkehrswesen* (General War Department 7, Transportation Section), from which title it drew its designation of A7V. Although the Germans had examined several of the British tanks and had taken some pointers from their weaknesses, the designers decided to base the German tank on a track system used by Holt farm tractors, for which production capability was already present. The prototype displayed for the Kaiser in July 1917 was accepted by the Army for production, and 100 chassis were ordered. The first vehicles were delivered to the army in December of the same year.

Weighing in at 30–33 tons (the two manufacturers, Krupp and Rochling, used different types and grades of armor-plate), the A7V was just over 24 feet in length; 10 feet, 5 inches wide; and 10 feet, 10 inches in height. It could span a seven-foot-wide trench and it had a top speed of six to eight miles per hour on hard, level ground. Mounting six machine guns and a single 57mm cannon in the bow, with a field-of-fire limited to the front, the A7V required a crew of 18 men drawn from at least three branches of the army! The commander and the 12 machine gunners were infantrymen; the two cannon gunners were artillerymen; the driver and mechanic were engineers; and there was also a "signaler," a position possibly detailed from the signal corps. The British, on the other hand, had created a new branch to operate their tanks—the Royal Tank Corps—thereby allowing the German army the distinction of creating one of the first combined arms teams to take the field in modern history.

Just about all of the attributes of the British Mk I were absent in the A7V, which possessed virtually no climbing ability (any obstacle more than a foot-and-a-half tall could stop it); was limited to movement over relatively hard, smooth ground (though sources differ on this subject, it had a very low ground clearance, somewhere between about 8 inches and slightly less than 16 inches); and could not fire its cannon to the sides (the Mk I, with two sponson-mounted cannon, could straddle a trench, train its guns to 90 degrees, and sweep the trench clean of enemy troops).

Mechanically, and in terms of crew comfort, the A7V was a nightmare. Two noisy, heat-and-smoke generating 4-cylinder in-line Daimler diesel engines were mounted side by side in the center of the vehicle. Though engine exhaust was piped outside, no ventilation was provided, either for the engines or for the crew, except through the various vision slits and gun ports. A deck above the engines supported seats for the commander and the driver, who were protected by an armored cupola projecting above the body of the tank. The un-muffled engines, track noise, and the general sounds of battle made voice communications a near impossibility, so a system of electric lights was installed near each of the seven gun positions through which the commander could instruct each gunner when to fire and when to reload. To supplement the system of lights, the signaler was charged with circulating around the confined interior, passing on instructions from the commander.

While the armor plate was superior in thickness to that used by the British, the A7V shared with its British counterpart the problems of spall and bullet splash. Large-caliber hits on the crude steel of the time often ripped shards from the inside wall of the plate and sent them flying through the interior of the vehicle (spall) with wounding and sometimes lethal force. Likewise, molten lead and steel from bullets striking at the imperfect joints of the plates spewed through to the interior of the tank (bullet splash). As protection against these hazards, the crew wore uncomfortable, heavy, thick leather clothing, helmets, and gloves.

Encapsulated with the guns, the enormous basic load of ammunition (500 rounds for the 57mm cannon and up to 36,000 rounds for the machine guns) and two huge, pounding engines, operation of the vehicle must have been something far less than a pure delight for the crew. The image of 18 men outfitted head to foot in thick leather, crammed into a 24-foot by 10-foot steel box rocketing along at 6 mph, their ears aching from the screech of the tracks and the roar of the engines, eyes burning from the engine smoke and exhaust, and with the signaler squeezing past and over them, pounding on them to get their attention before giving hand signals and shouting commands at the top of his lungs is bleak indeed. Add to that scene the need for the gunners to keep a sharp eye out through the narrow vision slits for targets, and at the same time give heed to the flashing light signals from the commander, and one gets something of the picture of life inside one of these monsters.

Less than a year after the Kaiser saw the prototype, the *Sturmpanzerwagen* A7V (the "armored all-terrain vehicle" designation having been dropped in favor of the much more aggressive "assault armored vehicle") saw its first combat. On 21 March 1918, near St. Quentin, France, five A7Vs, supported by five captured British tanks, attempted to take part in the "Michael Offensive." Three of the German tanks immediately rendered themselves useless due to mechanical problems, leaving only two A7Vs and the five captured tanks to carry out the attack. The British were unprepared to face German armor, and were quickly routed from that small part of the battlefield, whereupon the two A7Vs were withdrawn for overhaul. This first use of the A7V in combat resulted in only a minor tactical victory, as the terrain captured was soon regained by a British counterattack.

One significant claim the A7V has to its historical credit is that it participated in the first ever tank-on-tank engagement. Though accounts of the confrontation differ in minor details, it is safe to say that it ended in pretty much of a draw. This historic fight took place on 24 April 1918 as part of an attack by the German 2nd Army on Allied positions in and around Villers-Bretonneux. All 15 of the A7Vs then on hand (three units of five each) participated in offensive—or at least tried to participate— though they were committed in small groups spread over a large area. Two A7Vs broke down even before the attack began. The remaining 13 tanks were employed in three groups and had some successes, although two of them fell over on their sides while negotiating rough terrain, one suffered a seized gearbox, and at least one was put out of action by overheated engines.

Four A7Vs under command of *Leutnant* Steinhardt were detailed to support the 77th Reserve Division in its attack on the town of Cachy. The tanks quickly became separated in a thick fog and in efforts to maneuver around rough terrain. One tank ("Elfriede") fell over on its side; its commander, *Leutnant* Stein, was killed by infantry while defending the wrecked tank. Two of the remaining A7Vs penetrated the town, but the third tank, "Nixe" drifted in the fog—into the annals of history.

As "Nixe," commanded by *Leutnant* Blitz, screeched and rumbled down a road north of Cachey, the fog began to lift, revealing three British Mk IV tanks of 1st Section, 1st Battalion, Royal Tank Regiment. The lopsided engagement began immediately, and at close range. Fortunately for Blitz, two of the Mark IVs were "Females," armed only with machine guns, and his cannon fire quickly put them to flight. The "Male" Mark IV, commanded by Lieutenant Frank Mitchell, and "Nixe" concentrated on each other. They blasted away at each other for quite awhile, for it was Mitchell's twenty-fifth round that finally knocked a hole in "Nixe," leading Blitz to order the survivors to abandon the A7V.

How much damage was done to Mitchell's tank is unknown, but apparently there was some, for as Blitz and his crew huddled in a ditch, a German shell knocked out the Mark IV (There is confusion whether this shell was from a trench mortar or from another A7V arriving late on the scene), whereupon, Blitz and his men remounted "Nixe," which had been left on the road with engines running, and resumed the attack. The engines seized after a short time, however, and the tank was again abandoned.

Australian and British troops quickly regained all the ground lost to the German offensive, and as the Germans withdrew, three of the disabled A7Vs were in danger of being captured by the advancing Allies. Recovery vehicles were dispatched to retrieve two of the damaged tanks, but the third, "Elfriede," which had tipped over, was deemed too difficult to recover. A demolition squad was sent out to destroy "Elfriede." The same war god that had blessed the terrible contraption that became the A7V must have been on duty that day as well, for the demolition squad blew up "Mephisto" instead—"Mephisto" was behind the German lines and was in no danger of being captured.

Underpowered, top-heavy, with gearing problems and a tendency for the engines to overheat under just about all conditions, the A7V was a slab-sided, slow, ungainly ugly duckling, prone to operational and mechanical failure. And there weren't enough of them. While the British fielded well over 1,000 tanks during the war, deliveries of the A7V totaled a mere 20 by the Armistice.

As Christopher Chant recounted most aptly in *The Encyclopedia of the Tank*, the A7V "proved next to useless for any task other than boosting the morale of the German infantry." Whatever morale boost the German infantry got from viewing the A7Vs, however, must have been very transitory as they beheld the sight of hundreds of British, French, and American tanks rolling over their wire while they observed their own handful of lumbering steel boxes fall over on their sides, screech to a halt with seized engines, sit broken well behind the lines, or—in the case of "Mephisto"—be blown up by their own engineers! In sum, the A7V was pretty much a failure from the start and had approximately zero effect on the conduct of the war.

Although the German Panzer Museum in Munster has a full-scale model, only one original A7V remains in existence, all the others having been cut up for scrap after the war. Interestingly, the surviving A7V resides in Australia. Taken home as a war trophy, the battered hulk was painstakingly restored and is now on display in Brisbane. It is "Mephisto," apparently not-too-thoroughly blown up by German engineers.

## Largest Gun Ever: The Railway Gun Gustav

The German tendency towards gigantism is unbounded, but then again, it would have to be. From Frederick I and his obsession with his regiment of giants—which meant that no extremely tall man in Europe was safe—to German arms in WWII and various other projects, it was go big or go home. In fact, Demetrios the Besieger would have been right at home, if not welcomed with open arms, in Germany. Take, for example, the Panzer Maus super-heavy tank of WWII. *Maus* in German means mouse—who says the Germans have no sense of humor? Only two prototypes were built in 1944 and subsequently destroyed in April 1945, but what a machine! The frontal armor was 7.9 inches thick and sloped at 60 degrees at the nose. The turret armor was 9.5 inches at the front and 7.9 inches on the sides and rear, which was sloped 60 degrees. The turret roof was a mere 2.4 inches, which was one-third more than the thickness of the Panther's side turret armor. The main gun was the 150mm KwK 44 L/38 and it carried a 75mm KwK 44 L/36.5 gun and a 7.92 MG 34 co-axially mounted in the turret. In fact, the turret weighed as much as a Panther tank, but it had a second MG 34 on the roof. The main gun's ammunition weighed 154 pounds per round, so its 50 rounds were transported in a separate carrier. There were also 1,000 rounds for the 75mm. The 1,200-horsepower engine, fed by 1,056 gallons of gasoline, could propel this behemoth at 12 miles per hour on roads and 7 miles per hour cross-country. The operational range of 60 miles cross-country translates to 317 feet per gallon. Its weight of 188 tons meant that there were few bridges which could carry it, and at 33 feet long, 12 feet wide, and 12 feet high, there were few garages where one could park it. The fact that such a machine was designed and built demonstrates another extreme—the extreme inefficiency if not outright absence of rationality in Nazi planning.

So with this in mind, let us turn to the Gustav, the largest artillery piece ever built; fortunately. Ian Hogg provides us with the technical details: The Gustav was a railway gun without equal. None could equal its size, or its impracticability. Let us start with the gun. Its caliber was 800 mm or 31.4 inches. The barrel was 106.56 feet long and could be elevated from plus 10 degrees to 65 degrees; there was no traverse. In order to aim it you had to move the whole thing—kit, caboodle, and carriage. This was not as big a deal as you might think because you had to lay four sets of tracks at the firing site in order to assemble it anyway. So you would take into account that you might need to move it a little when it was time to fire. The gun and carriage took up two tracks and the other two tracks were for the cranes that put the thing together. Its size aside, the construction of the weapon was conventional by railway gun standards. Hogg tells us that the lower carriage was constructed of box-girders that sat on four twin trucks of five axles each; thus, the carriage rode on 80 wheels. The upper carriage, trunions, gun, and its cradle were then assembled on top. When the weapon was disassembled, the cranes loaded the upper components onto transport cars and the lower carriage was split length-wise so each part could travel on one set of tracks.

The Gustav took weeks to assemble and came with 1,420 men, a major-general, and its own anti-aircraft regiment for protection. The actual firing and control of the piece could not be trusted to anyone lower than a colonel and 500 men. All assembled, the Gustav weighed 1,328.9 tons and had an overall length of 141 feet. It fired two types of shell: the HE weighing 4.73 tons, and the CP weighing 6.99 tons; that is, HE, as in high-explosive, which was used for anti-personnel work, and CP, as in concrete-piercing, for when you just, absolutely, positively, have to penetrate 80 meters of concrete with three Volkswagens. The HE shell had a muzzle velocity of 2,690 feet per second and a maximum range of 29.2 miles. The figures for the heavier CP shell are 2,330 feet per second and 23.61 miles, respectively. Interestingly, the smaller German railway guns had greater range, but they were firing smaller shells. The reader should note that "smaller" is a relative term. The famous "Paris Gun" that the Germans used to shell Paris was fired from 68 miles away. This gun was the German Navy's, by the way, so in the 1930s, the army came up with a new design which could throw a 237-pound shell 71.46 miles. This was the 210 mm (8.31 inch) K12(E) railway gun. The K5(E) railway gun, however, with the barrel bored out to 310 mm (11.02 inch) and firing the Peenemünde Arrow Shell with special propellant had a maximum range of 93.8 miles. Hogg tells us that only two railway guns survived the war, both K5(E)s, one is in France and the other is at the Aberdeen Proving Ground in the U.S. of A.

The reader may be asking, "now why did the Germans build such a gun as the Gustav?" If the reader has been paying close attention, the answer is obvious: because they are German. The gun was dreamed up by Krupp in 1937. It was intended to attend the party in 1940 and blast apart the Maginot Line, but it was not ready in time. Thus, it saw its debut on the Russian front in the summer of 1942 where it bombarded the defenses at Sevastopol. It fired 30 to 40 rounds from Bakhchisaray at Sevastopol. In 1944, it set up at Pruskov about 18 miles from Warsaw and fired about 30 rounds into the city during the Polish uprising (August–September). After this, Gustav was never heard from again, although it is suspected that he fell into the hands of the Soviets. Gustav had a companion, by the way, Dora, but it is said that she never left the proving ground and her whereabouts are also unknown. A third gun was in the works, but the war ended before it could be completed. What there was of it fell into Allied hands and was later scrapped. This leads to some speculation. When the author was in his twenties, his grandfather gave him his old Cup Brand hammer, which was stamped as being made in the "Br Zone Germany," maybe he has a little bit of baby Gustav in his toolbox.

# Best and Worst Armored Fighting Vehicle Designs of World War II:
## The *Panzerkampfwagen* V "Panther" and the "Ferdinand"

The tank came into its own as a decisive battlefield weapon during the Second World War. From 1916 and the lumbering, mechanically unreliable "land battleships" which were developed to straddle trenches and kill the occupants with machine-gun and small-caliber cannon fire, to 1945 and the fast moving big-gunned weapons platforms developed to defeat other armored vehicles, tanks had become the capital land weapon for dominating open or rolling terrain.

For this entry, we frame the argument about "best" and "worst" by considering only tanks which were developed during the war. The technology of tank design and the doctrines of armored vehicle employment developed so quickly and markedly after September 1939, that most of the tanks with which the major combatants entered the war were obsolete by late 1940. In 1944, who would want to be in the best tank of 1939?

Each major belligerent nation developed a different philosophy about tank design during the course of the war and an understanding of this is necessary to comprehend why the Germans have the bipolar honors as producers of the war's best and worst armored fighting vehicle designs. To the reader familiar with the old saying that the Germans are either at one's feet or at one's throat, this display of bipolarism may be explained away as easily as saying that it is just an example of the Germans being German, but let us examine the main contenders and learn what we can.

Great Britain's early designs were either heavily-armored, slow, infantry-support vehicles, such as the Matilda and the Churchill series or the lightly-armored, fast "cruiser" tanks, such as the Crusader. From this, they moved to the middle ground of medium tanks, the Comet and, at the very end of war, the Centurion, that could play both roles. As a result, until the very end of the war, the British did not produce a tank that could possibly have dominated the battlefield.

The Americans, who entered the land war much later than the British, would have had a similar problem had they gone into combat in 1939 or 1940, as their tank design concept was quite similar to that of the British. By the time the US Army embarked on sustained land operations, however, they had settled upon a single design: the medium-weight, adequately-armed, and sufficiently-protected Sherman series.

The Americans upgunned many Shermans from the 75mm L/40 gun to the much more potent 76mm L/53.* They also improved the armor protection on some Shermans, such as the M4A3E2 "Jumbo" version. Ultimately, they were hampered in the quest to design a heavier, more powerful tank by fundamentally inescapable geographic realities. Wherever American built tanks went to fight, they had to be transported over great distances by sea, and, in cases such as the northern European mainland, the planners could not, necessarily, count on having the

---

*Expressions such as "L/53" denote the length of the barrel, or tube, in terms of multiples of the caliber of the gun ("caliber lengths"). Thus, a "76mm L/53" gun has a barrel that is 53 x 76mm (4,028 mm or 159 inches) in length. This notation is common because the length of a gun barrel is only really meaningful to its relationship with the size of the projectile. For example, a three-foot barrel would be very long for a .30-caliber rifle (a rifle firing a bullet that is three-tenths of an inch in diameter, such as the M-1 Garand), but extremely short for a tank main gun firing shells 76mm in diameter. Hence, rather than describe barrel lengths empirically, ordnance engineers describe them in terms of "caliber lengths," noted as "L/."

advantage of unloading at a developed port facility. The same factor also influenced British design, and constituted yet one more limitation for them. Thus, the Sherman had to be designed to be transportable in large numbers on existing ships, and furthermore, to be deliverable to enemy shores by amphibious vessels that could off-load tanks under primitive port conditions. Heavy, large, powerful tanks were out of the question for the Americans and British for this very practical reason.

In the years before the war, Soviet tank design was lamentable. Free from the geographical constraints which encumbered American and British designers, the Soviets possessed the world's heaviest tank, the T-35, which was useful for little more than impressing dignitaries during May Day parades in Moscow. The Soviets also possessed some of the world's most poorly-armed tanks—the T-60, for example, sported a meager 20mm gun. Armor-wise, some of the world's most thinly-armored tanks were Russian, the BT-5 and BT-7 had 13mm of frontal armor, while the T-26 had 15mm. Crew-wise, they had some of the world's most inadequately-manned tanks—the T-60 and T-70 had only two-man crews. Of course, if you are sending guys out in poorly-designed tanks, you may as well have just two men in them—why double your casualties with larger crews? Just before the war began, however, the Soviet Union began producing two tanks that were years ahead of their time in firepower, mobility, and armored protection. The KV-1 was armed with a 76mm gun that could destroy any German tank of 1941, while there was no German armored fighting vehicle that mounted a gun capable of penetrating the KV's three-inch thick frontal armor—at any range. Later versions of the KV had about five inches of frontal armor. The Germans had to bring up the very vulnerable and unprotected 88mm antiaircraft gun to penetrate the KV's armor. The other techniques the Germans developed were: trying to score a direct hit with an aerially-delivered bomb, a very hard thing to do when attacking a moving target; hiding in a deep hole hoping the KV broke down; hoping the KV got stuck; or just plain ran out of fuel.

The other Soviet design that gave the Germans fits was the T-34, destined to become the world's most manufactured tank and one of the longest lived. Its 76mm main gun could destroy any German armored fighting vehicle. Whereas its armor was lighter—the early version was just under two inches and so not as thick as the KV-1's— the effectiveness of this lighter armor was greatly enhanced by the fact that it was severely sloped. Sloped armor meant that a higher percentage of shots would strike the tank with glancing blows. The T-34 was also faster than any German tank, with a road speed just over 32 miles per hour. It was much more maneuverable, as well, due to in part to its wide tracks, which reduced the overall ground pressure exerted by the vehicle.

No German tank in existence in 1941 could deal with the KV-1 or T-34, no matter how heavily modified. Up through the initiation of Operation BARBAROSSA, the Germans had favored speed and reliability over armored protection or firepower as it fit better with their revolutionary combined arms, mobility-oriented tactical doctrine. Even when their heaviest design at the time, the 25-ton Panzer IV, with its two inches of frontal armor, was upgunned to the 75mm L/43 in 1942, or to the 75mm L/48 in 1943, all that was achieved was a rough gun-to-armor parity with the T-34. The KV-1, while not faster than the Panzer IV, could run rings around it in snow or mud, and let us not forget the significant armor advantage held by the KV-1.

To deal with the better and ever more numerous T-34s and KV-1s, the Germans had two choices: to continue to develop the two designs already in progress or go, literally, "back to the drawing board" and design an entirely new tank. In consonance with a trend that was all too common for the German armament industry, they chose to do both, which is to say, build the two new designs *and* design a new tank. In choosing not to choose, the Germans thereby diluted their industrial power, which was already inferior to that of the Soviets. Consequently, they never had enough of the newer generation tanks available, while managing to produce both the best and the worst armored fighting vehicles of the war, simultaneously.

The two new designs in progress had been requested in May 1941, just before the T-34s and KV-1s had so sourly surprised the *Wehrmacht*. They were both much heavier than anything the Germans had built to date. It mounted an 88mm gun, which was, at that time, the largest main gun in the world. The Henschel company produced one design, and the Porsche firm the other. The Henschel design ultimately became the famed Tiger tank, duly appearing on the battlefield in the late summer of 1942. After overcoming some mechanical reliability challenges, it became, arguably, the most important heavy tank of the war, but it was handicapped by its weight, size, and difficulty of manufacture; in two full years of production, only 1,350 were built. This quantity was clearly inadequate to handle the sheer numbers of enemy tanks it had to face. It was a good design, however, neither the best nor the worst.

The Porsche design, though, was a flop. Officially called the "Ferdinand" after the designer, Ferdinand Porsche, it was a huge, glacially-slow target without even the benefit of a rotating turret. This meant that if the vehicle became immobilized—a very likely event, given that it was only necessary to damage one set of road wheels to stop it—the crew could not defend themselves unless a target presented itself directly in front of the main gun.

The Ferdinand's maximum speed, on a road, was 12 miles per hour. Going cross county, it was about half of that. To attain even these speeds, the Ferdinand (*Sdkfz* 184) had two V-12 Maybach petrol engines producing a combined 640-brake horsepower. The engines were fed 210 gallons of gasoline which provided operational ranges of 93 miles on roads and 56 miles cross-country, that is 3.75 gallons per mile. Russian infantrymen found that one of the very best ways to immobilize the Ferdinand was to attach a magnetic mine to its enormous, boxy hull, or to lay a contact mine directly in front of its tracks. As long as accompanying Panzer-Grenadiers had been swept away by artillery, mortars, or machine-gun fire, this was not hard to do for several reasons. Twelve miles an hour is somewhere between a jog and a sprint, an infantry man could easily carry a 12-pound mine or shaped charge and run down the Ferdinand and place the explosive on the vehicle. If the Ferdinand was moving cross-country, even the author could manage it without risking a heart attack. Normally, attempting to knock out a tank with a mine would be a great way to get killed, because WWII tanks typically mounted a machine gun in the bow, and another in the turret, firing coaxially with the main gun. Either one could take out a would-be tank killer trying to affix or toss a mine, but the Ferdinand did not have any machine guns. Soviet infantrymen could cavort at will around the

The Worst Armored Fighting Vehicle Design of World War II—the Porsche "Ferdinand" tank destroyer. *NA*

vehicle, and commit every type of mischief, all to the detriment of the Ferdinand's crew.

Enemy action was not the only way Ferdinands could become immobile. The vehicle's tracks, though a massive 25.5 inches wide, were not sufficiently wide enough to distribute the vast weight of the Ferdinand in a fashion conducive to good mobility over soft ground. For perspective, the Ferdinand's ground pressure was 17 pounds per square inch; the T-34's was only 10; the KV-1's 10.5; the Tiger's 11.3; and the King Tiger's 13.7. Thus, even if Russian infantrymen didn't stop a Ferdinand, the notoriously soft soil or mud of the steppes almost assuredly would.

In addition to being extremely slow, easily disabled, and inadequately armed, the Ferdinand was an enormous target, and not nearly as well protected as its vast amount of armor should have allowed. It stood just shy of 10 feet tall, was 23 feet long and 11 feet wide. For comparison, the T-34 was 8 feet tall, 20 feet long, and 10 feet wide. Worse, although heavily armored, its box-like design included very little sloping, meaning that incoming projectiles were unlikely to be deflected, but would rather transfer their energy quite efficiently directly to the hull, optimizing penetration and spalling. Moreover, by arraying the armor horizontally rather than at an angle, the design made poor use of the armor it incorporated. For example, the two inches of steel on the front of a T-34 were sloped at 60 degrees; effectively, then, a projectile striking the armor dead on would have to penetrate about four inches of armor to reach the crew. The frontal armor on the Ferdinand, although eight inches thick in front, was not sloped at all, nor was the 3.2-inch-thick side hull armor. Only the sides and rear of the superstructure and gun compartment were sloped, and then only mildly. In short, the extremely thick armor—which accounted for a huge percentage of the vehicle's monstrous 71.7-ton weight and tortoise-like speed—was arrayed in the least effective manner.

Finally, the Ferdinand's main gun, although absolutely the most powerful, most accurate weapon mounted on any German armored vehicle produced in quantity during World War II, was mounted in a fashion that greatly limited its effectiveness. The reader may be interested to know that the same weapon was also mounted on the *Nashorn* (Rhinocerous) and *Jagdpanther* (Hunting Panther) tank destroyers and *Königstiger* (King Tiger) tank. The *Jagdtiger* (Hunting Tiger) tank destroyer mounted a 128mm L/55 main gun, but only 70 were produced. In the case of the Ferdinand, the gun was set directly into a built-up superstructure on the chassis, it had only 28 degrees of traverse, which is to say, 14 degrees either side of straight ahead. Thus, to make anything but very small changes in deflection, the entire vehicle had to turn. As alluded to before, if the vehicle threw a track (a common enough problem even without a tenacious enemy trying to blow them off), or a pair of road wheels were damaged, or the Ferdinand became stuck in a ditch or a tank trap, the design's very best feature was useless. In a static defensive situation, this would not be an insurmountable problem for a well-trained crew, but on the offensive, it was a nightmare. The vehicle had to stop, pivot in the general direction of the target, lay the main gun, and fire, all of which took time and gave the enemy, especially an enemy in a tank with a rotating turret, lots of time to engage first. If the target happened to be moving and the gunner missed the first shot, at all but the greatest ranges, the entire vehicle had to be pivoted still more, then the gun laid again, then fired.

The deeply-flawed design of the Ferdinand was only accentuated by the vehicle's initial employment. Ferdinand's baptism of fire was during the Germans' Operation ZITADELLE (CITADEL), the attack on the heavily-fortified Soviet salient at Kursk in the summer of 1943. The Germans used Ferdinands to lead their "panzer wedges," and echeloned their less-well-armed and well-armored tanks behind and to either side of the Ferdinands. This ensured that the speed of the entire formation would be dictated by the slowest, most unwieldy vehicles possible, the ones that took the most time to fire, and were the easiest for Soviet

The Best Armored Fighting Vehicle Design of World War II—the *Panzerkampfwagen V*, "Panther" tank. *NA*

infantrymen to engage and destroy with mines or other field expedient weapons. A worse combination of poor design and ill-advised tactical employment would be difficult to imagine.

Mercifully, only 90 Ferdinands were built, and after their debacle in the Soviet Union, they were withdrawn for modification. Zimmerit plaster was applied to the hull, which defeated magnetic mines by making adhesion much more difficult, and a bow machine gun was added. Perhaps equally importantly, now redesignated "*Elefants*," the heavy tank destroyer units equipped with them were transferred to Italy, where they faced a far less serious enemy tank threat in the hilly, rocky, terrain of the Appenine range. Here, at least, they were employed in defensive operations that allowed their excellent, long-range firepower to be used to greatest advantage . . . even if they were still huge (26 feet, 8 inches long; 11 feet, 3 inches wide), ponderous, sluggish targets for Allied tanks and tactical aircraft!

While the Ferdinand was clearly not the answer to the T-34 that the Germans so desperately needed, the design which sprang from their entirely new efforts commencing late 1941 definitely was. The design of the Panther struck the best balance of speed, armor protection, firepower, and agility of any tank in World War II. Its only technical disadvantage versus Soviet tanks was that it used gasoline rather than diesel fuel; this made it more flammable and shortened its combat radius. Contrary to popular notions, possibly initiated by a line spoken by George C. Scott's Patton to Karl Malden's Bradley in the movie "Patton," German tanks were not diesels, but rather were powered exclusively by conventional gasoline engines.

Once the earliest models' mechanical problems were addressed, it had no technical disadvantages versus American or British tanks. The following table outlines the G Model Panther's characteristics in comparison with the best Allied and Soviet tank designs.

The following technical data on the competing designs for "best" make the choices fairly obvious. (Table 1)

Lest anyone be fooled by the calibers and tube lengths of the guns, here are the comparative performance statistics for the main competitors for the "best design" title. (Table 2)

Thus, overall, the Panther's armor, speed, and horsepower-to-weight ratio were roughly similar to both models of the T-34, making its tactical mobility practically identical. Its armor was superior to that of the T- 34, and its hull armor superior to that of the T34/85. If not all of the Panther's armor was as thick as that of the T-34/85, it was still more than adequate in a one-on-one duel: because of the slope of the Panther's armor, the 85mm gun's projectiles could not penetrate the

**TABLE 1. Technical Data**

| Type | Armament | Armor (in.) Glacis/Hull sides/ Turret Front/ Turret Sides) | Max. Speed (mi./hr.) | Ground Press. (lbs./ sq. in.) | Cbt. Radius (mi.) (Road/ x-country) | HP/Wt. Ratio |
|---|---|---|---|---|---|---|
| Panther | 75mm L/70 2x7.92mm MG | 3.2@55° 2.0@30° 4.3@0° 1.8@30° | 30 | 12.5 | 124/62 | 14:1 |
| T-34 | 76mm L/41.5 2x7.62mm MG | 2.0@60° 2.0@40° 4.8@0° 2.5@30° | 33 | 10 | 280/161 | 15.6:1 |
| T-34/85 | 85mm L/53 2x7.62mm MG | 2.0@60° 2.0@40° 6.0@0° 3.5@0° | 33 | 10.8 | 250/155 | 14.5:1 |
| KV-1 | 76mm L/41.5 3x7.62mm MG | 4.9@20° 3.0@0° 7.8@0° 3.0@0° | 22 | 10.5 | 208/124 | 11.5:1 |
| JS-2 | 122mm 1x12.7mm 3x7.62mm | 4.3@45° 3.5@30° 3.9@0° 3.7@10° | 22 | 12.6 | 160/— | 12:1 |
| M4A3E8 | 76mm L/53 1x.50-cal. MG 2x.30-cal. MG | 2.0@46° 1.5@0° 6.5@0° 2.0@0° | 26 | 10.6 | 155/100 | 13.5:1 |
| Sherman VC | 76mm L/60 1x.50-cal. MG 1x.30-cal. MG | 2.0@46° 1.5@0° 4.0@0° 2.0@0° | 25 | 13.1 | 120/100 | 12.6:1 |
| Comet | 77mm L/50 2x7.92mm MG | 3.0@0° 1.7@0° 4.0@0° 2.5@0° | 30 | 13.8 | 123/— | 18.3:1 |

**TABLE 2. Performance Statistics**

| Weapon | Penetration at | | | |
|---|---|---|---|---|
| | 100m. | 500m. | 1,000m. | 1,500m. |
| Panther, 75mm L/70 | 7.6 in. | 6.9 in. | 5.9 in. | 5.0 in. |
| T-34, 76mm | 3.5 in. | 2.7 in. | 2.4 in. | — |
| T-34/85, 85mm | — | 4.4 in. | 4.0 in. | 3.7 in. |

Panther's glacis from a frontal aspect beyond 1,000 meters, nor its frontal turret armor beyond 500 meters. On the other hand, the Panther's 75mm could penetrate the T-34/85's glacis out to beyond 1,500 meters, and its frontal turret armor at almost 1,000. Given the superior optics on practically all German armored fighting vehicles, as well as the generally much better level of training of the crews vis-à-vis their Soviet enemies, hits at these greater ranges were also much more likely for a Panther.

Taken altogether, then, the Panther's mobility and agility allowed it to keep up with any T-34 or T-34/85 on the battlefield, but its firepower allowed its crews to knock them out at ranges about 500 meters greater than those at which even the T-34/85 could inflict similar damage on a Panther. Had German industry concentrated not on simultaneously manufacturing a huge variety of different tanks and tank destroyers, per the US and Soviet practices, its armored forces would undoubtedly have been far more effective. At one point in 1943, Germany was producing the Panzer III, Panzer IV, Panther, Tiger, Ferdinand, and tank destroyer or assault gun variants of all four, plus assault gun or tank destroyer variants of the Czech 38(t) and Panzer II! Of course, it would also have helped if they had not produced stinkers like the Ferdinand. Nevertheless, the roughly 5,000 Panthers built by the Germans were the best tanks of the war.

The best known Panther ace was Sergeant Ernst Barkmann of the 2nd *SS* Panzer Regiment, 2nd *SS* Panzer Division, *Das Reich*. Barkmann began the war as an infantryman in Poland, but later switched to tanks. He served with distinction at the battle of Kharkov where he won the Iron Cross, First Class in his Panzer Mk. III. He was among the first to fight in the Panthers when they appeared at Kursk. The capability of the Panther is demonstrated by Barkmann's exploits. The *Das Reich* was transferred to France in early 1944 and on 8 July, Barkmann recorded his first Sherman kill near St. Lo. On 9 July, he destroyed two more, then three more, then two so that by 14 July, when in a borrowed Panther fresh with the previous commander's blood in the turret, he had tallied another nine tanks. His next great test started on 26 July when his regiment was trying to hold back the Allied breakout in Operation COBRA. His tank was beset with mechanical breakdown, then damaged by air attack, and nevertheless, he managed to repair it during the night and set out to find his unit. Near Le Lorey, he attacked an American column and fought until his crew was wounded by spalling, his hatches jammed, his drive train was damaged, and his hull was battered. He managed to reverse out of the battle to his own lines. In this deadly fighting, he had destroyed nine more tanks. By the next day, his tank was sufficiently repaired for him to do battle again and rack up six more tank kills. On 1 August, Barkmann, who was wounded three days earlier, finally had his tank destroyed, but he led his crew back to the German lines. He was awarded the Knight's Cross for his exploits and some of the credit certainly had to go to the Panther.

# Personalities

## Biggest Officer Reduction in Forces (RIF) in History: Stalin's Purges of the Soviet and Polish Officer Corps, 1936–40

Reductions in force (RIF), especially among officers' corps, are almost inevitable after every major war. After WWI, for example, the United States cut its Army's strength by more than 95 percent, with almost proportional cuts in the size of its officer corps. Many of the officers who were allowed to stay on had to accept reductions of one or more ranks. George Patton, for example, was reduced from colonel to captain, and even though he was soon promoted to major, he and most officers languished for many years in their lower post-war grades. This was an attempt by the government to avoid having a large number of officers at higher pay grades, as occurred after the Civil War. Reservists—who had been called up, returned to reserve status, and resumed their civilian professions or vocations—were even more acutely subject to reductions in their wartime rank.

Thanks to the restrictions imposed at Versailles, the German Army was even more drastically cut. At the height of the Great War, it counted 11,000,000 soldiers, but was allowed only 100,000 after 1919. Reserve officers simply ceased to exist as a category, as Germany was allowed no reserves by the victors who imposed their will on the vanquished in 1919. Dozens of thousands of German officers had to settle for positions in local and state police forces for over 13 years, until Hitler gave them all jobs again when he threw what was left of the Versailles accords in the trash can and cranked up the *Wehrmacht*.

Hitler, however, was just following a traditional path of expansion and contraction with regard to the armed forces. Josef Stalin was the real trendsetter in many ways; he broke with tradition and managed to conduct drastic reductions in the size of two different armies' officers' corps in new and interesting ways, and under unique circumstances. In the case of his own army, he reduced his officer corps by 50 percent;

what differentiated this from other reductions in force is that Stalin did it before the greatest war his nation would ever face. Unlike the usual force reductions in history, in which officers lost prestige, career opportunities, and pay, Stalin contrived not having to pay any retirement costs. The best way to eliminate costs? Eliminate officers, with bullets. Here is what a homicidal paranoid can do when he has control of a totalitarian regime. He can get all the help he needs to liquidate: 3 of the 5 marshals, 14 of the 16 army commanders, and approximately half of the 80,000 men in the entire officer corps. The general officers were all but wiped out.

This created the conditions for the great defeats that the Soviet Army suffered in 1941. The Red Army lost 3,000,000 men killed, wounded, and captured in the first five months, an all-time loss record. The result of these losses created another new trend with which we can credit Comrade Stalin. In other countries—those that were not run by chess masters, ballet dancers, and brutes—the officer corps was drastically reduced after wars because there were not enough enlisted men left for them to lead. In contrast, in the Soviet Army, the enlisted corps was drastically reduced during a war because the officer corps had already been RIFed before the war had ever started. In fact, while the Germans were kicking in the front door of the Soviet Union, NKVD personnel, the Soviet secret police, were going up and down the front summarily killing soldiers who they thought were not where they were supposed to be.

Stalin, however, was not one just to sit around the Kremlin with a big foam finger proudly proclaiming that he was number one in reduction in forces. The other really innovative reduction in forces Stalin conducted was smaller, but no less unique. For centuries, western armies treated captured officers with special care; after all, in Europe, even through the Great War, officer prisoners could easily be related to the officers of the detaining side . . . or even the camp commandant! Moreover, since professional officers were bound to stay on in their army after the peace treaty was signed, it was a good idea to not engender especial hatred by abusing the ones unfortunate enough to be captured. Better not to give them something personal to fume over, don't you know? Furthermore, there was the simple reality that the officer-prisoners of today might turn out to be the camp commandants of the winning side tomorrow, so treating them well was also a hedge against future unpleasantness following an adverse outcome to the war.

Stalin changed all that. After pretending that his army invaded Poland in 1939 to "protect it" from the invading Germans, he "interned," rather than "captured" dozens of thousands of Polish officers. The invasion, by the way, was the secret part of the Nazi-Soviet Non-Aggression Pact, which most observers believed had just such a clause, especially the more it was denied. Stalin's "protection" included swallowing up 30 percent of the country in the process, none of which has ever been returned to this day.

Then, just after becoming "guests" of the Soviet Union, the officers were subjected to extensive questioning by NKVD officers, most of it quite friendly and chummy. In the process, Stalin was able to determine which officers were regulars—and therefore likely to be used most efficiently against the Germans and then to man a post-war Communist Polish army—and which officers were reservists. The reservists, of course, were mostly lawyers, doctors, scientists, minor government officials, and businessmen in civilian life. After the war, they would form the backbone of a free, stable, and capitalistic Poland. So, in a move unprecedented in history, Stalin wiped them out. Here is how he justified it at the time:

A large number of former officers of the Polish Army; employees of the Polish Police and intelligence services; members of Polish nationalist, counter-revolutionary parties; members of exposed counter-revolutionary resistance groups; escapees and others, all of them sworn enemies of Soviet authority full of hatred for the Soviet system, are currently being held in prisoner-of-war camps of the USSR NKVD and in prisons in the western provinces of Ukraine and Belarus.

The military and police officers in the camps are attempting to continue their counter-revolutionary activities and are carrying out anti-Soviet agitation. Each of them is waiting only for his release in order to start actively struggling against Soviet authority. These included:

14,736 former officers, government officials, landowners, police, gendarmes, prison guards, settlers in the border regions and intelligence officers [more than 97 percent are Poles] are being held in prisoner-of-war camps. This number includes soldiers and junior officers.
Included are:
– generals, colonels, and lieutenant colonels—295
– majors and captains—2080
– lieutenants, second lieutenants, and ensigns—6049

– officers and juniors of the police, gendarmes, prison guards, and intelligence officers—1030
– rank and file police officers, gendarmes, prison guards, and intelligence personnel—5138
– government officials, land owners, priests, settlers in border regions—144

18,632 detained people are being kept in the western region of the Ukraine and Belarus [10,685 are Poles]. They include:
– former officers—1207
– former intelligence officers of the police and gendarmerie—5141
– spies and saboteurs—347
– former land owners, factory owners, and government officials—465
– members of various counter-revolutionary and resistance organisations and other counter-revolutionary elements—5345
– escapees—6127

In view of the fact that all are hardened and uncompromising enemies of Soviet authority, the USSR NKVD considers it necessary:
1. To instruct the USSR NKVD that it should try before special tribunals:
a. the cases of the 14,700 former Polish officers, government officials, land owners, police officers, intelligence officers, gendarmes, settlers in the border regions, and prison guards being held in prisoner-of-war camps;
b. together with the cases of 11,000 members of various counter-revolutionary organisations of spies and saboteurs, former land owners, factory owners, former Polish officers, government officials, and escapees who have been arrested and are being held in the western provinces of the Ukraine and Belarus and apply to them the supreme penalty: shooting.

In all, 9,631 Polish officers were killed under this order. A total of 15,790 Poles of other ranks were also killed. Thus, long before the Germans and their allies rolled across their border in June 1941, the Soviets managed to conduct a kind of RIF that no one else had ever accomplished or perhaps even contemplated: wiping out an officer corps of an army which no longer existed.

## Most Overrated General of World War II:
### Erwin Rommel, the Desert Fox

Yes, that is right, Rommel. And no, this is not a trick category, the author knows that Rommel was ultimately a Field-Marshal. The author begins with a disclaimer, he has never met the Rommel family, although Rommel's grandson once stayed at the fraternity house of the author's cousin. The author moreover, has no personal axe to grind with the *Afrika Korps*, the author's father served in the Pacific and Rommel had nothing to do with the occupation of the Greek villages where the author's relatives resided during the war. In fact, to hear the author's assorted Greek uncles talk (first cousins once removed, for those who prefer to keep score in English), just ask them after the Canadian Club has been flowing for a while, they'll tell you how lucky the Germans were to leave when they did. Nor is it the author's intent to argue that Rommel was an incompetent commander, but he was rash and reckless throughout his career. Rommel strikes the author as the kind of guy who knows, no matter what he does, he will not be hurt. Guys like this act and have no concern about what happens ten seconds to ten minutes from now. And make no mistake about it, Rommel was one physically tough man. He was abstemious in food and drink and when his nerves gave him wrenching stomach pains, he had the mental fortitude to keep going.

Rommel is the best known German general of the war and why should he not be? Rommel has been mythologized beyond what his record merits and he was part of the process of adulation. He had the best publicity. During the war German propaganda pushed Rommel's image as hard as it could. He was a favorite of Hitler, and in turn, he supported Hitler as well. He remained loyal for most of the conflict, only becoming disillusioned with the *Führer* late in the war. He was not keen on the Nazis however from early on and he wondered why a great man such as Hitler would keep such questionable company. His opponents in North Africa spoke well of him, too.

The good impressions, post-war, of Rommel were boosted in the west when it became known that the Nazis coerced him into suicide by poison. Rommel had been implicated in the 20 July 1944 assassination attempt of Hitler and was told that if he took his own life, the lives of his family would be spared and he would be granted a full military funeral. Anyone making such a sacrifice deserves renown and this was certainly seized upon in the post-war period to demonstrate that Germans, too, were victims of Hitler. Moreover, the quest for German rearmament in the 1950s needed the image of a noble German soldier to be palatable to the public. Then came movies about Rommel and

testimonials about the *Afrika Korps* and soon one could not swing a dead
cat without bumping into a Rommel fan.

Rommel was born in 15 November 1891 at Heidenheim, near Ulm, he
was not, therefore, a Swabian and not a Prussian. He was, nevertheless,
a professional soldier and an excellent leader of men. As a junior officer
in World War I he was awarded the Iron Cross, First and Second Class,
and later the *Pour le Mérite* (the highest medal) for his battlefield
leadership and exploits at the battle for Mounts Mzrli (26 October 1917)
and Matajur in Italy. Awarded, one should add, after extensive lobbying
on his part to correct what he thought was a gross injustice done him
as he had been overlooked for the medal initially. After the war, he
also badgered the German official historian for recognition of his
accomplishment.

While war builds character in some men, it reveals character in all
men. In World War I he demonstrated that was a daring, dynamic, and
forceful leader who led from the front and was wounded at least three
times. There is not the space here for a full account of Rommel's war
record, but what emerges is that Rommel was hard on his men and

subordinates and prepared to sacrifice them as he pursued his objectives. On 29 January 1915 he led his company in diversionary action against the French in the Charlotte valley in the Argonne near Labordaire. Rommel led his men about half a mile into the enemy defenses where, after losing contact with the rest of the battalion, they were nearly surrounded. When they ran out of ammunition Rommel left his five severely wounded men behind and the survivors ran back through the wire to their original line. When writing up this action in his book, Rommel commented that neither the battalion nor the regiment could exploit his company's success! More than once in his book, *Infanterie Greift An*, Rommel described actions in which he pushed his men forward when they were outnumbered and, more tellingly, short on ammunition. Here Rommel demonstrated that while he had tactical skill he lacked strategic sense. This appraisal accurately describes assessments of his generalship in North Africa some 27 years later.

After the First World War he managed to stay in the *Reichswehr*, but he was passed over for a spot on the General Staff. Later as an instructor at the Infantry School, he wrote the lectures that were published in book form in 1937. Hitler told Rommel that he had read the book and been impressed with it. Hitler chose Rommel to command the *Führer's* escort battalion, which was tasked with protecting the Leader on his visits to military installations. It was from this association that Rommel would secure a coveted command for the Battle of France, the 7th Panzer Division. There is no doubt that this was a patronage appointment; Rommel, an infantryman, had had no time on the General Staff and now he received one of the most sought after commands in the army. Nevertheless, Rommel made the most of his opportunity and gave Hitler no cause to regret the decision.

This was an ideal command for Rommel, the mobility and firepower of the panzer division made it the perfect tool for a hard-charger. In the battle for France, 10 May to 25 June 1940, the 7th Panzer Division was given the assignment of driving as fast as it could go for the Meuse River and then beyond. On 13 May, elements of the 7th, or the Ghost Division, as it would soon be known, reached the Meuse River some 30 miles south of Liege. The Belgians opposed the crossing from prepared positions and German engineers built a bridge across under heavy fire. Waist deep in the water helping out was Rommel. This is inspiring leadership, but it is not responsible leadership. Rommel had no business exposing himself to such danger and the author is not alone in his assessment that there are better things for a divisional commander to be doing during an attack than leaving his headquarters to build a bridge. Regardless, guess who drove the first tank across? The reader may think that this was not the first time Rommel exposed himself to danger nor the last, and that is correct. The next day Rommel was nearly captured when his tank was disabled and he was slightly wounded. Only the timely arrival of support saved him and this was not the only time he was nearly captured. For the next weeks his division rampaged behind the French lines, cutting their communications and overrunning French positions. The battle for France was a triumph for Rommel and 7th Panzer, they captured nearly 100,000 prisoners and destroyed 458 tanks, 277 guns, as well as thousands of vehicles and other equipment, all at the cost of about 2,200 men and 42 tanks. These losses, however, were the highest sustained of the panzer divisions similarly engaged. The German press, nevertheless, loved Rommel and this was the start of his international celebrity; helped along by several important members of the Propaganda Ministry whom he had secured as reserve officers for his division. Rommel's memoir of the campaign, *The Ghost Division*, includes falsified diagrams designed to make him look good and he ignored or downplayed the contributions of others. He also appeared in Goebbels's cinematic production, *Victory in the West*. This and more may be found in Douglas Porch's *The Path to Victory*.

In September 1940 the Italians under Marshal Rodolfo Graziani invaded Egypt; in December the British under General Richard O'Connor struck back in a daring attack against far larger forces. They chased the Italians out of Egypt and captured 38,000 prisoners and much matériel. In January 1941 the British continued their offensive, captured Tobruk on 22 January, and by the first week in February they had secured the unconditional surrender of the Italians in Libya. The British took 130,000 prisoners, 400 tanks, and 1,300 guns at a cost of 1,900 casualties. They had achieved this with the 7th Armored Division, the famed Desert Rats, one infantry division, plus two infantry brigades and one tank battalion.

Hitler then sent support to Mussolini in the form of the *Luftwaffe*'s Tenth *Fliegerkorps* (Air Corps); some 500 aircraft arrived in Sicily from Norway in January. On February 12, Rommel arrived in Tripoli. The first elements of the *Afrika Korps*, 5th Light Division, started coming in two days later. On 16 February, these elements, Reconnaissance Battalion 3 and Anti-tank Regiment 39, gained contact with the British. The rest of the division arrived over the next weeks; in August it was re-designated as 21st Panzer. The 15th Panzer Division came over in April and May. Then various independent units in Africa were gathered up and when they were added to others from Germany became the *Afrika Division*, later designated the 90th Light Division. This, then, was the material basis of the *Afrika Korps* and Rommel would provide the legend. He was, at this time, the only German Army general in combat against a major opponent; all eyes would be on him until Operation BARBAROSSA was launched against the Soviets in June. The author has not forgotten the Balkan Interlude, by the way, but how much publicity did Wilhelm List get? Here the author wishes the reader to take note, Rommel was not chosen for BARBAROSSA. OKH (Army High Command) did not want him in Russia. They did not want him in Africa. But Adolf did.

The *Afrika Korps* was officially known as the *Deutsches Afrika Korps* or DAK, but most people think of it as the *Afrika Korps* and that is how it shall be styled. Rommel was under the Italian commander-in-chief, Garibaldi, but the *Afrika Korps* was to be a unique entity under Rommel's command. Rommel had the right to appeal any order given to him by any Italian to OKH. Rommel did not have control of the Tenth *Fliegerkorps*; Goering did. Rommel had to make requests for air support to the *Fliegerführer*, Fröhlich, who would see what could be done with whatever units of the Tenth were available. No wonder Rommel was to complain about a lack of air support throughout the campaign. That aside, Rommel was to have something which few other commanders ever experienced in the twentieth century—a nearly independent command. In Africa, he would have no superior closely supervising him, in fact his only superior in Africa was an Italian and given the mess the Italians were in, Rommel had little worry of interference. Moreover, he was able to ignore the orders he received from Germany as well with little repercussion.

The events of the North Africa campaign are detailed in many books and so the author will only offer the barest of summaries. On 24 March, Rommel went on the offensive against the wishes of his titular superior, Garibaldi, the German Commander-in-Chief, Walter von Brauchitsch, and Hitler. In April the British were pushed back, the 2nd Armored Division, divided and running out of gasoline, was captured. General O'Connor was captured as well. The 9th Australian Division reached the port of Tobruk and, though cut off from the rest of the British army, defended it against Rommel's haphazard attacks. The Royal Navy supplied Tobruk and this proved crucial to the campaign as Tobruk was the proverbial thorn in Rommel's side.

A British counteroffensive was launched in June on orders from Churchill and failed. Both sides built up their forces until November when the British launched Operation Crusader. The attacks were poorly coordinated and the offensive was checked. More than once in this theater the British were to suffer from their deficiencies in doctrine and training. Rommel then, typically, went on the offensive and created some panic in the British rear areas, but unlike his attacks in April, the

British did not fall back and the Germans and Italians were stopped. A counterattack by the British affected a junction with Tobruk when the New Zealand division cut through the rear of the German forces. The surrounded Germans had to break out, which they did, and Rommel retreated westward with the British forces applying pressure. By the end of December 1941, Rommel was back at El Agheila, which is where he was in April. The Italians and Germans had lost 61,000 men killed, wounded and taken prisoner, 386 tanks, and 850 aircraft. The British had lost 18,000 men. However, in December a series of naval disasters left the Royal Navy with only 3 cruisers and some destroyers in the Mediterranean. This allowed Rommel's resupply to proceed without much hindrance.

Rommel went on the offensive again in January 1942. The British retreated to Gazala, west of Tobruk and there the line stabilized in February. On 28 May the battle of the Gazala—Bir Hacheim line started and on 13 June, the British 8th Army was ordered to pull back into Egypt. Tobruk was taken on the hop by the Germans on 21 June in a stunning blow and by July Rommel was 60 miles from Alexandria. At the end of August Rommel attacked again and the battle of Alam Halfa lasted through the first week of September. Rommel could not effect a break through against 8th Army, now led by General Bernard Montgomery. This was to be Rommel's last offensive; by now the Germans had lost the logistic battle in the Mediterranean.

Montgomery did not attack until 23 October, when the 8th Army's strength had been greatly built up. The battle of El Alamein lasted until 4 November. Rommel was not there, he had gone to Germany for medical treatment and the blow fell on General Hans Stumme who had taken command. The defensive plan Stumme inherited was Rommel's. The *Afrika Korps* still existed, by the way, but it was now a part of the *Panzerarmee Afrika*, which had evolved from *Panzergruppe Afrika*. Anyway, Stumme died on 24 October under odd circumstances. He had been out reconnoitering on that morning to determine British progress in his northern mine field. While Stumme and an aide were away from their vehicle, they came under shellfire. The aide was killed and Stumme leapt on to the vehicle as the driver drove away. The strain on his heart was too much for Stumme and he suffered a heart attack and fell off the vehicle. The driver did not notice that he had lost the commander until much later. Stumme's body lay by the side of the road where it was found the next day. Why was Stumme up there? The British artillery bombardment and radio jamming had completely disrupted German communications and Stumme, getting no reliable information, had gone up to the front to see for himself.

Meanwhile, Rommel hurried back from Germany after only three weeks of treatment, still a sick man. He arrived on 25 October. The British ground down the German armor in sharp, attritive fighting and the Germans could not repair, fuel, or supply their vehicles. The 8th Army forced a breakthrough on 4 November and the Germans retreated; the *Afrika Korps* had 3 dozen tanks left and before much longer they were down to twelve. Montgomery did not pursue for nearly 24 hours but he had won a great victory, one of the decisive victories of the war. Four days later the Americans landed in Morocco and Algeria. The Axis would fight on as they retreated but the end came in May 1943 in Tunisia but by then Rommel was back in Europe.

The war in the desert covered distances greater than any industrialized armies had ever faced. The distance from the Axis base in Tripoli to Alexandria was 1,200 miles, twice the distance from the 1939 German border to Moscow or from the Normandy beaches to Berlin. Nor was there a railway line that could be used in a way to assist transport, thus everything had to go by road or what passed for roads. Along with the large distances to be covered was the increased strain on man and machine. Men needed more water in an area where there was far less. Engines designed to operate in Europe overheated in the desert and filters became clogged with fine dust. Maintenance requirements went up and when not performed, vehicle life went down.

Even diet affected mobility; the Italians had to carry more water than other nations because they cooked pasta. More water means less of something else. The German diet, lacking in fruit and vegetables but high in fat, also affected their morale and performance; many young men lost teeth. It was said that more than two years in Africa would permanently ruin one's health. The British, by contrast, had a much healthier and varied diet reflecting their collective experience in Northern Africa. The Germans, accordingly, relished grabbing British food stocks.

Other than Tripoli, the Axis had no ports adequate for the task of supply. The limits of Tripoli's harbor, so Martin van Crevald tells us in *Supplying War* was such that 45,000 tons a month could be landed. In practical terms, he tells us, a German motorized division at Sirte, some 300 miles from Tripoli, needed 39 columns of 30 two-ton trucks (1,170) to provide the 350 tons of supplies the division needed daily. If more reinforcements arrived or the front shifted eastward then the supply problem worsened exponentially. With Rommel calling for reinforcements for the *Afrika Korps* and when Hitler overrode the High Command and sent them, the threat of shortages was real. Thus Rommel was told not to start any offensives.

What did Rommel do? Disobeyed orders and went on the attack because he knew the British forces were dispersed and at the end of long supply line. He saw a tactical opportunity and created a logistical calamity. He refused to acknowledge that he was now in the strategic business. He scored a stunning advance and chased the British back into Egypt, which made him look good. It was hard to be hard on the guy publicly, but he had failed to take Tobruk. His attacks on it were not well-coordinated, but he passed the blame for that on to others. And quite a failure it was, for he greatly lengthened his supply line and did not knock out the British. Tripoli remained the major port for the Axis forces and it was 1,000 miles behind Rommel.

In fact, the supplies at Tripoli were piling up faster than they could be delivered. Rommel's complaints about not receiving enough matériel were not based on his transports being sunk, because by May 1941, the Axis had delivered 45,000 tons more of supply than the armies were using. As the weeks went on Rommel's situation worsened. He thought, wrongly as van Crevald tells us, that capturing Tobruk would solve his twin problems of not enough supply and protecting his reputation, but he could not take Tobruk with the forces he had. He wanted more panzer divisions for the task. There were none available, of course, because of *BARBAROSSA*. Moreover, even if there had been a couple of tank divisions lying around, their presence in Africa would only have made the supply situation worse. Rommel's response to the High Command as to how he would provide supply for all the armor he was asking for was, in essence, "that's your problem." From the perspective of OKH the situation appeared thus, "we have just invaded Russia in the largest military undertaking in history, if we lose this, as everybody from Hitler on down knows, we are finished, and here comes that ambitious self-promoter and Hitler pal, Rommel, asking for a couple of panzer divisions so that he can attack a place which is 700 miles from where he is supposed to be. Thanks, but no tanks for you." The Nazi solution was to rename the *Afrika Korps* the *Panzergruppe Afrika* and promote Rommel to panzer general. "Hey Rommel, congrats, you are the youngest man to achieve this rank." This did not go over well at OKH either.

Also in June most of the Tenth *Fliegerkorps* was moved to Greece and the RAF began sinking more and more of the supply ships leaving Italy. Despite the losses the Italians still managed to deliver enough to match consumption. The problem was it still could not reach Rommel. The reader undoubtedly realizes that the trucks taking the supplies to Rommel also used fuel. One thousand miles to Rommel and one thousand miles back and then factor in that perhaps one-third of the trucks are under repair or broken down at any one time, and you get the picture.

Rommel could not capture enough supplies to keep going. This, then, was the campaign that made Rommel famous. The situation for 1942 was essentially the same. Rommel advanced, ran short on supplies, tried to win the campaign with a bold stroke that was inadequately supported and then retreated before a powerful counterstroke. Of course by now he was a field-marshal.

The other factor often used to assess Rommel or rather mitigate his defeat in North Africa is the role of signals intelligence in the campaign. In fact at the beginning of the campaign the advantage lay with the Germans and did so for some time. The British took quite a while to develop an effective system for the collection and dissemination of the German super-secret Ultra traffic in North Africa. The Germans thought that any message encoded by this gizmo could not be broken by anyone. They were wrong. Nevertheless, the breaking of Engima took a good deal of time and a lot of brain power. Once the British achieved this, the problem became how to effectively disseminate the information and still keep the secret. This too was achieved in time.

The story of how the Axis gained their initial intelligence advantage is revealing of Allied signals security and also of the state of Germano-Italian relations. The Italians had snuck into the American Embassy in Rome in September 1941 and photographed the American "Black Code," so called as the binding was black. They did not tell the Germans. Meanwhile the Cipher Branch of the German Armed Forces (OKW/Chi) was also working to break the Black Code and when it did, the Germans did not tell the Italians. The object of all this attention was the American military attaché in Cairo, Colonel Bonner Fellers. He used the Black Code to send his reports to Washington and it seems that he was able to go pretty much everywhere and see pretty much everything. Thus when Rommel was retreating in November 1941 he knew the British intentions and what strength they were massing for the attack. Nor was this intelligence bonanza solely the result of a simple American code and poor security. John Hinsley in volume 2 of the official history, *British Intelligence in the Second World War* tells us that the Germans were reading the British War Office's high-grade hand cipher (wireless telegraphy) which gave access down to division level from August 1941 to January 1942. Moreover, British carelessness in use of radio telephony, tactical codes, plain language, and call-signs completed the chain down to frontline battalions. The upshot of all this was is that for his first campaign in Africa, Rommel received information daily as to the British order of battle and intentions. He knew, exactly where the British units were, and what they were likely to do. Moreover, he kept this information to himself. It was not confided to his subordinates or his diaries. The author believes that this was done for reasons beyond security. Rommel would appear less the tactical genius if his staff knew all that he knew. Similarly, as David Kahn tells us in *Hitler's Spies*, when Rommel was once again on the attack in January and February 1942 he knew the status of all British armor, the transfers of aircraft to the Far East from North Africa, the efficiency ratings of units, the defensive positions and intentions to establish same, where air and commando raids would be launched, and so on.

Rommel's offensives of May and June 1942 for the Gazala Line, which so dazzled friend and foe alike, were accomplished by a general who knew much of his enemy's moves before he made them. This did not guarantee Rommel of easy pickings however. There were times during the battle that the British could have destroyed the *Afrika Korps* but they did not co-ordinate their counter-attacks and attacked Rommel's gun line without first suppressing the anti-tank guns by shell fire. Nevertheless Rommel's rashness saw many of his tanks run out of fuel and units run so low on ammunition and water that they were close to surrender. However, Rommel's mammoth luck held and it was the British who retreated. Typically during this battle Rommel charged around the battlefield and personally commanded units, he even led his supply columns to his tanks. This was a dramatic demonstration of leadership, the kind he favored, but it also put him out of touch from his headquarters. In his absence, his subordinates had to make decisions.

Intercepted information kept on coming to Rommel through the spring and into the summer. Rommel could not have had it better if he was lunching at British HQ. Then it stopped. The Americans switched from the Black Code at the end of June suspecting that it had been compromised. How did it happen? The likely story is good ol' thorough intelligence work and analysis. David Fraser, in his biography of Rommel, *Knight's Cross*, states that it was Ultra decrypts of OKH signals. The unlikely story is too good to pass up, however. The author has seen only one explanation like this and implausible or not, here it is, compliments of Wilhelm Flicke in *War Secrets in the Ether*. Flicke served in various aspects of German signals intelligence from WW I through WW II. He tells us that on Saturday, 27 June 1942 at 6 p.m. he tuned in a broadcast called *Deutschlandsender*. The offering was a radio drama of scenes from the enemy information bureau. The location was North Africa, the subject—political and military matters. The dramatist personae included the American Military Attaché in Cairo who proceeded to discuss all the information he was sending to Washington and the means by which it was done! Thirty-six hours later the transmissions from Fellers to Washington stopped. When they resumed, the Germans were unable to break them.

In early July came another telling blow to Rommel, elements of the 9th Australian Division shot up and overran his radio intercept company. Its commander, the extremely talented Captain Seebohm, was killed. This unit had become adept at intercepting and breaking low-level tactical codes. Now, for once, Rommel would know less about what the British were planning.

What to make of Rommel? He won when he faced opponents who could not put up an effective fight and when he had an overwhelming intelligence advantage. Most commanders could win under these circumstances. Did Rommel win when he should have lost? No. When Montgomery won at El Alamein and pushed Rommel across North Africa, Monty had the advantage. Rommel was down on men and matériel. When Rommel lacked the intelligence insights into his opponents or rather, when he was as much in the dark than the other guy, he was no better than the other guy. Yet Rommel's decisions and actions ensured that his forces would be compromised. The blame for this, he thought, belonged to others, but it was all his. His aggressive tactics put the men entrusted to him in precarious and deadly situations. Nor were losses confined to the ranks. Ronald Lewin in *The Life and Death of the Afrika Korps* lists on one page 15 generals who were killed or wounded while following Rommel's established culture of frontline leadership. Rommel called it, demanding the utmost self-denial and continual personal example. His men respected the fact that Rommel shared these dangers but while it was forceful leadership, it was irresponsible generalship. Often Rommel was saved by phenomenal luck and bad decisions by his opponents, still the bill for these excursions was high and paid in blood and destroyed equipment. So, if your idea of a great general is a publicity crazy guy who is frequently out of touch with his HQ, who believes that tactical and operational success can overcome strategic shortcomings, who acts precipitately and with little regard for logistics or casualties, and who will blame everybody he can find for his failure in a side-show theater, then this is the commander for you.

## Most Underrated General of World War II:
### Alexander Patch

He was the first American commander to drive the Japanese off a major island; commanded soldiers from North America, Africa, and Europe in a stunningly successful invasion of the European mainland; led the first Allied units to successfully establish themselves along the Rhine; and defeated the last German offensive in the west. Other than Lucian Truscott, he was the only American to command a division, corps, and

field army in combat. He was the *only* American general to command
large forces in three distinct theaters, namely, a division and corps in the
Pacific Theater; an army in the Mediterranean Theater during the invasion of southern France; and an army in the European Theater. The field
army he commanded fought over the most diverse and difficult terrain
in all of western Europe, yet he never lost a major unit, and accomplished every mission assigned. Eisenhower rated him as "more valuable" than several of his much more well-known peers; Barry Goldwa-
ter said that he would have given his "right arm" to have served under
him. He was deeply admired by his men, and lost his only son, an
infantry captain serving under his command in combat.

Despite all of this and more, apart from the soldiers who served
under him, only the most serious of World War II buffs know Alexander McCarrell Patch, Jr. as more than a name on a unit icon of small-
scale maps of the European Theater of Operations. A variety of coinci-
dental events which overshadowed or obscured his achievements—

a consistent record of victory in battle without debacle or mishap; a quiet and unassuming personality; and the preoccupation of the press with disaster, obnoxious personalities, and other sensational news—all combined to ensure that he would be the most unknown and underestimated commander of World War II.

Born at Fort Huachuca, Arizona, in 1889, Patch was the son of a cavalryman and Annie Moore Patch, the daughter of Congressman William S. Moore of Pennsylvania. Of German and Scotch-Irish descent, the senior Patch was an 1877 West Point graduate and veteran of the Indian Wars who was retired in 1891 following wounds sustained in the line of duty. As a result, young Alexander grew up in Lebanon, Pennsylvania, where his parents raised their family of three boys and a girl in the comfortable surroundings made possible by the senior Patch's pension and his salary as a railroad executive.

As an adolescent, Patch was a pugnacious and high-spirited, never backing down from a fight, but never tolerating cruelty to animals or bullying of his friends. Although he was not excited by the idea of an Army career, in consonance with his disciplinarian father's desire, Patch applied for and earned an appointment to the United States Military Academy at West Point in 1909. As a cadet, he loathed the sometimes inhumane treatment of plebes by some upperclassmen; as a plebe himself, he rebelled against it, and as an upperclassman, he showed no interest in playing the plebe vs. upperclassmen game. Patch ultimately graduated near the bottom of his class, but was a solid intercollegiate baseball player and pole vaulter who was admired by many of his peers for his consistent refusal to curry favor with his superiors. Commissioned in the infantry on 12 June 1913, Patch was assigned to the 18th Infantry Regiment in Texas.

During duty on the Mexican border in 1915 and in his service in the Punitive Expedition against the *Villistas* in 1916, Patch's superiors noted a promising ability and sense of professional judgment. Later that year, in November, Patch married his "one and only" from cadet days, Julia A. Littell (a general's daughter), thus affirming a rock-solid relationship that endured through war, triumph, and tragedy for the rest of his life. During the Great War, Patch and his older brother, Dorst (who had enlisted in 1909 and secured a commission without attending the Military Academy), both deployed to France in June 1917 as infantry captains with the 1st Infantry Division.

Patch commanded the American Expeditionary Force's machine-gun school at Langres through the remainder of 1917 and most of 1918, but gained command of a battalion of the 18th Infantry Regiment in time for the final offensive of the Great War in October 1918. Thus, his combat experience in the Great War was limited, but it was meaningful, and it was in command. Further, it enabled him to make a direct link between his experience as a trainer and that of a combat commander.

Patch's Great War experience also included one ominous development: he suffered from a serious bout with pneumonia during much of his tour in France. It was not the last time that he would suffer from the disease that ultimately killed him.

In an army as small as the miniature US Army between the wars, (190,000 men in 1939), Patch managed to keep his hand in training combat troops as well as honing his skills as a coach and mentor of young men.

Between the wars, Patch spent eleven years, parsed out over three separate tours, as Professor of Military Science and Tactics at Staunton Military Academy, a private secondary school in western Virginia, not far from the Virginia Military Institute (VMI). Here, while Patch honed his skills as a trainer and groomer of young men, he met and befriended Withers A. Burress, the commandant at the VMI, who later commanded the 100th Infantry Division under Patch in Europe in WWII. Throughout what otherwise might have been a period of professional stagnation, Patch also maintained and enhanced his other professional abilities. Between the Staunton tours, which began in 1921 and finally ended in 1936, Patch graduated from the Field Officer's Course at the Infantry School at Fort Benning, was a distinguished graduate from the Command and General Staff School (as it was then called) at Fort Leavenworth, and attended the Army War College. While Staunton Military Academy was out of session, he served as Director of Training, and later Commanding Officer, of the ROTC training camp at Fort Meade, Maryland. More importantly, he commanded the 3rd Battalion, 12th Infantry Regiment at Fort Washington, Maryland, from 1928 to 1931.

After completing his last tour at Staunton, Patch contributed to the development of infantry tactics and ordnance with a tour on the Infantry Board from 1936 to 1939; trained the Alabama National Guard, from 1939 to 1940; and was finally assigned to command the 47th Infantry Regiment of the 9th Infantry Division at Fort Bragg, North Carolina. This assignment was a particularly fortuitous one, as the 9th's commanding general was Jacob Devers, a man who would later figure very prominently in Patch's WWII service. After receiving his first star in 1941, Patch was reassigned as the commanding general of the Infantry Replacement Training Center at Camp Croft, South Carolina.

Barely a month after the Japanese sneak attack at Pearl Harbor, Patch was promoted to major general and assigned to command Task Force 6814, a quickly tossed-together *ad hoc* assembly of roughly divisional size built around two National Guard infantry regiments (the 132nd from Illinois and the 182nd from Massachusetts). The task force was charged with the mission of defending the French colony of New Caledonia from what appeared to be imminent Japanese attack; with things going quite badly for the American Regular Army forces in the Philippines at the time, there was considerable question about the ability of US forces to defeat the Japanese on the ground. Patch was literally, therefore, the "man in the arena," the champion personally selected by Army Chief of Staff George C. Marshall to go to the southwest Pacific with whatever the Army could scrape together and stand between the rapidly-advancing Japanese and the frantically-preparing Australians.

En route, Patch was again stricken with pneumonia, but overcame it again to arrive in New Caledonia in early March 1942. Although this was literally his first acquaintance with his new command, he busily set about organizing and training them for the formidable task at hand: defending the 1,250-mile-long island. He requested augmentation by a complete horse cavalry regiment as well as another infantry regiment, but only received the latter, the 164th Infantry Regiment of the North Dakota National Guard.

As Patch painstakingly trained his polyglot division—which, at the suggestion of Private First Class David Fonseca became officially known as the "Americal Division," combining "American" with "New Caledonia"—other difficult challenges arose. As if organizing and training an entirely new outfit and preparing them for combat with the seemingly invincible Japanese were not daunting enough, the French government and military establishment on New Caledonia began squabbling. As the situation neared the point of explosion, Patch, who liked and respected the French from his Great War experience, provided tactful but firm military diplomacy to quell the situation. So outstanding was his intervention that the Army awarded him the Distinguished Service Medal, its highest award not requiring battlefield valor. He also gained General Marshall's further respect and confidence.

With New Caledonia secure, Patch's next mission as commanding general of the Americal Division was to relieve the 1st Marine Division and, on orders from Admiral Halsey, "eliminate all Japanese forces on Guadalcanal." Landing in August 1942, Marine Major General Archie Vandegrift's division struck the first American offensive blow on the ground against the Japanese who, up until that time, had been seemingly invincible in their defeats of the Americans in the Philippines, the British at Singapore, and the Dutch in the East Indies. Locked in desperate fighting in the pesthole that was Guadalcanal, the Marines and their US Navy supporting elements tenaciously fought a see-saw action that held on to the crucial perimeter around the key airstrip at Henderson Field, but were unable to make decisive headway against constantly-reinforced, aggressive Japanese forces.

Although infantry elements of Patch's division arrived on Guadalcanal as early as mid-October, it was not until 9 December that Patch and the Americal Division officially relieved Vandegrift and the 1st Marine Division. In preparation for a three-division offensive in January 1943, Patch's men conducted fiercely-contested limited-objective attacks to seize terrain that would posture them for success when sufficient combat power was present for the final offensive. In early January, as the 25th Infantry Division and 2nd Marine Division completed their deployment to Guadalcanal, Patch was promoted to command of the newly-created XIV Corps, the headquarters which controlled them all.

Patch launched the corps' attack on 10 January 1943, and in almost exactly a month of vicious jungle fighting, XIV Corps methodically and effectively cleared the Japanese from Guadalcanal. Although the combined Army-Navy-Marine forces engaged in and around the island failed to prevent over 11,000 Japanese from escaping to fight another day, it was an immensely important victory. For the first time in World War II, a major Japanese force (in this case, one which had amounted to over 36,000 troops in all) had been driven off a major island by American ground forces. Coming just a few weeks after a joint US/Australian force had defeated the Japanese in Papua, Patch's victory gave even greater impetus to the turning tide in the Pacific because it was proof that American ground forces could not only stave off defeat—as the 1st Marine Division had in the first four months of the Guadalcanal operation—but decisively clear the Japanese off a large island. With many dozens of such islands left to go on the long route to Dai Nippon, it was a fabulously important first step.

Typically, few people today associate Patch's name with Guadalcanal. Marine Major General Archie Vandegrift, who was awarded the Medal of Honor and later went on to become the Commandant of the Marine Corps, is the general officer whose name is usually associated with this battle. Partially, this is undoubtedly due to the Marines' legendary public relations talents, and partially, it is a function of timing. When it comes to fame, as with so many other endeavors, timing is everything.

When the Marines assaulted Guadalcanal in August, it was just six months after the British surrendered the "impregnable" fortress of Singapore; five months since the surrender of the Dutch Army in the Netherlands East Indies; and only three months since the surrender of US forces in the Philippines at Corregidor and the eviction of Allied forces from Burma. The German summer offensive was driving to the Caucasus oilfields, and the top British commanders in Egypt were being relieved for their failure to stop Rommel's offensive across Cyrenaica in the spring. The Anglo-Canadian "raid" at Dieppe, launched just nine days after the Marine landings on Guadalcanal, had been a complete disaster. When the 1st Marine Division was hanging on by its finger-nails around Henderson Field in the first half of October, it was still the only major American ground force in contact with the enemy anywhere in the world. American media focused on the dramatic, see-saw battle on Guadalcanal because it was the only show of its type at the time, and it provided hope to an American public which was in sore need of good news.

By the time Patch and the Army took over from the exhausted Marines on 9 December and cleared the island of Japanese two months later, many other momentous events had taken place. The tide had turned in North Africa with the British Eighth Army's offensive at El Alamein. The German offensive in Russia had been halted, and Paulus's Sixth Army had been destroyed at Stalingrad; a 300,000-man Axis field army had ceased to exist over a period of three months. Allied forces had landed in French Morocco and Algeria, among them five US Army divisions (1st, 3rd, 9th, and 34th Infantry and 1st Armored); *Panzerarmee Afrika* was being squeezed from two sides now and its days were num-bered. Closer to Guadalcanal, in late January 1943, joint American and Australian ground forces defeated the Japanese around Buna and Sanananda Point in New Guinea. On 4 February, less than a week before Patch could announce the "total and complete defeat of Japanese forces on Guadalcanal," and after a hero's return to the States, a speaking tour, and a national radio broadcast on the popular show "The March of Time," General Vandegrift was decorated by President Roosevelt with the Medal of Honor.

In short, public awareness of the exceptionally important and hard-won victory on Guadalcanal, skillfully engineered by Patch with many of the soldiers he personally trained, was largely lost in the hoopla sur-rounding his predecessor's publicity and the other major, positive developments in the course of the war. Although it was all fine with the self-effacing, quietly-professional Patch, it was far from the last time that this sort of phenomenon would obscure his magnificent achievements.

After Guadalcanal, Marshall recalled Patch to command IV Corps at Fort Lewis. Marshall had been apprised, accurately, that the campaigns in the southwest Pacific had severely degraded Patch's health, and, remembering his near-run bout with pneumonia en route to New Cale-donia, the Chief of Staff brought him back to a more hospitable climate. During Patch's command, he finished the training of the 91st, 96th, and 104th Infantry Divisions, which subsequently deployed to Italy, the Pacific, and northwest Europe, respectively. Patch's training expertise, developed in WWI and over long interwar years and honed by his recent combat experience, helped all of these divisions become more effective in the tasks that loomed before them. During the period at Lewis, Patch also built a staff, combining officers who had served with him in the southwest Pacific with many who had been already serving in IV Corps when Patch arrived. To a very great extent, this was the staff that Patch would take with him for the rest of the war, so they were a very cohesive and well-coordinated group indeed. Patton was not the only one to derive intense loyalty from his subordinate staffers.

In March 1944, Patch assumed command of the Seventh Army, then only a headquarters in North Africa. Formerly commanded—during the Sicily campaign—by George Patton, a man who was Patch's opposite in many ways, the Seventh Army would have tactical control of all allied troops during the upcoming Operation ANVIL (later re-dubbed DRAGOON), the invasion of Southern France. This operation was controversial for a number of reasons. The British, especially Churchill, preferred using the available resources for an operation in northeastern Italy. Such an alternative would relieve pressure on the Italian front; encourage German allies such as the Hungarians and the Romanians to switch sides; and place Allied troops into eastern Europe in advance of the Soviets.

An invasion of southern France would be of more immediate support to the landings in Normandy. It would force *Oberbefehlshaber-West* (the German high command in western Europe) into a series of undesirable choices: commit already thinly-stretched reserves, risk encirclement of forces in southwest France, or, at a minimum, be unable to use the divisions of Army Group G. An invasion in southern France would also allow swift support to the *FFI* (*Forces françaises de l'interieurs*), much of which was located in the Central Massif. Finally, the seizure of the port facilities at Marseilles and Toulon would relieve the massive pressure on the artificial docks in Normandy, especially if Cherbourg or other Atlantic ports could not be seized intact.

Ultimately, the southern France invasion was agreed upon by the Allied Combined Chiefs of Staff, and Patch and his staff prepared the final plans for the invasion. Under the command of the North African Theater (which became designated as the Mediterranean Theater in November) and using three veteran US divisions of VI Corps under the experienced and reliable Lucian Truscott (3rd, 36th, and 45th Infantry Divisions, all veterans of extensive mountain fighting in Italy) to make his main attack, Patch also had other important assets at his disposal. A provisional airborne division—with American and British parachute and glider troops—would land well inland of the beaches to prevent rapid reinforcement of the defenders, cut off German withdrawals, and interfere with the Germans' command, control, and communications systems. Commencing on D+1, the equivalent of two French corps would follow the American assault troops; these consisted of mostly soldiers from French colonies in northern and western Africa, led by white French officers. The political pressure on Patch to get these French troops into combat as quickly as possible had no parallel in the Normandy operation.

Thus, Patch would command soldiers from three continents in an invasion which, if not as complex as the OVERLORD landings, were nevertheless substantial and elaborate, and which posed some very different challenges from those encountered in Normandy. The choke points for the landing area were much further inland than the ones for the OVERLORD beaches, so the airborne landings would have to be much deeper (ten miles). This vastly increased the risk to both the airborne and amphibious forces. Also, the details of the airborne operation were planned in just five weeks and executed by an *ad hoc* unit whose subordinate formations consisted of one US parachute infantry regiment, three separate US parachute infantry battalions, a British parachute brigade, and numerous separate glider-borne units—some of which, such as the Anti-Tank Company of the Nisei 442nd Infantry Regiment and several 4.2″ heavy mortar outfits, had never even *seen* a glider before.

Apart from the amphibious and airborne landings of VI Corps and the Provisional Airborne Division, there were pre-H-hour assaults by American and Canadian commandos (the famed 1st Special Service Force, or "Devil's Brigade"), French Commandos, and French naval infantry. Patch's plan incorporated massive deception operations intended to mask the true location and nature of the main landings. A huge signals deception effort seemed to indicate a shift of forces in north Africa, and a variety of naval diversionary efforts suggested landings at locations as diverse as Genoa, Italy, Nice, and Marseilles. All of this was planned and executed by Patch's headquarters, which was only a fraction of the size of Eisenhower's in England, and had nothing like the all-out priority of OVERLORD from the Combined Chiefs.

Executed commencing 15 August 1944, DRAGOON and the Seventh Army's subsequent pursuit of German forces up the Rhône Valley were very successful. As late as 10 August, German intelligence was convinced that no landings would take place on the Mediterranean coast at all, and as late as 12 August—the day the invasion force put to sea—German intelligence could not predict whether the landings would be in France or Italy. Even on D-day—as the first Allied paratroopers hit the French earth and the French commandos began landing on the islands just off the invasion beaches—the commander and staff of the 19th Army could not determine the location of Patch's main effort.

As a result, unlike the Normandy landings, which failed to result in the capture of a single usable major port, the southern France invasion yielded two major deep-water ports—Marseilles and Toulon—which were put into use by early September. The especial rapidity of the American assault landings and the nimble arrival of the equivalent of two French corps assured the rapid expansion of the beachhead and the destruction of two German divisions, the 242nd and 244th Infantry. The rest of Army Group G was severely disorganized and quickly put to flight. Ultimately, over 88,000 Germans from Army Group G were captured by the Seventh Army during its pursuit of German forces up the Rhône River valley. This astounding total is all the more amazing when contrasted with the total German prisoner haul from the much more famous Falaise encirclement, which netted—depending on how one figures it—only 50,000–70,000 German prisoners.

Patch's Seventh Army's accomplishments are spectacular for more reasons than these. Far less air support was available, for example, than had been allotted to the OVERLORD efforts. Less than 10 percent of the 3,500 tactical aircraft that had been allotted to the Normandy landings were tasked by the combined Mediterranean Allied Air Forces for support of the DRAGOON landings. The mechanized and armored forces available to Patch were a mere shadow of those made available to Bradley. Aside from the very temporary use of one combat command (brigade) of the French 1st Armored Division (CC Sudre), Patch could only count on three US separate tank battalions (191st, 753rd, and 756th) three US separate tank destroyer battalions (601st, 636th, and 645th), and the VI Corps' mechanized cavalry reconnaissance squadron (117th). The next time additional armored forces would be made available to the Seventh Army would not be until XV Corps was allotted from Third Army in late September.

Nevertheless, Patch made optimal use of what he had. Attaching most of his armor to his three infantry divisions to enable combined arms operations for pursuit of German forces withdrawing northward up the Rhône Valley, Patch created Task Force (TF) Butler, commanded by the VI Corps Assistant Commanding General. Built around the 117th Cavalry Squadron, TF Butler also consisted of two tank companies, a company of tank destroyers, one battalion of truck-borne infantry (2nd Battalion of the 143rd Infantry, detached from the 36th Infantry Division), and a battalion of self-propelled 105mm howitzers. Before the end of August, in conjunction with the XII Tactical Air Command and elements of the 36th Infantry Division, this small *ad hoc* task force did much to cut off and bottle up German 19th Army units attempting to withdraw to the Vosges Mountains and Belfort Gap, their ultimate destination. German units such as the 198th and 338th Infantry Divisions completed the withdrawal from southern France with their combat strength depleted by about 80 percent, while American casualties amounted to less than 5 percent of the forces committed.

The Seventh Army's rapid progress northward forced all of Army Group G to withdraw to northeastern France, and resulted in the liberation of fully 65 percent of all French territory. As Eisenhower said after the war, "there was no development of that period [summer 1944] which added more decisively to our advantage or aided us more in accomplishing the final and complete defeat of German forces than did this attack coming up the Rhône valley."

Typically, Patch himself was very low key about all of this, and remained focused on the operations at hand. When his photo appeared on the cover of the 25 August 1944 *Time* magazine, the Seventh Army Public Information Officer rushed in to his office with a copy, only to have Patch ignore the story inside altogether. According to the secretary of his general staff during the war, Patch genuinely hated the limelight and avoided publicity for himself.

Apart from the *Time* article, however, Patch's accomplishments went virtually unnoticed by the press and, therefore, by the rest of the world. In the same week that his Seventh Army was routing German forces and beginning the end of the occupation of two-thirds of France, the fierce fighting around Falaise and Argentan was nearing a climax. The so-called "GI's General," Omar Bradley, commanded First Army in this important battle, and George Patton was commanding the recently created Third. The latter, famous for his filthy language, abuse of his own soldiers, and loud mouth, was always avidly watched by the press.

Ten days after the DRAGOON landings, as Toulon and Marseilles were on the verge of falling to the Seventh Army and the remainder of Army Group G was departing from southern France, the German commandant of Paris disobeyed his orders and let Paris be liberated by Jacques Leclerc and his soon-to-be-famous French 2nd Armored Division. On the same day, Germany lost an important ally as Romania switched sides, and declared war on Germany.

Although Patch's Seventh Army's accomplishment was, indeed, decisive for the liberation of France, once again, other momentous events, occurring simultaneously, grabbed the headlines and stole the thunder away from Patch and his consistent victories.

In mid-September, the two French corps under Patch's command were stripped away to form the new First French Army, and along with Seventh Army. This came under command of the newly-formed Sixth Army Group, commanded by Jacob Devers. At about the same time, the Sixth Army Group came under command of Supreme Headquarters, Allied Expeditionary Forces, and was thus no longer controlled by the

North African Theater of Operations. Left with only a single corps under his command, Patch nevertheless pushed forward, pressing back German forces into the western slopes of the High Vosges mountain range. By steadily forcing the Germans back from the Moselle River, he deprived them of choice defensive terrain, and compelled them to occupy their main defensive lines in the Vosges before the massive German engineer and labor forces committed there could complete them. Even as Operation MARKET-GARDEN—the airborne thrust through the Netherlands toward the Rhine—was grinding to a dismal conclusion and the British 1st Airborne Division was being reduced to combat ineffectiveness, Seventh Army was gradually, consistently, pushing ever forward.

In late September, XV Corps was transferred to Patch's control, and the Seventh Army's combat power doubled. Upon losing the corps, George Patton, ever the *prima donna* and supremely childish egotist, delivered these sour grapes to his Army Group commander, Bradley, "I hope [Devers's] plan goes sour." Eisenhower, who barely tolerated Patton but despised Devers, expected little or no benefit from gaining control (and responsibility) for his army group, beyond support for Bradley's Twelfth Army Group efforts.

Aside from Eisenhower's well-documented personal antipathy for Devers, however, there was a certain amount of logic to Eisenhower's attitude. The Seventh Army's logistical support originated 400 miles to the south, in Marseilles. A single rail line and a single highway, National Route 7, was the tenuous link to whatever supplies the Seventh Army could get from those far away docks . . . which were still under control of the North African Theater of Operations, and therefore competing with the needs of the more established Fifth Army in Italy. (This situation was not resolved until November, when the logistical support of the Sixth Army Group through Marseilles and Toulon became an ETO responsibility.)

Further, the terrain facing the Seventh Army was the most easily defensible in all of western Europe. The High Vosges mountains (differentiated from the low Vosges, which lie north of the Saverne Gap) had never before in the history of warfare been penetrated by attack. Neither Roman, nor Hun, Burgundian, Swede, French, Austrian, or German had been able to pierce the rugged, heavily forested, range that runs from the Belfort Gap in the south, parallel to the Rhine River, all the way north to the Saverne Gap. In World War I, some of the costliest fighting of the first year of the war took place there, yet the geographical crest of the Vosges remained, by and large, the political border, just as it had been since 1871. The Germans didn't even try to force the passes of the High Vosges in 1940, preferring the route through the Ardennes and the Low Countries.

Since the late summer of 1944, German military engineers had been using both volunteer and slave labor to construct a series of massive defensive lines on the western slopes of the Vosges. Thick barbed wire barriers, deep tank ditches, dense minefields, carefully sited pillboxes, and easily-executed abatis and log crib road blocks turned the High Vosges into a defensive maze that only contributed to the already naturally formidable defensive advantages of the terrain. With the fog and rains of autumn coming on, and the vicious Vosges winters not far behind, the German high command, OKW (*Oberkommando der Wehrmacht*) fully expected the Vosges Winter Line to hold until at least April 1945. Eisenhower expectations were about the same.

Patch and Devers were to surprise Eisenhower and *OKW*, however. As the Seventh Army's VI Corps ground its way into the western slopes of the Vosges in mid-October, and XV Corps simultaneously fought their way through the forested approaches to the Saverne Gap, they continually deprived the Germans of time and space for improving their defensive posture. By applying the kind of constant, steady pressure that his men used on Guadalcanal, Patch wore out German units faster than they could be rebuilt, while carefully maintaining his own units' strength and cohesion. In the month leading up to the Seventh Army's great autumn offensive in November 1944, the Americans were attacking in miserable weather conditions and in terrain that not only eliminated the effectiveness of tactical air support, but minimized the effectiveness of what little armor the Seventh Army possessed. Despite these disadvantages, the Seventh Army inflicted more than 24 percent more casualties on the Germans than they sustained themselves, an extremely unusual proportion for an army conducting offensive operations.

Despite the favorable casualty ratio, Patch still agonized over the casualties his men suffered. Although unanimous testimonials by his staff and subordinate leaders prove that Patch was deeply, personally moved by the casualties suffered by those under this command, the death, on 22 October, of the commander of Company C/315th Infantry Regiment had an especially severe impact on him. On that day, while leading an assault against entrenched German positions near the bloody Forest of Parroy, Captain Alexander M. Patch III was killed in action. The grief that losing his only son caused Patch was only paralleled by the sadness and frustration of not being able to comfort his wife, Julia, over the loss. Despite the profound shock and sorrow he felt, Patch buried his son at the American military cemetery at Epinal a few days after his death, and went back to the business of winning the war. As he pointed out to his wife in a letter, they were far from unique in their situation.

By the time three new divisions (the 44th, 100th, and 103rd) had arrived to bolster Seventh Army's combat power for its November offensive to penetrate the German Winter Line and gain the Vosges passes, Patch had postured his army for success in every way he could. The supply problems stemming from both the unexpectedly rapid advance up from the southern France beaches and the tenuously long lines of communication were largely solved by late October. More importantly, by steadily, if unspectacularly, pressing ahead against the German 19th Army's dwindling infantry reserves, Patch had created an opportunity for success entirely unexpected by Eisenhower or the pouting Patton to the north and west. What had, in October, amounted to a virtually even infantry battle (the Americans possessed no more than a 1.2 to 1 foxhole strength advantage) had become a much more advantageous ratio by November. Additionally, the Germans were now occupying their Winter Line positions; there was nowhere left for them to go if they withdrew, and besides, Hitler had decreed that there would be "no retreat" from the Winter Line. Patch had hamstrung the Germans into a do-or-die situations, with no tactical options but to stand, stationary, and fight it out.

Even with the pronounced numerical and tactical advantages produced by his own operations, however, there were numerous factors mitigating against the Seventh Army's success in its drive to penetrate the Vosges barrier. First, the weather was getting only worse, and the ice and sleet combined with the winding roads to eliminate the efficacy of armor support. Besides, German antitank defenses were well developed and effective; panzerfausts and other close-range antitank weapons were ideal for the Vosges terrain. Second, the Seventh Army was allotted only 72 P-47 fighter bombers for close air support during November, and the mostly overcast weather limited even those few aircraft to a handful of flying days. Finally, the Germans were fighting from prepared positions, on the doorstep of the *Reich*. As the historian/ veteran Gerhard Graser of the German 198th Infantry Division put it in the division history:

> "The fighting always consisted of small battles in the underbrush, man on man. The American infantryman, accustomed to the protection of superior airpower and artillery, and used to advancing behind tanks, suddenly found themselves robbed of their most important helpers. The persistent bad weather hindered their air force, and the terrain limited the mobility of their armor to a significant degree. here the individual soldier mattered the most. For the German soldier, there was the courage of despair that gave rise to the utmost resistance: After many years of combat all over

Europe, his back was to the wall of the homeland. On their side, the Americans believed that the banner of victory was already half-fastened to their colors and that it would take only one last energetic exertion for them to victoriously end the war. So both sides fought with unbelievable bitterness and severity."

To the north, things were not going well for Bradley's Twelfth Army Group. Elements of Hodges' First Army were dashing themselves to pieces against Germans dug into the Hürtgen Forest. Whole regiments and even entire divisions were being destroyed as the First Army failed to penetrate the forest barrier in its zone. Patton's XX Corps was slogging it out against Germans ensconced in the nineteenth- and early twentieth-century fortifications at Metz; between mid-September, when the attack on Metz began, and the end of November, when the final forts fell, three of Patton's divisions sustained stunning casualties in their efforts to move beyond the ancient fortress on the Moselle.

Unlike these failures and near-failures befalling his famous peers, Patch's army was on the verge of a historic achievement. Beginning 12 November, the northern division of VI Corps, the green 100th Infantry Division, commanded by Patch's old friend from Staunton days, Withers Burress, began clawing its way straight through the equally-green 708th Volks-Grenadier Division on the east bank of the Meurthe River, east of Baccarat. As the 100th's success forced the 708th's commander, Josef Krieger, to reinforce his southern wing, Patch launched the XV Corps into the weakened northern wing, along the boundary between the 708th and the 553rd Volks-Grenadier Division, to the north. Not only did the XV Corps attack fall on a newly-weakened sector, but it thrust between two divisions which belonged to two entirely different field armies; coordination between the two German divisions was practically non-existent as a result.

As the XV Corps plowed through uncoordinated opposition and approached the Saverne Pass—threatening to outflank the entire German Winter Line—Patch unleashed the rest of VI Corps, to the south, against the High Vosges passes. With every available reserve force committed to the north, the 19th Army had nothing with which to stem the tide of the attacking 3rd, 36th, and 103rd Infantry Divisions. By 23 November, Seventh Army elements had reached the Rhine at Strasbourg and were pouring through the Vosges passes onto the plain of Alsace. The German Winter Line was breached, the first Allied troops had successfully reached the Upper Rhine, and the 19th Army was being cornered in what became known as The Colmar Pocket. By refusing to engage in frontal attacks against dug-in German defenders on the doorstep of the *Reich*, but rather, creating opportunities for maneuver by cleverly and carefully phasing his own offensive strikes, Patch saved his men the ordeals endured by elements of Patton's and Hodges's armies to the north. He also, once again, quietly and competently produced an unprecedented victory. For the first time in history, an army crossed the Vosges barrier against bitter resistance.

The Seventh Army's stunning success also had another consequence; Eisenhower was presented with the very real option of jumping the Rhine between Strasbourg and Rastatt, and eliminating the last great geographical barrier to the conquest of Germany. Exactly why he decided against this electrifying opportunity—one which truly could have changed the course of the war in so many ways—has never been satisfactorily answered by historians, and the reasons expressed by Eisenhower himself in *Crusade in Europe* are nonsense. In any event, he ordered Devers to turn Patch's army 90 degrees to the north, to attack toward the southern border of the Palatinate, in support of Patton's flagging efforts toward the Saar. American forces would now not cross the Rhine until March 1945, and another opportunity for the world to recognize the brilliance of Sandy Patch was lost.

As the Seventh Army ground its way north, now partially traversing the easily-defensible Low Vosges range north of the Saverne Pass, XV Corps encountered the most heavily fortified sector of the Maginot Line. The fortifications of the so-called Ensemble de Bitche were built to withstand attacks from all sides. In 1940, the fortresses of this sector had been attacked by German forces from precisely the same aspect, that is, the south, as they were about to be again by elements of the Seventh Army in 1944. Indeed, they had held out until a full week after the rest of the French Army surrendered in that first spring of World War II. Such would not be the case when Patch's men attacked. Although aerially-delivered 500-pound bombs and direct fire from 240mm howitzers and eight-inch guns made no discernible difference to the German defenders, the Seventh Army penetrated the Maginot Line just west of Bitche by employing patient, methodical close assault by infantry and combat engineers. Unlike the Third Army, which was held up for two and a half months by the pre-World War I defenses at Metz, the Seventh Army punched through the most massive and modern fortifications in the world near Bitche in less than a week.

This tremendous accomplishment was, once again, overshadowed by disaster elsewhere. Just as the last German defenders of the great Maginot forts in the XV Corps zone were being cleared out of their steel-reinforced concrete fastness, three German field armies caught Omar Bradley, Courtney Hodges, and their subordinate leaders completely by surprise in the Ardennes Forest to the north. Despite the courageous efforts of the soldiers of several American divisions, the

First Army was blown back from its lines along a multiple corps front. Two of the three infantry regiments of the 106th Infantry Division surrendered to the Germans, and the rest of the division was knocked out of the war. For the second time in a month, the 28th Infantry Division was badly mauled. The 7th Armored Division was flung aside with heavy casualties, and, along with elements of the 10th Armored Division, the 101st Airborne Division was completely surrounded at Bastogne. Other outfits, such as the 2nd and 99th Infantry Divisions, were barely hanging on to their positions, locked in desperate combat with the attackers.

As the Third Army pulled out of the line to counterattack into the southern shoulder of the German salient, Eisenhower ordered Sixth Army Group to suspend offensive operations and shift westward to fill the gap left by departing Third Army units in the Saar. With some VI Corps units already engaged in the *Westwall,* and XV Corps moving northward to do the same, Patch ordered a withdrawal to defensible positions. To cover the vastly extended line, Patch improvised, using even an engineer group and a task force composed of disparate mechanized cavalry and armored infantry units.

As the First and Third Armies scrambled to recover from their disastrous intelligence lapse in the Ardennes, Patch's intelligence officer, Colonel Bill Quinn, announced the detection of a chilling development opposite XV Corps. Based on the few aerial photos taken during brief holes in the general western European overcast, patrol reports, and the disappearance of several important German formations not accounted for in the Ardennes or elsewhere, Quinn audaciously predicted another German offensive, aimed at Bitche, on the boundary between the XV and VI Corps. Although some senior Seventh Army commanders were highly skeptical, Patch was convinced by Quinn's argument. He directed that preparations be immediately undertaken to prepare for a major German offensive, expected on New Year's Eve.

That offensive, known as Operation NORDWIND, fell precisely when and where Quinn had predicted. With nothing less than the Saverne Pass as its terrain objective and the division of American and French forces in Alsace as the strategic goal, the attacking German XIII SS, XC, and LXXXIX Corps drove directly into carefully-placed American minefields, machine-gun protective fires, and artillery concentrations. Although the German units managed to achieve an overall infantry numerical superiority of almost exactly the same magnitude that the Seventh Army had enjoyed the previous autumn when the tactical tables were turned, they were unable to effect a breakthrough anywhere but in the sector of the mechanized task force Patch had arrayed in the most mountainous sector of the Low Vosges. Even here, despite the premature, precipitous withdrawal of one of the cavalry squadrons, elements of XV Corps' 45th Infantry Division, assisted by the infantry regiments of the newly-arrived 70th Infantry Division, sealed off the ten-kilometer gap between Bitche and Neunhoffen by 3 January. On the next day, the staff of the 17th SS-Panzer-Grenadier Division was relieved for the full-strength division's failure to break through the American lines along the boundary of the 44th and 100th Infantry Divisions. At the same time, the entire XC Corps called off its offensive operations. On 5 January, the German armored reserves intended for exploitation of the situation were withdrawn and sent toward Wissembourg, well to the east, and on 6 January, the last German offensive operations in the LXXXIX Corps zone were terminated. Outnumbered overall and, in some sectors, suffering from odds against them of 3–1 or more, the units of the Seventh Army completely frustrated the Germans' attempts to break through to Saverne from the northwest.

Although Patch and his men had won an important victory, the Germans were far from done with their offensive. On 5 January, Army Group Upper Rhine, personally commanded by SS Chief Heinrich Himmler, attacked across the Rhine at Gambsheim with the 553rd Volks-Grenadier Division of XIV SS Corps. While VI Corps attention focused on the bridgehead, XXXIX Panzer Corps attacked southward, down the Wissembourg Corridor on the Plain of Alsace, with the 21st Panzer and 25th Panzer Grenadier Divisions. Originally earmarked for exploiting the anticipated breakthrough near Bitche, these divisions now attempted to take Saverne from the east. Over the next two weeks, the Germans threw in the best formations they had left in the West, including the 10th SS-Panzer Division, the 7th Parachute Division, as well as various infantry formations, in the last, desperate attempt to split the Americans from the French and bring about a separate armistice.

Patch's response was both rational and effective. Although, for political reasons, he was overruled in his desire to withdraw American forces to the much more defensible eastern edge of the Vosges Mountains, Patch's forces conducted a series of delays and defenses that thoroughly wore out the attackers. At this point, Patch was saddled with nine incompletely trained infantry regiments that had been deployed without their parent divisions and concomitant supporting units and command and control headquarters. He had already attached the three belonging to the 70th Infantry Division to the 45th for use in plugging the gap left by Task Force Hudelson in the Low Vosges, and then parceled out the units of the 63rd Infantry Division's regiments to the 44th and 100th Infantry Divisions for use in reinforcing their defenses. Although the arrangement was far less than optimal and resulted in the wholesale loss of several rifle companies, it was infinitely preferable to the loss of entire divisions, as Hodges had with the inexperienced 106th in the Ardennes. Between 6 and 23 January, the regiments of the 42nd Infantry Division were attached to the 79th Infantry Division and, in concert with the 14th Armored Division, and later, the 12th Armored and 103rd Infantry Division (and, at the end, even the 101st Airborne Division), these combined units ended the Germans' last offensive in the west in what veterans of both sides termed some of the most savage fighting of the entire war.

To this day, little is generally known about this, the spectacularly successful rebuff of Operation NORDWIND. In *The Final Crisis* (Aegis, 1999), scholar and veteran of the campaign (as an assistant BAR gunner in the 42nd Infantry Division), Richard Engler postulates that a variety of factors combined to make the public unaware of this tremendous achievement. Among them were war weariness by an American public that had no stomach for a second crisis in as many months and a press that was preoccupied with the astounding near catastrophe in the Ardennes.

Bill Quinn had a more direct analysis. Referring to the far greater publicity received by other generals in other contemporaneous battles, he said, "The way to get recognition is to lose your ass—get the shit kicked out of you." There is undeniable merit to his argument. Perhaps exactly who had lost their asses when was what the Supreme Commander, Eisenhower, was thinking about on 1 February 1945 when he ranked the value of Patch's services ahead of Hodges and Simpson!

Patch spent the rest of the winter preparing the Seventh Army for its part in the final offensive to crush Germany. For the most part, this consisted of defensive operations and local patrolling, although Patch took advantage of the quiet weeks to integrate new outfits such as the (finally complete) 42nd, 63rd, and 70th Infantry Divisions, as well as the late-arriving 71st Infantry Division. (Second Lieutenant John S. D. Eisenhower led a rifle platoon in that outfit, briefly.) From late January to mid-February, Patch had to detach the recently-constituted XXI Corps to the French 1st Army to help wipe out the Colmar Pocket, but of the units which remained under Patch's control throughout the winter, defensive operations and training were the norm. A few limited objective attacks, such as the 70th's attack at Forbach in the Saar in late February, were conducted to better posture the Seventh Army for the commencement of Operation UNDERTONE, the drive into the Palatinate in mid-March.

On 15 March 1945, the Seventh Army began the drive that took it into the heart of Europe. Crossing the Rhine at multiple locations north and south of Worms, the Seventh Army drove into Swabia and across Bavaria. Ultimately, it was, fittingly, units from Patch's army which swarmed through the "National Redoubt," proving the fictitious nature of its existence; it was Seventh Army's 103rd Infantry Division which linked up, in the Brenner Pass, with US Fifth Army elements driving north in Italy; and it was Seventh's 71st Infantry Division which thrust furthest into eastern Europe, meeting elements of the Red Army east of Linz by 8 May.

The magnificent, and largely ignored, performance of the Seventh Army in Europe was not without its lost battles. The 12th Armored Division needlessly lost a full combat command to the 10th SS-Panzer Division on the Alsatian Plain near Herrlisheim on 16/17 January; five companies of the veteran 45th Infantry Division's 157th Infantry Regiment were wiped out in the hills above Reipertswiller in the Low Vosges by SS-Mountain Infantry Regiment 11 of the 6th SS-Mountain Division in late January.

There were, however, never any wholesale failures of whole corps, such as there were at Metz, in the Ardennes, or in the Hürtgen, or losses of whole divisions, as with the British 1st Parachute Division at Arnhem, or the US 28th Infantry Division in the Hürtgen or again, a month later, in the Ardennes, or the 106th Infantry Division in the Schnee Eifel. Patch's careful, yet forceful and aggressive, style of fighting prevented such debacles. Even in the pain of the grief caused by his son's death in combat while under his command, Patch never made foolish choices that resulted in the unnecessary deaths of his men. Sending a battalion task force 80 kilometers behind enemy lines to liberate his son-in-law from German captivity—as Patton did in March, 1945 with Task Force Baum—would never have even seriously occurred to Patch. Losing it in its entirety, save 15 men, as Patton did, would have been unthinkable for the Seventh Army commander.

Patch was the consummate team player. In sharp contrast to Patton's childish wish, upon losing XV Corps to Patch, for the Sixth Army Group's failure in upcoming operations, Patch behaved magnanimously when confronted with similar or worse disappointments. In March 1945, for example, when Eisenhower proposed that Third Army be assigned objectives within the Seventh Army's zone, thus causing massive command and control challenges for long-planned Operation UNDERTONE, Patch's response was, "We're all in the same army," and that the objective was to defeat the Germans.

Also unlike Patton, who verbally—and sometimes physically—scourged his soldiers, Patch was deeply caring and quietly compassionate. One of his senior staff officers recalled "Patch was compassionate more than any other commander in his love and care of the soldiers." He described him as "Lovable, kind. A modest man," and added, "I loved that man."

Despite all this, in his report of operations published after the war, Eisenhower rewarded Patch and his men with a total of eight pages of text, out of a total of 180 in the report. This obvious snub may have been prompted by Eisenhower's steadfast dislike of Patch's boss, Jacob Devers, but was nonetheless an inaccurate portrayal of Seventh Army's accomplishments, and was grossly unfair to Patch's soldiers, who were, after all, Eisenhower's, too.

It was undoubtedly this kind of ingratitude, combined with Patch's genuine commitment to his soldiers, that led Patch to his final significant act on behalf of the soldiers of the Seventh Army. Having left command at the end of May, 1945, Patch was slated by General George Marshall, Army Chief of Staff, to command an army in the upcoming invasion of Japan. However, with Japan's capitulation after the nuclear strikes at Hiroshima and Nagasaki, Patch was reassigned to organizational duties in the Pentagon. Even in the drudgery of the Pentagon assignment, however, Patch never relented in his loyalty to his men.

The Army had granted campaign credit for all participants in the efforts to defeat the German offensive in the Ardennes in December and January, but had not granted similar recognition to the soldiers of the Seventh Army for their much more successful repulse of NORDWIND. This had resulted, *inter alia*, in the award of another "battle star" to be proudly worn on their European-African-Middle Eastern campaign ribbons by every member of Third and First Armies who helped stem the tide of Ardennes thrust . . . but in no such recognition for soldiers of the Seventh Army. Indeed, the additional campaign credit had resulted in the receipt of additional "points" for the Ardennes veterans, which meant earlier transfer stateside for demobilization and the return to civilian life, the thing which meant the most in the world for most ETO veterans.

After failing in his attempt to convince Eisenhower of the justice of granting Seventh Army veterans a campaign credit for the defeat of NORDWIND, in the autumn of 1944, Patch went over his head to Marshall. His passionate and well-articulated plea resulted in a reversal of Eisenhower's decision, and later, the "Ardennes" campaign credit was changed to "Ardennes-Alsace;" every soldier of the Seventh Army who took part in defeating the last German offensive in the west was finally officially recognized for his significant contribution to victory in Europe. Unfortunately, by the time the decision became official, practically all of the men so affected had long been demobilized—late. However, to this day, Seventh Army veterans are still seeing to it that their military records are being amended to reflect the additional campaign credit . . . thanks to their quiet, compassionate, committed commander, Sandy Patch.

The final factor in ensuring that Patch would go unheralded and unrecognized occurred in November 1945. As had happened in World War I and twice in World War II, Patch contracted pneumonia on 14 November 1945 and succumbed a week later, just two days shy of his fifty-sixth birthday. In a small ceremony a few days later, his remains were interred in the cemetery at his *alma mater*, the United States Military Academy at West Point. Asked by Maxwell Taylor, the Superintendent at USMA, if she wanted a cadet honor guard for the interment ceremony, Patch's wife replied, "Absolutely not." She explained that as a cadet himself, the general hated being called out for details to bury generals of whom the cadets had never heard.

# Tactics

## Most and Least Effective Major Fortifications:
### *Westwall* and *Atlantic Wall*

Much has been made of the obsolescence of fixed fortifications during World War II and the dynamics introduced by the combination of reliable tracked vehicles, tactical radios, and combined arms doctrines. All of the European powers, however, to greater or lesser extents devoted considerable resources to the construction of major fortifications before and even during the war. The fortifications of Belgium, the Netherlands, Poland, and France failed to protect effectively their respective nations. The most extensive line of fortifications in the history of the modern world, moreover, was built after those failures and it failed most spectacularly of all.

In the aftermath of the Great War, every European power sought to avoid a reprise of the carnage of the Western Front between 1914 and 1918. The Soviets, Romanians, Czechs, Finns, and others all built significant lines of fortifications, all of which were completed to widely varying degrees by the time WWII began. Some, such as the Finns' Mannerheim Line, saw extensive use against the Soviets during the Winter War from 30 November 1939 to 1 March 1940. Others, such as the Czechs' incomplete fortifications, were given up without a fight. Thank you, Appeasers and Munich.

The Germans took a holistic approach to fortifications. In order to reintroduce battlefield fluidity and then to dominate it, they developed a carefully-coordinated joint and combined arms offensive capability centered around the panzer, light, and motorized divisions. It should be noted here that these divisions comprised a small minority of the *Wehrmacht's* otherwise WWI-style army in which about 85 percent of the German army's artillery were horse-drawn throughout WWII! The German Air Force, the *Luftwaffe*, with radio-linked tactical support capability and a limited parachute assault force, complemented and enhanced this revolutionary concept and provided unprecedented mobility for the first three years of the war. Nevertheless, the Germans built an extensive set of fortifications along their eastern and western frontiers to optimize the effectiveness of their new, small, mobile forces. In current military parlance, this would be described as an economy of force measure.

In the east, these fortifications consisted of complex, but linearly-arrayed positions intended to accomplish the following purposes: in East Prussia, designed to protect the approaches to the capital, Königsberg; in Silesia, to protect the industrially-significant areas there; and in eastern Brandenburg, to protect Frankfurt-on-Oder and Berlin. The most extensive and important German fortifications, however, were built along the frontiers of the countries whose powers represented the most important threats, namely, France and Belgium. Although Belgium itself was no threat to the Germans, a French thrust through Belgium was, so the *Westwall* (a.k.a., the Siegfried Line) was constructed along a 400-kilometer front from the point where the Rhine enters the Netherlands, then south along the Dutch, Belgian, Luxembourgian, and French frontiers almost to Switzerland.

Unlike most of the other lines of fortifications in Europe, the defensive works of the *Westwall* were arrayed in considerable depth. No individual *Westwall* work could compare in size, armament, or strength to even the smallest of the Maginot fortresses, but their collective effect was far greater.

The *Westwall* pillboxes—most of which were designed in 1939 to house machine guns and 37mm antitank guns—were arrayed, as terrain allowed, in a "checkerboard" fashion. This allowed optimal mutual support, and exposed attackers to frontal and flanking fires at all times. To enhance this effect, most of the *Westwall* positions were built in three belts: the first belt was at least two—but could be as much as 20—kilometers deep; the second belt, located just a few kilometers behind the first, was three to eight kilometers deep; the third, generally less shallow than the first two, was located only a few kilometers behind the second. In this way, when the defenders of the first belt were about to be overrun, they could withdraw to the second belt under the covering fires of their artillery, from the second belt, and similarly through the third belt. The effectiveness of the entire system was enhanced further

An American M-36 tank destroyer of the 645th TD Battalion (attached to the 45th Infantry Division) crosses through the Dragon's Teeth of the *Westwall* in a breach made by US Army engineers, March 1945. *NA*

by the addition of continuous tank ditches and miles of "Dragon's Teeth," armor obstacles, all of which canalized the armored support of any assault into kill zones heavily sown with mines and/or well covered by antitank guns. This arrangement proved extremely effective against the Americans in 1944–45 as it minimized the exposure of the defenders to attack while keeping the attackers under fire continuously and over a great deal of terrain.

The *Westwall* effectively served its purpose as an economy of force measure during the invasion of Poland in 1939 and the ensuing *"Sitzkrieg,"* or "Phony War" in which the Allies failed to mount a major offensive against western Germany. Despite the fact that the *Westwall* was scantily manned during the invasion of Poland, and far from complete for months thereafter, German deception and disinformation efforts succeeded in convincing many Allied analysts that the defenses were stronger than they really were. This, combined with Allied political leaders' reticence to take the offensive, resulted in the execution of no more than a handful of very localized, minor attacks against the German frontier, even after the commencement of the invasion of Western Europe in the spring of 1940.

During the German offensive in Western Europe in 1940, the fortifications of the defenders met with much more varying degrees of success. The imposing, but usually incoherent, defenses of Belgium and the Netherlands were either easily bypassed or quickly penetrated. The

American NCO inspects a recently neutralized *Westwall* pillbox. Unlike the Maginot fortifications—which ranged from simple machine gun blockhouses all the way to massive, 14-story-deep masterpieces of the military engineer's art—the fortifications of the *Westwall* were generally small, steel-reinforced concrete pillboxes, housing a machine gun crew and perhaps an artillery forward observer. These were built by the thousands, and were arrayed in a sort of checkerboard fashion, in depth, ensuring mutual support. *NA*

Dutch, in particular, had depended upon advanced notice of an offensive to be able to activate their system of water obstacles, but the suddenness of the German strike deprived them of that key requirement. Besides, German airborne and special operations forces achieved envelopments and penetrations so quickly that even the isolated fortifications were rendered untenable. In a few cases, notably the Belgian fortress of Eban Emael, which was neutralized by a *Luftwaffe* gliderborne *coup de main,* they were easy victims of the Germans' joint and combined arms mobility advantage.

The much-maligned Maginot Line of France actually had a great deal more success than many post-war critics have allowed. First, the presence of this enormous line of fortifications from Longuyon near the intersection of the Luxembourg-Belgian-French frontiers to the Rhine at Fort-Louis unquestionably had a profound effect on German strategy. The first plan was a reprise of the 1914 modified Schlieffen Plan through Belgium, and even after those plans were compromised, the main effort was still to be made through the Ardennes and not through the regions defended by the Maginot works.

Very different in design and concept from the *Westwall*, the Maginot Line was intended to provide a series of linearly-arrayed strongpoints to support the defensive operations of large infantry formations, mostly reserve divisions with limited offensive capabilities. These units, known as "troops of the interval," were to occupy the outlying pillboxes and other fortifications, providing close support of the garrisons in the forts. The Line's fortifications consisted of heavily-protected observation posts, casemates, and blockhouses (pillboxes) designed to slow or disorganize advancing infantry; carefully-sited, extensive shelters for the interval troops; and, most importantly, "small" and "large" fortresses, designed to provide indirect fires from impregnable positions close to the front. Although primarily oriented toward the German frontier, the Maginot works provided protection through 360 degrees for the Line's fortresses. Such protection was achieved by the fortresses' own rotating gun, mortar, and machine-gun turrets with commanding all-around fields of fire and/or observation, and by the construction of pillboxes in depth, in front of, beside, and behind the fortresses. The Maginot's depth never approached that of the *Westwall*, however, and was usually a single belt, three to five kilometers in deep.

The Maginot Line's fortresses undoubtedly represent the zenith of the traditional military engineer's art, and are fitting descendants of Vauban's great legacy. The small and large fortresses of the Maginot Line integrate disappearing steel turrets, massively thick steel-reinforced concrete walls, and deep subterranean galleries (often with electric narrow-gauge railways to transport gun crews and ammunition from the underground magazines) into the hills and mountains of the frontier regions, thereby taking the greatest advantage of the defensive possibilities of the terrain. Unlike the *Westwall*, which was an economy of force measure designed to facilitate offensive activity elsewhere, the Maginot Line was originally built as the main focus of French strategic effort, and was to be occupied specifically for the defense of France. Even when French strategic thinking began to change in the late 1930s—after most of the Line had been built—and the French General Staff began to prepare plans for sending the best French Army forces into Belgium upon commencement of hostilities with the Germans, the Maginot Line was still the bulwark of French strategy.

And while we are talking about it, not only did the Maginot Line succeed in diverting the 1940 German offensive through Belgium first, but it also stood up well when attacked. Contrary to common myth, the Germans did indeed attack the Maginot Line during the 1940 campaign. In mid-June, elements of the German 16th Army attacked several of the fortresses on the extreme western end of the line, and suffered

Troops of the US 103rd Infantry Division at Bloc 13 of the Maginot Line's Fortress Hochwald, ca. December 1944. This casemate mounted a 135mm gun, but, like much of the Maginot Line, was abandoned by the withdrawing Germans and fell to the Americans without a fight. NA

significant casualties without successfully reducing the forts. Near the other end of the line, *Luftwaffe* Stukas and a WWI-vintage 420mm howitzer managed to inflict some damage on Fort Schoenenbourg, south of Wissembourg, but the fort did not fall. Infantry elements of the 215th Infantry Division penetrated the pillbox line in the densely-wooded, craggy Low Vosges east of Bitche, but they were not able to secure a viable line of communication to exploit the success. The only penetration of the Maginot Line that carried operational significance was achieved by the German First Army in the Saar River Valley. Here, where the high water table had defied French attempts to build major fortresses, the sector was defended only by pillboxes, one small fortress (Haut-Poirier), and a series of water obstacles. The latter, like those of the Dutch, had to be created by purposeful flooding, which the French had failed to do, more than a month after the German invasion!

By the middle of June, as the Allied armed forces were collapsing elsewhere, practically all of the "troops of the interval" were withdrawn for commitment to the desperate combat elsewhere. The Maginot fortresses were thus no longer strongpoints of a coherent line, but more akin to partially- or completely-isolated yet fortified islands. This was the moment at which the German First Army struck. Nine German divisions burst through the Saar and fanned out to the west, south, and east between 15 and 22 June 1940. One, the Austrian 262d Infantry Division, drove east and seized Haut-Poirier by bombarding it with direct fire from its 150mm howitzers. Built without artillery or mortars of its own, and beyond the range of the guns of the larger forts nearby, the garrison of Haut-Poirier was helpless to resist and surrendered after a two-day battle. The 262d then went on to attack Welschhof, another fort without its own indirect-fire capability, which was the westernmost of the major works of the *Secteur Fortifié de Rohrbach*. After a similar pounding from directly-laid 150mm howitzers and 105mm high-velocity field guns firing special concrete-piercing shells, its garrison also surrendered, just less than three hours before the entire French Army laid down their arms.

About 20 kilometers to the east of Welschoff, the "Berlin Bears" of the 257th Infantry Division attacked the outer works of Fort Schiesseck, near Bitche, but it was bad news for them as they were rebuffed after suffering significant casualties. Although attacking from the rear of this fort, the 360-degree defenses of the so-called *Ensemble de Bitche,* including Forts Simserhof, Schiesseck, and Otterbiel, all rained indirect fire down on the attackers, who could not even penetrate the rearward pillbox or casemate defenses.

To the west of the penetration in the Saar, the German 167th Infantry Division also achieved mixed results. After several days of pounding Forts Bambesch and Kerfent, two small fortresses of the *Secteur Fortifié de Faulquemont* (the Maginot sector just west of the Saar), with direct fire from high-velocity 88mm antiaircraft guns, the Germans were able to secure the surrender of the garrisons. These, too, were forts without artillery or mortars, and it is significant that the 167th was not able to seize the other three forts in the Faulquemont sector. The four 81mm mortars in the rotating turrets of one of them, Fort Laudrefang, were able to protect the other three forts from the depredations of high-velocity weapons fired directly at close range. If just four mortars could achieve this sort of effect, the impact of the absence of the troops of the interval, with their integral artillery and mortars, can only be speculated upon. Certainly, they would have been more than adequate to prevent the sort of close-range artillery attack that brought about the surrender of Haut-Poirier, Welschhof, Bambesch, and Kerfent.

The garrisons of the over 40 other major Maginot Line fortresses held out at least until the armistice went into effect on 25 June. Some, notably

Soldiers of the 71st Infantry Regiment of the US 44th Infantry Division inspect a 75mm gun battery of Fortress Simserhof, ca. December 1944. The destruction of the concrete façade was inflicted by a bombardment by artillery of up through 240mm caliber and aerially delivered 500-pound bombs, but the they caused little interior damage; it still required infantry to attack with bayonet and satchel charges to root out the defenders. The 100th Infantry Division was forced into a similar assault on the nearby Fortress Schiesseck at exactly the same time. Both forts were among the largest of the Maginot Line, and had completely stymied German efforts to seize them in 1940. They were part of the group of Maginot garrisons that refused to surrender until a week after the capitulation of the rest of the French Army in 1940. NA

in the eastern end of the Line, but also some around Thionville, stubbornly refused to surrender until almost a week after the rest of France had capitulated. This alone wins laurels for the Maginot Line as the only fortifications in Europe in World War II to support the continued resistance of defenders well after the rest of their army gave up!

Overall, then, the Maginot Line achieved several, although not all, of its purposes. Strategically, it decisively deterred a German attack directly against the French frontier. Tactically, most of the works which were attacked were successfully defended; even the ones which fell did so most likely due to their isolation in the wake of the disastrous strategic situation, rather than from real tactical flaws. Operationally, however, the line failed to halt the First Army's multi-corps thrust through the weak Saar Valley defenses.

Aside from their breathtaking scale and marvelous engineering, the Maginot fortifications were—and in many cases, still are—works of an unsurpassed style. Not surprisingly, being designed in the 1930s, there are clearly art-deco influences in the stepped forms, rounded corners, and even striped decorative elements. With the passage of time, the works, which were always intended to blend with and take advantage of the natural defensive advantages of the surrounding terrain, have become subtle parts of their environments. Even if it was not the most effective line of fortifications of WWII, the defensive edifices of the Maginot Line were certainly the most visually appealing.

The incompleteness of the German victory in Western Europe was underscored by the construction of the most massive and lengthy set of fortifications in modern history. The Atlantic Wall, over 2,600 kilometers long and running intermittently from northern Norway to the southern reaches of the Bay of Biscay on the Spanish border, was built as a consequence of Germany's inability to bring about Great Britain's surrender. Strategically, this left the Germans' western flank open to attack, and, with the vast bulk of the *Wehrmacht* committed to the struggle in the Soviet Union, it was necessary to protect the Atlantic coast of the Nazi empire by other means.

At first, the fortifications of the Atlantic Wall served as protection against small-scale amphibious raids and were essentially an economy of force measure, much like the *Westwall*. The Germans never imagined that the war in the Soviet Union would drag on as long as it did, and so it was not until March 1942 that Hitler issued a formal directive to fortify the Atlantic coast even though work had begun in the late summer of 1940. Until the order by Hitler, the Atlantic Wall consisted of fortifications that were largely designed to protect ports, including the submarine pens in a few Atlantic ports such as Lorient and St. Nazaire; and the Channel Islands from which shipping was interdicted in the Channel. The open beaches, the main avenues of ingress for an invading force, received last priority.

In November 1942, the same month that the German 6th Army became encircled at Stalingrad, the Allies staged their first successful major amphibious operation of the war in the west, in North Africa. Just as the Germans were wasting their last great armored formations at Kursk in July 1943, the Allies staged an even more impressive landing in Sicily. In October 1943, Hitler ordered a second belt of fortifications to be built behind the main one on the coast, and although it received little more than lip service, it emphasized the German concern over the Allies' growing effectiveness at amphibious invasions. By late 1943, the Atlantic Wall was no longer an economy of force measure, it was a

Typical Atlantic Wall coastal artillery fortifications (above and below). Note how the guns are mounted in barbettes, well protected from air and sea bombardment, but fairly open to close ground assault. *NA*

major part of German strategic planning. The Wall was no longer intended merely to protect the coast from raids, or to serve as a temporary measure to discourage Allied landings until such time as the bulk of the victorious German Army could be brought back from its successful Eastern campaign and employed to defeat invading Allied forces. It was now intended to defeat Allied invaders on the beaches.

Until mid-1943, the Germans' main construction efforts had been centered on building the submarine pens themselves and on structures for coastal guns that could defeat naval vessels. In many cases, the armaments themselves came from a variety of captured French, Dutch, Belgian, and Norwegian weapons, as well as old German railway guns and guns from German fortifications on the Baltic. Even guns and turrets from laid-up naval vessels were sometimes used. There were local fortifications—pillboxes with machine guns to defend against landing parties and protected antiaircraft gun positions to ward off aerial attacks—but only after mid-1943 did work begin in earnest to defend against large-scale amphibious landings by ground forces.

These measures included a wide variety of works, from armored observation posts and pre-fabricated concrete machine gun bunkers to mazes of covered and uncovered trenchlines. These all provided excellent observation across fields of fire with acres of barbed wire; sea and land minefields; and steel anti-landing-craft obstacles. Areas featuring open terrain just behind the beaches were sown with large, upward-pointing stakes to prevent parachute or glider landings. Dummy positions were also built to deceive Allied reconnaissance and divert naval gunfire or aerial bombing efforts away from the real defenses. The amazingly rapid completion of hundreds of protected coastal gun batteries, tens of thousands of pillboxes and casemates, hundreds of miles of trenches, and thousands of acres of barbed wire obstacles and minefields was accomplished using German Labor Service (*RAD*), *Organisation Todt* (*OT*), and battalions of prisoners from the Eastern Front. Enormous quantities of concrete were consumed. According to J. E. Kaufmann and R. M. Jurga in *Fortress Europe*, from June 1942 to June 1944, at least 200,000 cubic meters of concrete were poured each month. The cost of the efforts cannot be calculated, but put simply, the construction of the Atlantic Wall was the Germans' main effort in preparation for defending against an invasion from the West.

So how did they do? Well, the fact that this book is written in English demonstrates that the German effort failed . . . hugely. In less than one day, the Allies pierced the Atlantic Wall and drove inland, obviating most of the remainder of the line. The hedgerows of Normandy and the tenacity of the German field forces' counterattacks held up the attackers for more than two months, but the Atlantic Wall had nothing to do with this lack of progress toward Germany. The fortifications around the major ports the Allies could have used to bring in supplies more rapidly and efficiently than through the artificial harbors in Normandy were also defeated; the Germans deprived the Allies of Brest and Cherbourg, for example, by simply destroying the port facilities just before their defenses failed. Although in a Maginot-like act of defiance, the German Atlantic Wall garrisons of Lorient and St. Nazaire did manage to hold out until (but not after!) the general German surrender on 8 May 1945. These fortifications contributed nothing to the accomplishment of the Atlantic Wall's mission.

If the Atlantic Wall succeeded in anything, it diverted the Allies from landing in the Pas de Calais, the shortest way across the Channel from England, and the closest route toward the Ruhr. While this diversion may have been an operational success for the Germans, however, it was certainly not a decisive one. Given the extent of the line, the effort expended in building it, and the magnitude of its failure, the Atlantic Wall must be adjudged the least effective line of fortifications of World War II.

The Germans also built the war's most effective series of fortifications. Not only did the *Westwall* serve its purpose well in 1939–40, but its effectiveness greatly exceeded the German expectations in 1944. After the conquest of most of Western Europe was completed in 1940, many of the armaments of the *Westwall* were stripped out for use elsewhere. As the German Army was collapsing in France in the summer of 1944, the *Westwall* was simply not ready for combat; its installations were poorly maintained, its armament was largely missing; and its fields of fire and obstacles had become overgrown or even partially dismantled in many sectors. Frantic efforts to re-arm and otherwise prepare the *Westwall* were only partially completed when elements of the US First Army reached the line near Aachen in early September 1944. Fierce combat raged there and at the other points of contact along the *Westwall* for months. The defenders benefitted from the fact that the US Army was at the end of a long logistical lifeline. The destruction of the Channel ports—events unrelated to the Atlantic Wall *per se*—had forced the continued Allied dependence on the artificial harbors in Normandy. The fuel, ammunition, spare parts, and other items of supply necessary for assaulting the *Westwall* had to be off-loaded, stockpiled, and sent forward over the road by convoy. Although in no shape to withstand a major offensive against it, the *Westwall*'s strength was sufficient to withstand the uncoordinated and incremental efforts that the Americans mounted until their resupply had been effected. By then, the hurried and desperate efforts to build up adequate defenses in the *Westwall* were sufficient to halt, or at least severely slow, the American attacks.

The course of the battles in the *Westwall* in places like Aachen, the Hürtgen Forest, and the Saar-Moselle Triangle throughout the autumn of 1944 and into the winter of 1945 are well known and need little further documentation here. Five years of essentially unchecked foliage growth and other natural developments succeeded in developing a patina of concealment for the pillboxes and other works that made them almost impossible to detect before engagement. Once covered by snow in one of the twentieth century's most bitter European winters, the firing positions of the *Westwall* were virtually undetectable at any but the closest of ranges. With artillery and rocket launchers in place to prevent the sort of direct-fire attacks that had had humbled a few of the Maginot's smaller fortresses, and with Dragon's Teeth to canalize American armor into kill zones full of mines, and covered by high-velocity 75mm and 88mm antitank guns, the defenses of the *Westwall* defied decisive penetration until the late winter of 1945. Whether stopping the First Army from September on, or the Ninth Army in November, the Seventh Army in December, or the Third Army in January, the defenders of the *Westwall* successfully conducted their defensive missions against active attacks longer than those of any other line of fortifications in World War II.

The *Westwall* was not the only series of fortifications faced by the Allies in late 1944. Taking advantage of their all-around defensive capabilities, the Germans used certain stretches of the Maginot Line to slow the American Seventh Army advance toward the Palatinate in mid-December. In the vicinity of Bitche, two of the great Maginot Line fortresses which had held out until after the rest of the French Army laid down its arms in 1940 were again defending against attack. Forts Simserhof and Schiesseck, as well as their outlying works, were tenaciously defended against the attacks by the 44th and 100th Infantry Divisions of the US XV Corps respectively. American divisional and corps artillery (up to 240mm howitzers) were fired at point-blank ranges against the casemates, and achieved only marginal destruction. Repeated divebombing by USAAF P-47s dropping 500-pound bombs also failed to do much more than chip the concrete and shake the steel reinforcing bars. Only closely-coordinated infantry and combat engineer teams, operating under cover of artillery and mortar-fired smoke, were able to assault the forts, blow holes in steel doors and air ducts, and work their way through the subterranean galleries with satchel charges, bayonets, and flamethrowers. After killing, capturing, or forcing the defenders into lower levels of the fortresses, bulldozers and tank dozers buried many of the turrets, closed off the firing ports, and filled in the air ducts of the great forts. Just after the forts fell, the Germans began their Ardennes offensive, and the Seventh Army's offensive toward the next belt of frontier defenses, the *Westwall* to the north, was postponed. Nevertheless, some of the Maginot forts had again proved their toughness, albeit in a way unimagined by the Line's builders! Even this was not the last time the works of the Maginot would be used during WWII. In January, when the Germans launched their last offensive in the West,

Operation NORDWIND, some of the casemates and pillboxes of the line were used as observation posts, aid stations, and command posts by the 44th and 100th Divisions against the thrust by XIII SS Corps. Further east, elements of the American 42d Infantry Division defended the line of Maginot pillboxes east of Hatten and Rittershoffen against the attack of XXXIX Panzer Corps' 21st Panzer and 25th Panzer-Grenadier Divisions.

For those readers who have not been keeping score, allow the author to recapitulate. The Maginot Line was built by the French and they fought the Germans from it. Then the Germans took the Line and fought the Americans from it. Then the Americans took the Line and fought the Germans from it. Thus, the Maginot Line has the distinction of being the only line of fortifications to be defended by three armies (the French in 1940, the German in 1944, and the American in 1945) and assaulted by two armies (the German in 1940 and the American in 1944). The German Army, of course, attacked it twice, four and a half years apart!

In the final analysis, the Germans built the biggest and least effective line of fortifications, the Atlantic Wall, as well as the most effective line of the war, the *Westwall*, respectively. True to stereotype, the French built the most artistically rendered; the most hopelessly and romantically defended; and the most fickle line of fortifications used in World War II.

## Largest Maneuvers in History: US Army, 1941

In 1941, the US Army conducted the largest peacetime maneuvers in history. During the period 1940–41, the US Army was trying to do in one year of peacetime what the German army had done in seven years of peace and war. The US Army was training men on an unprecedented scale in peacetime and, at the same time, engaging in a philosophical debate about the proper role, structure, and conduct of armored units. This was in response to the example the German army had shown the world in France 1940 and was about to show in Russia.

Large-scale maneuvers had not been practicable for the United States armed forces in the inter-war period. The principal reason for this was that the normal peacetime strength of the armed services was insufficient for such activities because of lack of funding. In time of war, when the army was of sufficient size, the exigencies of the situation usually precluded long-term, large-scale training exercises. In World War I, the military situation called for the urgent deployment of the American Expeditionary Force overseas and so no large-scale exercises or maneuvers were scheduled.

In the post-war era, the US Army was progressively pared by Congress from its authorized, though unattained, strength under the National Defense Act of 1920 of 280,000. In 1921, Congress cut the Regular Army to 150,000; in 1922, it was reduced to 137,000; and by 1927, it stood at 118,750. Only under the prodding of successive chiefs of staff, Generals Douglas MacArthur and Malin Craig, and the darkening international scene of the late 1930s, did Congress authorize an increase to 165,000 for fiscal 1938. The pressure of foreign events continued to affect American considerations, and with the outbreak of war in Europe, President Roosevelt raised the ceiling of the Regular Army to 227,000. The defeat of the Low Countries and France in June 1940 saw the enlisted strength of the army upped to 280,000. Moreover, the signing into law of the Selective Training and Service Act on 16 September 1940 permitted the induction of 630,000 draftees, the federalization of the National Guard for one year, and the raising of the ceiling on the Regular Army to 500,000 men. This meant that by 1 July 1941, 1,326,577 men were being trained.

There were three types of training exercises in the US Army in the inter-war period: command post exercises (CPX), field training exercises (FTX), and large-scale field maneuvers. The last mentioned involved exercises on a corps level, either corps versus corps or a corps against one of its divisions. The training of soldiers could easily and nearly adequately be conducted in exercises of the first two categories, but the training of high-level commanders, support elements, and operational staff members could not. Modern warfare had produced massive organizations and the problems of directing them could not be simulated. The best way—probably the only way—to provide the necessary training for divisional, corps, army, and support staffs was to engage in realistic exercises; in other words, make them do in peace what they would have to do in war. This meant that the maneuvers had to be true to the requirements of time and space. They lasted, therefore, for many days, even weeks, and were conducted over thousands of square miles. Only then could the many frictions of war be simulated and overcome. Many of the men involved in making these decisions adhered to the theory that the only way to see how the whole army would operate was to make the whole army operate.

The scope of these maneuvers is striking. For the first time in its history, the United States prepared for large-scale, peacetime maneuvers. And what is actually meant by large-scale? In 1935, it was 36,000 troops at Pine Camp, New York; in 1939, 50,000 troops at Plattsburg, New York. The First Army's maneuvers of August 1940 involved 81,010 men. The Second Army versus Third Army Louisiana Maneuvers of 1941 involved over 400,000 men. The area requirements were equally impressive. For the Third Army maneuvers of 1940, rights to 1,776,000 acres of Louisiana and 402,800 acres of private land in Texas were secured. It is a tribute to American patriotism that for 1940 and into wartime, 3,400 square miles of private land were made available to the army at no cost to the government. For the army-versus-army maneuvers of 1941, about 30,000 square miles were secured in Texas and Louisiana.

Perhaps the most important steps for peacetime training were taken in the summer of 1940. Major General Lesley J. McNair, chief of staff to General Marshall, was given command of General Headquarters (GHQ). On 26 July 1940, GHQ was given the task of speeding up mobi-

During late September 1941, Generals McNair (left) and Marshall (right) study the situation map for the ongoing Louisiana Maneuvers. *NA*

lization and supervising the training and organization of the field forces in the continental United States. This meant that McNair had the training authority over four armies; the air corps; the Armored Force, which was constituted on 10 July 1940; harbor defense troops; and other GHQ reserves. To meet this challenge, the Mobilization Training Program (MTP) was instituted. Under this plan, the average civilian was made into a soldier with 13 weeks of basic training, followed by several months of progressive unit training, from squad to platoon to company and so on, up to army versus army.

The training had to take place in hurried conditions, with too few officers and with equipment shortages, but it also took place in the shadow of German military prowess. Throughout the maneuver period, the leaders of the US Army were keenly aware of German military successes. The 1940 maneuvers were played against a backdrop of the conquest of France, and in 1941, against the spectacular German gains in Russia. Not only was the US Army trying to match the fighting and organizational excellence of the German army, but it was trying also to match it technically and materially. Training, therefore, was conducted with an eye to ensuring that if American and German soldiers faced each other in combat, the G.I. would have at least a fighting chance.

The maneuvers of 1941 were designed to be as realistic as possible. The Tennessee Maneuvers of June, the Louisiana Maneuvers of September, and the Carolina Maneuvers of November were classified as free maneuvers. This meant that the opposing forces received orders as to mission and force size. The respective commanders had to determine their own strategy, plan their movement into the maneuver area, compile their own intelligence, and issue their own orders. The battles would be fought with blank ammunition and signal flags; umpires would be responsible for enforcing the rules and deciding victory in the many skirmishes. The purpose of the maneuvers was to test the officer corps and men; the new equipment; and the new doctrine of the American army after a year of rearmament. Of particular interest—to the public and to GHQ—was the performance of the three new elements of the army: the armored force, the antitank units, and ground support aviation.

The war games were to be conducted according to new rules. The Umpire Manual had been rewritten by McNair for the maneuvers in order to enhance realism and ensure fairness. As actual combat involved movement, fire, and physical contact with the enemy, the goal of the manual was to recreate these elements as realistically as possible. Movement was to be real, therefore, and infantry or tanks had to be on the scene to be counted in an engagement. Fire was simulated, for obvious reasons, and hand-to-hand combat, as it could not be real, was not allowed.

The Louisiana Maneuvers were conducted in a series of corps-sized maneuvers and culminated with a two-phase war between the Red 2d Army of Lieutenant General Ben Lear and the Blue 3d Army of Lieutenant General Walter Kruger. Including the two Air Task Forces, one assigned to each army, the Red force had 130,000 men, including the 1st Armored Corps of 1st and 2d Armored Divisions to defeat the larger Blue force of 270,000.

The extent to which the Americans had one eye on Europe is demonstrated by McNair's statement that the purpose of Phase One of the maneuvers was to see whether a tank offensive could be stopped. While the US Army strove mightily to put 19 divisions into Louisiana, the Germans sent that many panzer divisions into Russia. The Louisiana Maneuvers were judged a success by the participants and organizers, and they were. McNair's criticism ran to 157 paragraphs, but in general, it was that troops were not aware enough of the threat from air attack; roads were often congested, which reflected poor staff work; reconnaissance and security were weak; not all weapons were employed; and units often attacked on frontages too large for their strength. Additionally, orders were too long and too detailed. On the other hand, air-to-ground cooperation was excellent, although there were many problems to work out to ensure fast and effective support. On the key issue of antitank defense, McNair was very pleased. He said that mobile antitank units, which were being developed, showed promise of success. The mobile antitank unit (battalion-sized) was McNair's baby.

Phase Two included the famous, although not entirely authorized, dash through Texas by Patton's armor. It showed some of the potential of tanks, but in the manuevers, armor had been under-utilized and its combat power was not fully brought to bear on the battlefield. The most important reason for this was that there was a fundamental defect in the structure of the armored division. The division lacked enough infantry and artillery. Moreover, the command structure for its use was fragmented. There was no direct chain of command linking the armored brigade with the infantry regiment and the reconnaissance battalion except the division commander. These and other features were not corrected until General Jacob Devers dealt with them in the reorganization of the armored division in March 1942. The correctives directly reflected the lessons learned in the maneuvers. The maneuvers also showcased the two existing infantry division organizational structures: the large, square division—still used by the National Guard—from WWI;

and the smaller, triangular division used by the Regular Army. The 28,000-man square division was organized into two brigades of four regiments with each regiment having three battalions. The 15,000-man triangular division had three regiments of three battalions. The latter was easier to transport and supply and clearly demonstrated its greater flexibility and speed in the wargames. All divisions were triangulated for the war.

The maneuvers cost in excess of $25 million dollars, but the price was not high when weighed against the results. The United States had, for the first time in its history, a large peacetime army on the eve of a great war.

## Most Important Development in Tactics and the Best Practitioners Thereof: Combined Arms Mobility Tactics and the United States Army

The battlefield deadlock that characterized the Great War in the west was broken by the appearance of combined arms mobility tactics, and the organizations for executing them. As such, these tactics were the most important development in land warfare during the Second World War. The Germans were the first to develop and implement tactics and build organizations for it; reporters dubbed it *"Blitzkrieg."* Using integrated mobile infantry, armor, and artillery units—sometimes supported by tactical air strikes—the Germans quickly defeated the Poles, French, Dutch, and Belgians in 1940. Although the Germans certainly inflicted heavy casualties in the process, the main impact of such mobility tactics was the deprivation of the Germans' adversaries will—not the means—to fight. For example, although the French lost 120,000 men killed in their catastrophic, six-week war in 1940, this loss was relatively little compared to their losses of over 1,359,000 dead in 1914–18.

Although the Germans inflicted millions of casualties on the Red Army during their offensives in 1941–42, they failed to eliminate the Soviets' will to fight. This was probably less due to a problem with their doctrine than with their overall organization of their ground forces. The German Army never fielded mobile, mechanized units that comprised more than 15 percent of their total ground tactical forces; the rest were no more mobile than their Great War antecedents. Quite literally, for all the bluster and bombast about *Blitzkrieg*, the vast bulk of the German Army moved on foot, with horse-drawn artillery and supply wagons. Well into 1942, company commanders in infantry battalions were still issued horses with which to lead their foot-borne soldiers. Thus, the *Wehrmacht* simply lacked the degree of mobility essential for the scale of maneuver required to knock the Russians out of the war. Certainly, there were political, industrial, economic, and other factors involved in the strategic outcome, but this is what it came down to at the tactical and operational levels.

While the *Wehrmacht* clearly led the world in the development and implementation of these sort of tactics and units in 1939–41, Germany's adversaries were watching intently, learning, and adopting their own tactical doctrine and organizations for the conduct of a similar type of warfare. The Soviets eventually developed an extremely effective and sophisticated *operational* doctrine, that is, a set of rules for combat at the campaign level, that allowed them to hand the Germans crushing defeats on huge scales in 1944–45, but their *tactical* doctrine and organizations (those intended to fight battles) remained more primitive than that of the Germans. This was due to a combination of economic, logistical, and even cultural factors, but the fact remains that the Red Army did not develop or possess units which integrated armor, mechanized or motorized infantry, and motorized (vehicle-drawn or self-propelled) artillery into units below the corps level (with the exception of their "destroyer divisions," which were mainly employed for defensive antiarmor, not offensive, missions). Notably absent from Soviet organizations were armored personnel carriers that allowed infantry to accompany tanks into battle with at least a modicum of protection; Soviet infantryman often rode into battle mounted on the outside of the tanks with which they were attacking. Few more dangerous ways can be imagined to arrive onto a battlefield full of high-explosive shells, antitank projectiles, and machine guns . . . not to mention the effects of the jinking, pivoting tanks and their ever-swiveling turrets!

By mid-1944, German and American tactical doctrines were the most advanced prescriptions for combined arms mobility tactics of any adopted by any combatant army. The organizations that the US Army built for the execution of these tactics, however—and the training they gave the soldiers who manned them—were far superior to those of the *Wehrmacht*.

## The Germans

### German Operational and Tactical Doctrine in Mid-1944

German doctrine for the conduct of attacks demanded swift, coordinated combined arms strikes designed to demoralize the enemy by encircling him, cutting his lines of communication, and denying him freedom of maneuver. Such offensive action was most effectively carried out by armored—or at least motorized—forces that could rapidly penetrate the enemy's weakest points, fan out behind his main defensive positions, and wreak havoc deep in his rear areas. To reduce the inevitable effects of what Clausewitz referred to as "friction"—or the things that inevitably cause plans to go awry in battle—the Germans encouraged independent action by their combat leaders, depending on their astute judgment to allow the German operational (corps- or division-level) commanders to retain the initiative in the rapidly-developing situations encountered in the offensive.

Of course, such principles assumed a high level of competence and responsibility on the part of subordinate commanders. German doctrinal literature specifically pointed out that although the commander should give his subordinates the greatest possible freedom of action, he must nevertheless not allow subordinates' activities to endanger the success of the whole operation. In addition, warned these manuals, the commander must not delegate those decisions for which he alone was responsible.

## German Offensive Operations

All offensive operations were to be preceded by extensive reconnaissance, including high-level aerial operations down through local patrolling.

At the start of World War II, German doctrine originally identified five distinct types of attacks. All were intended to accomplish—or at least significantly contribute to—the ultimate mission of the destruction of the enemy's forces. The type eventually chosen by a commander depended upon enemy dispositions, terrain (hence the criticality of reconnaissance), and what friendly forces were available. Each type of attack reflected the German belief in the value of maneuver: cutting the enemy's supply lines; preventing the enemy from reinforcing; paralyzing the enemy by preventing coordinating communications; threatening the enemy or preventing his retreat; and retaining the flexibility to attack individual enemy positions with superior forces. Eventually, seven different types of attacks were developed. The two additions were variations on the themes of flank attack or encirclement, and were developed during the war. Each type of attack also called for the execution of a main effort in a narrow sector (*Schwerpunkt*), normally directed against the enemy's flank or rear, and several supporting efforts. In all cases, combined arms cooperation was stressed and thorough coordination was considered essential.

The Germans considered the *flank attack* to be the most effective type of offensive maneuver. By attacking the enemy from the side, such operations maximized surprise and diminished the retarding effects of enemy fortifications, which were usually oriented to the front. Enemy forces could be rapidly cut up and destroyed by "rolling up" his defensive line without the danger of exposing one's own rear to counterstrokes.

The *envelopment* involved both a supporting frontal attack, designed to fix the enemy in place, and a main effort consisting of a flank attack from the side or, preferably, the rear to destroy the immobilized enemy. The coordination of such an offensive maneuver was difficult because it involved maneuver from two directions simultaneously, but the benefits were also considerable. To avoid being split by enemy counterattack, reserves had to be employed in depth, and this further compounded the complexity of the maneuver. Of course, as complexity increases, so do the factors leading to friction.

The most potentially costly of all attacks was the *frontal attack*. From their experience in the First World War, the Germans knew that this type of offensive operation required a clear superiority of forces and firepower if enemy positions were to be overwhelmed by direct assault.

Because of this difficulty, when faced with the impossibility of any type of attack other than frontal, the Germans preferred the *penetration and breakthrough*. By concentrating overwhelming force against the enemy in an extremely narrow sector, the Germans hoped to cause a rupture in the enemy's line that would then, in effect, create two new unprotected flanks. Once the penetration was achieved, the breakthrough took on the characteristics of a flank attack, with all of the advantages described earlier.

The *limited objective attack*, intended to fix the enemy in place or to gain a specific piece of ground, usually took place as part of a greater maneuver designed to bring about more decisive results. For example, the unit executing a flank attack could require that the enemy be immobilized or tied down to successfully move against his weak flank. The unit conducting the supporting attack would therefore conduct a limited objective attack to facilitate the flanking unit's maneuver.

During the war, two other types of attacks evolved, both of which were variations on two pre-existing themes. *Attacking an enemy wing* was preferred when the enemy's flanks were initially unassailable due to terrain or manner in which his forces were arrayed. An attack on the extreme end of an enemy position might possibly cause his forces to bend back, thus exposing a flank. Such a success would then be followed by a flank attack.

*Encirclement* was a variation on envelopment. This maneuver required only a weak, if any, supporting attack, and was designed to totally isolate the enemy. The development of this maneuver probably had its origins in the experiences of the 1940 campaign in France and the initial stages of the 1941 campaign in the Soviet Union. If the enemy chose to fight rather than to succumb to the pressures and fears induced by being cut off, then there would clearly be problems for the attacker—with unsubdued enemy left in the rear, the encircler could easily become the encircled!

Each of these attacks was preferably conducted by coordinated, combined arms teams. The composition and disposition of enemy forces generally dictated the roles to be played by the maneuver elements of armor (*Panzer*), mechanized/motorized infantry (*Panzer-grenadier*), and infantry (*Grenadier* or *Infanterie*) elements, all of which were to be supported by flexible, responsive artillery fires. The lowest level at which a permanent combined arms team could be found was indeed the division; below that level, only combat groups (*Kampfgruppen*) created on an *ad hoc* basis for the accomplishment of a specific mission, were formed. As a result, there was limited opportunity for the commanders and soldiers of these different units to become accustomed to working together. (The temporary and *ad hoc* nature of these combat groups would have a seriously negative effect on the conduct of many German operations as the Second World War continued, as will become evident later.)

If the enemy had well-prepared positions around which it was impossible to maneuver, these were to be battered and broken by artillery barrage and then assaulted by tank-led infantry formations until a penetration had been achieved. The armored element would then storm through and rampage behind enemy lines, and the infantry would "mop-up" remaining pockets of enemy resistance with the help of artillery.

In the event the enemy had not yet formed a solid, coherent defense (again, the need for thorough reconnaissance can be seen here), then the initial attacks were to be made by *panzer* and *panzer-grenadier* elements, allowing a rapid breakthrough and subsequent pursuit, with the infantry echelons following in the van for the conduct of their unenviable but inevitable "mopping up" tasks.

If the enemy was routed, the German pursuit maintained contact with the retreating enemy units with armored or armored reconnaissance elements so as to keep him from halting, consolidating, or "catching his breath." More armored and motorized infantry formations followed as quickly as possible, deployed in depth, with the forward elements of even these units constantly attacking the backpedalling enemy. Whatever enemy forces remained were bypassed, to be destroyed later by those friendly echelons constituting the "depth" of the pursuit effort.

Their experiences during the war served to diminish the Germans' prewar and early war tendency toward spectacular, slashing thrusts. After 1940, faced by enemies who did not lose their will to fight when cut off or bypassed by German armor, their tactics became more conservative. The authoritative compendium of American and other Allied experience and intelligence, the *Handbook on German Military Forces*, published by the US War Department in March 1945, states that:

> "The original German *Blitzkrieg* tactics were based on the belief in the irresistible power of tank formations operating independently with the support of dive-bombers. Considerable modifications have taken place in this theory over the past few years. At the present time, the offensive tactics of the Germans are less spectacularly bold than they were in 1939, but *the fundamental theory behind them has changed remarkably little* [emphasis added], though in their armored tactics they stress more tank-infantry coordination since unlimited air support is no longer at their command."

## German Defensive Tactics

As Clausewitz pointed out, "the defensive form of warfare is intrinsically stronger than the offensive" for numerous reasons. Conduct of the defense allows the commander to choose terrain and thereby make optimal use of whatever is available. It turns the passage of time to greatest advantage as defenses are prepared in greater and greater depth and complexity. The defense allows orchestration of the counterattack at the moment when the enemy's thrust has been parried, when he has taken unforeseen casualties, and when he is, logically, least prepared for a defense of his own. The defense is, in the final analysis, stronger because it facilitates the destruction of the enemy's forces while providing maximum opportunity for both protecting friendly forces and launching an attack under the best possible circumstances.

Accordingly, German doctrine called for the organization of defenses in great depth. They organized the battlefield into three areas: the advanced position, the combat outposts, and the main battle line.

Reconnaissance elements usually occupied the advanced position about five thousand to seven thousand meters forward of the main battle line, with the triple mission of gaining intelligence (information about the enemy's attacking strength, intent, direction of advance, and so on), delaying the enemy's progress (though not halting it at the expense of serious loss to friendly units), and deceiving him as to the location of the main line of resistance. To these ends, advanced positions were usually placed on hilltops, ridges, or at crossroads, where they were afforded optimal fields of fire and observation. From these locations, German forces in the advanced position could observe and report enemy activities; call for and adjust artillery fires; and engage attackers with antitank weapons and machine guns at maximum ranges before withdrawing along preselected covered and concealed routes to the protection of the main battle line.

Infantry, tank, and antitank units occupied the combat outposts, usually located two thousand to five thousand meters forward of the main battle line. These elements had the mission of breaking up the enemy's attack before it struck the main battle line, and so were dug in and concealed to the greatest extent possible. Here the mission also entailed deception, trying to make the enemy believe he had encountered the main defensive belt so he would deploy his units on line for the final assault, thus dissipating his momentum long before he hit the strongest part of the German defenses. The troops occupying the combat outposts would then fall back under the cover of friendly artillery fire, assemble behind the main line of resistance, and prepare to counterattack.

At the main battle line, all rearward movement of friendly forces ceased and positions were held at all costs. Positions were organized in depth with interlocking fields of fire designed to halt the enemy as far forward as possible. Obstacles—barbed wire, landmines, and antitank ditches—were employed both to impede the enemy's advance and to channel his forces into areas where maximum friendly fires could be brought to bear from well-protected, entrenched, and camouflaged positions. When the enemy had used his last reserves against this line and begun to fall back in bloody disarray, the counterattack would be launched, perhaps directly into the pursuit mode, to complete the destruction of his forces. For this purpose, it was critical to have a designated reserve (in the event that the combat outposts had been rendered ineffective or had been eliminated altogether), and that this reserve be positioned so that a swift and effective counterattack could be launched.

As the war continued, German defensive practices changed, even if their doctrine did not. Greater reliance was placed on linear "passive" defenses and, frequently, only scaled-down counterattacks were launched. Like the changes to offensive doctrine, this alteration of original prewar concepts was due largely to wartime exigencies. As the 1945 *Handbook on German Military Forces* put it:

"At present, more emphasis is placed on the construction of defensive positions, and counterattacks are frequently local in character.

It is most likely that this passive type of defense is only an expedient due to German shortages of mobile equipment and manpower."

## German Delay Doctrine

Delays enabled units to disengage from the enemy, move to the rear, and establish a defensive position before the enemy could effectively pursue and annihilate them. To accomplish this, lines of resistance were designated to coordinate the orderly movement of units to the rear. Rear-guard units were to take maximum advantage of long-range machine gun, mortar, and artillery fires to delay the enemy advance. Obstacles such as minefields and roadblocks were to be integrated into the scheme of maneuver to allow delaying units the maximum time possible to establish new defensive positions before the arrival of the pursuing enemy.

## German Land Forces' Organization

At the time hostilities commenced in 1939, the major combatant units of the *Wehrmacht* were organized in a fairly simple and straightforward manner. The lowest echelon at which the various branches (that is, armor, artillery, infantry, and engineers) were organized together on a permanent basis was the division. There were a few standardized types of divisions, and at the outset, most German divisions were uniformly equipped, trained, and organized. Such uniformity allowed commanders to understand the capabilities of subordinate echelons and enabled them to plan appropriately for their operational and tactical employment.

In 1939, there were basically six types of *Wehrmacht* divisions: the infantry division (*Infanteriedivision*), the armored division (*Panzerdivision*), the motorized infantry division (*Infanterie Motorisiertesdivision*), the mountain infantry division (*Gebirgsdivision*), the cavalry division (*Kavalleriedivision*) and the light division (*Jägerdivision*). Additionally, the *Luftwaffe* fielded parachute infantry divisions (*Fallschirmjägerdivision*).

An infantry division was organized with three infantry regiments of three battalions each. These regiments were supported, collectively, by three battalions of horse-drawn light artillery, equipped at full strength with twelve 105mm howitzers each, and by one battalion of medium artillery, equipped with eight 150mm howitzers and four 105mm rifles. No tanks, tank destroyers, or assault guns were organic to this type of division, but such units could be attached according to the requirements of a given situation. (The antitank battalion was equipped with towed antitank guns.) There were about five thousand more men manning the division reconnaissance battalion and the antitank battalion, as well as support troops, including signal, engineer, quartermaster, military police units, and the like.

With three major subordinate maneuver units (infantry regiments), each possessing three of its own maneuver elements (infantry battalions), the commander of an infantry division had considerable flexibility when planning for the deployment of his troops. When conducting a penetration and breakthrough attack, for example, he could choose to weight his main effort at the *Schwerpunkt* with two regiments while conducting a limited objective attack with his remaining regiment. In the defense, he could defend his assigned terrain with two regiments while keeping one in reserve for a counterattack. Each of the regimental commanders could then choose to defend their assigned sectors with two battalions, while holding one in reserve for their own counterattacks.

The panzer division was organized with a tank regiment of two tank battalions (about 1,700 men total) and with two panzer-grenadier regiments, each with about 2,200 men. One of the panzer-grenadier regiments consisted of a battalion borne in armored personnel carriers and one equipped with trucks; in the other panzer-grenadier regiment, both battalions were truck borne. Each tank battalion had about fifty tanks, which by 1944 would have been either Pzkw IVs or the more mobile and better-armed Panthers. Each division also possessed an armored reconnaissance battalion, which included companies equipped with heavy armored cars and armored personnel carriers; the latter could be and were often used to conduct infantry missions in conjunction with the panzer and panzer-grenadier battalions. These maneuver elements were supported by an armored artillery regiment (with about 1,600 men) comprised of one battalion of twelve truck-drawn 105mm howitzers, one battalion of twelve self-propelled 105mm howitzers, one battalion of truck-drawn 150mm howitzers and six additional self-propelled 150mm howitzers, and one battalion of towed 170mm heavy guns. The divisional armored reconnaissance, antitank, and engineer battalions, all of which were mobile due to the presence of motorized and/or armored transportation assets, and divisional support troops comprised the remainder of the division's roughly 13,500 soldiers.

In the attack, panzer formations would be accompanied by mechanized infantry in their own armored personnel carriers. These units would be followed by truck-borne motorized infantry who would consolidate on objectives seized by the armored echelons, or who could begin the task of mopping up bypassed enemy pockets of resistance.

While division organizations were, indeed, fairly flexible and manageable, even from the beginning there were some inconsistencies of organization and purpose that portended an ominous later trend. For example, the light divisions never had consistently defined organizations. At various times throughout the war, divisions that were classified this way included semi-mechanized formations and even light infantry divisions; many of the former were later redesignated as *Panzer* divisions, while many of the latter became *Jäger* divisions. Similarly, after 1941, many of the motorized infantry divisions received quantities of armored troop carriers (of a variety of types) and these were subsequently renamed panzer-grenadier divisions. In 1943, some infantry divisions were reorganized with only two infantry regiments. German Army mountain divisions *never* had more than two infantry regiments.

Each type of German division differed in organization, equipment, and purpose, but through uniform organization and equipment within a type, each could be employed to fulfill a clearly-understood doctrinal requirement. In the attack, for example, a panzer division would lead a flanking attack and, followed by panzer-grenadier formations, would continue to "roll up" an enemy's flank, while remaining pockets of enemy resistance (if any) would be engaged and destroyed by more slowly moving infantry divisions. Since each division was uniformly organized and had been similarly trained, such a maneuver could be carried out by any division in a universally-understood manner. The flexibility thus enjoyed by German commanders was great, and the friction resulting from misunderstandings or miscalculations of unit abilities or mission requirements was low.

As the war continued, the different types of German divisions proliferated. By 1942, the *Waffen-SS* began fielding divisions which, in many cases, received the best equipment and more of it than army formations—despite the reality that many of their higher-level commanders and other leaders were not trained to the same standards of tactical proficiency as those of the army. Some *Waffen-SS* divisions also were oversized, that is, their organizational structures included elements such as extra tank platoons, assault gun battalions, and rocket launcher battalions that the army equivalents simply did not possess. Others, particularly the divisions manned primarily by foreigners, were organized in completely different ways, sometimes with equipment and strengths that were considerably inferior to comparable Army units. All four *Waffen-SS* mountain divisions, for example, were differently organized, with the mostly-German 6th SS-Mountain Division being larger and more powerful than a standard Army mountain division, the 7th being roughly the same, and the 13th, 21st, 23rd, and 24th, consisting mostly of personnel of mixed or mostly non-German origins, being considerably weaker than their Army counterparts.

Often, *Waffen-SS* formations also had first priority of replacement equipment, and their leaders were even known to sometimes use their political connections to garner the lion's share of replacements and supplies originally intended for equitable distribution among German Army and SS formations. This not only prompted resentment among army officers, but also contributed in other ways to the increasingly strained relations between the Army and the SS at all levels.

To add to the confusion and difficulties for German field commanders, the *Luftwaffe* contributed a variety of ground maneuver elements, too, including 22 *Luftwaffe* field divisions, which were each organized and equipped almost in unique fashions, respectively. Most of the latter ended up with two three-battalion regiments, but rarely were any manned at full strength. These units helped siphon off quality manpower that would unquestionably have been better used by the Army in more uniformly organized, better trained units. The parachute divisions also belonged to the *Luftwaffe*, which even raised its own panzer division and a panzer-grenadier division!

Frequently, due in part to the considerably different ideological, political, and social backgrounds of the SS and German Army officer corps and in part to the differentials in training (particularly of the officers), quarrels arose between commanders of adjacent army and SS units—all adding to totally unnecessary friction on the battlefield.

By September 1944, OKW had decided to stop replenishing certain badly-mauled infantry divisions and to instead replace them altogether with new, differently organized and equipped formations called *Volksgrenadier* divisions. Sometimes, these were entirely new formations, built from former *Luftwaffe* ground personnel or *Kriegsmarine* crewmen no longer needed for a shrunken surface fleet. Sometimes, units which had been seriously degraded in combat were reorganized as volksgrenadier divisions. In either case, these divisions' three infantry regiments had only two battalions each. Additionally, they had diminished reconnaissance capabilities (a *Füsilier,* or elite infantry company with bicycles and trucks replaced the reconnaissance battalions of the 1939-pattern divisions) and reduced (by more than 30 percent) artillery assets. These volks-grenadier divisions eventually numbered fifty in all, and usually trained together for less than ten weeks before being deployed to the front.

In an attempt to compensate for fewer combat troops in these divisions, the infantrymen of volks-grenadier divisions were supplied with higher proportions of automatic weapons such as submachine guns, assault rifles, and machine guns. They were also frequently supported by corps-level *Nebelwerfer* units firing multi-barrelled rocket launchers which, although not as accurate as conventional artillery, nevertheless delivered an extremely high volume of high-explosive fires.

Still, although these volks-grenadier divisions' organizations were designed to make up in firepower what they lacked in manpower, their mobility and tactical utility at the operational level was hampered by lack of training and the almost total absence of organic transportation assets. Further, by reducing the number of infantry battalions within each regiment to two, the ability of such units to mount the counterattacks called for by doctrine and by necessity became severely limited. By opting for such expedient solutions to strategic problems, OKW was practically forcing its field commanders to rely on the stronger but less preferable mode of operations—the defense. As mobility, maneuverability, and tactical options became increasingly limited by the introduction of new types of divisions, it became increasingly difficult for commanders to estimate the capabilities of these units. Misunderstandings of such capabilities could only be furthered by the terse, mission-type orders favored by the Germans. As the multitude of new types of units increased, so also would the need for specificity of instruction. Either way, the structure of the German military organization did not fit with its decentralized system of tactical orders.

While the production of armaments such as armored vehicles actually grew until the middle of 1944 according to Albert Speer, the number of experienced tankers was vastly reduced by the disastrous (for the Germans) battles during the Normandy campaign. To compensate for these losses, the Germans created separate panzer brigades—an altogether new size and level of organization. A panzer brigade was smaller than a division, but larger and better supported than a regiment; there was, however, no established doctrine for the employment of such formations, nor was there any operational experience upon which to draw for their use. As with the other organizational changes initiated in 1944, the result was a loss of operational flexibility and increased friction in battle.

## German Army Training

Before the continuous ground combat phases of the Second World War in Europe were initiated by the Germans with the execution of Operation BARBAROSSA in June 1941, the organization and training of the soldiers and officers of combat formations followed a logical and highly effective pattern. Units were raised with recruits and, so far as possible, cadre, from discrete geographical areas of Germany, trained sequentially from individual skill instruction through corps-level maneuvers, and then committed to battle. Each division also maintained its own field training battalion, which helped hone the skills of arriving replacements and integrate the new troops into the division. This ensured not only a high level of technical and tactical proficiency, but also created a bond of camaraderie and trust between the officers, noncommissioned officers, and junior enlisted men that would pay great dividends of cohesion under the strain of battle conditions.

Typically, in peacetime, German regiments trained their own recruits during a 16-week period each year. When WWII began, this became impractical, but each regiment maintained its own training battalion at the regimental home depot, and the soldiers of each regiment were, as much as practicable, drawn from the same geographical area within Germany. The positive impact of such a system was considerable, particularly in a country where geographical origin corresponded so directly to ethnicity and religious background. Additionally, such a system ensured that each soldier felt that he was a member of his regiment from the outset, with all of the associated positive effects on cohesion.

As the war developed and lasted much longer than originally envisioned, however, the German replacement system required radical changes to keep up with the demands of attrition. After the autumn of 1942, the training of replacements for most regiments was no longer performed exclusively by those regiments' respective training battalions. Beginning at this time, the best that could be hoped for was that a training battalion from a particular military district (*Wehrkreis*) would be able to supply troops as replacements for several regiments from the same geographical area. The breakdown here is obvious, and, as a result, the cohesion derived from a feeling of belonging to a specific unit from the outset of a soldier's military service was diminished if not altogether lost.

Without a coherent strategy for mobilization, the German manpower replacement system developed in an even more erratic manner as the war progressed. By 1944, as the quantity of trained pilots and available fuel waned, *Luftwaffe* ground support personnel were provided as replacements to ground combat units, or organized into infantry battalions, regiments, and even whole volks-grenadier divisions for combat deployment to the fighting front. Often, these units had received scant training in infantry combat techniques. As the German surface fleet declined drastically in usefulness and size, naval ratings were also often pressed into combat as individual or small-unit replacements in army formations—with all of the problems of training, conditioning, and cohesion one might expect from such a policy. Try as they might, German division field training units simply could not bring such men up to speed in the few days or week that they typically had to train them.

As the Anglo-American Allies prepared for the invasion of France and the Soviets pressed ever closer to Germany's frontiers, even more pronounced changes to the German manpower and replacement system were instituted. By the time of the Normandy invasion in June 1944, there were a considerable number of "ethnic German" (*Volksdeutsche*) troops serving in German army units. What exactly constituted ethnic "Germanness" is difficult to ascertain, for such designation apparently was derived from the inconsistent and often bizarre National Socialist theories of race.

At the outset of the war, Austrians and Sudetenlanders (ethnic Germans from western Czechoslovakia, annexed in September of 1938) were included in units raised in the traditional way in the newly-created *Wehrkreise* XVII and XVIII (Austria) and *Wehrkreis Böhmen* (western Czechoslovakia). By the time the Allies invaded western Europe, Nazi doctrine had been expanded or reinterpreted to include Alsatians and non-Sudeten Czechs as ethnic Germans eligible for duty in army (*Heer*) combat formations.

Oddly, the *Waffen-SS* had even more liberal standards. By 1944, the ranks of the *Waffen-SS* included whole divisions of Albanians, Ustachi Croats, Poles, Ukrainians, Dutch, Danish, Belgian, and other types previously (and, undoubtedly still, behind their backs) classified as *Untermenschen* (subhuman). Of course, these units were usually officered by Germans and were employed, as much as possible, against the most appropriate enemies. For example, the Croatian divisions were employed in antipartisan roles against Tito's communist guerrillas in Yugoslavia; the Dutch, Danish and Belgian units, recruited heavily from particularly anticommunist sectors of the political right, were sent to the Eastern Front; and the Ukrainian and other Russian troops (often turncoat prisoners) usually fought in the west.

The degree of ferocity with which such ethnic German units fought—in the West, anyway—was usually not particularly high, and often resulted in the wholesale or nearly-wholesale surrender of such organizations. Equipment furnished to such units was practically thrown away in these cases. In situations involving the amalgamation of *Volksdeutsche* replacement troops with *bona fide* German (*Reichsdeutsche*) soldiers, or in cases of ethnic German units being brigaded together with all-German outfits, differing language, customs, and traditions played havoc with cohesion. What a far cry from the pre- and early war situations of ethnic and regimental homogeneity!

In addition to these variations from prewar norms, other replacement and manpower practices were adopted by the autumn of 1944 that only added to the troubles of the German army. In addition to the arrangement by which a single training battalion supported several regiments with replacements, by this late stage in the war, often the training units themselves were committed as tactical fighting entities. This situation left the supported units without a training and replacement base, and from that point on, there was only the most tentative, if any, relationship between field units and the organizations providing them with replacements.

Worse, in the fall of 1944 the German army instituted a system of straggler control that effectively destroyed unit cohesion altogether. Military police (*Feldgendarmerie*) operated straggler control points at which members of shattered units, troops who had been cut off or otherwise lost touch with their parent organizations, and other stragglers were herded together, placed under the command of a lieutenant or captain, and sent as a "unit" to the front. Obviously, this deprived some units of their returning troops; placed soldiers of no particular region, unit, or even skills or ranks together; and allowed no time for the bonding process of training so valuable and necessary for unit success on the battlefield. The effects this policy had on morale and cohesion were devastating.

## Summary of Wehrmacht Doctrine, Organization, and Training by Late 1944

German tactical and operational doctrine was theoretically sound and battle-proven, but this doctrine was not always reflected by the organization of army units for combat by 1944. For a variety of reasons, many new types of units were introduced by late-1944, each with varying organizations and types of equipment. Many of them were unsuited for the execution of doctrinal tactical or operational maneuvers, and this only added to the Clausewitzian friction always present in war. Further, the growing disparity between *Waffen-SS* and army units caused counterproductive rivalries that detracted from the common effort against the Anglo-American Allies and the Soviets.

By late 1944, these units, already handicapped by doctrinal and organizational inconsistencies, were often manned by ill-trained and sometimes unmotivated soldiers. In attempting to deal with the rapidly-worsening battlefield situation, the German army adopted measures that often redounded to its disadvantage. The failure to prepare a replacement system that could adequately cope with the demands of a protracted, high-intensity conflict resulted in the adoption of increasingly counterproductive stop-gap measures. The most brilliant of tactics and operational techniques are useless if they are not carried out by formations suited to the accomplishment of the required tasks; by late

1944, the German army in the west was suited neither by organization nor by personnel and training for the execution of its mission to hold back the Allies from the gates of Germany.

## The Americans

### US Army Tactical and Operational Doctrine in 1944

The primary document prescribing tactical and operational doctrine for the US Army in late 1944 was *Field Manual (FM) 100-5, Operations,* which was revised and updated in 1941 and again in mid-1944. The operational and tactical tenets and teachings of this manual were supplemented by a variety of others, all written as corollaries to the *FM 100-5* capstone. Additions and corollary practical hints were communicated to field commanders in training and in combat from July 1944 on through the distribution of a series of circulars known as "Battle Experiences." These publications consisted of "DOs and DON'Ts" contributed by officers and soldiers in combat against the Germans and edited for publication by officers at Supreme Headquarters, Allied Expeditionary Forces-Europe. The published American tactical and operational doctrine was so similar to the German army's that it shared its Clausewitzian validity almost point for point.

Like the Germans', American doctrine placed heavy emphasis on reconnaissance. US doctrine also classified reconnaissance operations into three categories, namely distant, close, and battle. These corresponded in their essentials to the Germans' categories of operational, tactical, and battle reconnaissance. As with their German foes', the Americans' doctrine called for "constant and intensive" reconnaissance efforts conducted by forces heavily-enough equipped to allow protection and exploitation of the situation. To reduce friction, the reports of these units, as well as other intelligence gathered from sources such as prisoners of war, signal intercepts, and aerial reconnaissance, among others, were collated, analyzed, and distributed as quickly as possible.

Like German doctrine, American doctrine stressed independence of action and the use of initiative at all levels. Indeed, the wording of *FM 100-5* on this point is extremely close to that of the *Truppenführung* manual. Orders should be "clear and concise" and should not "trespass upon the province of a subordinate."

> Orders must be as clear and explicit and as brief as is consistent with clarity. Short sentences are easily understood. *Clarity is more important than technique.* [Italics in original] The more urgent the

situation, the greater is the need for conciseness in the order. Any statement of reasons for measures adopted should be limited to what is necessary to obtain intelligent cooperation from subordinates. Detailed instructions for a variety of contingencies, or prescriptions that are a matter of training, do not inspire confidence and have no place in an order.

To stress the importance of initiative, *FM 100-5* went on to emphasize that subordinates' orders should be original, and not mere parrotings of their superiors'. Indeed, in the words of this manual:

"In spite of the advances of technology, the worth of the individual man is still decisive. The open order of combat accentuates his importance. Every individual must be trained to exploit a situation with energy and boldness and must be imbued with the idea that success will depend upon his initiative and action."

Given the experiences of previous generations of the US Army in the years of conflict on the western frontier and in the mountainous jungles of the Philippine Archipelago, it should not be surprising that initiative was so highly prized. Indeed, an army operating over the vast distances of the western plains and in the densely-vegetated, compartmentalized terrain of the Philippines had to develop a tradition of individual thought and action in order to succeed. As pointed out in *FM 100-5*, such attributes were ideal for success in the fast-paced environment of modern battle as well.

As in German doctrine, the preferred mode of wartime operations was the offensive. *FM 100-5* cites essentially the same justifications as the *Truppenführung* manual: decisiveness, maintenance of initiative, and so on. Unlike the German classification of such maneuvers, however, the US Army identified only two types of attacks, namely envelopments and penetrations (although there were two distinct types of envelopments specified; that is, turning movements and double envelopments). In each type of operation, attacking troops would be divided into two or more groups. One of these groups would constitute the main attack, into which the "greatest possible offensive power is concentrated to bring about a decision." The other group, or groups, conducted secondary attacks designed to "render maximum assistance to the main attack." This simplified classification may have allowed greater flexibility in the formulation of plans for offensive action, but basically paralleled German doctrine.

Main attacks were to be characterized by: narrow zones of attack; heavy fire support from artillery, tanks, and aviation assets; and deep echelonment of reserves. Such attacks were made to secure terrain objectives that facilitated the destruction of hostile forces. As with German doctrine, attacks were to be made by combined arms units, and thorough coordination between attacking echelons was stressed. Although the importance of firepower was emphasized, the decisive factor contributing to success of any attack was the "intelligent, energetic, and coordinated execution" of such assaults.

Envelopments involved a secondary attack against the enemy's front to prevent reactive maneuver, and a main effort directed against the flank or rear of the enemy. One type, the turning movement, sought to hold the enemy with a supporting attack and to maneuver around a hostile flank, intending to seize a vital objective in the enemy's rear. This tactic was very similar to the Germans' envelopment. The other type of envelopment specified in *FM 100-5*, the double envelopment, sought to simultaneously envelop both enemy flanks while preventing enemy reaction by the execution of a supporting attack. The successful conduct of such an attack required a considerable superiority of combat power, and was similar in concept to the Germans' encirclement.

The other basic type of attack described in *FM 100-5* was the penetration. The objective of a penetration was the "complete rupture of the enemy's dispositions," and the subsequent "roll-up" of the enemy's lines. Again, the character of such operations was clearly almost identical to the Germans' equivalent.

Interestingly, American doctrine did not call for frontal attacks, except inasmuch as penetrations were usually to be made from the frontal aspect of enemy positions. Wing attacks and flank attacks also received no recognition in the American manual; after all, a wing attack is but a penetration through the extreme end of an enemy line, designed to facilitate a subsequent envelopment. A flank attack is nothing more than an envelopment that does not require a limited objective attack to prevent enemy reactive maneuver. While the American lexicon of attacks may seem, at first glance, more limited than the Germans', it is, in fact, only less complicated.

If friendly attacks resulted in the enemy's withdrawal, American doctrine called for the conduct of pursuit operations. Such operations required the exertion of constant, direct pressure on retreating enemy units while highly mobile, combined arms teams attempted to envelop them and cut their line of retreat. Annihilation of fleeing enemy forces was the goal, just as it was in German doctrine.

The American doctrinal concept of the defense also closely resembled that of their German foes. The Americans organized their defenses in depth, and their doctrine called for responsive, violent counterattack. The defense sector was organized into four areas: the covering force area, the outpost line, the main line of resistance (MLR), and the reserve area.

The mission of the units in the covering force area was to delay the attacking enemy, deny him forward artillery observation, and to permit the strengthening of the defenses of the other friendly defensive echelons. After the covering force fell back, the mission of the units on the outpost line was not only to delay the enemy, but to impede his advance in such a way that he would be deceived into thinking he had found the MLR. This would hopefully cause the attacker to deploy his units for the assault and thus dissipate the greatest force of his attack before it reached the main defenses.

After completing their mission, units on the outpost line would retire to the main line of resistance to occupy reserve positions or, possibly, to participate as part of the defense. Under no circumstances were the positions along the MLR to be abandoned without permission from higher headquarters: defense required that battle positions be "held at all costs." Positions on this "line" (The authors of *FM 100-5* were very careful to point out that the MLR was only a rough "line," and really consisted of positions at irregular intervals in some depth) were to be so sited as to assure interlocking fields of fire, mutual observation, and mutual support in every way. Indirect fires were to be carefully coordinated to ensure maximum destruction of enemy forces in front of the MLR.

The units occupying the reserve area were to conduct counterattacks "without delay, on the initiative of the local commander." Since combined arms operations were so stressed, it was expected that these reserves would conduct their counterattack supported by tanks and other mechanized vehicles. Interestingly, *FM 100-5* emphasized that mechanized forces were not suited to the defense of positions, but rather to the role of counterattack. Holding ground remained a strictly dismounted infantry affair.

Overall, the American concept of defense closely resembled their German foes'; the precepts of Clausewitz were held to as closely as they were in offensive doctrine.

## US Army Tactical Organization

Although US Army doctrine closely resembled that of the Germans, US Army organization differed in several key respects. Unlike the Germans, who had many different divisional organizations, the Americans essentially developed only three—the infantry division, armored division, and airborne division—and stayed with them throughout the war.* This uniformity eased supply and other logistical support problems, and, most importantly, diminished the friction in command and tactics so prevalent on the German side. For an American corps commander and his staff, "what they saw was what they got," and they knew that each of their divisions and subordinate elements would be fully capable of executing doctrinal requirements. Of course, the quality of leadership and amount of experience always introduced variables, but that was as true for the Germans as it was for the Americans.

The US Army infantry division was organized in a fashion somewhat similar to that of the Germans' early-war organizations. The maneuver elements of the infantry division consisted of three infantry regiments, each with three infantry battalions. This allowed the "two-up, one-back" arrangement so conducive to the execution of both offensive and defensive doctrine. In the attack, for example, two regiments could conduct the main effort while one conducted a secondary attack; in the defense, two regiments could defend forward while one regiment remained in reserve to counterattack. These regiments were supported by three battalions of 105mm howitzers with twelve pieces each, and by one twelve-piece battalion of 155mm howitzers. A total of 2,123 troops comprised the remainder of the division, including combat support troops such as engineers, armored reconnaissance, and signal units, as well as service support units such as quartermaster, ordnance (maintenance), and other logistical groups. No tanks or tank destroyers were organic to a US Army infantry division, but there were habitual relationships developed that assured combined arms operations.

These relationships were prescribed in *FM 100-5,* which called for the formation of task forces known as "regimental combat teams," or RCTs. The US Army adhered to a system of "pooling" of assets such as tank battalions, tank destroyer battalions, heavy artillery battalions (155mm rifles, 8-inch howitzers, 8-inch rifles, and 240mm howitzers),

---

*Three armored divisions were organized in accordance with an earlier structure that was different from the way the other 13 were organized. Also, there was one mountain infantry division, a motorized division, and a light infantry division; the former was only committed to combat in 1945, and the latter two were reorganized into conventional infantry divisions and committed to combat as such in 1945 as well. One other, the Philippine Division, was comprised of a mixture of American units and Philippine Scouts, but it was destroyed on the Bataan Peninsula in early 1942. Otherwise, the US Army's 66 infantry divisions were identically organized. US Army airborne divisions were organized quite similarly to infantry divisions, so they will not be discussed separately here.

and specialized engineer units at the corps and even field army level. Supposedly, these units would be assigned on an "as needed" basis to infantry divisions in combat, and then released and reassigned upon completion of a particular mission for which their presence had been required. By mid-1944, it was common to assign particular tank and tank destroyer battalions to a specific division for the duration of combat, however, as it was recognized that combined arms operations were always superior to operations without such benefit. Furthermore, a habitual working relationship encouraged the development of trust, mutual understanding, and cohesion—which paid off on the battlefield.

Typically, an RCT would include a company of tanks (M4-series Shermans), a company of tank destroyers (these M-10 Wolverines or M-36 Sluggers, or, by the autumn of 1944, M-18 Hellcats) all of which were designed to carry a heavier gun than a Sherman at the expense of a degree of armor protection), a company from the divisional combat engineer battalion, and a battalion of 105mm howitzers from the division artillery. With the possible exception of the tank and tank destroyer units, all of these component outfits had trained together extensively in the United States prior to deployment, and a high degree of cohesion and cooperation was thus attained. The RCT system guaranteed that the combined arms operations so heavily emphasized in the tactical and operational doctrine of the day would regularly be carried out. While American doctrine also allowed the formation of battalion task forces, this practice of building semi-permanent RCTs provides a marked contrast to the German system of temporary, *ad hoc* combat groups, established and dismantled on a strictly situational basis.

The post-1942 US armored division provided another exceptional contrast to the German organization of units for combat. Each armored division consisted of three "combat commands," designated Combat Command A, Combat Command B, and Combat Command R, for "reserve." These divisions were superbly organized for the conduct of mobile, combined arms warfare. Each armored division possessed three tank battalions (each with three companies of M4 mediums and a company of M5 light tanks for reconnaissance), three armored infantry battalions (with three rifle companies mounted in M3-series armored halftracks to enable them to keep up with the tanks), three armored medium artillery battalions (with M7 self-propelled 105mm howitzers, which were really nothing more than M4 chassis carrying the standard M1 105mm howitzer, thus easing the logistics and maintenance requirements), and a mechanized cavalry reconnaissance troop with M8 armored cars and M5 light tanks. These units were controlled by three "combat command" headquarters, each of which could be (and frequently were) tailored for the mission at hand. Additionally, an armored combat engineer company was usually attached to each combat command to facilitate mobility; these troops were also carried into combat in armored halftracks. Clearly, this organization, marked by complete mobility and armored protection for all combat units, surpassed anything established by the German army during the Second World War.

Simplicity—of command, supply, and maneuver—was characteristic of American organization for combat in 1944. Units were identically organized and equipped to achieve a considerably greater capacity for combined arms warfare than their German counterparts. In addition, the cohesion inculcated by the American system of regimental combat teams in infantry divisions and combat commands in armored divisions far exceeded that of opposing German formations.

## US Army Training

Unlike the Germans, whose training system changed according to a considerable dynamic during the course of the war, the US system was largely fixed in 1941 with the introduction of the Mobilization Training Plan (MTP) by Army General Headquarters (GHQ). Although the quantity and number of types of divisions to be created diminished as the war progressed, the basic plan for the activation, training, and deployment of divisions remained unchanged throughout the war.

The MTP called for the activation of infantry divisions from three sources: the Regular Army divisions, already in existence at the outset of the war; the National Guard divisions, which consisted of reservists who trained for about thirty-nine days per year until mobilization; and the "new," or Army of the United States (AUS) and Organized Reserves (OR) infantry divisions, the soldiers of which were activated, trained, and deployed together according to a uniform plan.

Starting with the mobilization of 1940, the Regular Army and National Guard divisions participated in a series of exercises designed for the large-scale testing of doctrinal techniques and organizations that had been previously impossible under the fiscal constraints of the Depression-era American economy. By the time of deployment to combat theaters, these divisions had trained together for the better part of at least two, if not three or more years. Although numerous officers and noncommissioned officers (NCOs) were removed to serve as cadre in the AUS and OR divisions in mid-1942, the cohesion thus imparted was considerable.

Beginning in the middle of 1942, GHQ implemented the MTP to build an army that eventually included 89 divisions, of which 39 were

AUS or OR infantry divisions built according to the standard plan. This plan included a process by which recruits were brought to a training post and were subsequently trained in basic and advanced individual techniques for 17 weeks by a cadre of 1,500 experienced regulars. These regulars had themselves already served together for up to two months previously in various higher-level schools designed to prepare them for their upcoming assignment. The regulars in the training cadre then became the higher-level chain of command upon completion of individual training. By the time that a division embarked on its phases of unit training, the soldiers had already served together for more than four months, and been reduced in number as a result of training attrition by about 20 percent. By this process, the mentally and physically unfit or injured were reassigned or discharged prior to the commencement of unit training.

Unit training through the regimental level was conducted at the activation post for thirteen weeks. During this time, platoon, company, and battalion teams were built in both dry-fire and live-fire training exercises. This phase was followed by 14 weeks of combined arms exercises, in which each division was deployed as part of a corps to a maneuver area away from the activation post. As a result, this training was conducted solely in the field, with the goal of mentally and physically acclimating the men to protracted operations in a field environment.

Following the combined arms phase, during which regimental combat teams were formed and thoroughly tactically drilled in the field, there followed a movement to a garrison (usually a different one than had been used for activation and earlier training phases) for eight weeks' training in coordinated air, mechanized, and antimechanized warfare techniques. Upon the completion of this 52-week training program, the division was available for deployment to a combat theater. Eleven of the sixteen armored divisions ultimately created by the Americans during the war followed a similar training scheme, tailored appropriately for their different needs.

While the American system for creating and training divisions was effectively organized and systematically carried out, the problem of providing replacements to units already in combat caused significant turbulence for numerous divisions prior to deployment. Various replacement training centers had been established by branch (infantry at Fort Benning, Georgia; field artillery at Fort Sill, Oklahoma, and so on) for the provision of individual replacements for units that were sustaining casualties in combat. These centers never provided sufficient quantities of troops for the adequate replenishment of manpower to committed formations. Two factors influenced the decision to strip units already in various phases of training of certain percentages of their personnel rather than to increase the output of the replacement training centers. First, commanders in the field overwhelmingly preferred replacements who had been trained as part of a division. Such soldiers already understood the importance of teamwork and were generally more highly motivated. Second, replacements to units already in combat clearly needed to know the basic skills associated with their assignment (as an infantryman, artilleryman, and so on), whereas units still in training would have some time left to incorporate replacements who required additional training.

As a result of this reasoning, soldiers (mostly privates; commanders generally preferred to promote NCOs from within their own organizations) who had been with a division since activation were sometimes pulled out and sent to units already in combat. They were often replaced by reclassified soldiers who had previously been trained to be technicians or specialists of some sort under the Army Specialized Training Program (ASTP), by former USAAF trainees, or by soldiers who had originally been trained as antiaircraft gunners. (Army estimates regarding the number of soldiers needed for these programs had been much too high.) The Supplemental Training Period was thus added to the divisional MTP in recognition of the need to integrate these troops into the division's combat echelons. Divisions usually created Provisional Training Battalions to teach basic combat skills to these newly-arrived troops. After several weeks of such individual training, these replacements would be sent to the units with which they would deploy for integration into the fighting team. While some of the late-deploying divisions (those which sailed for Europe in December 1944 or later) did not have the advantage of this Supplemental Training Period, those which deployed prior to that did, and were thus much more cohesive, combat-ready units for it.

## Summary of US Army Doctrine, Organization, and Training by Late 1944

American tactical and operational doctrine closely resembled that of the Germans in its essentials by late 1944. As such, it adhered closely to those Clausewitzian precepts that were still valid. It stressed the importance of combined arms operations in both the attack and in the defense, and made considerable demands for initiative and good judgment on the part of its soldiers.

Unlike the Germans, however, whose organization for combat sometimes failed to accurately reflect the needs of tactical and operational doctrine, the Americans' organization was admirably suited to the task. By uniformly organizing and equipping their units and by the institution of carefully-tailored regimental combat teams in their infantry divisions and combat commands in their armored divisions, the Americans ensured flexibility and cohesion in the execution of their doctrine.

While American unit training was not ideally conducted due to the need for replacements for units already in combat, it nevertheless basically satisfied the requirements of cohesion and bonding by ensuring that most of the soldiers in combat formations had served and trained together for a considerable amount of time prior to deployment to a combat theater. In marked contrast to the German practice by mid-1944, the Americans integrated replacements from other branches and specialties into their new units, rather than create them wholesale, in short periods of time, from personnel originally trained for duty other than ground combat. During lulls in the action, US units conducted training designed to sharpen combat skills and to fully integrate replacements for men lost in combat.

Of course, strategic considerations dictated many of the differences in organization and training of the respective foes' armies by mid-1944. The *Wehrmacht* had been at war for five years (by its leaders' own choice). This meant that many of its leaders were highly seasoned, but also that many of its best men were gone. A huge percentage of the Germans' manpower were foreigners of questionable motivation, quasi-Germans, or men not accustomed to or well prepared for the rigors of infantry combat. On the other side, very few of the American soldiers who went to war through Normandy or southern France in 1944 had been in combat before, so they were generally green, but fairly fresh. It should be remembered, however, that both nations were conducting multi-front, coalition warfare, and that their strategic situations were mostly of their own making. Nevertheless, the fact is that by mid-1944, American doctrine was more clearly reflected in the organization of its troops for combat, and US soldiers were far better trained, collectively and individually, than most of their *Wehrmacht* counterparts.

This superior preparation stood the Americans in good stead to defeat the Germans even under conditions of numerical parity or logistical inferiority. While the USAAF and RAF shot the *Luftwaffe* out of the sky and wreaked havoc with German ground transportation systems, according to Albert Speer, German munitions and weapons production actually peaked in very late 1944/early 1945. Meaningful shortages of ammunition and fuel really did not affect German tactics until late in the war, while the Allies had enormous headaches with logistical support due to the very limited port facilities available to them until the late autumn of 1944. While there were certainly instances of lavishly supported US Army units overwhelming outnumbered German ones, until early 1945, there were also many instances of the battlefield odds being even. Overall, better training and better organization for the conduct of what was, after all, very similar tactical doctrine resulted in American superiority in the conduct of mobile, combined arms tactics—and that truly made the difference in World War II in the west in mid- to late-1944.

# Battles

## Best Example of the Viability of Maneuver in World War I: Tannenberg, 26–31 August 1914

The Battle of Tannenberg 1914 was part of the first clash of arms between the Germans and the Russians in World War I. The battle did not produce the far-ranging results of 1410, but it was a nice tactical victory just the same. The first battle of Tannenberg, referred to as the Battle of Grünwald by the Slavs, was part of the previous Great War of 1409–11. On that occasion, the Knights of a Teutonic monastic military Order, along with some Swiss and English mercenaries, were defeated by an army of Poles, Lithuanians, Czechs, Bohemians, and some Tartars and Russians. The Slavs fought to prevent the eastward expansion of the Order and this they accomplished in a victory so punishing that over 50 of the 60 senior leaders of the Order were killed along with 18,000 others, 14,000 were captured, and about 1,400 escaped. Slav losses totalled about 13,000 out of an army of 50,000. The defeat of the Russians in 1914 was seen as revenge for the loss in 1410. It was certainly seen as such by the German commander, von Hindenburg, and millions of other Germans.

Interestingly, the initial moves in August of the Germans on both fronts resulted in envelopments. In the west, the Germans executed the revised Schlieffen Plan which called for the right wing of their army to sweep through Belgium and France and drive west of Paris. In the east, the German army was to remain more or less on the defensive strategically but take advantage of opportunities. The German 8th Army under the command of General Max von Prittwitz und Gaffron protected East Prussia and it was opposed by the Russian Northwest Army Group under the command of General Yakov Grigorievich Zhilinski. The Russian Northwest Army Group was made up of the First Army under

General Pavel K. Rennenkampf and the Second Army under Alexander Samsonov. The Russian plan was to advance on two lines into Prussia; First Army would drive west from the Nieman River and the Second Army would advance northwest from the Narew River. The two armies were separated by the Masurian Lakes, swamps and forest, a distance of over fifty miles. The German 8th Army was based at the fortress of Königsberg on the Baltic, but spread out south from there to Frankenau some 90 miles away. In the south, 20th Corps covered the area around Tannenberg while in the north, 1st Corps, 17th Corps, 1st Reserve Corps, 1st Cavalry Division, and 3rd Reserve Division protected the *Reich*.

As always, geography dictated what the armies could do. The Masurian Lakes presented a very difficult obstacle and while the Germans had a score of rail lines they could use in Prussia, the Russians had only three running into Prussia. In the north, one railroad line ran from Vilna due east to Königsberg; a second line ran northwest from Bialystok through the center of the Masurian Lakes area to Rastenburg and then on to Königsberg; and the third line ran from Warsaw northwest to West Prussia. Moreover, the road network on the Russian side of the frontier was not as well developed as on the German side. This was not simply the result of Russian inefficiency, but was in part a security decision; it made any German advance into Russia more difficult. Thus, the Germans would have the advantage of interior lines, road, and rail for shifting their forces.

In this campaign, the commanders on both sides committed serious errors of omission and commission. There were prickly personalities, old grudges, faint hearts, lily-white livers, and weak knees on display. When all this is added into the usual mix of incompetence, friction, luck (good and bad), deception, desire, and the drastic consequences which attend many military operations, the reader may be amazed at why this battle achieved such prominence.

On 17 August, Zhilinski ordered his two army commanders to advance into Prussia. The Russians took 3,000 casualties at the ensuing battle of Stallupönen and fell back to the border; François then pulled back to Gumbinnen. These Russian armies were 15 days into their mobilization and far from ready, but Zhilinski had promised long ago that his armies would move on M+15. In the north, elements of Rennenkampf's Second Army met General Hermann von François's I Corps. Is it just the author or does the reader also think it ironical that the Russian general has a German name and the German general a French name? There are reasons for all this, of course—the Baltic Germans had long been in service to the tsars—but why go into this now?

Oh well, that is nothing, the Germans also had a general with a Scottish name—Mackensen. On 20 August, the battle of Gumbinnen, again involving François's 1st Corps, ended in a draw.

Meanwhile in the south, Samsonov's Second Army was still not doing much, but Prittwitz feared that the Russians might get onto his rear and threaten his communications. He was overreacting to Rennenkampf's advance and Samsonov's threat and he telephoned the Chief of the German General Staff, General von Moltke (the younger) and told him that the Russians were coming, so he was going to withdraw behind the Vistula River, thereby ceding most of East Prussia and, oh yeah, he needed more men. Now we should state at this point that the German 8th Army was outnumbered in divisions 9 to 22 and in men 173,000 to 485,000, but things at this point were far from hopeless. Moltke was deep into the battle of France and did not really want to hear this kind of complaint. He decided that Prittwitz had to be relieved and he ordered General Paul von Hindenburg, 67, out of the pub—in which he was passing his retirement—to go east, old man. General Erich Ludendorff, the hero of Liege, was picked to replace Prittwitz's chief of staff, Waldersee. Ludendorff began to formulate a plan to deal with the situation, he telephoned orders to the 8th Army Corps commanders, and when he met up with Hindenburg, he told him that he had given orders to mass against Samsonov in the south and hold against Rennenkampf in the north. Hindenburg approved.

They were not the only ones thinking, however. Lieutenant-Colonel Max Hoffmann, Prittwitz's chief of operations, and as capable a man as the Germans had, also came up with a plan. He realized that as the two Russian armies were so far apart, it would be possible to hold the Russian Second Army in the south with 20th Corps and move 1st, 17th, and 1st Reserve Corps by road and rail to surround and destroy Samsonov's army. All that would be left in the north would be the 1st Cavalry Division to oppose Rennenkampf. Prittwitz had regained some color in his liver by the evening of 21 August, and agreed to the plan. It was, however, too late for him to redeem himself in Moltke's eyes.

When Hindenburg and Ludendorff showed up to take command, they learned that Hoffmann had already put his own plan, which was similar, in motion. It was now clear to Prittwitz, Hoffmann, Hindenburg, Ludendorff, and others that things were not so bad in the east. Now why did they think so? Because they knew what the Russians were doing. Russian operational security was dreadful, so even German security could be bad and still have the advantage. In this war, radio and telephone came to the fore as communications devices to supplement and even supplant telegraph in some applications. Much has been made of the Russians sending some wireless messages in the clear rather than coding them, but the Germans did the same. When speed and accuracy were deemed essential, the commanders gambled that the message might not be intercepted or if it was intercepted, its utility might not be readily recognized or seized upon. Neither's codes were sophisticated, but the reader must remember that the armies were not yet set up for massive signals intelligence operations. Be that as it may, this was the first battle in history in which signals interception proved decisive. Thus, at the dawn of the use of radio and signals intelligence, interception was to prove its most decisive.

On the evening of 23 August, the German commanders had finished the arrangements for the encirclement of the Samsonov's Second Army. The plan was to allow Samsonov to come northwest with his army while the German 20th Corps blocked them and retreated if necessary. Meanwhile, the rest of the 8th Army was on the move. First Corps (François), opposite Rennenkampf in the north, was withdrawn and moved by rail to a position west and south of Second Army. Similarly, 17th (Mackensen) and 1st Reserve Corps marched south and west to arrive east of Russian Second Army. Now as Second Army advanced, the Germans were in position for a classic double envelopment of the flanks; another Cannae. In the end, that is almost how it happened. The battle commenced on 26 August and lasted until 30 August. In the battle, the Germans were superior in infantry by some 23 battalions (155 versus 132), in field artillery (690 pieces versus 608), and in heavy artillery (128 versus 12). The Germans destroyed two corps (XIII and XV) to the tune of only 50 officers and 2,000 men escaping. Sixth Corps was reduced to a division, say under 14,000 men, XXIII Corps to 3,000. The Germans claimed to have captured over 120,000 prisoners—95,000 of whom were unwounded—and 500 guns. Other sources give 92,000 as the total number of prisoners and 50,000 dead. German losses are placed at 10,000 to 15,000.

The Germans were confident of success and here, in part, is why. Intercepts on the morning of 24 August had alerted 8th Army that the Russian XIII Corps (part of Second Army) was ordered to outflank to the west the German 20th Corps that was opposing the Russians in the south. With this foreknowledge, the Germans were able to thwart this attack and maintain their positions. More was to come. On the evening of 24 August, German radio operators intercepted a plaintext message sent from General Rennenkampf to IV Corps. It contained a complete operational order that stated the speed of First Army's advance in the north and the lines it was to reach for the following days. From this message, Hindenburg learned that he would have all the time he needed in the north, thus a lone cavalry division was given the task of screening Rennenkampf's army. Hindenburg then proceeded to visit his subordinate, General François of 1st Corps. On the way, he received another intercept; this one, also in plaintext, gave the order of battle and movements of the Russian Second Army. This message was also sent to XIII Corps. Each day from 25 to 30 August, more radio intercepts chronicled the Second Russian Army's movements, objectives, and schedule.

Why were such important messages sent in plaintext? Wilhelm Flicke in his *War Secrets in the Ether* theorized that the Russian XIII and IV Corps lacked the cipher keys necessary to decrypt their communications; thus, there was no other option than sending radio messages in clear. Why not use the telephone or telegraph, you ask? Ah, that leads us to another failure for the Russians. Simply put, they did not have enough cable and that forced them to use the radio. Attached to Samsonov's Second Army was an independent telegraph company; repair troops; 25 telephones and operators; two field radio stations; and 80 miles of cable. It was thought that the existing government lines would be enough to maintain effective communications. The lines from Army to Corps were the corps' responsibility and each was given 50 miles of cable with which to connect to the government stations as need be. This usually left nothing for the Corps to connect to its Divisions; messages had to be messengered. The Russian inability to provide adequate field communications was to prove telling. Samsonov, when he moved up with his Field Headquarters on 28 August in an attempt to better direct the battle did no less than cut himself off from his own communications and so from most of his army. Later, on 29 August, as he tried to make his way from one Corps HQ to another, Samsonov saw the sad results of the battle. Shattered men and equipment jammed the roads and there was nothing he could do. Eventually, he and his staff tried to evade the Germans on foot. The asthmatic Samsonov was not up to it physically or emotionally. By nightfall they were cut off and wandering in the woods. No wonder with the full weight of his defeat realized that he walked off alone and shot himself.

Before leaving this section, another first should also be pointed out. In the follow-up Battle of the Masurian Lakes, wherein the Germans turned against Rennenkampf's First Army, the Germans purposely transmitted misleading and garbled plain-text radio transmissions to mislead the Russians about the strength and direction of German reinforcements. The Russians were enticed, thereby, to hold large reserves north and east of Königsberg.

As we have come to expect, mistakes, some serious, were made by both sides in this battle, but the Germans had superior organization, communication, and, ultimately, information. The commander of the Northwest Front, Zhilinski, did little to coordinate his two army commanders, Rennenkampf and Samsonov. These two army commanders could not communicate directly, which was not desirable even though each maintained a high level of personal animosity for the other. Rot at the top, inefficient supplies, and poor troop management doomed the Russians, and although there are numerous examples of the Russians fighting well and smartly, they could not overcome the immense limitations and inadequacies of their organization.

Tannenberg was the greatest defeat any army suffered in the war. Uniquely, Tannenberg was the lone major battle in Europe which was resolved by maneuver.

# Best Example of Slaughter in the Trenches . . . and the Worst Day Ever for the British Army:
The Somme, 1 July 1916

### Background

In 1916, the German High Command was led still by Erich von Falkenhayn, a favorite of the Kaiser. Falkenhayn had been made a general and Minister of War in 1913, and in November 1914, he had replaced von Moltke and added chief of the general staff to his resume. In 1915, the Germans went on the offensive in the east and achieved much success, but they did not drive Russia out of the war. For 1916, Falkenhayn decided to push for a decision in the west and to that end, he thought that if he engaged the French in a battle of attrition, then he could break French morale and either win the war or compel France to sue separately for peace.

The site chosen for the latest episode of meat-grinder was Verdun and the killing started on 21 February. The Entente powers (France, Russia, and Great Britain), or if the reader prefers, the allies, decided to coordinate their offensives for 1916 and launch them in the early summer. Falkenhayn, however, upset their timetables when he struck in February. In a series of attacks, the Germans made some progress, but did not break through. The French held in this contest of national will in which the German's used phosgene gas for the first time in war. The French rotated their units regularly through Verdun and by the end of the campaign, most of the battalions of the army had fought at Verdun. As scheduled, and in order to ease the pressure on the French, the Russians launched the Brusilov Offensive (4 June) in the east and the British attacked in the Somme. These attacks stripped off German troops from Verdun and by late summer, the Germans were no longer on the offensive. Falkenhayn was relieved of command on 29 August and replaced by von Hindenburg and Ludendorff. In the autumn, the French went on the offensive and by mid-December, the Verdun campaign was at an end. The French had sustained about 542,000 casualties and the Germans about 434,000.

## *The Battle*

The area of the Somme is south of Flanders and has a river of the same name. The British attack would be led by the Fourth Army under General Henry Rawlinson—which would carry the bulk of the assault—and a corps of the Third Army under General Edmund Allenby. The infantry attacks on 1 July, Dominion Day for the Canadians, were preceded by a week-long artillery bombardment during which some 1,738,000 shells (some historians say 1,500,000) weighing 21,000 tons were fired. The fire plan was to obliterate the barbed-wire, machine-gun emplacements; to collapse the trenches and dug outs in the first two German lines and whatever else was in between; and to suppress the German artillery way in the back. This was to be done along a 15-mile front and to a depth of 2,000 yards. Some 1,437 guns of various calibers were assigned to the task, one gun every 18 yards. This battle would also introduce the rolling barrage to warfare, whereby the infantry would advance behind a curtain of fire which was timed to move from objective to objective in 500-yard jumps.

The shelling lasted until about 7:30 on the morning of 1 July, then some 120,000 men from 14 British divisions started across. The distances they had to cover varied from a couple of hundred yards to over 800 yards. Some men already lay dead from German artillery fire which fell on their assembly areas. By the time the day's fighting ended, and for most that meant early afternoon, just over 19,000 men were dead, 38,470 were wounded, missing, or taken prisoner; the casualties totalled 57,470 and most of them came in the first minutes of the attack. Few of the objectives were reached and fewer were held. Three miles of the British right had advanced its front one mile; the left had barely advanced. The Germans had sustained only 8,000 casualties. What had gone wrong? Had anything gone right?

Where to begin? Let us start with the artillery bombardment. Two-thirds of the shells fired were shrapnel and one-third high-explosive. Why so much shrapnel, which is an anti-personnel weapon, and so little high-explosive? The destruction of the enemy trenches, strong points and dugouts, some of which were cut thirty feet deep into the chalk of the region, could only be accomplished with high-caliber high-explosives. The British factories, however, were not turning out enough high-explosive shells, so shrapnel was used. The shrapnel shells the factories were producing, moreover, contained a goodly proportion of duds, between one-quarter and one-third, and the high-explosive was also plagued. Thus, while shrapnel could cut wire effectively, it had to be targeted and fused precisely and then it had to go off. British industry was not quite up to the task as yet and ditto a good number of the artillerymen. The result was that on the day the infantry went forward (Z-day), the wire was still a great impediment to progress.

The statistics above and some simple arithmetic by the author yields the following understanding of the bombardment, if we average things out. Each ton of shells was spread over 2,380 square yards or roughly one pound per square yard. Another way to look at it is that each 100 square yards received three shells if we use the figure of 1,500,000, or just under three and one-half shells per 100 square yards if we use the higher figure. John Keegan in *The Face of Battle*, who provides many of our statistics, tells us that of large-caliber guns firing high-explosive shells, the British had only six 15-inch howitzers. Each 1,400-pound shell contained 200 pounds of explosive. The lightest artillery piece used in the bombardment was the 4.5-inch field howitzer which fired a 35-pound shell with less than five pounds of explosive. Keegan works it out that each square mile received 30 tons of high-explosive over days and contrasts that to Normandy in 1944 when the Allies put down 800 tons per square mile in minutes. All this is by way of demonstrating that the artillery preparation was inadequate to the task.

When the soldiers started across No-Man's Land at zero hour they were also heavily laden with 60 pounds of equipment. Half the troops involved were newly trained and thus inexperienced. The men moved in waves rather than in small groups by rushes with covering fire as it was thought by their staff officers that they did not yet have the capacity for fire and movement. Thus, each man in each company of 250 men lined up two to three yards from the next man. Each company formed a line 150 yards behind the one in front and these thousand men (one battalion) arrayed in four lines represented the first wave for this part of the front. Along the front, 60 battalions formed the first wave. Immediately, they came under concentrated artillery, machine-gun, and rifle fire and fell in rows. The German guns had not been suppressed; the machine gunners in their dugouts had not been obliterated; and the wire had, as often as not, been cut. The Germans were able to scamper out of their shelters and man their guns before the British were able to reach them. The result was catastrophic and none more so than the fate of the 801 men of the 1st Newfoundland Regiment. At 8:45 A.M., it was ordered to assault German positions some 650 to 900 yards away. The wire, some 250 yards away, was mostly uncut, so the attack was canalized by the few gaps there were, but these breaks were covered by German machine guns. Some of the men managed to reach and enter the German trench, but not many. By the time the attack was called off at 10:00 A.M., every officer in the regiment had been killed or wounded. Losses for 75 minutes of combat were 310 killed and 374 wounded or missing; a casualty rate of 85 percent. Only 68 men were not seriously injured.

The plight of all the wounded was horrific. So rapidly were men mutilated, maimed, and mauled; pounded, ripped, and torn that there was no possibility of evacuating them in a timely fashion. Each staging area for casualty treatment was overwhelmed. A battalion had only 32 stretcher bearers, which meant that they could move 16 men at a time, provided the stretcher bearers remained unwounded. On this day, it sometimes took up to an hour for the bearers to move one man to a dressing station. Thus, thousands of wounded died before they could be given aid; others lay for days in No Man's Land before they were reached. One man, Private A. Matthews of the 56th (London) Division, was shot in the thigh and sustained a compound fracture. He remained 14 days in No Man's Land in the unused trench into which he had been dragged by an officer. He survived by occasionally receiving food and water from other wounded soldiers who stumbled upon him. He was later partially buried by shell fire, but survived. Finally, he was rescued by a patrol from the London Scottish. His wound was not septic, but he took a year to recover. Even those wounded and in their own trenches were not safe. On 2 July, a rain storm flooded the area and the wounded who were unable to move drowned.

Overall casualties evened up greatly after the first day. By the end of August, however, the Germans were still ahead: the British had 190,000 in losses, the French 80,000, and the Germans 200,000. By the time the Somme battles ended on 14 November 1916, the British had lost 419,654 men, the French 194,451 men and the Germans 450,000 to 500,000.

## Most Decisive Battles of World War II:
Moscow, 1941; Stalingrad, 1942; Kursk, 1943

Let us examine the events in sequence. In 1941, Italy looses an army in Cyrenaica (Libya), and then the Afrika Korps comes in. Then the Germans invade Russia. Then the Germans and Italians lose another army each in Tunisia. Then the Germans and Italians each lose another army at Stalingrad. Then the Allies invade Sicily in July 1943 and the Italian people were asking, "which way is the exit?" Meanwhile Germany throws away more men and armor at Kursk. Then the Allies invade Southern Italy in September 1943 and the Italians say, "that is enough for us." But how did all this happen in the east?

Here is how it goes. The Germans attacked the largest army in the world in the summer of 1941 in Operation BARBAROSSA. In attacking and failing to knock the Soviets out of the war before the winter of 1941 ended, Hitler guaranteed that the Nazis would not win the war. Then, in losing the Sixth Army at Stalingrad in early 1943 along with the armies of their allies, Romania, and Italy, Hitler guaranteed that the Germans would lose the war.

The Eastern Front was the decisive front of the war. It tied up the bulk of the German army for four years and gave the Americans the time they needed (two and one-half years) to create their magnificent war machine. By attacking Russia, Hitler committed the greatest strategic blunder of the war; the Japanese attack on Pearl Harbor is second. Here is why: The guy who started the war would now not win it. The Japanese brought the US into the war, but the author is of the opinion that the Americans would have come into the war against Germany eventually, regardless of Japanese actions. As an undergraduate, the author had the honor of studying with Charles P. Stacey, the official historian of the Canadian army in the Second World War. Stacey, who was overseas for five years, told us that when Germany attacked Russia, he was relieved because it meant that we would not lose the war; and when Japan attacked the United States, he knew that we would win the war. To this the author adds that the "when" and "how" of how we won was determined for the most part on the Russian Front.

The scale of this conflict is greater than colossal: the number of divisions involved, men, materiel, atrocities, you name it. Imagine if Germany did not have over 230 divisions in Russia, just how were the Allies going to fight their way onto the continent at Normandy?

For the Operation BARBAROSSA invasion, the Germans massed some 162 divisions and three-quarters of a million men; the Soviets had 152 divisions and 1 million men. The Germans believed that if they could destroy the frontier forces of the Red Army, then the Soviets may not be able to stop the *Wehrmacht* before it reached Moscow. Assisting the Germans was Stalin who kept the best of the Red Army near the border and then gave orders keeping them there when they wanted to retreat. Nor should we overlook the contribution of the NKVD (state security forces), who roamed behind the battle zone killing their own soldiers who had become separated from their units. So not only had Stalin greatly compromised the Red Army's effectiveness with the Purges, but he helped the Germans capture some of the best of what was left of the officer corps. Stalin was not the only politician being true to himself, however; Hitler was still Hitler.

Hitler pushed an attack that the best logisticians of the German army knew could not succeed. He diverted large forces during the attack, which hindered the drive on Moscow. He issued orders to treat the subject peoples of the Soviet Union as enemies, thereby guaranteeing that they would fight the Germans rather than join them. And let us not forget that Hitler had seen to it that German industry was still not rationalized for war; civilian goods were still being produced. What ultimately did in the Germans was that there was no clear object for the campaign. Was it to be Moscow? That is what the General Staff wanted. Was it to be the Ukraine and Caucasus? That is what Hitler wanted. And what about Leningrad and Stalingrad? In the end, the Germans tried to do it all, and they did not have the resources. What would Clausewitz have said?

As most readers know, the Germans bagged hundreds of thousands of Russian soldiers in this campaign, but they did not knock the Soviets out of the war. Besides the mistakes committed by Stalin and Hitler was the famed Russian winter, and this one was one of the coldest ever. First, the autumn rains turned the roads and fields to heavy mud, and then the winter cold froze men and vehicles solid. The Russians, moreover, proved themselves more resilient than the Germans thought they would be and the Nazis obviously forgot that the Russian soldier can— and historically has—withstood more hardship and stupidity than any other soldier in the world. Those soldiers who did fight, fought bravely. On 6 December 1941, when the Russians counterattacked and stabilized the front, the Germans had managed to get within 25 miles of the Kremlin.

Hitler decided that for 1942, the army would strike for the Caucasus and the oil fields and push the assault on Leningrad. Hitler came to believe that the fate of the Caucasus would be decided in Stalingrad. During the summer offensive, he diverted some forces from the Caucasus operation to capture Stalingrad, thus weakening both operations. The drive to the Caspian would fail and the battle for Stalingrad would suck in more and more troops, becoming the meatgrinder of the Eastern Front. From August to the end of January 1943, thousands of men were abraded, erased, pulverized, and shredded. The Red Army counterattacked in late November and surrounded the German Sixth Army in Stalingrad. Besides trapping Germans, the Russians also destroyed the Italian, Hungarian, and Romanian forces supporting the flanks. The

Soviets knew that every Hungarian and Romanian soldier that they killed in Russia was one less to oppose them their own countries later. Clausewitz would have approved.

The Germans lost about 300,000 men in this campaign, losses they could never make up. This was one of the greatest battles of the war and one of the greatest victories for Russian arms. This success, coming just after the British victory at El Alamein in November 1942, boosted morale terrifically for the Allies.

The Germans were saved by Manstein, whose fabled mobile defense with Army Group Don (February–March 1943) managed, at great odds (up to 7 to 1), to beat back the Russian offensive. Both sides spent the spring building up their forces. Stalin wished to renew the offensive, but the Soviet High Command convinced him that the smarter thing to do was to absorb whatever German attack came and then strike back once the Nazi offensive power was blunted.

The Russian salient at Kursk was the most likely candidate for reduction and this was confirmed through Soviet intelligence. General Georgi Zhukov, the commanding general of the Soviet forces, tells us that the Red Army built up formidable defenses in three lines to a depth of over 150 kilometers and waited, for what it knew was coming. Although the reduction of the salient was seen as a limited operation by the Germans, it was going to be carried out by massive forces—50 divisions, 2,700 tanks, 2,600 aircraft—and still the Germans would not have enough. The Russians gathered over 1,500,000 men, over 3,200 tanks, 2,600 aircraft, and laid 3,200 mines for every 1,000 meters of front. The Soviets were prepared to throw back the German assault and then go on the offensive.

The battle began on the morning of 5 July 1943 with a pre-emptive Soviet artillery attack of German assembly areas. The Germans attacked the salient at two points, from the north and from the south against the respective shoulders of the bulge. The north attack managed to gain 12 kilometers by 12 July and the south attack penetrated 35 kilometers before being stopped. The south attack is well-known for it culminated in the biggest tank battle in history.

On Monday 12 July at Prokhorovka, about 900 German tanks—100 of which were Mark VI Tigers—encountered about 900 Soviet tanks. For 18 hours, most of these steel monsters plus self-propelled guns, other vehicles, and infantry battered one another within an area of twelve square miles. The terrain was far from ideal for armored combat—the land between the rail junction at Prokhorovka and Psel River was rolling countryside cut with ravines, and thickets of trees. The day was overcast with occasional rain.

Much of the fighting was in close as T-34s from the Fifth Guards Tank Army charged into the deploying German tanks in order to take away the latter's advantages in armor protection and firepower. Tanks were holed at point-blank range; turrets were blown a hundred feet from their hulls; and acrid black smoke and flame covered the battlefield. Overhead, the air forces fought an equally fierce struggle, in ground attack and air-to-air combat. The fighting stopped late at night. Across the battlefield was the detritus of wrecked war machines and shattered men. The Germans lost 350–400 tanks, 88 guns, and 300 trucks. Seventy of the Tigers were junk. The Soviets lost at least 450 tanks, but their line had held. This was the last great offensive the Germans would launch in the east; from now on they would be on the defensive as the Soviet High Command and the Red Army made war in a manner more sophisticated than most people realize. By the end of the Kursk battles, the manpower losses in the German units was substantial, regiments were the size of companies, and companies the size of platoons. After Kursk, the Germans had no chance to win the war.

So what was the most decisive battle on the Russian front? The author's view is this: the battle for Moscow was not decisive for the Germans because after it, they still had a chance to win. It follows then that the Russians still had a chance to lose. BARBAROSSA was a tremendous strategic error on the part of Hitler, but only because he was Hitler. If the Nazis had come as liberators and driven straight for Moscow, they could have pushed the Soviets out of European Russia and who knows what would have happened then? Would Stalin have accepted terms? Would he have fought on? The author is inclined to think that he would have fought on—given the American entry into the war and British success in North Africa—if had managed to hold on until then. However, Hitler was Hitler, and the Nazis were Nazis, so they turned potential Slavic allies into implacable enemies. The battle of Stalingrad cost the Germans more than they could replace and that has to be seen as decisive. What armored strength the Germans had left, they threw away at Kursk where the panzer divisions, the spear points of the *Wehrmacht*'s power, were ground down to blunt instruments. In fact, the panzer division itself was diluted in terms of tanks during the campaign. While the Germans created more panzer divisions, they did so by halving the number of tanks in them. It has been said that Stalingrad meant that the Germans would not win the war and that Kursk meant that they would lose it. To this the author adds the refinement that Kursk meant that the Germans would lose it sooner. In the way the war was fought on the Eastern Front, Stalingrad was *the* battle. Had the campaign been fought differently, Moscow could have been decisive.

## Cavalry's Last Charge: The Winner? It Depends

Rapid-fire gunpowder weapons spelled the end of cavalry, or did they? Here we can split hairs and produce quite a do. When was the last successful cavalry charge? When was the last cavalry-on-cavalry encounter? When was the last time horses were used in war? The last question is the easiest answered; turn on your television set and watch. In Afghanistan in 2003, the Northern Alliance is riding to take on the Taliban. Horses will always be used in areas where the terrain permits and the conditions are primitive, even when the armaments are sophisticated. Why? Because soldiers value mobility in war, they are sentimental about their horses, and you cannot eat a Humvee. Charging a tank or unbroken infantry from horseback is losing proposition and has been for over 100 years, but riding a horse in order to cover 60 miles during the night will always be of value. And it is in this role as a dragoon—who rides to the action and fights on foot—that the horse shall continue to be a feature in warfare. Otherwise, a soldier on a horse is just too big and too soft a target.

When was the last cavalry-on-cavalry action? The last one in western Europe came in 1870 during the Franco-Prussian War (1870–1871). As a point of interest, the *Official History of the War* by the German General Staff calls it the Franco-German War. Be that as it may, let us turn our attention to the events of 16 August 1870, a month and a day after the French declaration of war. In the fighting around Vionville, the French general Bazaine had an opportunity that he may not have appreciated. The German left wing north of Vionville was vulnerable. General Alvensleben was assured that help was on its way, but he feared that the French would fall on his left before his support arrived and it was already after noon. All he had over there was cavalry, and the dust clouds from the French lines indicated that the enemy might get there first. French artillery on that side was battering the German line; the reserve infantry had already been sent up and stopped. All that Alvensleben had in reserve was two divisions of cavalry. The unit closest was von Bredow's cavalry brigade, and he was ordered to attack the French guns. Cavalry charging artillery protected by infantry was usually a recipe for disaster but, Michael Howard tells us, von Bredow accepted his mission without complaint and set about preparing; by 2:00 P.M., his brigade was ready. The stage was set for what became known as von Bredow's death ride.

This is what von Bredow had to work with after part of his brigade, the 13th Dragoons, had been sent elsewhere: he had eight squadrons total, four in 7th Cuirassiers and four in the 16th Lancers. As his reduced brigade moved out, an officer from III Army Corps rode up with orders taking two squadrons for reconnaissance work elsewhere. Fine. Six squadrons it is. Von Bredow rode in column with the 7th Cuirassiers in the van and he had done his homework terrain-wise. North of Vionville is a depression, and along this he led his troopers unseen by the French. When he was a few hundred yards from the French gun-line, he wheeled right by squadron and formed into line as they approached the ridge of the heights. They crested the ridge and headed for the French in a sight unseen in 55 years. Major Count Schmettow led the 7th Cuirassiers on the left of the line and Major von der Dollen the 16th Lancers on the right. Covering them, at this point, was German artillery and rifle fire, the cavalry covered the open ground quickly and French line was ridden over. Once in amongst the gun-crews, the horsemen used sword and spear to dispatch their foe, so we are told in the *Official History*. The second French line is reached and ridden over and then the Germans see the guns on the heights limbering to take flight. They spur on and pursue for almost two miles when they are surrounded by French cavalry. Two brigades of Froton's Cavalry Division crash into the Germans. The 7th French Cuirassiers under Gramont strike the Prussian left flank and two squadrons of the 10th Cuirassiers attack the rear. Murat's brigade of the 1st and 9th Dragoons attacked the front of the Prussians. Also involved was the 4th and 5th Chasseurs and 7th and 12th Dragoons of Valabrègue's Cavalry Division. All told, less than 800 Prussians were now engaged in mêlée against 3,100 Frenchmen. Von Bredow ordered the recall sounded and the Prussians cut their way out. They rode back the way they had come, through the two French lines and pursued not by the French horse but by French bullets.

By the time the Prussians rallied at Flavigny, von Bredow had lost 16 officers, 363 men, and 409 horses. Major von der Dollen of the Lancers was captured when he was trapped beneath his dead horse. Captain Meyer was killed leading his squadron. The Prussians had succeeded, however, in stopping the advance of the French 6th Corps as General Bazaine called a halt. It was now 3:00 P.M.

World War I in Europe was a graveyard for cavalry and the commanding generals were the undertakers-in-chief. If one picks a year—any year—in the Great War, one will find a murderous futility in the employment of cavalry. John Ellis reports that the one nation which put the big "C" and big "F" in Cavalry Futility and dotted both "i"s was Austria. When the war started, it was discovered that their regulation saddle was unsuitable for war. While the regular horses had gotten used to the saddle over the years, the saddle rubbed the skin off the backs of the requisitioned horses. By the third week of August, the saddle and the heat had put half of the requisitioned horses out of action, he tells us.

In the four years of fighting, cavalry never gave up hope that the "G" would appear at a spot on the map. That was "G" as in *gap*, and if one was looking on a European map for it, one would never find it. The big gap never opened up on the Western Front—big surprise. The enemy sat behind a score of lines of wire, in reinforced entrenchments, in deep defensive positions.

If, however, one looked at a map of Palestine, then there were gaps galore and General Allenby made sure of it. He used cavalry to impart strategic mobility, but it often fought dismounted to give it more effectiveness tactically. Cavalry, for example, would reach the rear of an enemy position, dismount, and establish a line from which it could pour in fire. The bolt-action magazine rifle and the machine gun permitted a large amount of firepower to be laid down. Thus, the strategy was offensive, but the tactics were defensive. Nevertheless, there were some old-fashioned cavalry encounters and they will be detailed below.

On 31 October 1917 at the battle of Beersheba, cavalry showed it still had worth. Allenby attacked the town frontally with infantry and then sent the Mounted Desert Corps east of the city. At dusk, the Australian cavalry brigade charged the Turkish position. Leaping the wire and trenches, the Australians made it into the town and captured the water supply. Allenby then sent the Mounted Corps towards Gaza to the northwest in an attempt to cut off the Turkish Eighth Army, but the Turks moved quickly up the coast. The Turkish Seventh Army retreated towards Jerusalem. During November, the Turks, under the command of the German general von Falkenhayn, established a defensive line in the Judean Hills. Hard fighting pushed the Turks out of this position and on 9 December, Jerusalem fell to Allenby. For the first eight months of 1918, Allenby was limited in what he could take on because the crisis on the western front had taken two entire infantry divisions from him, the infantry of equivalent of two more, batteries of artillery, and machine-gun companies. When his replacements came, some were inferior troops in the sense that they were not trained to the same level. He received two good Indian Divisions from Mesopotamia, but the rest of the Indian troops were not trained up. Over the summer, however, they responded well to training. Two Indian Cavalry divisions were sent from France with the British regiment from each brigade replaced with Yeomanry. A very good French Cavalry regiment was sent and brigaded with the Australians. The Desert Mounted Corps now consisted of the 4th and 5th Cavalry Divisions, the Australian Mounted Division, the

Australian and the New Zealand Mounted Division (Anzacs). As summer came, Allenby planned the offensive by which the Turkish forces in Palestine would be defeated and cavalry would be given its last golden moment. It would all start in September.

General Allenby had 12,000 cavalry, 57,000 infantry, 540 artillery pieces, and the Turks as his opponents for this offensive. The plan was for the cavalry to line up on the left of the British line which was on the Mediterranean near Arsuf. The Desert Mounted Corps would launch three left hooks at the enemy's rear. The offensive began with the artillery opening up a gap in the Turkish positions along the sea coast. Through this "G," the Desert Mounted Corps poured with the 5th Cavalry Division on the extreme left executing the long hook aimed at Nazareth, the enemy GHQ. Next to them was the 4th Cavalry Division, the medium hook driving for Megiddo. To their right was the Australian Mounted Division, the short hook, which would head for Jenin and Sebustiye, south of Jenin. This would cut the rail line running north to south in three places and trap the Turkish Army. In the execution of this plan the cavalry would ride hard, but its commanders, as good horsemasters, would preserve their horseflesh to a remarkable degree. The cavalry would also fight hard, and in so doing, overrun, outmaneuver, and outwit the enemy. The cavalry would cover themselves in glory, but there would be few witnesses to Mars last gift to the horseman.

The 4th Cavalry Division began passing through the Musmus Pass on 19 September without opposition and moved to put itself behind the enemy. The 2nd Lancers exited the pass at 5:30 A.M. on 20 September and found a Turkish force blocking their way onto the Esdraelon Plain. The Lancers were under the command of Captain D. S. Davison because the commanding officer and the second-in-command were ill. He ordered the machine gunners and armored cars of one squadron to pin the enemy to the front while the reserve squadron maneuvered onto the enemy's flank. This was aided by the terrain—a depression—which protected the horsemen from fire. Watching this unfold was Davison's other squadron commander who, without orders, decided that he should attack the other side of the enemy formation. This was, of course, the right thing to do. The Turkish machine guns were not ready for a real fight and when the cavalry struck both lines of the Turkish position on the flanks, panic was not far behind. Cyril Falls, in his account of this action, tells us that 46 Turks were speared and 470 taken prisoner against the loss of one man wounded and 12 horses killed. In 34 hours, the 4th covered 70 miles, and foundered only 26 horses—how is that for mobility and know-how? Megiddo, by the way, is the same

Megiddo that our friend Thutmosis attacked some 3,387 years before and he, too, used the Musmus Pass.

The 5th Cavalry Division started off at 7:00 A.M. on 19 September along the coastal beach, and by pushing hard, covered a great deal of ground. Once they turned east, the terrain became rougher, which slowed the pace, and the leading regiment had had to kill several of its horses and leave others. By 3:00 A.M. on 20 September, elements of the brigade crossed the rail line which ran northwest from El Affule to Haifa on the coast. The engineers cut the line. Brigadier P. J. V. Kelly commanded the 13th Cavalry Brigade which reached Nazareth at about 4:30 A.M. He set the Gloucester Hussars in the van and they swept into the town looking for the German commander-in-chief, Liman von Sanders. They almost bagged him, too, but he got out just in time, dressed in his pajamas. There were a fair number of Germans in town as this was their GHQ and the fighting against the staff was intense, so Falls tells us. Kelly had been ordered to fight his way through the town or to cut the roads to the northeast and northwest beyond the town. Unfortunately for him, he did not have enough men because he had detached two squadrons to take a village and 200 Turks some four miles back. At 7:00 A.M., he sent a message for reinforcements, but was told at 11:00 that none could reach him. Accordingly, he was ordered to fall back to El Affule. Kelly was dismissed from his command for his error in judgment. Earlier, Brigadier Howard-Vyse of the 4th Cavalry Division had been dismissed for not finding the entrance to the Musmus Pass. Based upon his own covering of the terrain, Cyril Falls tells us that the southern entrance to the pass is not an easy thing to find in daylight let alone night. It was Howard-Vyse's job to find it, however, and his being late could have had serious repercussions.

From the Australian Mounted Division, our last example, is the 10th Australian Light Horse Regiment which was part of the 3rd Light Horse Brigade under Brigadier L. E. Wilson. They were sent to capture Jenin, which was about the mid-point of the Sebustiye to El Affule section of the north-south rail line. The commander of the 10th did not want to attack in darkness and as the day was getting on, he set the regiment to a gallop and covered 11 miles in 70 minutes, Falls reports. Furthermore, three miles from the town, a large body of the enemy, about 1,900 strong, was surprised by one squadron of the 10th and surrendered to a force one-fiftieth its size. At Jenin proper, the opposition was lighter than light and the town surrendered. Besides 3,000 prisoners, the new conquerors found a bullion wagon and 120 cases of German champagne.

There would be more success for the cavalry, but it should be stated that Allenby and his staff had crafted a plan that employed cavalry, infantry, and artillery in a magnificent harmony of a combined arms offensive. In two days, the Turkish Eighth Army had been defeated and the Seventh was in full retreat. Allenby chased his foe into Jordan and then Syria, taking Damascus on 1 October. On 30 October, Turkey signed an armistice. Note: the majority of Allenby's forces were Indian, not British; he had but one British division, the 54th Infantry.

Turkish casualties for the campaign: about 75,000 taken prisoner, of which about 4,000 were German and Austrian; 360 guns; and 89 locomotives. British casualties: 71 officers killed, 249 wounded, 3 missing; 782 from the ranks killed, 4,179 wounded, 382 missing. A total of 5,666. Losses from disease were higher for both sides as the medical staffs had to contend with the usual diseases of the area plus the Spanish Influenza.

Why was cavalry not eliminated from the order of battle of every army after the war? The usual reasons: hide bound-tradition and enough success somewhere. In this case it was Palestine.

In the Russian Civil War, cavalry was useful for moving bodies of soldiers over the vast territory, especially as much of the combat was more akin to large-scale raiding. The last of the cavalry-on-cavalry encounters was in the Russo-Polish War of 1920. Most of it was of the raiding variety, although the reportedly largest cavalry battle came at Zamosc, where brigade-sized units were involved. If one side was entrenched, however, then the cavalry was used only to turn the flanks, if possible.

The last cavalry charge of the American army was delivered by the 26th Cavalry Regiment (Philippine Scouts) and took place in 1942 at Morong in the Philippines. First, the big picture. General Douglas MacArthur was resolved to defend the Bataan peninsula and fight a delaying action down the peninsula against the Japanese troops under General Homma. Major-General Jonathan Wainwright's I Corps held the left of the line and Brigadier-General George M. Parker's II Corps held the right of the line. MacArthur was buying as much time as he could to build up the defenses and supplies in Bataan and Corregidor Island. The supply situation was precarious because the number of military and civilian personnel far exceeded the pre-war planning, and ample transport was not available to move what was there. The 26th Cavalry Regiment was actively involved in the defense of Luzon following the Japanese invasion. On 1 January 1942, after 11 days of fighting, there were only enough horses to mount three troops. The 26th was, on this day, attached to the 21st Philippine Division and assigned to patrol the extreme left flank of the American defensive line at Porac.

We now turn to Lieutenant Edwin Price Ramsey and 1st Platoon, Troop E, 26th Cavalry. Ramsey, who provides us with the details in his book, *Lieutenant Ramsey's War,* had been commanding Troop G, but he had made a fundamental mistake when his unit had been relieved after performing reconnaissance. Instead of going to the rear to rest, he offered to help Captain John Wheeler familiarize himself with the area. The maps Wheeler had were useless from the tactical standpoint. At noon, Wainwright came to the camp to tell General Fidel Segundo of the 1st Philippine Division that he should not have pulled back from Morong. The village offered a good defensive position on the Batolan River, the only one between the Americans and the Japanese. Wainwright wanted the village occupied pronto before the Japanese came across. At this point, he saw Ramsey and Wheeler. Wainwright remembered Ramsey because of the Lieutenant's participation in the big polo match at Fort Stotsenberg. He ordered Ramsey to take an advance guard up to Morong and secure the village until the 1st Philippine Division came up. Wheeler, to his credit, tried to have someone else lead the advance guard, but Wainwright told Ramsey to get moving.

And so Ramsey took the first platoon (27 men), Wheeler rode with the second, and the third platoon brought up the rear. Duly ordered by their commanding general, the troop mounted and head for Morong along a dusty, rutted, jungle path which was overgrown with underbrush. They rode up to the village about four miles away that appeared deserted; the huts on stilts and the animal pens beneath were empty. Ramsey tells us that he "deployed his platoon in column of squads of eight men each, and gave the command to raise pistols." The point riders entered the village. Just beyond it was a coconut grove, and a swamp and the sea was nearby. In the center of the village was a stone church. The rest of the platoon followed at a distance. As the point riders turned at the church, automatic-weapons fire crashed through the silence. The Japanese advance guard had just crossed the river and entered the village. Ramsey could now see the enemy in the center by the church and scores more wading the river and crossing the narrow bridge. He knew that he must act quickly to prevent the Japanese from establishing themselves in the village. Ramsey ordered his "troopers to deploy as foragers," he raised his pistol, and called for a charge. Here, in the middle of the twentieth century, Edwin Ramsey decided to resort to shock action to break the cohesion of the enemy. He did so because all of his training in the cavalry and his instinct told him that this was the only way to retrieve the situation. He deserves to have the next part of the story told in his own words:

> I brought my arm down and yelled to my men to charge. Bent nearly prone across the horses' necks, we flung ourselves at the Japanese advance, pistols firing full into their startled faces. A few

returned our fire, but most fled in confusion, some wading back into the river, others running madly for the swamps. To them we must have seemed a vision from another century, wild-eyed horses pounding headlong; cheering, whooping men firing from the saddles.

The charge broke clear through the advance unit and carried on to the swamp, where we dismounted and grabbed our rifles from the scabbards. I threw out a skirmish line of one squad along the river to keep the main column from crossing, and led the rest back into Morong to search for snipers. [Ramsey, *Lieutenant Ramsey's War*, 1990, p. 66.]

The fighting in the village was fierce as the Japanese poured fire in from the coconut grove and from the huts. The Japanese also began mortaring the village. Ramsey knew that he had to hold until Wheeler came up. His life was saved at one point by a horse frozen from fear, a mortar shell exploded in front of him but the animal took the brunt of the blast. Just after this, Wheeler came up with the other platoons; one went to the river and the other joined in the firefight for the huts. The fighting continued and the Japanese were forced across the river. Of those in the village, dozens were killed or wounded and captured. In the late afternoon, the 1st Philippine Division came up. Ramsey and Wheeler were both wounded, Ramsey's left knee had been punctured by shrapnel and Wheeler had been shot through the calf. Additionally, one of Ramsey's men had been killed and six wounded.

The cavalrymen were ordered to the rear to regroup and receive medical attention; most of them had to walk. The horses were temporarily abandoned because sniper fire near the river had made it too dangerous to retrieve them from where they had been tethered. Early the next morning, a fellow officer, Cliff Hardwick, who had not been in the battle, went up to retrieve the horses and was shot in the head by a sniper. His Filipino sergeant managed to get the horses. Not long after that, the animals were slaughtered for food.

Thus ended the last cavalry charge of the American army against an enemy. As an aside, the author offers the information that the last cavalry horse of the American army was named Chief. He was foaled in 1932 and entered the army in 1940 at a cost to the taxpayer of $183.00. He was retired in 1958 and was still alive in 1966.

The last successful charge of cavalry for the British came in 1953 in Kenya. John Ellis tells us, in his history of cavalry, that during the Mau Mau uprising, a unit of the North Tribal Police charged a guerrilla camp near Isolio and rode down the defenders.

The author takes this final opportunity to discuss, briefly, the most famous alleged cavalry action of the Second World War. Some historians have stated that Polish cavalry charged German tanks in September 1939. To them and to those non-historians who agree, the author says, "horse manure; it never happened; such musings are work of fiction."

## Best Example of the Superiority of American Combined Army Tactics: The Battle of Mortain, August 1944

The battle at Mortain in early August 1944 was the first major German attempt to mass combined arms formations in a counteroffensive against American forces in France. Since it occurred two months after the Allied landings, it is not a battle that is colored by the tremendous advantages initially owned by the Germans in Normandy, such as massive fortifications, numerical superiority, or the ideal defensive terrain of the Norman coastal hedgerow country. Also, because it occurred before the wholesale destruction of German forces in the Falaise Pocket, it is not a battle influenced by an overwhelming Allied advantage in combat power. Although only about 15 percent of the *Wehrmacht* consisted of mobile units with more than World War I-vintage horse-drawn artillery and foot-borne infantry, the German units committed at Mortain were all armored or mechanized, so even the materiel disadvantage at which the *Wehrmacht* usually operated was obviated. At Mortain, a variety of the very best divisions the German Army possessed engaged American units—largely from the National Guard—and utterly failed, due mostly to the superior execution of combined arms operations by the Americans. The American victory at Mortain helped set up the double envelopment of the German *7th Army* and elements of *5th Panzer Army* a few weeks later, a blow from which the German Army in the West never recovered.

The capture of the Pontaubault Bridge at Avranches by American forces on 31 July stunned the German High Command in France. Just when it appeared as if the *LXXXIV Corps* and *II Parachute Corps* had succeeded in escaping encirclement in the wake of the American breakout at St. Lô, loss of the critical Pontaubault Bridge meant that the southern flank of the entire *7th Army* was vulnerable to attack. The Americans, who also realized the advantage they gained by seizing Pontaubault intact, began pouring men and machines south through Avranches into Brittany. Caught at a severe operational disadvantage by the unexpected American advance, the Germans scrambled to assemble a blocking force under the command of *LXXXI Corps* to shield the southern flank of *7th Army*. Scattered elements of the *275th Infantry Division, 352nd Infantry Division, Panzer Lehr,* and *Sturmgeschütz (Assault Gun) Brigade 341* attempted to slow the unrelenting American advance. When it became obvious that *LXXXI Corps* would only be able to temporarily stem the worsening situation, Field Marshal Günther von Kluge, commanding general of German forces in France, decided on 2 August that a large-scale offensive effort designed to recapture the bridges at Avranches was needed to halt the American breakthrough.

Kluge choose to mount his planned counteroffensive from assembly areas located just to the east of the crossroads town of Mortain, which was currently unoccupied by American troops. The counterattack force, consisting of a reinforced panzer corps, would be assembled by *Waffen-SS Oberstgruppenführer* Paul Hausser, commanding general of the *7th Army*. Hausser designated *General der Panzertruppen* Hans von Funck's *XLVII Panzer Corps* as the tactical headquarters for the counterattack force. In addition to the *2nd Panzer Division* and *116th Panzer Division* already under von Funck's command, the *XLVII Panzer Corps* would be augmented with the *1st SS-Panzer Division, 2nd SS Panzer Division,* and elements of the *17th SS-Panzer-Grenadier Division*. The *2nd Panzer Division*, reinforced with Panther tanks from the *116th* and *1st SS-Panzer Division*, would initially penetrate the American defenses. The *1st SS Panzer Division* would follow in the wake of *2nd Panzer* to seize Avranches itself. The *116th Panzer Division* and *2nd SS-Panzer Division* were positioned to either flank with the mission of preventing American counterattacks against the main effort. *The 2nd SS-Panzer Division* was also tasked to capture the town of Mortain and the commanding heights to the east, designated as Hill 314, which dominated the *XLVII Panzer Corps* line of departure. The counteroffensive was slated to begin in the pre-dawn darkness of 6/7 August to avoid interference by Allied tactical aircraft. German planners calculated that the panzers would be able to punch through weak American resistance to reach their final objective of Avranches before daylight.

Unexpected changes to von Kluge's plan, however, occurred on almost a daily basis. Pressure on other parts of the front lines forced Hausser to divert artillery and self-propelled guns that were originally designated to support *XLVII Panzer Corps*. The most serious threat to the German plan came on August 4th, when Major General Clarence Huebner's 1st Infantry Division captured Mortain and seized Hill 314. In addition, VII Corps attached the 39th Infantry Regiment of the 9th Division to Huebner with the mission of attacking to the northeast to secure the town of Sourdeval. Unbeknownst to the Americans, the 39th

Infantry Regiment was heading straight into the middle of the assembly area for the German counteroffensive. To forestall premature discovery of his assembled forces, as well as the loss of crossroads town of Sourdeval, von Funck was forced to commit elements of the *2nd* and *116th Panzer Divisions* against the advancing Americans. Although *XLVII*

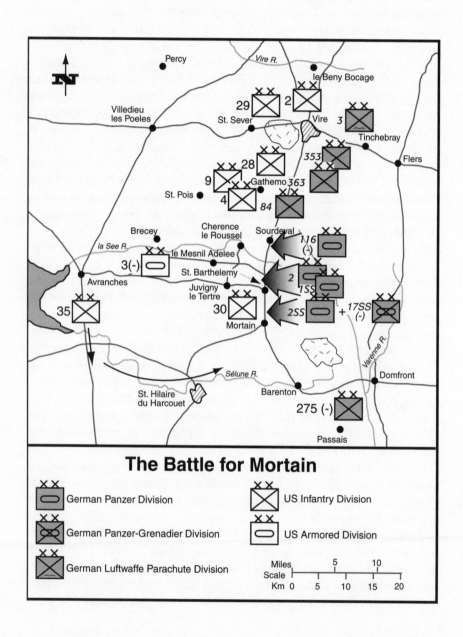

# The Battle for Mortain

German Panzer Division

German Panzer-Grenadier Division

German Luftwaffe Parachute Division

US Infantry Division

US Armored Division

Miles
Scale
Km   0      5      10     15     20

*Panzer Corps* succeeded in halting the 39th Infantry Regiment by 5 August, the Germans suffered significant losses to men and equipment they could ill afford.

On 6 August, First Army ordered the 30th Infantry Division to relieve the 1st Infantry Division at Mortain. Huebner's command, which included Combat Command B of the 3rd Armored Division as well as several attached tank and tank destroyer battalions, would move south to Ambriers le Grand and Mayenne while simultaneously securing crossings on the Mayenne River. The 30th Division, which did not possess combat power comparable to the heavily reinforced 1st Infantry Division, found itself spread thinly along the defensive line established by Huebner at Mortain. It did, however, enjoy the support of the attached 743rd Tank Battalion and 823rd Tank Destroyer Battalion. Both had been working with the 30th for about six weeks, and were fully integrated into the division's RCTs. Headquarters, VII Corps had already alerted the 30th Infantry Division to be prepared to send a regiment to Domfront during the early morning hours of 7 August. Unbeknownst to Kluge, the *Schwerpunkt* he had chosen was now perhaps the weakest sector within the American First Army's area of operations. Not only were there fewer American troops defending Mortain, but also the 30th Division did not have time to gain a good appreciation of the terrain.

The German counteroffensive, codenamed Operation LÜTTICH, lurched forward in an uncoordinated and haphazard fashion just after midnight on 6/7 August. Assembling their forces in a somewhat piecemeal fashion during the hours of darkness, a number of units transferred from other parts of the Normandy front had not yet arrived in time to participate in the opening assault. Panzer-grenadiers of the *116th Panzer Division* assaulted the 39th Infantry Regiment north of Mortain, but failed to overrun the defending Americans, who were supported by Company C/70th Tank Battalion. A combat group composed of mixed elements of the *2nd* and *116th Panzer Divisions* discovered an undefended gap south of Cherence le Roussel. The German armor succeeded in advancing five miles without meeting serious resistance, but halted in the village of le Mesnil Adelee to allow supporting units to catch up.

*SS-Panzer-Grenadier Regiment "Deutschland"* of the 2nd SS *Panzer Division*, assisted by a combat group of the *17th SS-Panzer-Grenadier Division*, launched a furious assault on Mortain and Hill 314, but could not overcome the defending 2d Battalion/120th Infantry Regiment, a North Carolina National Guard unit of the 30th Infantry Division. A similar effort by a combat group from the *17th SS-Panzer-Grenadier Division* against the 1st/120th Infantry on Hill 285 to the northwest also failed. In both instances, the attacking *SS* panzer-grenadiers received very little armor or artillery support. *The 2nd SS-Panzer Division* experienced additional problems when it was discovered that traffic jams caused by late arriving units of the *1st SS-Panzer Division* prevented *SS-Panzer-Grenadier Regiment "Der Führer"* from launching an attack against the crossroads hamlet of L'Abbaye Blanche located on the northern outskirts of Mortain. Forced to postpone its assault for five hours, *"Der Fuhrer"* advanced at dawn only to find itself facing fully alerted defenders. As a result of that initial failure, the crossroads village of L'Abbaye Blanche remained in American hands for the duration of the battle.

Since the Panther Battalion of the *1st SS-Panzer Division* had been assigned to reinforce the *2nd Panzer Division*'s assault, the late arrival of the former unit resulted in considerable delays for the main effort of *XLVII Panzer Corps*. Once again, the Germans found themselves thrust into combat against fully alerted American troops. The tactical disadvantage caused by a lack of surprise was exacerbated by the *XLVII Panzer Corps* prohibition on preparatory reconnaissance. The 30th Infantry Division's 1st/117th Infantry—a Tennessee National Guard outfit— which defended the village of St. Barthelemy, sat squarely in the path of the attacking *2nd Panzer Division*. Groping forward in unfamiliar terrain, the panzers advanced in single column along the fog-shrouded roads until they literally bumped into the defenders. In this manner, the presence of American defenders was normally disclosed only when the leading panzer exploded in flames. After seven hours of bitter fighting, the 2nd *Panzer Division* finally overcame the 1st/117th Infantry. Unfortunately for the Germans, the fog that had cloaked the opening phase of their counteroffensive lifted by early afternoon, allowing Allied airpower to make its presence felt on the battlefield.

British Typhoon fighter-bombers appeared over the village of St. Barthelemy at 1230 hours on 7 August. For the remainder of the day, the Allied planes attacked virtually any armored vehicle they could observe moving. While this led to several unfortunate instances of fratricide, the Allied addition of close air support to their combined arms team brought the German advance to a standstill, thus completing the process begun by the 30th Infantry Division's tenacious defensive stance. Lacking artillery support, the German combat group at le Mesnil Adelee was forced to withdrawal by a smaller American force.

The battle for Mortain continued inconclusively for several more days. The fighting that took place during the period of 8–12 August consisted primarily of American counterattacks intended to regain key terrain while simultaneously employing aerial and indirect fires to attrit the defending panzers. Lacking a coordinated reconnaissance effort, *XLVII Panzer Corps* failed to avert tactical stalemate once its initial assault had been halted. Most of the available German reconnaissance units were employed in combat roles in an effort to reinforce the assaulting tanks. As such, the Germans had no means of discovering a thinly defended five-mile gap between Mortain and Barenton. The Americans, however, were keenly aware of the difficulties they would face should the Germans take advantage of that gap. The 35th Infantry Division, a National Guard division with elements from Kansas, Nebraska, and Missouri, which had been enroute to Patton's Third Army, was diverted to seal off the gap before *XLVII Panzer Corps* could outflank the resolute defenders of Mortain. Like its sister unit, the 30th Infantry Division, the 35th had integrated a tank battalion (737th) and a tank destroyer battalion (654th) into its regiments, and was a powerful and effective addition to American combat power in the vicinity. By failing to integrate their reconnaissance effort with the scheme of maneuver, the Germans stumbled into a situation that quickly resulted in tactical stalemate. By neglecting to identify alternative maneuver options should their initial plan fail, the Germans also surrendered the tactical initiative to the defending Americans.

The battle for Mortain is instructive because it provides a unique opportunity to gauge the employment and organization of combined arms teams by American and German divisions in both offensive and defensive situations at the tactical level. Mortain also offers us an example in which superiority in combined arms operations clearly translated into battlefield success in that a single American infantry division defeated the offensive efforts of several German *panzer divisions*. The attacking Germans had all of the components of combined arms (infantry, armor, and artillery) present on the battlefield; however, *XLVII Panzer Corps* was unable to synchronize these components to present the defenders with a challenge with which they could not effectively cope.

Both sides were faced with limited planning time and forced to distribute a limited amount of troops and equipment over a relatively large battlefield. The Americans, however, had clearly mastered the ability to coordinate their available resources in a superior manner during the crucial opening stages of the engagement. Lacking sufficient maneuver forces, the Americans made excellent use of their artillery to blunt the German attack. In sharp contrast, the Germans failed at the outset to employ indirect fires effectively. Given the piecemeal efforts of the attacking panzers and infantry, effective artillery support may have made the difference in the opening phase of the German counteroffensive. *XLVII Panzer Corps*, however, was unable to assemble a significant amount of artillery until 9 August, which was far too late to have a significant impact on battlefield events. Failure to devise a means by which artillery support could be effectively provided to advancing panzer columns prevented *XLVII Panzer Corps* from capitalizing on the sole penetration it had achieved on the opening day of the counteroffensive when a combat group managed to secure le Mesnil Adelee.

Mortain also demonstrated that, having mastered the intricacies of combined arms cooperation amongst the deadly hedgerows of Normandy, American commanders would rarely relinquish that advantage during the eight months remaining in the campaigns in the European Theater of Operations. The Germans, who were also aware of the expert manner in which Americans synchronized their employment of airpower, infantry, tanks, and artillery, were increasingly forced to rely on natural countermeasures, for example, rough terrain and weather, or manmade obstacles such as cities and villages, rather than their own maneuver capabilities to offset the American superiority in combined arms warfare. In a defensive situation, there was little to choose from between American and German combined arms prowess. In an offensive situation however, the Americans were much more capable and expert at exploiting their combined arms advantage on the mobile battlefield. This latter achievement is the greater accomplishment. Offensive operations against a proficient and dedicated opponent is the more difficult form of war. Just ask Clausewitz.

# Notes

### The Ancient World

1. Herodotus, *The Histories*. 1954. Reprint. Trans. Aubrey de Sélincourt. Rev. ed. A. R. Burn (Markham, Ontario: Penguin, 1972), *passim*. Other references by Herodotus are taken from this work.

2. Victor Davis Hanson, *The Wars of the Ancient Greeks and Their Invention of Western Military Culture* (London: Cassell, 1999). See also his *The Western Way of Warfare: Infantry Battle in Classical Greece* (New York: Knopf, 1989); *The Soul of Battle: From Ancient Times to the Present Day, How Three Great Liberators Vanquished Tyranny* (New York: Free Press, 1999); and the edited volume, *Hoplites: The Classical Greek Battle Experience* (London: Routledge, 1991; 1993).

3. Thucydides, *History of the Peloponnesian War*, trans. Rex Warner, 1954. Reprint. Rev. ed. M. I. Finley (Markham, Ontario: Penguin, 1972).

4. Plutarch, *Lives of Noble Grecians and Romans*, 2 vols. ed. A. H. Clough. trans. John Dryden, 1992. Reprint. (Modern Library, 1992)

5. Frank E. Adcock, *The Greek and Macedonian Art of War*, Reissue ed. (Berkeley: University of California Press, 1974), p. 25.

6. Arrian, *The Campaigns of Alexander*, trans. Aubrey de Sélincourt. 1958. Reprint. Rev. ed. J. R. Hamilton (Harmondsworth, UK: Penguin, 1971).

7. Donald W. Engels, *Alexander the Great and the Logistics of the Macedonian Army* (Berkeley: University of California Press, 1978).

8. Livy, *The War with Hannibal* [*idem* Books 21–30 of *The History of Rome from its Foundation*], trans. Aubrey de Sélincourt. 1965. Reprint. Ed. Betty Radice. (Harmondsworth, UK: Penguin, 1972).

9. Edward Gibbon, *The Decline and Fall of the Roman Empire* (New York: Knopf, 1993).

### The Medieval World

1. William H. McNeill, *The Pursuit of Power: Technology, Armed Force and Society Since A.D. 1000* (Chicago: University of Chicago Press, 1982).

2. Kelly Robert DeVries, *Medieval Military Technology* (Peterborough, Ontario: Broadview, 1992).

3. Charles Oman, *Art of War in the Middle Ages, AD 378–1515* (Ithaca, NY: Cornell University Press, 1960).

4. Kelly Robert DeVries, *Infantry Warfare in the Early Fourteenth Century: Discipline, Tactics, and Technology* (Rochester, NY: Boydell, 1996).

5. Charles Oman, *A History of the Art of War in the Middle Ages,* 2 vols. 2nd ed. (New York: Burt Franklin, 1969).

6. Jean Froissart, *Chronicles,* selected, trans. and ed. Geoffrey Brereton. 1968. Reprint. (Markham, Ontario: Penguin, 1978).

7. J. F. C. Fuller, *A Military History of the Western World,* vol. 1 (New York: Funk and Wagnalls, 1954; Da Capo, 1987).

### *The Early Modern Era*

1. Archer Jones, *The Art of War in the Western World* (Urbana: University of Illinois Press, 1987).

2. Hew Strachan, *European Armies and the Conduct of War* (London: George Allen & Unwin, 1983).

3. Christopher Duffy, *Siege Warfare: The Fortress in the Early Modern World, 1494–1660* (London: Routledge & Kegan Paul, 1979).

4. Ian V. Hogg, *Fortress: A History of Military Defence* (New York: St. Martin's, 1977).

5. Geoffrey Parker, *The Military Revolution,* 2nd ed. (New York: Cambridge University Press, 1996).

6. Lynn Montross, *War Through the Ages,* 3rd ed. (New York: Harper, 1960).

7. R. Ernest Dupuy and Trevor N. Dupuy, *The Encyclopedia of Military History: From 3500 B.C. to the Present* (New York: Harper & Row, 1970). 4th ed. NYC: HarperCollins, 1993.

8. John A. Lynn, *The Wars of Louis XIV, 1667–1714* (London: Longman, 1999).

9. Christopher Duffy, *The Army of Frederick the Great* (New York: Hippocrene, 1974).

10. Norwood Young, *The Growth of Napoleon, a study in environment* (London: John Murray, 1910).

11. Auguste Frédéric de Marmont, *Memoires du Marechal Marmont, duc de Raguse, 1792-1841,* 9 vols. (Paris: Perotin, 1857). Extracts from this work appear in Brett James, ed. trans. and comp. *Europe Against Napoleon: The Leipzig Campaign, 1813 from Eyewitness Accounts* (London: Macmillan, 1970).

12. Lucian E. Henry, *Napoleon's War Maxims* (Aldershot, UK: Gale & Polden, n.d.).

13. David G. Chandler, *Campaigns of Napoleon* (New York: Macmillan, 1966).

14. Antoine Henri Jomini, *The Art of War,* trans. G. H. Mendell and W. P. Craighill. (Philadelphia: J. B. Lippincott, 1862; Westport, CT: Greenwood, 1971), p. 69.

15. Winston S. Churchill, *Marlborough: His Life and Times,* 4 vols. Abridged by Henry Steele Commager (New York: Charles Scribner's Sons, 1968). The battle of Blenheim is in volume 2.

16. Christopher Duffy in *The Army of Frederick the Great* cites C. Meyer, *Briefe aus der Zeit des ersten Schlesischen Krieges.* (Leipzig: n.p., 1902).

17. Henri de Catt, *Frederick the Great, the Memoirs of his Reader.* 2 vols., trans. F. S. Flint. (London: Constable, 1916).

18. Frederic N. Maude, *The Leipzig Campaign 1813* (London: Swan Sonnenschein, 1908).

19. J. F. C. Fuller, *A Military History of the Western World,* vol. 2 (New York: Funk and Wagnalls, 1955; DaCapo, 1987).

20. David G. Chandler, *The Art of War in the Age of Marlborough* (London: Batsford, 1976), pp. 261–262.

### Prelude to Cataclysm

1. Jonathan Spence, *God's Chinese Son* (New York:W. W. Norton, 1996).

2. Franz Michael, Taiping Rebellion: History and Documents (Seattle, University of Washington Press, 1972).

3. Charles J. Kolinski, *Independence of Death: The Story of the Paraguayan War* (Gainesville: University of Florida Press, 1965).

4. Gilbert Phelps, *Tragedy of Paraguay* (London: C. Knight, 1975).

### Modern Warfare

1. U.S. Air Force Dictionary (Washington, DC: Government Printing Office, 1956).

2. Frederick V. Longstaff, *The Book of the Machine Gun* (London: Hugh Rees, 1917).

3. *The Franco-German War, 1870–1871,* 5 vols. Trans. F. C. H. Clarke. (London: HMSO, 1874–84; Nashville: Battery Press, 1995–96). The battle of Gravelotte is described in volume 2 of this official history produced by the German General Staff.

4. Antulio J. Echevarria, II, *After Clausewitz: German Military Thinkers Before the Great War* (Lawrence: University Press of Kansas, 2001).

5. John A. English, *On Infantry* (Westport, CT: Praeger, 1994).

6. Christopher Chant. *World Encyclopedia of the Tank: An International History of the Armoured Fighting Machine.* (Nr. Yeovil, UK: Patrick Stephens, 1994).

7. Ian V. Hogg, *Twentieth-Century Artillery* (Etobicoke, Ontario: Prospero, 2000).

8. Stalin's order for the Katyn Forest Massacre, 5 March 1940, trans. David Paterson Mirams, http://www.katyn.org.au/beria.html.

9. Erwin Rommel, *Infanterie Greift An* (Infantry Attacks) (Potsdam, Germany: Boggenreiter Verlag, 1937). Rommel, Erwin. *Attacks*. 1937. Reprint. (Vienna, Virg.: Athena Press, 1979).

10. Martin van Creveld, *Supplying War* (Cambridge, UK: Cambridge University Press, 1979).

11. David Kahn, *Hitler's Spies* (New York: DaCapo, 2000). NYC: Macmillan, 1978

12. Wilhelm Flicke, *War Secrets in the Ether* (Walnut Creek, CA: Aegean Park, 1992).

13. Ronald Lewin, *The Life and Death of the Afrika Korps* (New York: Quadrangle, 1977).

14. Dwight D. Eisenhower, *Crusade in Europe* (Garden City: Doubleday, 1948), p. 294.

15. Gerhard Graser, *Zwischen Kattegat und Kaukasus: Weg und Kämpfe der 198. Infanterie Division, 1939–1945* (Between the Kattegat and the Caucasus: The Route and Battles of the 198th Infantry Division, 1939–1945). (Tübingen, Germany: Veterans' Association of the 198th Infantry Division, 1961), p. 322–323.

16. Richard Engler, *The Final Crisis: Combat in Northern Alsace, January 1945* (Bedford, PA: Aegis, 1999).

17. J. E. Kaufmann and R. M. Jurga, *Fortress Europe: European Fortifications of World War II* (New York: DaCapo, 1999).

18. US War Department, *Handbook on German Military Forces* (Washington, DC: Government Printing Office, 1945).

19. US War Department, *Field Manual (FM) 100-5, Operations.* (Washington, DC: Government Printing Office, 1945).

20. John Keegan, *The Face of Battle* (New York: Viking, 1976).

21. Michael Howard, *The Franco-Prussian War* (London: Rupert Hart-Davis, 1961; Methuen, 1981).

22. Cyril B. Falls, *Armageddon 1918* (London: Weidenfeld and Nicolson, 1964).

23. Edwin Price Ramsey, *Lieutenant Ramsey's War*. With Stephen J. Rivele (New York: Knightsbridge, 1990), p. 66.

24. John Ellis, *Cavalry: The History of Mounted Warfare* (Newton Abbot, UK: Westbridge, 1978).